FOREIGN AND COMMONWEALTH OFFICE

DOCUMENTS ON BRITISH POLICY OVERSEAS

EDITED BY

R. A. SMITH, PhD

P. SALMON, PhD

AND

S. TWIGGE, PhD

SERIES III

Volume VIII

LONDON AND NEW YORK

WHITEHALL HISTORIES: FOREIGN AND COMMONWEALTH OFFICE PUBLICATIONS

Series Editor: Patrick Salmon

ISSN: 1471–2083

FCO historians are responsible for editing *Documents on British Policy Overseas (DBPO)* and for overseeing the publication of FCO Internal Histories.

DBPO comprises three series of diplomatic documents, focusing on major themes in foreign policy since 1945, and drawn principally from the records of the Foreign and Commonwealth Office. The latest volumes, published in Series III, are composed almost wholly of documents still unavailable to the public.

Since the early 1960s, several Internal Histories have been prepared by former or serving officers, the majority of which concentrated upon international developments and negotiations in which the UK has been directly involved. These were initially intended for use within the FCO, but some of the more substantial among them, studies that offer fresh insights into British diplomacy, are now being declassified for publication.

Published DBPO volumes:

SERIES I: 1945–1950

Volume I: The Conference at Potsdam, July–August 1945
0 11 591682 2
Volume II: Conferences and Conversations, 1945: London, Washington and Moscow
0 11 591683 0
Volume III: Britain and America: Negotiation of the US Loan, 3 August–7 December 1945
0 11 591684 9
Volume IV: Britain and America: Atomic Energy, Bases and Food, 12 December 1945–31 July 1946
0 11 591685 7
Volume V: Germany and Western Europe, 11 August–31 December 1945
0 11 591686 5
Volume VI: Eastern Europe, August 1945–April 1946
0 11 591687 3
Volume VII: The UN, Iran and the Cold War, 1946–1947
0 11 591689 X
Volume VIII: Britain and China, 1945–1950
0 7146 5164 8
Volume IX: The Nordic Countries: From War to Cold War, 1944–1951
978 0 415 59476 9

SERIES II: 1950–1960

Volume I: The Schuman Plan, the Council of Europe and Western European Integration, May 1950–December 1952
0 11 591692 X
Volume II: The London Conference: Anglo-American Relations and Cold War Strategy, January–June 1950
0 11 591693 8
Volume III: German Rearmament, September–December 1950
0 11 591694 6
Volume IV: Korea, June 1950–April 1951
0 11 591695 4

SERIES III: 1960–

Volume I: Britain and the Soviet Union, 1968–1972
      0 11 591696 2
Volume II: The Conference on Security and Co-operation in Europe, 1972–1975
      0 11 591697 0
Volume III: Détente in Europe, 1972–1976
      0 7146 5116 8
Volume IV: The Year of Europe: America, Europe and the Energy Crisis, 1972–1974
      0 415 39150 4
Volume V: The Southern Flank in Crisis, 1973–76
      0 7146 5114 1
Volume VI: Berlin in the Cold War, 1948–1990
      978 0 415 45532 9
Volume VII: German Unification 1989–1990
      978 0 415 55002 4

DOCUMENTS ON BRITISH POLICY OVERSEAS

Series III, Volume VIII

The Invasion of Afghanistan and UK-Soviet Relations 1979–1982

First published 2012
by Routledge
2 Park Square, Milton Park, Abingdon, Oxon, OX14 4RN

Simultaneously published in the USA and Canada
by Routledge
711 Third Avenue, New York, NY 10017

Routledge is an imprint of the Taylor & Francis Group, an informa business

© 2012 Crown Copyright

The right of Richard Smith, Patrick Salmon and Stephen Twigge to be identified as editors of this work has been asserted by them in accordance with sections 77 and 78 of the Copyright, Designs and Patents Act 1988.

All rights reserved. No part of this book may be reprinted or reproduced or utilised in any form or by any electronic, mechanical, or other means, now known or hereafter invented, including photocopying and recording, or in any information storage or retrieval system, without permission in writing from the publishers.

Published on behalf of the Whitehall History Publishing Consortium. Applications to reproduce Crown copyright protected material in this publication should be submitted in writing to: HMSO Copyright Unit, St Clements House, 2–16 Colegate, Norwich NR3 1BQ. Fax: 01603 723000. E-mail: copyright@hmso.gov.uk

British Library Cataloguing in Publication Data
A catalogue record for this book is available from the British Library

Library of Congress Cataloging-in-Publication Data
A catalog record has been requested for this book

ISBN13: 978-0-415-67853-7 (hbk)
ISBN13: 978-0-203-12108-5 (ebk)

Typeset in Times New Roman

Printed and bound in Great Britain by
CPI Antony Rowe, Chippenham, Wiltshire

CONTENTS

		PAGES
PREFACE		ix
ABBREVIATIONS FOR PRINTED SOURCES		xxvi
ABBREVIATED DESIGNATIONS		xxvii
LIST OF PERSONS		xxix
DOCUMENT SUMMARIES		xxxvii
CHAPTER I	7 December 1979 - 1 December 1981	1
CHAPTER II	17 December 1981 - 9 December 1982	293
APPENDIX	JIC(80)(N) 4: Soviet Intervention in Afghanistan—An Interim Assessment, 10 January 1980	433
INDEX		436

PREFACE

This volume examines British policy towards the Soviet Union in a period dominated by the aftermath of the invasion of Afghanistan in December 1979 and the imposition of martial law in Poland in December 1981. The British government faced a dilemma: namely, how to express strong disapproval of Soviet actions while still attempting to maintain a constructive bilateral relationship and at the same time to keep British policy in line with the Western Alliance. The consistent aim during this period was to maintain Western unity and impress on the Soviets that stable and productive East-West relations were only possible on the basis of political and military restraint.

The UK's relations with the Soviet Union had been strained since the Second World War, punctuated by brief honeymoons, the last of which—the Wilson-Brezhnev 'new phase' of 1975—was coming to an end when the volume opens.[1] The first document, entitled 'British Policy in East-West Relations,' sets the scene for the period covered by the volume. Dated 7 December 1979, it was intended as a blueprint for handling relations with the Soviet Union and was circulated widely to overseas Missions. The paper stated that the Soviet Union sought to defeat the West by all means short of war, and détente was little more than a tactic to secure technology, grain and credits without slowing their military build-up, relaxing their internal repression, loosening their grip on Eastern Europe or renouncing their freedom to intervene in developing countries.[2] It was produced following a Heads of Mission conference on East-West relations, held at the Foreign and Commonwealth Office (FCO) in October 1979. However, East-West relations were not high on the agenda of the new Conservative government, led by Margaret Thatcher, which was preoccupied with domestic reform. The most pressing foreign policy issue for the Foreign Secretary, Lord Carrington, was Rhodesia. Talks aimed at securing independence began at Lancaster House in September 1979 and ran for the next three months. Lord Carrington resolved to turn his attention to East-West relations as soon as Rhodesia allowed.[3]

In the meantime Peter Blaker, Minister of State at the FCO, set out the approach he thought the government should adopt towards East-West relations, taking up the clear lead set by Mrs Thatcher in opposition.[4] It was the Soviets who famously

---

[1] The fluctuations in UK-Soviet relations have been examined in previous *DBPO* volumes including: Series III, Vol. I: *Britain and the Soviet Union, 1968-1972*, Vol. II: *The Conference on Security and Co-operation in Europe, 1972-75* and Vol. III: *Détente in Europe, 1972-1976*.

[2] This contrasted with a Planning Staff paper, circulated in July 1979, on 'Managing Russia' which concluded that the Soviet threat needed to be kept in proportion and was perfectly manageable by a healthy united West. 'More constructively, it still makes sense to pursue the overall aim which lay behind the more sober definitions of détente in the early 1970s: the creation of a network of practical East-West relationships, in which the Soviet Union has a material stake, and which multiplies the links between the two sides, reinforcing the trend when the overall relationship is improving, and cushioning the shock when it deteriorates, as it is bound to from time to time' (FCO 33/3839, WR 021/14).

[3] Record of a Heads of Mission conference on East-West relations, 19 October 1979 (FCO 28/3701, EN 400/2).

[4] During the 1970s Mr Blaker consistently urged a firmer line towards the Soviet Union and produced a pamphlet on the subject entitled *Coping with the Soviet Union*.

UK-Soviet Relations, 1979-82

dubbed her the 'Iron Lady'.[5] She had been sceptical of the value of the Helsinki Declaration[6] and had criticised the Labour government for cutting defence spending and expanding trade with the Soviet Union on subsidised credit terms. Mr Blaker believed British policy should aim to secure the respect of the Soviets rather than their good opinion. Britain should not necessarily seek to match what the Americans, French and Germans were doing, but should develop a businesslike relationship based on a realistic calculation of respective interests. This would require an active programme of exchanges and visits at all levels to meet the ideological challenge. Britain should also take on human rights cases, based on the Helsinki Final Act, and differentiate between the Soviet Union and Eastern Europe.[7] These sentiments were incorporated into the policy paper of 7 December, which clearly depicted the Soviet threat in belligerent terms.

The Soviet invasion of Afghanistan

The decision by the Soviet Union to intervene in Afghanistan had evolved gradually over the course of 1979.[8] The Soviet government had lost confidence in the communist regime of the Democratic Republic of Afghanistan (DRA), and by late 1979 suspected Prime Minister Hafizullah Amin, who had taken office in October after a power struggle, of drifting towards American influence. By the end of 1979 it also felt it had less to lose internationally, with the ratification of the SALT II treaty by the US Senate in doubt and NATO having taken the 'twin-track' decision to modernise its Theatre Nuclear Forces by deploying Pershing II rockets and Cruise missiles in Western Europe. The decision to intervene in Afghanistan was formally ratified by the Politburo on 12 December in a short handwritten protocol entitled 'Concerning the Situation in "A"'.[9] On Christmas Eve Soviet troops began to move into Afghanistan, and on the evening of 27 December they launched a coup in which Amin was killed and Babrak Karmal, brought from exile in Eastern Europe, was installed as head of a new government (No. 21).

The events leading up to the Soviet invasion did not go unnoticed in the West. In June 1979 the British embassy in Moscow anticipated a further strengthening of the Soviet military presence to defend the Afghan revolution, especially if a deteriorating internal situation could be blamed on external intervention and it could be argued that there was a threat to the 'security, independence and territorial integrity' of Afghanistan within the terms of article 4 of the Soviet-Afghan Friendship Treaty.[10] In November 1979 Christopher Mallaby, head of the FCO's East European and Soviet Department (EESD), considered how the UK should react in the event of a Soviet invasion. It was clear, he thought, that the West could not stop an invasion, so should avoid 'King Canute' statements that only revealed

---

[5] See her 'Iron Lady' speech—*Britain Awake*—made at Kensington Town Hall on 19 January 1976. Full text can be found on the Thatcher Foundation website: http://www.margaretthatcher.org/.

[6] Signed on 1 August 1975, it was the climax of the Conference on Security and Co-operation in Europe (see *DBPO* Series III, Vol. II). Her reservations about the Helsinki process are set out in Margaret Thatcher, *The Path to Power* (London: HarperCollins, 1995), pp. 149-53.

[7] Minute by Mr Blaker on East-West Relations, 9 August 1979 (FCO 28/3680, EN 021/2).

[8] For the history of Soviet involvement in Afghanistan see Rodric Braithwaite, *Afgantsy: The Russians in Afghanistan* (London: Profile, 2011).

[9] Translated Soviet and East German documents relating to the Soviet invasion are reproduced in Odd Arne Westad, 'The Situation in "A": New Russian Evidence on the Soviet Intervention in Afghanistan', CWIHP *Bulletin* 8-9 (Winter 1996/1997), pp. 128-184 and 'New Evidence on the War in Afghanistan', CWIHP *Bulletin* 14-15 (Winter 2003-Spring 2004), pp. 139-271.

[10] Moscow telegram No. 329 of 4 June 1979 (FCO 37/2131, FSA 020/2).

Preface

the impotence of the West. Instead the situation should be exploited to secure the maximum propaganda value in the developing world from the Soviets' 'cynical imperial behaviour'. The best outcome would be the slow escalation of the present situation which would ensure that the Russians 'are slowly and painfully educated in the limits of imperial power.'[11]

The invasion marked a watershed in East-West relations and confirmed perceptions of the Soviet threat set out in the 7 December despatch. This was the first occasion since the Second World War on which the Soviet Union had used armed force outside the borders of the Warsaw Pact, although it continued a trend for intervention established by using Soviet proxies, such as the German Democratic Republic (GDR, East Germany) in South Yemen, and Cuba in Angola and Ethiopia. The official Soviet explanation for the invasion—that they had intervened at the invitation of the Afghan authorities in response to outside interference in the country and had had no hand in the coup—was unconvincing. The message from Karmal, announcing that he was taking over the government, was broadcast on Kabul Radio's wavelength but from a transmitter inside the Soviet Union. Kabul Radio was still transmitting music at the time. The clumsy international presentation indicated to Sir Curtis Keeble, the British Ambassador in Moscow, either 'carelessness for detail or a remarkable contempt for international opinion' (No. 24).

The Soviet action was condemned by Western and non-aligned countries alike. US President 'Jimmy' Carter, already reeling from the Iranian hostage crisis,[12] called the invasion the greatest threat to world peace since the Second World War, and it brought about the sharpest downturn in US-Soviet relations since the invasion of Czechoslovakia in 1968. However, the British embassy in Washington reported that Soviet intervention had at least brought 'the relief of certainty' to an America increasingly uneasy about human rights, Indo-China, Yemen, Ethiopia and SALT II (No. 30). The British government's response was more measured, with Mrs Thatcher informing President Brezhnev by letter that she was 'profoundly disturbed at recent developments' and making clear her belief that the people of Afghanistan had a right to choose their own government without outside interference (No. 7). She also made it clear, in what must have been an uncomfortable forty minute meeting for the Soviet Ambassador, that she was aware of no external intervention or aggression towards Afghanistan as claimed by Moscow, apart from that carried out by Soviet forces (No. 17).[13]

For Sir C. Keeble, the Soviet action was carried out in classic style: 'with the Iranian problem deflecting attention, substantial force swiftly applied, immediate liquidation of political opposition, and a public presentation of Goebbels-like effrontery'. The aim was to preserve the Afghan socialist revolution without the loss of too much political capital (No. 10). For the Soviets to accept that they had miscalculated, the Western reaction needed to be tougher than they expected, sustained over a long period and shared by non-aligned countries. In the first week

[11] Minute to Mr White, 8 November 1979 (FCO 37/2132, FSA 020/2).
[12] On 4 November 1979 revolutionary students stormed the US embassy in Tehran demanding the return of the Shah, and dozens of US staff were taken hostage.
[13] In Moscow the Soviet foreign minister, Mr Gromyko, noted to the DRA foreign minister that representatives of Western countries, 'particularly Thatcher', were trying to draw a parallel between the change of Afghan leadership and the introduction of Soviet troops. He thought it should be emphasised in the UN debate that there was no link between the two events—'This is purely coincidental.' Record of a meeting between A. A. Gromyko and Shah. M. Dost, 4 January 1980. Reproduced in the CWIHP *Bulletin* 8-9 (Winter 1996/1997), pp. 161-2.

UK-Soviet Relations, 1979-82

of January 1980 both the FCO Planning Staff and the Joint Intelligence Committee produced assessments of Soviet motives for intervention and reached similar conclusions. Moscow could not risk losing its investment in a neighbouring country, particularly at a time when Iran was in chaos, and abandoning a 'socialist revolution' would have meant an unacceptable loss of face. It was doubtful whether the Soviets had plans for further expansion, but they were now well placed to extend their influence in Asia and advance towards the Indian Ocean and Gulf region. They could also seek to exploit border disputes that existed with Afghanistan and an increasingly unstable Pakistan. Another consideration for Moscow had been to avoid the prospect of having a second Islamic fundamentalist state on its border. The Soviet government had calculated that the effect on East-West relations was worth the risk, and that the Western response would be muted and short-lived. The danger was that the Soviets would consider their success cheaply bought and this would encourage similar future ventures (No. 23 & Appendix).[14] Retaliation was unlikely to force them to modify their intentions but would help determine the West's future credibility in Soviet eyes.

The response of the West

In early January 1980 Sir C. Keeble noted that the 7 December despatch read well in the light of the Afghan adventure and should remain the basis for dealing with Moscow—'a relationship of mutual respect founded on consistent firmness and courtesy, pursued in close concert with our allies and designed to make it plain that the Soviet Union cannot attain the détente it seeks if it continues its expansionist policies' (No. 24). In an attempt to establish a unified Western response, the US Under-Secretary of State, Warren Christopher, travelled to London for a hastily arranged meeting with representatives from Britain, France, the Federal Republic of Germany (FRG, West Germany), Canada and Italy (No. 11). On the eve of the meeting Sir Nicholas Henderson, British Ambassador in Washington, wrote to London that the United States was emerging from the 'post-Vietnam chrysalis': they were in the mood to shoulder responsibility abroad but did not want to do it alone.[15] The meeting proved a disappointment, with Douglas Hurd, FCO Minister of State, reporting that the US had no clear ideas on how to proceed and the French determined to block any action which threatened détente: 'A lot of hard work and clear thinking is required if this US initiative is to bear any fruit' (No. 13). On 4 January President Carter announced a series of unilateral measures against the USSR, including a grain embargo and limitations on high technology.

The British government also drew up a series of measures against the Soviet Union but was reluctant to act alone, preferring instead to press for discussion within NATO in an attempt to formulate a set of mutually consistent measures. All were agreed on the need to take action to prevent the Soviet Union from engaging in similar future ventures but some, notably the FRG and France, did not want to jeopardise détente by a hasty response (No. 22). Sir C. Keeble warned that 'a

---

[14] A US Defense Intelligence Summary, written around the same time, asserted: 'The broader implications of the Soviet invasion . . . lie in the significantly enhanced threat of destabilization of the countries of the region, notably Saudi Arabia and other oil-producing countries. Given the continued dependence on Middle East oil by the US and its allies, the Soviet occupation of Afghanistan translates into a direct threat to the West.' 'Soviet invasion of Afghanistan' by the US Defense Intelligence Agency', c.February 1980. Reproduced on the Digital National Security Archive at http://nsarchive.chadwyck.com/marketing/index.jsp

[15] Washington telegram No. 4407 of 30 December (FO 37/2135, FSA 020/9).

Preface

patchwork of minor gestures of irritation, with French dissent publicly registered, will weaken the effect of American action and encourage Soviet mischief making' (No. 32). Measures proposed by the Europeans tended to focus on diplomatic and political, rather than economic, sanctions. Members of the Cabinet were also sensitive to the effect any attempt to reduce credit or high technology exports might have on the British economy. Sir N. Henderson remarked that détente had been turned on its head. Rather than inhibiting the Soviet Union from taking hostile action through fear of disturbing the beneficial trade and cultural contacts it had built with the West, it was the West who had become fearful of losing important commercial relations with the USSR (No. 60). It was 15 January before a statement was issued recording the Alliance's view that the Soviet invasion could not fail to have a damaging effect on détente. Sir Clive Rose, the UK Permanent Representative to NATO, reported that if this statement were not followed quickly by practical measures the 'gap between the American and European reaction was likely to become all too apparent and exploited by the Russians' (No. 38).[16] On 24 January the British government announced measures against the USSR which included ending special preferential credit rates, not replacing the Anglo-Soviet credit agreement, cancelling military exchanges, applying the full rigour of COCOM restrictions to exports of sensitive technology and avoiding high level contact with the Soviets.[17] The big freeze had begun.

Sir N. Henderson conceded that the Europeans had grounds for complaint about the lack of adequate consultation from the Americans. The US had, for example, failed to consult before the State of the Union address on 23 January in which President Carter had announced a new commitment to the security of the Persian Gulf region. But the Ambassador pointed out that the criticism went both ways, with the US calling the European response irresolute. Although Britain was a conspicuous exception to this view, he added, 'that does not do us much good in Europe' (No. 52). Mrs Thatcher remained concerned lest the West's response was a 'nine-day wonder' as it had been in the case of Hungary and Czechoslovakia (No. 53) but she was also aware of European sensibilities. In her letters to President Carter she counselled that the FRG had 'considerable human, political and economic investments in Berlin and East Germany and are wary of losing ground' (No. 43). In discussions with Chancellor Helmut Schmidt she questioned whether the European reaction had been partly to blame when he expressed disquiet over the US failure to consult (No. 55).

In mid-January 1980 Lord Carrington toured Turkey, Oman, Saudi Arabia, Pakistan and India to look at ways of supporting countries in the region against any further Soviet encroachment. He returned home with a long list of actions which included encouraging non-aligned (particularly Muslim) countries to continue denouncing Soviet actions; accelerating the sale of defence equipment to Oman, Saudi Arabia and other Gulf states; providing friendly states with assessments of Soviet activities and intentions in the area ('Operation Commonsense'); providing counter-subversion assistance; and reviewing policy towards China, including arms sales (No. 41). At a meeting on 22 January the Cabinet's Defence and Oversea Policy Committee (OD) supported the Secretary of State's proposals. The

---

[16] The fact that there was little unity in NATO over measures towards the Soviet Union did not go unnoticed in Moscow where Gromyko reported to the Politburo that Western countries were not in agreement with, and were not following, the US in applying sanctions. CC CPSU Politburo transcript, 17 January 1980. Reproduced in the CWIHP *Bulletin* 8-9 (Winter 1996/1997), pp. 162-3.
[17] *HL Debs*, 24 January 1980, vol. 404, cols. 530-46.

UK-Soviet Relations, 1979-82

Committee also endorsed Mrs Thatcher's decision to write to the Chairman of the British Olympic Association, asking him to press the International Olympic Committee to change the venue of the 1980 Games, due to open in Moscow in July. Sir C. Keeble believed that a Western boycott was the single gesture that would most hurt the Soviet government. This view was shared by the Prime Minister and the Secretary of State for the Environment, Michael Heseltine. He contended that if a boycott meant that Britain would have to embrace the use of sport for the first time as a political weapon, 'the end would justify the means' (No. 39). They both recognised, however, that the British Olympic Committee was an independent body and could not be forced to follow government instructions. The Foreign Secretary thought the best outcome might be if the government recommended against participation but the various committees, and participants, decided to go anyway (No. 26). President Carter wrote to the US Olympic Committee making it clear that the US should not participate in the Games if Soviet troops were not withdrawn. The idea of moving the Games was pursued but ultimately deemed impractical.[18]

At the end of January EESD produced a paper on 'Soviet foreign policy after Afghanistan' concluding that the UK faced a difficult period in East-West relations in which Western resolve was indispensable. If the Soviet Union faced firm and consistent opposition to its aims, self-interest might lead it to be less assertive in pursuing them, and it might seek instead to look for agreement in areas of mutual interest (No. 47). A darker summation of the situation was offered by Mr Johnson of EESD:

'The Russians will have assessed the Western reaction to Afghanistan as riven by doubt and conflicting national interests. They will have weighed up Western countries as vacillating, self-seeking, unwilling to give up the good life, too ready to take an optimistic view of likely Soviet actions, too subject to electoral winds of change, and in general too weak and split to offer serious resistance to Soviet expansion . . . and may also reckon that an alliance of equals is in the final analysis no match for one dominated by a single, determined and ruthless directing force' (No. 61).

'Soviet foreign policy after Afghanistan' was sent to No. 10, along with a suggestion from Lord Carrington that the Prime Minister meet with FCO officials to discuss Soviet policy. The meeting that took place a week later was attended by Lord Carrington, Rodric Braithwaite, head of Planning Staff, and Mr Mallaby. It was an attempt—largely successful—by the Secretary of State to overcome the Prime Minister's scepticism of the FCO's ability to handle the Soviets firmly enough, and to ensure that she had an alternative view to balance against those of her academic advisers.[19]

---

[18] Mr Hurd called his role in attempting to frustrate the Moscow Games 'the most foolish task with which I was ever entrusted as a minister'. It was clear from the outset that athletes and administrators were unlikely to abandon for political reasons an event in which they had invested so much time and ambition. Douglas Hurd, *Memoirs* (London: Little, Brown, 2003), p. 262.

[19] See Lord Carrington, *Reflect on Things Past* (London: Collins, 1988), p. 285 and Rodric Braithwaite, *Across the Moscow River* (London: Yale, 2002), pp. 51-2. For further reflections on Mrs Thatcher's relations with the FCO see George Walden (at that time the PPS to the Foreign Secretary), *Lucky George: memoirs of an anti-politician* (London: Allen Lane, 1999), pp. 208-14.

xiv

Preface

Preventing future Afghanistans

In a letter of 16 January 1980 to Mr Mallaby, Sir C. Keeble expressed the view that beyond the short-term objectives of making the Soviet leadership recognise that a similar operation conducted elsewhere would be likely to prove both dangerous and ineffective, the invasion of Afghanistan offered the West an opportunity to develop a global policy which exposed 'the basic fallacy in the Soviet concept of détente'. The primary need was for consolidation of the UK's relationships amongst the Allies and with developing nations, who received little but arms and dogma from the Soviet Union. Though the idea of the UK holding a unique position between Europe, the US and the Commonwealth was un-fashionable, the UK was now in a position to exercise influence (No. 40). Even before the invasion of Afghanistan there was concern over Communist military interventions in the developing world, which had begun with the Cuban-backed installation of a Marxist regime in Angola. This was reflected in the 7 December 1979 paper which called for an examination of ways to prevent Soviet expansion in this area. A meeting was held in the FCO on 30 January 1980 to take the work forward. The aim was not to punish African countries close to the Soviet Union, but to seek to build on their need for links with the West in the hope of weaning them away from the Soviets. It was felt there was a need to identify possible future targets of Soviet opportunism and define the degree of Western influence in those countries with a view to working to prevent future 'Afghanistans' (No. 48). In addition, the overturning of the *de facto* understanding that Soviet forces would not fight outside the territories of the Soviet Union and her allies now meant that other neighbours looked vulnerable—in particular Yugoslavia and Iran (No. 37).

A final version of a paper on 'The Management of East-West Relations' was sent to Mrs Thatcher and discussed at a meeting with FCO officials on 20 May, before being submitted to OD Committee. The paper made a number of recommendations for restoring the coherence of the West, improving the North-South economic relationship, reviewing the scope for putting economic and other pressure on the Soviets, improving arrangements for giving military assistance in the Third World, developing capacity for long-range military intervention outside NATO, reviewing machinery for countering Soviet propaganda and developing links with Third World political organisations. In a covering letter Lord Carrington reiterated the view that the Soviet Union saw no incompatibility between détente and the continuation of the ideological struggle. The desire to equal the US as a world superpower drove Moscow to shift the world correlation of forces in their favour whilst being careful to avoid direct military confrontation with the West. The spread of Soviet economic, political and military power in the Third World was a threat to Western interests and must be checked if the East-West relationship was to be put on a more secure basis (No. 65).

This agenda was agreed by the OD Committee on 5 June 1980. In the course of discussion it was suggested that the large increase in Soviet power over the past decade was mainly a result of weak leadership from the US, with other contributing factors such as the insistence of the French on an independent posture and West Germany's growing economic interdependence with Eastern Europe, leading to 'disquieting political manifestations'. In these circumstances it was all the more important that Britain take a strong political and ideological lead. Though Britain's resources, particularly economic, were limited, the English language was a source of great influence and Britain's moral authority was respected in many countries, especially in the Commonwealth, where the settling of the Rhodesian

UK-Soviet Relations, 1979-82

problem had recently removed a major cause of contention (No. 67). Commenting on the paper from Moscow, Sir C. Keeble stressed that the Soviet presence in Afghanistan was a reality and could remain so for many years. Any insistence on withdrawal, as a precondition for progress in other areas, would condemn the policy to failure in advance. The government had to avoid an unrealistic choice between détente and a freeze in relations, and plan for the long-term management of continuing East-West tension in which various aspects of East-West relations were dealt with on their merits, 'recognising the essential malevolence of Soviet policy and exploiting its weaknesses' (No. 69).

Sir C. Keeble's views fed into a paper by EESD on 'UK Policy in East-West Relations' prepared in response to the Secretary of State's request for a short paper on where things stood on East-West relations, especially the resumption of contacts (No. 72). The paper, submitted in mid-July, noted that Western countries had already begun to drift back to business as usual with Moscow. In May 1980 French President Giscard d'Estaing and President Brezhnev had met in Warsaw for a one-day summit, and in June Chancellor Schmidt visited Moscow for talks. It was not in Britain's interest to be left out of East-West contacts (this was a theme that would increasingly occupy the FCO over the coming years). At the end of July 1980 EESD reflected on the West's response to Afghanistan in a paper entitled 'Warning, Actions and Threats to Deter Soviet Moves' which admitted that a range of measures had been applied in a partial and piecemeal manner and that although they had had some political and economic impact, it was not certain whether this had been significant. The paper tried to draw lessons and suggest how the West could act in a more timely and coherent manner in a future crisis (No. 74). With strikes about to break out in Poland such a paper would not gather dust.

Proposals for a Neutral and Non-Aligned Afghanistan

The greatest area of Soviet vulnerability was Afghanistan itself. In Kabul, the British Ambassador, William Hillier-Fry, voiced the question as to whether the Soviets had 'landed themselves in a mountainous and inhospitable Vietnam' (No. 21). The FCO thought there would be strong pressure to build up the scale of Soviet military intervention with the aim of the complete suppression of opposition but concluded: 'It is doubtful whether this aim can ever in fact be achieved, given Afghan history, terrain and social characteristics' (No. 9). However action was needed to try and change the situation in Afghanistan and at the end of January 1980 the Planning Staff drafted a note which concluded that a 'Treaty of Neutrality' for Afghanistan, guaranteed by the countries of the region including the Soviet Union, Iran, Pakistan, China and India, would be a good outcome of the crisis (No. 44). The proposal was fleshed out further by the Planning Staff as both a device for putting political pressure on the Soviets and a basis for a settlement. As the West could not force the Soviets to leave through military or economic pressure the neutrality proposal demonstrated that they were looking for a solution rather than confrontation, and could act as a rallying point for the non-aligned. One of the positive aspects of the invasion had been the hostile response from many non-aligned and developing countries (No. 59).[20]

---

[20] Moscow looked to use the interest in finding a political solution to create more favourable conditions for the stabilisation of the situation in Afghanistan but viewed the current Western proposals as thinly veiled attempts to achieve the rapid withdrawal of Soviet troops and regime change. CPSU CC 'Politburo decision on Soviet policy on Afghanistan', 10 March 1982, with

Preface

In pitching the neutrality idea to the Prime Minister, Lord Carrington noted that the demand for Soviet withdrawal would be more plausible if a positive solution to the Afghan problem could be found (No. 49). Despite initial misgivings from Mrs Thatcher—'It would be *useless*' was an early marginal comment—Lord Carrington put the idea to his colleagues at the European Council in February and the Nine launched the initiative as a positive step towards defusing the international situation. At this stage the idea was intended as a constructive proposal designed to allow the Soviets to withdraw without losing face and to demonstrate to Moscow that their fears of Western intervention in Afghanistan were groundless (No. 54). Sir C. Keeble thought it was unlikely to be accepted. If the Soviets could not subdue Afghanistan easily then the idea of neutrality might become attractive, but that point had not yet been reached. Nor would they welcome the implication in the concept of neutrality that their existing bilateral treaty with Afghanistan would cease and that the DRA government would be left to fend for itself (No. 56).

Lord Carrington floated his proposal for a neutral and non-aligned Afghanistan with the Soviet Foreign Minister, Andrei Gromyko, during meetings in Vienna in May 1980 and again at the United Nations in September. The only requirement from Britain was that a political solution must lead to the complete withdrawal of Soviet forces and to guarantees of non-intervention in the future by other states, including the USSR. The Soviets preferred to see the conclusion of bilateral treaties between Afghanistan and Pakistan and Iran, providing assurances of non-interference in Afghan affairs, namely the end of armed incursions. Complete withdrawal could not be discussed before guarantees of non-interference from outside were given and seen to be effective. Lord Carrington thought these positions were not irreconcilable, and that it should be possible to work out a formula which made commitments to both withdrawal and undertakings simultaneous, with a timetable settled at the outset (Nos. 59, 64, 77).

In May 1981 Lord Carrington decided to stimulate fresh diplomatic activity and picked up on a French idea for an international conference. The Prime Minister agreed to his proposal for a two-stage conference: stage one, involving the Permanent Members of the UN Security Council, Pakistan, Iran and India, would work out arrangements to halt external intervention and safeguard against future intervention; stage two, involving Afghan representatives, would reach agreement on the implementation of the international arrangements worked out in stage one. The proposals were presented as a serious attempt to move towards a peaceful solution and to maintain international interest. Around the same time the Soviets were putting out feelers for a visit to Moscow by Lord Carrington. In April 1981, the Soviet Ambassador in London handed him a note at Northolt airport, which stated that the Soviet Union was prepared unilaterally to halt the deployment of SS-20 missiles. The note also indicated a willingness to develop bilateral political dialogue 'by implication at a higher level' (No. 95). Nigel Broomfield, now head of EESD, felt that the visit could be linked to the initiative on Afghanistan. Experienced Soviet-watcher Tony Bishop, of the FCO's Research Department, thought the Soviet interest in dialogue with senior Western figures was aimed at drawing the US into talks with the USSR, regaining international respectability and restoring a peaceful image. The Soviets were 'devoid of ideas but hoping that somebody outside will step in and provide some' (No. 99).

report on 'Proposal by Fidel Castro to Mediate between Afghanistan and Pakistan'. Reproduced in the CWIHP *Bulletin* 8-9 (Winter 1996/1997), pp. 167-170.

UK-Soviet Relations, 1979-82

In June the European Council gave their approval to the idea of an Afghan conference, and Lord Carrington went to Moscow in his capacity as President of the Council of Ministers. The meeting between the two Foreign Ministers took place on 6 July. Following a morning of discussions Gromyko dismissed the proposal for Afghan neutrality as 'completely divorced from reality', largely over the question of DRA representation (No. 107). There was little surprise that the Soviets were not keen on the proposed conference, but there had been a hope that the wide international support for the initiative would make it difficult for them to reject it. Britain attempted to keep the initiative alive, stressing the offer remained on the table for negotiation. But, as Sir C. Keeble reported in October, 'there is no choice open to the Soviet Union other than that between soldiering on in a long colonial war or admitting defeat. They are not yet ready for the latter' (No. 114).

The response to martial law in Poland

If the Soviet Union was not ready to accept defeat in Afghanistan, it was also reluctant to accept to accept political change in Poland. Following the formation of the independent trade union *Solidarnosc* (Solidarity) in August 1980 Poland was paralysed by a political struggle that hovered between reform and repression.[21] On 13 December 1981 the government of General Jaruzelski decided to break the deadlock by declaring martial law, an act that once again posed problems for the Alliance over how best to handle East-West relations. There was little doubt that the Soviet Union bore a degree of responsibility for the repression in Poland. Moscow had placed political, military and economic pressure on the Polish government to deal with 'anti-socialist activities'. In Sir C. Keeble's opinion Poland was too crucial to Soviet political and security interests for the situation to be left to deteriorate, but the international penalties of direct intervention were judged to be so great that an 'internal' solution was preferable (No. 118). Again, the Western response was led by the US government, now led by President Ronald Reagan.[22] On 29 December, with little consultation, the US announced a series of economic and political measures, and put pressure on the European allies to follow suit. They made it clear that they wanted to see specific economic and political measures from Europe aimed at the Soviet Union as well as Poland.

The EC and NATO called for reconciliation in Poland through the lifting of martial law, the release of those detained, and the resumption of genuine dialogue between the Polish authorities and the Church and Solidarity. But the European allies were not fully convinced of the arguments for strong measures against the Soviet Union in circumstances short of direct armed intervention. There were wide variations in national positions and the measures proposed were largely political rather than economic. To shore up the Western position, Mrs Thatcher wrote to President Reagan expressing her support for a concerted European response and contending that the diplomatic focus should be directed at Soviet failures rather than differences between Alliance partners (No. 123). The Soviet Ambassador was called to the FCO on 5 February to hear the specific measures Britain had decided to take against the Soviet Union, including additional restrictions on the travel of

---

[21] UK relations with the Soviet bloc, including Poland, will be covered in a forthcoming *DBPO* volume.

[22] At National Security Council meetings held on 21, 22 and 23 December 1981 President Reagan was clear that the Soviets were behind the repression in Poland and that he wanted to take a tough line. There were also warnings from Mr Haig, the US Secretary of State, that pre-emptive US action risked splitting the Alliance (minutes reproduced at http://www.thereaganfiles.com/).

xviii

Preface

Soviet officials in the UK, a reduction of bilateral technical co-operation, a proposal to renegotiate the terms of the Anglo-Soviet Treaty on Merchant Navigation and the introduction of a licensing system covering Soviet factory fishing vessels in UK waters. The Ambassador claimed, as the Soviets had done with Afghanistan, that it was the reaction of the West that amounted to interference in Poland's affairs rather than any actions of theirs (No. 130).

One area of immediate concern was the future of the West Siberian gas pipeline project in which many European companies had significant involvement, including John Brown Engineering Ltd with contracts worth £104m at stake. The Americans were unsympathetic to this project, regardless of the Polish situation, thinking the Europeans would become too dependent on Soviet gas and provide the USSR with a future source of hard currency. The West German and French governments were determined to go ahead with the project, despite US sanctions, and Sir N. Henderson was warned that US interference in the pipeline would cause a major transatlantic row (No. 124). Lord Carrington was concerned enough to suggest that Mrs Thatcher send an urgent message to President Reagan to bring the situation to his personal attention. Just prior to this she made her views known to Mr Haig who made an unscheduled stop in London on his way back to the US from the Middle East.[23] She suggested that the Europeans exchange some commitment on future contracts and agree not to undermine US measures in the future in return for exemption of existing contracts (No. 127). Although her government was ideologically attuned to America's new determination to oppose Soviet expansionism, which began under President Carter and then toughened under President Reagan, she did not unquestioningly follow all the demands for diplomatic and economic sanctions made upon the Alliance by the US and often took a similar view to the European allies.[24]

The pipeline issue became caught up in the wider question of political and economic relations with the Soviet Union. The climate for East-West trade changed following the invasion of Afghanistan and this trend was reinforced by the Reagan administration. The US traditionally took the view that trade should be subject to political control, whereas the Europeans considered trade beneficial in its own right. Some members of the US Administration believed the weaknesses of the Soviet economy rendered it susceptible to pressure and wanted to use economic and trade measures to extract political concessions over Poland or even secure more far-reaching changes in Soviet internal and external policy.[25] The Americans were concerned about the export of advanced technology and Western credit to the Soviet Union. However, the British government agreed with other West European countries that the Soviet economy, though in difficulty, was more robust than the US believed. In a background paper assessing the impact of Western measures on the Soviet economy, officials concluded that trade with the West accounted for only a small proportion of Soviet GNP, many Western imports could be sourced

---

[23] Mr Haig recalled that Mrs Thatcher 'with her usual perspicacity' identified the fundamental issue, that it was too much for the Europeans to punish their own economies and interests in support of policies that would inflict no noticeable wound on the Soviet Union. Alexander M. Haig, *Caveat* (New York: Macmillan, 1984), p. 256.
[24] Mrs Thatcher called the pipeline issue, 'a lesson in how not to conduct alliance business.' Margaret Thatcher, *The Downing Street Years* (London: HarperCollins, 1993), p. 256.
[25] For example, at a National Security Council meeting on 24 May 1982 to review the December 1981 sanctions, President Reagan stated: 'The Soviet Union is economically on the ropes—they are selling rat meat on the market. This is the time to punish them' (minutes reproduced at http://www.thereaganfiles.com/).

from neutral countries and any shortfall accommodated by belt-tightening. The leverage available through the imposition of broad trade restrictions was limited.[26] At the time of the Afghan crisis Sir C. Keeble had acknowledged that there were few countries in the world less vulnerable to economic measures or more ready to suffer a severance of external links than the Soviet Union. Similarly, in September 1981 Andrew Wood, from the embassy in Moscow, concluded in a memorandum on the 'Soviet Union: Will It Change?' that despite the increasing problems faced by the Soviet leadership, radical change was unlikely in the short or medium term. Change would become progressively harder to achieve without sending the system into shock and with the Soviet political structure so rigid, successors to Brezhnev would have little choice but to follow similar policies even whilst problems mounted (No. 112). As the pipeline dispute rumbled on throughout 1982, the FCO worked on a paper, drawing views from across Whitehall, on 'British Policy in East-West Economic Relations in the 1980s'. It concluded that the overriding principle in trade with the Soviet Union should be commercial advantage. Trade should not be used as a political weapon; nor be artificially encouraged for political reasons.

In March 1982 the Planning Staff took stock in a paper entitled 'Western Response to the Polish Crisis: Assessment and Prospects'. They concluded that repression would continue for some time and that Western measures towards Poland and the Soviet Union would not reverse this. There was still a serious risk of a Western split over Poland but Britain should continue to act as a catalyst for unity (No. 134). US policy, according to an analysis by the British embassy in Washington in August 1982, was that the West should keep its military guard up, its purses closed and its granaries open. The embassy also talked of Britain having to help 'pull the Administration's chestnuts out of the fire which they themselves have stoked' over relations with the rest of the Alliance. This was a task in which Britain had no choice, as in the last resort the Americans could live without the Europeans but the reverse was not true (No. 155).

US-Soviet relations and the UK

Sir C. Keeble observed that the relationship between Britain and the Soviet Union had never been determined in isolation or on its own merits but was the product of a whole complex of other policies and relationships, especially that between the superpowers (No. 138). In February 1980 he examined the state of the relationship between the Soviet Union and the United States noting that the Soviet leadership needed a controlled relationship with the US in order to feel secure. Whilst the immediate US reaction to Afghanistan might prompt a greater degree of caution in the Soviet leadership, in the longer term the Soviet Union would pursue its objectives according to its perception of the strength of purpose of the American President (No. 50).

The election of Ronald Reagan brought a fiercely anti-Communist President to the White House who was determined to take a more assertive approach in dealing with the Soviet Union. Any assumption by Moscow that his anti-Soviet rhetoric was confined to the election campaign was soon dismissed. Mr Gromyko told Lord Carrington, when the two met in New York in 1981, that US-Soviet relations were in disarray but through no fault of the Soviet Union (No. 111). The Soviet leadership attempted to appeal directly to the governments and peoples of Western

[26] 'British Policy in East/West economic relations in the 1980s: The likely effect of Western economic/trade measures on the Soviet economy', 1 October 1982 (EN 091/1).

Preface

Europe who, they believed, still accepted the basic tenets of détente from the 1970s. President Brezhnev used his speech in February 1981, marking the opening session of the 26th Congress of the Soviet Communist Party, to launch the Soviet 'Peace Programme'. He called for a summit meeting with President Reagan and renewed his call for NATO to stop the deployment of US nuclear missiles in Europe, offering to freeze the deployment of the SS-20s in return (No.86). This initiative was followed by a letter from President Brezhnev to Mrs Thatcher, delivered by the Soviet Ambassador on 9 March. In her response the Prime Minister made clear that if President Brezhnev wanted to reduce the level of armaments, and if he was prepared to withdraw from Afghanistan and engage in 'two-way' détente, he would find HMG willing to discuss these matters. However she could only judge the Soviet government by its actions: if deeds matched words they would find the British willing partners (No. 87).

Reviewing the US-Soviet relationship in March 1982 Sir C. Keeble thought there were those in the Soviet leadership questioning whether US policy was attempting more than just containing and counterbalancing Soviet power in Europe. Even so, in an era of 'mutual hostility and abuse' both countries still needed to avoid an uncontrolled relationship and retain an interest in dialogue, however unfruitful (No. 140). US policy towards the Soviet Union was analysed further in a paper produced in August 1982 by the British embassy in Washington (No. 155). President Reagan was described as a conviction politician with 'exceptionally crude' views on international affairs and policies 'harking back to the relatively clear-cut black and white concepts of earlier eras'. Soviet-American relations were governed by a policy of neo-containment stressing the need for Soviet *restraint* (by rejecting intervention in other countries), *reciprocity* (in complying with undertakings like Helsinki) and *linkage* (where the Soviet Union must satisfy US requirements in other policy areas if it wanted a satisfactory bilateral relationship).

Sir C. Keeble was confident that control of strategic armaments by bilateral agreement was a policy objective for both the USSR and the US and an area where Soviet-American understanding was inherently possible. The outlook for East-West relations was bleak but the Europeans should press the Americans for strategic arms reduction talks (START) to begin and for INF negotiations to continue. The other half of the NATO 'twin-track' policy on INF deployment was to open negotiations for arms reduction. This was an important factor in Alliance relations as many European governments were under pressure from domestic peace movements. Mr Broomfield noted that whatever the current difficulties over the Siberian pipeline, these would 'pale into insignificance' if the European NATO allies thought responsibility for the lack of progress on arms control lay with the US rather than the Soviet Union (No. 158, note. 1). Sir Iain Sutherland, British Ambassador in Moscow from September 1982, observed that the Soviets did not like President Reagan but they had the US Administration they deserved and which they in part had helped to create in failing to realise that the US mood was changing and the imbalance inherent in the Soviet view of détente was unsustainable (No. 177). Although Mr Gromyko had characterised the position of the British government as no more than an echo of the US military (No. 89) Britain's close relationship with America was not always unhelpful to Moscow. As the Soviets struggled to develop a stable relationship with the Reagan administration they looked to Britain as a sensible interlocutor with standing in Washington. During a conversation with Francis Pym (Lord Carrington's

UK-Soviet Relations, 1979-82

successor)[27] in New York in September 1982, Mr Gromyko recalled there had been many examples since the war of Britain's helping to find a way round differences between America and the Soviet Union (No. 161).

Following the death of President Brezhnev on 10 November 1982 President Reagan stated that an opportunity to improve East-West relations existed so long as the Soviets abided by acceptable standards of international behaviour. The British government was represented at the funeral by Mr Pym who took the opportunity to have meetings with Mr Gromyko and the US Secretary of State George Shultz. Mr Pym also explored the possibility of a US-Soviet summit to steady public opinion. He was sceptical about the likelihood of any change in Soviet polices but equally firm that the opportunity for exploring possibilities for change should not be turned down. He wanted the December NATO meeting to issue a separate declaration on East-West relations setting out 'in an eloquent and eye-catching form' their basic approach (No. 173). This would emphasise President Reagan's point that more constructive East-West relations were on offer if the new Soviet leader, Yuri Andropov, would do what was necessary to grasp the opportunity. Mrs Thatcher could not see the merit of an early summit and indeed the idea was politely rebuffed by Mr Shultz.

'The coldest spell is before the dawn'

In March 1982 Mr Broomfield surveyed the state of UK-Soviet relations and concluded that they had 'been stripped of any fat'. He argued in a submission to Alan Goodison, assistant under-secretary, that a constructive bilateral relationship was needed to put across British views direct to the Soviet leadership and assess Soviet thinking and personalities at first hand (No. 135). At the same time Sir C. Keeble was dictating a despatch along similar lines, arguing that Britain had almost no contact with the world's second power and advocating a more positive attitude. He thought the government should take advantage of opportunities when they occurred, adding that political exchanges were 'not necessarily demonstrations of goodwill' (No. 138). This analysis was supported at all levels in the FCO. Julian Bullard, Deputy to the Permanent Under-Secretary and Political Director, thought there was a need to 'intersperse our current disapproving line with at least one or two concrete signs of interest' (No. 137). Lord Trefgarne, Minister of State, did not want to risk damaging Alliance solidarity or get out of step with major allies—especially the US—but did agree there were good reasons not to become too distant from the Soviets and endanger channels of political communication (No. 141).

The prospect of an immediate thaw was effectively put on hold during the Argentine invasion of the Falkland Islands. The initial Soviet attitude to the Falklands conflict was cautious, but became more hostile to the UK. Soviet propaganda avoided reference to Security Council Resolution 502 and instead portrayed the crisis as one provoked by the UK's colonialist intransigence, supported by US imperialist ambitions in South America. They also took umbrage at the suggestion that they were providing Argentina with information on British fleet movements. However, in July EESD returned to the theme of bilateral relations. In order to redefine UK policy, David Manning of EESD produced a draft paper (No. 151) which argued that the absence of bilateral political dialogue

---

[27] Lord Carrington resigned as Foreign Secretary following the outbreak of the Falklands War in April 1982.

Preface

was no longer in Britain's interest and was unlikely to persuade the Soviets to 'moderate their policies in ways we should like'. The main thrust of the paper, endorsed by Mr Broomfield, argued for political dialogue to be re-established on three levels—Foreign Minister, Deputy Foreign Minister and Political Director—with other exchanges at higher and lower levels on an *ad hoc* basis when in the British interest.

The idea of a visit by the Prime Minister was also mooted, with Mr Manning noting: 'Her ability to present the Western case forcefully and lucidly whilst eschewing false bonhomie, would be an educative process for the Soviet leadership.'[28] Given that East-West political exchanges were almost certain to increase it was considered important that a strong, independent British voice be heard in Moscow (No. 151). Sir J. Bullard was in no doubt as to who would carry off the honours in any meeting with Brezhnev (No. 156). In his valedictory despatch Sir C. Keeble noted that Britain was well placed to take the lead on the Western side in the East-West relationship—'the Prime Minister's standing is high and her words will carry weight here' (No. 157). But in the final analysis, proposing that Mrs Thatcher visit Moscow was felt to be a step too far and the idea was dropped from the final paper, entitled 'East-West Political Relations: UK policy towards the Soviet Union', sent by Mr Pym to No. 10 in September 1982. The paper also included a proposal to re-establish cultural exchanges in order to project Western values to the Soviet people.

Sir Iain Sutherland, on his arrival in Moscow (as Ambassador) in September 1982, noted his surprise and concern at the extent to which Britain had cut herself off from the USSR when Soviet policy was both more active and hesitant than for some time, economic difficulties more acute, the pace of social change accelerating and a new leadership imminent (No. 164). Mr Broomfield thought a number of developments had enhanced the UK's importance in Soviet eyes—pessimism over relations with the US, the cooling of relations with France since the accession of President François Mitterrand and uncertainty over the policies of Chancellor Helmut Kohl, the independent line the UK had taken from the US over the pipeline dispute, and the victory in the Falklands campaign (No. 163). Mr Pym was due to meet the Prime Minister to convince her that the change in tack was necessary but within the FCO there remained doubt over whether his arguments would carry the day. The strident position adopted by Mrs Thatcher towards the Soviet Union caused disquiet. Mr Walden, head of the Planning Staff, expressed his concern about the 'tough stuff' the Planners found themselves drafting for the Prime Minister's speeches on the Soviet Union (No. 166).

Mr Pym met Mrs Thatcher for the long awaited discussion on East-West relations following his return from President Brezhnev's funeral. Disappointingly for the FCO, she opposed the idea of a senior British minister visiting Moscow and expressed scepticism about the utility of expanding political contacts or cultural relations, believing they might harm Britain's whole stance on East-West relations. She was prepared to contemplate a visit at a lower level, provided that it had a clear purpose, was consistent with the various undertakings given in the wake of

---

[28] Mrs Thatcher met the Soviet Prime Minister, Alexei Kosygin, at Moscow airport in December 1979 during a refuelling stop *en route* to the G7 meeting in Tokyo. When Mr Kosygin tried to suggest that the boat people fleeing communist Vietnam were all drug-takers or criminals Mrs Thatcher asked disbelievingly: 'What? One million of them? Is communism so bad that a million have to take drugs or steal to live?' Margaret Thatcher, *The Downing Street Years* (London: HarperCollins, 1993), pp.65-6.

UK-Soviet Relations, 1979-82

the Afghan invasion and that the US had advance notice (No. 172). This led to the prospect of talks between the Planning Staffs in the two Foreign Ministries and an invitation for Deputy Foreign Minister Ryzhov to visit London in 1983. However the 'big freeze' was far from over.

The volume closes with a despatch from Sir I. Sutherland (No. 177) reflecting on the legacy of the Brezhnev years. The Ambassador concluded that under President Brezhnev the Bolshevik Revolution had finally run out of steam. In foreign policy the Soviet Union in 1982 was back to where it had stood in 1964: facing a new arms race, with weaknesses in the socialist camp. Economic growth had brought higher living standards and supported an expensive foreign and military policy but little had been done to overcome structural weaknesses, and inefficiency and inertia in the system. Soviet society had turned from Communism to consumerism, and grown cynical and apathetic. Ultimately, the man who had led the Soviet Union for the last 18 years was 'an uninspiring and at the end an unloved leader who has left more problems than he solved'.

Acknowledgements

In accordance with the Parliamentary announcement cited in the Introduction to the Series, the Editors have had the customary freedom in the selection and arrangement of the documents including full access to all classes of FCO documentation. There has, however, in the case of the present volume been one instance when it has been necessary to excise certain passages from a document. These omissions are indicated with square brackets and appropriate footnote references.

Some of the official documents published or cited in this volume are not yet in the public domain and will not be transferred to The National Archives (TNA) in advance of their due date, but they have been marked for permanent preservation and will be released in the usual way. Documents not released at the time the volume went to press (for 1981 and 1982) have been given their departmental file reference. Documents for 1979 and 1980 have also been given their TNA reference. Documents quoted or cited in footnotes have only been accorded a file reference where it differs from that of the printed document to which they refer. Telegrams have been given the date on which they were sent, which in a small number of cases differs from the date when they were drafted. Omitted from the headings and formulations at the end of documents are some classifications regarding administration and circulation but the main security classifications are included. Some minor typing errors have been corrected.

The main source of documentation in this volume has been the archives of the FCO held, pending their transfer to TNA, by the Information Management Department (IMD). I should like to thank Simon Fraser, the Permanent Under-Secretary, and Christine Ferguson, Head of IMD, for their encouragement and support of the project. I am also grateful for the help given by Martin Tucker, the Head of Corporate Records, and members of his team including Rachel Cox, Caroline Puddephat and Elaine King.

The volume also draws on records of the Cabinet Office and the Prime Minister's Office, and I am grateful to Roger Smethurst, Tessa Stirling, Sally Falk and Chris Grindall, in the Cabinet Office for their assistance. The Cabinet Secretary, Sir Gus O'Donnell, has kindly given permission for the publication and citation of documents from the Cabinet Office and Prime Minister's collections.

Preface

I am grateful to Tony Bishop, Jim Daly and Elizabeth Teague for their help and advice, and to all those current and former members of FCO Historians who have helped on this volume, in particular Patrick Salmon, Chief Historian, and Gill Bennett, former Chief Historian of the FCO. Additional valuable assistance has been provided by Rosalind Pulvermacher, Giles Rose and Jane Crellin. Above all, I am grateful to Dr Stephen Twigge, formerly of FCO Historians, for undertaking the original document selection and initial editorial work on the volume.

RICHARD SMITH
September 2011

ABBREVIATIONS FOR PRINTED SOURCES

Cmnd.	Command Paper (London)
CWIHP *Bulletin*	Cold War International History Project *Bulletin* (Washington: Woodrow Wilson International Center for Scholars, 1992f)
DBPO	*Documents on British Policy Overseas* (London: HMSO/ Routledge, 1984f.)
Parl. Debs., 5th ser., H. of C.	*Parliamentary Debates (Hansard), Fifth Series, House of Commons, Official Report* (London, 1909f.)
Parl. Debs., 5th ser., H. of L.	*Parliamentary Debates (Hansard), Fifth Series, House of Lords, Official Report* (London, 1909f.)
Public Papers: Carter (1979, 1980-81)	*Public Papers of the Presidents of the United States: Jimmy Carter* (Washington, 1981-82). Also available online through *The American Presidency Project* at: http://www.presidency.ucsb.edu/.
Public Papers: Reagan (1981, 1982)	*Public Papers of the Presidents of the United States: Ronald Reagan* (Washington, 1982-83). Also available online through *The American Presidency Project* at: http://www.presidency.ucsb.edu/.

ABBREVIATED DESIGNATIONS

2ED	Second European Department, Soviet MFA
ACDA	Arms Control and Disarmament Agency
AFP	*Agence France-Presse*
ALCOA	The Aluminium Company of America
APS	Assistant Private Secretary
ARMCO	American Rolling Mills Corporation (US Steel Company)
ASEAN	Association of South East Asian Nations
AUS	Assistant Under-Secretary of State
BAOR	British Army of the Rhine
BTU	British thermal unit
CBM	confidence building measures
CDE	Conference on Disarmament in Europe
CMD&D	Conference on Military Détente and Disarmament
CMEA	Council for Mutual Economic Assistance
COCOM	Coordinating Committee for Multilateral Export Controls
COI	Central Office of Information
COMECON	Council for Mutual Economic Assistance
CPSU	Communist Party of the Soviet Union
CRD	Cultural Relations Department, FCO
CSCE	Conference on Security and Cooperation in Europe
CTB	Comprehensive Test Ban
DOD	US Department of Defense
DoE	Department of the Environment
DOP	Cabinet's Oversea and Defence Committee
DRA	Democratic Republic of Afghanistan
DUS	Deputy Under-Secretary of State
EC	European Community
ECD(E)	European Community Department (External), FCO
ECGD	Export Credit Guarantee Department
EEC	European Economic Community
EESD	East European and Soviet Department, FCO
ERD	Economic Relations Department, FCO
ESSD	Energy Science and Space Department, FCO
FBS	forward based systems
FCO	Foreign and Commonwealth Office
FNLA	*Frente Nacional de Libertação de Angola*
FRD	Financial Relations Department
FRG	Federal Republic of Germany
FRUS	Foreign Relations of the United States
GLCM	ground launched cruise missile
HMT	Her Majesty's Treasury
IAEA	International Atomic Energy Agency
ICBM	Intercontinental ballistic missile
INF	Intermediate range nuclear forces
IOC	International Olympic Committee
IPD	Information Policy Department, FCO
JIC	Joint Intelligence Committee
LDC	less developed countries
MBFR	Mutual and Balanced Force Reductions
MED	Middle East Department, FCO
MFA	Ministry of Foreign Affairs
MIFT	My Immediate Following Telegram
MIPT	My Immediate Preceding Telegram
MOD	Ministry of Defence
MPLA	*Movimento Popular de Libertação de Angola*
MX	missile experimental
NAC	North Atlantic Council (NATO)
NAM	Non-Aligned Movement
NATO	North Atlantic Treaty Organisation
NENAD	Near East and North Africa Department, FCO
NNA	Neutral and Non-Aligned
NOFUN	No First Use of Nuclear Weapons
NSC	US National Security Council
OD	Cabinet's Oversea and Defence Committee
ODA	Overseas Development Administration
OECD	Organisation of Economic Cooperation and Development
OID	Overseas Information Department, FCO

UK-Soviet Relations, 1979-82

OPEC	Organisation of Petroleum Exporting Countries	START	Strategic Arms Reduction Talks
PAP	*Polska Agencja Prasowa* (Polish News Agency)	Telno	telegram number
		TNF	Theatre Nuclear Forces
PDRY	People's Democratic Republic of Yemen	TRED	Trade Relations and Export Department, FCO
POCO	Political Cooperation (EU)	TUR	telegram under reference
PPS	Principal Private Secretary	UIP	United International Press
PQ	Parliamentary Question	UKDEL	United Kingdom Delegation
PS	Private Secretary	UKMIS	United Kingdom Mission
PUS	Permanent Under-Secretary of State	UNDP	United Nations Development Programme
RSFSR	Russian Socialist Federative Soviet Republic	UNGA	United Nations General Assembly
SAD	South Asia Department, FCO	UNHCR	United Nations High Commission for Refugees
SALT	Strategic Arms Limitation Treaty	UNITA	*União Nacional para a Independência Total de Angola*
SCG	Special Consultative Group (NATO)		
SCR	Security Council Resolution (UN)	UNSSOD	United Nations Special Session on Disarmament
SLCM	submarine launched cruise missile	USA	United States of America
		USSR	Union of Soviet Socialist Republics
SPC	Senior Political Committee (NATO)	VS	Verbatim Series, COI
SSBN	Ship Submersible Ballistic Nuclear (submarine)	YAR	Yemen Arab Republic

LIST OF PERSONS

Abrasimov, Petr, Soviet Ambassador, Berlin, 1962-71, 1975-83
Acland, Sir Antony, Permanent Under-Secretary, FCO, 1982-86
Adams, William, AUS, FCO, 1980-84
Afanasiev, Viktor, Editor-in-Chief, *Pravda*, 1976-89
Alexander, Michael, Prime Minister's Private Secretary for Overseas Affairs, 1979-81
Alexandrov, I. 'Pravda journalist' (pseudonym for officially sponsored articles)
Amin, Asadullah, Head of KAM (Afghan secret police)
Amin, Hafizullah, Prime Minister and President of Afghanistan, Sept-Dec 1979
Andreani, Gilles, Director of the Policy Planning Staff, French MFA
Andropov, Yuri, Chairman of the KGB, 1967-82; General-Secretary of the CPSU, 1982-84
Arafat, Yasser, Chairman of the Palestine Liberation Organisation, 1969-2004
Arbatov, Georgii, Director of the Institute of US and Canadian Studies, Russian Academy of Sciences, 1967-95
Archer, Graham, South Asian Department, FCO, 1979-81
Armstrong, Sir Robert, Secretary to the Cabinet, 1979-87
Atkins, Sir Humphrey, Lord Privy Seal, 1981-82
Baker, James, White House Chief of Staff, 1981-85
Barre, Mohamed Siad, President of Somalia, 1969-91
Bayne, Nicholas, Head of the Economic Relations Department, FCO, 1979-82
Beel, Graham, Research Department, Soviet Section, FCO, 1972-94
Begin, Menachem, Prime Minister of Israel, 1977-83
Benyahia, Mohammed Seddik, Algerian Foreign Minister, 1979-82
Berlinguer, Enrico, General-Secretary of the Italian Communist Party, 1972-84
Bishop, K. Anthony, Research Department, Soviet Section, FCO, 1961-98
Blaker, Peter, Minister of State, FCO, 1979-81
Bone, Roger, APS to the Secretary of State for Foreign and Commonwealth Affairs, 1982-84
Braithwaite, Rodric, Head of Planning Staff, 1979-80; AUS, FCO, 1980-82
Brement, Marshall, staff member with the US National Security Council (USSR/East Europe/East-West relations), 1979-81
Brewster Jr., Kingman, US Ambassador, London, 1977-81
Brezhnev, Leonid, General-Secretary of the CPSU, 1964-82
Bridges, Thomas Edward, 2nd Baron Bridges, DUS, FCO, 1979-83
Brooke Turner, Alan, Minister, British Embassy, Moscow, 1979-82
Broomfield, Nigel, Head of the East European and Soviet Department, FCO, May 1981-85
Broucher, David Stuart, East European and Soviet Department, FCO, 1978-83
Brown, Harold, US Secretary of Defense, 1977-80
Brzezinski, Zbigniew, US National Security Advisor, 1977-81
Buckley, James, US Under-Secretary of State for International Security, 1981-82
Bullard, Julian (later Sir), DUS Europe, 1979-82; Deputy to the Permanent Under-Secretary and Political Director, FCO, 1982-84
Burges Watson, Richard, Head of the Trade Relations and Export Department, FCO, 1978-81
Burns, Robert Andrew, Private Secretary to the Permanent Under-Secretary, 1979-82

UK-Soviet Relations, 1979-82

Burt, Richard, Assistant Secretary for European Affairs, US State Department, 1981-83

Burton, Michael, Head of the South Asia Department, FCO, 1981-84

Butler, Sir Michael, UK Permanent Representative to the EC, Brussels, 1979-85

Bykov, Vladimir, Minister-Counsellor, Soviet Embassy, London, 1978-83

Callaghan, James, Prime Minister, 1976-79

Carrillo, Santiago, General-Secretary of the Spanish Communist Party, 1960-82

Carington, Peter, 6th Baron Carrington, Secretary of State for Foreign and Commonwealth Affairs, 1979- April 1982

Carter, James Earl 'Jimmy', President of the United States, 1977-81

Chatty, Habib, Secretary-General of the Islamic Conference, 1979-84

Chernenko, Konstantin, Member of the Soviet Politburo, 1976-84

Chernenko, Mr, Head of the Press Department, Soviet MFA

Chevènement, Jean-Pierre, French Minister of Research and Industry, 1981-83

Cheysson, Claude, French Foreign Minister, 1981-84

Christopher, Warren, US Deputy Secretary of State, 1977-81

Clifford, Clark, former US Defense Secretary and Presidential Emissary to India, 1980-81

Coles, (Arthur) John, Head of the South Asian Department, FCO, 1980-81; Prime Minister's Private Secretary for Overseas Affairs, Dec 1981-84

Cooper, Richard, US Under-Secretary of State for Economic Affairs, 1977-81

Coon, Jane, US Deputy Assistant Secretary of State, 1979-81

Cornish, James, Deputy Head of Planning Staff, FCO, 1979-80

Cortazzi, Henry, DUS, FCO, 1975-80

Cresson, Edith, French Minister of Agriculture, 1981-83

de Cuellar, Javier Perez, UN Secretary-General's Personal Representative on Afghanistan, April-Dec 1981; Secretary-General of the United Nations, 1982-92

Czyrek, Jozef, Polish Foreign Minister, 1980-82

Daoud Khan, HRH Mohammad, President of Afghanistan, 1973-78

Dean, Lesley, Second Secretary, British Embassy, Moscow, 1979-81

Deaver, Michael, White House Deputy Chief of Staff, 1981-85

Demirel, Suleyman, Prime Minister of Turkey, 1979-80

Desai, Morarji, Prime Minister of India, 1977-79

Dobrosielski, Marian, Polish Deputy Foreign Minister

Dobrynin, Anatoly, Soviet Ambassador, Washington, 1962-86

Dole, Bob, Republican Senator from Kansas, 1969–1996

Dolgov, Vyacheslav, Minister-Counsellor, Soviet Embassy, London, 1982-84

Dost, Shah Mohammad, Minister of Foreign Affairs, Afghanistan, 1979-86

Downing, David, Counsellor (Scientific), British Embassy, Moscow, 1978-81

Dubček, Alexander, General-Secretary of the Czechoslovak Communist Party, 1968-69

Duncan, Michael John, Counsellor, British Embassy, Moscow, 1982-83

Eagleburger, Larry, US Under-Secretary of State for Political Affairs, 1982-84

Falin, Valentin, Deputy Head of the International Information Department, Communist Party of the Soviet Union, 1978-83

Fall, Brian, Head of the East European and Soviet Department, 1980-81, PPS to the Secretary of State for Foreign and Commonwealth Affairs, May 1981-84

Fenn, Nicholas, Head of the News Department, FCO, 1979-82

Fergusson, Ewen, AUS (Europe), FCO, 1978-82

Follows, Sir Denis, Chairman of the British Olympic Association, 1977-83

List of Persons

Foot, Michael, Leader of the Opposition, 1980-83
Forlani, Arnaldo, Prime Minister of Italy, 1980-81
François-Poncet, Jean, French Minister of Foreign Affairs, 1978-81
Frost, Ellen, Deputy Assistant Secretary, US Defense Department, 1977-81
Gailani, Sayed Ahmad, Chairman of the National Islamic Front of Afghanistan, 1979-
Gandhi, Indira, Prime Minister of India, 1980-84
Garside, Roger, Deputy Head of Planning Staff, FCO, April 1980-81
Genscher, Hans-Dietrich, Foreign Minister and Vice Chancellor, FRG, 1974-92
Gierek, Edward, General Secretary of the Polish United Workers' Party, 1970-80
Giles, Frank, Editor of the *Sunday Times*, 1981-83
Gillmore, David, AUS, FCO, 1981-83
Gilmore, Sir Ian, Lord Privy Seal, 1979-81
Giscard d'Estaing, Valéry, President of the French Republic, 1974-81
Glaspie, April, US Embassy, London, 1977-81
Glitman, Maynard, US Deputy Chief of Mission to NATO, 1977-81
Goodison, Alan, AUS, FCO, 1981-83
Gordon, John, First Secretary and Cultural Attaché, British Embassy, Moscow, 1980-82
Gordon Lennox, Lord Nicholas, AUS, FCO, 1979-84
Gotlieb, Allan, Under Secretary, Canadian Department of External Affairs, 1977-81; Canadian Ambassador to Washington, 1981-89
Graham, Sir John, DUSS, FCO, 1980-82; UK Permanent Representative to NATO, 1982-86
Green, Andrew, Economic Relations Department, FCO, 1979-82
Grinevsky, Oleg, Head of the Near East Department, Soviet MFA
Gromyko, Andrei, Soviet Foreign Minister, 1957-85
Gusarov, Viktor, First Secretary, Second European Department, Soviet MFA, 1979-82
Gusaryev, Y. P., Interpreter, Soviet MFA
Gventsadze, German, Counsellor/Interpreter, Second European Department, Soviet MFA,
Haig, Alexander, US Secretary of State, 1981-July 1982
Hailsham of St Marylebone, Lord, Lord Chancellor, 1979-87
Hampson, Stuart, PPS to Secretary of State for Trade, 1980-82
Hartman, Arthur, US Ambassador, Moscow, 1981-87
Havers, Sir Michael, Attorney-General, 1979-87
Healey, Denis, Deputy Leader of the Opposition, 1980-83
Heap, Peter, Head of the Energy, Science and Space Department, FCO, 1980-83
Helms, Senator Jesse, Chairman of the Senate Committee on Agriculture, Nutrition and Forestry, 1981-87
Henderson, Sir Nicholas, British Ambassador, Washington, 1979-82
Heseltine, Michael, Secretary of State for the Environment, 1979-83
Hibbert, Sir Reginald, British Ambassador, Paris, 1979-82
Hillier-Fry, William Norman, British Ambassador, Kabul, 1979-81
Howell, David, Secretary of State for Energy, 1979-81
Howell, Michael, Head of Chancery and Consul, British Embassy, Kabul, 1978-81
Hua Guofeng, Prime Minister of China, 1976-80
Hulse, Christopher, Defence Department, FCO, 1981-83
Humfrey, Charles, Private Secretary to Douglas Hurd, 1979-81

UK-Soviet Relations, 1979-82

Hurd, Douglas, Minister of State, FCO, 1979-83
Hussein, Saddam, President of Iraq, 1979-2003
Ilychev, Leonid, Soviet Deputy Foreign Minister, 1965-86
Jackson, Elizabeth, Second Secretary, British Embassy, Moscow, 1981
James, Cynlais (Kenneth), Minister, British Embassy, Paris, 1976-81; British Ambassador, Warsaw, 1981-83
Jaruzelski, General Wojciech, Prime Minister of Poland, 1981-85
Jay, Michael, Private Secretary to the Permanent Under-Secretary of State, 1982-85
Jøergensen, Anker, Prime Minister of Denmark, 1975-82
Johnson, David, East European and Soviet Department, 1978-82
Joseph, Sir Keith, Secretary of State for Industry, 1979-81
Kádár, János, General Secretary of the Hungarian Communist Party, 1956-88
Kania, Stanislaw, General-Secretary of the Polish Communist Party, 1980-81
Karmal, Babrak, Prime Minister of Afghanistan, 1979-81, President of Afghanistan, 1979-86
Keeble, Sir Curtis, British Ambassador, Moscow, 1978-September 1982
Keline, Vladimir, Charge d'Affairs, Soviet Embassy, London, 1978-81
Kennedy, Richard, US Ambassador to the International Atomic Energy Agency and Special Adviser to the Secretary of State on Non-Proliferation Policy, 1982-93
Khomeini, Ayatollah Ruhollah, Supreme Leader of the Islamic Republic of Iran, 1979-89
Kirilenko, Andrey Paulovich, Member of the Soviet Politburo, 1957-82
Kirkpatrick, Jeane, US Ambassador to the UN, 1981-85
Kohl, Helmut, German Chancellor, 1982-98
Komplektov, Viktor, Head of US Department, Soviet MFA, 1979-82
Kornienko, Georgi, Soviet First Deputy Foreign Minister, 1977-85
Kostandov, Leonid, Soviet Deputy Prime Minister, 1980-84
Kosygin, Aleksei, Soviet Premier, 1964-80
Kovalev, Anatoly, Soviet Deputy Foreign Minister, 1971-85
Kuzentsov, Vasily, First Deputy Chairman of the Presidium of the Supreme Soviet, 1977-85
Kvitsinky, Yuli, Soviet Chief Negotiator, Intermediate Nuclear Forces Treaty, 1981-83
Kypriano, Spyros, President of Cyprus, 1977-88
Lankester, Tim, Private Secretary to the Prime Minister, 1979-81
Lavers, Richard, South Asian Department, 1977-81
Leusse, Bruno de, Secretary General, French MFA, 1979-81
Lever, Paul, APS to the Secretary of State for Foreign and Commonwealth Affairs, 1978–81
López Portillo, José, President of Mexico, 1976-82
Louis Jr., John J., US Ambassador, London, 1981-82
Lucas, The Hon Ivor, British Ambassador, Muscat, 1979-81
Luce, Richard, Parliamentary Under-Secretary of State, FCO, 1979-81; Minister of State, FCO, 1981-82
Lunkov, Nikolai, Soviet Ambassador, London, 1973-80
Lyne, Roderic, APS to the Secretary of State for Foreign and Commonwealth Affairs, 1979-82

List of Persons

Macgregor, John, Private Secretary to Lord Trefgarne and Malcolm Rifkind, 1981-83

McLennan, Gordon, General-Secretary of the Communist Party of Great Britain, 1976-89

Maitland, Sir Donald, Deputy to the Permanent Under-Secretary of State, 1979-80

Makarov, Visily, Principal Private Secretary to Mr Gromyko

Malfatti, Francesco, Italian Minister for Foreign Affairs, 1979-80

Mallaby, Christopher, Head of the East European and Soviet Department, 1979-80; Head of Planning Staff, Sept 1980-82

Maltsev, Viktor, Soviet First Deputy Foreign Minister, 1978-86

Manning, David, East European and Soviet Department, FCO, 1980-83

Marcos, Imelda, First Lady of the Philippines, 1965-86

Mazur, Yuri, First Secretary, Second European Department, Soviet MFA

Mengistu, Haile Mariam, Head of State/President of Ethiopia, 1977-91

Messe, Edwin, Counsellor to President Reagan and NSC member, 1981-85

Miers, Henry, Head of the Middle East Department, FCO, 1979-83

Miles, Richard, Head of the Near East and North Africa Desk, FCO, 1980-84

Mitterrand, Francois, President of the French Republic, 1981-85

Mladenov, Petar, Bulgarian Foreign Minister, 1971-89

Moberly, John Campbell, AUS, FCO, 1979-82

Moi, Daniel arap, President of Kenya, 1978-2002

Mondale, Walter, US Vice-President, 1977-81

Monro, Hector, Minister for Sport, 1979-81

Montgomery, Alan, East European and Soviet Department, 1981-82

Morgan, John, Head of the Cultural Relations Department, FCO, 1972-80

Morris, Robert, Minister for Economic Affairs, US Embassy, London, 1978-81

Munro, Colin, Private Secretary to Minister of State, FCO, 1979-81

Murray, Donald, AUS, FCO, 1977-80

Murrell, Geoffrey, Research Department, Soviet Section, FCO, 1978-83

Muskie, Edmund, US Secretary of State, 1980-81

Needham, Geoffrey, Private Secretary to the Secretary of State for the Environment

Norbury, Brian, PPS to the Secretary of State for Defence, 1979–81

Nott, John, Secretary of State for Defence, 1981-83

Nudel, Ida, Soviet human rights activist

Orlov, Yuri, Soviet nuclear physicist, dissident and a human rights activist

Osborn, John, Conservative MP for Sheffield Hallam, 1959-87

Owen, Dr David, Secretary of State for Foreign and Commonwealth Affairs, 1977-79

Pakenham, The Hon Michael, First Secretary, British Embassy, Washington, 1978-83

Palliser, Sir Michael, Permanent Under-Secretary, FCO, 1975-82

Palme, Olof, Prime Minister of Sweden 1969-76, 1982-86; UN Special Emissary for Iran and Iraq, 1980-82

Panjshiri, Ghulam, Minister of Public Works, Afghanistan, 1978-79

Papandreou, Andreas, Prime Minister of Greece, 1981-89

Parkinson, Cecil, Minister for Trade, Department of Trade, 1979-81

Parsons, Sir Anthony, UK Permanent Representative to the UN, 1979-82

Patolichev, Nikolai, Soviet Foreign Trade Minister, 1958-85

UK-Soviet Relations, 1979-82

Pavlovsky, Ivan, Commander-in-Chief of Soviet Ground Forces

Percy, Charles, US Senator and Chairman of the Foreign Relations Committee, 1981-85

Petrovsky, Vladimir, Director of the International Organisations Department, Soviet MFA, 1979-86

Pham Van Dong, Prime Minister of the Socialist Republic of Vietnam, 1976-87

Pincher, Chapman, journalist and author

Pompidou, Georges, President of the French Republic, 1969-74

Ponomarev, Boris, Head of the International Department of the CPSU Central Committee, 1955-86

Popov, Viktor, Soviet Ambassador, London, 1980-86

Posilyagin, Nikolai, Counsellor, Soviet Embassy, London, 1982-84

Puja, Frigyes, Hungarian Foreign Minister, 1973-83

Puzanov, Aleksandr, Soviet Ambassador, Kabul, 1972-79

Pym, Francis, Secretary of State for Foreign and Commonwealth Affairs, April 1982-83

Qaboos, bin Said al Said, Sultan of Oman, 1970-

Qadhafi, Colonel Muamarr, Leader of Libya, 1969-2011

Qotbzadeh, Sadegh, Iranian Foreign Minister, 1979-80

Rakowski, Mieczyslaw, Polish Deputy Prime Minister, 1981-88

Reagan, Ronald, President of the United States, 1981-89

Renwick, Robin, Counsellor and Head of Chancery, British Embassy, Washington, 1981-84

Rifkind, Malcolm, Parliamentary Under-Secretary of State, FCO, 1982-83; Minister of State, FCO, 1983-86

Rose, Sir Clive, UK Permanent Representative to NATO, 1979-82

Ruhfus, Dr Jurgen, FRG Ambassador, London, 1980-85

Ryzhov, Nikita, Soviet Deputy Foreign Minister, 1980-86

Sadat, Anwar Al, President of Egypt, 1970-81

Sakharov, Andrei, Soviet nuclear physicist and human rights activist

dos Santos, José Eduardo, President of Angola, 1979-

Schmidt, Helmut, German Chancellor, 1974-82

Semeonov, Viacheslav, Deputy Head of the Second European Department, Soviet MFA

Sharansky, Anatoly, Soviet-Israeli human rights activist

Sheinwald, Nigel, East European and Soviet Department, FCO, 1979-83

Shultz, George, US Secretary of State, July 1982-89

Shvedov, Aleksei, Head of the First African Department, Soviet MFA

Shahi, Agha, Foreign Minister of Pakistan, 1978-82

Sissons, Peter, television journalist

Smith, Sir Howard, British Ambassador, Moscow, 1976-78

Smith, Roland, East European and Soviet Department, FCO, 1982-83

Soames, Lord, Governor of Southern Rhodesia, 1979-80; Lord President of the Council and Leader of the House of Lords, 1979-81

Solomentsev, Mikhail, Chairman of the Council of Ministers of the Russian SFSR, 1971-83

Stirn, Olivier, Minister of State, French MFA, 1978-81

Strathcona, Lord, Defence Minister, 1979-81

Sukhodrev, Viktor, Interpreter, Second European Department, Soviet MFA

List of Persons

Suslov, Mikhail, member of the Politburo and Secretariat of the CPSU, Head of Ideology, 1947-82

Suslov, Vladimir, Head of the Second European Department, Soviet MFA

Sutherland, Sir Iain, British Ambassador, Moscow, September 1982-1985

Tabeyev, Fikryat, Soviet Ambassador, Kabul, 1979-86

Taraki, Nur Muhammad, President of Afghanistan, April-Sept 1979

Taylor, Sir John, British Ambassador, Bonn, 1981-84

Thatcher, Margaret, Prime Minister, 1979-90

Thomas, Derek, Minister, British Embassy, Washington, 1979-84

Thomson, Adam, Third Secretary, British Embassy, Moscow, 1981-83

Thomson, Sir John, High Commissioner, New Delhi, 1977-82; UK Permanent Representative to the United Nations, 1982-87

Tikhonov, Nikolai, Chairman of the Council of Ministers of the USSR, 1980-85

Tito, Josip Broz, President of the Socialist Federal Republic of Yugoslavia, 1953-80

Tolubko, Vladimir, Soviet Deputy Minister of Defence and Commander-in-Chief of the Soviet Strategic Missile Forces, 1972-84

Trefgarne, Lord, Parliamentary Under-Secretary of State, FCO, 1981-82

Troyanovsky, Oleg, Soviet Permanent Representative to the United Nations, 1977-86

Trudeau, Pierre, Prime Minister of Canada, 1968-79, 1980-84

Uspensky, N, Second Secretary/Interpreter, Soviet Embassy, London, 1977-82

Ustinov, Dimitriy, Soviet Defence Minister, 1976-84

Vance, Cyrus, US Secretary of State, 1977-80

Van Well, Günther, State Secretary, FRG MFA, 1977-81

Vest, George, US Assistant Secretary of State for European Affairs, 1977-81

Vile, Martin, Private Secretary to Sir Robert Armstrong, 1979-80

Walden, George, PPS to the Secretary of State for Foreign and Commonwealth Affairs, 1978-82; Head of Planning Staff, July 1982-83

Waldheim, Dr Kurt, UN Secretary-General, 1972-82

Walker, Peter, Minister for Agriculture, Fisheries and Food, 1979-83

Warnke, Paul, Director of the US Arms Control and Disarmament Agency, 1977-78

Watson Jr., Thomas, US Ambassador, Moscow, 1979-81

Watt, David, journalist, *The Times*

Weinberger, Casper, US Defense Secretary, 1981-87

Weston, P. John, Counsellor, British Embassy, Washington, 1978-81; Head of the Defence Department, FCO, 1981-84

White, William, Head of the South Asian Department, FCO, 1978-1980

Whitelaw, William, Home Secretary, 1979-83

Whitmore, Clive, PPS to the Prime Minister, 1979-82

Wilkinson, Richard Denys, Planning Staff, 1980-83

Wilson, Sir Harold, Prime Minister, 1964-70, 1974-76

Wilson, William, Labour MP for Coventry South, 1964-83

Wright, David, Private Secretary to Sir Robert Armstrong, 1980-82

Wright, Patrick, DUSS, FCO, 1982-84

Wright, Sir Oliver, British Ambassador, Bonn, 1975-81

Wood, Andrew, Counsellor and Head of Chancery, British Embassy, Moscow, 1979-82

Wordsworth, Stephen, Second Secretary, British Embassy, Moscow, 1979-81

Zagladin, Vadim, First Deputy Secretary of the International Department of the Central Committee of the CPSU, 1964-88

Zamyatin, Leonid, Chairman of the International Information Department of the Central Committee of the CPSU, 1978-86

Zemskov, Igor, Soviet Deputy Foreign Minister, 1973-82

Zhivkov, Todor, First Secretary of the Bulgarian Communist Party, 1954-89

Zorin, Valerian, Member of the Central Committee of the CPSU

Zia-ul-Haq, Muhammad, President of Pakistan, 1978-88

DOCUMENT SUMMARIES

CHAPTER I

7 December 1979 – 23 November 1981

	NAME	DATE	MAIN SUBJECT	PAGE
		1979		
1	TO SIR C. KEEBLE Moscow	7 Dec	'British policy in East-West Relations.'	1
2	MR MALLABY EESD FCO	21 Dec	Minute to Mr Braithwaite: 'The Prevention of Soviet Expansion in the Developing World.'	6
3	MR HILLIER-FRY Kabul Tel. No. 284	27 Dec	Reports on Soviet military intervention in Afghanistan and speculation that President Amin has been overthrown.	7
4	MR LANKESTER 10 Downing Street	28 Dec	Letter to Mr Lever detailing a telephone conversation between President Carter and Mrs Thatcher concerning developments in Afghanistan.	8
5	SIR N. HENDERSON Washington Tel. No. 4394	29 Dec	Reports on proposals for Mr Christopher to visit Europe to discuss with allies the Western response to Soviet invasion of Afghanistan.	9
6	SIR N. HENDERSON Washington Tel. No. 4395	29 Dec	Details meeting at State Department and conveys US assessment of events in Afghanistan.	10
7	TO SIR C. KEEBLE Moscow Tel. No. 800	29 Dec	Conveys message from Mrs Thatcher to President Brezhnev concerning Afghanistan.	13
8	SIR N. HENDERSON Washington Tel. No. 4401	29 Dec	Details meeting with Mr Brzezinski concerning President Carter's message to President Brezhnev and Mr Christopher's visit to Europe.	14
9	FOREIGN & COMMONWEALTH OFFICE	29 Dec	Extract from briefing paper for a meeting with Mr Christopher and others on 31 Dec.	15
10	SIR C. KEEBLE Moscow Tel. No. 872	30 Dec	Assesses the situation in Afghanistan as seen from Moscow.	17
11	RECORD OF MEETING FCO	31 Dec	Discussion between UK, US, FRG, Canada, France and Italy concerning future policy and next steps in response to Soviet action in Afghanistan.	19

UK-Soviet Relations, 1979-82

	NAME	DATE	MAIN SUBJECT	PAGE
12	MR BLAKER AND MR BREMENT FCO	31 Dec	Record of a conversation concerning the prospect for insurgency in Afghanistan, the Muslim dimension for propaganda and the renewal of Western credit subsidies.	28
13	MR HURD FCO	31 Dec	Minute to Lord Carrington expressing disappointment at the outcome of the six-power meeting (No. 11).	30
		1980		
14	SIR C. ROSE UKDEL NATO, Brussels Tel. No. 2	1 Jan	Reports NAC meeting with Mr Christopher and possible actions to be taken by the Alliance in response to the Soviet invasion of Afghanistan.	31
15	TO MRS THATCHER 10 Downing Street PM/80/1	2 Jan	Minute from Lord Carrington reporting developments over the holiday period and possible next steps, including a visit to region by the Secretary of State.	33
16	MR HURD AND MR BREWSTER FCO	3 Jan	Record of a meeting at which the US Ambassador supplied the UK with a list of US actions.	34
17	MRS THATCHER AND MR LUNKOV 10 Downing Street	3 Jan	Record of a meeting in which the Soviet Ambassador delivered a message from President Brezhnev stating Soviet action in Afghanistan due to 'acts of external aggression'.	35
18	TO HM REPRESENTATIVES OVERSEAS Guidance Tel. No. 2	3 Jan	Contains text of Mrs Thatcher's message to President Brezhnev and additional points concerning Soviet intervention.	39
19	TO SIR N. HENDERSON Washington Tel. No. 17	3 Jan	Reports the measures HMG is willing to take in response to US Ambassador's démarche (No. 16).	41
20	MR HILLIER-FRY Kabul Tel. No. 12	5 Jan	Details discussions with Soviet Ambassador in Kabul.	44
21	MR HILLIER-FRY Kabul	5 Jan	Details the origins and execution of the Soviet occupation, the formation of a new government and further developments.	45
22	SIR C. ROSE UKDEL NATO, Brussels Tel. No. 11	7 Jan	Reports outcome of Senior Political Committee meeting on Afghanistan.	49
23	MR MALLABY EESD FCO	7 Jan	Minute to Mr White covering a note entitled 'Why did the Soviet Union invade Afghanistan?'	51

Document Summaries

	NAME	DATE	MAIN SUBJECT	PAGE
24	SIR C. KEEBLE Moscow	7 Jan	Annual Review for 1979.	53
25	MR MALLABY FCO	7 Jan	Submission to Mr Fergusson outlining possible measures to be taken against Soviet Union.	58
26	MR ALEXANDER 10 Downing Street	8 Jan	Letter to Mr Lyne conveying Mrs Thatcher's view on participation in the Olympic Games.	59
27	TO MRS THATCHER 10 Downing Street PM/80/4	8 Jan	Minute from Lord Carrington urging stronger action by HMG in the economic field in response to Soviet invasion of Afghanistan.	59
28	SIR C. KEEBLE Moscow	9 Jan	Letter to Mr Fergusson discussing Soviet motives in Afghanistan. Suggests that the invasion could mark substantial reassessment of Soviet policy.	61
29	SIR C. ROSE UKDEL NATO, Brussels Tel. No. 20	9 Jan	Reports that allied consultations have been made more difficult as the US has already announced measures; France, Germany, Italy so far reluctant.	64
30	MR WESTON Washington	10 Jan	Letter to Mr Mallaby discussing the prospects for US-Soviet relations.	66
31	TO MR LUCAS Muscat Tel. No. 99	11 Jan	Reports current activity on Afghanistan in the UN, NATO, EU and the press.	69
32	SIR C. KEEBLE Moscow Tel. No. 30	11 Jan	Suggests this is not the time for anti-Soviet crusade as such, but contends that wedges could be driven between Russia and Eastern European states.	71
33	MR MURRELL Research Department FCO	11 Jan	Minute to Mr Mallaby considering implications for Soviet foreign policy, and the Soviet attitude to détente, of the Soviet invasion of Afghanistan and Western reaction to it.	72
34	TO SIR A. PARSONS UKMIS, New York Tel. No. 46	11 Jan	Relays text of proposed Parliamentary statement on Afghanistan.	75
35	MR ALEXANDER 10 Downing Street	14 Jan	Letter to Mr Lyne reporting a meeting between Warren Christopher and Mrs Thatcher at which text of a message from President Carter was conveyed.	77
36	MR HURD AND MR CHRISTOPHER FCO	14 Jan	Record of meeting covering Western responses to Soviet invasion of Afghanistan.	79

UK-Soviet Relations, 1979-82

	NAME	DATE	MAIN SUBJECT	PAGE
37	PLANNING STAFF FCO	15 Jan	Draft paper outlining Soviet threat to Iran, Yugoslavia and other neighbours.	83
38	SIR C. ROSE UKDEL NATO, Brussels Tel. No. 39	16 Jan	Reports first NATO Council meeting on implications of Soviet invasion of Afghanistan and the gap between US and European reactions.	87
39	MR HESELTINE Department of the Environment	16 Jan	Letter to Lord Carrington regarding a potential boycott of the Olympic Games.	88
40	SIR C. KEEBLE Moscow	16 Jan	Letter to Mr Mallaby suggesting that Soviet invasion offers the West an outstanding opportunity to develop a global policy which exposes the 'basic fallacy' in the Soviet concept of détente.	89
41	TO MRS THATCHER 10 Downing Street PM/80/5	19 Jan	Minute from Lord Carrington detailing the outcome of his visit to Turkey, Saudi Arabia, Oman, Pakistan and India. Contains an enclosure on possible Olympic boycott.	92
42	CABINET DEFENCE AND OVERSEA POLICY COMMITTEE OD(80)1st Meeting	22 Jan	Topics under discussion include the Soviet invasion of Afghanistan and possible responses, including a boycott of the Olympic Games.	96
43	MRS THATCHER 10 Downing Street	26 Jan	Letter to President Carter on measures to be taken against the Soviet Union.	98
44	PLANNING STAFF FCO	28 Jan	Note entitled 'Action on Afghanistan' suggesting support for patriots inside Afghanistan and organisations in exile, with Treaty of Neutrality guaranteed by all states in region.	100
45	SIR C. KEEBLE Moscow Tel. No. 94	30 Jan	Reports on meeting with Mr Zemskov covering Soviet relations with the US.	102
46	MR MALLABY, MR FERGUSSON AND MR BULLARD FCO	30 Jan - 5 Feb	Minutes on the development of dissent in the USSR.	104
47	EAST EUROPEAN AND SOVIET DEPARTMENT FCO	31 Jan	'Soviet Foreign Policy after Afghanistan.'	106
48	MR MALLABY EESD FCO	1 Feb	Minute to Mr Fergusson discussing possible Soviet and Cuban activity in Africa post-Afghanistan and the need to plan against further Soviet expansion.	109

Document Summaries

	NAME	DATE	MAIN SUBJECT	PAGE
49	TO MRS THATCHER 10 Downing Street PM/80/8	1 Feb	Minute from Lord Carrington detailing measures agreed at OD and how these actions can be put into place.	111
50	SIR C. KEEBLE Moscow	8 Feb	'The relationship between the Soviet Union and the United States.'	113
51	SIR N. HENDERSON Washington Tel. No. 696	13 Feb	Reports on the possibility of a four power meeting on Afghanistan.	118
52	SIR N. HENDERSON Washington Tel. No. 749	16 Feb	Discusses relations between Western Europe and USA post-Afghanistan.	119
53	RECORD OF MEETING 10 Downing Street	22 Feb	Mrs Thatcher, Mr Vance and Lord Carrington discuss a possible Olympic boycott.	121
54	TO HM REPRESENTATIVES OVERSEAS Guidance Tel. No. 20	22 Feb	Details EC proposals for a neutral Afghanistan 'to demonstrate that the Soviet Union's professed fears of western intervention in Afghanistan are groundless'.	122
55	MRS THATCHER AND CHANCELLOR SCHMIDT	25 Feb	Record of a discussion on the international situation in the wake of Afghanistan.	123
56	SIR C. KEEBLE Moscow	27 Feb	Letter to Mr Fergusson discussing how future Soviet policy might develop.	128
57	MRS THATCHER 10 Downing Street	3 Mar	Letter to President Carter covering Afghan neutrality as a way of allowing the Soviets to withdraw; the necessity of improving Western defensive capability; increasing aid to Pakistan and Turkey; review of defence policy outside NATO.	131
58	PRESIDENT CARTER Washington	17 Mar	Letter to Mrs Thatcher discussing position in Southwest Asia, Pakistan & Turkey and suggesting allied efforts to restrict high technology transfers.	133
59	TO SIR N. HENDERSON Washington	24 Mar	Letter from Sir D. Maitland enclosing a Planning Staff note on the Afghan neutrality proposal.	135
60	SIR N. HENDERSON Washington	3 Apr	Letter to Sir D. Maitland summarising the Western response to Afghanistan.	137
61	MR JOHNSON EESD FCO	15 Apr	Minute to Mr Mallaby: 'An alternative view of Soviet foreign policy after Afghanistan.'	141
62	LORD CARRINGTON AND MR GROMYKO Vienna	17 May	Record of a discussion of a proposal for Afghan neutrality.	143

xli

UK-Soviet Relations, 1979-82

	NAME	DATE	MAIN SUBJECT	PAGE
63	MR MALLABY EESD FCO	19 May	Minute to Mr Bullard on the prospect of the Soviets entering into negotiations on Afghanistan.	147
64	MR MALLABY EESD FCO	20 May	Minute to Mr Braithwaite recording a meeting between Mrs Thatcher and Lord Carrington on East-West relations and a future paper for OD.	149
65	LORD CARRINGTON OD(80)43 FCO	2 June	Memorandum to OD on the 'Management of East-West Relations', and enclosing a Planning Staff Paper on the same subject.	150
66	TO SIR C. KEEBLE Moscow Tel. No. 342	3 June	Conveys speaking notes for possible meeting with Mr Zemskov on a political settlement in Afghanistan.	157
67	CABINET DEFENCE AND OVERSEA POLICY COMMITTEE OD(80)15th Meeting	5 June	Management of East-West relations: agreement to carry forward recommendations in No. 65.	159
68	SIR C. KEEBLE Moscow Tel. No. 402	11 June	Reports meeting with Mr Zemskov on possibility of Soviet withdrawal from Afghanistan.	162
69	SIR C. KEEBLE Moscow	17 June	Letter to Mr Bullard contending that Soviet troops will remain in Afghanistan for several years and that HMG must prepare policy for long-term management of East-West tension.	163
70	SIR C. KEEBLE Moscow	25 June	Letter to Mr Bullard discussing reports of Soviet troop withdrawals from Afghanistan.	165
71	SIR C. KEEBLE Moscow Tel. No. 457	2 July	Reports meeting with Mr Zemskov on Soviet withdrawal from Afghanistan.	167
72	EAST EUROPEAN AND SOVIET DEPARTMENT FCO	15 July	Memorandum entitled: 'UK Policy in East-West Relations'.	168
73	TO MR BROOKE TURNER Moscow	21 July	Letter from Mr Fergusson reflecting on East-West policy after Afghanistan.	173
74	EAST EUROPEAN AND SOVIET DEPARTMENT FCO	28 July	'Warnings, Actions and Threats to deter Soviet Moves'.	177
75	MR WOOD Moscow	3 Sept	Letter to Mr Johnson giving the current position of KGB activity against dissidents.	181

Document Summaries

	NAME	DATE	MAIN SUBJECT	PAGE
76	TO HM REPRESENTATIVES OVERSEAS Guidance Tel. No. 95	8 Sept	Provides guidance on contacts with Soviet officials; some to be re-established 'without a wholesale return to business as usual'.	182
77	SIR A. PARSONS UKMIS, New York Tel. No. 1341	24 Sept	Reports Lord Carrington's talks with Mr Gromyko at the UN.	185
78	MR GARSIDE Planning Staff FCO	12 Nov	Minute to Mr Mallaby reviewing policy towards Afghanistan and enclosing note by Mr Coles.	186
79	SIR C. KEEBLE Moscow	13 Nov	Memorandum for Heads of Mission Conference analysing Soviet policy towards the West.	190
80	RECORD OF MEETING FCO	19 Nov	Heads of Mission Conference discusses relations with the Soviet Union and Eastern Europe.	193
		1981		
81	SIR C. KEEBLE Moscow	7 Jan	Annual Review for 1980.	195
82	LORD CARRINGTON AND MR POPOV FCO	21 Jan	Record of introductory call by the new Soviet Ambassador.	199
83	TO MR ALEXANDER 10 Downing Street	30 Jan	Letter from Mr Walden concerning relations with the Soviet Union and arguing that a new Cultural Agreement should be agreed as it works to advantage of UK in the battle of ideas.	201
84	TO HM REPRESENTATIVES OVERSEAS Guidance Tel. No. 15	3 Feb	Refers to press comment concerning recent trade talks with the Soviet Union and renewal of Cultural Agreement.	202
85	SIR J. GRAHAM FCO	12 Feb	Minute to Mr Humfrey advocating a new approach to Afghanistan, adopting French proposal for conference of neighbours and other concerned governments, but excluding the Afghanis.	204
86	SIR C. KEEBLE Moscow	5 Mar	Reports President Brezhnev's speech of 23 Feb to the 26th Congress of the Communist Party in which he announced a moratorium on development in Europe of new medium-range nuclear missiles.	207
87	MR ALEXANDER 10 Downing Street	9 Mar	Letter to Mr Walden reporting meeting between Mrs Thatcher and Ambassador Popov, and enclosing message from President Brezhnev proposing arms control measures.	212

xliii

UK-Soviet Relations, 1979-82

	NAME	DATE	MAIN SUBJECT	PAGE
88	TO MR ALEXANDER 10 Downing Street	16 Mar	Letter from Mr Walden proposing that Lord Carrington visit Moscow for meeting with Gromyko.	218
89	SIR C. KEEBLE AND MR GROMYKO Moscow	18 Mar	Record of a discussion covering the arms control moratorium and Afghanistan.	219
90	MR BULLARD AND MR KORNIENKO Moscow	27 Mar	Record of a discussion covering East-West relations, the new US administration, Africa (Angola/Ethiopia), Poland and arms control.	224
91	MR BULLARD FCO	28 Mar	Minute to Mr Burns reporting on his visit to Moscow: 'I got more out of this than I expected'.	230
92	MRS THATCHER 10 Downing Street T 59/81	3 Apr	Letter to President Brezhnev covering Afghanistan, arms control and Poland.	232
93	MR BULLARD AND MR POPOV FCO	9 Apr	Mr Bullard conveys HMG's concern over Warsaw Pact troop manoeuvres and possible military intervention in Poland.	233
94	SOVIET NOTE	23 Apr	Translation of text delivered to Lord Carrington at Northolt airport by Mr Popov stating that Soviet Union was prepared to halt implementation of its current plans for modernisation of medium range nuclear weapons in Europe.	235
95	TO SIR J. TAYLOR Bonn Tel. No. 164	23 Apr	Analysis of Soviet Note (No. 94).	238
96	TO MRS THATCHER 10 Downing Street PM/81/28	20 May	Minute from Lord Carrington proposing to stimulate fresh diplomatic activity on Afghanistan with a two-stage conference.	240
97	SIR M. PALLISER FCO	29 May	Minute to Mr Walden reporting a meeting with Mr Suslov regarding the Popov message (No. 94).	241
98	MR BROOMFIELD EESD FCO	2 June	Submission to Mr Fergusson setting out advantages of Lord Carrington's proposed visit to Moscow; linkage to Afghan initiative and UK Presidency of the EEC.	242
99	MR BISHOP Research Department FCO	8 June	Minute to Mr Johnson analysing the Soviet desire for dialogue and the Popov message (No. 94).	244
100	TO MR ALEXANDER 10 Downing Street	9 June	Letter from Mr Lyne reporting arrangements for proposed international conference on Afghanistan.	245

Document Summaries

	NAME	DATE	MAIN SUBJECT	PAGE
101	MR BROOMFIELD EESD FCO	11 June	Submission to Mr Fergusson on steps that Sir C. Keeble should take to further Lord Carrington's proposed visit to Moscow.	246
102	TO SIR C. KEEBLE Moscow Tel. No. 365	15 June	Instructions concerning Lord Carrington's forthcoming visit to Moscow.	248
103	TO HM REPRESENTATIVES OVERSEAS Tel. No. 81	24 June	Contains text (adopted by European Council) of agreed initiative on Afghanistan for an international conference and two stage solution.	250
104	SIR C. KEEBLE Moscow Tel. No. 373	25 June	Reports on a meeting with Mr Kornienko. Mr Gromyko agrees to meeting with Lord Carrington on the Afghan initiative.	251
105	SIR C. KEEBLE Moscow	25 June	Letter to Lord Carrington outlining the current state of Soviet foreign policy.	252
106	LORD HAILSHAM AND MR POPOV FCO	30 June	Record of a meeting discussing a message from the Supreme Soviet, Israel's bombing of Iraqi nuclear reactor and forthcoming visit of Lord Carrington.	255
107	LORD CARRINGTON AND MR GROMYKO Moscow	6 July	Record of a discussion on the international Afghan initiative.	257
108	LORD CARRINGTON AND MR GROMYKO Moscow	6 July	Record of a discussion covering TNF, CSCE, the Middle East and Poland.	262
109	SIR C. KEEBLE Moscow	16 July	Letter to Mr Broomfield outlining next steps to keep the Afghan proposal alive following Lord Carrington's visit.	268
110	TO HM REPRESENTATIVES OVERSEAS Tel. No. 95	21 July	Encourages Posts to build support for the EU initiative prior to the forthcoming UNGA meeting.	270
111	SIR A. PARSONS UKMIS New York Tel. No. 895	23 Sept	Reports Lord Carrington's meeting with Mr Gromyko at Soviet Mission in New York on US/Soviet relations.	272
112	SIR C. KEEBLE Moscow	29 Sept	Letter to Lord Carrington enclosing a memorandum by Mr Wood: 'The Soviet Union: Will it Change?'	273
113	SIR C. KEEBLE Moscow Tel. No. 657	27 Oct	Reports discussions with Mr Gromyko on Afghanistan, East-West relations, CSCE, Poland, Southern Africa, the Middle East and bilateral affairs.	279

UK-Soviet Relations, 1979-82

	NAME	DATE	MAIN SUBJECT	PAGE
114	SIR C. KEEBLE Moscow	28 Oct	Letter to Mr Broomfield commenting further on No. 113.	284
115	MR BROOKE TURNER Moscow	12 Nov	Letter to Mr Broomfield conveying his impressions of the ageing Soviet leadership.	285
116	LORD TREFGARNE AND MR POPOV FCO	23 Nov	Record of a discussion covering TNF deployment, trade, CSCE and Afghanistan.	287
117	MR GORDON FCO	1 Dec	Summary of his paper for Mr Broomfield on British cultural and information policy in the USSR.	290

CHAPTER II

17 December 1981 – 9 December 1982

	NAME	DATE	MAIN SUBJECT	PAGE
118	SIR C. KEEBLE Moscow	17 Dec	Letter to Mr Fergusson reporting declaration of Martial Law in Poland and speculating on the extent of Soviet involvement.	293
119	MR DUNCAN Moscow	17 Dec	Letter to Mr Roland giving the current position on dissidents.	295
		1982		
120	SIR N. HENDERSON Washington Tel. No. 3	2 Jan	Reports on US measures taken against the Soviet Union and the expectation from Washington of action by the European allies.	297
121	EAST EUROPEAN & SOVIET DEPARTMENT FCO	2 Jan	Brief for Lord Carrington for an informal meeting of foreign ministers in Brussels covering relations with the Soviet Union following events in Poland.	299
122	SIR C. KEEBLE Moscow	7 Jan	Annual Review for 1981.	300
123	MRS THATCHER 10 Downing Street	8 Jan	Letter to President Reagan expressing support for concerted action by the Europeans but concerned that focus should remain on Soviet failures and not on differences between Alliance partners.	302
124	TO SIR N. HENDERSON Washington Tel. No. 59	18 Jan	Expresses concern over US interference with existing European contracts for the Siberian gas pipeline.	303
125	MR GOODISON FCO	20 Jan	Minute to Mr Bullard on British action against the Soviet Union.	304

Document Summaries

	NAME	DATE	MAIN SUBJECT	PAGE
126	SIR N. HENDERSON Washington Tel. No. 206	23 Jan	Reports on US policy towards the Soviet Union and expresses concern that unless Europeans take strong action the Alliance will suffer 'significant damage'.	305
127	TO SIR N. HENDERSON Washington Tel. No. 154	29 Jan	Conveys text of a letter from Mrs Thatcher to President Reagan counselling that an accommodation on existing contracts is essential to allied unity over Poland.	308
128	TO SIR C. KEEBLE Moscow	1 Feb	Letter from Mr Goodison suggesting the Russians are embarrassed by a military takeover in a communist country and uncertain how to proceed.	310
129	MR HEAP Energy, Science & Space Department FCO	3 Feb	Minute to Mr Adams outlining the energy and political implications arising from the West Siberian gas pipeline project.	313
130	LORD TREFGARNE AND MR POPOV FCO	5 Feb	Record of a meeting outlining measures taken by HMG in response to the declaration of Martial Law in Poland.	315
131	TO MR WOOD Moscow	11 Feb	Teleletter from Mr Sheinwald reporting a meeting between Mr Broomfield and Mr Dolgov on the prospects for Anglo-Soviet relations following events in Poland.	317
132	MR BULLARD FCO	19 Feb	Minute to Mr Broomfield recording a meeting with Mr Dolgov.	318
133	LORD TREFGARNE AND MR POPOV FCO	22 Feb	Record of a discussion of latest Soviet initiative on arms control tabled at Vienna, and the US decision to commence production of new generation of chemical weapons.	319
134	MR MALLABY Planning Staff FCO	1 Mar	'The Western Response to the Polish Crisis: Assessment and Prospects.'	320
135	MR BROOMFIELD EESD FCO	2 Mar	Submission to Mr Goodison contending that a wholly negative attitude toward Anglo-Soviet relations would endanger UK's political and economic interests.	325
136	MR GOODISON FCO	2 Mar	Minute to Mr Bullard supporting Mr Broomfield's contention (No. 135) that the measures HMG are taking may be misjudged by the Soviets.	327
137	MR BULLARD FCO	4 Mar	Minute to Mr Macgregor for Lord Trefgarne, endorsing Mr Broomfield's thesis (No. 135) that Anglo-Soviet relations matter.	327

xlvii

UK-Soviet Relations, 1979-82

	NAME	DATE	MAIN SUBJECT	PAGE
138	SIR C. KEEBLE Moscow	4 Mar	'The Relationship between Britain and the Soviet Union.'	328
139	TO SIR C. KEEBLE Moscow	9 Mar	Letter from Mr Broomfield replying to No. 112: 'Your despatch has been a very useful contribution to our own mind-clearing exercise before engaging in these wider issues.'	334
140	SIR C. KEEBLE Moscow	11 Mar	'US/Soviet Relations.'	337
141	LORD TREFGARNE FCO	11 Mar	Minute to Lord Carrington contending that HMG should not distance itself so far from the Russians and advocating a number of possible initiatives and a less frosty attitude to the Soviet Embassy.	342
142	MR WESTON Defence Department FCO	17 Mar	Minute to Mr Gillmore analysing the announcement by President Brezhnev of a Soviet moratorium on SS-20 deployment in European USSR.	343
143	TO SIR C. KEEBLE Moscow	18 Mar	Letter from Mr Broomfield in reply to No. 138. Agrees that proposed initiatives are not very striking but 'should be enough to help sustain the dialogue whose importance you rightly stress'.	345
144	MR MONTGOMERY EESD FCO	8 Apr	Briefing paper for Mr Pym on East-West relations (following the resignation of Lord Carrington).	346
145	TO SIR C. KEEBLE Moscow Tel. No. 210	15 Apr	Reports a meeting between Mr Hurd and Mr Popov covering Moscow's reaction to the Falklands crisis.	349
146	MR BROOKE TURNER Moscow Tel. No. 202	17 Apr	Reports the position of Soviet MFA over the Falklands dispute.	349
147	MR RIFKIND AND MR POPOV FCO	21 Apr	Record of a discussion of the Falklands dispute and bilateral relations.	351
148	SIR C. KEEBLE Moscow Tel. No. 286	18 May	Reports on President Brezhnev's *Komsomol* speech covering nuclear weapons in Europe and strategic arms.	354
149	TO SIR C. KEEBLE Moscow	26 May	Letter from Sir J. Bullard in reply to No. 140.	355
150	TO SIR C. KEEBLE Moscow	24 June	Letter from Mr Broomfield assessing what Soviet youth are really like.	359
151	MR MANNING EESD FCO	2 July	Draft paper: 'East-West Political Relations: UK Policy'.	361

Document Summaries

	NAME	DATE	MAIN SUBJECT	PAGE
152	MR BROOMFIELD EESD FCO	13 July	Draft paper to Sir J. Bullard arguing that HMG should restore a dialogue to put across UK views and assess Soviet thinking at first hand.	364
153	MR WALDEN Planning Staff FCO	22 July	Minute to Mr Smith commenting on No. 151 and agreeing with its general line.	366
154	MR BROOMFIELD EESD FCO	26 Aug	Submission to Sir J. Bullard arguing that HMG should re-establish political dialogue with the Soviets and encourage the Prime Minister to visit Moscow.	367
155	MR THOMAS Washington	27 Aug	Letter to Sir J. Bullard enclosing a paper by Mr Pakenham on 'US Policy towards the Soviet Union: Theory and Practice'.	369
156	SIR J. BULLARD FCO	31 Aug	Minute to Mr Macgregor welcoming the suggestion that Mrs Thatcher be encouraged to visit Moscow to meet President Brezhnev.	380
157	SIR C. KEEBLE Moscow	8 Sept	Valedictory despatch.	381
158	TO MR THOMAS Washington	17 Sept	Letter from Sir J. Bullard in reply to No. 155. Complains of the 'fissiparous tendencies within the [United States] administration which make it peculiarly difficult to deal with'.	388
159	MR BROOMFIELD EESD FCO	22 Sept	Summary of a paper: 'British Policy in East/West Economic Relations in the 1980s'.	391
160	TO MRS THATCHER 10 Downing Street PM/82/79	27 Sept	Minute from Mr Pym covering a paper entitled: 'East/West Political Relations: UK Policy towards the Soviet Union', and arguing that HMG should re-establish a regular pattern of political dialogue with the Soviet Union.	392
161	MR THOMSON UKMIS New York Tel. No. 1483	28 Sept	Reports on Mr Pym's meeting (in New York) with Mr Gromyko covering bilateral relations, arms control, CSCE, Afghanistan and personal cases.	396
162	MR BROOMFIELD EESD FCO	4 Oct	Briefing note on policy towards the Soviet Union for Mr Pym's meeting with Mrs Thatcher.	398
163	MR BROOMFIELD EESD FCO	6 Oct	Minute to Mr Jay referring to No. 157 and speculating on the Soviet view of the UK.	399

xlix

UK-Soviet Relations, 1979-82

	NAME	DATE	MAIN SUBJECT	PAGE
164	SIR I. SUTHERLAND Moscow Tel. No. 598	14 Oct	Comments on the Soviet relationship with France, Germany, Italy and the US.	401
165	TO HM REPRESENTATIVES OVERSEAS Guidance Tel. No. 191	20 Oct	Provides background on the West Siberian gas pipeline and lines to take on the wider issues of East/West trade.	403
166	MR WALDEN Planning Staff FCO	28 Oct	Minute to Mr Broomfield conveying increasing disquiet about the continuing hard line the Prime Minister is taking with the Russians.	407
167	MR GILLMORE FCO	1 Nov	Minute to Mr Walden sympathising with his unease over Mrs Thatcher's stance.	408
168	SIR I. SUTHERLAND Moscow Tel. No. 665	5 Nov	Discusses whether there has been a recent change of direction in Soviet foreign policy.	408
169	MR SHEINWALD EESD FCO	11 Nov	Briefing note for Mr Pym discussing the consequences of President Brezhnev's death for Soviet Foreign policy.	412
170	SIR I. SUTHERLAND Moscow Tel. No. 724	15 Nov	Reports Mr Pym's meeting with Mr Shultz in Moscow following President Brezhnev's funeral.	412
171	TO SIR I. SUTHERLAND Moscow Tel. No. 676	15 Nov	Transmits Mr Pym's account of his meeting with Mr Gromyko.	414
172	MR COLES 10 Downing Street	17 Nov	Letter to Mr Fall recording a discussion between Mr Pym and Mrs Thatcher on East-West relations.	415
173	TO SIR N. HENDERSON Washington Tel. No. 2037	18 Nov	Contains message from Mr Pym to Mr Shultz on prospects for East-West relations, floating the idea of a US/Soviet summit to steady public opinion.	416
174	TO SIR I. SUTHERLAND Moscow Tel. No. 691	18 Nov	Informs him of HMG's intention to broaden contacts with the Soviet Union.	418
175	SIR I. SUTHERLAND Moscow	25 Nov	'The Funeral of President Brezhnev.'	419
176	TO SIR I. SUTHERLAND Moscow Tel. No. 717	30 Nov	Authorises an invitation to Mr Ryzhov to visit London and a proposal for talks between planning staffs.	425
177	SIR I. SUTHERLAND Moscow	9 Dec	'The Brezhnev Years.'	426

Document Summaries

NAME	DATE	MAIN SUBJECT	PAGE

APPENDIX

JOINT INTELLIGENCE COMMITTEE Cabinet Office JIC(80)(N) 4	1980 10 Jan	'Soviet Intervention in Afghanistan—An Interim Assessment'.	433

CHAPTER I

7 December 1979 – 1 December 1981

No. 1

Lord Carrington (FCO) to Sir C. Keeble (Moscow), 7 December 1979[1]
Confidential (FCO 28/3683, EN 021/2)

British Policy in East-West Relations

Sir,

1. The security of Britain and the democratic world requires the successful management of East-West relations. The Government need a carefully considered policy in this field. The Heads of Mission Conference in London on 19 October discussed this and the present despatch sets out my conclusions. They should guide the work of our Missions which are concerned with East-West matters and will help posts to counter deliberate misrepresentation by communist countries of speeches by British Ministers.

2. On its own admission, the Soviet Union seeks to defeat the West in a struggle waged by all means short of war. The Russians hope, with their military strength, one day to become the dominant factor in Europe. 'Détente' for them is a tactic to lessen the risk of nuclear confrontation and secure technology, credits and grain. In their view it does not require them to slow down their military build-up, relax their internal dictatorship, loosen their grip on Eastern Europe or renounce their freedom to intervene in developing countries.

3. Some of our Allies have specific interests in East-West relations. The US needs to manage its relationship with the other super-power in the new situation of nuclear parity. The Federal Republic of Germany seeks a reduction in East-West tensions in order to keep Berlin quiet, to promote the emigration of ethnic Germans from the East and to facilitate the development of its own links with the German Democratic Republic. France has had particular reasons for developing a special relationship with the Soviet Union, both to assert its independent role in international affairs and to blur the apparent contradiction between the existence of a large Communist Party and the maintenance of a nuclear deterrent and an expensive defence budget. The United Kingdom, by contrast, has no exclusively national interests in East-West relations. Our interest is the general but highly important one of trying to ensure that the West maintains the balance of power and minimises the risk of Soviet acts which could significantly upset it. We are thus better placed than some of our Allies to take a consistently objective view of

---

[1] Mr Bullard hoped this despatch would serve as the guidance H.M. Representatives Overseas needed in 'a tricky and active period of East-West relations'. It was drafted by Mr Mallaby, taking on board contributions from Ministers, a range of FCO departments, the Department of Trade and the Ministry of Defence. Commenting on an earlier draft, the Secretary of State asked for the despatch to be shortened and made more 'action orientated' and to bring out the fact that the UK was well placed to advocate sensible East-West policies in the Alliance.

UK-Soviet Relations, 1979-82

Soviet intentions and to be an active influence for realism in the Alliance's policies towards the East.

Elements for British Policy

I *Western Defences*

4. This is the key requirement. Western defences must cover the full spectrum from conventional to strategic deterrence. Indeed it is in the interest of progress in arms control that this should be so. The Soviet Union has no compelling reason to engage in negotiations in areas where the West is weak. Soviet military preponderance could undermine political self-confidence in the West, and the USSR could exploit the situation for political ends, seeking to isolate and demoralise the weaker Alliance countries and spread its influence towards the Atlantic. To withstand this we also need political unity in the Western Alliance and it will be a major British objective to promote it. The Long Term Defence Programme[2] and the undertakings to increase expenditure by 3 per cent a year in real terms are a demonstration of renewed resolve. The UK will play its part in implementing these decisions and will encourage others to do the same. We are also doing all we can to persuade our Allies to carry through the plans for modernisation of NATO's longer-range Theatre Nuclear Forces (TNF), without which the continuum of capabilities which NATO needs to deter political and military aggression would be broken.

II *The Struggle of Ideas*

5. The Soviet Union, as part of its duel with the West, has challenged the latter to a contest of ideas. We can win such a contest and our answer should be 'take you on'. We should not copy Soviet tactics, but should make the most of our own strengths. Our democracy, ensuring that policies rest on public consent, starts with a powerful advantage over a system which cannot tolerate dissent. Soviet fears of Western contamination are an admission of weakness. Our Alliance, based on common interests, is politically stronger than the artificial and unwelcome Warsaw Pact. We in the West must manage our own affairs successfully, particularly our economies, if our ideas and the kind of societies which derive from them are to prevail, not only in East-West terms, but in the struggle for influence in the Third World. Here too I believe we are the stronger, for the USSR despite its long-term economic potential faces chronic problems of inefficient allocation and use of resources and cannot satisfy its consumers. We should work to bring home to developing countries the real nature of the Soviet system, its economic and other failures and its inability or unwillingness to provide economic aid in anything like the sums offered by the West.

III *East-West Contacts*

6. The Prime Minister has called for contacts with the European communist countries at all levels. There are many purposes in this. One is simply to learn more about those countries, so that our assessments shall be as good as possible and our credentials for advocating policies to our Allies shall be strong. Another purpose is to explain our policies to the East, so that the Soviet Union may better understand the limits of what the West will tolerate. Contacts also enable us to explore shared

---

[2] At the Washington Summit of the North Atlantic Council on 30-31 May 1978, NATO leaders approved the recommendations in the Long Term Defence Programme to improve NATO readiness in a number of non-nuclear areas including air defence, electronic warfare, maritime posture and mobilisation of forces. They also noted with interest the work underway in the Nuclear Planning Group towards meeting needs for the modernisation of theatre nuclear forces.

interests, such as the prevention of the wider proliferation of nuclear weapons.

7. Another purpose of contacts is to promote trade. Although economic and energy problems may depress Eastern Europe's imports from the West for a time, there are still likely to be major capital projects on offer which will be important for some of our key industries. If the East Europeans overcome their immediate problems, the number of such projects should increase. The decision whether to go after projects and the outcome of commercial negotiations are the responsibility of industry, but, since the Governments of these countries are directly responsible for their foreign trade, political relations play a key role. We shall therefore continue to provide substantial Government support for the efforts of British firms to secure business. I accept that Ministerial contacts can play an important part and we shall develop them as much as possible. Political activity will not win us contracts when we are uncompetitive, but its absence may help us to lose them. There is one important limit to the extent to which Government should support the efforts of British firms. Export credit should be kept to the OECD's 'consensus' rates of interest. We are trying to persuade France and other countries which hitherto have offered over-generous rates to join us in applying consensus rates after the expiry of various bilateral credit agreements with the Soviet Union this winter.

8. East-West contacts are also part of our armoury in the contest of ideas. A major purpose is to do what we can to undermine Soviet power by encouraging the existing tendencies towards diversity within the Warsaw Pact, tendencies exemplified by Romania's foreign policy, Hungary's new economic mechanism and Poland's particular brand of pluralism which was eloquently demonstrated by the Pope's visit. We have no interest in provoking a crisis in the area, which would again be ended by invasion if the Russians thought it necessary. But the East European countries are generally the best judges of what contacts with the West are safe for them to undertake.

9. Many types of contact have a role. We should also exploit to the limit the licence provided by the Helsinki Final Act.[3] We should develop cultural exchanges as far as we can within the financial constraints, using the GB-USSR Association and the GB-East Europe Centre to promote non-governmental exchanges. Tourism is offering increasing numbers of people a glimpse of reality on the other side, a process which in both directions is likely to be to our advantage. 'Round Table' discussions between academics, journalists and others can be enlightening, as I know from personal experience. One of the fruits of the Helsinki process was that the Soviet Union felt constrained six years ago to stop jamming the BBC and some other Western radio services. The more alternative opinions are available and listened to, the greater the potential resistance to the official view. In the long run that must be an influence for evolution. That is why the BBC's services to Eastern Europe are being maintained.

IV *The Prevention of Soviet Expansion and the Management of Crises*

10. We need to be able to deter and prevent Soviet expansion and to manage East-West crises. Provided we maintain our defences sufficiently in Europe, the major risk is likely to be in the Third World. We need an effective diplomacy and presentation of our policies to help us deal with this. Here too the BBC External Services and the British Council will provide important support.

11. We cannot allow Soviet successes like that in Angola to go on happening, or the impression will gain ground that history is after all on the side of Marxism-

---

[3] For details, see *DBPO*, Series III, Vol. II.

UK-Soviet Relations, 1979-82

Leninism and developing countries' resistance to intervention will be weakened. The catalogue of Soviet ruptures with Egypt and others will not prevent this. Indeed, after Ethiopia, South Yemen and Vietnam, and the rather different case of Cambodia, the need for a Western stand has become pressing. However the current case of Afghanistan is assessed, the Soviet Union and its proxies sooner or later will contemplate another intervention in an area of importance. It is essential that the West, and the US in particular, should contrive to leave as little room as possible for Soviet miscalculation.

12. High level contacts are the best means for this. The most effective signals will be those which register the danger of provoking East-West military confrontation. We must try to persuade the Americans to make the risks clear in important cases. But the Russians would not believe threats of confrontation if they were made on lesser matters. Here other actions, such as cancellation of major planned events, may have some limited impact.

13. The West should also be fully aware of the leverage at its disposal. When East-West relations are going well the Russians may be more reluctant to upset them. The growing Western relationship with China is a strong constraint on the USSR which much dislikes the idea of a crisis on two fronts, although any deliberate attempt to exploit the Sino-Soviet dispute would be risky and its effects unpredictable. Economic levers exist; but technology transfers (outside the COCOM[4] field) and credits cannot be denied effectively unless a number of Western countries act together, and some seem unlikely to agree to do so; this is a field which requires further study. Grain sales to the USSR offer the Americans a potentially powerful unilateral lever, but commercial interests and other factors have prevented its use.

13. [*sic*] The other aspect of crisis prevention is to identify the countries where the Soviet Union might be tempted to intervene, and to do what we can to prevent a vacuum emerging. Negotiations like Camp David and our own efforts on Rhodesia are needed to settle regional problems. Western economic aid, and training facilities for the military and security forces of friendly states, have important roles. So have well-timed political gestures, like Ministerial contacts with potentially vulnerable states. The United Kingdom may propose a co-ordinated Western study of how we can try together to prevent more Angolas by leverage and other means.

V *Negotiations*

14. Balanced arms control can contribute to Britain's security. With our NATO Allies we have suggested an arms control approach to long-range TNF in parallel with modernisation. I believe that SALT III would be the right forum for this, provided that SALT II is ratified. The negotiation should be a strictly bilateral US/Soviet affair, but with the closest consultation among the Allies. I should like to see some result in the MBFR talks in Vienna. We are currently preparing in the Alliance new proposals for a simplified agreement on US-Soviet ground force reductions and for a package of associated measures. Our aim is that these proposals—together with those on TNF—should be ready for approval at the NATO Ministerial meetings in mid-December. This would enable the Alliance to

[4] The Coordinating Committee for Multilateral Export Controls was responsible for monitoring and approving the export of high technology equipment produced in the West to the Soviet Union and its allies.

7 December 1979 – 1 December 1981

make a convincing and balanced response to Brezhnev's speech of 6 October.[5]

15. The Helsinki Final Act was important, principally because it established humanitarian questions on the agenda of East-West relations. It will be our policy to support the CSCE process as a forum for East-West dialogue and in order to keep up the long-term pressure on the Warsaw Pact countries to improve their performance on human rights. We shall therefore work for a successful but realistic outcome of the Madrid review meeting starting in November 1980. We shall press for a thorough review of implementation of the Final Act. We shall seek to exploit the Eastern interest in confidence building measures in order to call for their application throughout the European USSR and also to secure progress over Basket III.[6] Thus our final agreement to a follow-up meeting on security issues, on the lines of Phase I of the European Disarmament Conference proposed by France, will depend on there also being a satisfactory package of other measures. In the coming months we shall explore the possibilities with the Warsaw Pact countries and stress the need for them to improve their implementation of the Final Act before Madrid and to avoid actions, such as the recent sentences of Charter 77 supporters in Czechoslovakia and restrictions on foreign journalists in East Germany, which are totally inconsistent with the Final Act.

16. The Final Act also strengthens our standing for raising individual human rights cases with the Warsaw Pact countries. We shall continue to press for resolution of all cases where there is a direct family connection with Britain. We shall raise selectively and at high levels some other cases, like those of members of Charter 77 in Czechoslovakia and of Helsinki Monitoring Groups, on which there are particularly strong feelings in Britain. When possible we shall do this jointly with the Nine. It is important that we should keep public opinion with us in this way, even if responding to it may sometimes cause difficulties with the Soviet Union and Eastern Europe, because without public support it would not be possible to maintain that thickening of contacts which is an important lever in managing East-West relations.

17. I hope that successes will be achieved in the negotiations between the EEC and the CMEA, though at present there is no sign of a breakthrough. The outcome we seek is an agreement which will not strengthen the position of the CMEA vis-à-vis its member states but on the contrary will open the way to direct contractual arrangements between the Community and the individual East European countries. This would accord with our objectives of fostering diversity in Eastern Europe and promoting trade and there is evidence that some of the East Europeans would join Romania in welcoming the chance to negotiate directly with the Community.

Conclusion

18. The policy which I have sketched out will be applied flexibly, taking full account of the diversity of the European communist countries. Because of its genuine independence and its growing importance as Tito's departure nears,[7] we shall give a very high priority to our bilateral relationship with Yugoslavia, the uniqueness of which in Eastern Europe is exemplified by substantial sales of British arms. We shall seek to increase Britain's scope for influencing East-West relations in our own interest and that of the West by promoting the co-ordination of

---

[5] In a speech in East Berlin, Brezhnev denounced the planned deployment of Pershing II and Cruise missiles in NATO Europe, proposed a reduction of Soviet tanks and troops in the GDR and offered to negotiate limits on Soviet medium-range missiles provided that NATO suspended deployment.
[6] Basket III of the Helsinki Final Act dealt with 'Cooperation in Humanitarian and other Fields'.
[7] Josip Broz Tito, President of Yugoslavia, was in ill health and died on 4 May 1980.

UK-Soviet Relations, 1979-82

policies in NATO and the Nine and ourselves advocating realistic policies based on the kind of informed analysis which we are well placed to undertake.

19. I am sending copies of this despatch to HM Representatives in the NATO and Warsaw Pact countries; in Belgrade, Madrid, Berne, Stockholm, Helsinki, Vienna, Tokyo, Canberra, Peking and Havana; and at NATO, the European Communities, the MBFR Negotiations, the CTB Negotiations, the Committee on Disarmament in Geneva and the United Nations in New York.

I am, &c,
EWEN FERGUSSON[8]
(For the Secretary of State)

[8] Assistant Under-Secretary of State (Europe).

No. 2

Minute from Mr Mallaby to Mr Braithwaite (Planning Staff), 21 December 1979
Confidential (FCO 28/3683, EN 021/2)

The Prevention of Soviet Expansion in the Developing World

1. Section IV of the Secretary of State's despatch of 7 December on British policy in East-West relations dealt with crisis management and the need to deter and prevent Soviet expansion in the developing world.[1] The final sentence of para 13 foresaw a possible UK initiative to stimulate a coordinated Western study of the range of actions which might be open to us.

2. We now need to consider how to proceed. Once UK views have been worked out, we shall need to consult the Americans, and then I think the French and West Germans. The four of us might conduct a study, or most of it, before consulting others in the Alliance. Japan, Australia and perhaps others have an interest and might be brought in at some stage.

3. But the first thing is to form a more mature UK position. As the next paragraph shows, MOD, ODA and other departments have an interest. So we shall need an interdepartmental working group chaired by the FCO or possibly the Cabinet Office.

4. The content of the study is indicated briefly in paras 12 and 13 of the despatch. One major area would be military measures, ranging from the establishment of a Western long-range intervention capability to the placing of forces on alert or the movement of ships when a crisis looms. The Americans are planning a long-range capability. The French evidently have a rudimentary one. Is it beyond hope that the UK could earmark some existing units and aircraft, e.g. in BAOR, to do this as a second role? The study would also cover non-military signals for use in warning the Russians not to intervene in a particular crisis. These include protests and warnings and the cancellation of events involving ourselves and the Russians. Then there is the question of coordinated Western use of leverage, on which as you know work has already been done.

5. Another section of the study, related to the need to be consistent in making the limits of Western tolerance clear to the Russians, would identify the LDCs [less

[1] See No. 1.

7 December 1979 – 1 December 1981

developed countries] most vulnerable to Soviet influence and also those most important to us. We would need to consider which we were able effectively to support, whether or not they matter individually to us, for we cannot allow the Russians to get a grip of large numbers even of lesser LDCs.

6. Then there is the wide subject of forestalling vacua and minimising the opportunities for Soviet intervention. This includes the lowering of tension and resolution of regional disputes (Camp David, Rhodesia); the reduction of poverty by aid and investment; development of closer relations between LDCs and the West; propagation of the Western way of life through exchanges and the media; and combating Soviet ideology and exposing Soviet failings in international fora.

7. Yet another section would consider policies to Cuba and potential Soviet proxies.

8. It might be useful to have soon a preliminary meeting of FCO departments to discuss the shape of an FCO paper—which might not be able to cover all the above areas—designed to form the initial basis for consideration among Whitehall Departments.[2]

C. L. G. MALLABY

[2] In a minute of 28 December Mr Fergusson indicated he was content to see the work taken forward. He suggested an introductory paper covering the sources of instability in the developing world, the likelihood of this increasing and what prospects there were, if any, of Britain being able to reduce it. He went on: 'I recognise that we face the dilemma that some of those regimes in the developing world who, for the time being, are most friendly to us are precarious, disagreeably authoritarian, indifferent to human rights, and may well not survive into the longer term because of the consequences of their own internal policies; our visible support for them leads internal opposition to turn, for practical as much as ideological reasons, to the Communist world for support. Yet it is difficult to see the advantage of sacrificing a present good against very hypothetical longer term benefits from change.'

In a reply to Mr Mallaby, dated 3 January 1980, Mr Braithwaite added that the recent events in Afghanistan, and the American response to them, underlined the need for a study on the lines outlined in the minute.

Mr Broucher of EESD added his endorsement, in a minute of 23 January, saying the traditional view that the Soviet Union had no 'master plan' for the Third World and Soviet policy was 'opportunistic' was no longer tactically wise or intellectually sufficient. 'If . . . we are denying that the Russians have a coherent philosophy of the Third World and a planned strategy for dealing with it, then I think we are seriously underestimating them. As I see it, they have both a philosophy and a strategy, which is more than can be said for the West. The fact that they cannot make the Third World dominos topple over in prearranged order does not mean that they will fail to grasp the strategic importance of influence in certain countries or that they do not have aggressive long-term aims. They may not always create the opportunities which arise but they do not wait passively for them either' (FCO 49/894, RS 021/7). For a record of the preliminary meeting see No. 48.

No. 3

Mr Hillier-Fry (Kabul) to Lord Carrington, 27 December 1979, 5.13 a.m.[1]
Tel. No. 284 Immediate, Confidential (FCO 37/2135, FSA 020/9)

Soviet Move into Afghanistan

1. During the night 24/25 December and then from nightfall on Christmas Day virtually non-stop for over 24 hours Soviet transport aircraft were landing at Kabul

[1] Repeated Immediate to MOD(D14); Information Priority to Moscow, Islamabad, New Delhi, UKDEL NATO, Washington and Saving Tehran.

UK-Soviet Relations, 1979-82

International Airport at three minute intervals discharging troops and transport including armoured cars and tanks. It is estimated that at least five thousand troops must have arrived during this time. Some are reported to be accommodated on the military side of Kabul airport, others at barracks around Kabul, notably at Darulaman (my telegram 283 para 3)[2] and Pul-I-Charkhi. Darulaman was already closed off by road blocks.

2. Kabul airport remained open for ordinary traffic and no attempt was made to disguise what was happening. At least six helicopters with Soviet markings have also been seen at the airport.

3. The operation has not (not) been reported so far by the Afghan media. However, the English language TV news and other broadcasts on 26 December announced the arrival in Kabul of Panjshiri, Minister of Public Works and member of Politburo of Khalq party, who went to Moscow for medical treatment immediately after the shooting of Taraki on 14 September. This has inevitably caused speculation that the Russians propose to replace Hafizullah Amin[3] by Panjshiri who was said to have been opposed to Amin during Taraki's time.[4]

4. It is generally believed here that Asadullah Amin[5] has died in Moscow. Eye-witnesses claim to have seen seven coffins being carried out from the Kabul Military Hospital after the shooting of 17 December and being buried with full Khalq Party honours. Names mentioned (without corroboration) among the victims are Jauzjani (Minister of Justice) and Mohammed Yaqoub (Chief of Staff).

[2] Not printed.
[3] President of the Democratic Republic of Afghanistan.
[4] Late in the evening of 27 December, the Soviet Embassy delivered a note to the FCO which stated that 'the leadership of the state of Afghanistan approached the Soviet Union for help and assistance in the struggle against outside aggression'. Soviet troops were invited into the country under the terms of the 1978 Treaty of Friendship and in accordance with Article 51 of the UN Charter, under which the Afghanistan government had the internationally recognized right to turn to the Soviet Union with a request for aid and assistance in repelling aggression aimed at overthrowing the democratic system established as a result of the April 1978 revolution. It was further stated that when the reasons that prompted this action no longer existed, the Soviet Union would withdraw its military contingents from the territory of Afghanistan (see FCO telegram No. 797 to Moscow of 28 December, not printed).
[5] Nephew and son-in-law of Hafizullah Amin and head of the secret police (KAM).

No. 4

Mr Lankester (No. 10) to Mr Lever, 28 December 1979
Secret (FCO 37/2135, FSA 020/9)

Dear Paul,

President Carter telephoned the Prime Minister at 17.45 hours today about developments in Afghanistan. The following is a summary of their conversation.[1]

The President said that he regarded the Soviet intervention in Afghanistan as an extremely grave development. It was similar in scope and permanent impact to their intervention in Czechoslovakia. They had in effect converted Afghanistan into a puppet nation, and this would have profound strategic consequences on the stability of the whole region. It was essential that this action should be made as

[1] A copy of the US summary of the conversation, from the Carter Library, can be found on the Margaret Thatcher Foundation website: http://www.margaretthatcher.org/.

7 December 1979 – 1 December 1981

politically costly for the Soviet Union as possible. It was likely to cause serious problems for the non-aligned countries of the area, and he intended to call upon them to speak out against it. The Administration did not intend to allow their concern about the signing of SALT II to interfere with their taking a strong stand against the Soviets for what they had done in Afghanistan. He would have been prepared to take this issue immediately to the Security Council; but because of the initiative over Iran, it would be better if other countries could do so.[2] Perhaps the United Kingdom, or China or some of the non-aligned countries could take the lead. He hoped that there could be a Council meeting on Afghanistan in the near future. Furthermore, he thought that an early meeting of the North Atlantic Council would be highly desirable. In order to discuss these possibilities, he proposed to send Mr Warren Christopher to Europe over the weekend. There was a real need for urgency since the Soviets had been allowed to get away with too much. He would probably make known to the American press later today his serious concern about the Soviet intervention. He had already spoken to Herr Genscher[3], who had said that the Germans shared the Administration's concern. They (the Germans) were particularly worried about the impact which the latest Soviet move might have on Romania and Yugoslavia, and the precedent which it might set in Europe generally. Finally, he intended to send a personal message to Brezhnev expressing deepest concern about this development. It would be helpful if the United Kingdom could do the same.

The Prime Minister said that she shared the President's concern about the Soviet move and she agreed that swift action was needed. She and Lord Carrington would be very happy to receive Mr Christopher over the weekend to discuss the possibilities of taking this issue to the Security Council and to the North Atlantic Council. She also agreed to consider immediately the President's suggestion that we should send a message to Brezhnev.

I am sending copies of this letter to Brian Norbury (Ministry of Defence) and Martin Vile (Cabinet Office).

TIM LANKESTER

[2] On 4 November 1979, Islamic students and militants stormed the American Embassy in Tehran and held dozens of American staff hostage for 444 days. Two resolutions (457 & 461) condemning Iran's actions and calling for the release of all US personnel were approved by the UN Security Council on 4 and 31 December 1979. The hostages were finally released on 20 January 1981.

[3] Hans-Dietrich Genscher, Foreign Minister and Vice Chancellor, FRG.

No. 5

**Sir N. Henderson (Washington) to Lord Carrington,
29 December 1979, 12.55 a.m.**[1]
Tel. No. 4394 Immediate, Confidential (FCO 37/2135, FSA 020/9)

Afghanistan: Proposal for Allied Meeting

1. This is to confirm the arrangements made that arose out of an approach that Vance[2] made to me today for transmission to you.

[1] Repeated Immediate to Paris, Bonn, Rome, Ottawa. This telegram was dated 28 December but not sent until early the next morning.

[2] Cyrus Vance, US Secretary of State.

UK-Soviet Relations, 1979-82

2. The President has announced that he is sending the Deputy Secretary of State, Warren Christopher, to Europe in the next day or two to consult with several other countries on how the world community might respond to the unwarranted Soviet behaviour in Afghanistan. The US therefore propose a meeting of the leading members of NATO, but not under NATO, i.e. the USA, UK, FRG, France, Italy and Canada, at Deputy Foreign Minister level to consider the following subjects, (though a more specific agenda could be worked out later):

(*a*) What are the current foreign policy objectives of the Soviet Union?

(*b*) What are they up to in Afghanistan?

(*c*) What is the effect of their invasion of Afghanistan likely to be upon the rest of the region? And

(*d*) In what way might the Allies best respond?

3. The meeting would be announced. Indeed one of the purposes would be to show that the West was not indifferent to the Soviet move. But the Americans are thinking in terms of a very bland communiqué at the end and they certainly do not want to build up expectations in advance about the outcome.

4. Vance has requested that the meeting will take place in London and you have agreed to this. It will therefore start at 10 a.m. on Monday 31 December in Carlton Gardens. I have told Christopher that we will provide lunch.

5. The State Department will do all the inviting. Apart from Christopher, they think that Van Well will attend from the FRG, and Minister Stirn from France.[3] The Americans obviously want the level to be high.

6. As regards the taking of the chair, this will be decided when the meeting opens. I have told Christopher that we are not particularly anxious to be in the chair. He does not think there should be any difficulty about reaching a decision on this in such a small gathering.

7. Resident clerk please pass this to Bullard.[4]

[3] Günther Van Well, State Secretary, Auswärtiges Amt; Olivier Stirn, Minister of State, French MFA.

[4] Julian Bullard, Deputy Under-Secretary of State (Europe).

No. 6

Sir N. Henderson (Washington) to Lord Carrington,
29 December 1979, 12.56 a.m.[1]
Tel. No. 4395 Immediate, Confidential (FCO 37/2135, FSA 020/9)

Afghanistan

1. Representatives from the embassies of NATO partners plus Australia and New Zealand were called to the State Department this afternoon for a briefing by Lorton (Afghan country officer). State Department are also briefing the Saudi, Japanese, Chinese and 'South Asian' embassies. Lorton explained that US embassies are also being instructed to make approaches along the same lines as below. Americans have also asked for a meeting of the North Atlantic Council

[1] Repeated Priority to Kabul, Islamabad, New Delhi, Moscow, Jedda, Canberra, Wellington, Peking, Dacca, Tokyo, Colombo, all NATO countries, UKDEL NATO, UKMIS New York, MODUK. This telegram was dated 28 December but not sent until early the next morning.

7 December 1979 – 1 December 1981

which, he said, has been convoked for the morning of 29 December (but see my tel 4394—not to all).[2]

2. Lorton first gave the US assessment of what had taken place in Afghanistan. President Amin had on 27 December been deposed and executed in a _coup d'état_ which clearly had been planned and executed by the Soviet Union. In the two previous days there has been a massive airlift (over 200 flights) of men and material from the Soviet Union to Kabul. Though the reason for this airlift had not been clear at the time, it was now apparent that its first task was to effect a coup against Amin who had come to be viewed by the Russians as ineffective, perhaps even embarrassing (Lorton said that the Americans' best guess on the number of Soviet personnel that had now been introduced into Afghanistan over the last month 'was 4-5,000, including the 1,500 moved earlier to Bagram airbase. The most noteworthy items of equipment that had been brought in were 150 armoured personnel carriers and a quantity of light artillery).

3. The Americans had reliable eye-witness accounts from Kabul that Soviet troops had fought against Afghan troops and civilians for control of the radio station. They had been seen to be taking Afghan prisoners and 3 Afghan tanks near the radio station had been destroyed. Convoys of Soviet troops had been seen moving towards the city and there had been fighting in the vicinity of Durulaman Palace, Amin's residence, over several hours (7.30 p.m. until midnight Kabul time) and the palace was still burning today. There were Soviet troops at key intersections in the city and in front of many government buildings.

4. Initial American findings indicate that the first announcements of the coup were made over transmitters situated inside the Soviet Union and not from Kabul. They had clearly been pre-recorded and were repeated on several frequencies purporting to be Radio Afghanistan.

5. Amin had been succeeded as President of the Revolutionary Council by Babrak Karmal, for many years Taraki's rival for the leadership of the Afghan Marxists and head of the Parchamist faction.[3] After the April 1978 revolution, Babrak had been made Deputy Prime Minister but in June 1978 had been exiled to Prague as ambassador. He had been ordered to return to Kabul in September 1978 but did not do so. He was thought to have remained in Eastern Europe and had not re-surfaced until his installation as the new President. (Lorton emphasised that the information about the appearance of Babrak and others in Kabul was based on the assumption that the radio broadcasts were true—the Americans had no reports of anyone having actually seen Babrak.) Babrak was known to be a dedicated Marxist. He had been close to the Soviet Union for years and was thoroughly amenable to Soviet direction. Given the circumstances of his accession to power, it was clear that he would be dependent on Moscow for survival.

6. The Americans had reports of Soviet airlifts continuing. In early December major elements of a regiment had reached Bagram and there were elements of at least five divisions north of the border. Their presence suggested that the Russians might have additional military objectives beyond a mere change of government in Kabul. The divisions north of the border had large numbers of combat aircraft and helicopters. According to information received today Soviet military aircraft— MIG 21s or 23s—had appeared over Kabul though they had not been involved in any action.

---

[2] No. 5.

[3] The communist People's Democratic Party of Afghanistan was split into two factions known as Khalq ('Masses') and Parcham ('Banner'), after their respective newspapers.

UK-Soviet Relations, 1979-82

7. The new regime had already made some conciliatory speeches in an attempt to make itself more palatable to the Afghan public and had said that it would be willing to negotiate with unspecified rebel groups. The Americans expected the insurgents to spurn the invitation since they would regard Babrak as even more of a Soviet puppet than Amin. The new regime could be expected to pay lip service to non-alignment but would be subservient to Moscow internationally. They could expect a difficult time in co-opting elements of the previous regime. The army was already demoralised and this would make things worse. The economic development programme was also in bad shape.

8. Lorton said that US embassies in capitals were being instructed to stress that Soviet military action in Afghanistan and their role in installing a new regime should be the subject of grave concern to the entire international community—not just to the countries of South Asia. The Soviet Union had militarily occupied a sovereign country and been party to the removal of a government that allegedly had invited them in. The Americans viewed this as a qualitatively new stage in the use of Soviet military power against other countries. There was first hand evidence of direct Soviet involvement in a coup which had installed Babrak and led to the removal and execution of Amin. This blatant Soviet action in imposing on the Afghan people through direct intervention a regime which had summarily executed the previous president raised fundamental questions about Soviet intentions. Their self-justificatory references to Article 51 of the United Nations Charter and the terms of the 1978 Treaty of Peace and Friendship with Afghanistan caused the Americans to wonder if Moscow was not seeking to apply the Brezhnev Doctrine[4] in wider areas. The extent to which they got away with this argument would depend heavily on the reaction of the international community. The US had not interfered in the internal affairs of Afghanistan and had consistently made known its opposition to any outside interference by others.

9. Lorton concluded by saying that the US would continue to share with its allies its information on developments in Afghanistan as it came in and would appreciate her allies doing the same. They would wish to consult on what the international community should do and would appreciate the allies' assessment of the significance for world peace and stability of the Soviet Union. The US wished to encourage others to make their concern clear to the Soviet Union both in Moscow and in capitals and through their public statements.

10. The following points emerged in the questions and answers session which followed:

(*a*) The US had taken no decision on its future relations with the new regime;

(*b*) The Americans would appreciate being informed of any efforts by the Soviet Union to present their side of the story in other countries—they already knew them to have done so in London, Bonn, Manila and Ottawa;

(*c*) It was open for discussion whether the UN provided the best option for international action. The Americans did not rule it out nor had they taken a decision to use that forum. They would welcome others' views;

(*d*) The Americans would shortly be protesting formally to the Russians about the events of 27 December either in Moscow or in Washington or in both (so far their protests had been directed to the earlier troop movements they had detected);

---

[4] The doctrine, enunciated in September 1968 to justify the invasion of Czechoslovakia, asserted the right of the Soviet Union to use military force to maintain the leading role of the communist party in neighbouring socialist countries. See *DBPO*, Series III, Vol. I.

7 December 1979 – 1 December 1981

(*e*) The Americans still made no direct connection between Iran and the recent developments in Afghanistan where they believed the Russians had acted for local reasons;

(*f*) Several leading personalities who had fallen foul of the previous regime at various stages had already re-surfaced (including Watanjur).

11. My immediate following telegram[5] gives the text of President Carter's statement (which also covered Iran) to which Lorton drew particular attention in answer to a question about the effect of yesterday's developments on US/Soviet relations.

---

[5] Not printed. In a television address in the press room of the White House, President Carter condemned the Soviet invasion of Afghanistan describing it as 'a grave threat to peace' and 'a blatant violation of accepted international rules of behaviour'. See *Public Papers: Carter (1979)*, Book II, p. 2287.

No. 7

Lord Carrington to Sir C. Keeble (Moscow), 29 December 1979, 1.29 a.m.[1]
Tel. No. 800 Immediate, Confidential (FCO 37/2135, FSA 020/9)

Afghanistan: Message from Prime Minister to President Brezhnev

I have been profoundly disturbed at recent developments in Afghanistan. The large scale deployment of Soviet troops has coincided with a coup led by someone who had been absent from Afghanistan, living in Eastern Europe for over a year, and who returned to the country at the same time as the arrival of the Soviet troops.

I have seen the statement[2] by the Soviet Government handed to the Foreign and Commonwealth Office late on 27 December by the Soviet Embassy in London and I am frankly puzzled by the assertion that recent Soviet action was at the invitation of the Afghan Government. After all, the new Government was only announced on 28 December. Nor can I see that Soviet action is justified in terms of Article 51 of the UN Charter. There is no evidence of which we are aware to substantiate charges of outside interference in the affairs of Afghanistan. The only country which has involved itself in recent years in Afghan internal problems is the Soviet Union.

It is clear that the Soviet Union has sought a pretext to impose its will on a smaller neighbour. And what you admit to be open Soviet military intervention in the affairs of another independent country has been undertaken without any mandate from the Afghan people as a whole. I believe that the people of Afghanistan have a right to choose their own government without outside interference. Recent Soviet action appears to limit this freedom. I should welcome your assurance that all Soviet troops will be withdrawn at a very early date, leaving the Afghan people to determine their own future.

---

[1] Repeated Immediate to Kabul, Washington, UKMIS New York, Islamabad, Bonn, Paris, Rome, Dublin, UKDEL NATO.

[2] No. 3, note 4.

No. 8

Sir N. Henderson (Washington) to Lord Carrington, 29 December 1979, 5.31 p.m.[1]

Tel. No. 4401 Immediate, Confidential (FCO 37/2135, FSA 020/9)

Your Telno 799 to Moscow (not Ottawa): Afghanistan[2]

1. Brzezinski[3] asked to see me today to show me the text of the President's message to Brezhnev. He asked that I should not take notes of it. The main points in the message, apart from predictably strong statements of condemnation, were as follows:

(*a*) The Soviet action could be a long-lasting turning point in relations between the USA and the USSR;

(*b*) Soviet action was incompatible with the terms of the 1972 treaty;[4]

(*c*) The President called upon the Soviet Union to take prompt action to end their intervention in Afghanistan; and

(*d*) The situation was reversible but only if action was taken soon.

2. In showing me the message Brzezinski said that the US Government wanted there to be no doubt about how grave a view they took of what the Russians were up to.

3. I showed him the text of the PM's message to Brezhnev.

4. In discussion with Brzezinski and subsequently with Warren Christopher, the following points emerged regarding Monday's meeting in London: Christopher will be providing ideas for an agenda. This will incorporate the points already conveyed to you in my Telno 4394[5] (now being repeated to Kabul, Moscow and UKMIS New York) as well as the following: the wider impact of Soviet action in Afghanistan on détente, China and arms control; and the handling of the issue in the UN. The US think it best to let two or three days elapse before discussing this subject in the UN forum. This could enable the Islamic and non-aligned reaction to build up. The idea is therefore that a resolution should be tabled between the first and the second Iranian resolutions. They appear to be thinking, following the PM's talk with the President, that the UK and other western allies will table it. Brzezinski is enlivened by the idea that the Chinese might join us in doing so.

5. In response to the suggestion I put to Christopher at Bullard's request he said that he would be prepared to take the chair at the London meeting if that was what the other representatives would like. He thought that one day should be sufficient but in order not to undermine the importance of the meeting perhaps the impression could be given that the parties would be ready to go on longer if necessary. Christopher would be prepared to fall in with the wishes of others about the size of the delegations, though he would want to have the chance to say one or two things in restricted sessions, perhaps limited to us and one or two other delegations.

---

[1] Repeated Immediate to Paris, Bonn, Rome, Ottawa, UKMIS New York, Moscow, Kabul and UKDEL NATO.

[2] Not printed. This telegram informed selected posts of the message from Mrs Thatcher to President Brezhnev.

[3] Zbigniew Brzezinski, US National Security Advisor.

[4] This is probably a reference to the joint declaration on Basic Principles of Relations between the Union of Soviet Socialist Republics and the United States of America, which was signed 29 May 1972. For further details see *DBPO*, Series III, Vol. I, pp. 474-77 and No. 50, para. 3.

[5] No. 5.

7 December 1979 – 1 December 1981

6. As regards informing NATO, Christopher thought that it might be useful if this was done. He himself might not be available, but Vest could take it on.

No. 9

FCO Briefing Paper on Afghanistan, 29 December 1979[1]
Confidential (FCO 37/2135, FSA 020/9)

A. *What are the Current Foreign Policy Objectives of the Soviet Union?*
1. There is no reason to revise fundamentally the analysis of Soviet foreign policy contained in the 'Alliance Study of East-West Relations' approved by NATO Heads of Government in Washington on 30-31 May 1978, CM(78)35(Revised).[2]
2. Recent events in Afghanistan do however illustrate three characteristics of Soviet policy which Governments and public opinion in the West may tend to underrate:

(*a*) *Opportunism*: the Soviet Christmas coup in Kabul was deliberately carried out at a moment when vigilance and the capacity to respond would be at their lowest in the West and in the world at large;

(*b*) *Ruthlessness*: having decided, evidently after some hesitation, that the Soviet interest required the removal of Amin, the Russians deployed and used the substantial forces necessary to secure this objective, with only a perfunctory attempt to claim legal or moral justification for their action. (The pattern of prolonged hesitation followed by intervention in decisive strength is exactly that shown in the case of Hungary and Czechoslovakia in 1956 and 1968.) The Russians were no doubt aware of the risks (e.g. to the standing of the Soviet Union in the Third World, to US-Soviet relations and to détente as a whole), but judged these to be acceptable in the interests of securing their aims in Afghanistan;

(*c*) *Secrecy*: the Soviet preparatory moves were on such a scale that they were bound to be (and were) detected by the West, but the true purpose of the intervention was effectively concealed until it had been successfully completed.

3. It should be assumed that these features would also be present in any future Soviet intervention in similar circumstances.

B. *What are Soviet Objectives in Afghanistan?*
1. Soviet objectives in Afghanistan are likely to be:

(*a*) to ensure that there is no reversal of the policies of closer alignment with the Soviet Union followed by Afghan governments since the toppling of Daoud in 1978;

(*b*) conversely, to deny any opportunity for the establishment in Afghanistan of a regime hostile to the Soviet Union—in particular a Nationalist Islamic Government that might pursue xenophobic and reactionary policies and might infect Muslims within the Soviet Union.

---

[1] The briefing paper was prepared by Mr Cortazzi and Mr Bullard for a meeting on 31 December (No. 11). The final section covering allied relations with the Soviet Union and Afghanistan, and action in the UN, the non-aligned movement, NATO and the EC has not been printed.
[2] Not printed.

UK-Soviet Relations, 1979-82

(*c*) in the longer term, to build up a position of strength in Afghanistan from which to influence events in Central and South Asia, especially in Iran and the Indian Sub-Continent, to Soviet advantage.

2. The December coup seems to have resulted from a Soviet realisation that, with Amin at the head of the government in Afghanistan, the situation was not developing in accordance with Soviet wishes. He was both unpopular and unsuccessful. Further unexplained killings on 16/17 December may have finally convinced the Russians that a change was essential.

3. In the immediate future the Russians are likely to concentrate on stabilising and consolidating the new regime, hoping that the *fait accompli* will be accepted. They will want to keep Kabul quiet, to establish as much normality as possible throughout the country and to secure maximum international recognition of the new government. For the moment they are likely to be cautious about any further commitment to military operations against the opponents of the regime in the field.

4. We nevertheless expect that the trend towards progressive Soviet military involvement will continue. The Parcham party is no more popular than the Khalq party and the new government will remain totally reliant on Soviet support. There will be strong pressure to build up still further the scale of Soviet military intervention with the aim of the complete suppression of opposition. It is doubtful whether this aim can ever in fact be achieved, given Afghan history, terrain and social characteristics.

5. If and when relative stability has been restored, the Russians may seek to tie Afghanistan more closely into the Soviet system. At that stage we could expect to see a series of steps up to and including the formal entry of Afghanistan into COMECON (the communist economic grouping), together with even tighter bilateral agreements than those existing already. On this scenario the ultimate destiny of Afghanistan could be that of a *de facto* Asian colony on the model of Mongolia. (The East European members might oppose formal membership of the Warsaw Pact if the Soviet Union were to propose it.)

6. A legal critique of the Soviet pretext for intervention is attached.[3]

C. *Effects of the Soviet Invasion in the Rest of the Region*
Iran

1. The Iranians have always been wary of the USSR, a distrust much increased by the professed dislike of the clergy for communism. They will be very concerned by the invasion: it will demonstrate their vulnerability to the super-powers. They will also see it as super-power suppression of a Moslem people struggling for its freedom. Khomeini's own reaction (extract from AFP attached)[4] has been to condemn the invasion as an unfriendly gesture to all Moslems as well as an excuse to use the crisis between Iran and the US to intervene in the affairs of weak nations. Iranian support for the Moslem opponents of the Kabul regime is likely to intensify, though such support is likely to be more in the nature of propaganda and encouragement than in any significant material form so long as the Iranians remain distracted by their own domestic divisions and problems.

2. However, in the short term the Iranians are likely to equate the Russian action with what they see as the US position in Iran, and may resist any suggestion that the USSR poses a more serious menace than the US. (The Foreign Minister, Qotbzadeh, has already said, at a meeting with the EEC Ambassadors on 28

---

[3] Not printed.
[4] *Agence France-Presse*, not printed.

7 December 1979 – 1 December 1981

December which closed with him losing his temper, that he sees no distinction between the USSR and the US.) But in the long term Iran may realise the need to think more seriously about the real threat which Soviet military action poses.

Pakistan

1. The Pakistanis have not yet commented on the Russian action. Their reactions may well be ambivalent.

2. Traditionally they perceive the Soviet Union as a threat. They are deeply concerned lest a pro-Soviet regime in Kabul becomes a source of Soviet inspired subversion in the sensitive province of Baluchistan.

3. The presence of over 300,000 Afghan refugees in Pakistan presents them with a major problem. At the worst there is now a prospect of a Russian attack on camps or villages within Pakistan, on the grounds that the refugees within Pakistan are supporting the rebellion in Afghanistan.

4. Conversely the Pakistanis would welcome a political settlement. They have cancelled a visit by the Pakistani foreign affairs adviser to Kabul that was due to take place on 30/31 December. But their relations with Amin had been difficult. They may hope for improvement and they will be reluctant to start off their relations with a new Afghan government on a bad footing. In particular they must be hoping that Karmal will achieve a political settlement which will enable Afghan refugees to leave Pakistan.

India

1. The Indians have tried to put a good interpretation on what has happened. They enjoy good relations with the Soviet Union and with an election pending in early January are unwilling to stick their necks out. If Mrs Gandhi with her pro-Soviet views were returned to power the Indians would be even less likely to be openly critical of the Soviet rule.

2. The Acting Indian High Commissioner in London told us earlier this year that India would find it easier to deal with the Parchamites than the Khalq leadership. The Indians would view any more Islamic-orientated government with suspicion and fear that the alternative to a Soviet-supported government would not be a government better inclined towards India.

3. Privately however the Indians must be aware that the extension, in effect, of the Soviet Union's border with the Sub-Continent from the Oxus to the Khyber has important implications for them as well as the Pakistanis.

No. 10

Sir C. Keeble (Moscow) to Lord Carrington, 30 December 1979, 9.30 a.m.[1]
Tel. No. 872 Immediate, Confidential (FCO 37/2135, FSA 020/9)

Your Telno 171 to UKDEL NATO: Afghanistan[2]

1. You may find it useful to have an assessment of the situation as seen from here, even though there are many unknown factors.

2. The Russians have been uneasy about the Afghan situation since Taraki fell. They may at first have reckoned they could control Afghanistan through Amin although he was not their choice. The decision to replace him was probably taken when they realised this hope was futile, but may have been planned for longer. In

[1] Repeated Priority to UKDEL NATO, Washington, UKMIS New York and Kabul.
[2] Not printed.

UK-Soviet Relations, 1979-82

any case, I think we can assume that they would rather have ensured their grip on Afghanistan by less blatant means than those to which they have resorted.

3. The Soviet action has been carried out in classic style, with the Iranian problem deflecting attention, substantial force swiftly applied, immediate liquidation of political opposition, and a public presentation of Goebbels-like effrontery. Their aim must be to ensure that the situation within Afghanistan can quickly be brought under control: that the Barak Karmal regime can be made self-sustaining: and that any anxiety among the non-aligned will either soon evaporate or can be diverted into opposition to any western response: and that western anger can be left to subside without harm to any wider Soviet interest. I hope our own response can be designed to match these aims.

4. The Russians must have calculated that any protests from neighbouring states, in the Middle East, and among the non-aligned in general will quickly fade. The continuing ASEAN refus[al] to acquiesce in the Vietnamese invasion of Kampuchea[3] gives some hope that they may be wrong. I trust we shall do all we can to ensure that the full story of Soviet actions is repeatedly made known in the Third World, perhaps by emphasis on the timing of the appeal for Soviet help, the swiftness of Amin's murder after the arrival of Soviet troops, and the circumstances of Karmal's return. The longer it takes other[s] to forget what has happened, and the longer it takes the Russians to consolidate their hold, the higher price the Soviet Union must pay.

5. It is possible the situation under Amin was deteriorating so fast they felt they had only the choices of abandoning the Afghan revolution or replacing him urgently, and chose the latter without careful consideration of the consequences for East-West relations. I suspect, however, they were more complacent than they should have been, and may believe they can have their adventures and détente too. The harsher the reaction from NATO—and especially its smaller members—the more clearly the Russians may understand the damage they have done both to SALT II and to their own hopes of delaying or frustrating Western defence measures, including TNF, and the less prospect they have of getting away with their concept of détente in future so, for the Russians to begin to think they have miscalculated, the Western reaction will have to be rougher than they expected, both in terms of what is said and what is done: will have to be sustained over a long period, and, ideally, will have to be concerted so far as possible with reactions among major non-aligned countries.

6. There are no doubt many areas of policy you will wish to consider and coordinate with our allies, and on which I can offer no useful comment from here, including action in the UN, relations with the new Afghan government and policy in respect of the rebels, the US Quick Reaction Force and the 'China card' (though if a Harrier deal were imminent it might be a good time to conclude it). The Russian aim will clearly be to try to create the illusion of 'business as usual' and hence the continuation of a normal programme of political, commercial, scientific and cultural exchanges. The principal allied visit is that proposed by Schmidt in the first part of 1980. So far as the UK is concerned the following may be relevant:

(*a*) You have invited Gromyko to London early next year, but no date is yet firm;

---

[3] In December 1978, Vietnamese forces launched an invasion of Cambodia (Kampuchea) capturing the capital Phnom Penh on 7 January 1979 and installing Heng Samrin as head of state. The Khmer Rouge forces under Pol Pot were driven into hiding near the Thai border. The international community continued to recognise the Khmer Rouge as the legitimate government of Cambodia.

(b) Anglo-Soviet official consultations at official level on disarmament, CSCE, Asian affairs etc;

(c) RAF Staff College visit in the spring and an exchange of naval visits under discussion;

(d) Discussions between a GB/USSR Association delegation led by Sir H. Wilson[4] and the Anglo-Soviet Friendship Society in mid-January;

(e) The question of bilateral credit agreements will be due for decision shortly, (not only by the UK).

The Russians set considerable store by a successful and well-attended Olympic Games in Moscow next July and also want a quiet Madrid CSCE meeting late in 1980.

7. Whatever measures we adopt, I see little chance that we shall persuade the Russians to remove their forces until they are satisfied that they have brought Afghanistan under an acceptable degree of control. What we can achieve is to demonstrate the real nature of Soviet foreign policy to any who have illusions about it, and try to deter the Russians from embarking on similar adventures elsewhere.

8. I have now seen Washington Telegram No. 4403.[5] I hope these comments may be helpful in relation to some of the items on the agenda. On item 1 my view is that this does not reflect a fundamental strategic reassessment. It is an extreme illustration of the way the Soviet Union understands détente. It happened because of:

(a) The failure to control Afghanistan by political means alone.

(b) The belief that the West had been brought to acquiesce in a Soviet concept of détente, under which localised extension of Soviet power was compatible with understanding at the strategic level.

The doubt over SALT ratification prospects and perhaps a feeling (expressed to me recently by the Foreign Ministry) that TNF had robbed SALT of much of its interest to the Soviet Union were factors and the preoccupation of the United States with Iran may have seemed to leave the field clearer for them.

---

[4] Sir Harold Wilson, British Prime Minister 1964-70, 1974-76.

[5] Not printed. This telegram contained the US draft agenda for the London meeting on 31 December.

No. 11

Record of a meeting held in the FCO, 31 December 1979, 10 a.m.[1]
Confidential (FCO 37/2236, FSA 020/1)

Heads of Delegation:
UK: Douglas Hurd MP, Minister of State, FCO[2]

---

[1] On the eve of the meeting Sir N. Henderson wrote to London 'Although the calling of the meeting by the Americans may seem half-baked in London and other capitals, given that there is no obvious and constructive outcome, I think we should welcome their readiness to open their minds to us and seek our views before they reach conclusions. In other contexts recently, particularly Iran, we have complained at America's failure to consult us sufficiently in advance. They are certainly doing that now. I also think that the choice of London for the meeting-place was not purely because of geographical convenience.' Washington tel. No. 4407 of 30 December (FO 37/2135, FSA 020/9).

[2] In addition to Mr Hurd, the UK delegation consisted of Mr Cortazzi, Mr Bullard, Mr White, Mr Mallaby, Mr Archer and Mr Lavers.

US: Warren Christopher, Deputy Secretary of State, State Department
Canada: Alan Gotlieb, Under-Secretary, MFA
France: Bruno de Leusse, Secretary-General, Quai d'Orsay
Germany: Dr Gunther Van Well, State Secretary, Auswärtiges Amt
Italy: Francesco Malfatti, Secretary-General, MFA

1. *Mr Hurd* welcomed other delegations. There was general agreement that Mr Christopher should take the chair.

2. *Mr Christopher* expressed appreciation that other delegations were participating. The United States had suggested consultations because of the very grave view that they took of Soviet action and the need which they saw for agreement between allies on an appropriate response. The United States saw this as a most important development as it was the first time since World War II that Soviet forces had been used outside the Soviet bloc. What had happened was naked aggression for which the Soviets had offered an unconvincing explanation. It was a travesty to suggest that the intervention had been invited by Amin. He and other members of his Government had been assassinated within hours of the attack. To instance the Soviet/Afghan Friendship Treaty as grounds for Soviet involvement was equally false. Similar grounds could be claimed by as many as ten countries with comparable treaties. The question that needed to be asked was why the Soviet Union had chosen the present time to make this direct and massive further escalation of their involvement in the country. It followed an attempt to get rid of Amin earlier in the year which misfired.

3. The Afghanistan rebels now appeared to have been operating more effectively than had been assumed. Amin had failed to win support and the Soviets had removed him. What was initially a massive Soviet airlift had been complemented by a massive cross border invasion bringing their troop levels up to 25-30,000. The Soviet troops were reaching out throughout the country and occupying strategic lines including the border area between Afghanistan and Pakistan. Babrak Karmal was not yet believed to be in Afghanistan. The Soviets could expect to have continuing trouble with insurgents. To deal with this they would probably need to bring in more troops from the substantial forces lined up inside the Soviet border. An increasing number of Afghans could be expected to cross the border into Pakistan. The present 350,000 refugees there might soon become 500,000. Pakistan faced a dilemma. Their traditional fears of Soviet intentions had been confirmed. They would wonder whether help from the West would be sufficiently strong to provide security. They might wonder whether they needed a rapprochement with the Soviet Union. The Pakistan Government was weak. However the Government was trying to bolster its position by stressing its Islamic commitment. The President and Foreign Affairs Adviser were thinking of calling for a meeting of the Islamic Conference. The United States wished to encourage them to do so but this would not be an alternative to the West providing assistance to Pakistan. Any Indian Government could be expected to follow a cautious approach in public but their underlying concern would be that South Asia was becoming an area for super power confrontation. Mr Desai had been careful about dealings with Pakistan. Mrs Gandhi might not be so cautious. Past relations between Mrs Gandhi and Babrak were reported to have been close. The Soviet action in Afghanistan might help us with US/Iran relations. But there could be no certainty. The Americans thought that Iraqi suspicions of Soviet motives would be increased. Elsewhere President Mengistu would be worried. The governments of

7 December 1979 – 1 December 1981

Somalia, Kenya and Djibouti would be reinforced in their anti-Soviet attitudes. The Chinese could be counted upon to speak out and even to take an initiative. They might offer more aid to Pakistan. Recent events would have a special message for Yugoslavia and Romania. The West should reinforce their contacts with them and watch their reactions. It was necessary to review the consequence of Soviet action on general East/West relations. The TNF modernisation programme seemed wise and necessary. Soviet arms control measures needed to be looked at with new scepticism. President Carter's desire was to push ahead with SALT II which he saw as in the interest of the West but the Soviet Afghanistan venture would make it much more difficult to achieve agreement in the Senate. Congressional reaction would be apparent only after Congress returned. The general American conclusion was that the events in Afghanistan reinforced the need for Western solidarity and vigilance. Did events mean that the Soviet Union would in future move to support pro Soviet regimes in other countries whenever they seemed threatened? Their intentions would be influenced by the reaction to them. If this was weak the threshold for Soviet interference would be lowered. A firm reaction would lessen the likelihood that the Soviet Union would pursue similar action in future.

4. *Mr Hurd* noted the elements of opportunism, ruthlessness and secrecy in the Soviet action. He said that the UK analysis of the situation was close to the American. We saw three main Soviet objectives: to ensure that there was no reversal of Afghan commitment to furtherance of the communist revolution of April 1978; to ensure that there was no opportunity for a regime hostile to the Soviet Union to be established in Kabul; and for the longer term to build up a position of strength in Afghanistan from which it would be possible to influence events in Central and South Asia. The Soviets had probably not yet decided how to use Afghanistan as a satellite. But it was not possible to dismiss the prospect that the Soviet Union would seek to tie in Afghanistan very closely to the Soviet Union. Karmal's prospects of acceptance by the Afghans had started badly because of the way he had come to power. The Soviet immediate priority would be to build up his regime. The opposition was chaotic and incoherent but the Soviet intervention had neutralised the Afghan Army. Hence the Soviet Union would need to carry through operations in the field themselves. This might be the reason for the size of the Soviet intervention. The prospects were for massive intervention over a considerable period.

5. Pakistan was seriously worried. They feared that the new regime in Kabul might revive the case for Paktunistan [*sic*] with which Karmal had in the past been closely identified.[3] The Soviet Ambassador to Pakistan had told the Pakistan Government that Pakistan was an external power whose interference in Afghanistan had necessitated Soviet intervention. Reports from other capitals however indicated that the Iranians and the Americans had also been named in some capitals as interfering powers.

6. The Indians could be expected to put the best face possible on what had happened. They would be concerned to see an Islamic regime in Kabul and might prefer a pro-Soviet Government. But there would be deep concern at the role that Soviet forces had played in the country even if this was not publicly expressed.

7. *Mr Christopher* interjected that he had seen a report that one Soviet Ambassador had commented, when asked to identify the third country accused of

---

[3] Pakhtunistan was the name given to the idea of an independent country constituting the Pashtun areas of Pakistan including the North-West Frontier Province, the Federally Administered Tribal Areas and the northern portion of Balochistan.

UK-Soviet Relations, 1979-82

interference by the Soviet Union, that he could not remember which country it was.

8. *Dr Van Well* analysed the situation at some length on similar lines to previous speakers. He said that the Germans doubted whether the Russians were intent on absorbing Afghanistan into the Soviet Union. But Afghanistan now provided a new platform for the Soviet Union to extend its influence in the region. The Alliance should take this new factor into account. The Russians would have difficulty controlling the tribal rebels. Although the opposition was disunited there was intense hatred of the Russians. Appeals for national reconciliation would have little attraction. Nonetheless, any reaction indicating acquiescence in the intervention would psychologically undermine the rebels. The West should be alert to this consideration.

9. He thought that the Soviet timing of their move had been influenced by the Iranian crisis. There were parallels with Hungary in 1956. Initially his government had thought that the Iranians must now recognise where their true interests lay. Unfortunately the climax to the Security Council debate had come at the same time. Meanwhile the Iranians still thought their battle with the Americans was the main priority.

10. Turning to other countries in the region, Dr Van Well commented on Pakistan's lack of direction and governmental weakness. On India, he thought it unlikely that a caretaker government would make strong statements. But the Russian action would have a deep impact on Indian policy planning. The Chinese would issue strong statements but were not in a position to do much else. The Germans thought that the Western response should be framed with the wider region in mind, including the Gulf and the Horn. A strong reaction would stiffen governments uncertain how to play things.

11. Détente had lost ground. The German press had strongly condemned the Russians. Confidence building measures would hardly seem appropriate now to German public opinion. The Russians would not wish to negotiate with the Americans while there was so much uncertainty in East/West relations.

12. *M. de Leusse* asked if the Soviet action was really a move over a completely new threshold. He accepted that there had been no intervention of this size in a non-Soviet bloc country since 1945 but the Soviet Union had supplied armed troops and military hardware in Vietnam and had used the Cubans as surrogates in Africa. There had been no protest over Soviet action in Eritrea.[4] He thought that the most appropriate response to the situation in Afghanistan would be from Third World countries. So far they had said very little. The idea of Pakistan convening a meeting of the Islamic Conference was extremely desirable. The reactions of Romania and Yugoslavia would be important.

13. *Sr. Malfatti* agreed with previous assessments. He pointed to the problems for the Soviet Union from the anti-Islamic policies of Presidents Taraki and Amin. He thought that one of the reasons for the timing of the Soviet intervention might be that they felt that the winter season would be a good opportunity to end the revolution while lines of supply were interrupted by winter. The Italians had considered that a suitable response to the present situation was to recall their Ambassador from Kabul immediately. They supported action in the Security Council.

---

[4] In November 1978, Ethiopia and the Soviet Union signed a Treaty of Friendship and Cooperation. Under the terms of the treaty, Moscow provided military support for Ethiopia's military offensive against Eritrean separatists. In July 1979, Soviet officers reportedly commanded Ethiopian field units in a renewed offensive against Eritrea.

7 December 1979 – 1 December 1981

14. *Mr Gotlieb* said that Canada agreed with views already expressed. He thought that the Russians had taken the opportunity to position themselves in the arc of instability. The Pakistanis were particularly worried. They saw a prospect that they might be sandwiched between two hostile countries that might establish a close cooperation if Mrs Gandhi won the Indian election. He agreed that Third World countries should be engaged in any action at the United Nations to the maximum extent possible.

Action at the UN

15. *Mr Christopher* said that he proposed that the meeting should now discuss the various possibilities for action at the UN. He thought that action under Chapter 6 would underestimate the gravity of the situation. Action under Chapter 7 involved the threat of a Soviet veto. Some might see some advantage in forcing the Soviets to that position. Taking action to the General Assembly tended to be sequential to Chapter 7 action. Another alternative would be a letter to the Security Council but the Americans believed that this also underestimated the gravity of the situation.

16. *Mr Hurd* said that the United Kingdom felt that there should be recourse to the United Nations through the Security Council. There was provision in the UN Charter for countries to have the right to choose their own governments and a requirement for members to refrain from use of force against independent states. This could provide the framework for an approach. The operative paragraph could condemn Soviet action. A call for a withdrawal of Soviet troops would be a necessary consequence of condemnatory action. Another operative paragraph could perhaps establish a commission of three members to examine progress by, for example, 1 February. Early action was important. It was essential to act when the tide of protest in non-aligned countries and particularly the Muslim world was flowing strongly. Indignation subsided quickly. Fears remained but the inclination to do or say anything faded. It would be a pity to wait until after the second stage of the Iranian discussion and better to use the window between stage one and two. He saw no hope of persuading the Soviet Union to reverse their action. The aim should be to make the Soviet Union uncomfortable about what they had done in order that it would be less likely that they would repeat similar action elsewhere.

17. *Mr Gotlieb* said that it would be logical to use Chapter 7, as Chapter 6 referred to the peaceful settlement of disputes. By referring to Article 51 as their pretext for action the USSR had themselves necessitated Security Council attention as the Article required a Council report. It would not be desirable to take action to the General Assembly under peace procedures without widespread support. He thought it would be more desirable for a non-aligned country or countries to sponsor a resolution than for the rest to take the lead. It would be worth a 24 or even 48 hour delay to see if this could be achieved.

18. *Mr Christopher* agreed that it was desirable to involve Third World countries but no dependence could be placed on them to be self starting.

19. *Sr. Malfatti* said that the best solution would be to persuade an Asian member of the Security Council to take the lead.

20. *Mr Gotlieb* commented that any one of the 150 members could bring a complaint.

21. *Mr Christopher* added that the Indonesians, Niger[ians] and the Philippines would be the new members of the Council from 1 January. Third World countries could play a very helpful role in a resolution. Nigeria had played an important role over Iran.

UK-Soviet Relations, 1979-82

22. *M. de Leusse* suggested that Permanent Representatives in New York should consult together and try to get a Third World country, if possible from Asia, to take the initiative.

23. *Mr Hurd* commented that Bangladesh was, in principle, in favour of action in the Security Council but it would be a considerable jump for them to take the initiative themselves.

24. *Mr Gotlieb* thought that Sri Lanka, Singapore and the Philippines might perhaps jointly be persuaded to take the lead.

25. *Mr Christopher* hoped that the other countries present would take action in capitals around the world to urge other countries to take action. He hoped other countries would make similar démarches to those which the US had issued.

26. *M. de Leusse* thought it important not to make Afghanistan just an East/West quarrel; it should be dealt with as a world problem.

27. *Mr Hurd* asked whether all could agree to work for an early meeting of the Security Council. He did not think there was any need to decide at the meeting how or by whom the action should be taken forward.

28. There was general agreement but the *French* said that they must reserve their position on a Western initiative in the UN at least until 1 January.

Recognition

29. *Mr Christopher* proposed that there should be an exchange of views on the question of recognition of the new Afghanistan government. The US Embassy staff were down to about 50. The US had not yet reached a decision on what to do. There were a range of possibilities from breaking relations, removal of Ambassadors without a break and the drawing down of staff.

30. *Dr Van Well* said that a consideration for the Germans was the number of the German technical experts, school teachers and UNDP staff. It would be difficult for them to withdraw their mission.

31. If one country withdrew its Ambassador that would increase the pressure on the others. The Italians were going to withdraw their representative. *Mr Hurd* said we did face a problem of recognition. We would not take an early decision. The British Ambassador had been asked not to have any political contacts with the new government. The UK would be ready to fall in with any consensus.

32. *Mr Gotlieb* said that Canada had no resident Ambassador to withdraw. Afghanistan had been virtually annexed. It created an exceptional situation for the legal criteria for recognition.

33. *M. de Leusse* said France recognised states not governments. Recognition was not, therefore, a problem. They had not made a decision on the future of their small embassy in Kabul. There was no question of political contacts yet.

34. *Dr Van Well* saw a dilemma. The Germans would like to withdraw their Ambassador but found his presence useful. They would be prepared to go along with the general consensus to withdraw.

35. *Mr Christopher* agreed with Mr Hurd that all should abstain from political contacts with the new regime.

Aid

36. *Mr Christopher* said that the Americans had cancelled their programme. Under Taraki the Afghans had been at least nominally non-aligned. The new government was a puppet. He asked for views.

37. *Dr Van Well* said his government would reassess their programme. They would be reluctant to provide money to multilateral organizations for projects in Afghanistan.

7 December 1979 – 1 December 1981

38. *Mr Hurd* said the British programme was small but diminishing. We might not terminate the scholarships of students in the United Kingdom. But it would now be hard to justify bilateral projects. He hoped international organizations would adopt a similarly critical attitude.

39. *Mr Gotlieb* thought his government should see whether the World Bank could suspend its aid.

40. *M. de Leusse* said the French programme now amounted virtually to nothing.

41. *Mr Christopher* said that all the countries represented had either suspended or were phasing out their programmes. They would continue to do this and would encourage multilateral institutions to re-evaluate their involvement in Afghanistan. The US Government would urge them to suspend programmes and not initiate new projects.

Bilateral Relations with Soviet Union, Pakistan and India

42. *Mr Christopher* said the United States had contemplated granting most favoured nation status to the Soviet Union. They were looking at that again now. They were also reviewing their policy on export licences, grain sales, scientific exchanges, and the whole gamut of social and official contacts. In effect this amounted to the totality of their bilateral relations. Mr Christopher invited comments on the intentions of other governments.

43. *Mr Gotlieb* said that the Canadians had not yet reviewed their position. He would advise his Ministers of the sense of the meeting. He envisaged two immediate possibilities. The first priority should be the suspension of visits in both directions. Secondly they could postpone signature of new agreements. Both were visible signs of good will. They bore re-examination.

44. *Sr. Malfatti* said his government would review the question. It was important that all the allies should adopt a common line. *Dr Van Well* outlined his government's intentions. Firstly they would reply to the Soviet communication about their intervention. The Germans planned to criticise the use of force against the Afghans, to call for the withdrawal of Soviet troops and to reject the pretext and arguments used to justify the Russian invasion. Thereafter they would examine the possibility for reprisals, starting with participation in the Olympics. Careful study was required in the context of East/West relations. His government had a tight schedule of visits, including Mr Schmidt's to the Soviet Union and bloc countries. Should the East Europeans be included in the West's disapproval? In the immediate future though it was more important to establish our attitude in the region with, for instance, visits to Pakistan. Pakistan was suffering from a refugee problem. His government was ready to join an international programme to help Afghan refugees. Another possibility was a conference on debt relief for Pakistan. His government was ready to consider an increase in aid. Moreover, these were signals which should be noted in Moscow. After a brief reference to Iran and the possibility of a community gesture, *Dr Van Well* commented that the West should not allow the Soviet Union to exert additional pressure to complicate an already serious situation.

45. *Mr Christopher* said the United States had re-stated its commitment to the 1959 Treaty with Pakistan (the so-called Eisenhower doctrine). They intended to speed up the supply of weapons in the pipe-line. His government would be more forthcoming to Pakistan in every way not prevented by the statutes on nuclear proliferation.

46. *Mr Hurd* described the public reaction here and the Prime Minister's

UK-Soviet Relations, 1979-82

message to Mr Brezhnev.[5] The United Kingdom would also reply to the Soviet communiqué. The range of contacts with the Soviet Union planned for 1980 would be reviewed. He cited examples such as the proposed delegation to be led by Sir Harold Wilson and the Royal Air Force Staff College visit. Mr Gromyko had been invited for February. That might be cancelled but any action had to be the same as taken by the others. It would be particularly important to know whether Mr Schmidt went to Moscow. Credits to the Soviet Union presented another possibility. Our own were due soon to expire. Britain was prepared to consider this weapon but it would only be sensible if all acted together. The Alliance also needed to think of ways of reassuring the Pakistanis without upsetting the Indians. Perhaps action could be categorised under the headings firstly of implications for contacts with the Soviet Union and, secondly, measures of support to Pakistan.

47. *Mr Hurd* mentioned that Mr Blaker would be in Delhi from 24-26 January which would provide an opportunity to speak to the Indians.

48. *Dr Van Well* said that a German Minister would also be going to New Delhi for discussions shortly.

49. *Mr Christopher* asked whether one way of following up the present discussions could be through a working group. He asked if there was a consensus that governments should increase aid to the refugees in Pakistan.

50. *The Canadians*, *British* and *French* commented that there could be difficulties because of the squeeze on bilateral aid programmes.

51. *Mr Gotlieb* commented that for Canada there was the problem with Pakistan of the nuclear issue. Nevertheless the Canadians thought that something should be done to help with Pakistan's sense of isolation. Ought they to be re-invited to join the Commonwealth?

Non Aligned Movement

52. *Mr Christopher* asked how best to approach the Non Aligned Movement. If the Movement stood by their principles they should be concerned at the overthrow of a non-aligned government.

53. *Mr Gotlieb* said that he was pessimistic about the NAM taking any firm action.

54. *Mr Christopher* thought that Yugoslavia and possibly India could be approached.

55. *Mr Hurd* thought that some members of the Movement might be prepared to raise the case for the Movement considering the suspension of Afghanistan.

56. *Mr Christopher* commented that there was already an Executive Committee set up after the Havana meeting which might cut back on the power of Cuba as the Chairman.

57. *Mr Gotlieb* suggested that it might be useful to contact countries supporting Cuba in the current stalemate with Colombia. If some of these, e.g. Islamic countries, changed sides, this would be a useful signal to the Soviet Union of the damage done by their Afghan venture.

China

58. *Mr Christopher* reported that Harold Brown, the US Secretary for Defence, would be visiting China in the next few days. The trip now had a new importance.

59. *Mr Hurd* thought that the Chinese might now see advantage in offering material support to Afghan rebels as an attractive option.

60. *Mr Gotlieb* said that the Canadians had heard from their mission in Peking

---

[5] No. 7.

7 December 1979 – 1 December 1981

that the Chinese were asking about action in the UN and about the present meeting. He proposed that the Chinese should be informed of the substance of the day's discussions. *Mr Christopher* agreed.

East/West Relations

61. *Mr Gotlieb* thought that it was important to consider the cost to the West of any action. The West had an interest in arms control, détente and the CSCE. Policies should not be abandoned where Western interests would suffer, but there might be areas where we could without damage adjust our approach to issues. The style, timing and substance of our approach to such issues should be carefully examined.

62. *M. de Leusse* thought that the West must be careful not to over react so as to damage their own interests. They thought that the West should abide by the principles that had guided them for the last 1-5 years or so.

63. *Mr Hurd* agreed that the framework of détente should be maintained. Countries should, however, look at their bilateral dealings with the Soviet Union. British and other credit agreements with the Soviet Union were expiring about now. The Russians would interpret the conclusion of the next few months as a signal of business as usual and none of the Western countries concerned should conclude an agreement without consulting the others. He suggested that two groups of officials might be set up in which other NATO countries could participate if they wished: one would study the implications of the Afghan crisis for our contacts with the Soviet Union, and the other the measures we should take to support regional countries like Pakistan. He also pointed to the need to consider means, including leverage, in which the West could try to reduce the likelihood of Soviet interference in yet more countries.

64. *Mr Gotlieb* said that no one was advocating not pursuing détente but the credibility of détente would be in question with the public.

Summing up

65. *Mr Christopher*, in summing up what had been agreed, made the following points:

(*a*) Our reaction should be sustained. It should be pursued by démarches, public statements, etc.

(*b*) All countries were considering what action they should take in their bilateral relations with the Soviet Union. Our displeasure should be shown in some way. We would keep in touch.

(*c*) Countries might decide to change the nature of their diplomatic relationship with Afghanistan. Not recognising, drawing down our Missions and recall of Ambassadors were among the possibilities discussed. The United States would be guided by what the rest would do.

(*d*) We should take the opportunity to point out the lessons of the Soviet action to the Iranians.

(*e*) Help should be given to Pakistan. This could be done through aid, possibly an early debt rescheduling meeting. Additional ways of easing the burden of the refugees should be considered.

(*f*) There was a need to bring to Indian attention the real significance of the Soviet move, and to point out that what we did to help the Pakistanis was not a threat to India.

(*g*) China could be expected roundly to condemn the Soviet Union and to support Pakistan and anti-Soviet groups in Afghanistan.

(*h*) The Soviet aggression should be taken to the United Nations without delay.

UK-Soviet Relations, 1979-82

(*i*) We should point out the anti-Islamic nature of Soviet policy, the disregard of non-alignment and the increasing threat to regional countries.
He concluded that it had been agreed that continuing action was necessary. Possibilities included an early meeting of Ministers or the establishment of a working group, or groups, but no agreement had been reached on how to proceed.

66. *Mr Hurd* noted that there was also general agreement with Mr Christopher's view that it was not in the Western interest to make threats about ending general arms control measures which were to the benefit of the West, and that the SALT process should be pursued.

No. 12

Record of a meeting between Mr Blaker[1] and Mr Brement[2] in the FCO, 31 December 1979, 11 a.m.
Secret (FCO 37/2135, FSA 020/9)

Present:　　　Mr Peter Blaker MP　　　　Mr Marshall Brement
　　　　　　　Mr C.L.G. Mallaby
　　　　　　　Mr C.A. Munro

1. *Mr Blaker* invited Mr Brement to compare the Soviet intervention in Afghanistan in 1979 with their invasion of Czechoslovakia in 1968 and with Angola in 1975. Secondly, he asked if the Americans viewed the Soviet intervention in Afghanistan as part of a pattern? *Mr Brement* said that there were differences of view within the American Government. He thought for his part that Afghanistan was part of a consistent pattern. The Soviet invasion was also a very ominous development. There were differences of view within the Administration as to how successful Soviet intervention would be but he thought that it would turn out to be the Soviet Union's 'Entebbe'[3]. On this analysis there was a danger that in future crises the military option would be considered favourably in Moscow. A successful operation in Afghanistan would be a boost all round for the Soviet military establishment.

2. *Mr Blaker* agreed with Mr Brement's analysis. Our Ambassador in Moscow had described the invasion as an extreme example of the Soviet view of détente. It was a typically opportunist move. The Soviet Union calculated that their interest in détente would not suffer as a result. *Mr Brement* said that the Soviet Union probably regarded a strong US reaction as inevitable but they hoped for a muted reaction by European countries. *Mr Blaker* commented that Britain would certainly react vigorously. Mr Blaker and Mr Brement agreed that the West should react more strongly than the Soviet Union expected. Mr Blaker commented that in situations such as this, the obvious first move was to cancel impending visits, but this had only a temporary effect.

3. Mr Blaker and Mr Brement discussed the prospects for continuing insurgency

---

[1] Minister of State for Foreign and Commonwealth Affairs.
[2] US National Security Council adviser for the USSR/ East Europe.
[3] This refers to the operation conducted by Israeli commandos to free over 100 mainly Jewish hostages held by pro-Palestinian hijackers at Entebbe airport in Uganda in July 1976. Carried out at a distance of over 3,000 miles, and with a minimum loss of life, the operation was considered a great success.

7 December 1979 – 1 December 1981

in Afghanistan. They agreed that the terrain seemed less favourable to insurgent activity than Vietnam had been. _Mr Brement_ pointed out the American forces had succeeded in controlling even Vietnam for a while. The Soviet Union was likely to have a considerable military success in Afghanistan. Mr Brement said that the Soviet Union had already deployed between two and three divisions. It seemed likely that they had decided to introduce whatever forces proved necessary to control key passes and the capital. _Mr Blaker_ agreed that it was in the West's interests that insurgency should continue.

4. _Mr Blaker_ said that an important question was how to stop the Soviet Union doing the same thing in another country. Had the Americans any ideas about possible ways of bringing pressure on the Soviet Union to behave better? _Mr Brement_ said that the Americans were considering what might be done. They would certainly welcome consultation and cooperation with the United Kingdom. The United States was in the process of examining what levers existed but had taken no decisions yet. They were considering whether stopping grain sales would be an appropriate and feasible lever. _Mr Mallaby_ commented that one of the attractions of grain sales as a lever was that it would need only a few countries to agree to deny grain to the Soviet Union to have an effect. In other economic and commercial areas the trouble was that Western countries were in the habit of competing against each other. _Mr Brement_ said that the United States would give great weight to the views of Britain and its other allies. Coordinated action would be vital. It would be better not to try than to try and fail. The Americans would welcome private talks with the British on the whole question of leverage against the Soviet Union and on the question of supporting insurgency in Afghanistan.

5. _Mr Blaker_ said that we should also keep up the propaganda effort. _Mr Brement_ agreed the Soviet Union had at least made it easy for the West this time. Their intervention in Afghanistan could be depicted as a move against Islam, and portrayed as such in Western propaganda. Mr Brement said that the United States had not so far detected any echoes of the troubles in Afghanistan and Iran in Soviet Central Asia but in the longer term, if only for demographic reasons it was inevitable that the Soviet Union would have problems with its Muslim citizens. _Mr Blaker_ commented that these longer term considerations were not relevant to the question of what to do now about Soviet intervention in Afghanistan.

6. _Mr Brement_ asked if France and Italy would be likely to cooperate in any Western effort to exert economic leverage against the Soviet Union. _Mr Mallaby_ said that in the coming weeks the French, Italian and Canadian credit agreements with the Soviet Union were due to expire. France was the key country. French officials and indeed French Cabinet Ministers were opposed to continuing subsidised credit for the Soviet Union but the final decision would be taken by President Giscard himself. _Mr Blaker_ said it would be a major signal of the wrong kind if all the Western countries whose credit agreements with the Soviet Union were due to expire renewed them following the Soviet invasion of Afghanistan, at the existing subsidised rates. _Mr Mallaby_ said that Italy and Canada would follow the French lead. Mr Hurd would be raising the credit point at the main meeting.

7. The meeting ended at 11.25 am.

No. 13

Minute from Mr Hurd to Lord Carrington, 31 December 1979
Secret (FO 37/2135, FSA 020/9)

Secretary of State,

Afghanistan

1. As already reported by telephone, the Allied meeting today[1] was disappointing. US ideas were not clear, and the French (de Leusse) were determined to block any action today—even an agreement that the West take the Soviet Union to the Security Council. As regards both the UN and possible restrictions of bilateral relations with the USSR our own position was well ahead of the field—but no harm in that.

2. Interesting ideas were produced over a wide range:

(*a*) *The UN.* We all agreed that it would be best if the non-aligned took the lead. All except the French agreed that if this was not quickly feasible, the West should take the initiative. I argued for action this week before anxiety died away and before the second stage on Iran. According to Sir A. Parsons[2] the prospects for this are not too bad, and (though he did not tell the meeting) Warren Christopher was telephoned this afternoon by President Carter, who wanted immediate action in the Security Council.

(*b*) *Kabul.* Everyone has different procedures. It was agreed that no one should have political contacts with the new regime for the time being.

(*c*) *Détente and contacts with the Soviet Union.* No one seems in favour of upsetting the framework of détente (European Security Conference, MBFR, Salt II and III etc). There was agreement that we needed to look restrictively at our bilateral contacts and concert a response. I mentioned visits and credit. No one else was specific, except Christopher who said the US would look at a range of these including grain sales.

(*d*) *Iran.* Christopher made the point that there was just a chance of getting the Iranians now to think straight about the world. The EEC Ambassadors in Tehran will be encouraged to speak accordingly.

(*e*) *Pakistan.* The need for encouragement was strongly stressed by the US, e.g. on debts and Afghan refugees. One Canadian suggested she should rejoin the Commonwealth.

(*f*) *China.* To be kept in touch, but handled with care.

(*g*) Christopher told me privately that the US would now step up covert help for the Afghan rebels, which up to now has been food and medicine only.

3. There were thus several loose ends, and our proposal for working groups to tackle specific areas of action was not taken up. A lot of hard work and clear thinking is required if this US initiative is to bear any fruit.

DOUGLAS HURD

[1] No. 11.
[2] UK Permanent Representative to the United Nations.

7 December 1979 – 1 December 1981

No. 14

Sir C. Rose (UKDEL NATO) to Lord Carrington, 1 January 1980, 5.15 p.m.[1]
Tel. No. 2 Immediate, Confidential (FCO 37/2236, FSA 020/1)

Your Telnos 173 and 174 (not to all): NATO Council Meeting: Afghanistan[2]

1. The Council met this morning to discuss Afghanistan. The US Deputy Secretary of State, Warren Christopher, opened the discussion with a statement of the US position. His main points were as follows.

2. Christopher said that the Soviet military intervention in Afghanistan was the first occasion since World War II on which Soviet troops had been used for military action outside the Warsaw Pact countries. In Ethiopia and Angola the Soviet Union had used proxies, Afghanistan represented a qualitative change in the Soviet approach. The justification provided by the Soviet Union was groundless. Christopher recalled the passage on Czechoslovakia in the North Atlantic Council communiqué in 1968.[3] The views expressed in that were equally relevant to Afghanistan and perhaps more so because of Afghanistan's history as a non-aligned buffer state.

3. As regards possible reasons for the Soviet action, it appeared that the Soviet Union was not satisfied in having Afghanistan as an ally but wanted full control over the Afghan regime and its policies because of its concern about the effect on its Moslem population of its possible emergence of [*sic* ?as] an Islamic state. The Soviet Union might have decided to act now in the belief that the possibility of US reaction was lessened by the difficulties the US was facing in Iran. If so the Russians had misjudged since, as a result of the Iranian crisis, US domestic opinion was more united than ever before. Timing was probably also related to the holiday season, the Soviet Union appeared ready to put SALT II at risk or had perhaps concluded that SALT II would not be ratified. The Soviet Union may also have calculated that hostility towards the US in the non-aligned movement would work to its advantage.

4. The significance of the events in Afghanistan for the future would very much depend on Western and world reaction. If the Soviet Union could be shown that its intervention was too costly it might be dissuaded from repeating it elsewhere and might remove its troops from Afghanistan.

5. As regards the present situation in Afghanistan, the US estimated that there were now 30 to 40 thousand Soviet troops in the country. They were occupying Kabul, forming a defensive perimeter around Kabul and moving out into the countryside where they were already believed to have clashed with Moslem insurgents and elements of the Afghan army. The US had unconfirmed reports of mass defection from the Afghan army. Babrak Karmal's regime was totally dependent on Soviet support and had a very narrow political base.

6. The events in Afghanistan would confirm the fears of many countries in the region about Soviet aims. Pakistan would look for Western support. President Zia would no doubt use the events to try to foster national unity. There were signs that

---

[1] Repeated Immediate to Washington, Paris, Bonn, Moscow, UKMIS New York, Priority to Ottawa, Rome; Routine to other NATO Posts, Warsaw, Budapest, Prague, Sofia, Bucharest, East Berlin, Dublin, Islamabad, Kabul, Delhi, Peking, Canberra, Wellington, UKDEL Vienna; Info Saving, Tokyo, Jakarta, Singapore, Manila, Bangkok, Kuala Lumpur.

[2] Not printed.

[3] See *DBPO*, Series III, Vol. I.

UK-Soviet Relations, 1979-82

Pakistan might mobilise a Moslem conference to condemn the Soviet intervention. Alliance members should encourage this. Although the initial Indian response to the Soviet action had been cautious there was no doubt that the Indians would be very concerned. They should be encouraged to recognise the dangers of the Soviet action.

7. Iran had already condemned the Soviet intervention. This would provide an opportunity for Western countries to encourage Iraq towards closer relations with the West. In the Horn, Mengistu might well be viewing events in Afghanistan with some alarm: the other countries in the area would be confirmed in their anti-Soviet position. China would be confirmed in its long held opinion of Soviet expansionism and might offer further assistance to Pakistan.

8. On the implications for the Alliance and East/West relations, the Soviet action had underscored the vital nature of allied defence programmes, specifically the need to pursue TNF and the Long Term Defence Programme and three per cent goal for increases in defence expenditure. There would be a heavy price to pay if the Soviet Union saw a disunited alliance, for example on TNF arms control proposals in the context of TNF and MBFR were at present in the Soviet court. The US intended to move forward on SALT II ratification because of its vital importance although it would now be much more difficult to secure this. It was for consideration however whether it would be right for the Alliance to agree to a European disarmament conference as a follow-up to Madrid.

9. The Soviet action in Afghanistan would have aroused considerable unease in Eastern Europe, notably in Romania and Yugoslavia. Western contacts with the governments of these countries should be reinforced. The US Ambassador in Belgrade had called on the Yugoslav government. The Americans hoped that other Western Ambassadors might follow this example. Yugoslavia would be important in the context of mobilising non-aligned concern about the Soviet action.

10. Christopher said that it was a time for solidarity and resolve by the Alliance. He hoped that alliance members would show a strong response to the Soviet action. Several possibilities should be explored. There was the question of relations with the new Afghan regime. The US had no Ambassador in Kabul and did not intend to have political contacts with the new regime in the near future. It might go further and reduce its Embassy staff or suspend relations. The US Administration was also considering action with regard to its bilateral relations with the Soviet Union in the economic and other fields. The Americans were also giving higher priority to their relations with India, and with Pakistan, including possibly military assistance to Pakistan compatible with legislation on nuclear proliferation as well as aid for Afghan refugees in Pakistan. The US intended to enhance its presence on Diego Garcia and was considering the possibility of a military presence in Somalia, Kenya and Oman. Soviet action should make it in the interest of Iran to solve the hostages problem quickly. The US would also review the position with China during Secretary of Defence Brown's forthcoming visit. Action in the UN would be necessary. It would be important to mobilise and sustain a strong public reaction in the non-aligned and Moslem countries.

11. At the end of the Council discussion, Christopher said that he would be having meetings with the President and others tomorrow 02 January to discuss Afghanistan. The views which had been expressed in the Council would be very helpful at these meetings. The US was not considering any immediate change of policy over the hostages in Iran as a result of events in Afghanistan. The UN Security Council resolution passed yesterday provided a breathing-space for the

7 December 1979 – 1 December 1981

UN Secretary General to mediate with the Iranian government. The US Administration naturally hoped that Dr Waldheim's efforts would be successful though they were not overly optimistic. As far as action in the UN on Afghanistan was concerned, the permanent members of the Security Council were consulting on how best this might be pursued. There were three possibilities: the UNGA, the Security Council under Chapter VI or under Chapter VII. Action in the Security Council would raise the issue of a Soviet veto. The US was determined however to proceed with some form of UN action.

12. MIFTs contain summary of Council discussion, and my comment.[4]

[4] Not printed.

No. 15

Minute from Lord Carrington to Mrs Thatcher, 2 January 1980
PM/80/1 Secret (FCO 37/ 2240, FSA 020/1)

Prime Minister,
Iran and Afghanistan[1]
Both you and my other colleagues in OD[2] will wish to know where we stand following developments over the holiday period.

Afghanistan

1. The Soviet aim seems to be to bring the whole country rapidly under their control, using whatever force may be necessary and hoping that Babrak Karmal will prove more acceptable to the population than Amin. To achieve this, they may tolerate apparent concessions to Afghan and Islamic feeling and soft-pedal Marxist measures for the time being.

2. The Russians for their own reasons might like to withdraw most of their troops once the new government is firmly established, and if the Afghan army later was capable of controlling the country. But we certainly cannot rely on this. They are more likely to be drawn into a prolonged anti-insurgent campaign. And the possibilities of using Afghanistan as a staging post for troublemaking elsewhere, for instance Pakistan or Iran, could in time prove attractive.

3. Afghan governments have long lived in the Russian shadow, and a change from one Marxist to another is in itself not significant. But the manner of the change is unprecedented and could have extremely serious repercussions. I think it is important that the West's response should be robust, lest the Russians are led to believe that such tactics pay off. The Prime Minister's letter to Brezhnev set the tone. We met Americans, Germans, French, Italians and Canadians in London on 31 December,[3] and we hope to get action in the Security Council this week. The meeting of 31 December produced a number of ideas we shall be pursuing; while no one spoke in favour of upsetting the framework of détente (European Security Conference, MBFR, Salt II and III etc), it was agreed that we needed urgently to bring the matter to the Security Council and to consider the implications for détente and bilateral relations with the Soviet Union. We are pressing for further allied consultations on this. On 31 December there was also agreement about the

[1] The section on Iran covering developments in the UN has not been printed.
[2] The Cabinet's Oversea and Defence Committee.
[3] Nos. 7 & 11.

33

UK-Soviet Relations, 1979-82

need to provide encouragement to Pakistan; my intended visit to Islamabad next week serves this end (see below).

4. The Russian move has angered some Non-Aligned and Islamic countries. We are doing what we can to encourage a robust response here too. There is even some hope that the Iranians may eventually begin to think straight about the world.

5. We are in touch with our European and Commonwealth colleagues on recognition. Meanwhile our Ambassador in Kabul has been instructed to avoid political contacts.

Next Steps

6. Against this background, it is important that the West should make clear its concern at the threats to stability in the region and that a coherent response should be made to the Soviet move. It may of course take time to work out the most appropriate positive steps to take. But as a first measure I have it in mind to advance to the middle of next week the date of my proposed visit to Saudi Arabia and Oman, and to extend it by including Pakistan and Turkey. My main objectives would be:

(*a*) to familiarise myself at first hand with the problems of the region;

(*b*) to discuss the threats to stability with the leaders of the countries visited;

(*c*) to reassure our friends that we view these threats with concern.

I am copying this minute to our colleagues in OD and to Keith Joseph and David Howell.

CARRINGTON

No. 16

Record of a meeting between Mr Hurd and the US Ambassador (Mr Brewster), 3 January 1980, 10.30 a.m.
Confidential (FCO 28/3996, EN 021/1)

1. The Ambassador gave Mr Hurd a photocopy with American instructions to seek our reactions, and those of other allies, on a list of steps the United States Government was considering in response to the Russian invasion of Afghanistan. The Americans sought a reply by the close of play today. He apologised for the short notice but stressed that no matter how preliminary our views they would be grateful to have them. The démarche reflected President Carter's desire to keep the ball moving. If no proper response were made the initiative begun with the meeting on Monday 31 December would wither. Those passages in his *bout de papier* mentioning the 'Allies' were the ones to which his Government attached greatest importance.[1]

2. *Mr Hurd* undertook to consider the American request and provide an initial reply the same day. A brief discussion followed on the London meeting on 31 December. *The Ambassador* agreed with Mr Hurd that it had been disappointing; only the Americans, the Canadians and ourselves had been willing to face the issues at stake. The NATO meeting in Brussels on 1 January had been better.[2] The Americans were grateful to the role played by Sir Clive Rose. Touching on specific issues Mr Brewster said that the Americans were recalling their Ambassador in

[1] See No. 19.
[2] See No. 14.

7 December 1979 – 1 December 1981

Moscow as much because of their wish to have his advice during the present discussions in Washington as for symbolic reasons. *Mr Hurd* said that up to now we had not considered recalling our Ambassador from Moscow. Mr Christopher had not mentioned this as a possibility in either London or Brussels. It would be added to the list for consideration. On missions in Kabul, *the Ambassador*, speaking personally, said he did not favour complete closure. Information would become very difficult to obtain. *Mr Hurd* said that there was discussion in the Foreign Office as to whether we could withhold recognition of the new regime indefinitely if we kept our Embassy there. The Afghans might force us to have a 'political contact', for instance, by arresting a British citizen on a trumped up charge. *The Ambassador* detected a dilemma here. Recognition was tantamount to acquiescence in the Soviet intervention. Yet closure of the Embassy could also imply acquiescence in the annexation of Afghanistan.

3. *Mr Hurd* said boycotting the Olympic Games was already a subject of lively controversy. The Olympics were a major political event; sport and politics could no longer be separated. But he doubted whether the Government could provide an early reply. *The Ambassador* hoped we could at least indicate the drift of our impressions. As for grain sales, the Ambassador foresaw problems. His government faced domestic political obstacles. Nonetheless, this could be a significant test for the credibility of the Administration's resolve. Canadian and Australian intentions would be critical.

4. *Mr Hurd* said the consensus within Whitehall on credits for the Russians was now more restrictive than it had been under Sir Harold Wilson five years ago. The issue had been discussed in Whitehall before the Afghan crisis began. Basically, our concern was to ensure that others were not left in a position to outbid us. Perhaps the problem should be considered on the lines firstly of making sure that Governments did not go beyond the proposed consensus; and secondly establishing how far below this generally agreed level they might be prepared to restrict themselves.

5. *The Ambassador* emphasised that his government was not trying to drive others into precipitate action. *Mr Hurd* concluded by raising the machinery to co-ordinate a response among the Allies. For example, some means was required of bringing together all the replies to the questions now posed by the Americans. Perhaps there was a case for a meeting outside the formal NATO structure if that would help bring the French along. In any case there should be another high level meeting soon to maintain the momentum. *Mr Hurd* mentioned that the Secretary of State was considering bringing forward his visit to Saudi Arabia and Oman and going to Pakistan and Turkey as well. The Ambassador welcomed this news.

No. 17

Record of a meeting between Mrs Thatcher and the Soviet Ambassador (Mr Lunkov) at No. 10 Downing Street, 3 January 1980, 3 p.m.
Confidential (FCO 28/3996, EN 021/1)

Present: Prime Minister   H.E. Mr N.M. Lunkov
Foreign & Commonwealth Secretary   Mr N.N. Ouspenski
Mr M.O'D.B. Alexander

UK-Soviet Relations, 1979-82

After Mr Lunkov had completed reading the message from President Brezhnev[1] which he was delivering, the *Prime Minister* asked him about the 'acts of external aggression' referred to in the message. She was aware of none. The Soviet Union constantly asserted in recent days that there had been external intervention or aggression but she could find no evidence of this. The only aggression of which the British Government was aware was that carried out by Soviet forces. The Prime Minister also enquired about the request which, according to the message, had been addressed to the Soviet Government by the Government of Afghanistan on 26 December. So far as she was aware President Amin had still been in power then. Had the invitation to the Soviet Government come from President Amin? *Mr Lunkov* said that information from the Afghan authorities confirmed that internal counter-revolutionaries in Afghanistan had been receiving unlimited support from external sources. The support included weapons, equipment and money and the sources included the United States, China, Pakistan, Egypt and other countries. Scores of centres for subversives had been set up in Pakistan. They were disguised as refugee camps. Armed formations had been prepared for despatch into Afghanistan in these centres and had returned to them for recuperation. Among the instructors in the camps were members of the CIA, and specialists in subversion from China and Egypt. The United States had sought the agreement of the Pakistan Government to an expansion of its activities. A good deal of evidence about these activities had appeared in the British media. There were relevant articles in *The Times* and *Telegraph* of the previous day. In an interview with Mr Peter Sissons on New Year's Eve, the Chinese Ambassador had practically admitted that his Government was interfering in Afghanistan.

The Prime Minister said that even supposing subversive activity was taking place in a country this did not justify others in intervening. After all the Soviet Union itself was responsible for subversive activity in many countries. Such activity should be dealt with by the existing authorities in the countries affected. The Prime Minister noted the sequence of coups in Afghanistan involving Messrs Da[o]ud, Tarakki [*sic*] and Amin and repeated her question about the timing of the request from the Afghan Government to the Soviet Government for help. *Mr Lunkov* said that the Soviet Government had had nothing to do with the coups in Afghanistan. He could only repeat what was said in President Brezhnev's letter. *The Prime Minister* said that it was remarkable that the Soviet intervention had begun while President Amin was still in power but that within a few hours of the arrival of the Soviet troops, President Amin had been shot and a man who was not even in the country at the time of the intervention placed in power. She could only assume that the new President was not the choice of the Afghan people but had been placed in power by the Soviet Army and was being kept there by 50,000 troops. *Mr Lunkov* replied that following President Tarakki's assumption of power in the spring of 1979, the Afghan authorities had warned the world about external intrusions into the country and asked that assistance should not be given to those responsible.

The Foreign and Commonwealth Secretary said that as he understood the position, President Amin had outraged the Muslims to the point where they had taken up arms against him. The opposition was internal. As a result President Amin had appealed to the Soviet Government. But no sooner had Soviet forces arrived than they had shot President Amin. *Mr Lunkov* disclaimed any knowledge of these

---

[1] See Enclosure.

7 December 1979 – 1 December 1981

events. They were internal Afghan matters with which the Soviet Government had nothing to do. The Soviet forces were limited in scale and had been sent purely to repel incursions. They had met no opposition within Afghanistan. On the contrary, some very influential Muslims had welcomed them. Their presence was entirely in accord with the Afghan/Soviet Friendship Treaty. Once a request for help had been made under that Treaty, the Soviet Government could not have rejected it. In any case the Soviet Government had a very long frontier in common with Afghanistan and could not be indifferent to what was happening there. Afghanistan might in some circumstances open a bridgehead for intervention in the Soviet Union. The Prime Minister interjected that this last point was the real reason for the Soviet Government's action.

Mr Lunkov said that many other Governments had troops from the United States on their soil. When the Foreign and Commonwealth Secretary observed that this was condemned by the Soviet Government, *Mr Lunkov* replied that this depended on whether or not the forces in question were present by invitation. Soviet troops had been invited to enter Afghanistan. *The Prime Minister* said that this was not the case. Soviet troops had marched with the intention of annexing Afghanistan and turning it, in due course, into a buffer state. President Karmal was a puppet and a considerable military presence would be required to keep him in power. There would probably be continuing trouble from the Muslim population. If the Soviet Union's own claims were justified, Soviet forces could presumably leave Afghanistan within days. *Mr Lunkov* agreed but declined to be drawn further when asked for a precise estimate of the length of time Soviet forces would remain in the country.

The Prime Minister said that this was the first time that the Soviet troops had entered a genuinely independent country. While their intervention in Hungary and Czechoslovakia had been appalling, it had been recognised that those countries were in the Soviet Union's sphere of influence. But heretofore Afghanistan had been regarded as a country which was free to choose its own destiny. Now it was occupied by 40,000 or 50,000 Soviet soldiers. *Mr Lunkov* said that he was unable to confirm the number of Soviet troops in Afghanistan. This was a matter for the Soviet and Afghan Governments alone. He asked the Prime Minister to look beyond the text of President Brezhnev's message and to recognise that if stability in the region were to be preserved, the Governments concerned would need to display qualities of soberness, equanimity and commonsense.

The Prime Minister said that the British Government had all these qualities but this did not diminish the gravity of the situation that had been created. There were many Governments in the world of which she did not approve but she did not attempt to use armed force to change them. There was only one large imperialist and expansionist power left in the world today. This was the Soviet Union. The Soviet Union was engaged in annexing territory and using its undoubted military power to impose a Government of its own choosing. This was the first time since the war that the Soviet Government had taken such action. Although the Soviet Government had used proxies and surrogates elsewhere e.g. the East Germans in South Yemen, and the Cubans in Angola and Ethiopia, their action in Afghanistan was something new. The Soviet Government should not be surprised that Western Governments regarded the situation as grave. Fresh light had been cast on the motives of the Soviet Government's enormous military expenditure. Nonetheless, the Prime Minister said that she was hopeful the Soviet Government would agree to withdraw from Afghanistan.

UK-Soviet Relations, 1979-82

Mr Lunkov said that the Soviet Government categorically rejected the Prime Minister's allegations about the situation in Afghanistan. He asked why the British Government pretended it knew better than the Soviet Government about the situation in the country. *The Prime Minister* said that the presence of massive Soviet forces and of a new Head of Government who required their presence to retain his office was obvious enough. Nonetheless it was of great importance for relations between the Warsaw Pact and the North Atlantic Alliance that the troops should be withdrawn soon. Their presence could only cause great alarm. She accepted that the Soviet Government was entitled to take measures to defend itself. So was the West. Both sides should be prepared to negotiate from positions of equal strength and to reduce that strength step by step. On that basis she was anxious to see as many contacts as possible between East and West. But recent events in Afghanistan cast doubts on the Soviet Government's motives and in the whole field of East/West relations.

The Foreign and Commonwealth Secretary asked about the implications of the statement in President Brezhnev's message that Britain 'could do something if it so wished' about the ending of armed invasions of the territory of Afghanistan. Did this mean that the British Government were being accused of involvement in these invasions? *Mr Lunkov* said that President Brezhnev was seeking stability and peaceful co-operation in the region. The message invited the British Government to appeal to those who were seeking to overthrow the new regime to desist from their efforts. Despite what had been said in the Press, Mr Lunkov was aware of no Soviet Government statement accusing Britain of involvement. Of course there had been some reports from Afghanistan of such involvement: the British Government would know best what weight to give these. *The Prime Minister* said that the British Government had not been involved in any way in activities of the kind referred to. *Mr Lunkov* said that this was a very important statement. *The Prime Minister* concluded the conversation by repeating her hope that Soviet troops would leave Afghanistan very soon. The Afghan people must be free to choose their own Government. *Mr Lunkov* said that he agreed.

The discussion ended at 15.40 hours.

ENCLOSURE IN NO. 17

Message from President Brezhnev (unofficial translation)

In connection with your message delivered in Moscow on 29 December[2] I must note that the picture it draws of what is happening in the Democratic Republic of Afghanistan is quite far from reality. We have already informed you about the facts of the matter and still stranger seem to look [*sic*] the assertions contained in your message.

You seem not to wish to notice the fact that the question is about the entry of limited Soviet military contingents on request of the government of Afghanistan, I emphasize, exactly on its request. Attempts to cast a doubt on the fact itself of the approach to us on this score by the Afghan side are totally groundless. For almost two years the government of Afghanistan has repeatedly made such requests to us, with one such request addressed on 26 December 1979. You can not fail to know recent public statements of the Afghan side itself which mention these approaches.

[2] No. 7.

7 December 1979 – 1 December 1981

The motivations of these requests are no secret as well. For a prolonged period of time acts of external aggression against the democratic Afghanistan have been taking place, and now at an ever greater scale. In these circumstances the approach of the government of Afghanistan to the Soviet Union for help and assistance in repelling the external aggression, as well as our positive reaction to this request are natural and lawful actions provided for by Article 51 of the UN Charter which clearly states the right of any state-member of the UN to not only individual, but also collective self-defence.

Totally unacceptable are the hints in your message to the effect that the Soviet Union allegedly did something to overthrow the government of Afghanistan. I must quite definitely stress that the changes in the Afghan leadership are made by Afghans themselves. Soviet military contingents took no military actions against the Afghan side and we naturally have no intentions to take them. The Soviet Union has not at all interfered and does not interfere in the internal affairs of Afghanistan which are settled by the Afghans themselves. The Afghan people express its will itself by its words and its deeds.

It has already been said to the British side—and I can repeat it once again—that as soon as the reasons which caused the request of Afghanistan to the Soviet Union cease to exist we intend to withdraw completely our military contingents from the territory of this country.

As to the Soviet Union, it invariably builds its relations with all countries on the basis of complete equality and mutual respect without dividing them to strong and weak, big and small.

In the light of all this any attempts of others to speak as if on behalf of the Afghan people, to determine what is better and what is worse for it can not be taken seriously. If a real care is to be taken about the interests of the people of Afghanistan, one should above all contribute to the ending of armed invasions from outside to the territory of this country. And it is here that Britain could do something if it so wished.

In conclusion I would like to emphasise—although this subject is not touched upon in your message—that despite obvious differences on a number of questions of the international politics, the Soviet Union favours that no excessive emotions and artificial complications are introduced in the Soviet-British relations, but that they should develop in the spirit of mutual understanding, détente and peace. We are convinced that this would be in keeping with the vital interests of the peoples of both countries.

No. 18

Lord Carrington to HM Representatives Overseas, 3 January 1980, 7 p.m.[1]
Guidance Tel. No. 2 Immediate, Confidential (FCO 37/2236, FSA 020/1)

Afghanistan

1. While world indignation over the Soviet Union's ruthless military intervention in Afghanistan remains high, the Soviet Union has resorted to a variety of specious arguments in an attempt to justify its actions.

2. You should take all steps possible to maintain and encourage the momentum of official and public condemnation of the Soviet aggression, and to expose the

---

[1] Although dated 1 January, this telegram was not issued until 7.00 p.m. on 3 January.

mendacity of the Soviet case drawing on paras 3-11 below and on Mr Hurd's interview on BBC radio on 1 January.

Prime Minister's message

3. The text of Mrs Thatcher's message to President Brezhnev has not repeat not been released but you may quote the PM's press office as saying:

Begins. Mrs Thatcher said that she was profoundly disturbed at recent developments in Afghanistan and that she was frankly puzzled by the assertion that recent Soviet action was at the invitation of the Afghan government. There was no evidence to substantiate Soviet charges of outside interference in Afghanistan: the only country which had involved itself in recent years in Afghan internal affairs was the Soviet Union. The Prime Minister told Mr Brezhnev that she believed that the people of Afghanistan had the right to choose their own government without outside interference. Ends.

4. The Prime Minister met the Soviet Ambassador to the UK, Mr Lunkov, today at his request to receive a reply from Mr Brezhnev to her letter.[2] You may say unattributably that the Prime Minister told Lunkov that she knew of no evidence of acts of aggression against Afghanistan or of anything that would have justified the Soviet Union's own armed intervention. She found it difficult to reconcile the sequence of events with the Soviet assertion that it had done nothing to overthrow the previous government of Afghanistan. She reaffirmed her very serious concern over the Soviet action and re-iterated the points she had made in her letter. The Prime Minister concluded by stressing once again the importance of early Soviet withdrawal from Afghanistan.

Additional points

5. The Russians are resorting to 'the big lie' by saying that they intervened at the invitation of the Afghan authorities as allegedly provided for in the Soviet-Afghanistan Friendship Treaty of 1978. It is not credible that the government of the former President Amin, which was in power when the Russians launched their invasion, invited the Soviet action which deposed it and led to [his] own murder. By all accounts the new president, Babrak Karmal, was still in the Soviet Union when the coup took place on 27 December. According to *Izvestia* of 1 January the invitation to intervene came on 28 December but the Soviet build up had commenced well before this.

6. There are reliable indications that initial radio reports of the coup were pre-recorded tape recordings broadcast from transmitters located inside the Soviet Union rather than from Radio Kabul as claimed. There is evidence that when news of the coup was first broadcast, Radio Kabul was transmitting its normal programmes.

7. The assertion in *Izvestia* of 1 January that the UK had instigated Pakistan's opposition to the Afghan 'revolution' is a transparent falsehood. It is absurd to suggest that the troubles in Afghanistan have been caused by any governments other than the previous Afghan regime and the Soviet Union themselves with their policy of imposing a socialist revolution from above.

8. The Soviet Union provided military advice and assistance to the government which they have now overthrown which Babrak, the man they themselves placed in office, described as a merciless tyrannical dictatorship and against which there was a widespread rebellion.

9. By its action, the Soviet Union has demonstrated that it is prepared to

[2] No. 17.

continue to ride roughshod over the interests of people in an independent state. It is evident that it was not satisfied in having Afghanistan as an ally but wanted full control over the regime and its policies. In so doing they are prepared to totally discount the wishes of the people of the country in the furtherance of the Soviet Union's own interests.

10. This is the first occasion since World War II that the Soviet Union has used armed force outside the borders of the Warsaw Pact, though it continues the trend established by Soviet proxies in Angola and elsewhere. The implications are far reaching. If the world does not make it clear by its actions that the Soviet behaviour is totally unacceptable the Soviet Union may be led to believe that the world is apathetic about such action. It is important to drive home to the Soviet Union that the consequences of such action are damaging to Soviet interests. Hence the importance of action in the United Nations.

11. Soviet attempts to justify the aggression on the basis of the UN Charter are a travesty of UN principles. Their action in invading an independent country without any mandate from its people is however in clear violation of the charter.

For your own information

12. British officials warned the Soviet Embassy in London about the military build up in Afghanistan as early as 20 December, i.e. well before the alleged Afghan invitation to intervene. There appears to be little hope of persuading the Russians to reverse their course but we should take every opportunity to make them uncomfortable and bring home to them the consequences of their actions. They should be made to realise that they have miscalculated. This can best be done in the UN where there are three possibilities: the UNGA, or the Security Council under Chapter VI or VII. Urgent consultations are taking place aimed at agreeing a letter addressed to the President of the Security Council which we hope will be signed by a large number of Islamic and non-aligned countries.

13. All posts, but particularly those in Islamic and non-aligned countries, are asked to report by telegram any significant official statements, broadcasts or articles in the media condemning the Soviet intervention. OID[3] will shortly issue a fuller background brief.

[3] Overseas Information Department.

No. 19

Lord Carrington to Sir N. Henderson (Washington), 3 January 1980, 7.40 p.m.[1]
Flash Tel. No. 17 Secret (FCO 28/3996, EN 021/1)

My Telno 12 (not to all):[2] Afghanistan and East-West Relations

1. In response to the US Ambassador's démarche to Mr Hurd on 3 January,[3] please tell the Americans today at a high level that the UK is willing to consider

[1] Repeated Immediate to UKDEL NATO, Paris, Bonn, Rome, Ottawa, UKMIS New York, Moscow; Routine to Warsaw, Prague, Budapest, Bucharest, Tokyo, Sofia, Belgrade, East Berlin, Peking, Dublin, Islamabad, Delhi, Canberra, Wellington, Dacca, other NATO Posts, Singapore, Kuala Lumpar, Bangkok, Manila and Jakarta.
[2] Not printed. This telegram gave details of the measures planned by the US administration in response to Soviet invasion of Afghanistan. They were announced by President Carter in an address to the nation on the evening of 4 January. See *Public Papers: Carter (1980-81)*, Book I, pp. 21-24.
[3] No. 16.

taking the actions towards the Soviet Union described below, as part of a concerted series of parallel actions by members of NATO. We hold to our view that two working groups are needed in NATO to concert the allies' actions.

2. One of the most important fields for consideration is high-level visits to and from the Soviet Union. Provided other members of the Alliance do likewise I am willing to let it be known that a visit by Gromyko, whom I had invited to London in February or March, is no longer convenient. Brezhnev and Kosygin have outstanding invitations to visit Britain, and we could let it be known that no dates were available for the time being. Sir Harold Wilson, who was due to visit Moscow in mid-January in his capacity as President of the GB/USSR Association has decided not to go.

3. The following paragraphs comment on the points in the US Ambassador's speaking note.

4. Withdrawal of Ambassadors from Moscow. This is a matter on which we would wish to act together with our partners in the Nine. We are consulting them.

5. There are no plans for British Consulates-General in the USSR. We could, however, freeze negotiations with the Soviet Union on exchanges on new Embassy sites in Moscow and London.

6. Broadcasting etc. The BBC Overseas Services are giving full coverage to events in Afghanistan and we are taking particular care to brief them fully. Our missions especially in non-aligned countries are being instructed to draw attention as widely as possible to the Soviet aggression. At home, the government will continue to give a lead to public opinion, notably in Parliament after it reassembles on 14 January. Publicity is being given to the Prime Minister's remarks to the Soviet Ambassador when he called today.

7. Our Mission at Kabul consists of only six UK based staff, but we shall consider some further reductions. The No. 2 in the Embassy is absent on leave, the five UK based staff of the British Council are being withdrawn.

8. Since 1971, we have maintained strict ceilings on Soviet diplomatic staff in the UK. We have begun applying our travel restrictions on Soviet diplomats in the UK with especial strictness.

9. There are relatively few Soviet media correspondents in [the] UK and few responsible British ones in Moscow. We would not like the latter to be reduced. Nor do we think that expelling Soviet correspondents from London would hurt the Russians much.

10. Olympics. If other allies did likewise, we would not exclude making the Government's views known to the British National Olympic Committee, but that committee is completely independent of government, which has no power to force it to take any action. We should be interested in US views on whether the International Olympic Committee might be prevailed upon to postpone the games or change the venue.

11. We are glad that the US is considering cancellation or restricting grain sales to the USSR. Britain does not export grain but considers that a decision on restriction by Western exporters would be a very effective lever against the Soviet Union. The UK could approach the European Commission about stopping butter sales to the USSR.

12. The Anglo-Soviet five year credit agreement expires next month. We believe that preferential interest rates, more favourable than those which would apply under the OECD consensus, should cease. We have made this view clear to France, Italy and Canada, whose bilateral agreements with the Soviet Union also

7 December 1979 – 1 December 1981

expire about now. If these other countries join us, we would moreover be willing to consider refusal to replace the existing agreement with a new one. ECGD export credit would then be available on a case by case basis to the USSR.

13. The UK would be willing to join in applying the full rigour of the COCOM system to sales of technology and equipment such as computers to the USSR. Moreover, the question of restricting exports of civil technology in key areas like chemical plant and advanced machine tools has never been studied jointly by Western countries. The UK would be willing take part with others in such a study.

14. Aid. We have terminated bilateral aid to Afghanistan and are cutting off aid in the pipeline (although students here may remain). We shall oppose any proposal for new allocations of aid under UNDP and other aid agencies, the World Bank, and the Asian Development Bank. We intend to ensure that no further EEC food aid goes to Afghanistan.

15. Civil Aviation. We expect like the Americans to be able to reduce special privileges granted to the Russians outside the bilateral air services agreement.

16. The number of Soviet nationals engaged in commercial activity in [the] UK has been limited by numerical ceilings since 1971.

17. Soviet fishing in UK waters is a matter for the EEC. There is none at present.

18. On other exchanges, depending on other allies' actions we shall consider:

(*a*) Cancelling a visit by the Soviet Coal Minister this month.

(*b*) Postponing the annual review of our medical exchange agreement, due in March with the participation or a Soviet Deputy Minister.

(*c*) Shelving planned consultations between senior foreign ministry officials on international subjects, for instance, CSCE, disarmament and UN matters.

(*d*) Cancelling plans for an exchange of visits by military staff academies and rejecting a Soviet proposal for an exchange of ships' visit.

(*e*) Holding up negotiations on a bilateral agreement on visa handling.

(*f*) Cancelling a visit to UK in May-June by the Red Army Choir.

(*g*) Cancelling the Anglo-Soviet agreement on agricultural research cooperation.

(*h*) Delaying issuing invitations for the next meeting of the Anglo-Soviet Joint Commission, due in May and led on the Soviet side by the First Deputy Minister of Foreign Trade.

(*j*) [*sic*] Rejecting a Soviet proposal for an Anglo-Soviet agreement on prevention of incidents at sea.

(*k*) Cancelling or delaying other exchanges which might attract public attention.

19. In the UN, following the President's request to the Prime Minister, the UK has taken the initiative in seeking action in the Security Council and has lobbied widely in capitals for support for a special or emergency session of the General Assembly after a Soviet veto in the Security Council, although any Western initiative of this type could have implications concerning Israel or South Africa.

20. In addition to the above, I am planning a visit between 9 and 16 January to Turkey, Oman, Saudi Arabia, Pakistan and probably India, which will provide good opportunities for demonstrating British support for the countries concerned.

21. We shall consider whether our bilateral relations with other members of the Warsaw Pact should be influenced by the degree to which each endorses the Soviet invasion of Afghanistan.

22. I consider that the important thing is for Western countries to act together and in concert after proper thought and preparation. An impression of allied disarray is highly undesirable. Whatever decisions the Americans reach

UK-Soviet Relations, 1979-82

unilaterally should therefore not be announced until further consultations take place.

No. 20

Mr Hillier-Fry (Kabul) to Lord Carrington, 5 January 1980, 11.40 a.m.[1]
Tel. No. 12 Immediate, Confidential (FCO 37/2238, FSA 020/1)

Soviet Intervention in Afghanistan

1. I took advantage of my meeting with the Soviet Ambassador[2] this morning about the two ITN men detained by Soviet troops (my telegram 14 not repeated)[3] to quiz him about the presence of Soviet forces. Without prompting he said they had been invited by Hafizullah Amin and had established themselves in Kabul by agreement. Their role on 27 December had been to ensure order in Kabul and incidentally to ensure there were no attacks on foreign embassies which could have caused trouble. In answer to my question, he said that Soviet troops had not suffered any casualties. The attack on the Darulaman Palace had been carried out by Parchamites and it was they who had captured Amin. The Parchamites had already a good following in the army and half of the troops guarding Amin turned against him when the Parchamites attacked.

2. In answer to further questions Tabeyev said that the only persons executed with Amin were some of his military aides. Some of his Ministers (he instanced Ziari and Panjshiri) had been set free and were active with party matters: others were in custody and would be brought to trial. There would be no (no) killings. Tabeyev was at pains to explosise [*sic* ?explain] that Babrak Karmal had declared a general amnesty and had guaranteed human rights. There was no reason why HMG should not recognise his government.

3. I asked whether the new government was satisfied with the security situation throughout the country. Tabeyev implies [*sic*] that this was well in hand. There were some Soviet troops outside Kabul but these were only there in order to defend Soviet development projects in the east and at Kandahar. He admitted there might be some Soviet troops in Herat but 'probably only a few armoured cars passing through'. There was very little fighting. Soviet troops would be withdrawn as soon as possible.

[1] Repeated Immediate UKMIS New York; Routine Moscow, Washington, UKDEL NATO, New Delhi and Islamabad.
[2] Fikryat Tabeyev, Soviet Ambassador to Kabul.
[3] Not printed.

7 December 1979 – 1 December 1981

No. 21

Mr Hillier-Fry (Kabul) to Lord Carrington, 5 January 1980
Confidential (FCO 37/2243, FSA 020/1)

The Soviet Occupation of Afghanistan

Summary . . . [1]

My Lord,

The Christmas 1979 occupation of Afghanistan by the Soviet Union has been reported in rather fragmentary fashion by telegrams from this post. I now have the honour to attempt a more coherent account of the happenings which encompassed the physical elimination of President Hafizullah Amin, the installation of a Government headed by a Soviet protégé, Babrak Karmal, and the occupation of the country by the Soviet armed forces.

2. It has indeed been a case of actions speaking louder than words, as words are still lacking to describe many of the key events, and many of the words offered by the principal participants in explanation of those events are palpably untrue.

Prologue

3. The origins of the Christmas 1979 action may lie in August 1978 when Babrak Karmal, then Deputy President of the Democratic Republic of Afghanistan following the Revolution of April 1978, was ousted from the Government together with the other Ministers of the Parcham (flag) Party—the Parcham favoured a purer pro-Moscow line than its fellow Communist Party forming the government of the Khalq (People's) Party. Babrak Karmal went to Prague as Ambassador but was relieved of that post after one month and then disappeared from view, presumably in Eastern Europe, until the Soviet occupation of his country.

4. The more recent story however may be said to begin in September 1979 by which time popular discontent with the regime of Nur Mohammad Taraki, who had been President since April 1978, was widespread and military activity by rebels in several provinces was hardly being contained. On his way back from the Non-Aligned Conference in Havana at the beginning of September Taraki was well received in Moscow, and it is generally believed that plans were then made to remove the Prime Minister, Hafizullah Amin, who was not only the object of much public hatred but also opposed to sharing power with anybody, including no doubt those whom the Russians had in mind. However, the planned action on 14 September in the People's House (the complex of old royal palaces, then used by the President) to which Hafizullah Amin went on the strength of an assurance of safe conduct by the Soviet Ambassador, Puzanov, went wrong: Amin escaped, although his escorting officer was killed in the shooting, and a few days later he announced that Taraki had died in hospital after a long illness. Amin became President as well as Prime Minister.

5. Against this background it was hardly to be expected that Amin should regard the Russians as his friends and supporters or that the Russians should regard Amin's Government as a client regime on which they could rely in the long run. Amin for his part set about strengthening his control of the party and government machine while paying lip-service to the Soviet Union as the best friend of Afghanistan. On their side, the Russians took steps to conciliate and reassure Amin such as replacing Ambassador Puzanov while no doubt finalising their plans for his

---

[1] Not printed.

UK-Soviet Relations, 1979-82

removal.

6. In early December the Russians landed a strike force of three battalions, about 2,500 men, at the military air base of Bagram, about 40 miles north of Kabul. As far as is known, these were the first Soviet combat troops sent to Afghanistan. No announcement was made regarding their arrival and the purpose in sending them is a matter for conjecture. At the time a favoured explanation was that they were intended to bolster any Afghan Army formation in danger of breaking under rebel pressure. It is not known what role they played in the 27 December coup.

7. On 17 December Asadullah Amin, the head of the Intelligence Service as well as being nephew and son-in-law of Hafizullah Amin, was seriously wounded in a shooting incident in his office in the People's House and was flown to the Soviet Union the next day. Seven people were killed in the incident, including according to unconfirmed reports, at least one Minister and the Chief of the General Staff. It may be that this loss of key members of the Amin Government, indicating also that rifts within the Government could no longer be contained, was the final proof to the Russians that Amin's days were numbered, and that they should move swiftly to replace him with someone of their own choosing. Another school of thought is that the shooting of Asadullah Amin and others was engineered by the Russians in order to deprive Amin of support so that he could be removed without resistance.

Arrival

8. During the night of 24/25 December Soviet transport planes began to arrive at Kabul International Airport and this movement continued virtually non-stop for over 24 hours from nightfall on Christmas Day with aircraft landing and taking off at three minute intervals. It is estimated that about 5,000 troops arrived during this time, mostly in light tanks/armoured personnel carriers with four or five men to a tank. Many were deployed in the vicinity of the airport but other contingents moved to the People's House in the centre of town and to various barracks on the outskirts, including the old Darulaman Palace which was now used by the Ministry of Defence (and which by an ironic coincidence was featured on the first post-Daoud banknote just issued to mark the 15th Anniversary on 1 January, 1980, of the foundation of the Khalq Party). Also perhaps by a coincidence, Hafizullah Amin had a few days earlier transferred his office and residence from the People's House to the Tajbeg Palace on the hill behind the Darulaman, the refurbishing of which had been ordered by President Daoud.

9. There was no opposition on the part of the Afghans to this move. There was, however, no report in the Afghan media of this massive arrival of Soviet troops which no attempt was made to disguise. On 26 December the media announced the return to Kabul of the Minister of Public Works, Panjshiri, who had gone to Moscow for medical treatment immediately after the shooting incident of 14 September. As Panjshiri was reputed to be opposed to Amin this naturally provoked speculation that the Russians proposed to replace Amin by Panjshiri.

10. After the coup, the Russians claimed that they had been asked by the Afghan Government to send troops to help them repel imperialist aggressors. The Afghan Government at the time of the first arrival of Russian troops was of course that of Amin. It is possible that he asked for combat troops since the capability or will of the Afghan Army to withstand rebel attacks in the provinces was becoming increasingly doubtful (as indeed was the personal loyalty to Amin of the Kabul garrison). On the other hand, senior officials of the Ministry of Foreign Affairs, including the Political Deputy Minister, Dost, who became Minister of Foreign

7 December 1979 – 1 December 1981

Affairs after the coup, told diplomatic enquirers that the Soviet aircraft were bringing urgently needed supplies because of snow in the north, and not combat troops. Whether the number and nature of the arriving troops surprised Amin or not, nothing was done to hinder their arrival and deployment. Possibly, the relatively small arrivals during the night of 24/25 December did not cause undue concern and then, by the time the main airlift started on Christmas night, control, e.g. of the airport, was firmly in Soviet hands. There is also evidence that the Soviet advisers, who were present certainly down to company level in the Afghan Army units in Kabul, had taken action to neutralize these units.

Coup

11. The coup itself began soon after dark on 27 December. At about 7.15 p.m. Soviet troops seized the Ministry of the Interior in the centre of the new town (slant across the road from the Indian Embassy where the Ambassador was still working, having just got back from his Consulate in Jalalabad). At the same time, we heard heavy gunfire coming from the direction of Darulaman, which only lasted an hour. The main Post Office in town was put out of action by tanks but the radio station, which is at the town end of the main airport road and which was guarded by Afghan tanks, was not attacked until about 9.30 p.m.—by which time the Indian Ambassador, whose residence is a few hundred yards from the radio station, had arrived safely home! The US Embassy is next door to the radio station but was not damaged except for a dozen or so bullet holes in the masonry. The Federal German Embassy, which lies behind the radio station, was also slightly damaged but none of the Embassies in the neighbourhood suffered any casualties.

12. When the first message from Babrak Karmal announcing that he had taken over the Government was broadcast on Kabul Radio's wavelength at about 11 p.m. (from a transmitter in Termez on the Soviet side of the Oxus) Kabul Radio was still broadcasting music on the same wavelength, so the announcement was not very convincing. This suggests that something had gone wrong with the timing of the operation. Apart from this hiccough, the coup seems to have gone very smoothly. All the evidence is that the military side of the coup was a purely Soviet operation without any Afghan military participation on their side.

13. In the early hours of 28 December, Kabul Radio broadcast another speech by Babrak Karmal in which he announced that Hafizullah Amin had been tried by a revolutionary court and executed for crimes against the people of Afghanistan. 'A few of his lackeys' were also executed but no names were given. There has been no announcement since then of the fate of other Ministers of the Amin Government, but there have been reports that some of them, including the recently returned Panjshiri, had been having discussions in the radio station with some of the new Ministers.

New Government

14. In the course of 28 December, the principal members of the new Government were announced. They include not only the Parcham Ministers of April-August 1978 but also the three Taraki Ministers who disappeared after the shooting of 14 September, 1979, and were reported to have taken refuge in the Soviet Embassy. There is also, for good measure, a Minister from Daoud's Government as well as the former Ambassador in London, Abdul Wakil. The new Minister of Foreign Affairs is Shah Mohammad Dost, a career diplomat who had been Political Deputy Minister of Foreign Affairs since the Revolution of April 1978, and who is said to be a long-standing supporter of Babrak Karmal. The appointments indicate an attempt by Babrak Karmal to implement his broadcast

UK-Soviet Relations, 1979-82

intention to re-constitute the unity of the Khalq Party, which is now given the fuller title of the Unitary Wahed People's Democratic Party of Afghanistan.

15. Babrak Karmal himself was not reported to have been seen in Kabul for two or three days after the coup and during this time it is believed that Shah Mohammad Dost acted as Head of Government. The first semi-public appearance of Karmal was on 1 January at a ceremony in the Chehel Sotun Palace to mark the 15th anniversary of the Khalq Party. This was a gathering of about 100 of the party faithful but it was televised (and re-broadcast on two successive days). Karmal appealed for unity, promised all the right things, attacked Amin for his crimes against the people of Afghanistan and also attacked the US as leaders of the imperialist aggressors.

Further Developments

16. In his broadcast message on 28 December Karmal said that on taking office he had requested the Soviet Union for assistance, including military assistance to repel imperialist aggression. Clearly the Soviet troops were already here but, whether by choice or necessity, they began deploying almost immediately to face the consequential threat of rebel attacks in various parts of the country. As indicated above, the Kabul garrison was largely neutralised as the coup was launched; troops, even those guarding Embassies, were disarmed and the Soviet forces assumed complete control, guarding key points but otherwise leaving the city to run itself. Nightfall, however, brought sporadic bursts of fire as Afghans who objected to the presence of Soviet troops sought to eliminate individuals on guard or patrol.

17. For the next few days supplies and reinforcements arrived in Kabul by air and road but there was a definite redeployment of troops towards the east, from where reports of engagements with the rebels soon began to emerge. Heavy movements of Soviet armour and troops by road into the northern provinces took place, as well as air landings in the western province of Herat and the military base to the south of Herat. The number of Soviet troops in Afghanistan is by now estimated to be upwards of five divisions or 50,000 men. Fighting is reported in several areas but it is not always clear whether it is the Afghan Army or the rebels who are opposing the Russians. Clearly, however, it is the Soviet intention to establish their control over the whole country by a physical presence. Equally clearly they have to be prepared to fight (and no doubt, they hope, to destroy) the rebels since the Afghan Army has neither the will nor the capacity to carry on that struggle in its present disorganised state. Inevitably the question in people's minds is whether the Russians have thus landed themselves in a mountainous and inhospitable Vietnam.

18. I am sending copies of this despatch to Her Majesty's Representatives at Moscow, Islamabad, Delhi, Tehran, Washington, UKMIS New York and UKDEL NATO.

I am, Sir,
Yours faithfully,
W. N. HILLIER-FRY

No. 22

Sir C. Rose (UKDEL NATO) to Lord Carrington, 7 January 1980, 4.40 p.m.[1]
Flash Tel. No. 11 Confidential (FCO 37/2238, FSA 020/1)

UKDEL Telegrams Nos. 7 and 8[2]: Afghanistan and East/West Relations.

1. The Senior Political Committee met this morning to consider the implications of the crisis for East/West relations, and possible reactions by Western governments. Most delegations reacted warmly to the lead given by the US and ourselves: but the French raised procedural difficulties over the form of the Committee's report to the Council. Few delegations had instructions on specific measures which their governments were taking or contemplating, all except the French and Germans said they were reviewing the full range of their contacts with the Soviet Union and expected to take decisions soon.

2. After introductory remarks by the chairman (Heichler), Glitman (US) gave a detailed catalogue of the decisions now taken by the US (copy of speaking notes by bag to EESD and Washington only). Scott (UK) drew on your telegram no 17[3] to Washington; as instructed in your telnos 4 and 7 to me and in telecon Scott/Mallaby.[4] He said that the Russians had probably calculated in advance what they thought the Western reaction to their intervention would be; and decided that the risks were worth taking. Our objective must be to show them that they had miscalculated: it was important that the new Soviet leadership which might now be in the process of emerging should learn that there was a heavy price to pay for such actions. He stressed the need for the Alliance to show solidarity, and for individual governments to take steps that were mutually consistent. Now that US measures had been announced, it was urgent for other allied governments to make similar announcements, and these should not be delayed until the Council meeting planned for 15 January: some measures should be announced this week. Quick decisions might be taken most easily in the area of contacts and other bilateral exchanges. In the UK view, it was also important to discuss official credits to the Soviet Union particularly since a number of bilateral agreements on preferential credit rates were expiring at about this time. We would welcome the views of other allies on these issues.

3. During the ensuing *tour de table* Bassett (Belgium) said that his authorities were preparing an inventory of bilateral relations in all areas. Speaking personally, it seemed to him that there were measures which could be taken individually by governments (the US decision on grain was an example), and those that could only be applied collectively, e.g. restrictions on credits. The Olympic Games was an awkward issue for the West because of our tradition of trying to separate sports from politics, and any measures would need to be weighed carefully. Belgium was anxious to avoid any action which might prejudice prospects for SALT III. Mawhinney (Canada) said Canadian Ministers were urgently considering what actions to take. There was considerable scope in the field of bilateral contacts, and it was likely that decisions would be taken to suspend some at least of these. He

---

[1] Immediate to Washington; Priority to Paris, Bonn, Rome, Ottawa; Routine to other NATO posts, UKMIS New York, Moscow.

[2] Not printed. These telegrams conveyed instructions that the Senior Political Committee, NATO (SPC) should as a first step take concerted action on export credits to the Soviet Union.

[3] No. 19.

[4] Not printed. These telegrams gave further instructions for the SPC meeting and stressed the importance of avoiding the impression of allied disarray.

UK-Soviet Relations, 1979-82

agreed with Scott that the question of credit arrangements should be actively considered among the governments concerned. Riis-Jorgensen (Denmark) said that there would be no Danish visits to the Soviet Union at the political level for the time being, and no official measures to stimulate trade. Action on the Olympic Games was not a matter for the Danish government. Governments should think carefully before taking measures in the CSCE context. Yennimatas (Greece) said that a number of measures were under consideration including postponement of negotiations on opening of consulates in Thessalonika and Odessa and the possibility of restricting the numbers of Soviet Embassy personnel and journalists. Iceland and Luxembourg supported the UK and the US and promised details of specific action by their governments.

4. Voorst tot Voorst (Netherlands) strongly emphasised the need to exact a higher price from the Soviet Union than the Russians had anticipated in their calculations. The objective was to restore the 'political deterrent', which had failed: otherwise there would be no future for détente. The Hague was making an inventory of contacts which would be circulated in NATO. Action over CSCE would have to be considered carefully because the Soviet Union was less than enthusiastic about the conference. As regards the Olympics, much would depend on success in mobilising public opinion to take the view that a boycott was an appropriate counter measure. Personally, he thought that his government should restrict the number of visas given to Soviet personnel, e.g. in the Trade Office at Amsterdam.

5. Pfeffer (FRG) agreed on the need to prevent the Soviet Union from engaging in similar ventures in the future. There was a clear need to co-ordinate alliance reactions but at the same time the *acquis* of détente should be preserved.

6. Norway, Portugal and Turkey also supported our line, and promised details of bilateral relations and government action in the near future.

7. Jessel (France) limited himself to a brief account of his Foreign Minister's statement on 6 January, stressing the need for cool heads, and the danger that détente might be sacrificed by hasty action. It was stated French policy not to use commercial relations for political purposes: nor would France profit from the action of others in the commercial fields.

8. There was an unresolved discussion on procedural questions. Jessel questioned the chairman's summary of the terms of reference agreed by the Council for the SPC, and made it clear that he could not accept a report to the Council couched in the form of recommendations (whereas most other speakers had said that the report should not merely be a catalogue of measures under consideration in the different capitals). This argument is likely to continue at the next meeting at 1400Z tomorrow.

9. At a parallel meeting of the Political Committee, to discuss Western relations with countries in the region and possibilities for their development in the light of the Soviet intervention in Afghanistan, Howells drew on the brief in your telegram No. 5.[5] Delegations were invited to exchange further views at the Political Committee meeting on 8 January (0930Z) and to circulate written contributions, before a further meeting on 9 January (1400Z), towards a paper to be prepared by the International Staff in the form of a Chairmen's Report. De Belenet (France) objected to such a report but was overruled by the chairman who said with strong support round the table, that he would seek confirmation of his instructions from

[5] Not printed. This telegram contained the text of a message delivered to the French and German MFAs stressing the need for concerted action and regret 'if our actions were much longer delayed'.

7 December 1979 – 1 December 1981

the Secretary-General.

10. Whatever form the report takes its value will be determined by the written contributions provided by delegations. We shall be drawing on telegrams already repeated to us but would be grateful to receive, if possible by 1800Z on 8 January, supplementary details of our bilateral and multilateral aid to the region, including military supplies, and an assessment of the influence that these events may have on our relations with China.

No. 23

Minute from Mr Mallaby to Mr White, 7 January 1980
Confidential (FCO 37/2239, FSA 020/1)

Soviet Motives in Afghanistan

1. I have today submitted separately a note for the Prime Minister on 'Why did the Russians invade Afghanistan?'[1] That note does not give fear of contamination by Moslem extremism as one of the reasons for the intervention. The Soviet leaders are inveterate makers of worst case assumptions and I have no doubt that they dislike Moslem extremism and fear that it could one day infect Moslem areas of the Soviet Union. To have had a Moslem extremist Afghanistan besides Moslem extremist Iran would have been uncomfortable. But Soviet control in central Asia, so far as we can tell, is very strong. It would have been possible, if fear of Moslem extremism was a prime motive, to react by new measures of internal control, without having to resort to all the complications [and] international odium of committing aggression. In other words, I believe that fear of extremist contamination may have been a background long-term consideration. The major, immediate causes were the ones given in my separate submission.

2. Needless to say, none of the above means that we should not point, in speaking to Non-Aligned Moslem countries, to the disregard of Islam which the Soviet Union has demonstrated by the invasion.

3. I may as well take this opportunity to comment also on the theory that the invasion of Afghanistan might mean that the Soviet leadership is now dominated by the military. If this were so, it would be a reversal of a tradition, dating from the inception of Soviet power, that the party leadership controls the military. When Marshal Zhukov, the great hero of the War and presumably a man of real popularity in the USSR, was thought to be showing Bonapartist tendencies, he was removed from office. The invasion of Afghanistan can be explained in terms of policies of the Brezhnev leadership, although it is the most 'hawkish' single act of that leadership so far. A more interesting question is whether a military success in Afghanistan will give the military leaders a somewhat greater say in the leadership after Brezhnev and Kosygin. This is possible but uncertain.

C. L. G. MALLABY

[1] See Enclosure. A note on this subject was requested following a conversation between Lord Carrington and Mrs Thatcher on 2 January. A similar appreciation was undertaken by the JIC and circulated as JIC(80)(N) 4: 'Soviet Intervention in Afghanistan—An Interim Assessment' (see Appendix). The JIC paper was chosen for inclusion in the Prime Minister's weekend box by Mr Alexander who noted that it 'seems to reflect many of the thoughts in the FCO paper' (PREM 19/135).

UK-Soviet Relations, 1979-82

ENCLOSURE IN NO. 23

Why did the Soviet Union invade Afghanistan?

Soviet Foreign Policy: Expansion and Opportunism

1. A major aim of Soviet foreign policy is to gain influence worldwide and to reduce and limit Western and Chinese influence. The cohesion of NATO, reinforced recently by demonstrations of resolve such as the decision on TNF modernisation, has blocked Soviet military expansion in Europe for the time being. So the Russians have been concentrating on amassing military strength which could be used for political arm-twisting in Europe, as well as on subversion, propaganda and diplomatic blandishment.

2. The main thrust of their expansionism has been in the developing world, where in recent years they have become much more assertive. In 1975, they correctly judged that the United States, after Vietnam, would not react strongly to the unprecedented military intervention by Cuban proxy forces in Angola. Then came the intervention in Ethiopia, much greater influence in South Yemen, and Vietnam's invasion of Kampuchea.

Motives in Afghanistan

3. The Soviet desire for greater influence is especially strong in relation to nearby countries. The Russians have steadily built up their influence in Afghanistan, particularly since 1973 when the monarchy was overthrown. In April 1978, they made a major advance through the installation of Taraki's communist regime. Although this was rapidly weakened by internal dissension, the Russians continued to support the government and gradually increased the numbers of Soviet civilians and military advisors. The crude doctrinaire approach of the government, aimed at increasing its power in the provinces, and a hurried land reform programme alienated the Muslim tribes. The Afghan army proved incapable of dealing with the insurgents. Russians began to be killed. The rebellion was very disorganised but the government began to crumble with purges and shootings. President Taraki tried to remove his Prime Minister Amin; but Amin, in whom the Russians seem to have had no confidence, came out on top. Moscow was soon faced with a dilemma; to risk the ousting of Amin by some group which might prove anti-Soviet and possibly pursue a nationalistic Moslem extremist line, or to intervene, install an alternative of their own choosing and try to end the revolt. Careful plans had clearly been laid in case the second course was chosen, and the infrastructure had been installed during many years of Soviet aid. The Russians used excuses for aggression that were even more breathtakingly untrue than on past occasions. The major reasons why they acted were that they thought they risked losing their investment in a neighbouring country, when Iran was already in chaos and, on the other side of Afghanistan, China was becoming a world power. In addition, abandonment of a 'socialist revolution' would have meant loss of face.

The Invasion

4. In undertaking this first use of Soviet armed forces outside the Warsaw Pact since the War, the Russians must have calculated that the advantages for their position in Afghanistan outweighed the risks in East-West relations and to Soviet standing in the world. They perhaps thought that Western protests and gestures would be short-lived and that there would be no retaliatory measures which would really hurt the USSR. They will have foreseen the risk of driving the West and

7 December 1979 – 1 December 1981

China closer together but may have judged that this process was in any case taking place. They presumably now intend to quell the rebels to a large extent but, despite the disunity and inefficiency of the rebels, this may require more Soviet troops. The Soviet political purpose will be to consolidate a lasting grip on Afghanistan, while maintaining the country's nominal independence and its membership of the Non-Aligned movement.

Implications

5. The Russians will hope, from their new base in Afghanistan, to be better placed to extend their influence in Asia, and to make further advances in Russia's long-standing search for access to the Indian Ocean. Pakistan is unstable and could be vulnerable. The Soviet Union could seek to exploit the border disputes between Afghanistan and Pakistan as a basis for political and military intervention. In Iran, the Russians have not so far been involved in the revolution, and their invasion of Afghanistan will add to Iran's distrust of the Soviet Union. But the latter has very strong power-political and energy motives for trying to gain influence in Iran if opportunities arise out of the current chaos there. The Russians will hope to increase their influence in India if Pakistan moves closer to the West.

6. New Soviet leaders may prefer to be cautious on the international scene for a time. But, if the present military intervention succeeds, the use of Soviet or proxy forces in developing countries will attract the Soviet Union even more in the future. At the same time, the Russians have reasons for pursuing a limited kind of détente with the West—notably the desire to avoid confrontation with the US and for technology and grain on credit. Whether the military option is actually adopted on future occasions will thus depend significantly on whether the West and the world react now to the invasion of Afghanistan more sharply and lastingly than the Russians have expected.

No. 24

Sir C. Keeble (Moscow) to Lord Carrington, 7 January 1980
Confidential (FCO 28/4194, ENS 014/2)

Soviet Union: Annual Review for 1979

Summary . . . [1]

My Lord,

1. This Review must be dominated by the Soviet military occupation of Afghanistan which began on Christmas Eve. It is difficult yet to offer even an immediate assessment of this operation, let alone the more reflective analysis which might be appropriate for an annual review. The Afghanistan campaign must however mark a new stage in the Soviet Union's relations with the rest of the world.

2. In my Review for 1978,[1] I said that the Afghanistan revolution represented a significant extension of Soviet influence and that the Soviet Union, with its Friendship Treaty, had put on to a formal basis what Brezhnev described as 'a qualitatively new relationship'. During 1979 the Soviet Union realised that political and economic means backed by limited numbers of military advisers might not suffice to hold Afghanistan firmly within the Soviet orbit. The resultant

---

[1] Not printed.

UK-Soviet Relations, 1979-82

military action demonstrated just what the qualitatively new relationship meant. The Soviet Union believed that in a situation where there was no risk of direct military confrontation with a major power it could afford to use substantial military force to achieve a political end, covering its action with pretexts, including prior foreign intervention, so flimsy as to constitute an added affront to the international community. There can scarcely be a country, even including the Soviet Union's closest allies, which does not feel anger, disquiet or both.

3. I must admit that I was surprised at the cold-blooded effrontery of the action in Afghanistan. I ought not to have been. When Soviet force is used it is used massively, swiftly and combined with political brutality. There was nothing in the Afghanistan operation which ran counter to the classic Soviet pattern. In Angola and Ethiopia it was convenient to use Cuban forces. Afghanistan required Soviet forces. So they were used. What I still find slightly surprising is the clumsiness with which the international presentation was conducted. A sequence of events under which Soviet troops are introduced on the 24th, and their introduction publicly justified by an appeal said by the Soviet Union itself to have been made on the 28th by a new puppet government, after the Prime Minister in power at the time the Soviet forces entered has been murdered, indicates either a certain carelessness for detail or a remarkable contempt for international opinion.

4. In assessing the occupation of Afghanistan it is well first to look back at the year's other major military operation, the Chinese punitive attack on Vietnam, a country bound to the Soviet Union in a treaty relationship if anything stronger than that with Afghanistan. Yet Brezhnev, having threatened China, committed no Soviet forces. His decision in relation to Vietnam must have been based on an assessment that China meant what it said when it declared the limited nature of the operation; that there was no absolute need to introduce Soviet forces in order to sustain the Government in Hanoi; and that military action against China itself could not have been quick, limited and decisive. So China administered the 'lesson' and in doing so probably heightened Soviet readiness to take military action in circumstances where it could do so with impunity. The Vietnamese occupation of Kampuchea served, however, to awaken awareness among the nations of South East Asia of the threat they might face. For their part, the Russians proved sufficiently realistic in their attitude to China to recognise its increasing importance in world affairs by beginning talks on normalising relations. The fact that discussions have not yet broken down represented a degree of progress in the unusual world of Sino-Soviet affairs.

5. In the context of the development of Soviet foreign policy during 1979 it is also appropriate to consider Iran. It was in November 1978 that Brezhnev issued his public warning against intervention. Since then as the revolution has developed, the Soviet Union, whatever its own irritation at the interruption of its gas supplies and its distaste for Moslem fanaticism, has been able to draw comfort from the loss of American influence, the change in the balance of power in the Middle East and the weakening of the West by the escalation of oil prices. After indicating, at a relatively early stage, that the Iranian revolution had a long way to run, the Soviet Union offered little direct comment, referred only occasionally to the Tudeh Party, concentrated on criticism of the US and appeared to be biding its time while the internal situation evolved. It was an interesting sign of the importance attached to total control over Afghanistan that to achieve it the Soviet Government was willing at the end of the year to accept the risk of prejudice to its influence in the Moslem world. Looking more widely it is perhaps not fanciful to hope that if the West

plays its cards well we may, in retrospect, see 1979 as the year when the events of Kampuchea and Afghanistan made the tide begin to ebb away from the Soviet Union in the politics of the Third World.

6. If Vietnam, Afghanistan and Iran were the principal points of concern in relation to the Third World, the consolidation of the Soviet hold on Ethiopia and South Yemen was not unimportant. There were no new Soviet initiatives in the Arab-Israel dispute.

7. The conclusion of SALT II and the NATO decision to modernise its Theatre Nuclear Forces in Europe made 1979 a significant year for the development of Soviet foreign policy at the strategic level. At the start of the year the Soviet Union enjoyed a remarkably satisfactory situation in respect of the nuclear and conventional balance with NATO. Parity in strategic intercontinental nuclear weapons had been established and, with the prospect of sustaining it at minimal cost, the Russians must have thought it worth while making some movement to secure signature of SALT II. At the theatre level the development of the SS-20 rocket and Backfire bomber had given the Soviet Union a qualitative if not quantitative superiority and with the Vienna negotiations on the reduction of forces stalled, the Soviet superiority in conventional forces in Europe remained substantial. With this comforting prospect the Soviet Union developed its relationship with the West, concentrating on high-level contacts with the US, France and Germany. President Giscard d'Estaing visited Moscow in April, Gromyko was in Bonn in November and Schmidt was to meet Brezhnev in Moscow early in 1980. As for the US, the meeting between Carter and Brezhnev at Vienna, with signature of SALT II, offered for a moment the hesitant promise of an easier bilateral relationship between the superpowers. But the underlying conditions were not such as to permit it. The Soviet Union believed that it was dealing with an indecisive and inconsistent American Administration. Over-confident after the success of the campaign against the 'neutron bomb', the extraordinary muddle over Soviet troops in Cuba and the acute American dilemma over the hostages in Tehran, it may well have miscalculated the will of President Carter to hold the NATO alliance together and to respond to the occupation of Afghanistan. By the end of the year, with the West reassessing its policies in the light of Afghanistan, the ratification of SALT II unlikely and NATO preparing, despite a Soviet campaign based on letters from Brezhnev to NATO Heads of Government and a major speech by Brezhnev in East Berlin, to install Cruise missiles and Pershing II rockets in Western Europe, the strategic prospect for the future was substantially less reassuring to the Soviet Union.

8. The Soviet actions in respect of Afghanistan, Vietnam and Iran and policy towards the West during 1979 provide an excellent illustration of the different facets of a complex but to the Soviet mind consistent foreign policy. The essence of that policy, misleadingly described as détente, has been to establish enough stability in the relationship between the major powers to allow the Soviet Union to pursue its proclaimed policy of shifting the balance of power in favour of 'socialism', or in other words, without risking its own security, to extend by covert or overt means its influence and ultimately its political control within the developing world—and, albeit more cautiously, within Europe itself. The tactics and the timing have been determined by a careful assessment of the risks and opportunities in each case. Where the risk of extended conflict was high or the time perhaps premature, caution and patience prevailed. In the case of Afghanistan, the inhibiting factors were absent. Soviet policy there had a double basis. The reversal

UK-Soviet Relations, 1979-82

of the April revolution could not be accepted and the Soviet Union would not permit a State bordering the Soviet Union 'to be turned into a bridgehead of imperialist aggression', i.e. such a State should accept subservience to Soviet policy, although the extent of that subservience, the means of attaining it and the timing might depend on the local circumstances. It is because the only wholly effective inhibiting factor is the security of the Soviet Union itself that the Soviet détente policy is so hard to contest effectively unless others are ready for a trial of nerve which in a nuclear world can seem reckless. In fact, because of the Soviet Union's obsession with its own security, Soviet expansion can, with firmness and patience, be contained. But this takes me beyond the bounds of an annual review.

9. If 1979 was a year in which the world had clearly revealed to it the nature of Soviet foreign policy, it was also a year in which the Soviet Union had to acknowledge the failings of its economic policy. A growth rate of about 2 per cent would not look bad for a developed economy but is not adequate in the present state of the Soviet Union. Day after day *Pravda* has come out with case histories of failure in different industries and, in his speech to the Central Committee in November, Brezhnev summed it up in an explosion of irritation and frustration, naming nine of his Ministers for various degrees of inefficiency, yet having nothing to offer except yet more exhortation. A former Pakistani colleague once said to me 'Communism is like a car with bottom gear only. It is good for getting you out of the mud, but not much use on the motorway'. The Soviet economy is no longer in the mud, but it cannot cope with the motorway and the driver's remedy of blowing his horn and cursing the passengers has little effect. In practical terms I have the feeling that the sheer problem of a Government trying to plan every detail of the economic life of a country of 260 million is just too much. One of our British visitors was recently received by the Deputy Minister of Foreign Trade, Mr Kuzmin. Explaining the production of consumer goods, Kuzmin said 'We know the breakdown of the population by age and sex and we can calculate easily enough the requirement for socks and stockings. But then you come along with tights and all our planning is thrown out'. *Pravda* comes out with an article 'Oh, those tights'. Brezhnev addresses the Central Committee on everything from nuclear power to nappies. The miracle is not that the economy creaks but that it functions at all, when every detail of it is a responsibility of the Government itself. Searching for remedies the leadership have castigated the lower and middle reaches of the Party. Their dilemma was well revealed by Scherbitsky, the Party Leader in the Ukraine, who was given a half page of *Pravda* at the end of the year to call for enthusiasm and creativity. 'I think I am not mistaken when I say that the prerequisite for a further development of the initiative of the masses and of the creativity of labour exists in the nature of our system of society, the economy and the State, in our conception of life.' His readers must have sighed as they reached for the vodka bottle.

10. Each winter the world has wondered whether Brezhnev would survive to the summer. This December again he is ill, but not too ill to congratulate his new Afghan protégé. Kosygin has been seriously ill for over two months. Whether and when the change of leadership will come I cannot predict, but the fact that the military occupation of Afghanistan was carried out when neither Brezhnev nor Kosygin was wholly fit makes it reasonable to conclude that there is no reason for optimism about the course of events when they are gone.

11. In March The Duke of Edinburgh paid a successful visit to Moscow in his capacity as President of the International Equestrian Federation. It coincided with

7 December 1979 – 1 December 1981

an improvement in Anglo-Soviet relations which continued in the early months of the Conservative Government. The Soviet leadership have a certain respect for plain speaking. They were much impressed by the Prime Minister's action in receiving Mr Patolichev, the Foreign Trade Minister, who arrived in London immediately after she had taken office and the frank discussion which Mrs Thatcher had with Mr Kosygin at Moscow airport on her way to Tokyo seems to have gone down rather well. Your own action in receiving the Deputy Foreign Minister, Mr Zemskov, was much appreciated and the subsequent political consultations at official level were developing satisfactorily in the second half of the year. The British export trade to the Soviet Union did not however flourish. Even in cash terms it looks like amounting to only about £420 million in 1979, the same as in 1978, while Soviet exports to Britain will rise from £688 million to about £800 million. I doubt whether in 1980 we shall even reach the 1979 figure.

12. With the intensification of the Soviet campaign against modernisation of NATO forces in Europe, the Anglo-Soviet relationship became more strained and Soviet hostility more apparent. It was focused first on the Prime Minister's Luxembourg speech of 18 October[2] and later on her reference to the need for the West to be able to negotiate from a position of strength. Now, the occupation of Afghanistan means that we and our allies must review the bilateral relationship and it is right that we should prepare for a further period of tension. There is always a temptation for an Ambassador to recommend measures to improve relations. Indeed he has a responsibility in this respect which is not just a matter of echoing the lady whom I heard say to her neighbour on the No. 11 bus 'You know, dear, it's nice to be nice'. I have in earlier despatches argued the case for our developing a more substantial relationship with the Soviet Union. I believe those arguments still to be valid. Our objective should be a relationship of mutual respect founded on consistent firmness and courtesy, pursued in close concert with our allies and designed to make it plain that the Soviet Union cannot attain the détente it seeks if it continues its expansionist policies. Your despatch of 7 December[3] reads well in the light of the Afghanistan adventure and I hope that the broad line of policy established by it can be maintained.

13. An annual review of the Soviet Union could become a review of the whole international scene. This has been a remarkable year, enlightening in the way that the essential features of Soviet foreign policy have been displayed, but heartening in the evidence it has given of the inability of the Soviet system to produce either prosperity at home or respect abroad. I am conscious that I have omitted much. For that the calendar of events[4] must suffice.

14. I am sending copies of this despatch to Her Majesty's Ambassadors at Washington, Bonn, Paris, Helsinki, Peking, Belgrade, Warsaw, Prague, Budapest, Bucharest, Sofia, East Berlin and Kabul; and to the UK Permanent Representative at NATO.

I am, [etc.,]

C. KEEBLE

---

[2] The Winston Churchill Memorial Lecture, 'Europe: the Obligations of History'. In this speech Mrs Thatcher criticised Soviet foreign policy and argued that if NATO did not station Pershing and cruise missiles in response to the Soviet deployment of the SS-20 'this might tempt the Soviet leaders to think they could exercise political pressure on Europe. Such a situation cannot be allowed to arise.' A copy of the speech can be found on the Margaret Thatcher Foundation website: http://www.margaretthatcher.org/.

[3] No. 1.

[4] Not printed.

No. 25

Submission from Mr Mallaby to Mr Fergusson, 7 January 1980
Confidential (FCO 28/4196, ENS 020/1)

Afghanistan: British-Soviet Relations

1. FCO telegram No. 17 to Washington[1] gives a first account of the actions we are prepared to take against the Russians. Guidance telegram No. 216 of 30 August 1968[2] describes our policy towards British-Soviet relations after the invasion of Czechoslovakia.

2. We now need to do, and be seen to do, what we can to damage Soviet interests, in concert with our Allies. I *recommend* that our policy in bilateral relations should be to:

(*a*) avoid generally contact with the Russians at Ministerial and Deputy Ministerial level for the next 2-3 months. This would avoid prominent events which might enhance Soviet prestige, attract criticism in this country, or enable the Russians to claim that business was proceeding normally;

(*b*) try to stiffen the conditions surrounding Soviet imports from the UK by action on export credit and in COCOM;

(*c*) but otherwise allow normal trade contacts to proceed as usual so as not to damage the competitiveness of British exporters;

(*d*) cancel exchanges and other contacts in the military field;

(*e*) freeze official consultations between Foreign Ministries and negotiations on mainly political matters;

(*f*) freeze cultural exchanges which are likely to enhance Soviet prestige but continue with other cultural contacts which may not be welcome to the Russians;

(*g*) allow contacts between experts under British-Soviet bilateral agreements to go ahead normally except where these are clearly more in the Soviet than the British interest;

(*h*) review urgently the possibilities of stiffening our policies in civil aviation and shipping. Consultation on this in Whitehall is in hand.

Our ability to achieve (*b*) will depend crucially on the attitudes of our Allies, and the desirability of fully implementing the other policies will also depend on our Allies' actions.[3]

3. On this basis, I have divided forthcoming bilateral events into four categories listed at Annex A.[4] The Annex contains some recommendations on particular events and I shall submit others as appropriate.

4. There is one event I have not listed which may cause particular difficulty. The Duke of Edinburgh is planning to visit Moscow for the Olympics in July-August in his capacity as Chairman of the International Equestrian Federation. This would attract attention. A decision on Ministerial advice can, however, await developments over the Olympics generally.

C. L. G. MALLABY

---

[1] No. 19.

[2] See *DBPO*, Series III, Vol. I, No. 17, note 2.

[3] Mr Fergusson minuted on 7 January that he was in general agreement with Mr Mallaby 'taking into account the difficulty of preserving the important criterion '*in concert with our allies*', on which further action is now proceeding.'

[4] Not printed.

7 December 1979 – 1 December 1981

No. 26

Letter from Mr Alexander (No. 10) to Mr Lyne, 8 January 1980
Confidential (FCO 13/966, PC 295/1)

Dear Roderic,

Afghanistan: Participation in the Olympic Games

When the Foreign and Commonwealth Secretary called on the Prime Minister this afternoon he raised the question of Britain's participation in the Olympic Games in Moscow this summer.

The Prime Minister said that she agreed with Sir Curtis Keeble that withdrawal from the Olympics by a substantial number of the Western nations would be the gesture that would hurt the Soviet Government most, at least in the short term. She asked whether there was any possibility of another city offering to host the Games. The Foreign and Commonwealth Secretary said that he thought this would be impracticable. He and the Prime Minister agreed that the role of Government in this question was limited. But the Prime Minister pointed out that it would be very difficult for the Government to avoid taking up a position, e.g. in dealing with Parliamentary Questions. The Government had expressed a view on the question of the British Lions Rugby Tour to South Africa and would certainly be asked to do the same in regard to the Olympic Games.

The Prime Minister made it clear that her own inclination would be to recommend against participation, but she agreed with the Foreign and Commonwealth Secretary that it would be important to co-ordinate our position with that of other Western Governments. The Foreign and Commonwealth Secretary said that perhaps the best outcome would be if the Government recommended against participation but the various committees, and the participants themselves, decided to go to Moscow none the less.

Given the Prime Minister's interest in this problem, I should be grateful to be kept in the picture as thinking develops.

I am sending a copy of this letter to Geoffrey Needham (Department of the Environment).

Yours ever,

MICHAEL ALEXANDER

No. 27

Minute from Lord Carrington to Mrs Thatcher, 8 January 1980
PM/80/4 Confidential (FCO 28/3997, EN 021/1)

Prime Minister,

Soviet Intervention in Afghanistan

1. Following my minute of 2 January to members of OD,[1] we have been pressing on with the discussion of British and Western reactions to the Soviet intervention. The UK took the lead in calling for discussion in the United Nations Security Council, which resulted satisfactorily in the USSR having to veto a Resolution sponsored by the Non-Aligned. In view of the new importance,

[1] No. 15.

UK-Soviet Relations, 1979-82

following Afghanistan, of developing our relations with countries in the region, I am off tomorrow on a visit to Turkey, Oman, Saudi Arabia, Pakistan and India. We are withdrawing our Ambassador from Afghanistan, reducing the Embassy staff, closing the British Council office and cutting off our aid apart from allowing Afghan students to stay in Britain.

2. I am firmly convinced that it is very important that Western countries should react to the invasion of Afghanistan in ways which will demonstrate to the Soviet Union, and to the Soviet people, that aggression brings penalties. The strength and durability of the Western reactions will influence the likelihood of further Soviet moves of this kind in the future. President Carter has already announced some important steps which should hurt the Russians, notably the restriction on grain sales. At British suggestion, discussion is taking place in NATO about the measures which the members of the Alliance could take in their relations with the USSR. Some of our Allies, notably the French, may well remain reluctant to do anything much.[2] A meeting of the NATO Council with ministerial participation, which Douglas Hurd will be attending on 15 January, should show whether concerted action is possible.

3. So far as the UK is concerned, I think there is interdepartmental agreement at official level that we can join in concerted moves by members of NATO to abstain from top level and ministerial and deputy ministerial contacts with the USSR for three months and perhaps longer; end the special preferential credit rates at present available to the Russians and not replace the Anglo-Soviet credit agreement which expires next month; cancel military exchanges, such as naval visits; and apply the full rigour of the COCOM restrictions on exports of sensitive technology to the USSR.

4. But I am not satisfied that these measures alone would meet the major need for a firm move against the Russians. I hope my colleagues will agree on further measures, in the economic field. I suggest that the UK should press in the European Community for moves to prevent any supply to the Soviet Union of grain which would help to replace that withheld by the United States; to halt butter exports to the Soviet Union by removing the much criticised export subsidy; and to consider restriction of sugar sales. I think we should also be ready to join with our Allies in a study of whether civil technology which the USSR needs from the West should be brought under restrictions. Officials, in urgently studying these measures, should also consider what scope the Soviet Union would have for counter-moves. It would of course be important, until joint decisions were taken in these fields, to take all precautions to prevent leaks to the press.

5. I believe that few things would hurt Soviet prestige more than the absence of a number of Western countries from the Olympic Games this year. But we face the major difficulty that the decision on British participation is not for the government. On the other hand, if we do not advise those concerned in Britain against participation in the Games, we could be criticised for inconsistency in the light of our advice that the rugby tour of South Africa should not go ahead. I should be interested to know Michael Heseltine's views on this problem.[3]

[2] In a meeting with Mr Palliser on 9 January, the French Ambassador confirmed that France was not contemplating any direct positive retaliatory measures against the Soviet Union and would not be prepared to take action on any of the measures so far put forward in NATO. The French justified this position by referring to France's special responsibility for détente and their different approach to East-West relations.

[3] See No. 39.

7 December 1979 – 1 December 1981

6. I am copying this minute to our colleagues in OD, to Keith Joseph, David Howell, Michael Heseltine, Peter Walker and Michael Havers, and to the Secretary of the Cabinet.[4]

CARRINGTON

[4] On 10 January the Cabinet expressed considerable doubt about economic measures against the Soviet Union (and Iran), given the vulnerability of Britain's position as a trading nation and the extent of the country's economic problems (see No. 41, note 1).

No. 28

Letter from Sir C. Keeble (Moscow) to Mr Fergusson, 9 January 1980
Confidential (FCO 28/3996, EN 021/1)

Dear Ewen,

Afghanistan

1. Though there are many unknowns, it may be useful for me to speculate as best I can on the background to the Soviet decision to intervene in Afghanistan.

2. One may go back beyond the April 1978 revolution, but there is no doubt that from the time of that revolution the Russians were resolved to control Afghanistan. Soviet involvement in Afghanistan affairs was increased, but the fundamental instability of the country was frustrating effective political control. This was true even under Taraki who purged erstwhile supporters as well as opponents and who was unable to prevent the spread of insurgency. The Russians must constantly have had to consider whether to increase their support or to let the regime founder. It was, however, the takeover by Amin which began the process leading to the military occupation. I do not know how much reliance to place on the story that Amin was invited by the Soviet Ambassador to meet Taraki in circumstances which were supposed to make possible his murder, but that the plot went wrong and it was Taraki who died. In any event, Amin (despite what the Pakistanis had to say) was not the Soviet choice and was at best on probation. The congratulatory telegram he received from Brezhnev and Kosygin, though prompt, was not notably warm. It probably seemed to the Russians in the autumn that their best bet for the time being was to hope Amin would succeed in stabilising the revolutionary regime and begin to defeat the rebellion, while remaining dependent on Soviet support. Ever since Taraki moved against the Parcham Group, however, in one of the moves which helped to narrow the basis of support for his rule, Babrak Karmal and his friends must have been held in reserve by the Russians with the aim of preserving the option of an Afghan leadership which would be more subservient than Amin to Soviet designs, and possibly more subtle[1] than Taraki or Amin in carrying them out. Indeed the decision to install Babrak Karmal could go right back, even before the Amin takeover, with only the timing and circumstances left open.

3. In this uncertain situation Soviet military planners must have been continually at work on a variety of contingency plans, ranging from a rescue operation for Soviet personnel in the event of a serious threat to Kabul to military support for Amin or full-scale Soviet occupation. In determining Western policies

[1] Marginal note by Mr Fergusson: 'and more moderate'.

UK-Soviet Relations, 1979-82

to deter the Russians from similar adventures in future, it is important to make as good an estimate as we can of the time when the occupation option was chosen. In this context the timing of visits to Afghanistan by General Pavlovsky, the Commander-in-Chief of Soviet ground forces, may be important. There is evidence he was in the country during August and September. Although his staff said he was recovering from an illness in the Crimea during October it is quite probable he was again in Afghanistan during that month. At any rate he cancelled a visit to France intended for October and, in apologising to the French Ambassador when he saw him on 7 November, the reason he gave was that he had been 'very busy recently'. The reports of Soviet troop movements began in October and it seems not unlikely that effective preparations for the occupation were begun very shortly after Amin took over, although the timing—and indeed the decision to move in—were left open until early in December.

4. As I understand it, however, the Russians were not faced in the autumn with an immediately critical situation from the military point of view. The main towns for example were in Government hands. It was in the longer term that the position was not encouraging (see for example Kabul telno. 281 of 20 December).[2] There appeared little prospect that the Afghan Army would be able to do much more in the face of rebellious tribesmen than hold its own: and even that was uncertain. Soviet soldiers were already being killed and possibly in some cases tortured. It is a fair presumption that the Soviet military adviser must have told his political masters by, say, early November that the mere staging of a Parcham coup against Amin would not suffice to guarantee Soviet control. It would need the support both of a small Soviet contingent at the time of the coup and of a major force to hold the country until the new regime was established and opposition crushed. He might well have added that if substantial forces could be made available it ought to be possible to lance the boil of the rebellion reasonably quickly. The present scale of the Soviet invasion suggests, however, that the Russians may not be too sanguine about their chances of achieving a rapid success. Although they will probably have a political incentive to withdraw some forces in a grand gesture to placate the non-aligned, they must now ensure total control and will be prepared if necessary to stay for a long time, using the Soviet-Afghan Treaty as a cover for doing so.

5. If the course of events was as I have suggested, the immediate cause of the Russian invasion has to be seen in the simple recognition that the April revolution could not be sustained without it. That said, external factors were also relevant and coincided to make the Soviet decision easier. There was no risk of a direct military confrontation with another major power and the Russians thought they could expect that Western reactions would be both ineffective and short-lived. So far as the immediate timing is concerned it looks from here as though the situation in Afghanistan left the Russians some latitude, but the Christmas period was tactically convenient. The United States was distracted with Iran—and Iran with the United States. The Russians may also have felt they had little to lose in terms of détente with the West. It may have seemed to them worth waiting until after the NATO decision on TNF but once that decision had been taken, any possible inhibition was removed. That said, TNF or no, the Russians would have been determined to control Afghanistan. NATO weakness over TNF might have encouraged them to go ahead, or if the European situation were uncertain, induced them only to defer action in Afghanistan while they exploited the situation in

[2] Not printed.

7 December 1979 – 1 December 1981

Europe.

6. So far as the United States was concerned the Russians must have reckoned that, with SALT II in difficulties and the Presidential election drawing closer, there would be a natural break in the process of détente during 1980. Towards the end of the year it would be possible to start preparing for a 1981 situation in which Afghanistan would have been effectively absorbed and the détente process could resume. I think the strength of the American reaction will have done a little to shake them and so too will the Third World response. I would also not ignore the reactions which they may evoke from their Warsaw Pact partners, acquiescent though these may be in public. But there is solace for the Russians in the French position. They may be encouraged by Mrs Ghandi's [*sic*] election victory[3] and I doubt whether they are yet drawing any political conclusions other than that the primary task is to accelerate the complete 'pacification' of Afghanistan.

7. Speculation on the process which led to the Soviet action is difficult enough. Taking that speculation into the future becomes even more hazardous. This first instance of the use of Soviet combat troops outside Eastern Europe must raise major questions about future trends. Must we now expect a more aggressive pursuit of Soviet expansion? Certainly the international climate has changed. The Chinese attack on Vietnam was a significant event. There are stories here that the Russians had a difficult time convincing Cuba that a military response was not necessary. It is possible also that the SALT II bargain in a post-TNF world looks less attractive and the challenge of increasing American naval and military concern with the Indian Ocean littoral more of a challenge. In short, I think that the Afghanistan adventure represented an extension of existing Soviet policy which may be bringing the leadership, by its conjunction with other events on the international scene, to the point of a substantial reassessment of policy. The outcome of that reassessment will be influenced by three main factors:

(*a*) success in effecting quick, total and lasting control of Afghanistan;

(*b*) the strength and duration of the reaction in the non-aligned countries; and

(*c*) the ability of the United States to sustain its initial strong reaction and the extent to which it can command NATO solidarity.

8. The absence, so far, of any Soviet Government or Party statement of policy in relation to Afghanistan may itself be indicative of the care with which the initial effects are being assessed.

9. I am conscious that this letter ranges far and in particular, covers ground on which Norman Hillier-Fry is better qualified to express an opinion.[4] I enclose a copy which I should be grateful if you would pass to him. I am not copying it elsewhere. May I leave you to do so if you think it appropriate?

Yours ever,
CURTIS KEEBLE

[3] Mrs Indira Gandhi became Prime Minister of India following victory for the Congress Party in the general elections held in early January.

[4] See No. 21.

UK-Soviet Relations, 1979-82

No. 29

Sir C. Rose (UKDEL NATO) to Lord Carrington, 9 January 1980, 3.15 p.m.[1]
Tel. No. 20 Immediate, Confidential (FCO 37/2240, FSA 020/1)

My Telnos 16 and 18:[2] Afghanistan and East-West Relations.

1. We have from the start played the leading role here in pressing for full Alliance consultation on the implications of the Soviet action and in seeking to concert measures to be taken by governments. Given the attitudes of the French and (so far) the Germans and Italians, this has meant we have found ourselves conspicuously out in front both as regards urgency and content of the measures we are considering. The Americans have of course supported our efforts, but they have been to some extent inhibited by the fact that President Carter has already announced a wide range of measures without waiting for allied consultation (or, so far as I have observed, making any public reference to the importance he attaches to this). They are also locally handicapped by the continued absence on leave (since mid-December) of the United States Permanent Representative, (which I find astonishing in a situation which President Carter has described as the most serious crisis since World War II) and the fact that as a result Glitman, as acting US representative, has had to leave the important study of East/West relations in the SPC to an ineffective political counsellor.

2. I hope your message to Genscher (your telno 11 to Bonn)[2] will help to stiffen the Germans. I am sure my German colleague will do his best over this at the meeting he is due to attend in Bonn on 10 January (para. 2 of my telno 16).[2] As regards the Italians, although the acting Permanent Representative has spoken bravely enough in the Council, his words have not been matched by any sense of urgency in the SPC. As regards the French, without a major change in instructions from Paris (which Sir R. Hibbert's[3] reports give us no reason to expect), I fear we shall have virtually to write off any hope of them cooperating within the Alliance in this exercise.

3. The SPC and Political Committee are meeting today and tomorrow and Council meetings have been arranged for the morning of 11 January and (with Mr Hurd and others present) on the afternoon of 15 January. I understand that the latter will follow a lunchtime Political Cooperation meeting in Brussels which Mr Hurd will attend as agreed with the department (my telecon with Fergusson). I will take the line at Friday's Council that we continue to attach urgency to this exercise and would have liked to be able to announce measures by the middle of this week. However we understand the problems some of our allies have had in reaching firm views on immediate measures and, because of the high priority we give to consultation within the Alliance, we propose to defer announcing measures we are taking until after the Reinforced Council meeting on 15 January. We hope our allies will be in a position to state at that meeting what their governments intend to do.

4. At the 15 January meeting, the Council will also have a report from the Political Committee on what governments are doing in relation to regional countries. On this the material in your telegram no. 31[2] is helpful and I hope others

---

[1] Repeated Immediate to Washington, Bonn, Paris, Moscow; Priority to other NATO Posts, UKREP Brussels, UKMIS New York.
[2] Not printed.
[3] UK Ambassador in Paris.

7 December 1979 – 1 December 1981

will produce similar information. But, especially given the French attitude, there is no chance of the report being anything more than a collation of national inputs. Discussion of policy and future action will depend on how far those attending on 15 January are prepared to go. I doubt whether the French (represented by their Perm Rep) will be willing to contribute much, but we might get more out of them at the preceding Political Cooperation meeting.

5. The SPC so far has been mainly concerned with immediate measures but we need now to move them on to consideration of medium and longer term action. As regards the measures not (not) included in the list in my telegram no. 17,[4] I have the following comments on items mentioned in your telno 17 to Washington[5]:

(a) Para 4: US and German Ambassadors have already been recalled and their return to Moscow is planned. I have seen nothing of the outcome of our consultations with the Nine on this subject, and would be grateful to be brought up to date. One possibility which you may wish to consider at the right moment would be to propose to our allies that all 15 Ambassadors in Moscow should be withdrawn at the same time for consultations, and should participate in a special meeting of the Council here to discuss the long term implications of Soviet actions in Afghanistan. This could have substantive value as well as being a dramatic gesture.

(b) Para 8: if you agree, I would propose to give our allies an account of the ways in which we have operated our restrictions on Soviet personnel in the UK since 1971 (Operation Foot)[6] and suggest to them that now is an excellent moment for them to follow our lead in this to the extent they can.

(c) Para 11: I hope it will be possible for the Council to be kept closely informed of what the Community is doing about agriculture exports to the Soviet Union (your telegram no. 37 to UKREP Brussels)[4] so that we can help to keep the pressure up on non-Community NATO countries. Presumably the Italians as Presidency should be asked to take this on.

6. On other points I should welcome guidance on your intentions with regard to:

(i) Lower level exchanges between foreign ministries, e.g. on disarmament questions and CSCE. In particular are we proposing to continue the dialogue with the Russians on CBMS in the present circumstances?

(ii) Action involving other members of the Warsaw Pact. I assume that in some cases (e.g. export of technology) measures will have to be applied to all Warsaw Pact or COMECON countries to avoid circumvention, but that in other cases you will wish to discriminate between those countries which have wholeheartedly endorsed Soviet action (e.g. the GDR) and those whose reluctance to do so has been more or less apparent. I should be glad to know what you wish me to say about this.

7. I should also welcome any assessment which has been made in London of Soviet motives and objectives, including our view of what calculations the Russians made about the possible consequences of their actions and the extent to which they may either have miscalculated Western and other international reactions or discounted them. It would also be helpful to know what light (if any) it is thought that recent events shed on the current leadership situation in Moscow. I found Moscow telno 872 of 30 December[7] most helpful in this context, but I

---

[4] Not printed.

[5] No 19.

[6] For details of Operation Foot see *DBPO*, Series III, Vol. I, pp. 298-428.

[7] No. 10.

UK-Soviet Relations, 1979-82

assume that more recent assessments have been made in London and I would find it valuable to be able to draw on these in Council.

No. 30

Letter from Mr Weston (Washington) to Mr Mallaby, 10 January 1980
Confidential (FCO 28/3984, EN 020/4)

My dear Christopher,

Prospects for US/Soviet Relations

1. You may find it helpful to have some thoughts on the implications of recent events for US/Soviet relations. These are largely personal and speculative. Even before the Soviet invasion of Afghanistan the prospects as a new decade opened were not rosy. For most Americans words like human rights, Indo-China, Ethiopia, Yemen, and Cuba in the 1979 headlines had left a bad taste. When it finally came, the Vienna Summit in June was a downbeat affair. The public debate on SALT II brought to the surface anxieties about military trends and balances which served only to accentuate the sense of vulnerability induced by the falling dollar and dependence on foreign oil. Electoral considerations heightened the effect while reducing the Administration's inclination to try to breathe new life into the relationship.

2. Against this background the Soviet intervention in Kabul came as a thunderclap to the doldrums, bringing at least the relief of certainty. While senior Administration spokesmen have drawn back from publicly pronouncing the death of détente, no-one disputes that we are now witnessing the sharpest downturn in Soviet/US relations since the invasion of Czechoslovakia in 1968. Indeed some argue that the present reversal is in fact more profound (cf. President Carter's briefing of Congress—'the greatest threat to peace since the Second World War'), and that it should not be followed by so complaisant a resumption of East/West contacts as occurred after 1968. The Administration, Congressional opinion and media comment all appear ready to contemplate a prolonged interruption of normal business with the Soviet Union and there is little sign that special pleading from the private sector interests most affected is impinging much on this consensus, at least for the present. To some extent of course, as commentators point out, such periodic oscillations have been characteristic of US/Soviet relations since the Second World War. Even President Carter's dramatic avowal that the scales have now fallen from his eyes as regards dealing with the Russians is by no means without precedent among post-war American Presidents. Once again faith in the personal touch and native American benevolence have proved no substitute in the White House for the recognition that differences of interest between States exist and cannot always be reconciled, and that the Russians do not play by American rules.

3. The immediate practical consequences were spelled out by the President in his 4 January broadcast[1] and in subsequent Administration briefing (Washington tels 68, 73 and 93).[2] These are not exhaustive. Further measures could be taken if it were judged necessary. But any such escalation would increasingly have to go

---

[1] These included restrictions on the sale of grain, high technology and other strategic items to the Soviet Union. See *Public Papers: Carter (1980-81)*, Book I, pp. 21-24.
[2] Not printed.

66

7 December 1979 – 1 December 1981

beyond short-term measures of immediate impact and to bite on institutional frameworks and procedures as such, e.g. abrogation of some or all of the formal bilateral agreements with the Soviet Union which cover many specialised areas of government activity. Any such piece-meal dismantling of the channels for intergovernmental relations would also carry implications for the likely time-span of the freeze. So far the Administration does not appear to have been tempted in this direction.

4. It has also been remarked (e.g. Bonn telegram 23)[3] that the President has not in his public response to Soviet action addressed the various multilateral aspects of détente, nor for that matter other bilateral arms control business beyond SALT II. Whatever his personal predilection, however, it is hard to believe that they will not all to some degree be adversely affected (and according to Richard Burt[4] in today's *New York Times*, ACDA [Arms Control & Disarmament Agency] have been put on hold till further notice by a White House directive). Despite SALT II signature, the arms control and disarmament constituency here was in evident decline as a determinant of policy during 1979. The deferral of SALT II ratification, together with the Soviet rejection on 3 January of NATO's TNF negotiating overture, will probably ensure the postponement of any meaningful exchanges with the Russians on the SALT III agenda throughout this year at least. This seems bound in turn to slow still further the comprehensive test ban negotiations (CTB). I doubt whether wider concern to present a respectable position on CTB at the 1980 non-proliferation treaty review conference will be enough to compensate for this. In MBFR the new Western package is on the table. If as seems likely the Russians are not disposed to pick it up, I would not expect there to be much support within the Administration to devise new concessions for the Western hand. It is also likely to prove more difficult to give the Russians the benefits of any doubts on CSCE, as the US considers what its policy should be for the Madrid Review Conference.[5] Wary counsels seem likely to prevail. Prospects for other ongoing bilateral arms control business such as conventional arms transfer limitations, anti-satellite arms control, the Indian Ocean and chemical weapons are also either nil or at very low ebb.

5. Then there is China. The Administration now has little incentive in the short run to take account of Soviet sensitivities in its relationship with Peking. The pretence to even-handedness has gone. If Brzezinski's advice is followed, we may expect the United States deliberately to play up the coincidence of US and Chinese world views and to encourage China's regional role as a counterbalance to Soviet pressure. Harold Brown's visit to Peking[6] has struck a note emphasising wider US/China cooperation in security matters which will undoubtedly be revealed to have some practical expression in defence-related fields. We may also expect the US to be less coy than hitherto about Western European sales of defence equipment to China. I do not however believe that the Administration will go overboard in its relationship with Peking, for example by means of a formal security or defence relationship or by reversing completely its policy of not selling arms as such. The President is undoubtedly aware that there is a point in US/Chinese relations beyond which he cannot go without inducing among the

---

[3] Not printed.

[4] Assistant Secretary for European Affairs at the US State Department.

[5] A review Conference on Security and Co-operation in Europe (CSCE) was due to begin in Madrid in November.

[6] Harold Brown, US Secretary of Defense, visited China from 5-13 January 1980.

UK-Soviet Relations, 1979-82

Russians the most deep-seated anxieties which could risk provoking unpredictable responses and a major destabilisation of the international scene. He will wish to avoid any action that could appear to be an irrevocable step in that direction.

6. The question arises: what result is the Administration aiming at? No-one here really expects the Russians to withdraw their forces from Afghanistan in the very near future, given the history of Soviet military intervention in East Europe, or indeed to mend their ways in other areas of current involvement. It is more a matter of demonstrating that the Soviet Union cannot, as the President put it, 'commit this act with impunity': that there is a cost which Moscow may have underestimated: and that the United States will act to defend its interests and its allies around the world. What is not yet clear is the extent to which Americans are prepared to translate applause for rhetorical calls for a more assertive posture vis-à-vis the Russians into acceptance of the costs which this may involve. It is therefore largely a matter of political judgment, rather than objectively demonstrable results, when enough is enough. But as seen from here the chill in US/Soviet, and consequently in East/West, relations is accepted as likely to be a determinant of international life for many months, probably until a new administration (even if the same President) here and possibly until a change of leadership in Moscow.

7. But there is also a feeling that compared with the cold war of earlier decades, as one commentator has put it, 'the world is more complex now, the margins of Soviet safety and patience are thinner and international life is more difficult to manage'. The new impetus for military spending on both sides, the danger of proxy wars sucking in the super-powers as the competition for scarce resources gets fiercer, and the ever-present risk of nuclear proliferation are all cited as contributing factors. In addition the still unsolved crisis over the hostages in Iran remains in the short run a mercurial element whose effect at any moment could be magnified by renewed East-West tension.

8. There therefore remains an underlying sense here that in the longer perspective both the United States and the Soviet Union are ineluctable partners in their responsibilities toward the maintenance of world order. The prime arguments remain valid for stopping short of active nuclear confrontation: and détente remains a policy imperative—at least in Kissinger's sense of 'a process of managing relations with a potentially hostile country in order to preserve peace while maintaining our vital interests'. Although undoubtedly angered and disappointed at the latest evidence of Soviet recidivism into the old pattern of narrow national self-interest, the Administration and most informed commentators here are assuming that no recent decisions in the Kremlin have been taken to invalidate this common ground.

9. Paradoxically, the present pause has already given rise to speculation about the new opportunity it provides for the major parties to find a fresh degree of consensus on what a non-partisan US policy toward the Soviet Union should be. In terms of hawks and doves both sides might be prepared to make some concessions toward each other for the sake of what Kissinger has called 'a settled view of what we are trying to accomplish'. But even if force of circumstances seem to draw the President and his Republican challengers closer together in practice, the exigencies of an election campaign in which foreign policy looks like being a major issue make it less likely that any such consensus would be publicly acknowledged short of the onset of a major East/West crisis.

Yours ever,

P. J. WESTON

7 December 1979 – 1 December 1981

No. 31

FCO to Mr Lucas (Muscat), 11 January 1980, 7.34 p.m.[1]
Tel. No. 99 Immediate, Secret (FCO 13/967, PC 295/1)

Afghanistan: Personal for Private Secretary from PUS

1. The Secretary of State may like to have the following thoughts on the picture as seen from London, to supplement the telegrams which have been and will continue to be repeated to you.

UN Aspect

2. This has been a success so far from the Western point of view. The vote in the Security Council, and many of the speeches too, could not have been bettered. It was a fair spread of the non-aligned who then decided to convene a special session of the General Assembly, and it is non-aligned speeches which will occupy the debate for the next day or two. This will incidentally give the Nine an opportunity to make their first public statement through the mouth of the Italian Presidency. Tony Parsons will be speaking tomorrow, Saturday. As yet we do not know what the chances are of getting the two thirds majority which it looks as though the resolution will need to pass.

Regional Aspects

3. The report of the Political Committee of NATO is not likely to be very helpful, although it will go through the motions of covering the points that need to be covered. I have repeated to you a separate exchange of telegrams showing that the Americans have already drawn the conclusion that the quadripartite forum is the only effective machinery for carrying this forward, and that we are responding positively to this suggestion. The obvious problem in all this is to help Afghanistan's neighbours, and especially Pakistan, without feeding the anti-Pakistani and anti-American sentiments in India to which John Thomson has drawn attention so clearly. The China angle (see para 9 below) is very relevant here.

East/West Aspects

4. The Secretary of State was pessimistic about the likely outcome of the work in the Special Political Committee of NATO: and I am afraid he will be proved largely right. The word from the various capitals is that this, that and the other measures have been considered but that all kinds of practical difficulties stand in the way of their being implemented. Nevertheless the French position has become noticeably more robust under the impact of French public opinion (François Poncet has been sharply criticised for wetness by the French media), of the mood in New York and probably of German advice. The German position is going to be not too bad. Some of the smaller allies are staunch. The result will be a catalogue of national measures which will look variegated but not too divergent, and which in total will be quite substantial in public relations terms, even though it is not likely to hurt the Russians much or for long. As regards the Olympic Games, we have told Tony Parsons to stimulate discussion of the possibility of mass withdrawals and/or transfer of the games from Moscow to somewhere else. But the prospects of this happening are not good: the Canadians have said definitely that Montreal will not be available. I have discovered that in 1940, when the Games were due to be held in Tokyo, the Japanese invasion of Manchuria resulted in their transfer to Helsinki—though World War Two stopped play. I am having this precedent

---

[1] Between 9-18 January Lord Carrington visited Turkey, Oman, Saudi Arabia, Pakistan and India.

UK-Soviet Relations, 1979-82

studied. Nevertheless there are signs of doubt amongst the Secretary of State's colleagues. In Cabinet yesterday the case for a strong response to the Soviet move was accepted, but attention was drawn to the likely economic consequences for Britain of any attempt to cut down on credit or high technology exports. This too is being studied. There has been some quite useful work on the EEC side—grain etc: see para 8 below.

UK Public Opinion

5. There is a lot of press interest, but scattered amongst the various targets in Afghanistan, New York and elsewhere. Curiosity is building up about what America's allies may eventually do, but I think this can be contained until after the NATO and Community meetings on 15 January.

Events in Afghanistan

6. Howell has arrived and Hillier-Fry has left for consultations. The telegrams from the post have added little to what has been in the press. Among the reports of interest are those of summary executions of supporters of Amin, lack of resistance to the Soviet troops by units of the Afghan armed forces and the build-up of Soviet forces to something in the region of 100,000.

Next Steps, 14 January

7. Mr Hurd will make a statement in the House of Commons on Monday condemning the Soviet action, describing events in the UN, referring to your trip, mentioning the discussions amongst the allies—both NATO and the Community— about how to respond and promising a further statement later in the week. Also on 14 January we expect a visit from Warren Christopher, on his way to the NATO meeting in Brussels the next day, together with Cooper of the State Department whose interest is in sanctions against Iran, and also possibly other American officials if President Carter accepts the Prime Minister's advice that the situation in Iran needs to be looked at as a whole and not exclusively from the angle of the hostages. Mr Hurd will see them and appropriate officials are available for talks.

Next Steps, 15 January

8. The Council of Ministers (Foreign Affairs) of the Community will take an hour or two off from Community subjects to consider Afghanistan and possibly Iran. They are likely to issue a public statement and will also consider possible actions in the regional and East/West fields—i.e. the two areas already being studied in NATO, but perhaps with a better chance of a constructive contribution by the French, The North Atlantic Council is to meet at Deputy Foreign Minister level on the same afternoon to take stock of the work done since Christopher's meeting in London on 31 December.[2] The Lord Privy Seal[3] will attend the first of these meetings and Mr Hurd the second.

9. There are 2 wider aspects on which we shall want to make progress as soon as possible after your return. The first is China, on which Harold Brown has been saying some rather wild things in Peking: we are trying to find out from the Americans to what extent they have really taken a conscious decision to change the nature of their relationship with China, and if so, what this could mean in practice. Secondly there are the possible implications for Yugoslavia. We are having the JIC paper on Soviet intentions towards Yugoslavia updated[4] and have put this on the agenda for the quadripartite meeting of Political Directors on 31 January/1 February.

[2] No. 11.
[3] Sir Ian Gilmore.
[4] Not printed.

7 December 1979 – 1 December 1981

No. 32

Sir C. Keeble (Moscow) to FCO, 11 January 1980, 11.31 a.m.[1]
Tel. No. 30 Immediate, Secret (FCO 28/3997, EN 021/1)

Afghanistan

1. This is not a time for an anti-Soviet crusade, which will consolidate the most dangerous elements in the Kremlin, but if we are to influence future Soviet policy in the right direction we have to demonstrate with clarity that the Afghan adventure has damaged both the standing of the Soviet Union and Soviet interests, internal and international. The direct American measures and the Security Council action have been most useful, but some of the actions under consideration by European members of NATO in the field of bilateral relations are mere trivia. They might serve as a gesture if they were pursued whole-heartedly, unanimously and as a corollary to a substantive response in other fields, but a patchwork of minor gestures of irritation, with French dissent publicly registered, will weaken the effect of American action and encourage Soviet mischief making.

2. I hope there is room for more effective action in relation to the countries threatened by Soviet expansion to the south. My French colleague is very pessimistic about Pakistan, but my own view is that the threat there may not be as immediate as it now appears, although there is certain to be friction over Afghan refugees (if only as a justification for the continued presence of Soviet troops in Afghanistan) and a certain attempt at intimidation. It will take time to digest Afghanistan and a more important Soviet objective may well be the establishment of a pro-Soviet regime in Iran. For this they are dependent on events which they cannot control, so the timing must be left open, but if the circumstances were right they would act and it is peculiarly difficult to envisage an effective Western response.

3. The area of greatest Soviet vulnerability could be Afghanistan itself. If Soviet forces are tied down there with sporadic fighting going on indefinitely this will be the best possible deterrent to a similar adventure elsewhere. It will also maintain the exposure of Soviet policy to the non-aligned countries, although the latter objective will of course be frustrated by any identification of external support for the rebels. The Soviet media are already carrying interviews with captured rebels telling of their training in Pakistan by US and Chinese instructors and their use of foreign including British weapons.

4. Looking more widely at areas where the Soviet Union is vulnerable to pressure or has objectives which we may frustrate, the kind of gesture which would be most effective would be a withdrawal of the Dutch and Belgian reservations on the TNF decision. If it is politically unrealistic to expect this, does the Madrid conference[2] offer more room for manoeuvre? Certainly the Soviet objective is a quiet meeting on the basis of which Soviet objectives in the field of military détente will be pursued. It is at least arguable that the West should now prepare for a substantially rougher conference, designed to damage the Soviet facade of international respectability which has already suffered from the Afghanistan action and which they will be the more anxious to repair. The argument that Afghanistan is irrelevant to CSCE is exactly what we need to disprove if we think that détente really is indivisible. Eastern Europe too is an area of Soviet vulnerability in both

---

[1] Repeated Priority to Washington, UKDEL NATO, Paris and Bonn.

[2] See No. 30, note 5.

UK-Soviet Relations, 1979-82

political and economic terms and one where there might be some chance of a degree of harmony in the Western response. Possibly some discreet harmonised and effective driving of wedges between the Soviet Union and her East European partners? Possibly too some publicity—though not in ministerial speeches—for past Soviet use of the Afghanistan technique, e.g. the attempt to install Kuusinen at the head of a People's Government of Finland in 1939 and his eventual installation as President of the Karelo-Finnish Republic within the Soviet Union (*Pravda* December 4, 1939: 'The Red Army is approaching Finland's borders at the request of the Finnish People's Government. As soon as the People's Government requests it, it will leave Finnish territory.').

5. I recognise that various of our allies will recoil in anxiety from the thought of robust action in any particular area; that the French will continue to run détente their own way; and that there is indeed a serious risk that heightened confrontation may damage our interests by frightening off the non-aligned. I cannot try from here to weigh all the factors. The point I want to make is simply that Soviet policy is world-wide; that it may be at a critical stage of development; and that in our search for a response we should look widely for the areas in which Soviet vulnerability may make our influence effective. At the same time I hope our public theme will be that the safety of the world requires a measure of East-West understanding; that this is what we seek; but that it is not compatible with the arbitrary extension of Soviet power.

No. 33

Minute from Mr Murrell (Research Department) to Mr Mallaby, 11 January 1980
Confidential (FCO 28/3998, EN 021/1)

Afghanistan: Possible Implications for Soviet Foreign Policy and the Leadership

1. The following are some preliminary thoughts about the implications of the Soviet invasion of Afghanistan and of the Western reaction to it for Soviet foreign policy and in particular the Soviet attitude to détente.

2. Does the Soviet action in Afghanistan represent a shift in Soviet foreign policy, perhaps associated with some change in the balance of forces within the Soviet leadership?

(*a*) There has been no evidence of any dissension in the leadership (not that we would necessarily expect it to be apparent). However there has been nothing unusual about the recent activities of the leadership. Brezhnev was indisposed due to a cold and made no public appearances between 20 December and 8 January when he received the French CP leader Marchais[1]. Appearances by other Politburo members have been few but not abnormally so and there have been no recent occasions which would have called for a full Politburo turnout. On the other hand the press has as usual reported nominations of all the Politburo members for seats in the Republic Supreme Soviets with Brezhnev receiving 4 or 5 times as many nominations as anyone else.

(*b*) There has been speculation that Kosygin's serious illness and Brezhnev's reduced vigour could have changed the balance of forces within the leadership in favour of a hard-line faction led by Suslov. We can see no basis for this

[1] Georges Marchais, head of the French Communist Party, 1972-1994.

theory. Suslov's considerable influence on foreign policy is a permanent factor and it can be presumed that he has consistently supported Brezhnev's line. There is a solid majority in the Politburo of those who are closely associated with Brezhnev.

(c) It is reasonable to suppose that the views of the leadership were not identical and that some may have argued against the invasion. But on an issue of this nature involving the use of Soviet military force we would expect the final decision to be taken unanimously and the leadership thereafter to maintain solidarity (as happened in the case of Czechoslovakia when opinions in the leadership are believed to have differed).

(d) Military advice must have played an important part in the Soviet decision but the nature of the Soviet system is such that the possibility can be excluded that the military imposed their will on the leadership on this issue or that there is any serious likelihood that they have achieved or will achieve a dominant role in Soviet foreign policy.

3. Leaving aside this kind of speculation there seems to us no reason to adduce a sudden shift in policy or a change of forces within the leadership in order to explain the Soviet action in Afghanistan. Contingency plans for Soviet intervention must have been in preparation for a considerable period (at least since Pavlovsky's lengthy visit to Afghanistan in August). The Soviet action is not inconsistent with previous moves by Cuban proxy into Africa or with the known evolution of Soviet attitudes, shared by the leadership as a whole including Brezhnev, i.e. an increasing exasperation and disillusion with United States policy; and a vigorous assertion of the Soviet right to intervene in the Third World coupled with a rejection of any linkage of such action with détente. These views were clearly reflected in speeches by members of the leadership during the Supreme Soviet election campaign early last year. Moreover it was becoming clear that for the Soviet leadership as a whole the constant inflation of the political price for the ratification of SALT II had gone far enough (they probably drew the line at the Cuban brigade episode): no-one in the Soviet leadership including Brezhnev would have been prepared to argue again that the Soviet Union should refrain from a foreign policy action in defence of Soviet interests because of its possible effect on SALT II whose ratification had in any case become problematical and whose value had been reduced by the NATO decision on TNF. Détente had also been eroded in Soviet eyes by the human rights campaign, the indefinite delay in the ratification of SALT II and the TNF decision to the point where even the firmest supporters of détente in the Soviet leadership may have concluded that there was not much more to lose. The additional cost of the grain embargo, the ban on technology exports and American-Chinese consultations on defence matters were probably not anticipated.

4. Why did the Russians take such drastic and large scale military action instead of building up their forces gradually? The Russians evidently sponsored an attempt by Taraki in September to get rid of Amin. Had this attempted coup succeeded it is reasonable to speculate that the Soviet policy thereafter would have been 2-fold: a moderation of the policy of the Afghan regime and a broadening of its base accompanied, if this still seemed necessary, by a gradual build-up of Soviet forces in the country at a pace which might not have aroused a sharp world reaction. The fact that Amin turned the tables on Taraki and the Russians and thereafter presumably rejected Soviet advice and offers of troops forced the Russians to change their plan. They could not risk another bungled coup and needed to control

the country before taking steps to remove Amin. One cannot exclude the possibility that feelings of personal resentment against Amin together with an emotional reaction to reports of the public torture and beheadings of Soviet advisers and the exhibition of their heads on pikes were an important factor in the Soviet decision to move into Afghanistan in force. They may well have had more effect on the minds of the Soviet leaders than the eventual possibilities of access to a warm water port or the prospects for destabilising Pakistan (one has only to consider the enormous repercussions on the American political scene of the hostages issue). It is for consideration that the Russians felt that they were acting in their own backyard and did not expect the West to see their action in such stark terms as a strategic threat. This is not to say that the strategic implications of their move into Afghanistan are not important or that the military advice which they received on the necessity for Soviet intervention in order to preserve the Afghan régime was not coloured by the professional perception by Soviet military leaders of the strategic advantages of Soviet control of Afghanistan.

5. In the light of this analysis of Soviet motives it is worth considering the possible effects on Soviet policy of what is evidently a much fiercer Western response to their action than they had expected. The American measures which have been announced may well deter them from future action of a similar nature as intended. But is there not a danger that if the dismantling of détente goes too far it could leave from the Soviet point of view too little left of détente to be worth salvaging and persuade some Soviet leaders at any rate that it would be better not to enter into political and economic agreements which are made permanent hostages to Soviet international behaviour? Some of the more dramatic statements by US spokesmen implying a radical reassessment of Soviet intentions and of American policy towards the Soviet Union and China could have a considerable impact on present and future Soviet leaders and their attitude to détente. Moreover if all available political and economic levers are used now there will be little left for any future occasion (until they are reversed or relaxed) except military action and in the short-term the Russians could conceivably decide that there is little more to be lost in terms of East-West relations if they were to repeat the exercise in the area e.g. Iran.

6. This is not to say that the present Soviet leadership is likely to throw caution to the winds: it must be assumed that perceptions of the strategic importance to Western interests of particular countries and areas, and the need to avoid military confrontation with the USA, are still major constraints. Moreover, in the present climate any increase in Soviet aggressive behaviour in the Third World, even in areas of less than vital importance to the West, is bound to carry an increased risk of exacerbating East-West relations still further. It is at this point that the question of whether the Russians wish to persist with those elements of détente which serve Soviet interests comes in. The evidence so far suggests that the Russians will try to salvage what they can of their relations with Western countries including the USA. It is nevertheless possible that a prolonged period of cool East-West relations (let alone something approaching a new cold war) which meant that the USSR economy suffered from an inability to gain access to Western technology and grain, and that Western suspicions of Soviet intentions meant that Soviet disarmament and related proposals were unlikely to make any headway, could provide the opportunity for those in the leadership who may have entertained doubts about the advantages of détente, or who may have ambitions for power, to seek to bring about a reversal of Brezhnev's policies. The 'Russia firsters' could

7 December 1979 – 1 December 1981

argue that 'détente' is effectively dead, that it has not brought sufficient gains in terms of Western technology etc and that the Soviet Union can no longer rely on being able to get what it wants from the West, and that in the new circumstances the best thing for the Soviet Union to do is to turn in upon itself and rely on its own resources in a 'siege economy' (relatively speaking). At a time of imminent leadership change this can by no means be ruled out.

7. None of the Soviet leaders has spoken publicly since Afghanistan, so there is no evidence of any kind to go on to support the above speculation. We shall of course be on the lookout for pointers. The irony is however that the more sustained and damaging Western pressure is, the greater the chance of the kind of reaction outlined above.[2]

G. D. G. MURRELL

[2] Mr Johnson, in a minute of 16 January, thought there was much in détente the Russians would wish to preserve. The danger he saw was that their reaction to the worldwide censure of their intervention would be one of defiance and introspection. The conjunction of global criticism of foreign policy and economic difficulties at home could all too easily lead to a state of mind 'in which the predominant sentiment is one of standing on ceremony, hurt dignity and indigenous Soviet economic possibilities.'

No. 34

FCO to Sir A. Parsons (UKMIS New York), 11 January 1980, 7 p.m.[1]
Tel. No. 46 Immediate, Confidential (FCO 37/2241, FSA 020/1)

My Telegram Number 43 (not to all): Parliamentary Statement.[2]

1. Following for your background information is text of proposed statement to be made on 14 January. As this may be changed before delivery you should not release the text at this stage.

1. [*sic*] In the view of Her Majesty's Government, the Soviet invasion of Afghanistan of the 27th of December was an unprovoked act of aggression against an independent country. It represents an unprecedented development in the history of post-war Russian expansion. The Soviet Union acted, to establish a military hold on a sovereign country, in violation of the international principles which the Soviet Union constantly calls on others to observe. The Soviet Union justified its act by alleging prior foreign intervention. Yet the only intervention has been the Soviet invasion.

2. In our view it is essential that we and our allies should draw the right conclusion. The Russians have shown, more vividly than ever before, that, when they have the chance of gaining positions of power in developing countries, they are willing to put at risk their relations with the West. Non-alignment is no protection against their appetites. We can expect further Soviet interventions elsewhere unless the international community shows clearly that acts of this kind cannot be undertaken with impunity.

3. With these considerations in mind we are developing our own response. First, we fully supported the action taken in the United Nations Security Council. The

[1] Repeated Immediate to UKDEL NATO, all NATO posts, UKREP Brussels, Kabul, Islamabad and New Delhi.
[2] Not printed.

UK-Soviet Relations, 1979-82

letter to the President of the Council was signed by fifty-two states (the Soviet Union had to resort to the veto to prevent the passing of the resolution sponsored by the non-aligned). Now a number of Third World countries intend to press their arguments in the General Assembly using the Uniting for Peace procedure.[3] This rallying of opinion in the Third World is a new and important factor. Second, in Afghanistan itself, we have recalled our Ambassador in Kabul for consultations. We have ended our aid programme in Afghanistan, though Afghan students now in the United Kingdom may complete their courses. We have provided relief aid—tents, blankets and medical supplies—to help the Afghan refugees in Pakistan, who now total about four hundred thousand. Thirdly we are considering the necessary firm and calculated response to the Soviet Union. The Government welcome the measures announced by the President of the United States. The United States must not be alone in its firmness. Her Majesty's Government have been reconsidering all aspects of British-Soviet relations. On the 31st of December the United States presided at a meeting in London attended also by the United Kingdom, Canada, France, the Federal Republic of Germany and Italy to discuss what steps might be taken.[4] Discussion has since continued in Brussels among the members of the North Atlantic Alliance. The measures which the United Kingdom has suggested might be undertaken by individual Western countries include curtailment of high-level and Ministerial meetings and other important contacts with the Soviet Union. Significant measures in the economic field are also being considered. It is highly desirable that measures by Western countries should be concerted, especially in the economic field, where solidarity with our community partners will be particularly important.

4. These matters will be discussed tomorrow at a meeting of Ministers of the European Economic Community in Brussels and later tomorrow at a meeting of the North Atlantic Council, which I and Ministers from some other member countries will attend. We will of course keep the House informed.

5. We saw an urgent need to consult and express support for our friends in the area. My Rt Hon. Friend the Foreign and Commonwealth Secretary is at present visiting Turkey, Saudi Arabia, Oman, Pakistan and India. He will discuss the current situation with their leaders, see the problems of the region at first hand, and reassure our friends and consult them about the right response. He is due in Islamabad this evening (i.e. Monday 14 January) and will be going on to Delhi before returning to London later this week.

6. In our judgement this is not a time for either panic or weakness. The Soviet Union has launched into an unprecedented foreign adventure. The chances of such an adventure being repeated will be reduced if it is met with a firm and concerted response. The Soviet Union cannot expect the process of détente to continue unchecked in Europe while it invades and subjugates independent countries of other continents.[5]

[3] On 3 November 1950, the UN General Assembly adopted Resolution 377 A, which was given the name 'Uniting for Peace'. The resolution stated that in cases where the UN Security Council fails to act in order to maintain international peace and security due to disagreement between its members, the matter shall be immediately addressed by the General Assembly. The resolution was initiated by the US as a way of circumventing the Soviet veto during the Korean War.

[4] No. 11.

[5] The Government statement on Afghanistan was delivered by Mr Hurd on 14 January. For text see *Parl. Debs., 5th ser., H. of C.*, 14 January 1980, vol. 976, cols. 1222-33.

7 December 1979 – 1 December 1981

No. 35

Letter from Mr Alexander (No. 10) to Mr Lyne, 14 January 1980
Confidential, Secret (FCO 49/893, RS 021/6)

Dear Roderic,

Call by Mr Warren Christopher

As you know, Mr Warren Christopher called on the Prime Minister this morning. He was accompanied by the US Ambassador, Mr Kingman Brewster. Mr Hurd was also present.

Afghanistan

At the beginning of the meeting, Ambassador Brewster handed over the enclosed message from President Carter to the Prime Minister. Commenting on the letter, Mr Christopher said that the United States Government needed the help of the British Government on both the punitive and the affirmative aspects of its policy on the Afghan crisis. In regard to the punitive measures, President Carter had taken a number of decisions which were, in domestic political terms, very risky. Mr Christopher mentioned the grain embargo, the action on the export of high technology and the action on fisheries agreements. The United States hoped that its Allies would produce parallel action. He would be exploring steps that might be taken in London and thereafter in Rome, Brussels and in other capitals. On the affirmative side, Mr Christopher said that he had just had a good meeting with a Pakistani delegation headed by Agha Shahi. The United States Government would be offering the Pakistan Government $400 million of new aid. There would be $200 million worth of economic aid and $200 million worth of foreign military credits. Half of the aid would be included in the 1980 budget (a supplementary appropriation would be necessary) and half in the 1981 budget.

The Prime Minister said that her views on the Soviet Union in Afghanistan were well known. She had been warning for a long time that the Soviet Government were capable of behaving in this way. The Western Allies would now have to work out what could be done. She asked about the United States Government's attitude towards a boycott of the Olympics. She thought that this would have the biggest impact on the people of the Soviet Union. Mr Christopher commented that there was a ground swell of opinion in the United States in favour of moving the Olympics. This was, of course, an issue where governments had to be responsive to public opinion. The Prime Minister agreed and said that the difficulty was that many sportsmen wanted to participate in the Games. It would be much easier to get opinion moving if there was an alternative venue. In any case, an early decision was needed. The British Government had made its views clear on the British Lions tour of South Africa and it would be difficult for it not to take a position on the Olympic Games.

Iran...[1]

I am sending copies of this letter, and its enclosure to John Wiggins (HM Treasury), Brian Norbury (Minister of Defence), Stuart Hampson (Department of Trade), Bill Burroughs (Department of Energy) and to Martin Vile (Cabinet Office).

Yours ever,
MICHAEL ALEXANDER

[1] This section is not printed.

UK-Soviet Relations, 1979-82

ENCLOSURE IN NO. 35

Dear Margaret,

As I know you will agree, the Soviet Union's invasion and occupation of Afghanistan are matters of the gravest concern. In my view, the Soviet action represents one of the most serious security challenges which our countries have faced in the post-war era. This naked aggression has implications in Southwest Asia and the Middle East, as well as globally, in the bilateral relationship between each of our countries and the Soviet Union, and in the multilateral relationships which have developed among the countries of the West and the Warsaw Pact involving European matters in the past decade. A failure on our part to respond adequately to the Soviet challenge in Afghanistan can only encourage Moscow to move in the future even more aggressively. Pakistan, Iran, the Gulf, Yugoslavia and even Turkey come immediately to mind. By the same token, a strong united Western response can correct Soviet perceptions, restrain Soviet behavior and ultimately advance the cause of détente to which both our countries are dedicated over the longer term. I know that you share my view that in these circumstances, it is imperative that you and I and our representatives in Washington and London maintain close and continuous consultations and coordination.

You are already familiar with the measures which I announced on January 4 involving our bilateral relations with the Soviet Union, and I appreciate your support for these actions. I had previously announced my decision that the SALT II Treaty not be called up for Senate action in light of the Soviet invasion and occupation of Afghanistan. I did not withdraw the Treaty because I believe its ratification would be in the interest of the West, and I hope that circumstances will, in time, make it possible for me to request that the Senate proceed with action on the Treaty. Further, I believe that it is important to continue our efforts in MBFR to reach agreement with the East which will lower military forces and tensions in Europe and to pursue vigorously our TNF arms control proposal. In my judgment we should also continue to participate in the CSCE process which if carefully managed promotes Western interests.

However, I feel strongly that we would be making a grave error should we, in the interest of preserving an atmosphere of détente, attempt to separate developments in Southwest Asia involving the Soviet Union from the bilateral or multilateral relations which we have with the USSR. The process of détente can continue only if we, collectively and individually, make clear to the Soviet Union that actions such as its invasion and occupation of Afghanistan must have serious consequences for the Soviet Union in other areas of the world, including Europe.

The Soviet Union's invasion of Afghanistan is simply not consistent with détente in Europe, and this must be made clear to the Soviet leadership. If Moscow does wish to pursue détente, then in the wake of Afghanistan it must give us evidence of such a desire. The most convincing confirmation of Moscow's desire to retrace its steps back to policies consistent with the principles of détente would be an early and total withdrawal of Soviet troops from Afghanistan. To this point, I regret to say that we have seen no evidence that that is Moscow's intention and the continually growing USSR deployment in Afghanistan appears to us to suggest that the Soviet Army went to that small and defenceless country to stay. And in the light of other Soviet activities in the region—especially in Ethiopia and the Yemens—we would have to regard a prolonged Soviet occupation of Afghanistan as part of a calculated strategic thrust against the West's vital interests.

7 December 1979 – 1 December 1981

We have already noted a predictable tendency in the Soviet Union's propaganda to try to divide the United States and Western Europe over the matter of Afghanistan. Indeed, I think we can expect the Soviets to launch a 'peace offensive' in Europe in the near future. Moscow will undoubtedly hope that by offering various inducements to West European countries they can secure a 'business-as-usual' approach by these countries, a tacit agreement to let concern about the Soviet occupation of Afghanistan fade away. I know that you will be particularly sensitive to this Soviet objective and will work with me and our colleagues from the other Western European countries to ensure that this Soviet aim is not realized.

Finally, I want to assure you that I am prepared to commit the United States to take the necessary steps to enhance security in Southwest Asia and the Middle East, not just because of US interests, but because of the broad stakes the West in general has in this region's stability and the flow of oil. In this effort, it will be important for the United States to have the support—and some cases the direct involvement of our European allies. The challenge to our common and crucial interests in this area is unprecedented; it calls for an unprecedented and coordinated Western response. This includes support for Pakistan, intensified political involvement with specific nations stretching from Southwest Asia to the Eastern Mediterranean, increased security involvement and military presence, increased economic assistance, as appropriate, and arms support to friendly nations. The United Kingdom's role in this effort will be particularly important and I look forward to learning of Peter Carrington's impressions after his visit to the region.

I want to thank you for your support in these trying times. I will be anxious to have your views in the coming period on the posture that we should adopt to convince this Soviet leadership and the following one that they cannot undertake naked aggression such as in Afghanistan without the most serious penalties for them.

Sincerely,
JIMMY CARTER

No. 36

Record of a meeting between Mr Hurd and Mr Christopher at the FCO, 14 January 1980, 10.30 a.m.[1]
Confidential (FCO 37/2243, FSA 020/1)

Afghanistan

1. *Mr Christopher* reviewed action taken by President Carter. Action on SALT had been deferred but it remained on the Senate's calendar. An agreement was in the national interest but ratification was not appropriate at present. The Americans did not intend to halt preparations for CSCE but inevitably the Soviet intervention

---

[1] The record of the meeting covering sanctions against Iran has not been printed. In addition to Mr Hurd and Mr Christopher, those present at the meeting included: for the UK, Mr Bullard, Lord Bridges, Mr Fergusson, Mr Murray, Mr Mallaby, Mr Bayne, Mr Miers, Mr Burges Watson, Mr Archer, Mr Green, Mr Lavers, Mr Barratt (HMT) and Mr Hancock (HMT); and for the US, Mr Brewster, Mr Cooper, Miss Coon, Miss Frost, Mr Morris and Miss Glaspie.

UK-Soviet Relations, 1979-82

in Afghanistan cast a shadow. Bilateral talks on CSCE with the Soviet Union were unlikely to be fruitful. Mr Christopher said the same applied to MBFR and CTB.

2. Ambassador Watson had not yet returned to Moscow. The Americans were considering cutbacks in the Soviet Embassy in Washington to bring about rough reciprocity. They were not going forward with the Consulates in Kiev and New York. Senior exchanges were being cut back although some would continue at the working level. Parliamentary delegations were being cancelled. Aeroflot flights were being reduced from 3 to 2 weekly. Most important, President Carter had reduced grain sales from 25m tons to 8m tons per annum, the minimum required by their legal obligations. This had been a painful decision, and had been attacked by other candidates in the US primaries. Mr Christopher described the meeting of grain exporting countries as a success. Other exporters would not take up the slack, directly or indirectly, left by the American embargo. Grain prices in the US had fallen. Nonetheless, the administration had promised that the ban on grain sales would not affect producers. Alternative uses were being examined, such as a gas alcohol programme.

3. The President had suspended all high technology sales and shipments to the Soviet Union. The Americans would also review exports for which licences had been granted but which had not yet been shipped. The Americans would ensure that their national action was co-ordinated with the actions of their allies. Mr Cooper would be following up the COCOM aspect. Finally, restrictions on fishing in American waters meant that the Russians lost some 360,000 tons per annum. Mr Christopher emphasised that all this was an attempt to bring home to the Soviet Union that their adventure was costly. They had to understand that comparable action elsewhere would also involve penalties. He sought an assurance that the UK would be prepared to take similar measures, for instance over export credit.

4. *Mr Hurd* said our analysis and aims were similar. We would have taken unilateral action, but we had to take account of the Community angle and of the need to concert within NATO. Tactics were important. It would be helpful if the Americans could stress to the French and Germans that the US proposals left the framework for détente intact. Perhaps Mr Christopher could stress in Brussels the next day that on CSCE no-one wanted to pull out altogether, but it had to be recognised that progress would be slower. Mr Hurd explained how Mr Gromyko's visit in February had been cancelled. We had not withdrawn our Ambassador in Moscow. But we were looking at an idea that all EEC Ambassadors in Moscow might be withdrawn simultaneously for joint consultations in the political co-operation context. That would bring home to the Soviet Union that the Community as such was concerned. Mr Hurd was worried that the Soviet Union should not be able to register a gain over NATO disunity to set against the ground they had lost elsewhere.

5. Mr Hurd accepted Mr Christopher's comments on grain sales. He agreed that credit was an important area for action. The UK's own credit agreement would expire in February. The Government wanted to concert with the French, the Italians, and the Canadians so that all would take a joint restrictive line. The Germans were sensitive on limiting high technology exports. He discerned here a need for detailed discussions. Some response was still possible from other Europeans. The Government would do its best to prevent sales of subsidised butter from the Community to the Soviet Union. One problem was the lack of control by the Commission over the destination of food exports.

6. *Mr Bullard* noted that President Carter had said détente was not dead. We

7 December 1979 – 1 December 1981

agreed and saw no reason to modify the NATO doctrine of 'defence and détente'. Over the next few months the public attitudes adopted by Governments should reflect public opinion as expressed in the media. We had to ensure that when the Soviet Union calculated the costs of its invasion in Afghanistan they would discover they were higher than originally expected. On arms control, the case for taking the Soviet Union on trust had been weakened. Thus, verification made more sense than ever before.

7. *Mr Hurd* asked for views on the Olympics. *Mr Christopher* said that President Carter felt the Olympics should go forward in some form. He described how public opinion in the United States had initially surged in favour of the Games continuing, but was now (at least in the press) concentrating on shifting the Olympics somewhere else. This was favoured by Vice-President Mondale. Moving the Olympics would impose the highest penalty on the Russians. It would be a blow to them both financially and in foregone opportunities favourable to influence world public opinion. Moreover, the news of not holding the games in Moscow would get through to the Soviet people in a unique way. On this the truth could not be cloaked. The Americans wanted to explore the possibility of finding an alternative site or sites. Not much time remained if we were to go for the latter opinion [*sic* ?option]. Mr Christopher personally favoured shifting the games from Moscow to another venue or several different venues. He hoped the allies could concert ideas.

8. *Mr Hurd* said that the general British attitude was similar. But this was not a matter for Governments to decide. It was [for] the Olympic Committees. The UK consider[ed] that the subject should be further examined. Public opinion in the UK was not yet definite. *Mr Christopher* had no suggestions on the mechanics of consultation. He commented that governments had the power to prevent their citizens going to the Olympics but were reluctant to use it. This was an essentially private problem. *Mr Fergusson* said the views of our Community partners would be important. It was easy for governments to express a view to Olympic Committees but more difficult to ensure that they took account of such views. He did not know where there were suitable alternative venues for the Games. The Canadians were reluctant to use Montreal. *Mr Cooper* commented that naming alternatives would have a catalytic effect and focus attention within the Olympic Committees. Canada and Germany were obvious choices. *Mr Fergusson* thought a non-aligned country would be preferable to Germany, with all its sensitivities over relations with the USSR. *Mr Hurd* said that if the search for an alternative site came to nothing, governments would need to consider how to handle the publicity-generating activities that went with the Games, such as attendance by senior Ministers etc.

9. *Mr Christopher* described recent US contacts with the Pakistanis. A delegation led by Agha Shahi had been received on Saturday 12 January. The Pakistanis now seemed to have decided that they could accept assistance from the West. Their earlier ambivalence had dissipated. The Americans had discussed and confirmed the 1959 Treaty of Co-operation: they would consult with Pakistan if Pakistan's territorial integrity were threatened by a Communist power. Perhaps there was a need to update the treaty. Mr Christopher considered that this might best be done by a presidential statement of re-affirmation. Because of the Symington and Glenn Amendments, the Administration needed to submit legislation to Congress. The draft would incorporate such a presidential affirmation.

UK-Soviet Relations, 1979-82

10. President Carter was prepared to ask Congress for $200m for economic support and 200m of credits for military purchases. The money would be supplied during what remained of the 1980 financial year and during 1981, i.e. over 18 months. The US would also increase its assistance to refugees from Afghanistan. They planned to use the UNHCR which the Pakistanis preferred to bilateral channels. Items of military equipment currently in the pipeline would be delivered more rapidly. In particular, they wanted to provide material for the defence of Pakistan's western frontier. This, on Pakistan's own admission, badly needed strengthening. Mr Christopher hoped other countries would also be helpful. The Pakistanis were overcoming their embarrassment about accepting assistance from the West. They would be interested in their allies' views on what could be in a package.

11. *Mr Hurd* said we would be able to provide information on the help we could offer once Lord Carrington returned. He stressed the importance of the Indian dimension. That was the reason why Lord Carrington was going there. Mrs Gandhi was not easy to deal with but she should now at least be open to ideas. It was vital not to drive the Indians into a position more favourable to the Soviet Union. *Mr Christopher* said the first indication of Mrs Gandhi's attitude, expressed by their statement in the General Assembly, was disconcerting and discouraging. Such a line did nothing to calm Pakistan's fears about a Moscow/Kabul/Delhi axis. The Americans had been giving thought to a special emissary. Ambassador Gohun would be returning.

12. *Mr Christopher* briefly described Mr Brown's visit to Peking. The Americans would supply technology for defence purposes but not arms. The Chinese were also interested in bolstering Pakistan. He thought this assistance might best be provided bilaterally and not through a consortium. *Miss Frost* said that the visit of Mr Brown had been planned for a long time. Any equipment sold to the Chinese would have to be approved by COCOM. She added that the equipment they had in mind would be used for surveillance.

13. *Mr Hurd* concluded by outlining what we had done over Afghanistan including the withdrawal of our Ambassador and the further reduction of the small Mission in Kabul. Aid was being cut off and the British Council were closing down. *Mr Murray* asked whether the Pakistanis had said anything to the Americans about the importance of Western Missions staying in Kabul. *Mr Christopher* said they had not mentioned it in Washington although the point had been made elsewhere.

7 December 1979 – 1 December 1981

No. 37

Draft Planning Staff Paper on lessons from Afghanistan, 15 January 1980[1]
Confidential (FCO 49/893, RS 021/6)

1. The Soviet military intervention in Afghanistan overturned the understanding that has prevailed since 1945 that Soviet forces would not fight outside the territories of the Soviet Union and her allies. The *de facto* understanding had previously given a degree of security to non-communist neighbours. Some of these will now feel more vulnerable. This paper looks at countries bordering the Warsaw Pact, and examines what can be done by the West to reduce their vulnerability.

Is Afghanistan a Special Case?

2. The Soviet leadership, in deciding to impose Babrak on Afghanistan by Soviet military power, acted out of a mixture of state and ideological interests. The Russians had built up in Afghanistan over the years, at considerable cost, a dominant position. The country is of defensive and offensive strategic importance to them. They probably thought that their position was threatened, and acted to preserve it. They no doubt saw the military and political consequences as manageable. They had a (flimsy) legal pretext in the Treaty of Friendship. And they probably regarded Afghanistan since the April 1978 coup as a country moving towards socialism, and therefore falling under the principles enunciated by Brezhnev in 1968, when he sought to justify intervention where socialist development is subject to internal and external threats from forces hostile to socialism (the 'Brezhnev doctrine').

3. No other neighbour of the Soviet Union is likely in the short term to exhibit a similar mixture of threatened socialism and military weakness. What must be guarded against is therefore not a second Afghanistan elsewhere, but rather an increased Soviet willingness to throw over *de facto* understandings, particularly those that have in the past affected the Russians but not the Americans, as in the case of the use of troops in the Third World.

Vulnerable Neighbours: Iran

4. An important Soviet goal in the 1980s is likely to be to secure access to Middle East oil and control over oil-producing countries in the area. Iran must be the most tempting target, with the possible break-up of the country, military weakness, and the opportunities offered by economic chaos to the Tudeh party. The Soviet instinct may be to let the situation develop in the expectation that Khomeini will eventually discredit himself and his brand of Islam, leaving the field

---

[1] This paper was produced by the Planning Staff following a meeting of Deputy Permanent Under-Secretaries on 10 January at which the PUS asked for a paper on ways of countering the ill effects of events in Afghanistan on some of the Soviet Union's neighbours. It was prepared by Mr Cornish, deputy head of the Planning Staff, based on Mr Braithwaite's account of views expressed at the meeting. This version of the paper reflects comments from the PUS. On 15 January Mr Braithwaite wrote to Mr Mallaby suggesting he take over the draft: otherwise, as so much was being written on Afghanistan, there was 'some danger of crossing of wires'.

In a reply of 17 January Mr Mallaby suggested amendments but it is doubtful whether the paper was taken any further. Mr Mallaby had suggested instead a study on the whole question of levers to stop Soviet interventions in non-aligned countries, as set out in the despatch of 7 December (No. 1), in conjunction with a small number of West European countries. Mr Hurd had raised this at the meeting on 31 December (No. 11). Mr Mallaby also proposed a British study on how to deter Soviet interventions in less developed countries, which would feed into the Allied study (see No. 48, note 3).

UK-Soviet Relations, 1979-82

open to progressive and in the longer term communist governments. But the Russians might be tempted to intervene militarily before then, e.g. to exploit the Azerbaijani situation or to stop Iranian military help to anti-Soviet forces in Afghanistan. A pretext is to hand in the Soviet-Iranian Treaty of 1921; the Soviet Union has not accepted the recent Iranian attempt to denounce it unilaterally.

Yugoslavia

5. While Tito lives, the Russians are unlikely to try to intervene decisively in Yugoslavia, though they will be encouraged by current economic difficulties there. When he dies, his initial successors will try to keep the country together, but the Russians will try to stir up trouble, particularly between the rival nationalities, in order to justify intervention. Yugoslavia is vulnerable as a former member of the Socialist camp which broke away in 1948; her best defence is the presumption that the Yugoslav armed forces would bitterly resist an invasion. Tito has probably never regarded a Soviet invasion as excluded if the Russians thought they could get away with it. The Yugoslav concern will be that the Afghanistan precedent might make the Soviet leadership more confident that a Soviet intervention in Yugoslavia, perhaps in alleged support of a group in one of the Republics, could be carried out without unacceptable costs.

Other Neighbours

6. Events in Afghanistan have not directly altered East-West rules of conduct in Europe, or made a Soviet attack on the central front, on Berlin, or on the more vulnerable northern and southern flanks more likely. It is in the Soviet interest to encourage the view, especially in the Federal Republic, that excessive Western reaction over Afghanistan will endanger *Berlin*, but it is more likely that the Russians will continue to seek to maintain the European balance, while winning a free hand elsewhere. Soviet pressure on *Norway* will no doubt continue, but is very unlikely to lead to an attack as a result of events in Afghanistan. *Finland's* situation is likely to be satisfactory to the Soviet Union. If the Finnish Communist Party were to achieve power on its own and subsequently be threatened by non-communists, the Afghan situation might be repeated, but the Finns are likely to be able to continue to avoid this sequence of events. *Austria* is not threatened, nor under the present government is *Greece*. A more promising Soviet goal may be *Turkey*, whose eastern-most provinces were claimed by the Russians in 1946. The desired order of events from the Russian viewpoint is however likely to begin with the Turks leaving NATO, and premature military pressure would have the opposite effect. The only other Soviet land neighbours are *China*, which the Soviet Union would presumably like to invade but cannot because of the size of the military task, and *North Korea*, an orthodox communist country, perhaps regarded as too friendly to China but not at risk.

The Western Response

7. The weakening of *de facto* understandings about the limits on Soviet military intervention is therefore of greatest concern to Iran and Yugoslavia. The West have very strong interests in the continuing independence of both countries. It is therefore important to consider ways of strengthening them.

8. One way of doing so would be by trying to buttress what is left of the ill-defined system of understandings which has hitherto limited Soviet intervention abroad. As a first step, the understandings should be stated more clearly, and sanctions against their infringement suggested. In particular, the West should consider how to bring home to the Soviet leadership that they cannot expect to be able to send Soviet troops to another non-Warsaw Pact country, or further erode

7 December 1979 – 1 December 1981

the system of *de facto* understandings in other ways harmful to important Western interests, without paying a price for it. It must be noted that the West in most cases is unable to inflict serious sanctions on the Soviet Union without some cost to the West in turn. Cutting US grain sales to the Soviet Union hurts Iowa farmers, the Administration's budget, and presidential prospects. Conversely, cancelling ministerial visits to the Soviet Union, while less painful to Western countries, also makes less impression on the Soviet leadership. If Soviet foreign policy is to be changed by Western actions the internal economic and political cost of such actions should indeed be calculated, but due weight should also be given to the expected foreign policy gains.

9. It is not, however, desirable to drive the Soviet Union into a position where all the sanctions in Western hands have already been enforced. The Soviet leadership would not welcome a return to the Cold War, an all-out arms race with the United States, and the increased dangers of nuclear confrontation that would be entailed. But for the West simply to impose these burdens would make the world a much more dangerous place without moderating Soviet policy; it would probably on the contrary become wilder. The task is therefore to make clear to the Soviet leadership that they can still avoid a return to unrestrained Cold War if they limit their behaviour in the appropriate way.

10. What are the sanctions at the West's disposal for this purpose? This paper will not give an exhaustive catalogue, but instead will sketch two sanctions which seem to meet the need. Both would be based on statements by Western leaders making clear that, if the Soviet Union proceeded with its course of breaking existing *de facto* understandings, the West would feel bound to relax certain understandings which have hitherto governed Western behaviour. In the first place, the West's relationship with China over the last three years has been conducted on the basis that Western help to China would stop short of military sales and cooperation which would make a decisive difference to China's strength. There are Western reasons for continuing wariness about China's long-term future, but interests of Western-Soviet relations have also played a part. It could be made clear, e.g. in speeches by Western leaders, that, if the Soviet Union continues on its present course in the Third World, Western military cooperation with China would become much more intense. There could also, it might be said, be closer cooperation between threatened Third World countries, China and the West in the training and supply of national liberation movements directed against Soviet imperialism, e.g. in Afghanistan. This sanction would have particular relevance to Iran.[2]

11. Secondly, concentrating on Yugoslavia as a European country, Western leaders could make clear that an upsetting of the rules in Europe would be inevitable if the Soviet Union destabilised Yugoslavia. If this happened, other rules affecting Europe would also be at risk in a way which would hurt the Soviet Union. In particular, the presumption that the Warsaw Pact countries of Eastern Europe were an exclusive Soviet preserve would be put in question. While the military realities would be respected (the West is not in a position to change them) it could be made clear that substantial efforts would be made to encourage the genuine independence of countries like Poland. No details would be given, but possible fields for study include the use of Eastern European indebtedness to the

---

[2] In a minute of 16 January, Mr Broucher commented that the Far East department believed Britain's relationship with China was too fragile to be switched on and off in response to external factors—'the China card, if it exists, is best left to play itself' (FCO 28/3998, EN 021/1).

UK-Soviet Relations, 1979-82

West as a means of leverage, e.g. to bring about greater implementation of the CSCE Final Act.

12. In giving warning of the possible use of such sanctions if the Soviet Union continued to transgress *de facto* understandings, Western leaders should have in mind particular actions which they would be prepared to take if the contingency arose, and were not going to take if the Soviet Union stayed in line. It would not be desirable to specify the particular actions publicly. The aim is to avoid a position in which the Soviet leadership were confident that they could transgress without serious long-term consequences. It would be sufficient to ensure that they know that something harmful would happen, without knowing its precise nature. The lack of specificity about Western sanctions would also make it less easy for the Russians to try to retaliate by counter-threats. The sanctions suggested above do not in any case make specific Soviet retaliation likely, though the West would once again be accused of frustrating the hopes placed in détente.[3]

13. Two further considerations need to be borne in mind. The first is that a positive result of the Soviet action in Afghanistan has been increased Third World and non-aligned willingness to condemn the Soviet Union. Western actions need to be calculated to avoid giving an excuse to the Third World to relapse into their past passivity and willingness to give the Russians, but not the Americans, the benefit of the doubt. For this purpose it is important that the Americans, for example, should avoid responding militarily to the continued plight of their hostages in Tehran in a way which would be equated with Soviet action in Afghanistan. The perceptions of individual important Third World countries also need to be taken into account. India is a country in which the Russians have invested a great deal, and it is important that the net results of the Afghanistan events should, if possible, be to widen the gap between Delhi and Moscow, rather than narrow it as a result of Indian reactions to the West's strengthening of Pakistan and closer relations with China.

14. Secondly, part of the potential vulnerability of Yugoslavia and Iran lies in their weakness. Yugoslavia's economic difficulties exacerbate her internal divisions. The West, in particular the countries of the European Community, have it in their hands to help the Yugoslav economy by trade and other concessions. These will inevitably hurt the givers, but a certain amount will have to be paid in order to strengthen Yugoslavia. A major effort should be made now. As far as Iran is concerned, the priority inevitably given to the hostages cuts across any Western efforts to help pull the country together. It should, however, not be forgotten that the long-term Western interest is in a stronger, independent Iran.

15. If the line recommended in this paper is agreed, the first step should be to float it among our immediate allies, the Nine and NATO—the United Kingdom cannot act alone. The French and Germans are likely to be more cautious than the Americans, given that for internal political reasons both Schmidt and Giscard do not want to be seen to be putting détente at risk. United States support would be more likely. It would not be necessary to work out agreed sanctions, but it would be reasonable to seek agreement to deliver warnings to the Soviet Union. The contents of the warnings could differ according to the country delivering them. Suitable British occasions would be the next foreign affairs debate in Parliament,[4] and the speech which the Secretary of State is considering giving to Chatham

---

[3] The last two sentences of this paragraph were handwritten additions to the original manuscript.

[4] See No. 45, note 3.

7 December 1979 – 1 December 1981

House.[5] Measures to help the Yugoslav economy would be less controversial, at least among Foreign Ministries. They would have to be worked out both in capitals, and among the Nine.

[5] See No. 73, note 7.

No. 38

Sir C. Rose (UKDEL NATO) to FCO, 16 January 1980, 10.10 a.m.[1]
Tel. No. 39 Immediate, Confidential (FCO 37/2244, FSA 020/1)

My Telno 38:[2] NATO Council Meeting on Afghanistan

1. This meeting was the first occasion on which the Alliance has met to hear the considered views of member governments on the implications of the Soviet invasion and to discuss the measures they are taking. Only Portugal and Iceland did not speak. Several speakers welcomed our initiative in calling the meeting and the contributions showed that a good deal of progress had been made since the Council met to hear American views from Warren Christopher on 1 January.[3]

2. Most of those who spoke had prepared statements and this inevitably involved a good deal of duplication. Nor did it leave any time for discussion after the initial tour de table. But it was at least satisfactory, even if not surprising, that there was a large measure of agreement with the analysis presented by Mr. Hurd, who spoke first. Arnaud (France) was at pains to emphasise points on which the French were in agreement with their allies, although [he] offered little hope that the French would concert action within the Alliance.

3. The statement issued after the meeting (my telno 37)[4] is satisfactory as far as it goes. It puts firmly on record the Alliance view that the Soviet action cannot fail to have a damaging effect on détente and that steps need to be taken to bring this home to the Soviet government. It also records the agreement, confirmed at the meeting, that consultations on all aspects of the situation should continue in the Alliance.

4. It has however taken the Alliance two weeks to get to this point. Meanwhile the Russians have persisted in their invasion, their contempt for the United Nations and their disregard for the effect on détente. The statement will have little effect unless it is seen to be followed up soon by determined practical measures. We originally pressed for announcement of some immediate measures to be made by all governments a week ago. Our allies were not ready by then and we agreed to defer action until after yesterday's meeting. Most of the measures which our allies are now considering or proposing to take are based on the original list we gave them. I hope it will now be possible for us to announce those relating to high level contacts, cultural and military exchanges and other similar events straight away. If others announce in parallel the measures in these fields (lists in my telegram under reference) this would have the effect of making it clear to the Russians that the Alliance is not prepared to continue business as usual. But we will need to go further than this if we are to show that we mean to take action which will have

[1] Repeated Immediate to Washington, Paris, Bonn, Moscow, UKMIS New York.
[2] Not printed. This telegram of 15 January reported the statements made by individual representatives on the NAC.
[3] No. 14.
[4] Not printed.

UK-Soviet Relations, 1979-82

some real bite in it. This would mean at least pursuing the proposals on credit terms and on tightening up the application of COCOM rules for high technology transfer. I hope that, even if the French will not join us, we shall follow up these points urgently.

5. As regards the Olympic Games, several of our allies supported our view, which the Americans share, that cancellation, transfer or boycott would be a major political blow for the Soviet government. This is a subject which I could, if you wish, pursue further with my colleagues. But I should need more detailed guidance on how you think we should proceed with regard both to the Games themselves and the supporting activities, e.g. ceremonial, high level attendance. It would be helpful to be informed of any reactions to lobbying in the United Nations on the basis of your telno 32 to UKMIS New York.[5] In particular, what signs are there of support among Islamic countries for the Saudi withdrawal? Presumably the Saudi foreign minister will promote this idea at the Islamic Conference.

6. By arrangement with us in advance, the Americans kept a low profile at the Council meeting, Warren Christopher speaking after Italy, France and Greece. Apart from emphasising the importance of firm action, he did not press for any specific measures. The American record so far on consultations in the Alliance on these measures has not been good. But if the allies do not now move fast at least to the extent indicated in paragraph 4 above, the gap between American and European reactions is likely to become all too apparent and will be fully exploited by the Russians. I hope therefore that we can continue to play a leading role in encouraging our European allies to take firm and immediate action.

[5] Not printed.

No. 39

Letter from Mr Heseltine (DoE) to Lord Carrington, 16 January 1980
Confidential (FCO 37/2244, FSA 020/1)

Dear Peter,

Soviet Intervention in Afghanistan

My Office passed to Ian Gilmour's Office last week my immediate thoughts on your note on 8 January to the Prime Minister.[1] I understand you would now like something more substantial.

Let me say immediately that I wholeheartedly agree that few things would hurt Soviet prestige more than the absence of the majority of Western countries from the Olympic Games this year or, alternatively, if the International Olympic Committee (IOC) saw fit, even at this late stage, to relocate the Games. But a major difficulty, as you go on to say, is that Western governments have no direct role in matters concerning the Olympics. However, I do not believe that this should deter us from pressing with our major allies for the inclusion of this weapon in the current discussions on possible sanctions against the Soviet Union for her aggression in Afghanistan.

This aggression has nothing to do with sport. It is a political move which needs to be countered by whatever means at our disposal, political or otherwise. If this means that we have to embrace the use of sport for the first time as a political

[1] No 27.

7 December 1979 – 1 December 1981

weapon, I feel that the end would justify the means.

But I do not believe that any unilateral approach to either the IOC or the British Olympic Association is a viable option. Either or both would be certain to meet with a rebuff in the light of very recent statements by their leaders. Like all governing bodies of sport, they are both autonomous; and the Government has no obvious financial hold on either body since they both rely on sources of finance other than through governments. Nor do we have any powers to prevent British athletes going to Moscow for the Olympics.

I believe we must therefore join with our allies either in a direct approach to our several national Olympic Committees to persuade them against participation—but after 4 years of preparation and build up it is unlikely that many would respond favourably—or to work through the General Assembly of the United Nations for a concerted appeal by most of the world's nations to the IOC to remove the Olympics from Moscow.

If we do nothing we could, as you suggest, be criticised for inconsistency in the light of our advice that the Lions tour of South Africa should not go ahead. I am therefore in no doubt at all about the need to support a major political initiative in the context of Afghanistan in conjunction with our allies.

I will leave it to Hector Munro at today's meeting at No. 10 to deal with this matter in more detail.

I am copying this to the Prime Minister, to members of OD, to Keith Joseph, David Howell, Peter Walker, Michael Havers and to Sir Robert Armstrong.

Yours ever,
MICHAEL HESELTINE

No. 40

Letter from Sir C. Keeble (Moscow) to Mr Mallaby, 16 January 1980
Confidential (FCO 28/3998, EN 021/1)

Dear Christopher,

1. It was thoughtful of you to write on 11 January and give us as much as possible of the background to thinking in London.[1] With the first round of allied consultations now nearly at an end and the tone of the initial reaction determined, it is not a bad moment to take stock. Hence this letter, which, inevitably goes over some of the ground covered in earlier letters and telegrams.

2. Our subsequent policy needs to be determined in the light of a long-term assessment of Soviet policy and its international effectiveness. This in turn must depend in part on our assessment of the cause of the Soviet decision on military occupation of Afghanistan and leads on to consideration of the extent to which we may be able to influence the determination of future policy by this leadership or its successors and the international reaction to it.

3. On the factors involved in the Soviet decision I have little to add to what I have already said. I have had, as you can imagine, lengthy discussions with my American, French and German colleagues. There may be differences of emphasis

---

[1] In this letter Mr Mallaby reported on developments within NATO and Mr Hurd's proposed statement to the Commons. He also sought Sir C. Keeble's view of the relative influence of the military in the formulation of Soviet policy.

UK-Soviet Relations, 1979-82

among us, with the French for instance inclined to put a little more emphasis on the effect of the TNF decision, but there is not much doubt that the Soviet decision was dictated primarily by developments in Afghanistan itself. On timing, however, there was a certain amount of latitude and it happened that various non-Afghanistan factors coincided to make the end of the year favourable. The TNF decision had been taken, so although there was still a lot to play for in Europe the risk of immediate prejudice was relatively low; the fate of SALT II was uncertain anyway; the first half of 1980 could not show major new initiatives, given the approach of the German and American elections; and the Americans were handicapped by the Tehran Embassy seizure. As 1980 wore on some of these factors would diminish and indeed begin to operate the other way. A major crisis at the time of the German and American elections could produce a commitment to harsh Western policies. There would be less time before the TNF plans began to be effective and as the Olympics approached the case for a sparkling Soviet international image became much greater. So, if there was to be a military occupation the end of the year must have seemed clearly the best time.

4. The substantive decision must have been the subject of considerable debate. We can probably take Brezhnev's statement that it was 'not a simple decision' as an understatement.[2] I do not however think that we can see the issue as one between a dove-like Brezhnev and his military hawks. We simply do not know how individuals lined up. In any case what matters for the future is not so much the identification of individuals as the identification of the issues which may sway their policies. Their calculation—or miscalculation—must have had the following elements:

(*a*) The military conditions in Afghanistan would not be easy, but, given an adequate Soviet force and a compliant Afghan regime it would be possible to crush any significant rebel opposition with a few months and leave a stable political situation;

(*b*) Western interests would be so diverse that there would be no counter measures which would significantly damage the Soviet Union itself;

(*c*) By the time any progress on disarmament was possible the West would be weary of confrontation;

(*d*) Reaction in the developing countries could be ignored;

(*e*) A show of strength might indeed be salutary in relation to the Arab world, and possibly outside it;

(*f*) Relations with China need not be substantially affected. Indeed it might be a good thing to show the Chinese that the Soviet Union too was capable of using force against its neighbours.

5. If these were some of the considerations which led to the decision to use force they will also be relevant to the Soviet estimate of the rightness of that decision. We should therefore have them in mind in assessing the Western response. On the basis of Soviet theory and practice we may take it that the long-term Soviet objective is the extension of national power and influence, primarily by political means but with a readiness to deploy force where this is both necessary and safe. Our own objectives should be:

(*a*) to make the leadership recognise that they miscalculated in several if not all

---

[2] President Brezhnev made the statement on 13 January to the party newspaper, *Pravda*. For records of Soviet discussions leading up to the invasion see Odd Arne Westad, 'The Situation in "A": New Russian Evidence on the Soviet Intervention in Afghanistan', CWIHP *Bulletin* 8-9 (Winter 1996/1997), pp. 128-184.

7 December 1979 – 1 December 1981

respects when launching the operation; and

(*b*) to demonstrate that a similar operation conducted elsewhere would be likely to prove both dangerous and ineffective.

But going beyond these short-term objectives we have the longer-term objective of constructing a safe and stable set of international relationships.

6. What measures will best help to attain our objectives? I initially advocated a response which would surprise the Russians by its harshness. I think that the United States action, particularly in relation to grain supplies, has had that effect. The display of unanimity among the non-committed countries in the General Assembly must also have made some impression and so too, quite possibly, has the expression of popular concern within the Soviet Union. The last is difficult to determine, but there have been some signs of it and I am fairly sure that it was a major reason for Brezhnev's statement. Prior to the statement, for instance, Zorin, in a television programme, referred to the very substantial volume of correspondence which he received and said that he hoped his answers would have helped to explain the Government's action.

7. In my telegram No. 44,[3] I said that we ought to keep the bilateral response in perspective and not regard our measures as sanctions. In saying that, I had in mind that the measures themselves will not, with the possible exception of technology and the grain embargo, have a substantially adverse effect on Soviet interests. There can be few countries in the world which are less vulnerable to economic measures or more ready to suffer a severance of external links than the Soviet Union. Not merely will the bilateral measures fail to cause substantial damage; many of them are necessarily of a short-term character. If they are seen by the Soviet Union as the principal feature of the Western response, it will be concluded that the response is not a significant factor for the future. Consequently, if the West wants to exercise an effective influence over future Soviet policy we have to devise a longer-term strategy using different weapons. It must have many elements. Some of them can be inferred from paragraph 4. But I hope it is not otiose if I say that the primary need is the consolidation of our relationships among the allies and with the developing world. It is a long time since the idea of Britain holding a unique position in relation to Europe, the United States and the Commonwealth was fashionable. But Brezhnev's statement shows just how keen the Soviet Union is to drive wedges between the United States and Europe and in this respect we are, I believe, in a position to exercise some influence. In the consolidation of relations with the developing world the solution of the Rhodesia problem may add to the effectiveness of Commonwealth cooperation. We need of course to provide military support for those non-communist Third World governments who may come under direct threat, but this by itself is not an adequate policy. Iran, surely, demonstrated to us that a military superstructure is no use if the political base on which it rests is unsound. If we are to build on the awakening of the developing world to the realities of Soviet foreign policy, we need to offer them a concept of relations with the West which has a certain consistency and a genuine appeal. In real terms we are well placed. The developing world receives much from the West and scarcely anything except arms and dogma from the Soviet Union. What is now needed is a consistent effort to formulate and at every turn to emphasise that it is with us, not with the Soviet Union, that the developing countries have a genuine community of interest; that it is the Soviet Union which has to rely on old-

---

[3] Not printed.

UK-Soviet Relations, 1979-82

fashioned imperialist force and we who have the political vision; that it is we who not only seek a relaxation of the strategic tension, but can offer a sound international structure of security and prosperity, on which it can alone be built. In short, there is now an outstanding opportunity for Western statesmanship to go beyond the negative response which was the necessary first stage and to develop a concept, world-wide in character, which strikes at the basic fallacy in the Soviet concept of détente and exposes the sterile hostility which is its essence. Apart from the intrinsic need for this kind of positive political response, it should enable us to place the emphasis on policies where there is a reasonable chance of Western unity and prevent the development of too large a gap between the Americans and the Europeans. The Prime Minister is in a good position to take the lead.

Yours ever,
CURTIS KEEBLE

No. 41

Minute from Lord Carrington to Mrs Thatcher, 19 January 1980[1]
PM/80/5 Secret (FCO 13/967, PC 295/1)

Prime Minister
Afghanistan
1. On 9-18 January I visited Turkey, Oman, Saudi Arabia, Pakistan and India, primarily to discuss with the governments of these countries the Soviet invasion of Afghanistan and their reactions to it. I had discussions with the Foreign Ministers and Heads of Government of all these countries. I also had a brief meeting during a stop-over on my return journey with the Foreign Minister of Bahrain. The following are my impressions and conclusions.

A. *Impressions*
General
2. All the countries I visited, except India, agreed broadly with our own analysis of Soviet motives for their invasion and with our estimate of the dangers to the security and integrity of other states in the region, and with the need for a significant and sustained response, both from the West and from those countries which feel threatened. The Western reaction so far has disappointed them. Oman, Saudi Arabia and Pakistan probably underestimate the threat of internal subversion. India's attitude is influenced by her traditional tendency to give the Russians the benefit of the doubt and her distrust of Pakistan.

Individual Countries
3. (*a*) *Turkey*: The Turkish economy is in a parlous state and internal security is bad. The Turks are especially concerned about the maintenance of the integrity

---

[1] This minute was requested following an *ad hoc* meeting on South West Asia chaired by the Prime Minister on 16 January which 'invited the Foreign Secretary to put forward a paper on issues for decision on the Afghanistan crisis'. In his covering minute to Mrs Thatcher, Sir Robert Armstrong commented that the minute was 'strong on general diplomatic and political measures. But it skates lightly over economic measures against the Soviet Union (over which the Cabinet on 10 January expressed serious doubts, in relation to Lord Carrington's earlier minute of 8 January) [No. 27].' The Cabinet Secretary went on to note that 'in most of these areas, the policy recommendation is blameless but its *implementation* will be far from easy' (PREM 19/135).

of Iran. They fear that Khomeini's policies could lead to the country's disintegration, stimulated by Soviet subversion in Azerbaijan and elsewhere. The Turks will require large-scale financial help over the next few years.

(b) *Oman*: [...][2] Oman is prosperous and Qaboos is likely to survive for some time longer. He remains anxious about the threat from the PDRY. The Omanis are discussing the possible provision of facilities for US forces but do not want Western personnel on Oman's territory. Their initiative for the establishment by the Gulf States of a minesweeper capability in the Straits of Hormuz was mishandled, but this could be rectified.

(c) *Saudi Arabia*: The Saudis are ready to help Turkey, e.g. over oil. They are also prepared to offer financial help for strengthening the military capabilities of the countries in the region under threat, though they are opposed to any Western military presence. They are playing a leading role, together with Pakistan, in mobilising Moslem opinion against the Soviet action in Afghanistan. But they regard the Camp David Agreement as an obstacle to full-hearted co-operation between the countries of the region and the United States. They look for a new move on the Middle East problem when, as they expect, the Camp David process runs into the sand in April/May; (this view was shared by the Bahraini Foreign Minister). The Saudis are concerned about Soviet influence in both the PDRY and the YAR and about possible subversion through the many expatriates in their own country. The Mecca incident was a shock to them.[3]

(d) *Pakistan*: The Pakistanis are deeply concerned at the new threat on their western frontier. They feel squeezed between the Russians in Afghanistan and the Indians on their eastern border. They particularly fear the possibility of Soviet 'retaliatory' raids from Afghanistan into their own territory. They are painfully aware that their military equipment is out of date. They were affronted by the meagreness of the US offer of credit. In both respects their attitude is justified. Moreover, the refugees from Afghanistan, who they think may number one million by the Spring, are an increasing burden. But their reaction to the Soviet invasion was dominated by their complex over India, who, they are convinced, still wants to establish hegemony over the sub-continent. Nonetheless, they are ready to resume the process of 'normalising' relations with India as a means of sanitising their eastern frontier. President Zia is in a dilemma over elections: if he holds them, the Bhutto faction will win; and if he does not, popular discontent will grow.

(e) *India*: The Indians accept that the Soviet invasion of Afghanistan poses a danger to the sub-continent. But they are anxious to find excuses for Soviet behaviour in the policies and activities of Pakistan, China and the United States, by whom they profess to feel surrounded. They resent the possibility of a super-power confrontation so close to India, not only on grounds of national security, but also because of the effect on the Non-Aligned Movement and India's role in it if she had to make a choice. They were somewhat shame-faced and defensive over the Indian statement at the United Nations and apprehensive about the Islamic line-up against the Soviet action. They are also preoccupied with their domestic economic problems and with unrest in their north-east and eastern

---

[2] A sentence is here omitted.

[3] On 20 November 1979, a group of armed militants occupied the Grand Mosque in Mecca. In the ensuing battle to retake the Mosque approximately 250 people were killed and 600 wounded. The US Embassy in Pakistan was burnt down by a mob following allegations that America was involved in the occupation.

UK-Soviet Relations, 1979-82

border areas. They are ready to talk to the Pakistanis but with little enthusiasm or hope of success, given the weakness of Zia's position and above all their congenital distrust of Pakistani promises against the background of three Indo-Pakistani wars, which leads them to express apprehension about any revival of a closer US/Pakistan military relationship.

B. *Conclusions*

4. My talks in the capitals I visited confirmed my view that the Soviet invasion of Afghanistan is a most serious challenge and unless the West reacts with vigour, any repetition of it, e.g. in Yugoslavia, could be disastrous. We must urgently pursue our discussions with the Americans and with our principal European allies. The following are among the actions we might undertake:

(*a*) We should pursue the political and economic measures directed at the Soviet Union which we have been discussing in NATO, even though for the most part, apart from a boycott or the removal of the Olympic Games (see Annex), these are unlikely to cause the Russians major difficulties or embarrassment.

(*b*) We should encourage the non-aligned countries, and particularly the Moslem countries, to continue their denunciation of the Soviet action and, if possible, to take measures against the Afghan regime. We should continue to urge the Americans to handle the Iran crisis in such a way as not to hinder this.

(*c*) We should encourage the United States formally to guarantee Pakistan against aggression from Afghanistan and to meet Pakistani legitimate military requirements up to a level which would give the Indians no justifiable grounds for concern. We should also support the Americans in their search for suitable defence facilities in the region.[4]

(*d*) We should conclude as rapidly as possible negotiations over our own sales of defence equipment to Oman, Saudi Arabia and other states in the Gulf and to Pakistan.

(*e*) We should prepare a European initiative amending Resolution 242 to provide for the acknowledgement of the Palestinians' rights in return for their recognition of Israel. This proposal could be put forward when, as seems likely, the Camp David process comes to an end in April/May.

(*f*) We should provide friendly states in the Gulf and Pakistan with more information about our assessments of Soviet activities and intentions in the area.

(*g*) We should also provide these states with assistance in counter-subversion.

(*h*) We should encourage closer co-operation among the Gulf States, e.g. over the security of the Straits of Hormuz.

(*i*) We should work carefully for an EEC/Gulf dialogue.

(*j*) We should increase Western and Saudi/Omani influence in the YAR.

(*k*) [...]⁵

(*l*) We should participate to the extent possible in further financial help for Turkey.

(*m*) We should encourage the Indians and Pakistanis, despite their pathological distrust of one another, to normalize their relationship.

(*n*) We should review with others our policy towards China including arms sales.

(*o*) We should review with the others concerned possible support for

---

[4] The Prime Minister commented: 'On reflection I am a little unhappy about such a guarantee. It would look as if we were guaranteeing President Zia's regime rather than the territory' (PREM 19/135).

[5] A sentence is here omitted.

Yugoslavia.

5. I am copying this minute to the members of OD and to Sir R. Armstrong.

CARRINGTON

ANNEX

Olympic Games

1. Following the meeting of Ministers on 16 January, we have asked the Germans and Italians whether they would join us in a formal approach to the International Olympic Committee to suggest moving the Games. The Germans are very cautious but Dr Genscher is expected to discuss the Olympics with Mr Vance when they meet on 21 January. The Italians have yet to react. Sir N. Henderson will put the matter to Mr Vance on 19 January.

2. The Canadian Prime Minister said on 18 January that Canada would approach the IOC about moving the Games and that the practical difficulties at Montreal might be less than the city authorities have said. The Japanese would probably be extremely reluctant to accept part of the Games. The Mexicans and the Germans would also be likely to see political objections to using their Olympic facilities. The Australian Government is reviewing the subject and the difficulties at Melbourne might be less than elsewhere.

3. The chances of getting the Olympic Games moved are very slight. On the other hand the Russians might be glad to have Britain excluded from the Games on the grounds of our sporting contacts with South Africa.

4. The Winter Olympics begin next month in New York State, but the United States Government do not intend to take any action on this front, such as denying visas to the Soviet team.

5. Another idea, not yet discussed with our Allies, would be a Western proposal to the International Olympic Committee that the Olympic sailing events should be moved from Tallinn in the Baltic States to another country. This would have political attractions. Summer 1980 is the 40th anniversary of another Soviet act of aggression, the annexation of the Baltic States. A number of Western countries, including the UK, France, Germany and the US, do not recognise the annexation *de jure*. Moreover, the relocation of the sailing alone would present far fewer practical difficulties than moving the entire Games. On the other hand, the response of the International Olympic Committee would probably be negative.

6. Yet other options include a Western boycott of the Moscow Games, or a boycott by the Western contingents of ceremonial events such as the opening and closing parades and official Soviet receptions. The British Olympic Committee would resist the first and probably the second. One thing in the Government's power is to decide that the Duke of Edinburgh and the Minister for Sport should not go to Moscow.

UK-Soviet Relations, 1979-82

No. 42

Extract from Conclusions of a meeting of the Defence and Oversea Policy Committee, 22 January 1980[1]
OD(80)1st Meeting Confidential (CAB 148/189)

Item 2. *Afghanistan*

The Foreign and Commonwealth Secretary said that the four major conclusions from his visit to the Middle East were that the threat lay in Soviet subversion rather than overt aggression; that Arab and other Moslem opinion saw the Camp David agreement as an obstacle to the development of a more unified response to the Soviet danger; that opinion in the area increasingly feared the break-up of Iran; and that American action against Iran was deplored both for contributing to this danger and for detracting from the condemnation of Soviet aggression by providing an alternative target for local criticism.

In discussion there was general support for the proposals in the Foreign and Commonwealth Secretary's minute of 19 January,[2] and the following points were made:

(*a*) In the light of President Carter's skilfully worded pronouncement on the Olympic Games, the Prime Minister would need to write to the Chairman of the British Olympic Association without delay and in terms designed to have maximum public impact.[3] While the Government would not need to go as far as President Carter had in all respects, it was important to convince the Russians that Britain fully supported the United States. The immediate aim should be to bring maximum pressure upon the International Olympic Committee to transfer the Games away from Moscow, to another or possibly to several other locations. If that failed, it would be necessary to do everything possible to damage the prospects for the Moscow Olympics. As well as ensuring that there were no British official visitors, this would involve considering whether British athletes should be advised not to attend. Such advice would be more likely to be heeded if it came from Parliament as well as from the Government. Subject to the advice of the Chief Whip on the prospects of securing a convincing majority, therefore, the Government might seek a formal Parliamentary vote endorsing its attitude to the Olympics. Useful suggestions had also been put forward in recent letters to the Press from Sir William Hayter[4] and others: these suggestions could be reflected in the Prime Minister's letter to the British Olympic Association. The British Olympic Committee's need to appeal for funds might provide a

[1] Those present were Margaret Thatcher, Lord Carrington, William Whitelaw, Lord Hailsham, Geoffrey Howe, David Howell, Michael Heseltine, Sir Keith Joseph, Francis Pym, Earl Ferrers, Sir Michael Havers and Cecil Parkinson.

[2] No. 41.

[3] On 20 January President Carter wrote to Robert Kane, President of the US Olympic Committee, informing him that, unless the Soviet Union withdrew their troops from Afghanistan within the next month, he could not support US participation in the Olympic Games in Moscow and that the Committee should work with others to seek to transfer or cancel the Summer Games. See *Public Papers: Carter (1980-81)*, Book I, pp. 106-7.

[4] The former British Ambassador to Moscow, 1953-57, whose letter to *The Times* was published on 21 January. In the letter, Sir William recalled the Soviet invasion of Hungary in 1956 and the subsequent cancellation of a visit to Moscow by the Sadler's Wells Ballet 'who would have been dancing on the grave of Hungary'. He expressed the hope 'that British athletes will have as much good sense and as much patriotism as British dancers'.

7 December 1979 – 1 December 1981

means of pressure; but it would not be right to involve The Queen in her capacity as the Committee's patron.

(*b*) There was general agreement that the Government should continue to oppose subsidised food sales to the Soviet Union by the European Community; should pursue with Britain's allies the possibility of tightening and widening the restrictions imposed by the Co-ordinating Committee on the International Strategic Embargo (COCOM), while recognising that agreement on significant steps was unlikely and that unilateral British action could not be contemplated; and should refuse the Soviet Union credit terms more favourable than the Organisation for Economic Co-operation and Development's Consensus, provided that other relevant members of the European Community did the same.

(*c*) Caution was expressed about giving too much political or military support to Pakistan, given the weak internal position of General Zia's regime, and the danger of adverse Indian reaction. The threat to Pakistan was in any case not primarily military. On the other hand, the first consideration must be to enable Pakistan to preserve her territorial integrity. The United States Government had reaffirmed the guarantee given to Pakistan under the 1959 Agreement: Her Majesty's Government were not called upon to do more than noting this guarantee.

(*d*) There was no doubt that the Pakistani armed forces were badly under-equipped, and their morale was important. United States military aid was likely to be inadequate. Since there were difficulties over financing any British arms supplies by means of an increase in the Export Credits Guarantee Department's cover limit, it would be worth exploring the possibility of Saudi money being made available.

(*e*) As regards Turkey, it was noted that the present Prime Minister's plans for restoring the economic situation were sensible but unlikely to command the necessary support in Parliament; the result might be a take-over by the Army.

The Prime Minister, summing up the discussion, said that the general case for supporting the Americans in response to the Afghanistan crisis was strengthened by the need to be less forthcoming towards current American policy over Iran. Her message to the British Olympic Committee would be redrafted in the light of the discussion, and she would arrange for it to be delivered as soon as possible.[5] She would at the same time inform President Carter as proposed. Further thought should be given to the possibility of seeking Parliamentary endorsement for the Government's attitude to the whole Olympic problem. The Government would continue to oppose subsidised food exports to the Soviet Union by the European Community; would explore with other countries concerned the possibility of tightening and widening the COCOM restrictions; and provided others did the same would not go beyond Consensus terms for credit. The Foreign and Commonwealth Secretary would pursue the various proposals for political action in the area, and would bring forward a separate paper on the possibilities of a European initiative on the Palestinian question. Certain of the proposals would require further consideration between the Foreign and Commonwealth Secretary and herself. The Foreign and Commonwealth Secretary would revise his proposed statement in the House of Lords, which would be postponed until 24 January when the Lord Privy Seal would be available to make a corresponding statement in the

[5] See No. 43, note 2.

UK-Soviet Relations, 1979-82

House of Commons.[6] She herself would meanwhile arrange for an announcement, either in Parliament or in the Press, about the Government's approach to the British Olympic Committee.

The Committee:

(i) Invited the Secretary of State for the Environment, in consultation with the Foreign and Commonwealth Secretary and Prime Minister, to redraft the proposed letter to the British Olympic Committee and to discuss with the Chief Whip the possibility of Parliamentary endorsement for the Government's Olympic policy.

(ii) Invited the Foreign and Commonwealth Secretary, in consultation with the Prime Minister and other Ministers as appropriate, to arrange for the other measures proposed in paragraph 4 of his minute to be pursued in the light of the Committee's discussion.

(iii) Invited the Foreign and Commonwealth Secretary and the Lord Privy Seal to report the Government's position to Parliament on 24 January.

(iv) Invited the Foreign and Commonwealth Secretary to draft a reply for the Prime Minister to send to President Carter's message of 14 January.[7]

---

[6] The agreed measures, including the suspension of high level and Ministerial contacts, were announced in Parliament by the Lord Privy Seal, Sir Ian Gilmour, on 24 January (see *Parl. Debs., 5th ser., H. of C.*, 24 January 1980, vol. 977, cols. 655-59) and conveyed to Posts in FCO Guidance Telegram No. 11 of 23 January 1980. This stated that 'these measures are designed to demonstrate to the Russians that aggression cannot be committed with impunity. If the Soviet leaders are not shown this in lasting and practical ways, the chances of their intervening elsewhere will remain high. The Russians may have calculated that the reaction to their invasion would be neither serious nor of long duration. We wish to bring home to them that the consequences of their actions and the damage to their interests will be both greater and more sustained than they believed' (FCO 28/4001, EN 021/1).

[7] No. 43.

No. 43

Letter from Mrs Thatcher to President Carter, 26 January 1980
Secret (PREM 19/136)

Dear Mr President,

Thank you for your letter which Warren Christopher handed to me on 14 January.[1] I was very glad to talk to him and Ambassador Brewster about the situation resulting from the Soviet invasion of Afghanistan. They will have reported my views to you. I deliberately delayed this written reply until Peter Carrington had returned from his tour of the area and we had considered the action we ourselves could take. Peter Carrington announced a number of measures in the House of Lords on 24 January, and you will have seen a report of his statement. We are also taking other measures, which I shall describe later in this letter.

You will already know that I fully agree with your analysis. A central principle of great strategic importance is at stake. For many years now, the West has sought to develop a sensible relationship with the Soviet Union which could minimise the risk of war, lower the level of armaments and develop mutually beneficial changes in the field of trade and human contacts. The Russians have chosen to interpret

---

[1] No. 35.

7 December 1979 – 1 December 1981

'détente' much more narrowly, and have continued to pursue a policy of expansion and subversion wherever they felt they could get away with it. They may well have thought that they could nibble away at our interests indefinitely. They need to be reminded in clear terms that this is not so. I therefore welcome and support the various measures that you have taken, including those you announced in your State of the Union message on 23 January.

For our part, Peter Carrington has announced that the British/Soviet Credit Agreement which expires on 16 February will not be renewed. Credit will in future be considered case by case and—assuming that the other Western countries take the same position—will not be provided at rates more favourable than those set by the international consensus. We are ready to study with you and our other partners the tighter application of the COCOM rules for controlling the transfer of sensitive technology to the Soviet Union. The European Community has decided not to export food to the Soviet Union which directly or indirectly would replace supplies denied by the United States. The United Kingdom is also pressing for an end to subsidised butter, meat and sugar sales from the Community's surpluses. We will avoid high level and Ministerial contacts with the Soviet Union for the time being; military exchanges which were under consideration will be cancelled, and certain cultural and other events will be avoided.

I have sent you a copy of the letter I have written to the Chairman of the British Olympics Association.[2] I believe that the move to shift the Olympic Games from Moscow will grow in strength following the arrest of Professor Sakharov.[3]

These are the immediate political and economic measures which we intend to direct at the Soviet Union. We also intend to encourage the non-aligned countries, and particularly the Muslims, to continue their denunciation of the Soviet action and if possible to take measures against the regime in Afghanistan. This will require some delicacy, lest some amongst the non-aligned accuse the West of trying to introduce the cold war into the Third World. We will accelerate negotiations over the sales of British defence equipment to Oman, Saudi Arabia and other States in the Gulf. We shall do what we can in this field for Pakistan, though there are technical difficulties over credit guarantees. We intend to provide friendly States in the Gulf, Pakistan and India with more information about our assessments of Soviet activities and intentions in the area: it was clear from Peter Carrington's trip that many of the Governments there are not well informed. This is an area where you too might wish to act. I should add, however, that Peter Carrington was struck by the deep conviction expressed by the Saudis and others that the whole Western position in the area was undermined by the Arab/Israel conflict and the failure to solve the Palestinian problem.

For our part we shall encourage closer cooperation among the Gulf States, for example, over the security of the Straits of Hormuz. We shall work for an EEC/Gulf dialogue, though here again there are a number of commercial and industrial policy difficulties and it may take the Community some time to work out its position. We shall do what we can to increase Western influence in the Yemen

---

[2] On 22 January the Prime Minister wrote to Sir Denis Follows, Chairman of the British Olympic Association, asking him to approach the IOC urgently to propose that the Summer Games be moved from the Soviet Union. A copy of the letter can be found on the Margaret Thatcher Foundation website: http://www.margaretthatcher.org/.

[3] On 22 January, Dr Andrei Sakharov, nuclear physicist, Nobel Peace Prize winner and leader of the dissident movement was arrested, charged with anti-Soviet activities, and exiled to the closed city of Gorky.

UK-Soviet Relations, 1979-82

Arab Republic, and encourage the Saudis and Omanis to be more active there as well: the threat of Soviet subversion leading to an amalgamation of the two Yemens cannot be ignored, and this would represent a further major gain by the Russians. We are looking at sensible ways of strengthening our links with China, including arms sales, on which our people are having early talks with yours.

We are also looking at a variety of possibilities for covert action.

Peter Carrington was much impressed by the difficulties we face in the Sub-Continent. There is deep distrust between India and Pakistan. Both countries have an obsession, almost indeed a paranoia, about encirclement. I know that the Pakistanis have been talking to you about strengthening the security guarantee you made in 1959. For her part, Mrs Ghandi [*sic*] speaks too readily for the Russians in her public statements. But she cannot relish the prospect of Russian forces on India's borders. She must know that any such development would seriously disturb the Muslim population in India itself. Nevertheless, if we do not handle the Indians carefully, they might slip further towards the Soviet Union. They speak of an axis linking Pakistan, China and the United States, and fear that the super-power confrontation will simply be imported into the Sub-Continent. Nonetheless we must do all we can to strengthen our relationship with the Indians. It was fortunate that Peter Carrington was able to see Mrs Ghandi [*sic*] so soon after her election. President Giscard is in Delhi now. I am glad to know that Clark Clifford will soon be there.

You spoke of the need for Western unity. We recognise that this is a prime condition for bringing effective pressure to bear on the Russians. At the same time our immediate preoccupations do not necessarily coincide. It is understandable, for example, that the Germans should be nervous at the prospect of losing some of the ground which they have made over Berlin and East Germany in the last decade. They have considerable human, political and economic investments there. We are aware not only of the need for unity, but of the importance of the effective American leadership which you are providing. We have already detected an evolution in European attitudes as the full significance of Soviet actions is becoming clearer.

Finally, there is the problem of Iran. I believe the Iranians are coming to see for themselves where the real threat to their interests lie. I very much hope that the discreet exchanges in which you are engaged will be fruitful. And I continue to admire the restraint with which you are handling this difficult and sensitive issue.

Warm personal regards,
Yours sincerely,
MARGARET THATCHER

No. 44

Note by the Planning Staff on Action on Afghanistan, 28 January 1980
Secret (FCO 49/893, RS 021/6)

1. This note suggests possibilities for further action to affect the situation in Afghanistan itself, as opposed to the wider actions which are needed to deal with the Soviet threat to our interests in the region and beyond. There are possibilities for immediate action (the first stage); and longer term action (the second stage).

7 December 1979 – 1 December 1981

First Stage

2. Two ideas have been suggested:

(*a*) Support for the patriots inside Afghanistan itself. This involves the covert supply of arms. The routes presumably lead over the Chinese, Pakistani and perhaps Iranian borders. The suppliers could be the Chinese, Western countries, or Islamic countries. Finance could come amongst others from the Islamic countries. The Western action should be disavowable. But this might not be possible, and in any case the Russians would proclaim it whether they had evidence or not.[1]

(*b*) The 'PLO Solution'. The Afghan patriots should be encouraged to set up an organisation in exile, which could claim representation in Islamic and regional organisations, and perhaps at the United Nations. The initiative for such a body should come from the Afghans themselves, encouraged by the Islamic countries. Further support should come from the Islamic countries. But the idea could perhaps be discreetly suggested by the West.

3. The purpose of these actions would be to keep up military pressure on the Russians inside Afghanistan; demonstrate more widely that the Russians were not having things all their own way on the ground; and maintain an alternative Afghan regime, even if the prospect of achieving it were remote.

Second Stage

4. A Treaty of Neutrality for Afghanistan, guaranteed by the countries of the region including the Soviet Union, Iran, Pakistan, China and India, would be a good outcome of the crisis. At the least, once the proposal for a Treaty entered the public domain it would substantially increase political pressure on the Soviet Union.

5. One model for such a Treaty is the Austrian State Treaty of May 1955, under which the Powers—including the Soviet Union—declared that 'they will respect the independence, and territorial integrity of Austria as established in the present Treaty'. This was matched by a Resolution of the Austrian Parliament which said: 'Austria declares of her own freewill her perpetual neutrality, and is resolved to maintain and defend it with all means at her disposal. Austria, in order to secure these objectives, will join no military alliance and will not permit the establishment of military bases of foreign states on her territory.'

6. It would be better if the proposal for such a Treaty came from an Islamic source: Saudi Arabia, Pakistan, or above all (if conditions permit) Iran would be possible candidates.

7. Any action to contain the Soviet presence in Afghanistan will depend for its effectiveness to a considerable extent on the role of India. The Indians will not be reliable as long as they fear the Chinese (and Pakistan). There is therefore additional reason to seek a real improvement in Indo-Chinese relations. Would this involve agreement on the frontier issues? Could China be persuaded to make some comparatively painless concessions to India, e.g. over Bhutan? Would the Chinese respond to suggestions that such a concession would be justified by the need for a joint struggle against 'hegemony'? Who should put these ideas to the Chinese?

---

[1] Sir Robert Armstrong, the Cabinet Secretary, discussed the question of support for Afghan resistance at a Quadripartite meeting in Paris in mid-January. It was agreed that so long as the Afghans were able to fight and Pakistan was willing to see its territory used as a base for guerrilla operations, it was in Western interests to support the resistance (letter from Sir R. Armstrong to Mr Alexander, 16 January 1980, PREM 19/136).

UK-Soviet Relations, 1979-82

Public Position

8. Our assessment is that it will be a long time before the Russian soldiers leave Afghanistan, if they ever do. But this does not mean that we should not continue to call loudly in public for a Soviet withdrawal. We need to bear this in mind for Ministers' speeches.

No. 45

Sir C. Keeble (Moscow) to Lord Carrington, 30 January 1980, 6.01 a.m.
Tel. No. 94 Immediate, Confidential (FCO 28/4196, ENS 020/1)

Your Telno 57[1]: Zemskov[2]

1. Zemskov evidently saw our lunch on 29 January mainly as an opportunity to sound out British reactions to Soviet policies. He had little to say except to develop without great enthusiasm the standard allegations against the US. The only reference to Anglo-Soviet relations was a sorrowful comment on the temperature—around minus 20 today. I spent most of my time trying to make him realise the depth of the reaction in the West and indeed world wide and arguing that while the world needed détente this was not compatible with Soviet attempts to deploy force.

2. Zemskov claimed that US policy towards the Soviet Union was extremely variable. A militant group of advisers associated with Brzezinski was not [*sic* ?now] in the ascendant. Militaristic American policies dated back a long way and if Afghanistan had not happened some other pretext would have been found to quarrel with the Soviet Union. He could understand US irritation at losing the investment in terms of money and prestige they had made in attempting to over-throw the Afghan revolution. The British government had reacted so forcefully as to suggest, although he was making no such allegation, that they too had made an investment in counter-revolution like the US government. For its part, the Soviet Union remained devoted to détente and was confident of its ultimate triumph. Recent events had clarified which other countries were similarly devoted to relaxation of tension and which took their cue from the United States. The USSR would take such clarification into account in formulating its future policies.

3. I pointed out that it was strange to hear now that Afghanistan had been subject to US interference. When the Americans had raised the matter a few days before the Soviet intervention they had been told that the question of Soviet troops in Afghanistan was purely a bilateral Soviet/Afghan question and as such no business of the United States. I had agreed to have lunch in the hope that we could have a serious talk. The allegations Zemskov had made, including the insinuation against Britain, were not serious, they were propaganda. Zemskov intervened to repeat that he had not meant to imply British involvement in external aggression against Afghanistan. I repeated that these allegations were simply not to be taken seriously. The Afghan affair itself was. I was curious to know what the real reason had been for Soviet actions.

---

[1] Not printed. This telegram stated that a return to normality in British/Soviet relations would depend entirely on Soviet behaviour in Afghanistan and that the main points of Lord Carrington's statement in Parliament (*Parl. Debs., 5th ser., H. of L.,* 24 January 1980, vol. 404, cols. 530-46) should form the basis of discussion.

[2] Soviet Deputy Foreign Minister.

7 December 1979 – 1 December 1981

4. Zemskov said that the Americans claimed Afghanistan was a vital interest for them. It was much more vital for the USSR. Afghanistan was the Soviet underbelly, a question of security. He repeated that the Soviet Union saw no alternative to détente and that the USA too needed peaceful co-existence. The Americans should realise how much they had lost in terms of Soviet public opinion. He said several times that any attempt to negotiate from a position of strength was counterproductive.

5. I told Zemskov that I believed it was at least questionable whether a correct assessment had been made in Moscow of Western reactions to Soviet policies. It was not only a question of Afghanistan but also of earlier problems raised by Soviet military expansion. There was a real concern in the West that the USSR had sought to build up a position of superior strength and to act from that position. Their nuclear missile policy had forced the West to improve its defences in Europe. Now the use of Soviet troops in Afghanistan had produced a profound reaction in the United States, in Europe and world wide. Zemskov had talked about American zig zags. This was not a zig zag. The Soviet Union should understand the extent of the concern it had aroused in the world. Zemskov replied by claiming that the United States had recognised the approximate parity of US/Soviet military strength during Carter's talks with Brezhnev in Vienna last summer. NATO's TNF decision of December had been an attempt to upset this. Afghanistan had been no threat to the United States and the USSR would continue to act to defend the security of its allies and friends.

6. I told Zemskov I thought it important that in times of stress we should be able to talk frankly. The world was too dangerous for the kind of policy the Soviet Union had pursued. Both sides would now have to reconsider what a policy of détente should mean. I drew his attention to the Prime Minister's speech of 28 January[3] (the full text of which I have now sent him) with its emphasis on the need to build a safer world. I added that I had been asked to remind him of what Mr Luce had said to the Soviet Ambassador about Sakharov.[4] This was a further reason for British disquiet about Soviet policies. Zemskov said that if he was to reply officially he would have to say what had already been said to others, including the Italian Ambassador (my telno 79.)[5] He wondered whether we in the West really knew what sort of man Sakharov was. It sometimes happened that a man who had done good things in the past, as Sakharov had done in the field of physics, went astray later in life, for example, through alcohol. In consideration of his past services the Soviet government had treated him with very great humanity. I repeated that their actions had made the worst possible impression in Western Europe.

---

[3] Opening the debate on East/West relations in Parliament, Mrs Thatcher endorsed the stance taken by President Carter and warned Soviet leaders that they would be gravely miscalculating the determination and unity of the Western alliance if they used their new position in Afghanistan as a launching pad for further advances into the oil rich Gulf States (*Parl. Debs., 5th ser., H. of C.*, 28 January 1980, vol. 977, cols. 933-45).

[4] The Soviet Ambassador, Mr Lunkov, was summoned to the FCO on 22 January and informed by Mr Luce that HMG deplored any action taken against Dr Sakharov which contravened the Helsinki Final Act and its provisions for civil and political rights.

[5] Not printed.

UK-Soviet Relations, 1979-82

No. 46

**Minutes by Mr Mallaby, Mr Fergusson and Mr Bullard on dissent in the
Soviet Union, 30 January-5 February 1980**
Confidential (FCO 28/4195, ENS 015/1)

1. I regret that pressure of other events has delayed the submission of Sir C. Keeble's interesting despatch of 4 December 1979.[1] This arrived shortly after Research Department issued their excellent memorandum on 'The Development of Dissent in the USSR',[2] which I also attach, along with the EESD's note on the arrest of Sakharov.[1] I have sent the despatch for printing in the General series and have written to thank the Ambassador.

2. There are two essential features of dissidence in the Soviet Union today. First, it is unlikely to be eradicated as once was possible under Stalin. Second, it poses no foreseeable threat to the regime, although a trickle of individual views, played back to the USSR by foreign broadcasters, might in the long term have some influence on larger numbers of intellectuals. Recent Soviet leaders have recognised the first of these propositions. They have dismissed the dissidents as a tiny minority representing only itself, but have shown acute sensitivity to dissidence, which suggests that they do fear it in the longer term. One reason for the fear is that the Bolshevik revolution had some of its origins in successful dissidence. Another is that totalitarian regimes aspire to total power and feel any exceptions as a loss of face.

3. The reason why dissidence succeeded under the Tsars, whereas under communism it has not, is essentially in the numbers and ruthlessness of the internal security forces. The OKHRANA[3] was not a patch on the KGB. But, given the reluctance of recent Soviet leaders to unleash the full repressive force of the internal security apparatus—reluctance caused by world opinion and possible internal public opinion—there is no reason why dissent should not continue to exist, fitfully and disjointedly. The deportation of Sakharov will greatly weaken the dissenters. No one of equal stature is likely to emerge soon. At lower levels, however, new recruits will probably continue to replace those who are arrested and expelled. The aim of the authorities nowadays is to contain dissent, to fragment it, to subject it to harassment and uncertainty and, above all, to isolate it from the mass of the population. In this, as the Ambassador points out, the regime has been successful. It has been helped by the attitude of the mass of the population. The average Soviet citizen has little sympathy for political and intellectual dissent. He is interested in his standard of living, regards the activities of dissidents, whether intellectuals or workers, as having little bearing on his own life style and is more inclined to regard them as parasites on society.

4. As to numbers of dissidents, according to Peter Reddaway of [the] LSE, a leading Western expert, there are a few hundred human rights activists and perhaps a couple of thousand who occasionally co-operate with them. Some hundreds of thousands of Jews and Germans may wish to emigrate. The nationalists are the most numerous, especially in Lithuania, where Mr Reddaway estimates from dissident writings that a majority of the population of 3 million may be politically

---
[1] Not printed.
[2] This memorandum, dated 24 October 1979, can be found in FCO 28/3848, ENS 015/1.
[3] The pre-revolutionary Russian secret-police organisation.

disaffected. But the KGB is helped to keep on the lid because of the fragmented nature of dissent.

5. The Soviet leadership is concerned about the effects of dissent, in all its forms, on the Soviet image abroad and on the achievement of foreign policy objectives. Soviet dissidents will continue to appeal to world opinion for support. Western governments must react, for public opinion will expect them to support the real achievement of freedom of thought, expression, belief and movement in the Soviet Union. Most Soviet dissidents maintain that active Western support for their cause has been instrumental in achieving the minor advances of the past 15 years. There is no reason to dispute this. At the same time excessive public intervention by Western Governments on behalf of individual Soviet dissidents could be counter-productive: we should beware of engaging Soviet 'machismo'.

C. L. G. MALLABY

1. I was much struck, at the Eastern European Heads of Mission Conference, by the distinction—now brought out very clearly by Sir C. Keeble's despatch—between the Russian response to dissidence and that in the other Eastern European countries. In the latter, the dissatisfactions with the Communist regimes are fed not only by the inheritance of many centuries of Western liberalism, the concept of individual liberty and of private rights against the State, but also by historical fears about and antagonisms against Russia. It is possible in Hungary or Poland (and in Lithuanian Russia) to be, in the eyes of one's peers, both a dissident and a patriot. But the central Russian tradition was profoundly alien: 'a social system which allowed no-one to dispose of his time or his belongings . . . serfdom was only the most widespread and most visible form of bondage which pervaded every layer of Muscovite society creating an interlocking system without room for personal freedom' (R. Pipes): and, as a sixteenth century traveller said 'All the people consider themselves to be Kholops, that is slaves of their Prince'.

2. Dissidence in the form of human rights activism is an alien flower. And yet it is not surprising in so large and diverse a country that some draw on Western traditions to challenge the regime on human rights grounds, even if their protest is on a relatively small scale. And (as Ginsberg[4] told Mr Blaker three weeks ago) Soviet repression does not seem to cause the spring to dry up. Nevertheless, in Russia as a whole human rights activism is a peripheral phenomenon and our own response must not exaggerate their possible impact. A new situation would arise if other forms of dissent mentioned by Sir C. Keeble, especially of regional nationalism, were to become more significant—especially if, however implausible it may now seem, they were to start to call in question the integrity of the Soviet State (in the longer term one cannot exclude the fashionable topic of Islamic revival). This, however, would raise much larger issues—whether our own self-interest lies in the internal stability of Russia or in working to upset it. I raise the point only to suggest that forces of this kind are potentially far more disruptive to Russia than any likely manifestation of Western style individualism. We protest about human rights violations not because we think that we can bring about significant change, but because a combination of individual conscience and collective public opinion requires that we do, and because pointing to the evils of

---

[4] Alexander Ginsberg; Russian journalist, poet, human rights activist and dissident. He was expelled from the Soviet Union in 1979.

UK-Soviet Relations, 1979-82

Soviet society is one of our most potent weapons in the struggle for the Third World.

3. Finally, I note the paradox mentioned by Sir C. Keeble—that outside encouragement of dissent may impair the opportunities for internal change to develop, and yet his recommendation that we should maximise the opportunities for the individual Russian 'to be exposed to Western ideas through . . . direct personal contact'. This is a factor to take into account in judging our own responses to 'Afghanistan'.

E. A. J. FERGUSSON

1. I concur in the general belief that dissidence is a largely superficial phenomenon in the USSR, neither shaking the regime nor touching the majority of the people. Its influence has been mainly on the way dissidents themselves are treated by the authorities. Foreign radio stations, foreign correspondents in Moscow and dissidents interact a good deal upon each other. But the phenomenon of dissidence, now as in the 19th Century, is part of the (slow) evolution of Russian society and political structure. And now as then one admires the individuals concerned and the nation that produces them.

2. Mr Peter Reddaway has a rival view, namely that political, economic, social and regional strains will sooner or later produce a Revolution. I am doubtful about that.

J. B. BULLARD

No. 47

Memorandum by East European and Soviet Department on Soviet Foreign Policy after Afghanistan, 31 January 1980[1]
Confidential (FCO 28/3987, EN 020/7)

1. The main aim of Soviet foreign policy is to accumulate power and influence in the world while also preserving the security of the Soviet State. The Soviet Union recognises that this will lead to its being engaged in continuing competition with the US, and to a lesser extent with China whose emergence as a world power the Soviet Union wishes to slow down. One of the Soviet purposes in seeking

---

[1] The paper incorporated suggestions by HM Ambassador in Moscow and other FCO Departments, as well as the Assessments Staff in the Cabinet Office. It was sent to No. 10 on 1 February along with a letter from Mr Walden to Mr Alexander stating that Lord Carrington suggested that 'the Prime Minister might wish, following the Soviet invasion of Afghanistan, to meet a small number of FCO officials who deal with Soviet affairs and who have worked in the Embassy in Moscow'. A meeting was subsequently arranged and attended by the Prime Minister, Lord Carrington, Mr Braithwaite and Mr Mallaby. For an account of the meeting see Rodric Braithwaite, *Across the Moscow River* (London: Yale University Press, 2002), pp. 51-52.

This paper was the first to be circulated under 'Operation Common Sense', a scheme whereby assessments of Soviet policy were sent to heads of government and people of similar standing in Middle East and Asian countries, as personal messages from the Secretary of State. The system was initiated by Lord Carrington who was struck, during his tour of the Gulf and the sub-continent, 'by the naivety and ignorance about Soviet aims and intentions exhibited by many of the leaders' (FCO 28/4030, EN 021/24).

7 December 1979 – 1 December 1981

influence in developing countries is to win ground in this competition. But the need to preserve Soviet security means that the USSR must avoid actions which might provoke an uncontrollable process leading to nuclear confrontation with the US. The USSR under Brezhnev has sought reasonable relations with the US and Western Europe, partly to reduce the risk that the East-West contest would produce such crises. The Soviet leaders also have an interest in obtaining Western technology to help modernise the sluggish and inefficient Soviet economy, and grain to compensate for the great failures of Soviet agriculture.

2. To reconcile their security needs, and their wish to have reasonable relations with the West, with their aim of increasing their power and influence in the developing world, the Soviet leaders propounded their own version of 'détente'. Their idea was that East-West relations could be improved in certain fields, so that they would get the things they wanted and also would secure, in negotiations with the US, the recognition which they coveted that they were now one of two super-powers. But the Russians never thought of détente as being comprehensive. They excluded from it their freedom to maintain dominance in Eastern Europe and dictatorship at home, to wage a struggle of ideas against the West and to acquire power bases in the Third World.

3. After the Vietnam war the US was far less willing to resist actively Soviet encroachment in the developing world. The Russians exploited what seemed to them weakness by proxy interventions in Angola and Ethiopia. Vietnam took over Cambodia. Although there were strong local reasons for the Russian move over Afghanistan, the Russians will have added to them the potential strategic gains from a decisive move on their part. The Western failure to react on earlier occasions, except by words, probably encouraged the Russians, after years of steadily building up their influence in Afghanistan, to believe that the West would not be unduly disturbed by Soviet military intervention there, even though it would be the first use of Soviet combat forces in the developing world. The Soviet leaders probably also calculated that there would be few dividends in 1980 from their relationship with the West, so that the cost in that regard should not be great. The invasion was thus an extrapolation of existing Soviet foreign policy. The West's failure was to realize in advance how selective was the Soviet concept of détente and that the Russians would exploit to the maximum whatever latitude for aggression in the Third World Western behaviour and local circumstances seemed to allow.

4. The Russians will persist in their drive for influence whenever possible. There will be further occasions when they will consider the use of force. They will assess carefully what latitude exists for this in the light *inter alia* of Western and world reactions to Afghanistan. At the same time, they will have reasons for wishing in due course to return to reasonable East-West relations, notably their desire to avoid hostilities with the US coupled with their need for Western technology. Since they cannot readily find substitutes for this, their need will persist whether or not the flow of technology from the West is seriously interrupted as a result of Afghanistan. The Russians will probably also want arms control negotiations to get going again (although not in earnest until after the US elections), since they fear that the US, with its greater economic and scientific resources, would suffer less from an all-out arms race; they will also want to avoid the greater international instability which an all-out arms race might create. The question is whether they can be convinced that détente, if the West is to play ball, must be reciprocal and global, and that the aggressive pursuit of Soviet aims in the

UK-Soviet Relations, 1979-82

developing countries will put an end to it.

5. While a firm and lasting Western response to Afghanistan would have a fair chance of causing the Russians to be more cautious, the short term Soviet reactions will be truculent. The Soviet leaders are intensely sensitive to the risk of appearing to give way under pressure. They are therefore likely to take some steps designed to show that they are not taking punishment lying down. There is still no question of a sudden Soviet attack on the West, and armed intervention in another developing country is unlikely, at least in the short term, for the Russians will be wary while the non-aligned and the West remain vigilant and critical after Afghanistan. The most likely Soviet steps are ones which the Russians want to take anyway and the cost of which is reduced because East-West relations are at present bad. The deportation of Sakharov from Moscow can be seen in this light. A reduction in the recent record flow of Jewish emigration, a resumption of full-scale jamming of Western broadcasts or cancellation of some cultural events like book exhibitions in the USSR are possible. So is an attempt to reduce the freedom of manoeuvre of some of the East European countries. They may well increase the pressure in sensitive and vulnerable areas; e.g. in Berlin, by restricting the return of ethnic Germans, in the Northern Seas, and on the Bulgarian/Macedonian question. Though the Helsinki Final Act is still regarded as a major achievement of the Brezhnev era, and the Soviet Union will want the Madrid Review meeting to be held next winter as planned, the value to them of Madrid is not such as significantly to inhibit such actions if they are thought desirable on other grounds.

6. The Soviet leaders will also wish to exploit differences among Western countries about how to react to Afghanistan. Brezhnev in a *Pravda* interview has sought to do so. But Soviet actions have not been well calculated for this purpose. Sakharov was arrested when the President of the French Assembly was in Moscow. Although West Germany's special interests have made it hesitant about following the US and UK in reacting to the invasion of Afghanistan, high level meetings planned by the Federal Republic with Hungary, Czechoslovakia and East Germany have been postponed, no doubt at Soviet instigation. The reason is probably that Moscow anticipates that the West will try to develop its relations with Eastern Europe while freezing those with the USSR. Soviet wedge-driving tactics could involve a move towards the French on their proposal for a European Disarmament Conference (however unattractive to them it may be in its present form) or the dangling of major export contracts in front of French or West German firms.

7. Soviet relations with China were already bad before Afghanistan. These factors will intensify Soviet fears that any crisis with the West or with China could become a crisis with both. This arouses long-standing fears of encirclement. The Russians are likely in the long run to seek a stable and controlled relationship with China as well as with the West. But for at least some years to come the balance of advantage for the Soviet Union will lie in developing its relationship with the West rather than with China.

8. In pursuing their drive for influence in the developing world, the Soviet leaders will seek, subject to the need to avoid East-West confrontation, to make new gains whenever opportunities arise. When they consider this necessary and the risk acceptable they will continue to be prepared to use force. Opportunities for new influence may grow if the Arab-Israel dispute continues, particularly since, despite the inherent antagonism between Islam and Communism, the Russians may see their best opportunities, after the furore over Afghanistan subsides, in the

7 December 1979 – 1 December 1981

unstable Islamic countries of the Middle East and South West Asia. From their established base in South Yemen they already are making efforts in the Yemen Arab Republic. They have strong motives for seeking influence in Iran, because of its oil and strategic location, but will also be conscious that the Western reactions would be far greater than over Soviet intervention in Afghanistan. Border troubles between Afghanistan and Pakistan, which they may not instigate but which are likely to drag them in, will offer opportunities to intimidate and infiltrate the latter. There will be a major effort to consolidate Soviet influence on India under Mrs Gandhi. The Russians will also hope for further opportunities in Southern Africa. They will support Cuba in its efforts to gain strong influence in other Caribbean and Central American countries.

9. The Soviet leaders are not likely to invade Yugoslavia when Tito goes. They will seek to play on economic problems and the differences between the nationalities, in the hope of creating opportunities for reintegrating Yugoslavia into their sphere of influence, even in time by invasion, although the Russians will be watching carefully for a military response by the West.

Conclusion

10. Before Khrushchev became top dog, he seemed as colourless as Stalin's other henchmen. In a totalitarian oligarchy, change can be arbitrary. It is possible that Brezhnev's successors will adopt a different foreign policy. It is possible for instance that they will reckon that détente has not produced enough results for the USSR and that, with the West and China coming closer together and the West taking more trouble about its defences, a Soviet policy of assertiveness in the developing world and no détente should be tried. But the leaders would fear that such a policy could increase the risk of East-West escalation, and might think that the absence of détente would not enable them to gain ground faster in the developing world. So the likelihood remains that the next leadership will be influenced by the same factors as the present one and that foreign policy will not radically change course. We are in for a difficult period in East-West relations. Western firmness will be indispensable. Provided that the Soviet Union faces consistent and determined opposition to its aims, its own self-interest may lead it to be less assertive in pursuing them, and more anxious to look for agreement in areas of mutual interest. In this way, it could be brought in time to accept a more balanced view of détente.

No. 48

Minute from Mr Mallaby to Mr Fergusson, 1 February 1980
Secret (FCO 49/894, RS 021/7)

Soviet Activity in the Third World Post-Afghanistan

1. This is a note of key points made at your meeting on 30 January.[1]

2. We should not attempt to punish the African countries which are close to the Soviet Union; rather we should seek to build on their need for links with the West in the hope of weaning them away from the Russians.

3. There was no mileage in helping the insurgents in Ethiopia or Angola. Rather

---

[1] The meeting was attended by Mr Fergusson, Mr Mallaby and the Heads of the Central African, East African, Middle East, Mexico and Caribbean and South Asian Departments and Planning Staff.

UK-Soviet Relations, 1979-82

our interest was in stability which might remove the regimes' need for the Cuban presence.

4. There was little use in backing insurgency in the PDRY. This was a country of venal, untrustworthy intriguers and attempting to influence them was a lottery. The Russians might find this too. We had been quite successful in helping Oman to quell the Dhofar rebellion.[2]

5. The Russians were unlikely to leave Afghanistan. If they had any sense, they would stick to towns and roads and to containing insurgency at manageable levels but would not try to eliminate the insurgents in the mountains. They would look for opportunities in Baluchistan and Pushtoonistan; the West had little choice but to back Zia.

6. The Afghanistan operation had cost the Cubans dear in the UN and NAM. There was unlikely to be scope for wooing the Cubans away from the Russians while they remained dependent on the $6 million per day Soviet subsidy.

7. Further Cuban military intervention in Africa was unlikely in the near future but there were good opportunities for the Cubans in the Caribbean and in Central America. Economic assistance from the West was not enough and we were putting together a package of assistance to local security forces with the US and Canada.

8. While the Soviet policy of seeking influence in the developing world would not change because of Afghanistan the non-aligned had been alerted as well as the West, and our chances of taking measures to deter further Soviet interventions had improved.

9. We needed to press ahead with work to identify possible future targets for Soviet opportunism in the Third World and to define the degree of Western interest in these countries with a view to working to prevent further Afghanistans.

10. I suggest that the Planning Staff should now do a first draft of the proposed paper on preventing Afghanistans[3]. The substantive need for such a paper needs no restating. The tactical moment for launching the exercise with a few of our allies, following Mr Hurd's statement to the Six Power (Christopher) meeting in London on 31 December,[4] should be favourable. While I understand the need to consider overall policy towards the Third World, I believe the paper can be written without a long introductory exercise on the wider subject. I should be glad to attend a meeting to discuss the contents of the paper.

C. L. G. MALLABY

[2] Originally a separatist movement directed against the conservative rule of Sultan bin Taimur, the Dhofar Rebellion (1962-75) soon attracted support from both China and the Soviet Union.

[3] A paper entitled, 'The Prevention of Soviet Expansion in the Developing World', was subsequently prepared by the Planning Staff, with contributions from across the FCO, and sent to the Prime Minister on 1 April. It was intended as a basis for discussion and attempted a broad survey of Soviet activities throughout the Third World and possible measures for countering them. The paper, with annexes, was eighty-eight pages long. It was refined under a new title, 'The Management of East-West Relations,' and sent to the Prime Minister on 2 May ahead of a meeting with FCO officials on 20 May (see No. 64).

[4] No. 11.

7 December 1979 – 1 December 1981

No. 49

Minute from Lord Carrington to Mrs Thatcher, 1 February 1980
PM/80/8 Secret (PREM 19/136)

Prime Minister,

Afghanistan: The Next Steps

1. In our discussion at OD on 22 January[1] we agreed on a number of measures proposed in my minute PM/80/5 of the previous day.[2] Action to put these into effect is now in hand, in concert with our European partners and the Americans where appropriate. We should now look at the next stage and consider what further action we need to set in train.

2. The decisions we have already taken were intended to promote two major objectives:

(*a*) to secure widespread condemnation of the Soviet invasion of Afghanistan, and to impose certain penalties on the Soviet Union;

(*b*) to find ways of supporting the countries of South West Asia and the Middle East against further Soviet attempts to secure advantage by subversion, if not by force. I shall shortly be circulating an analysis of the situation in the countries under threat.

3. These two objectives remain valid and need to be sustained. I am looking into a second series of actions which might be taken when NATO stocktaking is complete and when we have been able to judge the effect on the Soviets of the West's initial response.

4. Our ultimate aim should be to create a situation in which the Soviet Union concludes that it has nothing to gain[3] from further adventures. This must be part of the process of putting the East/West relationship on to a more stable basis, free of the illusions which characterised the 1970s.

5. Within this framework, there are a number of other objectives which we should pursue. All contribute to our ultimate aim; some would be of value in themselves. I have the following in mind:

Afghanistan

6. First, the future of Afghanistan itself. Two ideas are already being pursued. The first is support for patriots inside Afghanistan through the covert supply of arms and training, amongst other things. French officials favour this; the Chinese are also interested; and the US are already active in this respect. Moslem money is already flowing, and may be sufficient. There is a risk that the Russians would see this as a pretext for raiding over the Afghan frontier. The Pakistanis are understandably nervous.

7. Secondly, the various Afghan patriotic organisations announced a few days ago that they were setting up a joint organisation. They have asked for representation in the Islamic Conference. This may be a sign that the Afghans are trying to overcome their chronic disunity. This new body may not survive. But in so far as we can see, we should encourage the Islamic countries to support a united 'Afghan Liberation Organisation'.

8. The purpose of these actions is to maintain military pressure on the Russians inside Afghanistan; to demonstrate more widely that the Russians are not having

[1] No. 42.
[2] No. 41, dated 19 January.
[3] In a marginal comment, Mrs Thatcher replaced the words 'nothing to gain' with 'much to lose'.

111

UK-Soviet Relations, 1979-82

things all their own way there; and to maintain an alternative Afghan regime. The prospect of an early Russian departure is, of course, remote. But both for our immediate purpose and with a view to the longer term we should, at least in our public statements, continue to demand this, and encourage others to do the same.

9. The demand for Soviet withdrawal would be more plausible if a positive solution to the Afghan problem could be proposed. One possibility would be a Treaty of Neutrality for Afghanistan, guaranteed by the countries of the region, including the Soviet Union, Iran, Pakistan, China and India. At the least, once such a proposal entered the public domain, it would substantially increase political pressure on the Russians. There is a model to hand in the Austrian State Treaty of 1955, which the Russians signed amongst others. The idea might best be promoted by the Islamic countries, or by one of the countries of the region. I have set studies in train.[4]

Sino-Indian Relations

10. The effectiveness of action to contain the Soviet presence in Afghanistan will depend to a considerable extent on India, and on the extent to which India continues to rely on the Soviet Union for diplomatic and military support. This in turn will be affected by the state of Sino-Indian relations. The Indians will not be reliable, nor detach themselves from the Russians, as long as they fear the Chinese. Both the Chinese and the Indians have an interest in a gradual process of rapprochement. But mutual suspicions remain; each regards the other as its natural enemy and rival for influence in the area; and the recent Soviet actions will polarise them still further, particularly over their differing attitudes towards Pakistan. I have asked my officials to consider what we can do to encourage both sides to look at each other more objectively. But we have to accept that the Chinese will not be ready to offer the Indians much, until they see from evidence that they are distancing themselves from the Soviet Union; and whatever the Chinese offer, the Indians will in practice continue to cleave to the Soviet Union.

Western Unity

11. Finally, the present crisis has demonstrated yet again how difficult it is for the Europeans to unite effectively with the United States and even among themselves. Despite our basic community of interest, our perceptions and our short-term needs inevitably differ. The secret four power talks between British, French, German and American officials in London last week showed that it was not too difficult to reach agreement on the analysis.[5] But the particular interests of the French and Germans lead them to differing conclusions about policy. We need consciously to exploit the present crisis in East/West relations to strengthen unity amongst the European countries rather than the reverse. President Carter has suggested a new *ad hoc* body; and the Italians have pressed that they should be included. I am not sure that a proliferation of groups will help much. But none of

[4] Mr Alexander thought the idea of a Treaty of Neutrality for Afghanistan was an interesting one but in the margin Mrs Thatcher commented: 'It would be *useless*'.

[5] A Quadripartite meeting of Political Directors took place on 24/25 January and discussed allied action in Afghanistan and Iran. Mr Bullard, the British representative, noted: 'There was wide agreement on the analysis and on the need for allied unity; and a rueful acceptance that unity could not be absolute, and that effective action will cost money.' The meeting was also notable for a French and German 'frontal attack on the American decision over the Olympic Games' as it was believed that such action 'would cause the Russian people to rally behind their government, and that if the Americans were not widely followed the outcome would be an evident defeat for the West'. Mr Bullard also floated the idea 'that Madrid should be scrapped now that the Soviet Union had violated all ten of the Helsinki principles: it got no support' (FCO 37/2248, FSA 020/1).

7 December 1979 – 1 December 1981

the present bodies include the Japanese, apart from the Economic Summit, whose purpose is different. There may be room for something which would include them. My officials are studying this matter.

12. When the studies which I have commissioned on these and other related issues are complete, I shall make more detailed proposals for further action by ourselves. These seem bound to cost money, but pending further discussion with our Allies it will be possible only to give very rough figures.[6]

13. I am sending copies of this minute to other member[s] of OD, the Secretary of State for Energy and to Sir Robert Armstrong.

CARRINGTON

[6] The Chancellor of the Exchequer wrote to the Prime Minister on 6 February to express concern about the potential costs of any such action: 'I take it that no new proposals for action by ourselves in the Afghanistan context will be advanced in discussion with our allies before we have decided whether, and how, such costs could be met'. The Prime Minister's marginal comment read: 'Poppycock!'

No. 50

Sir C. Keeble (Moscow) to Lord Carrington, 8 February 1980
Confidential (FCO 28/3987, EN 020/7)

Summary . . . [1]

My Lord,
The Relationship between the Soviet Union and the United States

1. One effect of the Soviet move into Afghanistan has been a sharp deterioration in relations between the Soviet Union and the United States. In this despatch I consider the essential features of that relationship and the prospects for its development as seen from Moscow.

2. It is not easy to consider the bilateral relationship without dealing with Soviet foreign policy as a whole. For the purpose of this despatch however it must suffice to identify at the outset the two main bases on which that policy rests. Its ideological base is the global struggle between socialism and imperialism, a struggle in which the Soviet Union sees the United States as its principal adversary. In that struggle there may be tactical pauses, but the essential relationship is one of confrontation and there can be no true cooperation. The other base of policy is the practical interest of the Soviet state. This the Soviet Union can best pursue by a mixture of competition and cooperation with other countries, among which the United States by its size and the range of its interests must be prominent. It will rarely happen that on any substantial issue the two elements of policy, ideology and interest, can be separately identified. What matters is that the analysis of Soviet-American relations must take account of both.

3. The present state of relations can perhaps best be judged by reference to the Brezhnev/Nixon Agreement of May 1972 on the Basic Principles of Relations.[2] This spoke of 'a common determination that in the nuclear age there is no alternative to conducting mutual relations on the basis of peaceful co-existence'. It

[1] Not printed.
[2] See No. 8, note 4.

committed the parties always to 'exercise restraint in their mutual relations' and to 'negotiate and settle differences by peaceful means'. It further recognised 'that efforts to obtain unilateral advantage directly or indirectly are inconsistent with these objectives'.

4. The latter condition was of such imprecision that it could scarcely be expected to have a practical effect. In real terms, the extent to which the Soviet Union will go in pursuing policies hostile to the interests of the United States and the West as a whole is governed by its perception of what its opponents are prepared to tolerate. That perception is frequently faulty. There is a whole institute studying the United States, but although the specialists know every byway of the American political scene I wonder how well they understand it. They examine it from afar, rather like a satellite photograph. They can see what is there, but they do not know why it is there. Policy is decided at a higher level by a group of men conditioned by an ideological conspiratorial tradition, lacking any sense of how a democratic government works and largely isolated from contact with the West. It is not surprising that the Soviet leadership should still seem curiously blind, not to say complacent, about the effects of its policies on others.

5. The history of the 1970s illustrated the point. Seen from Moscow, it must have looked like a decade in which American power was gradually being tamed. The Politburo may well have seen the American defeat in Vietnam as a turning point in American willingness to deploy military force to resist communist expansion and the Soviet Union's own growing nuclear and conventional capabilities as providing a more secure strategic background for further pressure on the West. The fall of President Nixon may have seemed to them to demonstrate a weakness at the core of the American system. After the Cuban missile crisis, Kuznetsov, then a Soviet Deputy Foreign Minister, said 'You Americans will never be able to do this to us again'. By 1976, as Brezhnev put it at the 25th Party Congress, there had been 'a change in the correlation of world forces'. Complacent in his views of the relative weakness of the West, he presented the prospects for Soviet-American relations in constructive terms, claiming that very great attention had been devoted to their improvement and that the document on Basic Principles, together with the other agreements with the United States, laid 'a solid political and legal foundation for greater mutual beneficial cooperation'.[3] There were of course 'influential forces' in the United States struggling against this process, but the Soviet Union was firmly determined to seek further improvement. At the same time however it would support 'the struggle of other peoples for freedom and progress'. To the Soviet mind there is no obvious contradiction between a policy of cooperation with the United States at one level and Soviet backing for 'liberation struggles' at another.

6. The Russians did not know quite what to make of President Carter when he came to office. Brezhnev told Vance in Moscow in March 1977 that he was puzzled by the new Administration. He talked sharply about the President's concern for human rights and warned that the Russians would accept nothing under duress. The first American proposals on SALT were brusquely rejected. Nevertheless during the first three years of the Carter Administration it was the SALT negotiations which dominated the relationship with the Soviet Union, as indeed they had done for many years beforehand. Control of strategic armaments by bilateral agreement is a policy objective for the Soviet Union as for the West. It

---

[3] For details see *DBPO*, Series III, Vol. II.

7 December 1979 – 1 December 1981

is therefore an area in which Soviet-American understanding is inherently possible, albeit with a restricted objective. In the SALT II negotiations, both sides had to make concessions for the sake of agreement and in one respect the Russians probably took a gamble. They failed at the outset to secure acceptance of the concept that a weapon was strategic if it could strike the territory of one party, regardless of its location, and acquiesced in the exclusion of the American forward based systems from the main Agreement. Once the Treaty was signed, it became clear that the Protocol would not automatically be extended by the United States beyond 1981, that the Senate opposed extension, and that ground launched cruise missiles were likely to be deployed as early as 1983. At this point, it probably began to seem to the Soviet leadership that the gamble had failed and that a deal which might have stabilised for them a uniquely favourable situation of long-range equality and medium-range superiority would not work out as well as they had hoped. They affected to believe that the United States was taking advantage of its position in Europe to move the strategic balance against them. In fact they had bid too high and gone down. But their failure rankled and will constitute a significant factor in Soviet-American relations for some time yet.

7. In other respects there was little of substance. The lack of any mutual dependence other than in the field of strategic arms is one of the dominant factors in the Soviet-American relationship. Although the various bilateral activities, stemming from the Kissinger days, continued to provide an appearance of business, they had little relevance to the essential interests of the two parties. The initial Soviet puzzlement about the Carter administration turned increasingly to sourness. The one international area in which there seemed momentarily to be the possibility of cooperation was the Middle East, but the 1977 Agreement led nowhere.[4] Given the essential conflict of interest it probably could lead nowhere, but the existence of the Agreement no doubt increased the bitterness and sense of exclusion with which the Soviet Union still regards Camp David. At the same time the developing American relationship with China constituted a potentially serious change in the balance of forces. Unaware of, or impervious to, the reaction building up in the West the Soviet Union for its part continued to strengthen its conventional forces, proceeded with the production and deployment of the SS-20 and, convinced that the United States was in no mood to oppose it, pursued the extension of its power in the Third World. The episode of the Soviet troops in Cuba in the autumn of last year must have helped to confirm the Soviet leadership in the view that in Carter they were dealing with a rash but weak man who might commit himself quickly to a course of action which he would lack the strength to implement. For this in the Soviet book there is a simple answer. Hold firm and wait for the other man to back away.

8. The CSCE process provided another point of friction. The Russians regarded Helsinki primarily as setting the seal on their sphere of influence in Europe and in second place as a base for its further extension by 'military détente', or in other words a reduction of the American commitment to European security. The American emphasis on human rights and Basket III no doubt seemed a logical part of the bargain in Washington: for Moscow it was subversion, with the President's expression of support for Sakharov as a major symbol.

9. Soviet policy throughout these three years was not incompatible with the

---

[4] In October 1977, Cyrus Vance and Andrei Gromyko attempted to reconvene the Geneva Conference to negotiate a comprehensive Middle East peace but the Israeli government turned down the proposal.

UK-Soviet Relations, 1979-82

rules of détente as Moscow saw them. The SALT process was necessary in order to ensure Soviet security. The other arms control negotiations might serve the same purpose. Trade, scientific and technological exchanges could be useful. But the Soviet leadership was consistently frank in declaring that détente could not alter or abolish the laws of class struggle and that there was no question of 'freezing the status quo'. This, in Soviet terminology, meant that the Soviet Union regarded itself as free to promote the spread of Soviet-aligned socialist states whenever the circumstances seemed appropriate.

10. It was against this background that the Soviet Union took the decision to employ its own military forces in Afghanistan, seeing this as a necessary move to secure a newly-consecrated Socialist state on its own borders which was threatened with disintegration. It had already noted American acquiescence in the use of Cuban forces in Ethiopia and Angola. In the case of Afghanistan the geography made the use of Soviet troops appropriate. Concerned though the leadership was about developments at the strategic level, there may have seemed little to lose. There was no risk of a military clash with the Americans and the political reaction would no doubt prove ephemeral. The Russians, in other words, failed to realise that the American mood was changing, that the imbalance inherent in the Soviet concept of détente would at some point become unsustainable and that the occupation of Afghanistan might be seen as a direct challenge.

11. The American reaction is, I believe, still being assessed here. Soviet analysts rationalise it by looking back to Brezhnev's warning of 1976 about the 'influential forces' in the United States opposed to a relaxation of tension and by constructing a scenario in which these forces, inspired by the military-industrial complex and the doctrines of Brzezinski, have gradually gained the upper hand, their first decisive victory coming at the NATO meeting in May 1978 and Carter's final identification with them being signalled by the suspension of the SALT ratification process. The Politburo themselves may indeed see things this way. I doubt whether even now they assess the change in the American approach to relations with the Soviet Union as being of a fundamental or indeed wholly surprising character. For them the essential quality of the relationship has always been and still is determined by the struggle between the two systems. The American response to Afghanistan they see as the kind of over-reaction to be expected from time to time from an adversary who is unsure of himself. I suspect that they in turn are unsure of the potential of American power. They know that the Soviet Union has attained strategic parity, they see the economic troubles of the West and the dependence of the United States on Middle East oil, but still they are uneasy. As with the episode of the brigade in Cuba, they will probably hold firm over Afghanistan, calculating that Western fears of nuclear confrontation and the disintegrating tendencies of Western politics will in time combine to weaken the opposition to the further pursuit of Soviet interests. They will strenuously avoid any appearance of succumbing to Western pressure. Nevertheless, for the moment, President Carter's State of the Union message[5] has I think brought back a degree of caution which otherwise they might have lost.

---

[5] In this message delivered to Congress on 23 January, President Carter declared that any attempt by an outside force to gain control of the Gulf region would be regarded as an assault on the vital interests of the United States and would be repelled by the use of any means necessary including military force. See *Public Papers: Carter (1980-81)*, Book I, pp. 194-200. The speech was condemned in a *Pravda* editorial on 29 January which accused President Carter of fanning up a 'hysterical militaristic campaign' against the Soviet Union.

7 December 1979 – 1 December 1981

12. How then will the Soviet Union expect the relationship to develop? In the short term they will await the outcome of the Presidential election and meanwhile will busy themselves with political manoeuvres to discredit the present administration and frustrate its policies. The bilateral American measures, notably the ban on grain exports, will cause short term difficulty, but they will hope partly to circumvent them and in time to see them removed. To an Olympic boycott by the United States, even if not widely supported, they will have no effective answer, but their resentment will be deep and the Politburo will do its best to mobilise jingoistic support. The increase in American military expenditure will be met by renewed calls for détente, intensive attempts to disrupt relations between the United States and her allies, a tightening of discipline within the bloc and leaks about the likelihood of an increased Soviet and Warsaw Pact defence effort. In relation to the developing countries, propaganda will be concentrated on the military aspects of the American response, in the hope of awakening a reaction which might offset the damaging effect of Soviet intervention in Afghanistan and prevent the development of a common resistance to further expansion. I do not think the Gulf area is a short-term objective and in the longer term the Soviet hope will be that political developments will make the American guarantees irrelevant. Meanwhile nothing will be allowed to interfere with the consolidation of the Soviet grip on Afghanistan.

13. In the longer term, Soviet objectives will not change. The next President, whether Carter or a successor, will be dealt with according to the perception which the Soviet leadership form of his own strength of purpose and his ability to command the support of his own country and its allies. That perception will be formed on the basis of his response to a mixture of threats about the consequences of 'warmongering' and blandishments about the prospects for détente. Behind it all, the paramount concern of the Soviet leadership will continue to be the preservation of Soviet security. This will continue to require a safe and controlled relationship with the United States, a relationship in which the central item of bilateral business will once again be the control of strategic arms, first in terms of revival of SALT II and then in terms of a Soviet effort to repair the breach represented by the forward based medium-range American systems. At the same time, as well as the other aspects of arms control and non-proliferation, the Soviet Union will pursue the security concept of surrounding its own territory with a belt of subservient or at least compliant states, the gaps in which are at present Turkey and Iran. Expansion elsewhere will have a lower priority, but only if the Soviet Union is convinced that expansion is not compatible with security will it leave expansion for tomorrow. These are not policies on which there can be any expectation of genuine cooperation between the Soviet Union and the United States. If, however, as Sir N. Henderson has indicated in his telegram number 443,[6] there is now a new realism in American policy, and if this is quietly and firmly maintained and supported by the West as a whole, it is the more likely to be matched by a realistic acceptance by the Soviet Union of the limits to further expansion. The confrontation will be more controlled, limited and safer.[7]

[6] Not printed.

[7] In a minute of 18 March, Mr Blaker commented that the despatch was 'balanced and perceptive' and brought out 'the danger to the West resulting from the steady pressure of the Soviet Union to expand its areas of control and from its opportunism and the [resultant] need for a sustained and firm response'. He further observed that 'some of our allies do not seem to be prepared to act on these lessons or perhaps have not learnt them (France, Germany). The American system throws to

UK-Soviet Relations, 1979-82

> I am, My Lord,
> Yours faithfully,
> CURTIS KEEBLE

the top people unfamiliar with international affairs who have been brought up in a society where one expects the best of one's neighbours, and who therefore start by making mistakes. All this throws a particular responsibility on us, who seem to see the truth more clearly and feel freer to respond to the threat appropriately. The despatch does not provide much reason to hope for success for our neutrality initiative for Afghanistan [No. 54], but we must persevere.'

No. 51

Sir N. Henderson (Washington) to Lord Carrington, 13 February 1980, 4.35 p.m.[1]
Tel. No. 696 Immediate, Confidential (FCO 37/2263, FSA 021/2)

Your Telno 91 to Bonn:[2] Afghanistan: Possible Foreign Ministers' Meeting.

1. Vance is grateful for your message. He has had a talk with the French Ambassador which he thinks has cleared some of the air. His aim in making a trip to Europe will of course be to achieve a unifying, not a divisive, effect. He will let me know later today or tomorrow what his latest suggestions are, but my impression is that they are moving in the right direction.

2. In this connection I should tell you of a discussion I had with Warren Christopher on 11 February. Before your telegram arrived he asked to see me to exchange views very informally about how to get the allied wagon going in the right direction. Without in any way being acrimonious, he said that the French were being very difficult, but then they always were.[3] Apart from the things I would know from the press including the extremely hostile briefing in Paris, he mentioned the French complaint that the US had not consulted them about postponing the regulations imposing sanctions on Iran. I interjected that I also had been expecting some US notification on this point particularly as the US Government had been pressing us so intensively to introduce sanctions. On the French attitude generally I tried to explain the political and historic background that affects the French stance on relations with the United States. As regards the technique of dealing with them it was crucial to respect confidentiality: it was impossible if things leaked in the *New York Times* before the French government had been consulted. This question of [...][4]—when in doubt always consult—and I added that the same golden rule could also be applied to us however much we might seem tolerant and reasonable. Even if all these principles were followed, however, the French would probably continue to find it difficult to reflect publicly the reality of their belief in the importance of the Atlantic Alliance.

---

[1] Repeated Priority to Paris, Bonn, Rome.

[2] Not printed.

[3] Writing to Mr Bullard on 11 February the British Minister in Paris, Mr James, reported that 'the French official line is that dialogue with the Soviet Union must continue and that the French government will continue to make efforts in this direction'. It was further reported that the main objective of French diplomacy and, by implication, German diplomacy, was to get the Russians to withdraw their troops from Afghanistan and that they might be persuaded to do so if they could be provided with guarantees covering Afghanistan and some face saving formulae.

[4] Approximately half a line of text is corrupt and unreadable.

7 December 1979 – 1 December 1981

3. Christopher asked me what I thought ought to be done about the present impasse over a meeting of Foreign Ministers. He was frankly at a loss to know how to proceed. I said that I had no instructions but my own view was that if they were to have the French involved they must think in terms of a four-power meeting: and the other essential was that whatever was decided should be kept confidential. If they were skilful the Americans would so conduct proceedings that the French were able to persuade themselves that it was their idea that there should be a meeting.

4. Christopher said that it would be very difficult to keep a four-power ministerial meeting confidential. I said that the precedent and pattern had been set by the four-power meetings on Berlin. These were acceptable to the French. They managed to remain secret, though of course they always took place in the shadow of NATO ministerial meetings. He undertook to discuss the whole subject with Vance in the light of our talk.

5. By the way, it is unthinkable that the US would have a trilateral meeting with the French and Germans without us: indeed they were a bit amazed that I should think it necessary to clarify the point.

6. I asked Christopher how he saw the idea of a framework or web of security cooperation for the Middle East and South West Asia developing. He repeated what we know about the idea of a division of labour and a series of bilateral arrangements and facilities. But it was evident to me that he does not think that anything is going to come of any idea linking them. Nor do I believe that he thinks that this matters. Even if it were desirable, I am sure that he sees the subjects involved as being so disparate and complicated that there is no single rubric under which they could be assembled.

No. 52

Sir N. Henderson (Washington) to Lord Carrington,
16 February 1980, 8.45 p.m.[1]
Tel. No. 749 Immediate, Confidential (FCO 13/973, PC 295/1)

US/West European Relations and Motives of US Policy Post Afghanistan

1. Before your meeting with your European colleagues this coming week[2] I should like to highlight one or two general features of the above.

2. I am sure that the European leaders have grounds for complaint about the way the USA have conducted their policy since the Soviet invasion: the lack of adequate consultation and the plenitude of leaks. But they would be wrong if they thought the grumbles were just one way. There is much criticism here of the irresolution of the European response: both the lack of uniformity and the impression of a fear to stand up and be counted alongside the Americans, in contrast to American forthrightness to declare itself ready to defend Europe when the latter was threatened: and it is pointed out by government and press here that Europe's interests are menaced in the Gulf just as much as America's through their dependence on oil. HMG are gratefully acknowledged as a conspicuous exception to this widespread feeling here, a favour, I realise, that does not do us much good in Europe.

[1] Repeated Priority to EEC Posts, UKDEL NATO and Moscow.
[2] EC Foreign Ministers met in Rome on 19 February (see No. 54).

UK-Soviet Relations, 1979-82

3. It strikes one that the European Community needs to attend to its relations with the USA: and it should seek to do so collectively. There is a serious hiatus here which begins with a failure in the United States to appreciate not only the vulnerability of Europe, but the latter's defence contribution. Ignorance here is widespread in both press and Congress, and even the administration could well be reminded of what Western Europe stands for—provided Europe can get its act together. I am sure too that the US administration would welcome a lead from Europe on how in future the necessary consultation and coordination across the Atlantic could be effected to meet situations outside the European/Atlantic area.

4. I am struck too by what seems to be an inadequate interpretation in Western Europe of current US motives. Punishment may, to be sure, be among the springs of American action against the Soviets. But it is not now the only or the main one. Put synoptically and over-simply the following seem to me to be the main US objectives in their new policy that stretches from the grain embargo to the Gulf guarantee via the Olympics, base facilities in the Middle East, a framework of security and an embargo on high technology:

(*a*) to warn the Soviets that they cannot act again in that way. There cannot be another time, so far as the Americans are concerned, because a further move by the Soviet Union would immediately jeopardise fundamental Western interests, i.e. oil. The US government believe that their previous signals should have been sufficient to deter the Russians from such aggression: the fact that this did not prove to be the case explains why now they have to be so conspicuous (e.g. Olympics). Yet they cannot be precise about what would bring about a US military response or indeed about how that would be effected because to do so would be to leave the Soviets with the initiative and to remove the element of uncertainty that lies at the heart of deterrence;

(*b*) insofar as punishment features in the US armoury, it is applied in relation to the future as a foretaste of what will happen should the Russians move again. What is not understood here is the view prevalent in Europe that the Russians will take the Western response to Afghanistan seriously even in the absence of action that really hurts Soviet interests;

(*c*) to reassure the countries in the region threatened from within or without that they can rely on US support. Washington knows that anything in the nature of a NATO for the Middle East and Southwest Asia is out of the question. They are aware of their own unpopularity, of the sense of national pride and of the force of Moslem revivalism. Nothing must be imposed from outside. Yet the countries concerned need help. They feel threatened and insecure. The countries of the West have the most direct interest in helping to thwart any step that could eventually lead to the further curtailment of Middle East oil or its diversion to the Soviet Union;

(*d*) to provide for the requirements of the US forces if they are to meet (or be credible in deterring) a military threat: hence the search for bases euphemistically described as facilities. The US hope that other European countries will collaborate in this—the UK in Oman, for instance. Even if the forces that could be brought to bear in the region in the event of a Soviet threat would be insufficient to prevent the inevitably much larger Soviet forces from overrunning much of the area, the US believe that they will, within a year or two, be able to position quite a respectable force quickly and that, on the tripwire analogy, the fact that the Soviets will be overrunning cowboys from Kansas will make them realise what it is that they may be eventually taking on.

7 December 1979 – 1 December 1981

5. Given the disposition in Europe to see us as a Trojan horse for the Americans, I can see that it is difficult to decide how best to make use of the above. But, in fulfilment of the suggestions in paragraph 3, it does look from here as though we could usefully urge upon the Nine the need for a concerted voice, which complements, even though it does not coincide with, that of the USA.

No. 53

Record of a meeting between Mrs Thatcher and Mr Vance at 10 Downing Street, 22 February 1980, 7.45 p.m.
Confidential (FCO 37/2250, FSA 020/1)

Present:
Prime Minister
Foreign and Commonwealth Secretary
Mr M. O'D. B. Alexander

Mr Cyrus Vance
HE Mr Kingman Brewster

Mr Vance said that he had found his trip to Europe extremely useful. So far as he could see there was a common assessment of the threat and a common assessment of the objectives which the allies should be pursuing. There were, however, still some differences about the precise way those objectives should be achieved. The *Prime Minister* said that she was concerned lest the reaction to the invasion of Afghanistan should be a nine-day wonder. It was essential that the West's response should be sustained and should not dwindle after six months as it had done in the case of the invasions of Hungary and Czechoslovakia. *Mr Vance* said that President Carter entirely agreed with the Prime Minister on this point.
Saudi Arabia . . .[1]
Olympic Games
The *Prime Minister* said that if the boycott of the Olympic Games was to be effective, it would be essential that there should be alternative events in which the athletes could compete. *Mr Vance* agreed and said that the American Government had this much in mind. It looked as though Montreal would in many ways be a more satisfactory venue than Los Angeles. Although the defeat of Mr Clark in the recent Canadian election had created a problem, it seemed likely that Mr Trudeau's view would not be so very different from that of Mr Clark. He had rung President Carter earlier in the day to indicate that it was his intention to withdraw from the position he had taken on this issue during the election as quickly as possible. The *Prime Minister* said that Her Majesty's Government would be prepared to find some money to finance alternative games. *Mr Vance* said that in his view the key to the situation lay in the hands of the International Federations dealing with the respective sports rather than with Olympic committees. He said that it was not the intention of the American Government to stage national games in the United States. He commented that President Moi had said that he would like to stage one or two events in Kenya. The *Foreign and Commonwealth Secretary* said that not too much attention should be paid to the disagreements at the Political Co-operation meeting in Rome. The Germans had made it clear that they would not go to Moscow if the United States did not go. It was very probable that the French would stay away if the Americans and Germans were absent. M. François Poncet

---

[1] The sections dealing with Saudi Arabia and Turkey have not been printed.

UK-Soviet Relations, 1979-82

had hinted that France's attitude in Rome had been connected with the fact that the American deadline for Soviet withdrawal from Afghanistan expired the day after the Rome meeting.

Turkey . . .[1]

The discussion ended at 20.15 hrs.

No. 54

Lord Carrington to HM Representatives Overseas, 22 February 1980, 6.30 p.m.
Guidance Tel. No. 20 Restricted (FCO 13/976, PC 295/1)

Proposals for a Neutral Afghanistan

1. At the European Council meeting in Rome on 19 February, Foreign Ministers of the Nine launched the idea that the crisis in Afghanistan could be overcome constructively through an arrangement which allowed a neutral Afghanistan to be outside competition between the powers.

2. This initiative, conveyed in a Presidency press briefing, is based on an idea put forward by the Secretary of State and welcomed by his colleagues. At a briefing for journalists, Lord Carrington explained that Ministers had tried to contribute once again to the lessening of tensions and to make a positive step forward in defusing a dangerous situation. The Community is well placed to float this idea. It has strongly condemned the Soviet invasion but communications with the Soviet Union remain open. Europe has special interest in détente. This could be an example of détente in action. The Nine have a vast fund of experience and traditional ties in the region.

3. You may draw on paras 1 to 8 in answering general questions on the proposal supplementing them with points in the Secretary of State's press briefing (VS 022). In securing the interest or support of governments you may use paras 9-12 at your discretion.

Line to take

4. The idea is not a propaganda ploy but a genuine and constructive proposal. We believe it offers possibilities for progress. You should commend it to governments, especially those belonging to the non-aligned movement and the Islamic Conference. We regard it as important that the idea should generate support from these groups and not be seen incorrectly as a Western suggestion fired as a shot in an East-West exchange.

Further points

5. The proposal is made within the spirit of the UN General Assembly Resolution of 14 January which appeals to all states to respect the sovereignty, territorial integrity, political independence and non-aligned character of Afghanistan and refrain from any interference in the internal affairs of that country.

6. The idea is not a rigid proposal. The Nine are urgently meeting next week to flesh it out. They will concert their position on the subject with allies and friendly countries and with all countries having an interest in the equilibrium and stability of the region.

7. The Nine adhere to the analysis of the situation and its implications set out in their declaration of 15 January. The withdrawal of Soviet troops from Afghanistan remains their principal objective. The new initiative aims to establish a framework

7 December 1979 – 1 December 1981

for such a withdrawal.

8. Though some ideas have been culled from the Austrian State Treaty of 1955, it does not offer an exact parallel to Afghanistan. We are not wedded to any particular approach, and our intention is to be flexible.

9. The proposal is designed *inter alia* to demonstrate that the Soviet Union's professed fears of Western intervention in Afghanistan are groundless. The Russians have repeatedly said that their troops will withdraw when the reason (alleged Western and Chinese interference) for the intervention no longer exists and Mr Gromyko stated on 18 February that 'there is no disputed issue of intergovernmental relations, no major international problem, upon which we would not be ready for negotiations, for negotiations on an equal basis'.

For use with governments

10. The proposal establishes a specifically European position. (It has not been made within NATO machinery.) While the Nine have condemned the Soviet invasion, they have also kept their lines of communication open to Moscow.

11. The best way of proceeding is under discussion. One possibility might be a UN conference convened by the Secretary-General. Another could be an *ad hoc* conference called by a third party.

12. The Italians in their Presidency capacity will be briefing the Soviet Union fairly soon.

No. 55

Partial record of a meeting between Mrs Thatcher and Chancellor Schmidt at 10 Downing Street, 25 February 1980[1]
Secret (FCO 28/4003, EN 021/1)

Present:
Prime Minister   Chancellor Schmidt
Mr M. Alexander   HE Dr. Jurgen Ruhfus

International Situation in the Wake of Afghanistan

The *Prime Minister* said that the need to settle the British budgetary problem was given additional urgency by the present international situation. It was a bad time for Europe to be divided: the more so since there were signs both that the European reaction to events in Afghanistan was becoming better coordinated and that the situation in Afghanistan itself was deteriorating. *Chancellor Schmidt* said that he strongly agreed. The *Prime Minister* asked whether there was any truth in the stories in the morning's newspapers that Herr Brandt[2] had been asked to act as a mediator between the United States and the Soviet Union. *Chancellor Schmidt* said that he did not believe there was any substance to the stories. He had seen the text of a message which Herr Brandt had recently received from Mr Brezhnev. He had also seen the record of Herr Brandt's talks with President Carter. Neither supported the newspapers' reports. They appeared to have been invented by *Der Spiegel*. Despite its reputation, *Der Spiegel* was a thoroughly unreliable journal. The *Prime Minister* said that she was glad to learn this. She would have felt

---

[1] For a German record of the meeting see *Akten zur Auswärtigen Politik der Bundesrepublik Deutschland 1980* (Munich: Oldenbourg Verlag, 2011), Vol. 1, No. 61.
[2] Willy Brandt, West German Chancellor, 1969-74.

UK-Soviet Relations, 1979-82

uncomfortable had a German as prominent as Herr Brandt been cast in the role of a neutral between the US and the Soviet Union on this issue.

Chancellor Schmidt expressed his disquiet at the repeated failures of the Americans to consult with their allies in the course of the present crisis. They would not always be able to find sufficient people who were prepared to clap their hands on hearing the latest American policy decisions on the radio. The present American tendency to ignore the fact that other Governments had their own priorities and domestic considerations was thoroughly dangerous. The effect in Germany of the recent threat by Dr. Brzezinski to use nuclear weapons in response to further Soviet moves in South West Asia was a case in point. The threat, in particular the way it had been made, was preposterous, the more so since there was an indication that the weapons would not necessarily be used in the area where the Soviet move had been made. The effect of such statements in the Federal Republic, which had more than 5,000 nuclear weapons on its soil and was an obvious target for a pre-emptive strike, could readily be imagined. The American performance on the Olympic Games had been similarly thoughtless. The Germans had checked with the Americans twice in the period immediately before President Carter's statement on this subject and had been told that no policy announcements were in prospect (one of the checks had been made personally by Chancellor Schmidt with Mr Christopher). The Americans had consulted the Federal Republic neither about the impact of their announcement in Germany nor about its desirability. One consequence had been that Chancellor Schmidt had delivered a major address to the Bundestag the day before the American boycott was announced[3] and had made no mention whatever of the Olympic Games. As a final example, Chancellor Schmidt said that he had asked Mr Vance during his visit to Bonn the previous week whether the Americans had invoked the Nixon/Brezhnev doctrine[4] with the Russians during the early stages of the Afghanistan crisis. Mr Vance said that the Americans had done so. This was the first that Chancellor Schmidt had heard of it. Had he known earlier on, he would have seen more consistency in the American reaction in January.

Chancellor Schmidt said that there was an undercurrent of feeling in the Federal Republic that there is now a clear and present danger of a Third World War. Many leaders in Eastern Europe, notably Messrs. Gierek and Kadar[5] were deeply frightened. One consequence of the present situation was that they were losing what little independence they had achieved in the last 15 or 20 years. Mr Kadar had been told that his Foreign Minister should cancel his impending visit to Bonn if the Hungarian Government wished the Soviet Government to observe an agreement on energy supplies which had just been negotiated. The East Europeans, including the East Germans, deeply resented the invasion of Afghanistan, but were anxious that the West should not react in a way that led the Soviet Union to forcibly reassert their authority. The situation in Poland was in any case likely to get worse. The recent sacrifice of the Prime Minister there would make no

---

[3] On 20 February a White House statement announced that as Soviet troops had still not withdrawn from Afghanistan the US would not be sending a team to the Moscow Games. See *Public Papers: Carter (1980-81)*, Book I, pp. 356-7.

[4] This is probably a reference to the US-Soviet Declaration on Basic Principles of Mutual Relations of 29 May 1972 (see No. 8, note 4). In particular clause 2 stated that the two countries would do their utmost to avoid military confrontations and would exercise restraint in their mutual relations and refrain from 'efforts to obtain unilateral advantage at the expense of the other, directly or indirectly'.

[5] Respective leaders of the Polish and Hungarian Communist parties.

7 December 1979 – 1 December 1981

difference.

Chancellor Schmidt made it clear that he thought that the American reaction to the situation was inadequate. They had not analysed the situation that lay ahead with sufficient care and seemed unaware of the need for and nature of consultation with their allies. (Chancellor Schmidt noted with regret the disappearance of the old East Coast establishment figures and the absence of any credible replacements.) The Americans were inclined to talk about punishing the Russians. This was an erroneous idea. Punishment should not be an element in the international policy of a major power. The object now was to get the Russians out of Afghanistan and prevent them trying the same thing again. Boycotting the Olympic Games was a pinprick. What was necessary was to make it clear beyond doubt that if the Russians were, for instance, to move against the Yemen Arab Republic, something serious would happen. The Americans had also failed to show sufficient subtlety and sensitivity in their handling of the Third World. They should, for instance, already be working to ensure that the idea of neutrality for Afghanistan was taken over and promoted by Third World countries. The American failure to take into account the sensibilities of the countries in the Gulf region when announcing their guarantee had been glaring. The United States after all had had no fewer than three special Ambassadors dealing with Middle East problems in the last two years. It was not surprising that their policies lacked finesse. It was a pity that they had not sought the advice of e.g. the British whose expertise in the area was so much greater than their own.

Chancellor Schmidt said that this was by no means the first crisis that he had lived through. But he could not recall a previous instance where there had been so much muddle. He accepted that the Americans had a difficult hand to play. They had, simultaneously, to be clear in their own minds what they wanted to do; to act as leaders of the West; and yet to disguise the fact that they were doing so. Nonetheless, it was disastrous that matters had been allowed to get so far without a process of active and continuing consultation having been put in hand. The recent visit of Mr Vance had been very important in this context. But how was it going to be followed up? He had suggested that Mr Vance should have regular consultations with the British, German and French Ambassadors in Washington. This was a sensible idea in itself but did not overcome the fundamental difficulties caused by the fact that so many decisions were taken in the White House without the prior knowledge of the State Department.

The *Prime Minister* said that she agreed with many of the points made by Chancellor Schmidt but wondered whether the European reaction had not itself been partly to blame. She had been bitterly disappointed by the slowness with which the other members of the Nine had acted. *Chancellor Schmidt* said that he accepted this, but that much of the blame should be laid at the door of the Presidency. It had been for them to act. Perhaps they should have been pushed, but there was a natural reluctance to do so. The prospect in the autumn of Luxembourg being in the Chair, was not much more cheerful.

The Prime Minister asked what advice, assuming they had been asked, the Europeans would have given President Carter in January. She believed that President Carter had been right to advocate the boycotting of the Olympics. It was the best way to bring home to the Soviet people the gravity of what had occurred in Afghanistan. She accepted that it was wrong to think in terms of punishing the Soviet Government but presumably it was not wrong to speak of bringing pressure to bear on them. What kind of pressure would Europe have been advocating? Was

UK-Soviet Relations, 1979-82

a cut-off in exports of technology part of the stick with which the Russians should be threatened? *Chancellor Schmidt* said that he did not disagree with what the Prime Minister had said about the Olympics. He did, however, disagree about the way the card had been played. Now that the United States' deadline had expired, it no longer had any value. Moreover, it was not in itself enough. As regards technology, he might have been prepared to have seen this brought into the equation. But the Americans should show more awareness of the implications of this for the Federal German Government. One per cent of the German workforce was directly affected by trade with the Soviet Union. The trade had been built up for good political reasons. The Americans for their part had never sold anything of major importance to the Russians (the only exceptions admitted by Chancellor Schmidt were computers and drilling equipment: it was very debatable whether it would be to the advantage of the West to cut off supply of the latter given that it might lead to increased Soviet competition for oil resources elsewhere). Exports in any case played, relatively speaking, a tiny part in the US economy. Chancellor Schmidt said he was not prepared to make sacrifices simply for the sake of doing so. He was not only critical of the line the American Government had taken on this issue: he deeply resented it.

On the question of giving advice to the Americans, Chancellor Schmidt said that it was not easy for his Government to do so. Had he been sitting in the White House he would have been in little doubt as to what to do. As it was, he was representing a power which had a burden of guilt from the last war; which had 60 million[6] hostages in East Germany and 2 million in Berlin; and which was in a militarily untenable geographical position. The *Prime Minister* said that she saw no reason why the Federal Republic should not tender advice. The events of the last war were no longer a factor of major significance in this context. Moreover, everyone knew that the defence of the West depended on the reaction of four powers, the US, the UK, France and the Federal Republic. As regards Germany's exposed position, this in many respects made it easier for her to give advice and have it listened to rather than the contrary.

Chancellor Schmidt acknowledged the points the Prime Minister had made. He said that the West's response to events in Afghanistan would have to be a combination of stick and carrot. The dialogue between the American and Soviet Governments had to continue. The need for the Russians to save face had to be borne in mind. There should be no pinpricking and no sabre rattling. At the same time the West should find a way of doing something that really hurt the Soviet Union. This meant pushing them out of some country in which they were already established—Angola, Ethiopia, the PDRY or some similar country (Chancellor Schmidt noted that this was the kind of point that he could not put to anyone in writing: he asked that it should not be recorded or disseminated).

The *Prime Minister* said that she agreed with Chancellor Schmidt's approach. She was sceptical about the chances of pushing the Russians out of Afghanistan (Chancellor Schmidt agreed), but thought it might be done elsewhere. However, this clearly could not be done hamfistedly. The fact that there were election campaigns underway in the United States and the Federal Republic was a complicating factor. *Chancellor Schmidt* said that he would put his own election campaign out of his mind when dealing with the international situation. But he hoped that allied governments would bear the election campaign in mind. He was

[6] The German record of the meeting has this figure as 16 million.

7 December 1979 – 1 December 1981

grateful to the Prime Minister for the way she had handled Herr Strauss' letter about the cultural centre in Berlin. Notwithstanding the election campaigns and some recent public pronouncements, he hoped that the United States would not be under any misapprehension about the position of the Federal Republic and indeed of France. Both were very strong allies indeed. Both would support the Americans. Indeed they would support the Americans even where they thought the policies were wrong, e.g. on the boycott of the Olympics. Chancellor Schmidt said that in discussing the political dangers, the looming dangers in the economic field should not be overlooked. If, as a result of developments in the Gulf, the West's supply of oil was interrupted, even for a short period, the international banking system could easily collapse. The Euro currency market was inadequately supervised and a chain of bankruptcies could be set off. The economic actions of the Arab governments were not predictable. Taken as a whole, the prospects were frightening. Finance Ministers should be discussing questions such as how to cope with a crisis of confidence in the Euro currency market.

Future Action

At various points in their discussion the _Prime Minister_ and _Chancellor Schmidt_ touched on the question of action in the weeks ahead. They agreed that the Summit meeting in Venice[7] was an obvious opportunity for substantial discussion of the West's reaction to events in Afghanistan but that it was a long way off. They therefore envisaged a timetable including the following elements:

(_a_) Trilateral discussions, perhaps at official level, between France, the FRG and the UK to prepare comments on the American paper recently circulated by Mr Vance. (Recent British and German papers would provide a good starting point.) For the most part these comments should be conveyed to the Americans in written form, but it should be envisaged that some of the comments might have to be oral;

(_b_) Co-ordination of the European viewpoint at the meetings of the Council of Ministers (Foreign Affairs) in Brussels on 10/11 March and, possibly, at the subsequent meeting of Foreign Ministers of the Nine in April. It was for consideration whether the Americans could be associated with one of these meetings in some way. Whether or not this was possible there should be:

(_c_) At least one and possibly two meetings of the Foreign Ministers of the Four (US, UK, FRG and France) before the Venice meeting.

(_d_) A meeting of the Four Heads of Government, together with their Foreign Ministers, immediately before the Venice summit. The meeting should allow for several hours' discussion. It should be either in Italy or, if this proved impossible to arrange in view of Italian susceptibilities, before the Heads of Government concerned arrived in Italy. Chancellor Schmidt and the Prime Minister were both prepared to envisage Italian participation but thought that this was unlikely to be acceptable to the French. It was agreed that urgent thought would be given to this proposal in the next few days and that a considered British view would be communicated to Chancellor Schmidt before his visit to Washington next week.

(_e_) The Venice summit should not be exclusively devoted to a discussion of economic problems, serious though these were. The first day should be devoted to political problems and the second to the usual agenda. While recognising that there might be difficulties with the Japanese, both Chancellor Schmidt and the

[7] See No. 57, note 3.

UK-Soviet Relations, 1979-82

Prime Minister considered that it was time the Japanese were involved in discussion of the political issues.

(*f*) The *Prime Minister* hoped that the communiqué of the Venice summit would be short and could be limited to the subjects actually discussed at the summit. *Chancellor Schmidt* agreed.

[The above summary of the discussion on future action has been agreed with Dr. Ruhfus.][8]

[8] In a covering minute to Mr Walden, dated 25 February, Mr Alexander commented: 'For reasons that will be obvious, I should be grateful if the record could be given an extremely limited circulation. You told me that you had in mind to produce a bowdlerized version for telegraphing to Missions: clearly, this will have to omit most of the Chancellor's comments about the Americans.'

No. 56

Letter from Sir C. Keeble (Moscow) to Mr Fergusson, 27 February 1980
Confidential (FCO 37/2250, FSA 020/1)

Dear Ewen,

1. Brezhnev's speech of 22 February[1] marks a convenient point at which to consider where the Soviet Union has got to in Afghanistan and how its future policies may develop.

2. There is a good deal in the immediate outlook which must be discouraging for the Soviet leadership. The Russians may well have expected resistance to continue in Afghanistan itself and have calculated that they would not be able to undertake a serious effort to wipe it out until the spring. They appeared to start out with an effort to set Babrak Karmal up as someone who would unite the country under a relatively liberal communist regime and they must be disappointed at what looks from Moscow like his complete failure to attract support, compounded by the failure of the Afghan Army to give any useful account of itself. The latest rioting in Kabul[2] and other cities points up these failures and, even for those who depend on *Pravda* for news, it must seem to add a new and dangerous possibility of urban resistance, compounding the problems raised by tribal warfare. (I find it hard to believe that even Soviet propagandists can take seriously the allegation that these disturbances were provoked by the CIA or the Pakistanis.) If public indications are any guide, the Soviet leadership are beginning to recognise the failure of Babrak Karmal to make any mark on the situation. He is rarely mentioned in the Soviet press and for some time now contacts with him and his government, apart from an interview with his brother on TV last night as he was passing through Moscow en route for Ethiopia, have been given no publicity by the Soviet media. The impression I am left with is that the Russians are faced with the need to use a greater measure of force for longer than they had expected in trying to establish the control of an increasingly ineffective government. But I see no sign that having

[1] In this speech, delivered to delegates of the Supreme Soviet in the Kremlin Palace of Congresses, Brezhnev stated that the Soviet Union would be ready to withdraw its troops from Afghanistan as soon as all forms of outside interference directed against the government and people of Afghanistan were fully terminated. Brezhnev further contended that American hysteria over Afghanistan was a pretext to allow Washington to broaden its expansion in Asia and that American inspired subversion was making it impossible for Moscow to withdraw.
[2] On 22 February martial law was imposed in Kabul following outbreaks of rioting and arson.

7 December 1979 – 1 December 1981

embarked on a policy of establishing control by force, they will not be prepared to carry it through. They may look for a better way forward but do not—at least as yet—seem to be looking for a way back.

3. The Russians must still be disappointed at their failure so far to win much non-aligned support and especially at Gromyko's failure in New Delhi. They may take some heart from Mrs Gandhi's recent speeches (Manning's teleletter of 22 February to Pearce, SAD)[3] and they will undoubtedly continue to do what they can both to flatter the Indians (as Brezhnev did on 22 February), and possibly to bribe them with economic and military aid, but their main tactic up to now has been to try to distract non-aligned attention from Afghanistan by heaping all the blame for the world's evils on to American shoulders and by pointing to the real or imagined sins of the imperialists in Israel, Rhodesia, Micronesia[4] and so on. They must expect that the larger and harsher their own military involvement in Afghanistan the more they will antagonise Third World opinion and they may fear that the idea of a neutral Afghanistan could begin to gain force. As I suggested in my telegram No. 162[3] it may have been this, coupled with an attempt to ingratiate themselves with the Indians, that lay behind Brezhnev's 22 February remarks about a guarantee of non-interference from Afghanistan's neighbours. This has not yet been further developed by the Soviet press or by authoritative Soviet spokesmen, nor has there been any substantive comment on the idea of a neutrality treaty. On the latter, I cannot usefully add to the thoughts in my telegram No. 145 (not to all).[3] It is of course easy enough and attractive enough for the Russians to encourage the idea that Afghanistan's borders should be sealed, particularly since this carries the implication that the cause of the troubles has indeed been outside interference and offers a handy *droit de regard* over the policies of Afghanistan's neighbours. They will however certainly have nothing to do with the unwelcome implication in the concept of neutrality that the provisions of the existing bilateral treaty under which Soviet forces were introduced should cease to be effective and that the Revolutionary Government in Kabul should be left to fend for itself against its own population. Hence Brezhnev's gloss, on the usual formula about Soviet troops being withdrawn when the conditions which led to their introduction no longer apply, to the effect that this can only be done when the Afghan Government, too, agrees that the time is right. This would provide them with an escape hatch in the event that a guarantee of non-interference failed to induce tranquillity within Afghanistan. In short, the Russians can be expected to argue that a guarantee of non interference must precede a withdrawal of forces: that it must be effective; and that its effectiveness will be demonstrated by the ability of the Afghan Government to say that Soviet forces are no longer necessary.

4. Moscow also has significant problems to consider after Afghanistan in Europe. There are I think now scraps of evidence from which one may conclude that most Eastern European countries resented the way the Soviet Union took such cavalier action, cutting across their fundamental interest in détente, without consultation or any apparent regard for the interests of its partners. At any rate the Russians have had to make an effort to bring the Eastern Europeans into line. Their policy towards Western Europe has betrayed uncertainty. In general they would obviously hope, so far as they can, to isolate the United States. Soviet propaganda

---

[3] Not printed.

[4] Micronesia consists of some 600 islands extending 1,800 miles across the western Pacific grouped into four federated states: Kosrae, Pohnpei, Chuuk and Yap.

seizes on any sign that this may be about to develop. But the Soviet effort has been largely confined to propaganda. They have failed to offer much of a carrot to Western Europe and their stick has been used against their neighbours in Scandinavia and Turkey rather than against the main Western European countries. Even the treatment of the UK has not been noticeably more hostile than usual.

5. Internally, the adventure in Afghanistan is not without its economic cost. We do not have the resources here to put a price upon it but it must be an irritating extra burden on a Soviet economy which seems itself to be causing a growing degree of concern to the leadership through its poor performance. It is after all not just a matter of paying for Afghanistan but also, among others, Vietnam, Cuba, Ethiopia and the PDRY. In the wider context it has been a distinct feature of the election speeches by the leadership (Andrew Wood's letter of 12 February to David Johnson)[5] that the politicians have felt the need to explain what is going on to their own public opinion. I was also struck by the speed and relative fullness of the reporting in the Soviet central press of the Kabul riots, and by the stress Brezhnev laid in his speech on the need for unity.

6. None of the above means we are likely to see an early or significant change in Soviet policies towards Afghanistan. Brezhnev referred to an increase in US interference. What I think it does mean is that the Russians have for the time being at any rate bitten off at least as much as they can chew. If their intervention in Afghanistan was intended to be swift and surgical it has failed. Though I believe they would dearly love to mount a peace offensive which might ideally include some token withdrawal of troops they are not in a position to do so. Indeed *they are in no position in their own eyes to do anything which might be misinterpreted as weakness.*[6] On the contrary, because they have considerable problems they will be concerned to show strength. I remarked when I wrote on 9 January[7] that the prime cause of Soviet action probably lay in developments in Afghanistan itself. I believe we must still look to that country to explain present Soviet policies. Though Soviet propaganda against Pakistan has taken on a fresh degree of strength recently and Gromyko's remarks in India were distinctly threatening, it is hard to believe that Pakistan will come under early, direct military pressure. It is noticeable that the recent Soviet line on Iran has been bland and they have even been careful about China. Although the Russians have, as for example in the case of Schmidt, seemed keen to avoid top level contacts with the West and have directed a propaganda barrage against the Americans they have even there been careful also to signal that they wish détente (on their terms) to continue. Hence perhaps the proposal for a fresh exchange of data in MBFR, which may be meaningless but sounds good, and Brezhnev's recognition on 22 February of a US interest in oil supplies.

7. What happens in the longer term will depend in the first place on how successful Soviet arms may be in Afghanistan. If the Russians run into real difficulties they feel they may not be able to overcome except at great cost, then the idea of neutrality in some form may begin to prove attractive. But this would scarcely happen until, say, the autumn. The more easily they subdue Afghanistan, on the other hand, the more tempting any other opportunities which may open up, whether in Iran or Pakistan, will be. Signs of Western irresolution, for example

[5] Not printed.
[6] Emphasis in the original.
[7] No. 28.

7 December 1979 – 1 December 1981

over the Olympics, where the Soviet reaction to the IOC's decision[8] has been predictably smug, will encourage the Russians in the belief they can overawe or seduce the opposition.

8. Meanwhile in relation to NATO it is noticeable that the Soviet line is now that TNF modernisation is directed at the Soviet Union 'and its allies' so it would seem likely that the Warsaw Pact Anniversary in May may be used as the occasion for a Soviet version of modernisation coupled with arms control proposals.

Yours ever,
CURTIS KEEBLE

[8] On 12 February the President of the International Olympic Committee, Lord Killanin, announced that the 1980 Summer Games would take place as planned in Moscow. Recognising the difficulties this presented to the US, Lord Killanin stressed that the IOC could not solve the political problems of the world and called on the major powers 'to come together to resolve their differences.'

No. 57

Letter from Mrs Thatcher to President Carter, 3 March 1980
Confidential (PREM 19/137)

Dear Mr President,

Thank you for your letter of 10 February about the Western response to the Soviet invasion of Afghanistan.[1] I have delayed this reply in order to take into account Peter Carrington's discussions with his European colleagues in Rome on 19 February and with Cy Vance in London on 21 February.[2] He found Cy Vance's exposition of the next steps particularly clear and constructive. The Alliance is drawing closer together both on the analysis and on the action which should flow from it. We shall do all we can to push this process still further.

I believe that, first of all we should make it clear that we do not accept the Soviet invasion of Afghanistan as an accomplished fact. The idea for Afghan neutrality which we put to our colleagues in Rome was designed both to maintain pressure on the Russians to withdraw and to allow them a way out. We are now studying the proposal in detail with our European partners and as you know, have made it clear to the Russians that we hope they will consider it seriously. Cy Vance thought this was an appropriate initiative. Our people will keep in close touch with yours about the next steps.

I too hope that the Afghan crisis will serve as a catalyst in meeting some of the most urgent challenges which face us. On the need to improve the Western defensive capability inside and outside Europe we are at one. I agree, too, that we should seek to reduce the industrialised world's dependence on Middle East oil, and that measures to reduce consumption are the key to this. We shall continue to work closely with you and other major Western consumers. The oil crisis, and indeed the wider implications of the Afghanistan crisis, would I suggest be a

[1] In this letter, President Carter warned against Soviet attempts to split the Western Alliance and sought assurances that Britain would increase economic aid to Pakistan and Turkey, expand its military presence in the Gulf and further restrict the export of high technology items to the Soviet Union.
[2] Nos. 53 and 54.

UK-Soviet Relations, 1979-82

suitable subject for discussion when the seven of us meet in Venice in the Spring.[3]

I now turn to the particular points you raised.

Aid to Pakistan

We are, as you know, considering increased economic assistance to Pakistan in our next financial year (1980-81) when economic aid and debt relief will be worth about £30m. (For subsequent years forecasting is less easy, partly because the 1980-81 total includes special aid for ships.) Any aid to Afghan refugees would be additional. Apart from our initial consignment of emergency aid, we are providing our share, amounting to £1.1m, of the European Community response to the appeal by the UN High Commissioner for Refugees.

The Pakistanis do not often look to us for major items of military equipment. If they should now turn our way (and they may be interested in some items, e.g. radar, artillery, communications equipment, and military engineering equipment) we would do our best to help. But since we, like you, do not have a military hardware grant aid programme, much will depend on funds being made available to Pakistan by her Moslem friends. Meanwhile, I am glad that your military survey team has been counselling the Pakistanis. It is important that the Pakistanis concentrate on the Soviet threat—military on the NW Frontier, and subversive—and equip themselves appropriately. To purchase arms beyond their limited needs would waste scarce resources and alarm the Indians, who would move closer to the Russians.

Of paramount importance, it seems to me, is the scope of the military guarantee you have given to Pakistan, and whether it is properly understood in Moscow. I was glad to hear that Cy Vance told Peter Carrington that the extent of your commitment has been made clear to the Russians. Political anxieties in the Sub-Continent should lessen in consequence and the practical problems of supporting the countries of the area, militarily and economically, should become more manageable.

Aid to Turkey

I shall naturally consider what kind of contribution to the exercise being led by the Germans we can make within our own financial constraints. I certainly agree with you about the importance for us all of Turkey's position in the region.

Defence Policy Outside NATO

We are as you know reviewing our defence role outside the NATO area in order to see how the UK can best contribute. I think that it should be possible to use our resources more flexibly and thus to help out a little more in other areas without any major diversion from our efforts in NATO. Your suggestion that we could draw on US logistical assistance for deployments in the Indian Ocean and the Gulf area is an attractive one which we shall certainly want to explore fully. We, for our part, will be as helpful as we can over the use of our facilities by your forces. My people have already told yours of our agreement to the first stage improvements for Diego Garcia. They will be getting together again early in March to take matters further.

Export Credits and Transfer of Technology to the Soviet Union

A decision by the Alliance to restrict further the supply of equipment and technology to the Soviet Union and to toughen the terms on which it is exported would, I am sure, be the right kind of signal. But if the West's measures to this end are to have a substantial impact, they must be closely coordinated and rigorously applied by all the COCOM partners. The European countries have a proportion-

---

[3] The G7 World Economic Summit took place in Venice on the island of San Giorgio Maggiore between 22-23 June.

7 December 1979 – 1 December 1981

ately larger commercial stake than the United States in trade with the Soviet Union, much of it in long term projects, and tougher controls will cause added problems at a time when economic conditions are already difficult. Some COCOM partners may not be willing to go as far along the road as you would wish. In the export credit field, for example, not all our partners in the Community have agreed to move as far as we have and our discussions in the Foreign Affairs Council do not suggest that there would be sufficient support for a ban on new official export credits.

On high technology, several countries have expressed willingness to tighten COCOM's rules for exports to the Soviet Union. Restrictions on the submission of general exceptions cases to COCOM—while allowing for cases such as hardship or security interest, as you propose—would seem the most profitable area in which to seek collective agreement. Cy Vance and Peter Carrington agreed that we should push ahead on this. As an interim measure, we are not submitting applications to COCOM under the General Exemptions Procedure, and in the particular case of computers which you mention, we shall continue to operate on the 1976 lists.

I have noted with interest what you say about widening the scope of the COCOM embargo. We will consider this carefully. We have since received through your Embassy further proposals which we are studying. My officials will be in touch with yours to seek some clarifications.

Similarly, we shall need to look at the implications of your decision that ALCOA and ARMCO should withdraw from major projects in the Soviet Union. I think it unlikely that in these cases British companies would be taking part in competing bids.

Yours sincerely,
MARGARET THATCHER

No. 58

Letter from President Carter to Mrs Thatcher, 17 March 1980
Secret (FCO 37/2251, FSA 020/1)

Dear Prime Minister,

I appreciate your thoughtful and informative letter of March 3[1] concerning the critical issues confronting both our countries. I am pleased to see that by and large we agree about what steps should be taken next. As you know, Helmut Schmidt and I discussed these same subjects at length during his visit here last week. In the hope that you will find them helpful, I want to share with you some further thoughts directly related to the situation in Southwest Asia.

On the question of aid to Pakistan, I fully agree with you on the importance of encouraging the Pakistanis to concentrate on the Soviet threat, and I am certain that your efforts to this end will effectively promote overall Western interests.

The Government of Pakistan appears to be engaged in making fundamental decisions about its external orientation in light of the new situation created by the Soviet invasion of Afghanistan and the return to power of Mrs Gandhi. You have probably read the speech of General Zia's foreign affairs adviser who stated that my offers of support were insufficient in scale and duration and too restrictive in

[1] No. 57.

UK-Soviet Relations, 1979-82

their conditions. Evidently General Zia has concluded that the disadvantages of a close security relationship with the United States outweigh the advantages of the aid that I was prepared to offer. This is probably not the final word on the matter of United States aid. Prime responsibility for financing military aid for Pakistan by other, primarily Moslem, nations is not an unsatisfactory prospect for us.

In his speech of March 5, Agha Shahi appeared to suggest an approach which would entail dropping any military assistance, which Pakistan would seek elsewhere, and emphasizing economic aid along with a Congressional reaffirmation of our 1959 bilateral agreement. We are currently exploring an approach along these lines with the Pakistan government. In that context, it continues to remain of utmost importance that the Western and Islamic nations strengthen their relations with Pakistan, particularly with regard to economic aid and provision of defense equipment.

On a matter of more direct interest to the Alliance, Helmut Schmidt and his associates made a persuasive case during their visit here for accelerated and increased aid to Turkey. Demirel's economic reform program certainly deserves our admiration and support. I have agreed, therefore, to supplement our planned $200 million cash loan to Turkey with substantial aid in the form of export credits and food.

The Export-Import Bank also is expediting use of the credit line it extended to Turkey last year. I mention these details in the hope that you will find similar action to be feasible.

As to the question of high-technology transfers, I much appreciate your support for tightening COCOM rules on exports to the Soviet Union. A strong allied effort in this area will make it more difficult for the Soviets to acquire the technology and equipment they need to support their military establishment. I agree completely that the allies must act together for maximum impact. I recognize that some of our partners are reluctant to ban new official export credits or guarantees. From a strictly commercial point of view, this is understandable. Yet we must not lose sight of the overall objective of our economic sanctions: to force the Soviets to pay a concrete price for their aggression. The Soviets need export credits to purchase the Western goods and technologies essential to their economic development. By borrowing abroad—almost always on exceptionally favorable terms—the Soviets have been able to modernize their industrial plant while still devoting enormous resources to the military sector. At the very least, we should strive to increase the USSR's cost[s] by raising interest rates and shortening repayment terms. It is difficult to understand why Western governments should subsidize Soviet industry, especially under the present circumstances.

I look forward to discussing these and related issues with you in person when we meet later this year in Venice. In the meantime, of course, I continue to attach great importance to our personal correspondence; the breadth and candor of this exchange is very helpful to me.

Sincerely,
JIMMY CARTER

P.S.[2] Our efforts to convince the Soviets that they have made a serious mistake in Afghanistan and should withdraw will be continued as a firm and constant policy.

---

[2] This was a handwritten addition to the letter.

7 December 1979 – 1 December 1981

We need all the help we can get, and allied unity is crucial. Your efforts to achieve the same goals are beneficial. Let us stay close and stand together.

No. 59

Letter from Sir D. Maitland[1] to Sir N. Henderson (Washington), 24 March 1980[2]
Confidential (FCO 49/893, RS 021/6)

[No salutation]

Afghanistan: Neutrality Proposal

1. I enclose a copy of a note[3] on the Afghanistan neutrality proposal which has been approved by the Secretary of State.

2. I hope that you will find the note useful background to our present thinking. The note distinguishes between the use of the neutrality proposal as a device for putting political pressure on the Russians, and its eventual usefulness as the basis for a settlement. For the time being our intention is to place our emphasis on the first of these purposes, while we see how the political situation develops. We are of course continuing work on the substance of a neutrality arrangement: you already have a copy of the paper which has been handed to the Americans, the French and the Germans; (and the Department are sending you separately the revision of paragraphs 7 and 8).

3. To judge from the Americans' latest statement, we should have little difficulty in agreeing with them on the use of the neutrality proposal as a mechanism for exerting political pressure. They may be less clear about the feasibility of using it as a basis for a settlement, which could involve the West as well as the Russians in some difficult choices (see paragraph 8 of the enclosed note).

4. You should, therefore, not give the Americans a copy of the paper, nor reveal its existence to them. But you may use it as background in discussing the Afghanistan problem on a personal basis.

5. Reg Hibbert and Oliver Wright should be guided similarly.

Yours ever,
DONALD MAITLAND

ENCLOSURE IN NO. 59

Afghanistan: Neutrality Proposal[4]

1. This note discusses the background to our neutrality proposal, and makes some suggestions about handling.

Soviet Objectives in Afghanistan

2. The Russians have made a major political and military investment in sustaining in Afghanistan a regime which is both compliant and 'socialist'. To provide ideological justification for their action, they have by implication

---

[1] Deputy to the Permanent Under-Secretary of State (and Political Director).
[2] The letter and note were copied to HM Ambassadors in Paris and Bonn.
[3] See Enclosure.
[4] Note prepared by the Planning Staff dated 21 March 1980.

UK-Soviet Relations, 1979-82

expanded the geographical scope of the Brezhnev 'doctrine', under which they consider they have a right to intervene by force to support a Communist government in trouble: hitherto the scope of the doctrine has only applied to the countries of the Warsaw Pact. And they have invented the myth of 'outside interference' to provide a political justification.

3. The Russians will not voluntarily withdraw their troops unless:

(*a*) they have stabilised the situation in Afghanistan;

(*b*) they can be confident that the Afghan regime remains compliant and preferably 'socialist'.

4. But if the cost of remaining in Afghanistan became too high they might settle for withdrawal if they were sure that the Afghan regime would remain pliant, even if not 'socialist'. That is, they might be prepared to settle for a 'Finnish' solution.

Western Objectives

5. The West's objective is simple: to draw the clearest possible line against Soviet expansion in the Third World. In the Afghan context, this means:

(*a*) getting the Russian troops out of Afghanistan;

(*b*) securing the Russians' abandonment (no doubt tacit) of the 'extended' Brezhnev doctrine.

This objective will be fully achieved only if the Russians withdraw unconditionally.

6. The West cannot force the Soviet troops out of Afghanistan through military or effective economic pressure. There remain:

(*a*) political pressure, not so much from the West directly (the Russians will have largely discounted that); but from the non-aligned, among whom the Russians seek to pose as champions of national liberation.

(*b*) military pressure exerted by the Afghans themselves (to be the subject of a separate note).

The Neutrality Idea

7. The neutrality idea is designed to serve these Western purposes on two levels. It can be used to underline the message that it is the presence of Russian troops (and not 'outside interference') which is responsible for the crisis. It is the only constructive proposal in the field, and can help to demonstrate that the West wants a solution rather than a super power confrontation where none has previously occurred. It is thus a useful political weapon to rally non-aligned support and put pressure on the Russians.

8. The neutrality idea could have substantive value as well, as the nucleus for an eventual settlement, perhaps following an international conference. The Russians might eventually welcome this as a way of cutting their losses in the non-aligned world, and inside Afghanistan itself. But the West would not want to accept responsibility for a settlement which did not meet strict criteria, namely:

(*a*) all Soviet troops are withdrawn;

(*b*) the numbers of foreign civilian advisers are limited;

(*c*) India and other non-aligned countries are involved in the political arrangement, so as to make further Soviet military interventions harder;

(*d*) some form of international observation;

(*e*) the Afghan people can endorse their internal arrangements freely (e.g. through a national assembly convoked on traditional lines).

The Russians, as yet, are far from accepting any such arrangement. In their eyes, it would doubtless fall short even of a 'Finnish' settlement. The ultimate choice might thus be between Soviet withdrawal leaving a puppet regime and no Soviet

7 December 1979 – 1 December 1981

withdrawal. The judgement would turn, both for the Russians and for the rest of us, on whether the puppet regime could long survive popular Afghan pressure for something more nationalist and representative.

Handling

9. The neutrality idea has already served a useful political purpose. In principle it is acceptable to the Europeans and the Americans. Reception among the non-aligned has been more varied. Some are doubtful, but a growing number are showing interest as they come to understand it better. In so far as we avoid being specific, we can more easily respond to non-aligned suggestions on substance and presentation (as we have done on the avoidance of the word 'neutralisation', and the incorporation of the idea of non-alignment).

10. It is too early to see precisely how the idea could be worked out to our satisfaction at a conference. We would certainly need:

(*a*) to avoid premature negotiation with the Russians, which could erode our minimum position (paragraph 8) even before the conference met;

(*b*) to be clear before entering a conference about the risks to our interests if it broke down.

Conclusion: Next Steps

11. This leads to the conclusion that we should, at this stage, concentrate on using the neutrality idea primarily as a political weapon, rather than attempting to push towards actual negotiations. This means that we should:

(*a*) go no further into substance with the Russians for the time being, but confine ourselves to advocating the merits of the 'elements' we have already given them and countering their arguments;

(*b*) continue lobbying the non-aligned in order to develop a world-wide intellectual climate in its favour;

(*c*) encourage any tendency among the non-aligned to carry the idea forward;

(*d*) secure the public endorsement of the European Council for Afghan neutrality;

(*e*) lobby Islamic countries in the run-up to the next Islamic Conference;

(*f*) review progress regularly with the French/Germans/Americans;

(*g*) stimulate publicity for what is happening in Afghanistan.

No. 60

Letter from Sir N. Henderson (Washington) to Sir D. Maitland, 3 April 1980[1]
Secret (FCO 46/2179, DPN 061/18)

Dear Donald,

Western Response to Afghanistan

1. I have been thinking for some time that I ought to try to pull together some of the threads of our many reporting telegrams and see if there is not some theme emerging and certain conclusions so far as our own interests are concerned. But on reflection it seems to me too early to do this; so I will give you some tentative impressions and comments in this letter.

2. I am sure there is no need for me to spell out the untidy and uncoordinated method by which the US arrives at its foreign policy, except to say that they are probably worse now than ever before, but that really we can do absolutely nothing

[1] Copied to HM Ambassadors in Bonn, Paris, UKDEL NATO and Moscow.

UK-Soviet Relations, 1979-82

about it. We have to live with it and I believe that from the point of view of British interests we can do so, though there are no hard and fast rules about how we in this Embassy can best play the hand on any particular issue. The thought keeps striking me that the very unsatisfactory nature of the US policy-making process and indeed the great handicaps imposed upon them in their policy should give Europe the chance to put its act together so as to have more resonance in the world. But, looked at from here, Europe has not responded in a very profitable way over the past few months to the opportunities that might have been open to them.

3. The first question that I find people want to know who arrive in Washington from Europe in these very turbulent times is what on earth the Americans are trying to achieve by their uncoordinated responses to the Soviet invasion of Afghanistan. They have taken certain specific actions against the Soviet Union by way of punishment or warning, e.g. the grain embargo, limitations on high technology and the Olympics. So far as the arc of crisis area is concerned they have promulgated the need for a framework of cooperation involving the countries of the area and others outside who are also affected by the Soviet threat; and they have given a new commitment, however undefined to the security of the Gulf area. They are also engaged in trying to create a plausible deterrent in the Middle East and to establishing means by which they could actually provide for military defence in the area if need be. They have specific schemes for setting up military facilities in Oman, Somalia and Kenya. They are hoping to expand the facilities in Diego Garcia. Although we have had no authentic detail about it, I think they may also be nourishing ideas for providing themselves with a considerable military presence in Egypt and Saudi Arabia. But in the two countries which as it were are in the front line, Pakistan and Iran, the prognosis for the USA looks bad. The Pakistanis have rejected the American offer of a new relationship and however much Brzezinski may have persuaded himself about the good faith of the Pakistanis in their commitment to the West, I think it would be going too far to assume that they will never be prepared to accommodate themselves to the Soviets' presence in Afghanistan. In Iran it is difficult to see how, even if the hostages problem can be solved, the Americans are going to be able to make an impact there such as will help prevent the spread of anti-Western influence, in the foreseeable future.

4. What is painfully apparent to me here, after every conversation I have with the Americans in the White House and the State Department, is that they really have no coordinated plan for responding to the new Soviet threat. They see the need to do something and they see certain pieces that must be put into place but they have no overall concept, which partly I think explains why there is all this talk of inadequate consultations; because they are not really clear what exactly it is they want to consult about, except of course to get the rest of their Allies into line on specific matters, such as those referred to in the second sentence of the previous paragraph.

5. This does not stop them being very ready to complain about the inadequate European response. This complaint is made up I suggest partly of scapegoatism, partly of ignorance and partly of genuine disappointment. A constant theme of the American complaint is that the interests of Western Europe are now threatened in the Middle East just as much as are American interests. Why then have the Europeans failed to respond adequately? If anything the German attitude is more perplexing to the Americans than the French, partly because not much is hoped for from the latter. But at first sight it looks here as though the hoped for benefits from

7 December 1979 – 1 December 1981

détente are being stood on their head. The original idea was that the Russians would become so enmeshed in trade and cultural contacts with the West that they would be inhibited from taking action that might disturb this. But what appears to be happening is that it is the West who have developed such important commercial relations with the Soviet Union etc. that they do not want to do anything that may threaten them.

6. Schmidt made an impact here, at least initially, by stressing the vulnerability of Germany in face of the Soviet Union—the problem of Berlin, German refugees from the East, trade dependence, etc. This was linked with his theme that Germany is not a super-power and cannot therefore be expected to play in the big league by purporting to 'punish' the Soviet Union. But here again the Americans are wondering what this really amounts to and what it means for alliance solidarity. Is not the whole point of the Alliance to enable its individual members to withstand Soviet pressure? If Germany is inhibited by potential Soviet pressure on these weak points from taking part in a concerted Western response to Soviet aggression elsewhere, and if that response must therefore be handled entirely by the United States as the only Western super-power with the muscle to face the Soviet Union, has not one arrived at an apparent justification for a division of labour under which the United States alone carries the burden and faces the dangers of responding to Soviet aggression, whilst Germany signs the odd cheque? As regards the feeling of not being big enough, even as part of an alliance, to play a full part in standing up to the Soviet Union: does this not have within it the seeds of the dreaded Finlandisation?

7. I mentioned a failure here to understand European attitudes and this I think certainly relates to *Ost-Politik*. I am sure that Oliver Wright would agree with me that underlying much of the Federal Republic's belief in détente is their unexpressed conviction that without détente there will never be reunification; and although reunification is not something that can be talked about, nor is it something that can be renounced.

8. Whatever the uncertainties about Schmidt's attitude, the fact remains that his preoccupations look here to be less than totally convincing, or at any rate less than immediately relevant when set against the fundamental problem that affects us all: that the United States must be ready for armed conflict with the Soviet Union in South West Asia if there is to be a guarantee of the security of the oil supplies on which the economies of Western Europe and Japan are dependent. And I am sure that we are going to hear increasingly from the Americans about the need for Europeans to shoulder a bigger defence burden in Europe so that the American effort there can be reduced to enable them to play a bigger part elsewhere.

9. Although I absolved France from being the main butt of US criticism at the moment, I must not give the impression that their behaviour is in any way condoned. Giscard's apparent inability to distinguish between independence and non-alignment has caused consternation. If France's principles require them never to be aligned with the United States, what is the value of their supposed attachment to the Alliance in any situation short of total war? I have always been struck by the capacity of the French to infuriate the Americans and for the latter eventually to turn the other cheek and to do nothing that impairs French interests. I think that despite all the irritations here this is probably still the case. But I do think that there is a danger to the interests of Western Europe generally arising from common misunderstandings and annoyances and that the French are certainly able to make a very healthy contribution to this.

UK-Soviet Relations, 1979-82

10. As I have already indicated I do not think it matters too much that our consultative process is faulty. The real problem is not that we do not have adequate machinery, but rather that none of us has a very clear idea on where we ought to be going. There are two contributions that I should like to make towards this problem. Firstly that we ourselves should come to a fairly clear understanding of what the Americans are up to; and second that we should try to get closer together with our main Allies on Soviet intentions.

11. As regards the former, I believe that the essence of what the Americans are trying to do is:

(i) to create a concerted Western response to the Soviet invasion of Afghanistan in order to reassure the countries in the area that they have not been abandoned by the West and that, indeed, it is the West rather than the Soviet Union who are their friends;

(ii) to create this concerted response not merely through discussion with traditional Allies, important though that is, but also through discussion with the Islamic countries and the non-aligned countries generally in order to help them to see where their interests lie and what threatens them; and insofar as possible to encourage them to take initiatives in responding to the enhanced Soviet threat;

(iii) to strengthen the will and capacity of the countries in the area to resist Soviet pressure or an eventual military threat;

(iv) to reduce the likelihood of subversion which could be likely to lead to forms of government that would threaten Western interests;

(v) to create a plausible deterrent against further Soviet military action and to ensure that in the last resort there is a credible defence against it;

(vi) to stimulate a response to the invasion which will convince present and future Soviet leaders that action like that in Afghanistan creates unacceptable damage to Soviet interests;

(vii) and to bring about a situation by which the Soviets either withdraw forces from Afghanistan or suffer heavy damage from remaining there.

12. As regards the idea of an analysis of present Soviet intentions, this I am sure would help to bring closer together European and American viewpoints on what should be done in response. We may perhaps have focussed too narrowly on Afghanistan itself. We have to look at Soviet intentions regarding the flow of oil from the Middle East, whether in their direction or ours; the likely responses of the Middle East oil producers to Soviet threats regarding their oil; the likely trend of developments in Iran and the capacity of the Soviet Union to intervene there directly or indirectly. If there were a common assessment of the medium-term danger to the West arising from the threat to oil supplies, one might move closer to a common view of the significance of the invasion of Afghanistan and of the appropriateness of particular responses to it. I have been left with the feeling here that the Americans see more of a looming cataclysm than most Europeans do and are more disposed to try to avert it. This may be because the French and Germans are wiser than the Americans, or it may be because they prefer to keep their eyes shut. In either case, a closer look at the real nature of the dangers might reduce the gap and increase the response.

Yours ever,
NICKO

7 December 1979 – 1 December 1981

No. 61

Minute from Mr Johnson to Mr Mallaby, 15 April 1980
Confidential (FCO 28/4005, EN 021/1)

An alternative view of Soviet foreign policy after Afghanistan

1. I have been considering whether a case can be made for an assessment of the likely development of Soviet foreign policy over the coming two years or so which would differ somewhat from that in our own FCO paper[1] and that of the JIC. I do not disagree with those assessments, but it may be useful to have an analysis of a darker shade against which to measure our previous evaluations; and in order to see whether the measures recommended in the Planning Staff paper[2] would meet the Western need should Soviet policies take a more aggressive turn than expected. The alternative analysis would run on the following lines.

2. In the Soviet view the effects of the Western response to the invasion of Afghanistan have been no worse than expected. The measures which Western countries have taken collectively (or piecemeal because of conflicting national interests) will have little lasting impact on the Soviet Union. The US grain embargo has been largely circumvented, and the determination of some Western European countries to continue to trade with the Soviet Union will render largely ineffective any attempt to tighten significantly the rules governing the transfer of sensitive technology. The other measures were purely cosmetic and designed more as a sop to public opinion than with any hope of affecting Soviet actions. The Olympics boycott will be incomplete and will do more to show up Western disunity than to harm Soviet interests. It can in any case be used as a rallying point for the Soviet people.

3. The Russians will also consider that the West is unlikely to take further measures over Afghanistan. Iran has shown how the diversity of interests among NATO members can develop into damaging and public discord. Furthermore, the Russians may feel that criticism from Third World countries can easily be tolerated. They may calculate that memories are notoriously short and that the Third World will soon be looking for active support from the Soviet Union and its allies over issues such as South Africa, the new international economic order, US support for dictatorships in Latin America etc. The Russians can also rely on the Arab/Israel dispute placing an effective damper on Islamic criticism of the Soviet action in Afghanistan. They may already expect the next meeting of the Islamic Conference to demonstrate that the participating countries partly climbed down from their high horse and are now looking to mute their criticism of the Soviet Union for fear of losing the latter's active support against Israel.

4. The Russians see the Non-Aligned Movement in disarray, with no respected leader to follow Tito, India playing its own game (not necessarily unwelcome to the Soviet Union) and Cuba able in time to re-assert influence to swing the Movement leftwards.

4. [*sic*] In short, the Russians may feel that there are plenty of issues in international relations affecting what the Third World sees as its vital interests to mean that the furore over Afghanistan will soon subside—or at least will come to be seen as essentially an East-West issue irrelevant to the concerns of developing countries. This will leave the Soviet Union with a free hand to pursue the

[1] No. 47.
[2] See No. 48, note 3.

UK-Soviet Relations, 1979-82

elimination of all opposition to Babrak (or whoever they choose to put in his place); to ensure that the Afghan/ Pakistani border is no longer used to supply the rebels with equipment and fresh recruits; and then, after a period of consolidation, to look for the right time and place to make another forward move. In the meantime there is no need to get involved in serious talks about a political settlement of the Afghanistan affair.

5. All this means that there is no need for the Soviet Union to take any action which might be seen as appeasing the West. It is true that continuing imports of high technology, supplied on credit at rates below those commercially available, and the resumption of overt grain sales to the Soviet Union, would be welcome. But, even supposing that embargoes become more effective than seems likely at the moment, the Russians will be able to get by without supplies from the West. The major elements of the Soviet economy will be given additional investment and the retrenchment which will then be necessary in other areas (e.g. consumer goods) will not be particularly damaging, nor of long duration; it will in any case be accepted by the Soviet people if carefully presented as arising from actions by the United States.

6. In addition, the Russians can calculate that the West will still be eager to obtain supplies of Soviet oil, gas and other essential raw materials; and that the movement of world prices for these commodities will ensure that the Soviet Union's hard currency receipts will not fall by too much. On this view, economic constraints are unlikely to affect Soviet policies to any marked degree.

7. If the Russians are able to ride out the Afghan storm as suggested above, they will be encouraged to pursue their attempts to change the world balance of forces in their favour. They will realise that, while the natural course of events may offer them opportunities to exploit, standstill is not progress and they cannot afford to wait for apples to drop into their lap. They will therefore actively seek to engineer situations, preferably far from the NATO area, which can be manipulated in order to allow Soviet or proxy troops to move in, where possible with a fig leaf of respectability, but where necessary without this. They will see numerous countries where this kind of situation could be brought about, notably in Africa and the Middle East, but also in South East Asia and Latin America where the Cubans can be used to foment civil unrest leading to the emergence of strong left wing movements.

8. The Russians will have assessed the Western reaction to Afghanistan as riven by doubt and conflicting national interests. They will have weighed up Western countries as vacillating, self-seeking, unwilling to give up the good life, too ready to take an optimistic view of likely Soviet actions, too subject to electoral winds of change, and in general too weak and split to offer serious resistance to Soviet expansion. The Russians will regard the West's relative prosperity as its greatest weakness, and may also reckon that an alliance of equals is in the final analysis no match for one dominated by a single, determined and ruthless directing force.

9. The Russians will probably have recognised that their action in Afghanistan has had one unlooked for result in that it has driven the United States to abandon its policy of balance between the Soviet Union and China. The Russians may calculate that the Chinese have greater respect for a strong country or alliance which is prepared to pursue its interests single-mindedly, and if necessarily by military means, than for one which while potentially strong is politically weak. On this analysis the Russians could be tempted to sway the Chinese by further demonstrations of Soviet strength and will power, and thus of Western lack of

7 December 1979 – 1 December 1981

toughness. They may believe that the Chinese will come to see that it is only the Soviet Union which is prepared to be tough when the chips are down, and may therefore decide that their best hope of winning the Chinese away from the West is by further demonstrating that China's dependence on assistance from the self-seeking West is worthless.

10. This assessment contains many points which can be challenged. It is also simplistic. But, while believing that the other papers which have been written recently are probably more accurate, I would not wish to rule out completely a scenario along the lines of paras 2-9 above.

11. The measures identified in the Planning Staff paper to prevent further Soviet expansionism would be appropriate should Soviet policy take this rather more aggressive form; but the need for them to be agreed and set in hand quickly would be the more urgent.[3]

D. J. JOHNSON

[3] Commenting in a minute of 22 April, Mr Murrell agreed the Russians might not be impressed by Western counter-measures but he thought they were worried by the more militant mood now coming from the United States following its 'post-Vietnam torpor'. Moscow would also have to be careful in actively looking for new clients in the Third World to ensure they did not drain their economic and military resources without gaining much political or strategic advantage. He added that he would not underestimate the inhibiting effects on Soviet foreign policy of the fact that problems within Afghanistan had been worse than anticipated. In a minute of 29 April, Mr Broucher took comfort from these factors and concluded: 'The lesson which I draw from all of this is that the present depressing picture is more a result of Western flagellation than of Soviet success . . . The need may be less for a paper about Soviet foreign policy than about the failure of Western coordination and will.'

No. 62

Record of a meeting between Lord Carrington and Mr Gromyko at the Soviet Embassy in Vienna, 17 May 1980, 9 a.m.[1]
Confidential (FCO 37/2252, FSA 020/1)

Present:

Secretary of State	Mr Gromyko
Mr J. Bullard	Mr Dobrynin
HM Ambassador, Vienna[2]	Soviet Ambassador, Vienna
Mr G. Walden	Mr Sukhodrev
Mr P. Lever	

1. *Lord Carrington* said that Soviet ideas on the disarmament aspects of the CSCE seemed not dissimilar to those of the French. It might therefore be possible to take a step forward at Madrid.[3] There were however other baskets involved as well. He had noted Soviet statements that Foreign Ministers themselves should only be involved in the CSCE if, after careful preparation, their participation seemed useful. He himself agreed with this.

[1] Lord Carrington was in Vienna to mark the 25th anniversary of the signing of the Austrian State Treaty.
[2] Mr Donald Gordon.
[3] See No. 30, note 5.

UK-Soviet Relations, 1979-82

2. *Mr Gromyko* said that it was indeed the Soviet view that the CSCE should be well prepared. It was necessary to generate a good atmosphere at Madrid and not to permit the kind of demagogic statements which had been made at Belgrade.[4] As regards the idea of a disarmament conference, the Soviet leadership attached great importance to this. In the Soviet view such a conference should cover questions of military détente and disarmament. But it might be possible to tackle the two tasks separately, with a first stage of confidence-building measures and a second stage of measures of actual disarmament. It would be useful if the Madrid meeting could come out in favour of giving life to this idea. But the Soviet Union did not rule out the option of achieving something concrete at the Madrid meeting itself. If this was not possible, the Madrid meeting should give a mandate to a follow-up conference which would open up positive prospects for the future. Agreement on the idea of convening a Disarmament Conference would be an important catalyst to détente and so inject a warm breath into the general atmosphere in Europe.

3. *Lord Carrington* commented that the warm breath generated in Madrid would be less warm if it did not prove possible to find a solution or accommodation to the problem of Afghanistan. *Mr Gromyko* interjected that he had been surprised that Lord Carrington had not raised this issue at the beginning of their conversation. *Lord Carrington* continued that Britain had a special perspective on Afghanistan for historical reasons. Britain and Russia had been the two countries most involved in Afghanistan in the past: indeed Britain had fought three Afghan wars. (Mr Gromyko asked at this point whether Toynbee would agree with what Lord Carrington was saying). These had stemmed from a distrust of Czarist Russia's intentions towards the warm water ports of the Indian Ocean and the Gulf on the part of British India, and parallel suspicion by Russia of British intentions. Eventually a tacit agreement had been reached that Afghanistan would be a buffer state where neither power would seek to exercise influence to the detriment of the other. This arrangement had continued beyond the British withdrawal from the Indian sub-continent and its partition into India and Pakistan. In the present situation however there was a revival in the West as a whole, not just in Britain, of the fears which had been present in the 19th century. The British government realised that the Soviet Union was self-sufficient in oil, just as was the United Kingdom itself. Nonetheless the Soviet leadership should understand that such fears existed and that they equated in essence with those of the 19th century.

4. This was the background to the British proposal for a neutral and non-aligned Afghanistan which had been reasonably well received in the Third World and among the Islamic countries. Against the background of this proposal, it might be possible to build on the suggestions which had emanated from the present Afghan regime. The germ of an arrangement involving a neutral and non-aligned Afghanistan and guarantees of non-interference from outside seemed to exist.

5. *Mr Gromyko* said that there had in recent times been a number of propaganda statements from various Western capitals, particularly London and Washington, that the Soviet Union was brandishing some kind of dagger aimed at the heart of the Persian Gulf area. Such ideas were sheer nonsense. He was surprised that London had surrendered first prize to Washington in promoting such propaganda. (Lord Carrington said that we might still recover it.) He could assure Lord Carrington categorically that the Soviet Union had no interest whatever in interfering in the Gulf area or in Iran in such a way as to affect the interests of the

---

[4] President Tito's funeral had taken place in Belgrade on 9 May.

7 December 1979 – 1 December 1981

West in the region insofar as oil was concerned. As regards Iran, the only Soviet interest was ensuring the country was maintained as an independent state. It was astonishing that allegations about Soviet intentions in the Gulf area could be made. He could not believe that those responsible for spreading them really believed what they were saying.

6. As regards the historical background, it was possible to draw all sorts of analogies from history. He had taken note of the British statements on Afghanistan's international status and the references to neutrality or neutralisation (*Lord Carrington* interjected that the British government had never used the term 'neutralisation'). If he had understood this idea correctly, it seemed that a large element of the proposal reflected a wish to interfere in Afghanistan's internal affairs by deciding in advance what the international status of the country should be. If so, the Soviet Union categorically rejected such an idea. If, however, the British government thought in terms of the Afghanistan whose regime existed by right and by will of the people—something for example which it would be difficult to say of the regime in Pakistan—and whose international status was accepted as a matter for the Afghan government itself, then Mr Gromyko could say that the Soviet Union had no objection to the assumption by Afghanistan of the status of a non-aligned country. A non-aligned Afghanistan suited the Soviet Union perfectly well.

7. *Lord Carrington* said that he took note of and welcomed Mr Gromyko's assurances about Soviet intentions in the Gulf. But what made people in the West suspect otherwise was the scale of the Soviet military intervention in Afghanistan. The lesson of history was that Afghanistan wanted to be an independent and neutral country. Britain had no wish to interfere internally in the affairs of Afghanistan but could not accept interference by other countries either. *Mr Gromyko* said that statements had been made in London concerning the need for a change of regime in Afghanistan. He asked whether the British government was in favour of the existing regime or whether it necessarily wished to see that regime changed. *Lord Carrington* replied that his only wish was to see a regime chosen by the Afghans themselves free from machinations and interference from the outside. As seen from London it was primarily the Soviet Union who were interfering in Afghanistan. He did not believe that the Afghan people would, if free to choose for themselves, opt for the kind of regime which existed at the moment. He could however be proved wrong. If so this was the Afghans' own business and the British government would respect their choice. It was a fact however that a million Afghans, who were now refugees, had voted with their feet on the subject.

8. *Mr Gromyko* said that there existed in Afghanistan a regime and a leadership. He wanted to know whether the British Government accepted it or believed that it must necessarily be changed. The Soviet Union believed that on historical and scientific grounds there would come a time when the present capitalist and economic formation would be replaced by another system of the kind which the Soviet Union believed in. They did not however expect Western governments to endorse this view: time would show which interpretation was correct. It would however be quite another matter if the British government held a deeply-rooted non-belief in the regime in Afghanistan and was convinced that it must be replaced. It was the British Government's business how it saw the problem. But in the Soviet view what was needed was an agreement between the countries concerned, namely Afghanistan, Pakistan and Iran, which would provide for appropriate assurances of non-interference in Afghanistan's affairs. In this case the

UK-Soviet Relations, 1979-82

conditions would be created for the withdrawal of all Soviet troops and the Afghans would be capable of deciding for themselves on the internal and external orientation. [It is not certain that Gromyko used the word 'all'; Sukhodrev's interpretation was a trifle casual and impressionistic at some points.] He could assure Lord Carrington that the Soviet troops in Afghanistan were not there to interfere in the country's internal affairs. Even with the aid of a lantern in broad daylight it would be impossible to see Soviet troops in action in Afghanistan.

9. *Lord Carrington* said that he wondered whether the two countries' views were so far apart. He did not himself believe that the Babrak Karmal regime represented the wishes of the Afghan people, but if they did so he was willing to recognise this. He agreed on the need to stop interference with Afghan affairs whether from the Soviet Union or anywhere else. If the Afghans chose freely to endorse the Babrak Karmal regime this was their affair and the British government would accept this: there were plenty of governments of which the United Kingdom might not necessarily approve but which it recognised as representing the wishes of the people in the country concerned. The British government's only object was to avoid the imposition of a regime on Afghanistan from the outside whether from the Soviet Union or anywhere else.

10. *Mr Gromyko* said that there must be agreements between Afghanistan and Pakistan and between Afghanistan and Iran, although the Iranian angle was less topical since there had been fewer armed intrusions into Afghanistan from that country. Such agreements must provide for the termination of armed intrusion into Afghanistan and the provision of appropriate political guarantees. The Soviet Union would not object to the participation of certain other states in the provision of these guarantees if this was the wish of the countries directly concerned. Such agreements could also deal with the doubts which the Pakistan government seemed to have about its frontier with Afghanistan. Once agreement had been reached the question of Soviet troop withdrawals could be resolved as well. The Soviet military contingent in Afghanistan could not be withdrawn in a matter of seconds: withdrawal was a process, and time would be needed. But Pakistan could, if it wished, raise this question during the negotiations with Afghanistan. The result of the agreements could be that Afghanistan would adopt the status of a non-aligned state. This should suit both the United Kingdom and the United States; he had noticed that Mr Muskie[5] had not objected to an idea of a non-aligned Afghanistan. He hoped however that the British government would explain clearly to the Pakistan leadership the need for them to enter into negotiations with the Afghanistan government.

11. *Lord Carrington* said that guarantees of non-interference into Afghan affairs and guarantees on the withdrawal of Soviet troops would need to proceed hand in hand. Actual withdrawal of the Soviet military forces might take some time but the decision to withdraw them could be taken in seconds. It was important that there should be no delay in this respect. He repeated the need for an independent Afghanistan to be able to select a government of its own choice without any interference from outside. This meant that there should be no interference from the Soviet Union through troops or through political advisers.

12. *Mr Gromyko* said that the contingent of Soviet forces had been introduced into Afghanistan in accordance with agreement between the Soviet and Afghan governments and would be withdrawn in accordance with this agreement. Its

---

[5] Edmund Sixtus 'Ed' Muskie, was appointed US Secretary of State on 8 May 1980 following the resignation of Cyrus Vance.

7 December 1979 – 1 December 1981

withdrawal was not a matter for formal negotiation with Pakistan. Nonetheless the Soviet and Afghan leaderships had made statements that the contingent would be withdrawn if appropriate international guarantees were achieved. He was sure that Lord Carrington could accept Soviet assurances on this point.

13. Mr Gromyko said that he had one other matter to raise. He had seen reports from London that the British government had approved a plan to set up a fund for a memorial to the so-called victims of Yalta.[6] The British government had itself been a participant in the Yalta Conference. He found it impossible to believe that the British government could be involved in a project of this kind but had been told that the Prime Minister herself had sanctioned it. He would be grateful for Lord Carrington's comments.

14. *Lord Carrington* said that he had two observations to make in reply. Firstly, the proposed memorial was funded by private individuals in the United Kingdom. The Government was involved only in the sense that its approval was required for the erection of the memorial on Crown land and the Prime Minister had decided not to withhold such approval. Secondly, there was a different interpretation of history in the United Kingdom to what there was in the Soviet Union: a large number of people in Britain took a different view from the Soviet leadership of the events in question.

15. *Mr Gromyko* said that having heard this explanation, he could only regard the British government's decision as a hostile act in respect of the Soviet Union which the Soviet leadership would have to take into account, and 'would not remain in our debt'. He had nothing more to say on the matter. *Lord Carrington* said that he did have some more to say: the erection of the Yalta memorial was not intended as a British hostile act towards the Soviet Union, rather it was a memorial to those who had died.

16. In an informal conversation after the end of their meeting Lord Carrington suggested to Mr Gromyko that the UK and Soviet positions were not as distant as they might seem, and that we should keep in contact over the Afghan problem. *Mr Gromyko* agreed.

[6] The Yalta memorial was erected in Thurloe Square South Kensington in March 1982 and dedicated to the peoples forcibly repatriated to the Soviet Union and Yugoslavia between 1944 and 1947. It was severely damaged in October 1982 in an attack using an electric masonry saw. A new work entitled *Twelve Responses to Tragedy* was completed in 1986.

No. 63

Minute from Mr Mallaby to Mr Bullard, 19 May 1980
Secret (FCO 28/4005, EN 021/1)

Soviet Position on Afghanistan

1. It is hard to be sure, following the Vienna meetings, whether the Soviet position on a peaceful settlement has changed in substance. Since the beginning of the year, Moscow's position in essence has been that Soviet troops would be withdrawn once the reasons for their presence had ceased to exist, i.e. once all intervention had ceased. The Afghan proposals of 14 May[1] and Gromyko's

[1] The proposals put forward by the Afghan government called for bilateral agreements with Pakistan and Iran to normalise relations and for political guarantees, provided by both Moscow and Washington, for an overall settlement acceptable to Kabul. A precondition of the plan was that the

UK-Soviet Relations, 1979-82

remarks to Mr Muskie set out basically the same position. Instead of talking merely of the cessation of everyone else's intervention as a pre-condition for Soviet withdrawal, the Russians are talking of bilateral agreements between Afghanistan and Pakistan and Afghanistan and Iran and a US 'commitment to ban subversive activities against Afghanistan including those being launched from the territory of other countries.' As noted in FCO teleno 117 to Vienna,[2] there is nothing in the present Soviet position to suggest that there would be any undertakings about withdrawal before the Russians had had time to see whether armed resistance ceased after the conclusion of agreements with Pakistan and with Iran. I think it certain that armed resistance would not cease, since it is far from dependent upon the present situation on the Pakistani (and Iranian) borders. The continuation of resistance would enable the Russians to say that interference had not ceased and therefore that the pre-conditions for withdrawal had not been created.

2. We have also considered whether the Russians have any particular reason at the present moment to decide to negotiate more seriously. Here, of course, our knowledge is incomplete. It is very likely that they under-estimated world reactions and the military difficulties before they invaded Afghanistan. But that will have been clear to them for several months now. While non-aligned pressure for negotiations has recently been growing, this may give the Russians a reason for more seeming [sic] willing to negotiate than for serious negotiations involving concessions. It is only several weeks since the spring in Afghanistan enabled the Russians to begin to use their invading forces more effectively. Until they have had the summer to see what they can achieve by military force, it seems unlikely that they will have any military reason for recourse to serious negotiations.

3. On the other hand, Gromyko, in his talk with Lord Carrington, seemed to be a little more explicit about the possibility of withdrawal than before. He said the Russians would definitely withdraw once agreement was reached; and that the process of withdrawal was open to negotiation and could be raised by Pakistan in talks with Afghanistan (paragraph 5 of Vienna telno 177)[3].

4. The question whether the Russians are willing to contemplate serious negotiations can only be answered if their views are actively investigated. We should persist in our dialogue with the Soviet Union, to maximise any chance of real negotiations. At the same time as doing so, we and the West should maintain the pressure on the Soviet Union designed to make the occupation of Afghanistan uncomfortable and should step-up actions to assist the resistance in Afghanistan.

5. As soon as we have an account of President Giscard's meeting with President Brezhnev today, and of the conclusions reached on Afghanistan by the Islamic

US should express a clear commitment not to engage in any subversive activity against Afghanistan, including from the territories of third countries.

[2] Not printed. This telegram of 15 May set out the main elements of the Afghan proposal and suggested a number of questions which the Foreign Secretary might wish to raise at his meeting with Mr Gromyko. These were: '(a) would the Soviet Union give, during the Afghan negotiations with Pakistan and with Iran its undertakings to withdraw? And would this involve a timescale for complete withdrawal? Or would the decision on withdrawal come only after the two bilateral negotiations had been completed? (b) The Afghan proposals speak of Soviet guarantees. What undertakings would the Soviet Union be prepared to give in this connection? (c) Is the USSR willing that negotiations for a peaceful settlement should consider the security of Afghanistan's borders with other states than Pakistan and Iran?'

[3] Not printed. This telegram reported the meeting between Lord Carrington and Mr Gromyko (see No. 62).

7 December 1979 – 1 December 1981

Conference, I will submit a telegram of instructions to the Ambassador in Moscow.[4] This will revert to the questions in FCO teleno 117 to Vienna and add some others. The additional questions would explore further the question of Soviet withdrawal and whether the Russians would be willing not only to discuss withdrawal during Afghan-Pakistani negotiations but also whether the entry into force of an Afghan-Pakistani agreement and some US undertaking could be interdependent with binding Soviet undertakings to withdraw within a certain time-scale. Another question would be about the Afghan remark that the issue of Soviet withdrawal 'relates specifically to the solution of the question of effective guarantees in connection with bilateral agreements between Afghanistan and Pakistan and Afghanistan and Iran'. We could ask whether this means that the guarantees which the Soviet Union has said it would give of these two bilateral agreements would include guarantees to withdraw on a specified time-scale.

6. I suggest that we should inform our partners, when we are ready, that we propose to have another round with the Russians and give a brief account of the sort of questions we shall be asking.

7. SAD concur.[5]

C. L. G. MALLABY

[4] No. 66.

[5] Mr Bullard commented that he agreed the right course was to continue on the same three lines as at present: '(*a*) Help to the Afghan resistance movement, including efforts to ensure that the facts reach the general public, so that Gromyko cannot continue to maintain that the Soviet troops are not doing any fighting . . . (*b*) Bring political pressure on Moscow through the Third World, maintaining and elaborating our own ideas for a political solution. (*c*) Pursue the dialogue with the Soviet Union direct . . .'

No. 64

Minute from Mr Mallaby to Mr Braithwaite, 20 May 1980
Secret (FCO 49/895, RS 021/7)

Meeting with the Prime Minister on East-West Relations
1. This minute records the main points arising from the 30 minutes of discussion of East-West relations in the Prime Minister's office this morning. The Secretary of State, the PUS, Mr Alexander, Mr Walden, you and I were present.

2. The Prime Minister said she had found the FCO papers fascinating and extremely interesting.[1] She had read every word. She saw great similarity between FCO views and those in the paper written by her academic advisers, although the academics of course knew less than the officials and could not put as much flesh on their ideas.

3. There was some discussion about the BBC Overseas Services. The Prime Minister displayed some sympathy for those who argued that the BBC should broadcast in Ukrainian. The Secretary of State said that news about Britain on the BBC World Service presented far too black a picture of this country. The Prime

[1] Papers by the Planning Staff entitled 'The Management of East-West Relations' and 'Destabilising of Soviet Client States' were sent to No. 10 on 2 May. The Prime Minister also had a paper entitled 'Western Strategy in the Wake of Afghanistan' written by her academic advisers: Michael Howard, Elie Kedourie, Leonard Schapiro and Hugh Thomas (PREM 19/238).

149

UK-Soviet Relations, 1979-82

Minister mentioned twice the need to boost the signal of the BBC overseas broadcasts.

4. In a discussion of signals and levers for use against the Russians, there was general agreement that we needed to review the subject in the light of experience since Afghanistan. One of the ideas mentioned was that we might develop a range of moves which could be made when the Russians were seen to be preparing a military move, i.e. *before* the event rather than after it. It was relevant that the Russians had twice prepared for a military move which they had not carried out; the most important case was in 1973 after the American nuclear alert; the other case was during the Chinese 'lesson' against Vietnam.

5. I have recorded separately the main points made about 'destabilisation' of states in the Soviet orbit.

6. The meeting concluded with the decision that three papers should now be written in the FCO:

(*a*) a sanitised version of the paper entitled 'The Management of East-West relations' for OD,[2] which if possible should meet in the first week of June. Sub-para 3(*f*) and other references to 'destabilisation' would be deleted. Sub-para 3(*d*) and the other references to propaganda would be recast, to avoid the word 'propaganda' (the Prime Minister's point) and to bring out the need to disseminate the truth about Western countries as well as about the USSR, Cuba etc.

(*b*) a paper on our aims in the political discussions at the Venice summit.

(*c*) a first draft of what the Prime Minister would say at Venice.

7. We are discussing para 3 today with Lord N. Gordon Lennox. I will write a paper on levers etc. and the draft needed under 6(*c*). You will do 6(*a*) and (*b*).

C. L. G. MALLABY

[2] No. 65. The original version of the paper had the classification 'Burning Bush'—the code words covering all papers referring to Quadripartite discussions (between the US, UK, FRG and France), in particular the restricted format of 'Heads of Government Representatives' initiated by Mr Brzezinski in January 1980. The sanitised version omitted references to covert action and to Tripartite and Quadripartite discussions (PREM 19/238).

No. 65

Memorandum by Lord Carrington for the Defence and Oversea Policy Committee on the Management of East-West Relations, 2 June 1980[1]
OD(80)43 Secret, UK Eyes Only (CAB 148/191)

1. The Soviet invasion of Afghanistan was the latest in a series of Communist military interventions in the Third World which began in 1975 with the Cuban-backed installation of a Marxist regime in Angola. The invasion highlighted the difference between Western and Soviet expectations of 'détente'. The Russians have always made it clear that they saw no incompatibility between 'détente' and the continuation of what they called the 'ideological struggle'. But the use of

[1] A paper on the management of East-West relations was originally drafted by Mr Braithwaite of the Planning Staff and sent to the Prime Minister on 2 May. Following a meeting on 20 May (see No. 64) the paper was modified by Mr Braithwaite for discussion at OD and the covering letter added.

7 December 1979 – 1 December 1981

considerable Soviet forces outside the countries of the Warsaw Pact marked a new departure, and justifies a renewed look at the basis on which the West seeks to manage the East-West relationship.

2. The Russians' ideology, and their aspiration to rival the American superpower, mean that they will persist in their drive to shift the world balance of power (the 'correlation of forces', as they call it) in their favour. But they have always flinched from a direct military confrontation with Western forces. Despite their growing military power, there is no evidence that they have now abandoned this fundamental caution. But they will undoubtedly continue to probe for new opportunities and pick up new client states where they can. They affect to believe that history can only work one way—in the direction of Communism—and will try to establish 'socialist' regimes in client states, and, unless the risks are too great, to defend such regimes by force.

3. In Europe, and in the Far East, the West has long been aware of the need to contain the Russians. Since the late nineteen forties we have constructed a network of military and economic relationships which have successfully contained the Russians and prevented them from expanding in Europe beyond the limits set by the advancing Soviet armies in 1945. But in Latin America, Africa and Asia we have been less successful. The military organizations which we and the Americans set up in the nineteen fifties on the analogy of NATO have collapsed or faded away. The Baghdad Pact, SEATO, CENTO have all fallen victim to local politics. Issues such as the Arab-Israel dispute, Southern Africa, economic tensions between North and South, seem to the countries of the Third World more directly threatening than the Russians.

4. Yet the spread of Russian economic, political and military power in the Third World is a real threat to our own interests. If the East-West relationship is to be put back on to a more secure basis, free of the illusions which characterised the 'détente' of the 1970s, we need to find ways of countering Russian influence in the Third World, as well as making it clear to the Russians themselves that we regard many of their activities there as illegitimate.

5. I have no illusion that this will be easy. The methods that worked in Europe are not applicable elsewhere. Much depends on our ability to improve our political, military, and economic relations with the developing countries, and to help them solve their pressing political problems—things we would be interested in even if the Russians did not exist. But the West as a whole, and we in particular, are hampered by the consequences of world recession and straitened resources. These also limit our capacity to respond directly to the Russian threat by military and other means.

6. Yet there are a number of things which we are doing, or could do, which could improve the situation. The attached paper by officials[2] sets these out. It calls for no new decisions, but is intended both as a basis for discussion at our meeting in OD on 5 June, and as a guide for further work in Whitehall and in consultation with our allies, much of which has already been set in hand.

---

[2] See Enclosure.

UK-Soviet Relations, 1979-82

ENCLOSURE IN NO. 65

The Management of East-West Relations

Summary of Conclusions and Recommendations

1. We need above all to restore the coherence of the West. This means improving the existing arrangements for consultation, and perhaps devising new arrangements to bring in the Japanese and Australasians (paragraph 10).

2. We need to improve the North-South economic relationship and to seek solutions for political problems of particular concern to the Third World (paragraph 15).

3. In addition we should:

(*a*) Review the scope for putting economic and other pressure on the Russians (paragraph 13);

(*b*) Develop our capacity for long range military intervention outside the NATO area (paragraphs 17-20);

(*c*) Improve our arrangements for giving military assistance in the Third World (paragraph 21);

(*d*) Review our machinery for countering Soviet propaganda (paragraphs 22-24);

(*e*) Develop our links with Third World political organizations (paragraphs 28-29).

4. Work is already in hand on some of these. Only modest changes in existing arrangements may be needed: we have in any case few resources available. For this and other reasons, we need effective cooperation with our allies, and an appropriate division of tasks. Some possibilities are indicated in the body of the paper.

Background

5. The West has developed a number of arrangements for managing the relationship with the Soviet Union and its allies, covering defence, the negotiation of political and arms control agreements in the mutual interest, the development of political, commercial and other links. These arrangements remain adequate in principle for managing the direct East-West relationship. They depend, however, on the West's cohesion, its determination to maintain adequate forces, and its willingness in a crisis to use both its levers of pressure on the Soviet Union and its channels of communication. Recent events have called these in question: paragraphs 7-14 below therefore consider how existing arrangements might be improved.

6. But in the 1970s existing arrangements were insufficient to prevent repeated Soviet intervention in the Third World. Here the problems are more complex. In the 'North', the East-West confrontation is explicit, Soviet ambitions are contained, and most countries know well enough which side they are on. In the 'South', most countries hope to evade being caught up in the East-West conflict. They feel considerable resentment toward the West, partly because of past history, partly because of their continuing economic dependence on the developed West for their markets, industrial products, aid and education. Because the West is also to some extent dependent upon them they hope to extract concessions through political and economic pressure. By contrast the Russians have ambitions rather than real interests in the Third World: they can move into (or out of) situations and countries at little cost, provided they can avoid a direct military confrontation with

7 December 1979 – 1 December 1981

Western (or overtly Western-backed) forces. They offer military assistance and an ideology which is attractive to guerrilla movements and to authoritarian regimes in newly dependent countries. They have hitherto been little criticised for their poor economic aid performance. But their invasion of Afghanistan may lead to a more clear-sighted view of Soviet policies in this and other fields. Paragraphs 15 to 30 below consider what policies the West should pursue to reinforce such a trend.

The Management of East-West Relations in the 'North'

Western Consultation and Coordination

7. The essential basis for all our dealings with the Russians has always been the healthy functioning of relationships within the West itself, combined with clear and purposeful leadership by the United States.

8. These relationships are managed formally within the Atlantic Alliance and the European Community; and less formally through the irregular Summits of the Seven and other *ad hoc* gatherings. These arrangements have a number of weaknesses. NATO is precluded by its terms of reference from dealing with (or— for the most part—even discussing) issues arising outside the 'treaty area'. Some of its members have strongly resisted change, and the French insist on independence. The European Community, though a powerful influence in international affairs because of its economic weight, is rarely able to agree on effective political action, and is precluded from dealing with defence issues. The Summits of the Seven, an important function of which is to involve the Japanese beyond their narrow relationship with the US, meet too seldom and have hitherto dealt with economic issues. Apart from the US link, there is no arrangement for involving the Australians and New Zealanders, despite their concern with Soviet ambitions in the 'South'.

9. As long as the West did not face a divisive crisis, these weaknesses did not matter much. The situation has been changed by the crises in Iran and Afghanistan, and by the vacillation, confusion, and ineptitude of the present US administration. The lack of a clear and consistent lead from the Americans, and their preoccupation with their hostages in Tehran, risks greatly increasing the scope for Soviet meddling in Iran, and encouraging the Germans to develop policies in Eastern Europe which go beyond or cut across the policies of the West as a whole: this it has been the object of all post-war policy to avoid. In the interests of solidarity with the Americans, which all recognise as an overriding interest, the Europeans have adopted policies in which they do not believe. The multiplication of 'consultations' has hardly helped: it has done little to reduce misunderstanding between the Americans and the Germans, and too often the Americans have failed to follow through their own proposals, either through muddle or because they have changed their minds.

10. In these circumstances we need:

(*a*) to strengthen our relationship with the French and Germans. This will be a frustrating and painful process, for well-known reasons. It will need much patience. But the Europeans will not be able to function effectively unless they are reasonably united; and this depends on the maximum possible convergence of British, German and French views.

(*b*) to strengthen our direct links with the Americans, and to encourage them to consult fully, not only with us, but with the French and Germans as well.

(*c*) to develop the political cooperation of the Nine. The FCO has been

UK-Soviet Relations, 1979-82

examining ways of improving the administration of political cooperation (e.g. by strengthening the Presidency). This might be pursued, though it is unrealistic to expect dramatic improvements in the present cumbersome way of doing business.

(*d*) to continue to nudge NATO towards discussing issues outside the treaty area; and to get the Americans in particular to make more genuine use of the North Atlantic Council for political consultation (their Permanent Representative was not even in Brussels for the first weeks of the Afghan crisis).

(*e*) to devise better ways of involving the Japanese and Australasians. Bilateral relations will continue to be important. The network of meetings between officials for preparing political discussions could be maintained beyond the Venice summit of the Seven. The recent meeting between the Japanese Foreign Minister and the Nine set a useful precedent: the Presidency might be instructed to follow it up both with the Japanese and the Australasians when issues became ripe for useful discussion. It would probably be unnecessarily cumbersome to formalise the political consultations of the Seven by setting up new institutions, and the French have said they are against it.

Defence Arrangements in Europe

11. Despite the obvious connexion between the two, the defence arrangements of the Alliance are, for the present at least, in a slightly better state than its political arrangements. Provided that members of the Alliance stand by their existing decisions and meet their commitments, then the increase in defence budgets, the adoption of new programmes by the United States, the agreement of theatre nuclear forces, will all help to sustain the essential minimum military means for deterring Soviet adventures in the NATO area. But there are signs that even on these military issues Alliance resolution may be wavering; and the French refusal to participate in the integrated military structure is still a stumbling block. The chief problem, however, (discussed in the previous paragraph) is to ensure that the political basis is not eroded. Military arrangements outside the NATO area are discussed in paragraphs 17-20 below.

East-West Links: Threats and Levers

12. The East-West political links developed in the 1960s and 1970s worked well enough in the past as an instrument of crisis management. The most important channel was the secret link between Presidents Nixon and Ford (and Dr Kissinger) and Mr Brezhnev. As far as we know, this channel is not working at present, partly perhaps because of disarray in Washington, and partly because the Soviet leadership is moribund. Public exchanges (East-West summits, visits to Moscow etc) are less effective for crisis management because they can give opportunities to the Russians to divide allies and put pressure on Western opinion. The severance of such public exchanges as an expression of displeasure at Soviet actions or a warning to Moscow against actions in preparation is a gesture which can have value but cannot easily be long sustained: their resumption is a matter of timing.

13. In recent years the Soviet Union has ceased to strive for economic autarky: it is beginning to become dependent on the world economic system. To some extent, East-West trade can create a two-way dependence (e.g. Germany's interest in East European trade and gas supplies may affect her political judgement, as Poland's may be affected by her current debt problems). But the West has some real economic levers (grain, credit, and technology) and used them after Afghanistan. It is not clear how far these sanctions have affected Soviet actions, or

7 December 1979 – 1 December 1981

will deter the Russians from future adventures. But they have presumably raised the cost of the invasion to the Russians; they could be further extended in the current crisis; and they could be used again. One possibility for a future crisis would be for key Western countries to impose a selective embargo to hit Soviet industries particularly dependent on imported technology. The commercial and political problems are substantial, and the West is unlikely to agree on a completely effective embargo short of a near total breakdown of East-West relations. But we need to review our experience over Afghanistan, and to consider future possibilities in discussion with our allies if we are serious in trying to create leverage against the Russians. Work has already begun on this question within the FCO.

14. Other East-West links—professional, cultural and human—may have an intrinsic value, and are certainly welcome to the peoples of Eastern Europe and the Soviet Union. Their contribution to political evolution in those countries is likely to be slow and uncertain. Their severance in a crisis is unlikely to weigh much with Soviet policy makers, though it may be a necessary public gesture of displeasure by the West.

Soviet Expansionism in the 'South'

15. A new policy is needed to contain Soviet expansionism in the Third World, as a major addition in the 1980s to Western policies towards the Soviet Union. This will require measures both to constrain the Russians and to influence the actions and attitudes of the Third World countries themselves. This latter element would be designed to strengthen the resistance of the developing countries to Soviet infiltration and intimidation. It would involve, in the first instance, tackling problems with which the Russians have little direct concern: the overall economic relationship between the developing world and the developed West; the need to reduce the West's dependence on uncertain oil supplies by conservation and the development of alternative sources of energy; the Arab-Israel dispute; racial disputes in Namibia and South Africa. These and others are problems to be handled separately and on their merits, rather than as part of on[e] overall plan for countering the Russians. But if these problems could be solved, or mitigated, the Russians would lose much of their scope for making trouble where the West, but not they, have real political and economic interests at stake; and Western coordination would be made easier by the removal of points of dissension, e.g. on policy towards the Palestinians.

16. In our dealings with the 'South'—on aid, in the North-South dialogue, and in our political exchanges—we therefore need to keep the East-West aspect in mind. And in addition there are a number of things the West can do to counter Soviet influence in the Third World more or less directly.

Military Measures: Long Range Intervention Forces

17. A Western capacity to use force at a distance can have three purposes:

(_a_) to intervene locally to protect our interests, or our friends;

(_b_) to deter or oppose military action by a Soviet proxy;

(c) to deter a Soviet military move in the Third World by posing the risk that a direct local clash could escalate.

18. The West's capacity to do these things has declined since Vietnam and the British withdrawal from East of Suez. But the French regularly intervene in local quarrels, and American plans for a Rapid Deployment Force will substantially increase their capacity especially in the Indian Ocean. And because people are always worried when a superpower intervenes, there may be a particularly useful

UK-Soviet Relations, 1979-82

role here for modest European forces.

19. Ministers have agreed that we should improve our capacity in a modest way, and the Ministry of Defence are conducting studies. When these are completed we should consider military discussions with the French and Americans about the cooperative use of our forces before or during a crisis (the French have already shown some interest in talks) and about a possible role for the Australasian forces in South East Asia and the South Pacific.

20. We might also examine the scope for more extended military cooperation with the Japanese: Japanese domestic politics may become slightly less of an inhibition in future.

Military assistance

21. Military aid to developing countries is an effective way of influencing their policies, as the Russians have found. It should be a central element in our own policies. Military aid consists of:

(*a*) Training assistance (on which we will spend only £5.2 million in 1980-81);

(*b*) The provision of loan service personnel e.g. to Sudan (which will cost £2 million in 1980-81);

(*c*) Very occasionally, the provision of cheap, or free military equipment (e.g. to Zambia in 1978/9 at a cost of £7 million).

A review of overall policy in this field is being undertaken. The first priorities will be to establish an adequate scale for our assistance programme and to reach conclusions about its nature and financing. Once this has been achieved, the review should also consider the possibility of increasing our efforts to achieve a sensible division of tasks between ourselves and our allies.

Political Measures: the 'ideological struggle'

22. The Russians have always proclaimed the right to conduct the ideological struggle despite 'détente'. They attack Western domestic arrangements and foreign policies. They strongly resent Western counter-propaganda as an illegitimate interference in their affairs.

23. Ministers have said in public that they do not accept this 'one way option', and that we welcome the ideological struggle. But our machinery has been run down. We do not need elaborate or extensive arrangements of the kind we had in the past. In any case, we do not have the money. But within the limits of our resources we need:

(*a*) arrangements to produce high quality and carefully tailored material angled towards audiences in the Soviet bloc and the Third World;

(*b*) arrangements to disseminate this material, if appropriate by covert means.

Modest work is being done, especially following the Afghanistan invasion. The External Services of the BBC play an important role. So do Ministerial speeches disseminated by the COI.

24. We should review:

(*a*) whether the existing arrangements could be streamlined to get better value for money;

(*b*) whether more money is needed, and where it might come from;

(*c*) whether there is scope for cooperation with allies.[3]

Non-Alignment: Third World Political Organizations

25. Soviet relations with the Third World have come under increased strain not only as a result of Afghanistan, but as developing countries look beyond

---

[3] A paper on the 'Management of East-West Relations: countering Soviet propaganda', dated 1 December 1980, was subsequently produced (FCO 28/4011, EN 021/2).

7 December 1979 – 1 December 1981

propaganda and at, for example, the inadequacy of Soviet economic aid.

26. We cannot expect the Third World to abandon non-alignment. But we can hope to undermine its earlier bias towards the Soviet Union. Some of this is a matter for the ideological struggle (see above). Among other things Ministers have made appropriate references in recent speeches. But we also need to get close to Third World policymakers, and their own institutions for coordinating foreign policy. There is some scope for cooperating with the Non-Aligned Movement (NAM) and our Ambassadors are under instructions to be positive about the movement and to the philosophy of genuine non-alignment. The Islamic Conference is another important vehicle of Third World opinion; our discussions in April with the Secretary-General, Mr Chatty, about Afghanistan are an example of the cooperation we are seeking to develop. Relations with ASEAN are developing well.

27. No new decisions are needed in this field for the time being.

Economic Measures: Aid

28. Massive and carefully directed economic aid buys political support, as the Russians have demonstrated in Cuba, Afghanistan and Vietnam. Ministers have decided in principle to give greater weight to political and commercial considerations in framing our current Aid Programme. The cuts in our aid will fall particularly heavily on our bilateral programmes. We are trying to concentrate where we can on politically vulnerable countries, e.g. Turkey, Pakistan and Zimbabwe, though the sums we now have available are unlikely to make a dramatic difference.

29. The Americans, Germans, French and Japanese all give more aid than we do. We should examine what scope there is for persuading our allies to move in where we cannot (the Germans are already increasing their aid to Turkey and Pakistan for example).

No. 66

Lord Carrington to Sir C. Keeble (Moscow), 3 June 1980, 9.40 a.m.[1]
Tel. No. 342 Priority, Confidential (FCO 28/4006, EN 021/1)

MIPT: Representations to the Soviet Union on Afghanistan[2]

1. Following is text of speaking note:

The talks between Mr Gromyko and Lord Carrington in Vienna[3] were positive evidence of the scope for a continued dialogue about Afghanistan. The UK starts from the premise that the Soviet Union is willing to seek a political solution to the problem of Afghanistan. The UK shares this objective and continues to believe that a good basis for a settlement would be the resumption by Afghanistan of its traditional status of neutrality and non-alignment. The problem of Afghanistan has badly damaged East/West relations. A political settlement would make possible the resumption of progress in East/West relations which the UK desires. However, the

---

[1] Repeated for Information to Washington, Paris, Bonn, UKDEL NATO and Rome.

[2] Not printed. This telegram reported that recent Western contacts with Soviet leaders had not demonstrated any change in the Soviet position but that HMG wished to probe further to establish whether there was any hope of moving towards serious negotiations. Sir C. Keeble was directed to seek a meeting with Mr Zemskov and to convey the points contained in the speaking note.

[3] No. 62.

UK-Soviet Relations, 1979-82

British and Soviet views about the elements for a settlement have so far been very different. Our purpose now is to see whether there is scope for progress in bringing them closer together.

A positive outcome is likely only if the pre-conditions on all sides are reduced to a minimum. For the UK, the main requirement is that a political solution must lead to the complete withdrawal of Soviet forces and to guarantees of non-intervention in the future by other states, including the USSR. These elements must be organic parts of a political settlement, interdependent with the other elements, not something to be added afterwards on the basis of unilateral decisions. The UK has noted statements of Soviet willingness to envisage withdrawal if certain conditions are fulfilled and that the process of withdrawal is open to discussion. For example Mr Brezhnev said on 27 May that the date for the beginning of withdrawal and for further steps in this direction could be decided in the framework of a settlement. It would materially assist the search for a political solution if the Soviet authorities could say whether this means that discussion of a timetable for withdrawal could take place at the same time as discussions on other aspects of the problem and that undertakings by other countries on the other aspects could come into effect simultaneously with withdrawal.

As the above shows, the UK recognises that, if Soviet forces are to be withdrawn, the Soviet Union will expect certain obligations from others. The UK believes that there is no Western government which would not be prepared in the framework of an acceptable settlement to give firm undertakings, in parallel with the Soviet Union, of non-interference in Afghanistan. The UK would be interested to learn the Soviet position on this and on the statement by Afghanistan on 14 May that the issue of Soviet withdrawal relates specifically to the question of effective guarantees.

The UK does not wish to determine the political complexion of a future Afghan government: indeed it is essential that the government in Afghanistan should be chosen without outside pressure. The present regime was installed after a military coup, in circumstances which give rise to doubts about its popular mandate, not to speak of its legality. Internally the regime faces strong opposition. Externally, it has failed to win the approval of the international community. Insistence that a political solution must start with the present leaders is likely to block progress, since it does not address the causes of the discontent in Afghanistan or the concern of the international community. Does the Soviet Union agree that the future of the Afghan government should be decided and, seen by the international community to be decided, by the Afghan people themselves, without outside interference?

The Warsaw Pact's statement of 15 May called for a summit of world leaders to remove 'hot-beds of tension'. The Islamic Conference in Islamabad called for a conference on Afghanistan. In the British view a summit of all states would be too cumbersome for effective negotiation and would unnecessarily duplicate the role of the UN General Assembly. What are Soviet views on the possibility of an official conference, the likely participants, the terms of reference and the location?

7 December 1979 – 1 December 1981

No. 67

Extract from minutes of the Cabinet Defence and Oversea Policy Committee, 5 June 1980
OD(80) 15th Meeting Secret (CAB 148/189)

The Management of East-West Relations

The Committee[1] considered a memorandum by the Secretary of State for Foreign and Commonwealth Affairs (OD(80)43)[2] on the management of East-West relations in the light of the Soviet invasion of Afghanistan.

The Foreign and Commonwealth Secretary said that the Soviet invasion of Afghanistan demonstrated the need for a fresh approach to the management of East-West relations. In Europe, a system had evolved under which each side knew and observed certain basic rules of restraint. Elsewhere, experience had led Soviet leaders to believe that no such rules applied. The lack of effective response to their moves in Angola, Ethiopia, and the People's Democratic Republic of the Yemen had no doubt persuaded them that the West would not react differently to their invasion of Afghanistan. They had probably been astonished by the strength of the actual reaction, involving not only the United States but also the unprecedented condemnation of the Soviet Union by 104 members of the United Nations. It was necessary to build on this in order to improve the West's capacity to meet the continuing Soviet challenge in the world. The modest proposals summarised in paragraphs 1-4 of the Note by his Officials[3] annexed to his memorandum were the outcome of long discussions about how Britain should contribute to that process.

In general discussion, it was suggested that the large increase in Soviet power relative to the West which had occurred over the past decade was largely a result of weak United States leadership. But there were other reasons for Western disarray: e.g. the insistence of the French on an independent posture; and the growing West German economic interdependence with Eastern Europe, which was beginning to have disquieting political manifestations. It was therefore all the more important that Britain, despite her more limited economic resources, should continue to contribute a strong political and ideological lead. The English language gave British spokesmen great influence; and Britain's moral authority was respected by many countries particularly in the Commonwealth, where settlement of the Rhodesian problem had removed a major cause of contention and distraction. There was also increasing evidence that Third World countries were coming to recognise the irrelevance of Soviet ideology and Soviet weapons, to the solution of their real problems. The failures of the Soviet system were evident in the flow of refugees from Vietnam and Cuba and in the resistance of the Afghan tribes. At the same time, it had to be recognised that Britain's resources were limited. At a time of little real growth she was already allocating 5 per cent of her Gross Domestic Product to defence and planned additions which could bring this proportion to 6 per cent over the next 5 years. Yet even this represented less in total than the Germans could produce with their present expenditure of 3.3 per cent on defence. For the same reason, Britain was not well placed to give a lead in meeting the economic aspirations of developing countries. They sought trade opportunities

---

[1] Those present were Mrs Thatcher, Lord Carrington, Lord Soames, Lord Hailsham, Geoffrey Howe, Ian Gilmour, John Nott and Lord Strathcona.
[2] No. 65.
[3] Enclosure in No. 65.

UK-Soviet Relations, 1979-82

even more than aid. This meant openings for their exports in sensitive sectors and contributions to the proposed Common Fund for commodities, which Britain could not afford to provide. At the same time it was suggested that the British could do more to present themselves as sympathetic to the aspirations of the 'South'. More substantively, the impact of aid should not be underestimated. The Russians' total aid-giving might be small, but their take-over in Afghanistan, for example, had been preceded by a large civil aid programme over a long period. The United Kingdom aid programme was less flexible and less effective politically because of the high proportion allocated to multilateral assistance; at present this was about one-third of the total, but planned reductions would fall disproportionately on our bilateral aid programmes. A further important weakness was that in rigidly separating the defence, aid and overseas budgets, the British Government tended to lose sight of the fundamental links between defence, aid and foreign policy objectives.

In further discussion of the specific proposals put forward by the Foreign and Commonwealth Secretary the following points were made:

(*a*) Efforts at mobilising Britain's allies, on the lines proposed in paragraph 10 of the Note by Officials, in spite of the difficulties referred to, could make a contribution to greater political coherence in the West. There were impediments to using the North Atlantic Treaty Organisation (NATO) as a forum for facing Soviet challenges in the Third World; for example political nervousness on the part of Nordic member states, the independent attitude of the French, and constitutional limitations for the Germans, as well as the geographical limits written into the Treaty. But to accept these impediments as overriding would allow the Soviet Union to bypass the West's political defences. The forthcoming 7 power Summit Meeting in Venice would provide a good opportunity for discussion of these fundamental issues.

(*b*) There were many complexities in our relations with developing countries which had an indirect bearing on the Soviet threat. In the Caribbean, for example, governments had come to power which were so subject to Communist influence that we had been obliged to abandon our aid programmes. There was also a close connection between the political and economic turmoil in the West Indies and the tensions felt by the West Indian communities in Britain.

(*c*) In considering the scope for bringing economic pressure to bear on the Soviet Union while encouraging trade with selected countries in Eastern Europe, a number of conflicting factors, had to be kept in mind. Although the West as a whole would benefit from restricting trade credit, a country which broke ranks, as France had recently done, could expect advantages at a time when most of Western industry was short of orders. Studies within the Department of Trade had also shown that the United Kingdom would be far more vulnerable to a trade embargo than the Soviet Union, which was the source of supply for certain key minerals otherwise only obtainable from South Africa. Restraint on the supply of technology to the Soviet Union could lead to a diversion of Soviet technical effort from military to civilian purposes; but it might also tempt the Russians to take by force what they were prevented from buying. The American grain embargo, though only partially successful, had had considerable impact. It was unfortunate that the Olympic boycott, which entailed no economic cost, had not been more complete.

(*d*) Good progress was being made in the work to develop our capacity for long range military intervention outside the NATO area. Only a modest diversion of

7 December 1979 – 1 December 1981

resources would be involved; and talks would be held with the Americans and French to co-ordinate planning without creating new administrative structures. It would be necessary to exchange views with the United States before broaching with the Japanese (as suggested in paragraph 20 of the Note by Officials) the idea of more extended military co-operation.

(*e*) The link between defence and foreign policy objectives was demonstrated by the arrangements for providing military training assistance. Such assistance did not guarantee that the recipients would confine their purchases of equipment to the United Kingdom, as India's and Zambia's large deals with the Soviet Union had shown. But it could make a valuable impact on the attitudes of recipient governments and, as with the provision of Loan Service Personnel to Oman, could serve our defence interests as directly as by maintaining troops in Germany. The Ministry of Defence should not seek to recover from the Foreign and Commonwealth Office Vote more than, at most, the marginal cost of military training assistance. Accounting changes apart, some additional resources might need to be provided for this type of assistance; since this should fall within the approved total of Government expenditure, it would probably have to be at the expense of other forms of defence expenditure.

(*f*) In considering the scope for countering Soviet propaganda, the independence of the British Broadcasting Corporation (BBC) from political direction, and its impartiality, were recognised as important assets. But the Overseas Service tended to give a generally gloomier picture of events in the United Kingdom than the domestic services. It would be in the British interest, and without risk to the BBC's independence from partisan political control, for the Government to appoint as Governors of the BBC persons having both a keen interest in the Overseas Service and the time to bring their influence to bear at the level where day-to-day editorial decisions were taken.

The Prime Minister, summing up the discussion, said that the Committee agreed with the objectives outlined in the Foreign and Commonwealth Secretary's memorandum. Their discussion had brought out the essential unity of purpose in the Government's defence and foreign policies, including aid policy. Expenditure decisions, within the overall limits agreed, should reflect this unity. While there were clear economic and other constraints on the action the United Kingdom could take to counter the effects of Soviet power, many countries looked to the United Kingdom to give a political lead. The studies and initiatives proposed by the Foreign and Commonwealth Secretary should provide a suitable basis for action to this end. While the Committee would need to consider further any proposals which entailed an increase in public expenditure (e.g. in relation to the minor expenditure mentioned in paragraph 24f of the Note by Officials attached to OD(80)43) it should be possible to meet the costs of the Government's military training assistance programme, including a modest increase in it, by the introduction of more realistic methods of financial adjustment between the Ministry of Defence and the Foreign and Commonwealth Office.

The Committee:-

1. Took note, with approval, of the Prime Minister's summing up of their discussion.

2. Invited the Foreign and Commonwealth Secretary to carry forward the proposals set out in paragraphs 1-4 of the Note by Officials attached to OD(80)43.

3. Invited the Chancellor of the Exchequer, in consultation with the Foreign and

UK-Soviet Relations, 1979-82

Commonwealth Secretary and the Defence Secretary, to consider how to introduce more realistic methods of interdepartmental accounting which would leave the basic costs of service personnel participating in the United Kingdom military training assistance scheme to be met from the defence budget.

4. Invited the Foreign and Commonwealth Secretary and the Defence Secretary to consider jointly, in consultation with the Chancellor of the Exchequer, how to ensure that the agreed resources available for foreign policy objectives (including aid) and defence policy objectives were treated as a single 'pocket' from which expenditure could be flexibly directed towards meeting the requirements of national security in the broadest sense.

No. 68

Sir C. Keeble (Moscow) to Lord Carrington, 11 June 1980, 2.31 p.m.[1]
Tel. No. 402 Priority, Confidential (FCO 28/4006, EN 021/1)

Your Telno 342[2] (not to all): Call on Zemskov.

1. Zemskov received me at midday today. I prefaced my remarks by saying the events of the past few days had shown the situation in Afghanistan to be deteriorating and added to the urgency of a political solution.[3] I then took him through the points in your telegram under reference, emphasising that the link between undertakings and a withdrawal was crucial to us. I left a speaking note behind.

2. Zemskov undertook to report what I had said. Meanwhile his personal impression was that some of our premises were unrealistic, and that what I had said took matters no further than your conversation of 17 May with Gromyko in Vienna.[4] Two points in particular struck him. First, it was time to stop talking about a change of government in Afghanistan. To do so was unrealistic. The Soviet Union would not interfere in Afghan internal affairs.[5] Secondly, he thought a mutual understanding had been reached in Vienna about the non-aligned status of Afghanistan but here we were harping on our old 'neutral and non-aligned' theme again. So far as withdrawal was concerned, the Soviet position was clear. First, there would have to be guarantees of non-interference, and then withdrawal on the basis of agreement with the Afghan government. This was not a pretext for delay. The fact was Soviet troops were in Afghanistan at that government's request and it was therefore a juridical necessity that the Afghans should ask for their withdrawal, as no doubt they would once guarantees were made. I would know, he continued, it had not been easy for the Soviet government to accede to the 14th [of May] Afghan request.[6] Lastly, he wanted to take me up on my assertion that the situation had deteriorated. It was true that interference had spread and intensified, but the internal political situation had in fact improved. He made no comment on the question of a possible conference, nor did he refer to the Afghan proposals of 14 May.

---

[1] Repeated Routine to Washington, Paris, Bonn, Rome and UKDEL NATO.
[2] No. 66.
[3] Probably a reference to the death of 16 Soviet soldiers killed in an ambush in Kabul on 8 June.
[4] No. 62.
[5] A large exclamation mark has been inserted into the margin of the text at this point.
[6] See No. 63, note 1.

7 December 1979 – 1 December 1981

3. In reply, I repeated what you said to Gromyko in Vienna, that what government the Afghans should have was for them to decide. Not for Britain or the Soviet Union. If they wanted the present regime, well and good. But the evidence was they did not. On neutrality, I said I did not wish to add to what had been said in Vienna. On his final point, I emphasised once again that what mattered was the precise link between withdrawal and undertakings. It ought to be possible to work out a formula which would make commitments to both simultaneous with a timetable for withdrawal settled at the outset, to be followed by implementation of the timetable and the undertakings. We had seen a possible gleam of hope in this respect in some of Gromyko's remarks. I urged him to consider this part of the problem with particular care and to observe in relation to the situation in Afghanistan the realism he was urging on us. Despite his fairly trite comment— which was all to be expected—Zemskov seemed to take the communication seriously, saying that it would be studied carefully and a reply given in due course.

4. FCO please pass saving to Kabul, New Delhi and Islamabad.

No. 69

Letter from Sir C. Keeble (Moscow) to Mr Bullard, 17 June 1980
Confidential (FCO 28/4008, EN 021/2)

Dear Julian,

Western Response to Afghanistan

1. I was unfortunately not able to comment at the time on Donald Maitland's letter of 24 April[1] and its enclosures and now, on my return from leave, I hesitate to offer a belated intervention. So far as the Planning paper[2] is concerned, it is perhaps enough to say that you will have known from my letter of 16 January to Christopher Mallaby[3] that the main thrust is one which I welcome. I agree with most of the comments you have already received and on the detail I would mention only two points:

(*a*) The resumption of China's activity in the developing world is an element which could in part offset Soviet influence. It would of course raise a host of separate problems, particularly in South-East Asia, and would not be easy to deal with adequately in a paper, even of the length of the enclosure to Donald's letter, but it does rate a mention.

(*b*) I was struck by Donald's statement (paragraph 7 of his letter) that where a pessimistic and a relatively optimistic view of Soviet intentions are possible, policies should be based on the worst assumption. I have some doubts about this. The worst contingency in many instances would be direct Soviet military involvement. It is right that we should prepare for this, but only as one of a number of possibilities and in most cases an unlikely one. I would prefer to see policy based not on the worst assumption, but on the most probable.

2. My main purpose in writing now is to consider not so much the detailed matters dealt with in the April paper as the broader philosophy for the future conduct of East/West relations. In my Annual Review for 1979[4] I said that I

[1] Not printed.
[2] Enclosure in No. 65.
[3] No. 40.
[4] No. 24.

163

UK-Soviet Relations, 1979-82

thought the Secretary of State's despatch of 7 December[5] still read well in the light of the Soviet occupation of Afghanistan and I was glad to see from Donald's letter that it still forms the basis of our policy. Afghanistan does however make it necessary for us to take policy further. I start from the assumption that the Soviet Union will, within say the next year or so, neither attain such a degree of control over Afghanistan that it can afford to withdraw leaving the situation stabilised in its favour, nor recognise failure and withdraw in circumstances which will lead to the replacement of the Babrak Karmal regime by one which is not subservient to Soviet interests. In the long run the latter may well happen, but I would have thought it would more probably be a matter of ten years than of one year.

3. If my assumption is right, we have to prepare for a period of several years during which Soviet forces will remain in Afghanistan and there will be no logical case for relaxation of the measures adopted by the West at the beginning of this year. Indeed in logic there would be a case for their intensification. But we must all recognise that, unless there is a major new development of Soviet aggressive policy elsewhere, or an intensification of activity in Afghanistan to the point of arousing an even greater degree of international abhorrence than was expressed in January, the tendency will be for counter-measures to fade and for Western policy on direct relations with the Soviet Union—as distinct from our policies in the third world—to begin to revert to the 1979 state. I would not have thought it worth while writing now to make these rather obvious points had I not seen Washington telegram 2168.[6] The risk which I see is presumably what worries Brzezinski. What we need to do if we are to reduce to a minimum the potential policy divergence between the United States and Europe is to analyse the probable state of East/West relations during the next year or so in terms of realistic policy options. If we do so we may find that the divergence is not nearly as wide as it appears from the analysis in paragraph 6 of that telegram. If we do not we may saddle ourselves either with a divergence from which only the Russians will gain, or with policies which we cannot sustain.

4. Most people would agree that Soviet foreign policy, of which the occupation of Afghanistan is only an example, albeit an extreme one, is constructed on a philosophical basis of struggle which must produce a state of tension with those who resist that philosophy. It has often enough been pointed out in our own policy studies that the concept of détente has not been applied and is not intended to be applied by the Soviet Union so as to enable two different types of society to move forward in harmony. It is applied in order to enable Soviet communism to win. (At one's kindest one might say that it is reminiscent of the doctor relaxing his patient before the operation.) Détente, misleading though it is, is a term too hallowed by use and too cherished by the French and Germans, to be dropped. But the reality is that so long as Soviet policy remains as it is, a state of tension in East/West relations is inevitable. It is a situation not of our making and not flowing just from Afghanistan. For this reason I find it unrealistic to talk in terms of 'a return to détente' (paragraph 11 of Donald's letter). The contrast is not as absolute as that. What we have to do is in fact, so to manage a situation of tension as to minimise the risk to Western security and to promote Western interests. We have done this in the past. It is as reasonable to regard the progress which has been made over the years in inner-German relations as the product of successfully-managed tension as 'the *acquis* of détente'. But realism also means that, while the management of a

[5] No. 1.
[6] Not printed.

164

7 December 1979 – 1 December 1981

tense relationship may on occasion require the gesture of a breaking of contacts (which is itself more effective if in normal times there is a web of contacts), over a longer period it requires, even when the tension is extreme and perhaps particularly then, an active policy, one which involves contact at all levels and mutual accommodation where this can be negotiated on satisfactory terms. This is not a soft policy. The objectives and tactics can and should be hard. But it can be compatible with SALT II ratification, with subsequent negotiations on nuclear weaponry, with the pursuit of German _Ostpolitik_, with French self esteem and with a hard line at Madrid. Continued pressure for a full Soviet withdrawal and a genuinely independent Afghanistan are essential elements. We should not break the link between Soviet policy in Afghanistan and Western policy elsewhere, but should make it clear to the Soviet Union that in the field of direct East/West relations it is now the more necessary for them to demonstrate their good faith. However, if we are to be realistic we should probably not present a Soviet withdrawal from Afghanistan as a precondition for progress in other areas, because to do so may be to condemn ourselves in advance to an apparent short-term failure.

5. To try to develop these ideas further would be to range over all the current and prospective areas of East/West negotiations. That I cannot do. In any case there cannot be any one prescription which will reconcile all the conflicting Western interests. All I would argue is that we may make it a little easier to maintain Allied solidarity on the basis of sensible policies if we can get away from the unrealistic choice between freeze and détente; avoid making a Soviet withdrawal from Afghanistan the price for a so-called 'return to détente'; and prepare instead for the long haul management of a state of continuing tension, in which the various aspects of East/West relations are dealt with on their merits, recognising the essential malevolence of Soviet policy and exploiting its weaknesses.

6. I am sending copies of this letter to Nicko Henderson, Oliver Wright, Reg Hibbert and Clive Rose.

Yours ever,
CURTIS KEEBLE

No. 70

Letter from Sir C. Keeble (Moscow) to Mr Bullard, 25 June 1980[1]
Confidential (FCO 37/2259, FSA 020/8)

Dear Julian,

Afghanistan Troop Withdrawal

1. It is already beginning to be a little easier to assess the significance of the announcement about the withdrawal of certain forces from Afghanistan.[2]

2. Looked at from a Western point of view it seemed at first that the timing

---

[1] Copied to British Ambassadors in Bonn, Paris, Washington, New Delhi, Islamabad and Chancery in Kabul.

[2] On 22 June, TASS issued a statement that a number of military units whose presence in Afghanistan was not essential had been withdrawn to the territory of the USSR by agreement with the Afghan government.

165

UK-Soviet Relations, 1979-82

must have been influenced by the Venice meeting and the imminent Schmidt visit.[3] The Russians may also have had the Islamic Committee meeting in Geneva in mind. Brezhnev's action in writing to Giscard clearly showed a desire to exploit the move *vis-à-vis* the West and this tendency is taken a little further in an authoritative *Pravda* article today, which we are reporting to the Department separately, contrasting the welcome allegedly given by 'leaders in France and a number of other European countries' to this indication of the Soviet Union's serious intention to work for a political settlement and American attempts to belittle the move in order that they may continue to support the 'armed aggression' against Afghanistan.

3. The desire to influence Western opinion cannot however be the full explanation. It was not without significance that apart from the preparations for the XXVI Party Congress, Afghanistan was the only question dealt with, in Brezhnev's statement to the Central Committee, at any length. The statement and the resolution (my telno. 431)[4] smelt as though they covered a difficult discussion and I have now heard from the Americans that they have received two separate reports indicating dissension in the Plenum, one from someone said to have been present at the meeting. The American Embassy are doubtful how much credence they should give to these reports, but it is probable that internal considerations played a significant part in the Soviet decision and that the date of the Plenum itself was decisive for the timing of the announcement. Some of the language used in the Central Committee statement reflected language used by Falin when he spoke to the German Ambassador a week or so ago. Falin, after claiming that the main rebel groups had been broken up had said that it was now a matter of extinguishing those who would be left and using the most modern methods to achieve this in order to avoid loss of life among Soviet forces. Not unnaturally the last part of his statement has not been reproduced in public. It may however be that the line of argument within the leadership went something like this: The Afghanistan campaign has gone badly, from both the political and the military point of view. The Soviet forces were constituted too much on the Hungary-Czechoslovakia model, designed to subdue and exercise swift control over an organised State but unsuitable for prolonged guerrilla warfare. A choice had to be made between massive conventional reinforcement in an attempt to control the whole country or an intensification of aerial operations combined with an attempt to improve the internal political situation. With the prospect that concern among the Soviet population about the level of casualties might rise if the campaign proved prolonged, it was necessary to present an appearance of Soviet success and willingness to make peace combined with a justification for continuation of the operation and a strategy designed to minimise future losses. Whatever the arguments may have been I am sure the conclusion was that the Soviet Union could not afford to concede defeat in Afghanistan and that there could be no prospect of a substantive withdrawal in the foreseeable future. This would explain the treatment of the withdrawal itself in the Soviet press: it has certainly not so far been presented as the first stage in fulfilling the Soviet promise to pull out when Babrak gave the word. But presumably the announcement of the withdrawal in Kabul will itself necessitate an intensification of the campaign if those who may

---

[3] On 30 June Chancellor Schmidt and Hans-Dietrich Genscher visited Moscow and held discussions with the Soviet leadership on the situation in Afghanistan and the deployment of medium range nuclear weapons in Europe.
[4] Not printed.

7 December 1979 – 1 December 1981

still find themselves on Babrak Karmal's side are not to start hedging their bet. So it is natural that today's *Pravda* article drives home the final point of Brezhnev's statement, arguing that not only was the United States organising intervention in Afghanistan, but that certain circles in Pakistan and Iran were trying, through the 'so-called Afghanistan Committee' to justify intervention in the internal affairs of Afghanistan and concluding that although the enemies of the Afghan people were not prepared to lay down their arms, 'democratic Afghanistan had true friends who had shown their solidarity and would help Afghanistan in future with its defence'.

4. One may, in short, conclude that the withdrawal announcement reflects concern about the whole operation and a certain vulnerability to both internal and external criticism, but that there is as yet no indication whatever that the Soviet Union will do other than seek to achieve and sustain by military means effective control over Afghanistan.

Yours ever,
CURTIS KEEBLE

No. 71

Sir C. Keeble (Moscow) to Lord Carrington, 2 July 1980, 1.41 p.m.[1]
Tel. No. 457 Priority, Confidential (FCO 28/4006, EN 021/1)

Your Telno. 397[2] (not to all): Afghanistan

1. Zemskov asked me to call at mid-day today to receive the Soviet answer to my representations of 11 June (my telno 402).[3] The text of what he had to say, which effectively ignored our own points and was totally negative is in MIFT.[4]

2. I told Zemskov I would report his statement. I did not think it could be received with anything other than deep disappointment. I had noted in his remarks and in other Soviet statements repeated references to the need for realism. In the British view, a realistic assessment of the position in Afghanistan would be that there had been a largely unsuccessful attempt to impose an alien form of government on a people who were not prepared to accept it. As this became increasingly apparent the USSR had decided to use Soviet forces in an attempt to ensure by that means the success which had eluded it when it had tried to achieve its aims by other methods. I had to say this bluntly because repeated Soviet statements sought to present the matter in the unreal terms that the problem arose because of foreign interference. Zemskov said he rejected my interpretation of events and my assessment of the nature of the Afghan government. Soviet views were well known and he had nothing to add to what was contained in his oral statement. I said I had one more point to make at the present time on the latter.

[1] Repeated for Information Routine to Kabul, Washington and UKDEL NATO; Saving to UKMIS Geneva, Paris, Bonn, Islamabad and New Delhi.
[2] Not printed. This telegram reported the joint statement issued by President Brezhnev and the Indian Foreign Minister which made no reference to Afghanistan and stated that on major international problems, the views of the Soviet Union and India were close.
[3] No. 68.
[4] Not printed. This telegram reported the oral statement made by Zemskov which reiterated the Soviet position that withdrawal of troops would only take place after armed attacks from outside Afghanistan had ceased and that the British government 'could help in ensuring that the governments of Pakistan and Iran adopted a more realistic position'.

UK-Soviet Relations, 1979-82

This was that the ideas put forward by the Afghan authorities for a political settlement had also to be judged in the light of what was really happening. The British position was founded on the British view of the realities.

3. I took the opportunity to say I had been struck by the reference in what the Soviet Ambassador in Kabul had said to the Italian chargé on 24 June (Kabul telno 206)[5] to further troops being sent into Afghanistan if necessary. This had come oddly at a time when the Soviet government was talking in public about withdrawal and when the rest of the world was hoping that those statements reflected the first steps leading towards a total Soviet withdrawal. Zemskov said that everything depended on whether or not external aggression was stepped up. The Soviet side had taken a positive step and would naturally expect others to reciprocate. I commented that this brought us once again back to our difference on the realities of the situation.

4. This latest Soviet statement fits well into the policy already established by Brezhnev at the Central Committee plenum, in the exchange with Schmidt, in Gromyko's handling of my American colleague and in the *Pravda* editorial. It confirms that there is no desire for serious discussion of measures which could lead to definitive Soviet withdrawal, but that, on the contrary, the Soviet government is determined to do whatever is necessary to bring Afghanistan under its control. In that situation it seemed as well to leave no doubt on the Soviet side about the reality as we see it. It was interesting that Zemskov was not really prepared to argue the point. His brief was fairly clearly to discourage any attempt to continue a dialogue on other than Soviet terms.

[5] Not printed.

No. 72

Paper by East European and Soviet Department on UK Policy in East-West Relations, 15 July 1980[1]
Secret, Confidential (FCO 28/4009, EN 021/2)

Introduction

1. The Russians, barring a reversal of policy, will not withdraw from Afghanistan unless they can leave behind a government which they can rely upon

[1] This paper was written following a request from Lord Carrington's Private Office 'for a short paper on where we stand in East-West relations, particularly with regard to the resumption of East-West contacts; and what role the UK should seek to play in the next half year or so'. It was later endorsed by Lord Carrington as a 'useful piece of work'. Although he agreed with the principles he did not see himself actively promoting them but rather talking round them in routine contacts. He also commented that the paper 'if anything understated the importance of developing contacts with Eastern European countries' and more could be said about cultivating relations with Third World countries as a means of strengthening Britain's position when dealing with the Soviet Union.

Mr Blaker agreed with the broad lines of the paper but had reservations about the proposal to resume contacts in paragraph 7(*b*). He thought Dr Kissinger's notion that the West should develop levers for use against Russia by increasing trade was in danger of rebounding on the West. 'The Franco/German desire for trade with the Russians will make it more difficult (i) to get Western agreement on a more effective use of economic levers against the Russians (except perhaps in the event of a direct and serious threat in Europe) and (ii) consequently to propagate the idea that détente is indivisible' (Minute by Miss Marles, APS, 29 July 1980).

Guidance Tel. No. 95 (No. 76) informed HM Representatives of developments in the approach to East-West relations.

7 December 1979 – 1 December 1981

to be both durable and compliant. No such government can at present be established. The Russians seem intent on pursuing a military solution, and probably believe that the West will come to live with the Soviet military presence as it has with the one in Czechoslovakia since 1968. It therefore seems clear that Afghanistan will remain the major factor in East-West relations for some time and that this situation is more likely to end because the West acquiesces than because the Russians withdraw.

2. The Western Alliance has so far been united in insisting on complete Soviet withdrawal from Afghanistan. There is no risk that this position will soon be abandoned. But major Western countries have differed about the attitude to be adopted in relations with the Soviet Union since the invasion and these differences have recently been highlighted by Giscard's meeting with Brezhnev,[2] Schmidt's visit to Moscow,[3] signature of the Soviet/German Long Term Economic Programme and news of negotiations on a gas deal which may increase from 16 percent to 25 percent the Soviet share of the gas consumed in the FRG. At a less exalted level, a difference has again developed between the credit rates offered to the USSR by France on the one hand and the other members of OECD on the other. There is an obvious risk that Western countries, while continuing to condemn the invasion in words, will drift back towards business as usual with the USSR and fail to take all the feasible steps to deter Soviet expansionism. What Western policies should the UK promote?

British Objectives

3. The Secretary of State's despatch of 7 December 1979 to Moscow[4] concluded that the United Kingdom has no exclusively national interests in East-West relations but a general interest in ensuring that the West maintains the balance of power and minimises the risk of Soviet acts which could significantly upset it. This suggests that the UK should try to ensure that the West (*a*) does everything it can to maintain the pressures on the Russians to withdraw from Afghanistan and to prevent them from concluding that they have got away satisfactorily with the invasion, and (*b*) develops a convincing strategy for preventing more Afghanistans. This implies that the West should maintain and if possible strengthen the measures taken against the Russians after Afghanistan; and that the UK should seek to apply the brakes if our European allies start trying to return to normal. In practice, however, from the start there have been significant differences of approach between the French and Germans on the one hand and the Americans (followed by the UK) on the other, about how far pressure over Afghanistan should require the sacrifice of specific interests in Europe; not only are these differences unlikely to be resolved but, for the time being, the Americans show signs of being resigned to the eclipse of their own approach. Nevertheless, while as a rule avoiding the thankless and sometimes impossible role of transatlantic honest broker, especially during the current pre-electoral period,[5] we should try to promote the maximum agreement that circumstances allow, within NATO and among the Nine.

4. The first two lines of policy in the 7 December despatch—the maintenance of Western defences and acceptance of the Soviet challenge to a struggle of ideas—

---

[2] On 19 May, Presidents Giscard and Brezhnev met in Warsaw for a one-day summit to discuss Afghanistan and East-West relations.

[3] See No. 70, note 3.

[4] No. 1.

[5] i.e. before the 1980 US Presidential election.

UK-Soviet Relations, 1979-82

apply *a fortiori* after the invasion of Afghanistan. The questions for consideration concern the other three main lines of policy: developing East-West contacts, deterring Soviet expansion in the developing world and pursuing East-West negotiations.

East-West Contacts

5. High level Soviet-Western contacts have been re-established by Gromyko's visit to Paris in April, his meetings with several Western foreign ministers in Vienna in May, Giscard's meeting with Brezhnev in Warsaw and Schmidt's visit to Moscow. The avoidance of such contacts from Christmas until April helped to demonstrate, not least to its own public opinion, Western disapproval of the invasion of Afghanistan, though with the inevitable sacrifice of communication during a period of crisis. As time went by, the need to talk to the Russians about Afghanistan rightly came to prevail over other arguments. High level contacts will now continue. It is not in Britain's interest to be left out. The UK needs such contacts to explain our views to the Russians, to explore shared interests and not least so that our views on dealing with the Russians will carry weight with our Allies. But the political climate in the UK and the relative lack of content in British-Soviet relations mean that we need such contacts, in particular at head of government level, less often than do other Europeans.

6. Brezhnev and Kosygin have invitations to visit the UK dating from the last Anglo-Soviet Summit, which took place when Sir H. Wilson visited Moscow in February 1975.[6] A renewal of their invitations now, against the background of our statements in January that we would avoid high level contacts with the USSR, would be criticised in the UK (and the US) and would probably not lead to a visit by Brezhnev or Kosygin. Gromyko too has an outstanding invitation: dates were under discussion before Afghanistan but the Russians postponed the visit after the invasion. The best next step may be for the Secretary of State to meet Gromyko again in the traditional way during the UN General Assembly (i.e. at least one and a half months after the Olympics) and to consider in the light of that whether to renew the invitation to Britain.

7. We and some of our Allies have avoided certain types of contacts with the USSR at other levels, from Ministers responsible for technical subjects to discussions between officials about CSCE. Half a year after the invasion of Afghanistan, some contacts are being revived. For instance, Soviet Deputy Prime Minister Tikhonov has visited Bonn and several of our partners are discussing preparations for Madrid bilaterally with the Russians. The UK cannot prevent this. The best tactic is to advocate, and ourselves apply, certain realistic principles:

(*a*) Resumption of all the contacts with the USSR which existed before Afghanistan would imply that we had accepted the occupation of that country;

(*b*) Contacts which deal with real substance and routine scientific, academic and cultural exchanges and also Round Tables can resume/continue as long as they are in Western countries' interests. The presumption in marginal cases should be against resumption and publicity should not be encouraged;

(*c*) Other less substantive contacts, for instance major cultural events, and goodwill visits like Parliamentary exchanges, should be avoided so long as the problem over Afghanistan remains: so should military exchanges, for obvious reasons;

(*d*) Any contacts that do take place should be used to reiterate the Western

---

[6] Prime Minister Harold Wilson's visit to Moscow is documented in *DBPO*, Series III, Vol III, Chapter IV.

7 December 1979 – 1 December 1981

position on Afghanistan;

(*e*) The measures taken against the USSR after Afghanistan should be fully maintained.

8. The reference to Western countries' interests in (*b*) above is relevant to a series of cooperation agreements which the UK (and others) have with the Soviet Union. The most important of ours is the Long Term Agreement on Economic, Scientific, Technological and Industrial Cooperation of 1974 and the related annual meetings of the Anglo-Soviet Joint Commission led on our side by Mr Parkinson. The 1980 meeting in London was postponed from May. The policy outlined above would allow it to take place in due course. Our Allies are certain to pursue such meetings and there is no advantage to the UK in avoiding them. But some of our lesser cooperation agreements, such as those on Environmental Protection, Agricultural Research and Medicine are of far less value to us and have given unreciprocated benefits to the Soviet Union. Activity under them has virtually lapsed since Afghanistan. Some Whitehall Departments would like to take the opportunity to scrap these agreements because of their lack of concrete value, especially against the background of UK expenditure cuts. But Anglo-Soviet political relations would suffer badly if we cancelled a number of agreements. Other countries are not likely to do so. We are conducting a review of each; one approach might be to tell the Russians that certain selected agreements must be renegotiated on the basis of reciprocity and that we will not maintain them unless there is a balance of advantage.

9. Eastern Europe is a different matter. As the 7 December despatch said, we need contacts with Eastern Europe in order to encourage diversity. We also need now to put across our views on Afghanistan: not for many years has there been an issue which divides the East Europeans so much from the Soviet Union. In any case there is no reason to blame the East Europeans for Soviet misdeeds which they do not welcome. Our contacts with Eastern Europe are running at a higher level than usual this year: the Prime Minister is going to Yugoslavia; the Secretary of State has been to Romania and is going to Poland and Hungary in October; and Mr Blaker intends to visit the GDR, Czechoslovakia and Bulgaria. There will be a good case for the Prime Minister to visit Poland next year. We should maintain the level of activity thus established rather than increasing it further to keep pace with France and Germany. These two Allies have frequent high level contact with Poland, the GDR, Hungary, Czechoslovakia and Romania, including visits at head of government level. But our own interests are less great than theirs and we need not try to match their activity. Nor are the prospects for increased trade sufficiently good to argue for this. East European hard currency indebtedness is already so great that they usually insist on generous credit terms and substantial compensation trading arrangements. And there is pressure from the Treasury to cut back on further credits to countries such as Poland and Romania where ECGD is already heavily extended. Indeed the long-delayed advance in our relations with Poland comes at a time when the Poles may seek to use it largely as an opportunity to press for more credit.

The Prevention of Soviet Expansion and the Management of Crises

10. The major gap in Western policies towards the Soviet Union in the late 70s was the lack of a strategy for countering Soviet expansionism in the developing world. The policy on this which was approved by Ministers in June[7] foresaw a

---

[7] See Enclosure in No. 65.

UK-Soviet Relations, 1979-82

greater effort by the West, Japan and Australasia to develop their relations with the Third World, so as to reduce the scope for Soviet opportunism. More specifically it was agreed that HMG should:

(*a*) Review the scope for putting economic and other pressure on the Russians;

(*b*) Develop our capacity for long range military intervention outside the NATO area;

(*c*) Improve our arrangements for giving military assistance in the Third World;

(*d*) Review our machinery for countering Soviet propaganda;

(*e*) Develop our links with Third World political organisations.

11. There were some exchanges about policy towards the Soviet Union at the Seven Power Summit in Venice. Chancellor Schmidt advocated a general approach which is not incompatible with our ideas. We should now pursue the latter actively in Ministerial and senior official contacts with our principal allies. A more coherent Western approach is much needed anyway, and the need could be even greater if Mr Reagan were elected President.

12. Meanwhile the UK should insist on the maintenance of the measures taken against the Russians because of Afghanistan (which, incidentally, were very much greater than the cancellation of a few events which, apart from words, was all the West did after the invasion of Czechoslovakia). When the interest rate under the new Franco-Soviet Credit Agreement comes up for review in September 1981, we should press the French to return to consensus rates. Without getting out in front of our Allies, we should continue to participate constructively in discussion of extension of the COCOM lists and should argue if necessary for the continued suspension of the exceptions procedure.

13. We should continue actively to encourage Islamic and other Third World opposition to the occupation of Afghanistan. Our proposal on neutrality and non-alignment should remain on the table. Together with our allies, we should exploit all suitable opportunities for further pressure on the Soviet Union in regional and international meetings. We should continue to have actively in mind that the efforts of the Afghan resistance offer the best hope both of maximising the cost to the Russians of their Afghan adventure and of maintaining Third World and Islamic interest.

14. The further development of British and Western relations with China will have the important side effect of increasing the international pressure on the Russians. The recent Carter/Hua meeting in Tokyo, Mr Pym's visit to China earlier this year and the Secretary of State's in the autumn are very timely.

East/West Negotiations

15. Afghanistan has not destroyed the case for seeking balanced and verifiable arms control as part of an integrated security policy. It has merely underlined the need for a hard-headed approach. The Soviet moves on TNF and MBFR during Chancellor Schmidt's visit to Moscow confirm that the Russians recognise that they have an interest in discussion of arms control with the US and the maintenance of the SALT process. On TNF, the UK should encourage the US to probe Soviet intentions and should welcome any indication that genuine progress is possible. We should continue to work for progress in MBFR by recommending to our Allies a cautious but not unwelcoming response to the new Eastern proposals, designed to explore the details of the latter.

16. The Madrid CSCE Review Meeting will be the first major East-West event since the invasion of Afghanistan. The Russians will want to use it to demonstrate that 'détente' is back on the rails and for launching the conference on 'military

7 December 1979 – 1 December 1981

détente' proposed by the Warsaw Pact. Western policies are still evolving, but it is clear that there are substantial differences of view on the Western side which will create renewed dangers of divisiveness and Soviet wedge driving. The Americans, like ourselves, want a full review of implementation of the Final Act, in effect amounting to an indictment of Soviet shortcomings. They are hesitant about the Conference on Disarmament in Europe (CDE) proposed by the French. The latter have been taking a more robust line recently, with assurances (though possibly only for tactical reasons within NATO) against compromising on the essentials of a CBM mandate even if this means Soviet rejection of the proposed Conference. But the political importance of a distinctive French role in détente (especially as their election draws nearer) will not have vanished. The Germans are concerned above all to prevent any worsening of the atmosphere that could jeopardise the gains of *Ostpolitik*; they want to pay special attention to Basket II[8] and hope for a decision on an early High Level Meeting on Energy. A composite Western policy incorporating elements satisfactory to all sides is being worked out but this may merely paper over the cracks temporarily.

17. The British interest is to keep the Alliance together; to secure a thorough review of implementation; to reaffirm our view that détente and expansionism are incompatible; and to keep the CSCE process going. While we share the Western interest in Phase I of a CDE if it is on the right terms, we have no interest in a CDE for its own sake and should be ready with the Americans and others to withhold our agreement if necessary. It is important that the West should not make unrequited concessions to the Soviet Union merely in order to have a 'successful' meeting or to reaffirm détente.

[8] Co-operation in the fields of economics, of science and technology and of the environment.

No. 73

Letter from Mr Fergusson to Mr Brooke Turner (Moscow), 21 July 1980[1]
Confidential (FCO 28/4009, EN 021/2)

[No salutation]

East-West Policy after Afghanistan

1. We were very grateful for Curtis Keeble's letter of 17 June[2] to Julian Bullard and Moscow telegram No 408[3] of the same date. You have set out most clearly a line of argument which has helped to stimulate further thought here about East-West policy. I enclose a submission[4] and paper by EESD,[5] now on their way to Ministers, which, as you will see, reflect much of your analysis. The rest of this covering letter deals with more general issues arising from Curtis Keeble's letter and related correspondence,

2. First, 'détente'. As a catch-phrase it inevitably represents the over-simplification of a complex proposition, suggesting that East-West relations can be set out in terms of black-and-white, and leading to the exchange of slogans about

[1] Copied to HM Ambassadors at Paris, Washington, Bonn and UKDEL NATO.
[2] No. 69.
[3] Not printed.
[4] Not printed. The submission written by Mr Mallaby expressed the view that the paper, if approved, would be the basis of UK policy for the next half year.
[5] No. 72.

UK-Soviet Relations, 1979-82

whether détente is 'indivisible', 'reversible' or something else. As you know, we have preferred to use the phrase 'the management of East-West relations'; a phrase which is defined admirably in the last sentence of Curtis Keeble's paragraph 5. But that does not dispose of 'détente', which many people think has a real meaning, and to which some—particularly in continental Europe—have a particular attachment. We decided as early as 1976 in the very thoroughgoing planning paper on East-West relations[6] that we could not simply drop the word. President Ford tried to do so and failed. Afghanistan makes the word harder to stomach but not easier to abolish. We have therefore attempted to elaborate a more sophisticated explanation of what the word means to HMG, which is perhaps best set out in the speech which Lord Carrington made at Chatham House on 22 February.[7] This was distributed in the London Press Service but I enclose a copy for ease of reference. This has not, however, got us out of the wood. Although the French and Germans' private analysis of the significance of the Soviet invasion of Afghanistan is, as you imply, not too different from ours or the Americans', they have real and legitimate interests in what is popularly understood by 'détente', and need to demonstrate continued attachment to 'détente' in public. Otherwise—as Herr Genscher has found out—they get into domestic political trouble. An American, or a Western, policy which does not recognise these real interests will be built on sand. It is the need to make some accommodation in this direction which led us into using the phrase 'return to détente' in Donald Maitland's letter of 24 April[8] without sufficient qualification.

3. By contrast, it seems to us that Brzezinski (Washington telno 2168)[8] has over-simplified the issue, and failed to take account of the European realities. The Afghanistan crisis is a very serious one, and the use of Soviet force outside the Warsaw Pact represents a qualitative change. There is room for debate, however, over the scope of that change. It is not, for instance, self-evident that the present crisis is as serious as the Cuban missile crisis or the Berlin airlift. And it is cavalier, however 'reasonable' it may be, for the Americans to expect the continental Europeans to put very important relationships with the East (of a kind which are not shared with the US) at risk in a situation which seems to them somewhat less than a confrontation on the brink of war.

4. Another weakness in the American case is that the Americans do not seem to have a clear idea of how they propose to work for the resolution of the crisis. They are right to put all the pressure they can on the Russians both directly and indirectly; and right to expect their allies to do the same within the limits of the politically and economically feasible. But as you say, the Russians may well stay

[6] A summary of the paper, entitled 'Détente and the Future Management of East/West Relations', can be found in *DBPO*, Series III, Vol. III, No. 93.

[7] In this speech, Lord Carrington focussed on the Soviet invasion of Afghanistan and the consequences for the Western alliance, the Third World and the future of détente. In his concluding remarks, Lord Carrington stated that the West's view of détente as an 'irreversible, one-way option to a safer world' was naïve and that following the invasion of Afghanistan the West could no longer 'accept the Brezhnev doctrine that the frontiers of what the Russians call 'socialism' can only advance and never retreat. History does not work that way. And if the Russians try to help history by subversion or by force they will stumble into confrontation not only with the West, but also with the genuinely non-aligned who have no desire to be dragooned into either camp. In a nuclear world, that is the path of danger. It is not compatible with any meaningful kind of détente . . . There is no need for the East-West relationship to be a zero sum game. Indeed, détente, like the Caucus Race in 'Alice in Wonderland', should be a game which everyone can win and where everyone has a prize. But we need to see some changes in Soviet attitudes before we can be sure that is true.'

[8] Not printed.

7 December 1979 – 1 December 1981

in Afghanistan for a very long time. Some sort of East-West business will nevertheless need to go on. The next American President may feel the need to meet the next General Secretary of the Soviet Communist Party while Russian soldiers are still in Kabul, just as Muskie has already met Gromyko and just as Brezhnev received Kissinger in Moscow while the Americans were mining Haiphong. The ability to operate a double-barrelled policy of this kind is, we think, part of what is meant by crisis management. The present American Administration has not shown itself adept at this.

5. Nicko Henderson has however drawn attention to a particular difficulty which we ourselves face. This is that the Americans regard the British as being on 'their side' in the present Transatlantic argument over East-West relations and will be correspondingly upset if it appears that we have defected and adopted what they think is the Franco-German 'détente' approach. We face several difficulties here:

(*a*) The Americans and others also accuse us of speaking big and acting small; we have to guard against this in our rhetoric if we are not to diminish our credibility in other ways;

(*b*) Like the French and Germans, though less so, we have interests in East-West trade which we cannot lightly sacrifice;

(*c*) The nature of our domestic public opinion allows the Government to adopt a public line rather closer to that of the Americans. But—as Reg Hibbert and Oliver Wright have pointed out—our major need for a healthy working relationship with the French and Germans requires that we should not get too far away from them either;

(*d*) Our real interest is to devise a policy which can unite both America and Western Europe.

6. The ideas we have been developing in the various papers you have seen are meant to meet these complexities, and to avoid the 'either/or' trap into which discussion about East-West relations so often seems to fall. They are based on the propositions that:

(*a*) The mechanisms for dealing with the Russians in Europe and in the Far East, which have been developed in the past three decades, remain adequate. These include military arrangements on the one hand; and the development of political and economic relations with the Russians and their allies on the other—i.e. the policy summed up in the NATO slogan 'deterrence plus détente'. These arrangements have prevented Soviet expansion in Europe and the Far East. They have created useful political and economic links. They remain valid provided the Alliance remains healthy.

(*b*) The situation in the rest of the world is more complex. The Russians seek to profit from political and economic difficulties in the developing world which are not primarily of their making. The Western attempt in the 1950s to apply elsewhere the mechanisms which worked in Europe (e.g. CENTO and SEATO) did not work. The West's prime aim is therefore to help developing countries overcome their problems so as to give the Russians less scope. This needs to be supplemented on a world wide scale by measures of political, military and economic assistance similar to those being adopted in South West Asia, and by clear indications to the Russians that we will not accept direct assaults by them on Western interests in the Third World. Hence the importance of President Carter's statements earlier this year about the American interest in the Gulf.

(*c*) The link between the policies for the Southern and Northern Hemispheres is the proposition that the West should try to agree on measures in its relations

UK-Soviet Relations, 1979-82

with the USSR which might be taken before the event if and when we next have evidence that the Russians are getting ready to invade a non-aligned country. We are writing a separate paper on this[9]—the hypothesis, which is an ambitious one, will be carefully argued.

We think (*a*) and (*b*) at least should be acceptable on both sides of the Atlantic. We certainly regard it as a major objective of current policy to reduce the damaging divergence of views particularly between the Americans and the Germans, to which you draw attention and which, like you, we believe has been unnecessarily exaggerated. Indeed, the Americans themselves seem recently to be taking a more resigned and more realistic view of the 'Franco-German philosophy'.

7. Your point about China is well taken and is now reflected in EESD's enclosed paper. 'Worst Case' analysis (Curtis Keeble's para 1(*b*)) is a necessary aid in defining one limit of the problems to which policy has to address itself. It leads rapidly into the argument which so often dominates the discussions of military planners about the difference between capabilities and intentions. In the past we have rarely had the means to deal with Soviet capabilities (remember NATO's call in the early 1950s for 70 divisions to oppose the Russians—which were not forthcoming). The trouble is that whereas worst case assumptions rest on evidence which appears to be quantifiable (military hardware and numbers of men under arms), argument about intentions rests on less easily demonstrable judgments about the nature of Soviet and Warsaw Pact politics, the tensions between the military and civilian sides of the economy and so on. In the end, one is bound to strike an uneasy balance. Thus—to take the current example—a Soviet force securely in place in Afghanistan would indeed pose a new military threat to our oil supplies whether or not the Russians intended to use it for that purpose. The measures proposed to strengthen the American military presence in South West Asia may never be militarily adequate to stop a determined Soviet attack across the Iranian border. But they will—mostly for political reasons—make such an attack less likely. They are thus a reasonable response to the threat even if they are not adequate for the worst case.

8. Finally, though you will hardly need me to say this, we are very well aware that Summer 1980 is a difficult time for working out a reassessment of how to manage our relations with the Soviet Union in the face of at least two major variables—the elections in the FRG and the United States, not to speak of next Spring's French Presidential election. What has been set out above must therefore be seen as a contribution to a continuing discussion, an important element in which will be the East-West's Heads of Mission meeting in the autumn.[10] By then some things may be clearer!

Yours ever,
EWEN FERGUSSON

[9] No. 74.
[10] See No. 80.

7 December 1979 – 1 December 1981

No. 74

Paper by East European and Soviet Department on Warnings, Actions and Threats to Deter Soviet Moves, 28 July 1980[1]
Secret (FCO 46/2180, DPN 061/18)

Introduction
1. Since the Soviet invasion of Afghanistan, Western countries have taken a number of measures against Soviet interests, ranging from the American grain embargo to the Olympic boycott. These measures have however been applied in a partial and piecemeal manner; and, although they have had some political and economic effect on the Soviet Union, it is not yet possible to say whether this has been significant. An interim account of them is at Annex A.[2] Though it is perhaps rather soon, this paper attempts to draw some lessons from these events, and to suggest ways in which the West might be brought to act in a more coherent and timely manner in a future crisis. It does not, however, attempt to discuss next steps in handling the present crisis.

Lessons from Afghanistan
(a) Political warning time
2. Neither we nor the Americans examined in advance the full implications of a Soviet military occupation of Afghanistan. We undertook no contingency planning, and made no attempt to work out a combined strategy with other allies. This was not a failure of intelligence: by the middle of last year there was plenty of evidence that the Russians thought Afghanistan very important, and that they might be tempted and would be able to invade it. In the weeks before the invasion of Afghanistan the US apparently warned the Soviet Union five times against military action. The UK did so once, at official level. It was only after the invasion took place that its full implications dawned on the West, particularly the Americans.

3. Much the same thing happened in the period before the Soviet invasion of Czechoslovakia. As NATO's military planners regularly point out, the West's difficulties in resisting Soviet pressure lie less in our material arrangements than in our willingness to activate them in time, i.e. to consult, and then to take or threaten action (some of it painful) before the Russians have themselves acted, and indeed while their intentions are still unclear.

(b) Nature of assessment
4. America's allies (including France and Germany) came quickly to share the view that the Soviet invasion was a qualitatively new development with serious implications for East/West relations. They did not share President Carter's view that it was the most serious crisis in East/West relations since 1945. They therefore found it hard to accept the need to sacrifice important political and economic interests in order to contribute to the response which the US was demanding.

(c) Crisis management
5. The principles of crisis management include having a clear idea of how to resolve the crisis even when one is deliberately escalating it; leaving loopholes for

[1] This paper was written following the meeting of OD on 5 June (No. 67) which invited the Secretary of State to carry forward the proposals set out in paragraphs 1-4 of the paper under discussion on the management of East-West relations (Enclosure in No. 65).
[2] The paper also contains Annex B which lists a range of possible measures which might be taken in future if the Russians seem to be contemplating 'unacceptable moves'. Neither annex is printed.

one's adversary to retreat without losing face; and ensuring that confidential communication with the adversary continues even when tension is at its height. These principles were observed by the Kennedy brothers during the Cuban missile crisis. The Germans have criticised the Americans for having no coherent plan for the management of the Afghanistan crisis. The evidence is that this criticism is justified.

(*d*) *American leadership and allied consultation*

6. Crisis management cannot easily be practised by a coalition: the problems of risk, nuance, and timing are such that undivided responsibility and control are highly desirable, if necessary at the expense of some temporary deterioration in relations among allies.

7. This principle was followed by the Americans in 1962 and 1973 (Yom Kippur) and indeed by the British in the Rhodesian negotiations. In an East/West confrontation, the Americans are bound to bear a primary responsibility, though they may not like it. The allies may complain or be fearful: but they have in the past been satisfied by a demonstration of clear American purpose (and, of course, by a successful outcome), to which they can eventually rally. Even the French have done so; cf. de Gaulle in October 1962: 'You may tell the President that France will support him.'[3]

8. Over Afghanistan, however, the Americans have argued that their allies' response has been as important as their own, and have criticised its raggedness. But this raggedness is in part the consequence of the Americans' own failure to consult properly before they themselves acted, or to convince their allies that their approach was consistent and soundly based; and in part a result of their failure to accept that some of their allies had legitimate East/West interests at stake which did not entirely coincide with their own.

(*e*) *Differing interests*

9. These interests are both political and economic/commercial/political. The French have long displayed an interest, caused partly by the large communist vote, in playing a demonstratively independent role in East/West relations. The major factor highlighted by Afghanistan is that the West Germans have a major national interest in the continuation of policies which reduce the barriers between the two halves of Europe and of Germany. This is reflected in their domestic political opinion, which no Federal German politician can ignore (any more than an American politician can ignore the Jewish vote or the gas-guzzling lobby, despite the distortions these introduce into American policy). In a confrontation in Europe on the brink of war there is no reasonable doubt that the Germans would stand loyally by the Atlantic Alliance, whose unity is a national interest still easily superior to their interest in relations with the East. In any lesser crisis, it is bad policy to try to make them choose.

10. The economic and commercial interest of the Europeans in East/West relations reinforces the political interests of the Germans, the French and others. This makes and has always made the Europeans less willing than the Americans to use trade as an economic weapon: it was a Conservative British Government in the 1950s that argued—against strong American scepticism—in favour of Summit meetings and greater East/West trade. Since then important commercial interests have been created, and economic and trade Ministries in most European countries will remain reluctant to jeopardise them except in a major crisis in Europe.

---

[3] A reference to President de Gaulle's support for the US during the Cuban missile crisis.

7 December 1979 – 1 December 1981

11. The interest of Germany, France, and Italy in energy supplies from Eastern Europe creates a particular dependence, which has been described as 'reverse leverage'. This is bound to make those countries additionally cautious in the approach to a crisis. It is not so far offset to any significant extent by the dependence on the West of many East European countries (especially Poland) and even the Soviet Union for finance, technology and grain.

The Future

12. The Afghanistan crisis has shown up the West's difficulty in acting coherently in advance of an impending crisis; the weakness of the present US administration in managing a crisis relationship with the Russians and providing effective leadership to its allies; the uselessness of mere warnings to the Russians without threats or actions as well; the unwillingness of the French and Germans to put their own interests at risk in a situation which they judge to be less than a full scale crisis; and the extreme difficulty of imposing a comprehensive set of economic sanctions on the Soviet Union. Some of these failures stem from political or economic facts which can be neither removed nor ignored. Others could be avoided or minimised in future if the Western countries primarily concerned (America, Britain, France and Germany) could agree in advance on the measures which might be adopted, and on the circumstances in which they might be applied. The chance of preventing a major crisis will be much increased if agreed measures can be taken while the Russians are preparing an unacceptable act, rather than after they have moved and their prestige has been irrevocably engaged. A range of possible actions to prevent a crisis is briefly listed below. A fuller review is in Annex B.

(*a*) *Warnings*. These include everything from discreet US and allied warnings to the calling of high level consultations among the allies and perhaps China; they need to be backed up by some of the actions below;

(*b*) *Military actions*. i.e. US measures, such as alerts or the despatch of rapid deployment forces, to convince the Russians that the action they are contemplating could lead to war. There are also lesser military moves, e.g. naval deployments and exercises in the relevant part of the world;

(*c*) *Threats*. In circumstances where military moves are neither credible nor practicable, the West may have to fall back on non-military threats, e.g. to cancel agreements; suspend current negotiations; cancel major East/West events; and, most difficult of all, deny key types of technology.

(*d*) *Public actions*. These include public warnings about Western vital interests, publicity about Soviet intentions, action in the UN, withdrawal of Ambassadors, etc.

13. To be effective, these arrangements need to be carefully calculated and planned in advance. They need to take account of the need for a realistic plan for resolving as well as initiating a crisis; the likelihood that economic sanctions will have little early economic effect, even though they may usefully drive home a political point; the inadequacy of any policy which does not take full account of the interests of those who are to implement it; and the disadvantages of public disunity and of publicly announcing a policy which several allies may be unable to put into practice.

14. The Western measures against the Russians after Afghanistan, whatever their actual effects, were more concrete than the mere words, or at most cancellation of bilateral events, with which the West reacted to previous Soviet and

UK-Soviet Relations, 1979-82

Cuban invasions from Hungary onwards. In the light of this, the Soviet leaders cannot discount the possibility of some actions being taken against them by the West in future crises. This will add credibility to Western warnings made when the Russians appear to be contemplating dangerous moves. If as a result of Western contingency planning, a package of threats can be used to back up clear warnings, including threats of selective denial of technology and other possibilities mentioned above, the Russians will at least realise that to move forward would cause an East/West crisis. There can be no guarantee that they would therefore desist, but the chance would be far greater than if the West again issued mere warnings without threats.

15. The non-military threats suggested above pre-suppose that in times of relative normality Western relations with the Soviet Union will be fostered. A thin relationship provides little in the way of potential leverage or inducements, and is in any case difficult to slim further without severing relations completely. The development of a full range of East/West contacts and business, on the other hand, makes possible a graduated response and should permit some modulation of threats or actions in the light of subsequent Soviet behaviour.

16. One problem with the idea of advance warnings and threats to the Soviet Union, when it appears to be contemplating aggression, is that the Western countries concerned will need to be convinced that the Russians really are preparing a dangerous move. The Americans have the necessary intelligence sources. The UK has access to US intelligence, as well as having sources of its own. France and Germany, however, are likely to be relatively uninformed about Soviet preparations for action. Their willingness to take measures to deter the USSR would depend in part on the amount of intelligence the Americans would give them.

17. Annex B shows that the effectiveness of Western threats in support of warnings to the Russians will depend critically upon the US. Yet US willingness to discuss contingency planning for future crises will depend on European willingness to consider joining in warnings and threats. France and Germany are the key. The case for their participation will need to be deployed very skilfully. It rests, in essence, on these considerations:

(a) The next time the Russians are contemplating aggression, the potential victim, unlike Afghanistan, may well matter crucially to Western Europe—for instance Iran.

(b) The best way of avoiding in future the Western disagreements which followed the invasion of Afghanistan, and of inducing the US Government to engage in advance thinking and thus behave more steadily in another crisis, is for the Europeans to show themselves willing in certain contingencies to make threats about, and if necessary to sacrifice, certain discreet and carefully chosen elements of their relations with the Soviet Union.

Next Steps

18. These issues are suitable for covering in Quadripartite discussion. We should suggest to our three partners a programme of work covering the following questions:

(a) How can we ensure that effective and timely signals are sent to the Russians before a future crisis develops too far?

(b) What is the range of possible actions to back up warnings to the Russians?

(c) What is the role of economic sanctions against the Russians? Is it economic,

7 December 1979 – 1 December 1981

or primarily political?

(*d*) Is it possible to develop highly selective, and therefore effective, technological sanctions? Can Western countries agree on a range of such sanctions for use before a crisis begins and on the kind of circumstances in which they would be applied? Would the knowledge that such agreement had been reached in itself deter the Russians, or would they assume that in the event Western solidarity would break down under the pressure of economic interest?

19. Work on (*d*) is in hand in the FCO. It needs to be carried further before we can make our full contribution to Quadripartite discussion. The next quadripartite meeting will discuss policy for relations with the Soviet Union while Soviet troops remain in Afghanistan. We should seek to lead our partners on from that subject to examination of the questions in the previous paragraph.

No. 75

Letter from Mr Wood (Moscow) to Mr Johnson, 3 September 1980
Confidential (FCO 28/4195, ENS 015/1)

Dear David,

Contact with Dissidents

1. I promised you when I wrote on 10 June to review our ideas later this year. My hope then was that we might get a clearer insight into the way Soviet policies would develop and that this would make it easier to adopt a more forward attitude than in the past. We have since then, as you know, arranged for Lesley Dean[1] to seek admission to the Yakunin and Velikanova trials[2].

2. The prospects at the moment do not look particularly encouraging. There has been little let up since the Olympics in KGB activity. One can I suppose hope that the trials of dissidents are taking place now in order to get them out of the way before the main Madrid Meeting begins in the middle of November. My own prejudice however—and it can be little more than that at this stage—is that we are in for a longer period of unpleasantness than that. I do not yet know what will be the effect of Poland, but even apart from that, there has been a continuing series of ill-tempered articles in the press about dissidents (Lesley Dean's letter of 2 September to Stephen Band)[3] and Western personalities and organisations which take an interest in them, and Western Embassies have noticed an increase in the attention paid to them. I do not wish to exaggerate the latter point, and I am not suggesting we should allow ourselves to be frightened off by such indicators of greater KGB activity. But you should know we are having to operate in an atmosphere which is much frostier than was the case in 1979, that the dissidents themselves are under unusually strong pressure and that we must therefore be especially careful not to put them in further danger. I hope you will let me know

---

[1] Second Secretary, Moscow.

[2] Father Gleb Yakunin, a Christian dissident, and Tatyana Velikanova, a mathematician and human rights activist, were tried, and eventually convicted, for 'anti-Soviet agitation'.

[3] Not printed.

UK-Soviet Relations, 1979-82

whether our present efforts are satisfactory or whether there is anything more you would like us to attempt.[4]

Yours ever,
A. M. WOOD

[4] Mr Johnson replied on 19 September thanking the Embassy for their reporting on the dissident scene and the contacts they had managed to maintain against an increasingly hostile background. He went on: 'I do not need to tell you that public and parliamentary interest here in human rights in the Soviet Union remains high and is given added stimulus whenever trials of prominent dissidents occur . . . The Government are expected to translate their expressions of concern into specific action and little thought is given to the fact that, particularly in a period of cool Anglo-Soviet relations, our ability to influence the Soviet authorities is minimal. It is therefore useful to be able to point whenever necessary to action by the Embassy to demonstrate HMG's sympathy with those in the Soviet Union who campaign for human rights.'

No. 76

Lord Carrington to HM Representatives Overseas, 8 September 1980, 6 p.m.
Guidance Tel. No. 95 Confidential (FCO 28/4009, EN 021/2)

UK Policy in East/West Relations

Introduction

1. Your attention is drawn to my speech at Stockholm on 19 August on East-West relations (Verbatim 105/80).[1] It draws in part on the conclusions of a paper prepared in the department[2] which reflect some development in the policy which we have followed in East-West relations since the invasion of Afghanistan. It is in our interest that Western allies should so far as possible adopt a common attitude, particularly over contacts with the Soviet Union, and should understand the reasons for our own actions.

Line to Take

2. You should draw on paragraphs 3 to 9 below in discussion with trusted Western contacts. Paragraphs 1 and 10 to 12 are for your own information only.

3. The West's avoidance of high level contacts with the Russians from Christmas until April was one of the measures taken to demonstrate disapproval of the invasion of Afghanistan. However, a resumption in due course of high level discussion was inevitable. It was not possible to pursue our initiative on Afghanistan without talking to the Soviet Union and, in that context, I met Gromyko in Vienna on 17 May.[3] I shall expect to see him during the UNGA in New York.[4] Vienna in fact confirmed the resumption of high level contacts on the part of other major Western partners.

4. We and some of our Allies have also been avoiding various other types of contact with the USSR, from visits of Ministers responsible for technical subjects

[1] In this lecture entitled 'East-West Relations', delivered at the Swedish Institute of International Affairs, Lord Carrington contended that in invading Afghanistan, the Soviet Union had violated all ten principles of the CSCE Final Act. Despite this, 'practical discussion between East and West must go on . . . or future crises could escalate through misunderstanding, and we could never hope to resolve the problems which now face us'.
[2] No. 72.
[3] No. 62.
[4] See No. 77.

7 December 1979 – 1 December 1981

to discussions between officials about CSCE. Seven months after the invasion of Afghanistan guidelines are needed which will allow some contacts to be re-established without a wholesale return to business as usual. These should be:

(*a*) There should be no resumption of all types of contact which we had with the USSR before Afghanistan, since this would imply that we had accepted the occupation of that country;

(*b*) Contacts which deal with real substance, mutually beneficial commercial contacts, and routine scientific, academic and cultural exchanges which are in Western countries' interests can resume/continue. The presumption in marginal cases should be against resumption and publicity should not be encouraged;

(*c*) Other prestigious contacts, for instance major cultural events or national exhibitions, and goodwill visits like Parliamentary exchanges, should be avoided so long as the problem over Afghanistan remains; so should military exchanges, for obvious reasons;

(*d*) Those contacts which take place should be used to reiterate the Western position on Afghanistan;

(*e*) The measures concerning technology, credit, etc, taken against the USSR after Afghanistan should be fully maintained.

5. We should carefully differentiate our treatment of Eastern Europe: there is no reason to blame the East Europeans for Soviet misdeeds which, whatever their public pronouncements, they have clearly not welcomed. Contacts here should continue and will be expanded. I shall be visiting Poland and Hungary in October.

6. The continuing efforts of the Afghan resistance represent probably the most effective way of increasing the cost to the Russians of their Afghan adventure. We shall continue actively to encourage Islamic and other Third World opposition to the occupation. It suits us that Islamic countries are in the forefront in handling this issue; we shall maintain close contact with Habib Chatty, Secretary-General of the Islamic Conference, and other Islamic leaders. Our proposal on neutrality and non-alignment will remain on the table.

7. The Russians seem intent on pursuing a military solution in Afghanistan, and no doubt calculate that the West will come to live with the Soviet military presence, as it has with the one in Czechoslovakia since 1968. Barring a reversal of policy, they will not withdraw unless they can leave behind a government which they can rely upon to be both durable and compliant; and no such government can at present be established. We shall not be prepared to acquiesce in such a situation and it seems clear that Afghanistan will remain the major factor in East-West relations for some time.

8. Afghanistan has not, however, destroyed the case for seeking balanced and verifiable arms control as part of an integrated security policy. It has merely underlined the need for a hard-headed approach. The Soviet moves on TNF and MBFR confirm that the Russians recognise that they have an interest in discussion of arms control with the US and the maintenance of the SALT process.

9. The Madrid Conference on Security and Co-operation in Europe (CSCE) Review Meeting will be the first major East-West event since the invasion of Afghanistan. The Russians will want to use it to demonstrate that business can go on as usual in Europe despite Afghanistan, to show that 'détente' is back on the rails and to launch the conference on 'military détente' proposed by the Warsaw Pact. We continue to see advantage in maintaining the CSCE process; but the British objective is to secure a thorough review of implementation, to reaffirm our view that détente and Soviet expansionism are incompatible, to avoid the adoption

of propagandist declaratory measures and to support a limited number of new proposals to the extent that they are clearly in the Western interest.

For Your Own Information

10. The Western Alliance is united in insisting on complete Soviet withdrawal from Afghanistan. There is no risk that this position will soon be abandoned. But major Western countries have differed about the attitude to be adopted in relations with the Soviet Union after the invasion and these differences have been highlighted by Giscard's meeting with Brezhnev, Schmidt's visit to Moscow, signature of the Soviet/German Long Term Economic Programme and negotiations on a gas deal which may increase from 16 percent to 25 percent the Soviet share of the gas consumed in the FRG. There is an obvious risk that the international community will gain the impression that the West, while continuing to condemn the occupation of Afghanistan in words, will drift back towards business as usual with the USSR and fail to take adequate steps to deter further Soviet expansionism.

11. Inevitably the question will be raised whether, seven months after the invasion of Afghanistan, the West wishes to return to détente. As a catch-phrase 'détente' over-simplifies a complex process. We have preferred to talk of 'the management of East-West relations' and what we need to find is a more effective way of managing them; but we cannot abolish the word 'détente', which many people think has a real meaning, and to which some—particularly in Continental Europe—have a particular attachment. For instance, the French and German analysis of the significance of the Soviet invasion of Afghanistan is similar to the British or American one, but France and Germany have real and legitimate interests in what is popularly understood by 'détente' which affect the practical measures which they are prepared to undertake. It is essential that we should try to devise a coherent Western policy which at the same time recognises this.

12. The policy which we shall be advocating (given here in very summary form) will be that:

(*a*) The mechanisms for dealing with the Russians in Europe and in the Far East, which have been developed in the past three decades—i.e. the NATO doctrine of 'Deterrence plus détente'—have prevented Soviet expansion in Europe and the Far East and have created useful political and economic links. They remain valid provided the Alliance remains healthy, which will continue to be the cornerstone of our policy;

(*b*) In the developing world at large, we face an increasingly complex situation, in which we need to find ways of preventing the Russians profiting from political and economic difficulties and instabilities which are not primarily of their making. We cannot repeat the Western attempt in the 1950s to reproduce elsewhere the mechanisms which worked in Europe (e.g. CENTO and SEATO). If we are to reduce the number of potential trouble spots so as to give the Russians less scope for exploiting them, opportunistically or deliberately, the West's prime aim should now be to help developing countries to overcome their problems, to stabilize their governments and their economies and, so far as possible, to prevent political vacua from arising. This requires measures of political, military and economic assistance, backed up by clear indications to the Russians of the response which they will face if they continue to assail Western interests in the Third World. The complexity of this task, in conditions of economic recession and, in our case, of severe budgetary constraint, can hardly be under-estimated.

7 December 1979 – 1 December 1981

No. 77

Sir A. Parsons (UKMIS New York) to FCO, 24 September 1980, [1]
Tel. No. 1341 Immediate, Confidential (FCO 58/1998, UNP 026/3)

Following from Private Secretary

Secretary of State's talk with Gromyko, 23 September[2]

Iraq/Iran

1. Lord Carrington sounded out Gromyko's attitude to the possibility of Ministerial participation in Security Council consultations, and to a Security Council call for a cease-fire. Gromyko was reluctant on both counts. The situation was unclear, and there was a lack of information. Everyone might be wiser tomorrow. He was not sure that a Security Council meeting would be wise even then. Moreover, fighting might have stopped by then.[3] Saddam Hussain [*sic*] had said that Iraq had no territorial claims against Iran: it was strange that the fighting should continue in such circumstances. He suspected that the 1975 agreement on Shatt al-Arab had been too hastily concluded, and was not a reliable agreement.

2. Gromyko's general attitude on this subject was evasive and non-committal, though the Secretary of State also thought there might be an element of genuine uncertainty in his mind about what was going on on the ground, and about how the Russians would respond.

Afghanistan

3. Lord Carrington said that he did not propose going over the ground on Afghanistan once again, having heard Gromyko's speech. But he was afraid that the whole situation in the Middle Eastern area was becoming dangerous. Gromyko re-stated the Soviet position on Afghanistan in crisp terms. There had been no response to past proposals. There could be no political solution without agreements between Afghanistan and Pakistan and Iran. Even without a solution Afghanistan would continue to develop as an independent state, and encroachments from outside would continue to be repulsed. Soviet troops would remain in Afghanistan even though there was no real force for them to match their strength against. These troops were a stabilising factor, who would leave only when there was a complete end to outside interference.

4. Lord Carrington said that Ag[h]a Shahi was disappointed at the Soviet rejection of his suggestion for a conference, even though some people thought that a conference might be beneficial to people they were not anxious to recognise. Gromyko said that there was nothing for a conference to do, least of all discuss a possible change of regime. What was needed was an end to interference. Afghanistan was already non-aligned. In the past Britain had played a role in the settlement of disputes in various parts of the world, but she was now following in the footsteps of those who sent arms to Afghanistan, instead of appealing for realism. The Afghans had no territorial claims, but nobody would talk to them about the need to live in peace and friendship. If the Pakistanis had territorial claims against Afghanistan, they must be wrong in the head.

---

[1] Repeated Immediate to Washington, Moscow, Paris, Bonn, Baghdad; Priority to Islamabad, New Delhi, Madrid, UKDEL NATO. Lord Carrington was in New York for the 35th meeting of the UNGA.
[2] Prior to the meeting Lord Carrington wrote on his briefing note: 'Do I always have to call on Gromyko?'
[3] Hostilities between Iran and Iraq had begun on 22 September.

UK-Soviet Relations, 1979-82

5. Lord Carrington said that we did not wish to see a government hostile to the Soviet Union in Afghanistan. Nor did we wish for disturbances on Soviet borders. The difference between the Soviet and British view was not all that great: we wished for a neutral non-aligned government without outside interference, which included help given to the resistance in Afghanistan, from wherever it came, and Soviet forces. Gromyko must understand that the presence of large numbers of Soviet troops frightened the Pakistanis and Iranians. Last time they had met[4] Lord Carrington had been glad to hear Gromyko's assurances that the Soviet Union had no designs on oil in the Gulf, and would like to hear confirmation of this. Gromyko said that he was ready to repeat these assurances a hundred times. The Secretary of State was tilting at windmills: he could not possibly believe that Soviet forces would remain in Afghanistan after agreements had been reached with Iran and Pakistan. Either we were under a misapprehension or we were merely following our American allies, which was worse. Obsolete concepts about Soviet policies clearly prevailed in London. How was it possible to think that the Russians might after all go for the oil and the Persian Gulf, despite their assurances to the contrary?

6. Lord Carrington hoped that the Russians could understand that genuine differences of opinion sometimes arose, and referred to Gromyko's dismissive attitude to the possibility of a Rhodesian settlement when they had met in New York last year. There were a million Afghan refugees in Afghanistan [*sic* ?Pakistan], and the border was difficult to police. What was needed was reciprocity, and there was not sufficient trust. The essential problem was one of timing. It should not be beyond the wit of man to overcome this.

7. Finally, Lord Carrington asked Gromyko to stop jamming the BBC. Gromyko tried to turn this aside with a laboured joke. The Secretary of State persisted, pointing out that jamming was irreconcilable with the Helsinki agreements. Gromyko argued that the Final Act at Helsinki did not permit interference in internal affairs. He hoped that everyone would keep their cool in Madrid. The Soviet Union did not want demagogy or propaganda, and would rebuff anyone who took this attitude. Lord Carrington said that a review of implementation of the Final Act in Madrid would be essential. It was not a good basis for understanding between states to ignore things that had happened, and to paper over cracks.

[4] No. 62.

No. 78

Minute from Mr Garside (Planning Staff) to Mr Mallaby,[1] 12 November 1980
Secret (FCO 49/893, RS 021/6)

Afghanistan: Future Policy
1. A review of our policy on Afghanistan would be timely.[2] Mr Coles's short paper (attached) is therefore welcome[3].

[1] Mr Mallaby had been appointed Head of Planning Staff in September 1980.
[2] On 4 November, Ronald Reagan was elected President of the United States defeating Jimmy Carter by almost 10 percent of the popular vote. Carter's loss was the worst defeat for an incumbent President since Herbert Hoover lost to Franklin Roosevelt in 1932.
[3] See Enclosure.

7 December 1979 – 1 December 1981

2. Put in the very general terms of Mr Coles's para 1, our present policy is unexceptionable, and the tactics for maintaining international pressure sensible, although I doubt that it is worth devoting much effort to refining our proposal for a 'neutral, non-aligned Afghanistan' unless and until there is the least sign of Soviet readiness to contemplate withdrawal.

3. The question which calls for attention now is what to do about the Afghan Resistance.

4. It may be that the Pakistanis would much rather we stayed out of the business of arming, training or financing the Resistance lest it provoke greater Russian wrath. But we have not tested that assumption, and when discussing support for the Resistance with our Prime Minister, President Zia said that with better equipment they could do more.

5. It may be that the incoming Reagan administration would prefer to be the only Western government actively to help the Resistance. But I doubt it.

6. It may be that the Resistance consider they are getting all the material and moral support they need. But that is not what they say.

7. If these considerations are inhibiting us from helping the Resistance then I think it is time they were tested against actuality. Meanwhile a number of other things are clear enough:

(*a*) Admiration and support for the Afghan Resistance is very widespread indeed in the Western democracies, with the probable exception of our pro-Moscow minorities. There would be no significant domestic opposition to a policy of arming the Resistance. Serious daily and weekly papers including *The Times* and the *Economist* have made their editorial position quite clear: they regard support for the Resistance as the right policy. (See, for example, the *Economist's* editorial of 25 October and 8-14 November.)

(*b*) I find that people of my acquaintance who have been studiously 'liberal' for years, Guardianesque to the point of being tiresome, say that they darn well hope we are aiding the Resistance, and that it would be shameful if we were not.

(*c*) There is no question of our offending the French or Germans: President Giscard made it clear to the Prime Minister in Paris that he did not have many inhibitions on the principle of supplying the Resistance and thought the whole question should be reviewed 'by the Allies'. It is worth recalling that it was the French who took the lead in making Afghanistan the main political focus at the Venice 7-power summit this June. In the Quadripartite Political Directors' meetings the Germans have said they are inhibited by their constitution from considering such aid but they have never expressed opposition to the idea.

(*d*) The Afghans are the only people who are actually fighting direct Soviet imperialism in the world today. How long can we go on writing speeches for the Prime Minister to deliver at the Guildhall proclaiming the need to stop Soviet expansion in the Third World if we are not prepared at least to *offer* aid to the Afghan Resistance? We cannot plead money shortage because we could show our colours for a fraction of the amount by which inflation has increased our civil aid programme this year. To shrink from this test to our resolve to halt Soviet expansion would, in the long run, induce cynicism, at home and abroad, about our own seriousness of purpose. And by the same token it would encourage the Soviet Union and its allies.

(*e*) Aid to the Afghan Resistance would not conflict with our sponsorship of proposals for a political settlement, because that sponsorship has never been made from a position of neutrality as between the Russians and the Resistance.

UK-Soviet Relations, 1979-82

(*f*) Any aid from us would add little if any justification to Soviet accusations of external interference in Afghanistan because it would be a minor part of what is already a fairly substantial operation. (President Sadat, according to *The Times* of 11 November, has acknowledged Egypt's aid for the Resistance.)

(*g*) The Reagan administration is coming to power with a high regard for HMG's tough line with the Soviet Union. There is some danger of their being disillusioned if they find the UK failing to meet its commitment to a 3 percent increase in NATO spending. A declaration of readiness on the part of HMG to consider aid to the Resistance would go quite a way in mitigating that disillusion—and at a very modest cost. If we were to make such an offer it would be preferable to carry the French with us.

8. Willingness on the part of the French and ourselves to take a genuinely hard anti-Soviet line on Afghanistan would help considerably to still American fears (which have been strongly expressed by the Republicans) that Western Europe is 'going neutralist'. However unfair that accusation may be, it has gained wide currency in America and is a real, long-term danger to the essential base of popular support on which the Alliance rests.

9. Having accepted the principle of UK aid for the Resistance we would have to decide whether to acknowledge it, like President Sadat, or deny it like the Americans. This would depend largely on the views of our allies. Mr Wilkinson[4] has given some reasons for challenging the assumption that any aid should be covert. There might be diplomatic advantage in the position taken by the Soviet Union over its aid to the Vietcong. They were glad that people believed they were giving it but they never acknowledged it.

R. R. GARSIDE

Enclosure in No. 78[5]

Afghanistan

1. *We should stick to present policy*:

(*a*) Maintain international pressure on the Soviet Union, letting the Islamic countries take the lead so far as possible.

(*b*) Encourage the Afghan Resistance.

International pressure

2. The next step is the UNGA debate (20 November?). We and others are lobbying for the Pakistan resolution. Its main operational feature is the appointment of a Special Representative of the Secretary-General to explore a political solution.

3. When it is adopted, *we should consider the US proposal of a démarche* (joint or separately by the US, UK, Saudi Arabia and China) to Waldheim, emphasising that the Representative must not be dragged into a settlement on the basis of the 14 May proposals.[6]

4. Then, we shall wish to see the outcome of Madrid.

5. The conference of the Non-Aligned in Delhi in January may come up with an

---

[4] Richard Denys Wilkinson, Planning Staff.

[5] This paper by Mr Coles, head of South Asian Department, was dated 10 November 1980. The sentences in italics were possible conclusions for discussion at a future office meeting with Lord Carrington.

[6] See No. 63, note 1.

7 December 1979 – 1 December 1981

unhelpful initiative.

6. *We should consider whether our proposal for a neutral, non-aligned Afghanistan can be refined.* Perhaps more detail on the linkage between Soviet military withdrawal and steps towards a political solution. *A speech by the Secretary of State in the New Year* on these lines might help to sustain interest and pressure. We should discuss the main features first with Pakistan and perhaps the EC and the Americans.

The Afghan Resistance

7. It is very difficult to know what shape they are in. Reliable information is hard to come by. *We should now* ask (*a*) the Pakistanis (*b*) the Americans for a considered and detailed assessment. The Pakistan Foreign Secretary (PUS) is likely to pass through London shortly. I have suggested to the Embassy that we should try to arrange a couple of hours of talks.

8. No reason to believe the Resistance are a lost cause. They have kept going for ten months. Earlier Russian claims that the situation is returning to normal are unsubstantiated (and the Russians seem to talk now more of foreign interference, perhaps as a justification for their failure so far to bring the situation under control). We believe that considerable quantities of weapons are getting through. The Russians are thought to have lost about 60 helicopter gunships (some though by no means all due to Resistance attacks).

9. Military activity likely to fall off during winter. The Resistance need to be put in the best possible shape to resume activity during the Spring. Much depends on Reagan's attitude. *We should explore this as soon as we can and should seek an up-to-date US estimate of Resistance needs.*

10. *We should meanwhile maintain present policy on arms.* No overt or direct supply. *We should explore other ways of helping. But US should stay in control of operation.* French and Germans not likely to be able to help effectively.

Pakistan

11. Soviet or Soviet-inspired Afghan raids into Pakistan worrying. Latest went 25 miles into Pakistan. Virtually no Western response. Russians may be tempted to think they can go further. Pakistanis may be reluctant to raise the stakes, e.g. by taking a complaint to the Security Council. *We should now ask the Pakistanis how they view these raids and at what point they would go to the UN. We should compare notes with the US, the French and the Germans.*

12. Talk of more Western help for Pakistan is in the air but little is happening. Following Zia's visit to Washington the US are lobbying for more help for Afghan refugees. *We should now get an estimate of needs from the UNHCR and might then consider prompting an EC response.* A smallish bilateral UK response may also be possible.

13. Pakistan's main need is substantial financial aid. We cannot help but we should try to avoid cutting our aid by 50 percent next year as is envisaged under present framework estimates. We do not know whether the Saudis are giving or intending to give Pakistan money. *We should ask Jedda for a new reading and should ask Prince Saud when Ministers next meet him.*

14. *We should see whether the French and Germans propose doing anything more. We should consider giving them a short paper on Pakistani problems and need for aid.*

No. 79

Memorandum by Sir C. Keeble (Moscow) on Soviet Policy towards the West, 13 November 1980[1]
Confidential (FCO 28/4067, EN 400/2)

1. The occupation of Afghanistan brought the sharpest crisis in East/West relations since the invasion of Czechoslovakia in 1968. The crisis has not yet worked itself out, but with the election of Mr Reagan and the approach to the Soviet Party Congress in February, Soviet policy towards the West must now be at a point of review. There has been no definitive Soviet reaction to the change of administration nor any indication of new trends in policy, but much can reasonably be inferred from the experience of 1980.

2. In my paper for the 1979 Conference I said that the Soviet Union must be considering major policy options:

(*a*) contingency planning for unacceptable deviation in Eastern Europe, for a collapse of the Amin Government in Afghanistan and for a second Chinese strike against Vietnam;

(*b*) how to prepare for SALT III or for failure to ratify SALT II;

(*c*) how to frustrate modernisation of Western nuclear forces in Europe and/or how to respond to it;

(*d*) how to deal with future instability in the Middle East if it reaches the point of endangering American oil supplies.

Many of these issues became real in 1980. None of them was definitively resolved and they will continue to dominate East/West relations. The way the Soviet Union handled them illustrated both the more aggressive and the more cautious aspects of Soviet policy, as well as the order of priorities:

(i) The decision to occupy Afghanistan reflected no genuine strategic need, but rather a determination to sustain a political gain already made and a willingness to deploy military force in circumstances where no effective Western opposition seemed likely. But the occupation caused a harsher international reaction than had been expected and produced neither a stable government nor a military solution. The Soviet Union had to recognise that 'linkage' existed, but it was committed and would not change its policy. It is difficult to see how Soviet forces can be withdrawn without complete loss of political control. It must therefore be assumed that the occupation will continue. The Soviet Union will calculate that counter measures will fade. Their policy will be based on the expectation of eventual international acquiescence and they will be prepared to wait for it.

(ii) Control of Poland by contrast must be seen by the Soviet Union as essential to its own security and therefore in the last resort taking priority over virtually all other external considerations. The signs are that, temporarily at least, the Soviet Union gave the Polish leadership more latitude than might have been

---

[1] This paper was written for the Heads of Mission Conference on East/West Relations held at the FCO on 19 November (No. 80). Other papers circulated included 'The Reagan Administration and East/West Relations' submitted by Sir N. Henderson and 'Ostpolitik, Détente and Inner-German Relations' submitted by Sir O. Wright.

7 December 1979 – 1 December 1981

expected in resolving the struggle with the free unions.[2] This suggests a proportionately greater desire to avoid the need for intervention and a greater opportunity for internal liberalisation in Poland; but it also carries the risk of a worse crisis later if the Polish authorities cannot stabilise the position and begin to re-establish their control. The stakes are much higher than in Afghanistan and it must be assumed that, if military action were necessary in order to sustain control by a Moscow-aligned Communist party, the Soviet Union would have recourse to it, calculating that, as in the case of Afghanistan, the Western reaction, harsh though it might be, would not take the form of a military challenge.

(iii) Iran matters more to the Soviet Union than Afghanistan, but the revolution, which had first achieved a major Soviet objective by destroying a strong point of American influence, was not a socialist revolution, did not produce the 'qualitatively new relationship' of Afghanistan in 1978, and must have seemed progressively less valuable. At no time in 1980 did matters develop in a way which would have made direct Soviet intervention a desirable means of obtaining control and it now looks as improbable as ever. The fighting between Iraq and Iran has been difficult to exploit, even politically, without prejudicing the Soviet position, either in Iran or in the Arab world and the Soviet Union seems to have been content to stand aside, despite having to see a strengthening of the Western position in the Gulf, to which it has been unable to make any response.

(iv) In relation to arms limitation, the Soviet agreement to talks on theatre nuclear forces (albeit with the possible addition of forward-based systems) signalled a recognition that, while pressure against NATO modernisation might be sustained, it might be impossible to frustrate Western plans without at least putting equivalent Soviet weapons on the table. The cautious handling of this issue and of the delay in SALT ratification suggested a Soviet recognition that some price might have to be paid to avoid escalation of nuclear arms.

3. In short, a decision to take the more adventurous course in Afghanistan produced stalemate, but a decision to pursue more cautious policies in Poland and the Middle East still left the Soviet Union marginally worse off, and in relation to arms control, options were held open, but the initiative passed to the West. To make matters worse the Soviet harvest was bad, industrial inefficiency became more manifest and the need to divert resources from the military to the civil sector was recognised. Looking back to the 1976 Party Congress, the balance of success is in striking contrast. Then, Nixon's disgrace, victory in Vietnam, conclusion of Helsinki and recognition of the GDR left the Soviet Union confident that it could define détente on its own terms. It is against a very different background that Soviet policy for the next five years will be developed for the 1981 Party Congress. The primary concern will be with internal policy. Decisions in that area will have significance for foreign policy, but go beyond the bounds of this paper. In foreign policy, relations with the West will be significant in so far as ideologically, the struggle with 'imperialism' must be a central feature. The Soviet objective will still be to sustain strategic nuclear parity and military superiority in Europe; to maintain the integrity of the Soviet empire; and to expand elsewhere, if this can be done with safety. (This, when translated, comes out as 'to bridle the forces of war and

---

[2] The independent Trade Union *Solidarnosc* (Solidarity) was formed in Gdansk on 31 August 1980. The issue of UK relations with the Soviet bloc, including Poland, will be covered in a forthcoming *DBPO* volume.

UK-Soviet Relations, 1979-82

aggression, to consolidate world peace and assure the peoples' right to freedom, independence and social progress'.) So much for the medium-term theory. What of the short-term practice?

4. In some ways, for the past five years détente with the West has for the Soviet Union been a residual, a matter of manoeuvring to secure such advantage as could be attained while prior requirements elsewhere were met. In few, if any, of the areas outlined in paragraph 2 above does the Soviet Union now hold the initiative. The same is true if the area is extended to include the relationship with China and the Arab/Israel problem. It is not surprising that in these circumstances the initial Soviet reaction to Reagan's victory should be to wait and see what it portends. They may hope that they have a more reliable negotiating partner, but in most of the world the change offers them little prospect of movement unless the new Administration first makes false moves. They may see this possibility in relation to the Middle East, the Third World, China or even Western Europe, and may try to open it up. But these will be essentially tactical moves. They may well hope at the same time to move towards a balanced accommodation with the United States on arms control. A significant effort is likely to be made to keep the TNF talks going if only in the hope of delaying deployment of Cruise and Pershing II. There could be a readiness for progress in CTB and MBFR and some bait on arms control in the CSCE context if the Madrid conference does not collapse in acrimony before that stage is reached. A balanced SALT II renegotiation to take account of the lost time could be acceptable to the Soviet Union, but it is difficult to see Soviet acquiescence in a new treaty which would offer a better deal to the United States than the treaty already negotiated. On a rational assessment Soviet objectives would be well served by a wider *modus vivendi* which would enable the Soviet Union, in a potentially dangerous period, to hold its defence expenditure at a tolerable level, secure full Western economic cooperation and stabilise its own empire within the present boundaries, leaving expansion for later. It is, however, difficult to see any real basis for this. The Nixon/Brezhnev agreement of May 1972 on 'Basic Principles of Relations' had little, if any, practical effect and the prospect now is that third country crises, although neither the Soviet Union nor the West may control them, will tend to become polarised in East/West terms and lead to increased tension. The Soviet Union will probably expect this and, while maintaining a posture of reasonableness, will prepare for a lengthy period of tension which it will hope to contain, while concentrating upon internal (including bloc) control and manoeuvring for tactical advantage elsewhere. During such a period of tension we can expect a fluctuating attitude towards the West, with alternating periods of apparent reasonableness, and pressure; a harsh response to Western measures whether in Europe as TNF modernisation progresses, or in the Third World; and an attempt to break politically what it sees as a hostile encirclement. In Europe the Soviet Union will still seek to pursue a détente policy designed to split Britain and America from the Continental European countries. Although they may retain hopes of exploiting the CSCE process to this end, and have not given up the prospect of achieving progress towards a European Disarmament Conference through Madrid, they probably now see their main task at that meeting as damage limitation.

5. The USSR will alternately threaten and woo the Federal Republic, but the Soviet political position in relation to central Europe is inherently weak, and its primary interest there is to ensure stability. It will not abstain from Third World political subversion, but will continue to be cautious in the Middle East, while

7 December 1979 – 1 December 1981

hoping to pose as a protector of the Arabs. The avoidance of direct military conflict with the United States will continue to be an essential and the Soviet Union will seek to avoid the use of its own forces other than in order to sustain the areas which it already controls—in which respect Poland will remain the point of principal risk.

No. 80

Record of a meeting between Lord Carrington and participants in the East-West Ambassadorial Conference, 19 November 1980[1]
Secret (FCO 28/4067, EN 400/2)

Relations with the Soviet Union and Eastern Europe

1. *Lord Carrington* said that we should do some thinking about the content of our relations with the Soviet Union and Eastern Europe. The truth was that we had stood off from the Russians in the past, in a different situation. But we should now re-examine the problem. *Sir Michael Palliser* said that this problem had been on the minds of many people in the office for some time. Much could be done in thickening up our political contacts without getting into substance. *Lord Carrington* foresaw a new chapter in US/European relations. The Prime Minister had a certain political affinity with Mr Reagan, and both Giscard and Schmidt knew this. We might find ourselves more closely involved in the politics of the Four than we had in the past, and the Franco-German relationship might not be so exclusive. To get the most out of this situation we needed more serious contacts with the Soviet Union.

2. *Sir Curtis Keeble* agreed. It would be especially important to do this at a time when Soviet/US relations could start to develop. *Sir Nicholas Henderson* thought, however, that relations with Moscow were a less powerful card in dealing with the Americans than relations with Eastern Europe, where there was more scope for Western European activity. *Sir Michael Palliser* recalled that the climate of US/European relations had changed since the time of Kissinger, and the 'Year of Europe'. *Sir Oliver Wright* thought that more active contacts with the Soviet Union and Eastern Europe would help our relations with the Germans. *Sir Reginald Hibbert* said that the French would attack us for poaching on what they saw as their preserve, though it was agreed that this was not a problem.

3. *Lord Carrington* said there seemed to be general agreement on this theme. He agreed with Sir Michael Palliser that the Republicans were not in so dominant a position *vis-à-vis* Europe as they had been last time round. He himself might have to face the prospect of going to Moscow to see Mr Gromyko. But it was not wise to ignore the Russians, and one could not play a role on the world scene if one did so.

Poland

4. On Poland, *Sir Curtis Keeble* thought that the Russians would be prepared to intervene only in the last resort. There might be some possibility of deterring them,

---

[1] Those present included Lord Carrington, Ian Gilmour, Mr Blaker, Sir M. Palliser, Mr Bullard, Mr Walden, Sir N. Henderson, Sir C. Keeble, Sir O. Wright, Sir R. Hibbert, Sir C. Rose, Sir J. Thomson, Heads of Mission at Islamabad, Luxembourg, UK Deputy Perm Rep to the UN and the Minister Tokyo. The issue of UK relations with the Soviet bloc, including Poland, will be covered in a forthcoming *DBPO* volume.

UK-Soviet Relations, 1979-82

or of postponing intervention—perhaps even indefinitely—if this were done in the right way. *Lord Carrington* recalled that he had been told at a lunch for US Ambassadors to Europe that Mr Reagan would turn the economic screw on the Russians. *Sir Oliver Wright* thought that this would bring the Americans up against the Germans. *Sir Curtis Keeble* thought that it was also the wrong logic to use with the Russians, who were locked into Afghanistan whether they liked it or not. Moreover, it was a pity to use the economic weapon where it was unlikely to be effective. *Sir Michael Butler* thought we might be able to deter the Russians at the margin by warning them privately that existing food exports would also be stopped if they intervened. We might get the French and Germans to go along with this, if the Americans committed themselves too.

5. *Lord Carrington* thought that the Germans might be pushed, despite themselves, into following the West on sanctions, though Chancellor Schmidt had made it clear to him that relations between East and West Germany would continue. *Sir Oliver Wright* thought that the Germans would want to continue contacts with the Russians too, e.g. on arms control. *The Lord Privy Seal* remarked that the Governing Mayor of Berlin had given him the impression that he would put up with anything in order to maintain relations with the GDR. *Sir Reginald Hibbert* thought that President Giscard would take a hard line with the Russians more because of French public opinion than to help the Poles. Giscard's underlying sympathies lay with Schmidt, and he would be anxious to keep contacts with the Russians in some areas, particularly once he had been re-elected.

6. *Lord Carrington* doubted whether in fact the new American Administration would want to start its relations with the Russians by tightening the economic screw, unless they intervened in Poland.

NATO

7. *Sir Clive Rose* was convinced that we needed a review of NATO, if we wanted financial savings, however unpopular such a review might be. It could also help to achieve some specialisation. *Lord Carrington* welcomed the prospect of further specialisation, but said that the main thing at the moment was to get rid of the present Secretary-General.[2] He described Chancellor Schmidt's negative reaction to the proposal for a review (though there was some doubt about how fully this had been put to the Chancellor). *Sir Reginald Hibbert* thought that it was not a good time to propose a review. *Sir Nicholas Henderson* thought that the Americans would smell a rat, and see our proposal as an attempt to get off our 3 percent hook. *Lord Carrington* thought that we needed to give the issue much more thought, and this should be done quickly. He himself would be very reluctant to pursue the proposal as it now stood. *Sir Michael Palliser* thought that we needed a rather different proposal, and different tactics. But we should not throw away the good elements in the idea.

The Third World

8. *Sir John Thomson* thought that India, and much of the Third World, had long had the feeling that the Americans had been losing ground. Despite their own complaints they would therefore be impressed by a new American presence in various regions of the world, including the Indian Ocean, provided this were combined with evidence of a readiness to go on talking to the Russians. He thought the West should be prepared to keep up pressure on the Afghanistan issue. Otherwise the Indians might be even less inclined to bother themselves.

[2] Joseph Luns, NATO Secretary-General 1971-84.

7 December 1979 – 1 December 1981

9. *Lord Carrington* said that it was important that Mr Reagan should stop talking about military superiority over the Russians. This would never be accepted either by the Russians or the Third World. *Sir Nicholas Henderson* thought that the Americans would stop talking in this way. The main problems for us were firstly, the commercial and military consequences for us of the new American presence in the Gulf area; and secondly, how the new threats to the West outside NATO would be met.

10. *Sir Oliver Wright* thought that the Germans too would want to see the latter point discussed. We should smoke the Germans out on this issue. At present they were refusing on a constitutional pretext to take any action. It should, however, be possible for the Germans to take up some of the slack in NATO if others became more active outside the NATO area. *Lord Carrington* expressed irritation at the American tendency to compliment the French for their activity in the Gulf, which in effect was to reward them for bad behaviour in NATO. He wondered whether the Americans would like us to rat on our obligations to NATO in the same way. *Sir Reginald Hibbert* thought that we should discuss all these issues frankly in Quadripartite, however reluctant the French were to see them raised.[3]

---

[3] Following further discussion amongst officials in London, the Secretary of State decided that Mr Bullard should 'spy out the land' on the prospect of a high level meeting when he visited Moscow in March (see No. 90).

No. 81

Sir C. Keeble (Moscow) to Lord Carrington, 7 January 1981
Confidential (ENS 014/2)

Soviet Union: Annual Review for 1980

Summary . . . [1]

My Lord,
Zagladin[2] in *New Times* (November 1980, No. 45): 'The 63rd year of the first victorious socialist revolution has been a year of intense unceasing struggle between two worlds, two opposite ways of life, two essentially antagonistic outlooks.'

1. Afghanistan and Poland. I could almost leave an annual review for 1980 at that. This was to be the year of success, a smiling Moscow as host to the world for the Olympics. With the admiration of the developing world, the loyalty of the Socialist brethren, the grudging respect of the West, it was to be a climax to *Pax Sovietica*, the apogee of the Brezhnev years. As the Soviet troops landed at Kabul in the last days of 1979 it all began to go wrong. By the end of 1980 a part of the Soviet army was still entangled in a colonial war in Afghanistan while another was poised to suppress the Polish workers. At home the harvest was bad and the economy in a mess.

2. Zagladin was right to call it a year of struggle and I wonder whether we, in Western Europe and North America, preoccupied by the problems of inflation and unemployment, realise to what an extent we had the better of it. The occupation of

---

[1] Not printed.
[2] Vadim Zagladin, First Deputy Secretary of the International Department of the Central Committee of the Communist Party of the Soviet Union.

UK-Soviet Relations, 1979-82

Afghanistan took place because that country, welcomed after many years as a member of the Socialist community, threatened to slip out of control. Brezhnev said that the decision to intervene had been a difficult one. He and many of his colleagues might well now say that it was a wrong one. What was planned was no doubt a campaign of a few months, after which a pro-Soviet Afghan Government would be able to remain in power with the backing of a residual Soviet garrison. Politically and militarily it was a miscalculation. Politically it heightened Western understanding of the Soviet concept of détente and alerted the Third World, as no earlier Soviet intervention had done, to the nature of Soviet imperialism. Militarily it led to the virtual collapse of the Afghan army and left the Soviet army to fight an unwinnable war against guerillas whom it could defeat but could not extinguish. Economically, on top of the direct cost, it frustrated the ratification of SALT II and opened up the prospect of increased military expenditure at a time when the civilian sector was openly recognized as needing a transfer of resources from the military.

3. Ill-coordinated though the Western reaction to the occupation of Afghanistan was, it served its purpose. The Olympic boycott was wide enough to rob the event of its triumphal aspect from the Russians. I doubt whether the embargo on high technology exports or even the grain embargo did significant damage, but they indicated that the United States at least was prepared, even at the expense of some of its domestic interests, to begin the process of deterring the Soviet Union from further expansion. President Carter's vaguely worded guarantee of the security of the Gulf area began to take on more substance over 1980, with the result that by the end of the year the Soviet Union found itself not only struggling to hold Afghanistan but facing a strengthened Western position in the Gulf. The fighting between Iraq and Iran faced the Soviet Union with a situation in which the only available policy was a cautious non-intervention, in the hope of avoiding damage to Soviet interests in one or other of the combatant countries. In the course of the year there were only two Soviet initiatives in relation to the Middle East, the signature of a friendship treaty with Syria in October and the plan for the Gulf and Indian Ocean launched by Brezhnev when he visited India in December. The former appeared to do little more than codify the existing state of affairs: the latter consisted of a rehash of old proposals, the effect of which would be to remove Western forces from the Gulf area, while leaving the Soviet forces to control Afghanistan. The Indian visit was played up hard by Soviet propaganda, but seemed to have little substantive effect. Soviet relations with China remained sour throughout the year, and in Africa the Soviet Government, having backed the loser in Zimbabwe, has been trying with indifferent success to make up lost ground.

4. The internal troubles in Poland must have increasingly dominated Soviet policy-making in the final months of the year. In Soviet psychology Eastern Europe brings together the twin complexes of ideology and security. Having used the Soviet army to sustain control in East Germany in 1953, Hungary in 1956 and Czechoslovakia in 1968 there can have been little doubt that the leadership would have been ready to use it again in Warsaw in 1980 if it had been clear that the situation would otherwise go out of control. At the beginning of December, with the Solidarity Union having forced concession after concession from the Government, we must have been very close to the point of intervention. There was however a general recognition, when the Warsaw Pact countries met in Moscow,

7 December 1979 – 1 December 1981

that Kania's Government[3] was as good as any the Soviet Union could expect in the circumstances and that it was likely to be more successful if Soviet troops were kept out than if they were put in. So the decision was taken to give Kania a probationary period within which to harness the new unions to the Party. I think the severity of the international reaction to Afghanistan and the warning statements by Western leaders about Poland also helped to deter the Soviet Union from intervention so long as there was a hope of controlling Poland without it. By the end of the year tension had subsided slightly, but there was little basis for optimism in the longer term.

5. With Afghanistan and Poland as focal points for a confrontation between the Soviet Union and the main body of world opinion and with President Carter in his final year, the direct superpower relationship remained frozen. SALT II having remained unratified, the other arms control negotiations slowly withered and although by the end of the year preliminary talks on TNF negotiations had been instituted as a result of Chancellor Schmidt's visit to Moscow, nothing of substance could be achieved. We therefore ended the year with the Soviet Union preparing to confront the incoming Reagan Administration, professing a desire for a constructive relationship, but doing so against a background of clashing interests in many areas and with no major negotiations at a point at which swift results seemed likely.

6. The Soviet leadership no doubt counted it a success that Chancellor Schmidt visited Brezhnev in Moscow in the summer and they rewarded him by offering to negotiate with the United States on theatre nuclear forces, without requiring prior abandonment of the NATO modernisation programme. The visit could also fairly be counted as a success from the Western point of view in that it exposed the Politburo to a forceful and reasoned exposition of the Western position on Afghanistan. The Giscard-Brezhnev meeting was of substantially less significance and the gradual hardening of French policy, particularly in relation to Poland, must have been a source of no small irritation to the Russians. Even the European Communist parties offered little consolation. The Italians, Spaniards, Yugoslavs and Rumanians all absented themselves from the Paris meeting of European Communist parties, and Berlinguer and Carrillo visited Peking.[4]

7. Relations with Britain were at a low ebb throughout the year. Gromyko found, not surprisingly, that it would be inconvenient to accept the pre-Afghanistan invitation to visit London in March. Neither your meeting with him at the time of Tito's funeral nor your subsequent meeting at the United Nations provided any basis for a fruitful exchange. The Soviet Union did not altogether refuse to discuss your proposals for a neutral and non-aligned Afghanistan, but it was swiftly made plain that the Russians would not seriously consider proposals other than those designed to legitimise the Government of Babrak Karmal and the continuation of Soviet occupation. The Joint Economic Commission remained in suspense. Contacts were negligible in the cultural and scientific areas and the jamming of the BBC Russian service was resumed. British exports to the Soviet Union in the first eleven months of 1980 were slightly above the 1979 level, while imports fell slightly, but the trade reflected contracts concluded in earlier years and we must expect a decline in exports in 1981. Civil aviation negotiations led to a more balanced flight ratio but at a lower level. Even so, with contacts in most areas still

---

[3] Stanislaw Kania, General-Secretary of the Polish Communist Party.
[4] Enrico Berlinguer, General-Secretary of the Italian Communist Party; Santiago Carrillo, General-Secretary of the Spanish Communist Party.

UK-Soviet Relations, 1979-82

very limited, the four remaining British Airways' flights each week are nearly empty.

8. Internally, only Brezhnev went from strength to strength. His health much improved, he was clearly able to handle long discussions in a decisive manner, as he demonstrated during the visit of Senator Percy.[5] One sensed more and more the presence of Brezhnev on the public scene and the absence of significant public appearances by his Politburo colleagues. With Kosygin's death in late December Brezhnev's pre-eminence was further emphasised. The grain harvest, always of psychological as well as economical importance in this country, was bad and with the introduction of the new Five Year Plan at the end of the year failings in other sectors of the economy received much public attention.

9. There was a further thinning of the ranks of dissidents, especially human rights activists. The removal of Sakharov to Gorky at the beginning of the year proved to be a particular blow to the effectiveness and the morale of others. There are now only five members of the Moscow Helsinki Monitoring Group.[6] Since the invasion of Afghanistan, the leadership has felt less need than usual to consider Western reactions, and arrests and trials, particularly numerous in the pre-Olympic period, continued throughout the year, even during the Madrid Review meeting. The movement is now quiescent. But it has lived through similar, if not quite such severe waves of repression in the past, and shown itself resilient enough to survive. In the short term, however, the Soviet leadership no doubt congratulate themselves on having reduced the effective voice of human rights protest.

10. The prospect for 1981 must be that the grinding, sterile struggle against the Soviet imperial machine will continue. There are no areas in bilateral or multilateral relations where I can identify opportunities for a major turn for the better. Yet, preoccupied as they are with Poland and Afghanistan, the Soviet leaders will not, I think, be in a mood for adventure and could conclude that it is worth making some effort, by agreement with the United States, to avoid a further nuclear arms spiral. It is a dreary prospect, but substantially less hazardous than we sometimes suppose.

11. I am sending copies of this despatch to Her Majesty's Ambassadors at Washington, Bonn, Paris, Helsinki, Peking, Belgrade, Warsaw, Prague, Budapest, Bucharest, Sofia, East Berlin and Kabul; and to the United Kingdom Permanent Representative at NATO.[7]

I am, etc,

CURTIS KEEBLE

[5] On 28 November Charles 'Chuck' Percy, the Republican Senator for Illinois and Chairman of the Foreign Relations Committee (1981-85), paid a private visit to Moscow where he had a series of meetings with Brezhnev, Gromyko and Ustinov. His meeting with Brezhnev lasted two hours and forty minutes.

[6] A human rights group founded in 1976 to monitor the Soviet Union's compliance with the Helsinki Final Act of 1975, which included clauses calling for the recognition of universal human rights.

[7] Mr Blaker minuted: 'Sir C. Keeble brings out the reasons why the Soviet rulers should be disappointed with the way 1980 has evolved, but the picture doesn't look too good from our side either.' Mr Fergusson similarly noted: 'The Soviet Union is still in Afghanistan. Western leverage has yet again been shown to be generally ineffective. It is true that the economy may be in poor shape and that the harvest has been poor, but there are no signs of internal disaffection and the growing relative importance and consequent leverage of Soviet energy sources has been maintained.' On a different note, Mr Fall observed: 'Brezhnev's recovery is enough to get one believing in Georgian faith healers. Perhaps it is the stimulus of having indisputably out-run the other two horses in the troika?' (minutes of 19-22 January).

7 December 1979 – 1 December 1981

No. 82

Record of an introductory call by the Soviet Ambassador (Mr Popov) on Lord Carrington, 21 January 1981, 10 a.m.
Confidential (ENS 400/1)

Present:

Lord Carrington   Mr Popov, Soviet Ambassador
Mr Walden   Mr Dolgov, Counsellor, Soviet Embassy
Mr Fall, EESD
Mr Cummins, EESD

1. *Lord Carrington* began by saying that 1980 had been a bad year for East-West relations and hoped that 1981 would see an improvement. *Mr Popov* said that his instructions were to work to strengthen cooperation and develop friendly relations with the UK. What Brezhnev had said in May 1979 remained true. The Soviet Union advocated a policy of peaceful co-existence, effective measures to strengthen detente, and the elimination of obstacles to the development of relations. If the UK was prepared to play its part, the Soviet Union would like to see closer ties with the UK particularly in the field of Parliamentary visits, trade and culture. Such links were always easier to disrupt than to re-establish. The Soviet Union was also interested in large scale projects. Soviet long term plans would involve a broadening of economic relations with their partners. They wished to find ways of cooperating with all countries under mutually beneficial conditions. He was well-known in the Soviet Union for his championing of the development of good Anglo-Soviet relations.

2. *Lord Carrington* replied that the UK also wished for an improvement in relations. There was already some activity—the Joint Commission, Mr Bullard's visit to Moscow, the Economic and Industrial Review and the cultural negotiations. He had had talks with Mr Gromyko in New York and in Vienna and hoped that they would have occasion to meet again. There was not as much contact as we would like, but there were difficulties. The Afghanistan problem must be solved. It was possible to do this to the satisfaction of the Soviet Union and of the people in the region. Until a solution to this problem could be found we could not develop Anglo-Soviet relations as we would like, but we still favoured maintaining bilateral contact.

3. *Mr Popov* emphasised that the Soviet Union were in favour of a political solution to the Afghanistan problem. It was sometimes said that giving help to the opponents of the Afghan regime could play a useful part. In fact, the supply of arms by outsiders only prolonged the conflict. When the situation in Afghanistan had appeared a little better, some of the Soviet troops had been withdrawn.

4. On bilateral relations, Mr Popov thought that the level of trade and cultural contacts was not high enough. He would like to see, for example, more Soviet actors and artists visiting the UK and vice versa. The British side should make proposals—it had not been the Soviet side which had taken measures to reduce exchanges. On trade, he feared that the UK's competitors would find themselves better placed, though he would like to see Anglo-Soviet trade relations develop.

5. *Lord Carrington* drew a parallel between the current situation in Afghanistan and the era of the 'great game': there remained fears about expansionism, and the West had particular concern about the Gulf. But we understood also that the Soviet

UK-Soviet Relations, 1979-82

Union needed to have Afghanistan as a friend. It was not impossible to find a solution which would take account both of Soviet concerns and of those of the other countries of the region. We had no wish to impose on Afghanistan a government hostile to the Soviet Union. The need was to leave Afghanistan alone, to guarantee its independence and to leave it neutral and non-aligned.

6. *Mr Popov* picked up the reference to the Gulf and asked the Secretary of State for his reaction to Mr Brezhnev's proposals of 10 December.[1] These included provisions on no military bases, no nuclear weapons, a guarantee of independence of the countries of the region and a guarantee of free shipping. The last point should be of particular interest to the United Kingdom. The Soviet Union were also ready to discuss any proposals for stabilising the position in the area. *Lord Carrington* said that this was not the time for a detailed discussion of the proposals. He had not seen anything very new in what Mr Brezhnev had said, and the proposals had been received with caution by countries in the area. The proposals seemed a bit one-sided. The presence of Soviet troops in Afghanistan was not in accordance with the philosophy said to underline the proposals.

7. *Mr Popov* said that the proposals reflected not only the interests of the Soviet Union. They were compatible with the proposals for an Indian Ocean Zone of Peace which had been put forward by regional states. Further consideration of the proposals was needed: they were not intended as an 'ultimatum', but as a basis for discussion. Lord Carrington replied that if proposals of that kind were to be looked at seriously they should appear to be even-handed and not one-sided.

8. *Lord Carrington* raised the question of Embassy sites in London and Moscow. A new broom would be useful. Could Mr Popov not help to solve this problem as one of his first tasks? *Mr Popov* replied that he was familiar with the problem and had made enquiries in Moscow before his posting. He was under the impression that proposals had already been made to the British Ambassador in Moscow. When told that it was our understanding that no acceptable proposals on a site for the Ambassador's Residence in Moscow had been received, Mr Popov replied that it would be necessary to continue to study the problem and to discuss together what was needed in London and in Moscow.

9. *Mr Popov* then went on to say that he had been glad to note from his talks with Mr Blaker and others in the FCO that the UK was ready for a dialogue, but wondered whether the UK wished to 'have talks for the sake of talking' or whether they had any concrete proposals to make. *Lord Carrington* replied that we wished to improve relations and could not do this without doing something concrete like building up trade and cultural links, for example. But this would depend on the overall international picture. 1981 would have to be an improvement on 1980 for relations to develop as we would wish.

10. The meeting closed at 10.45 a.m.

[1] President Brezhnev had proposed a Persian Gulf Zone of Peace during a visit to New Delhi in December 1980.

7 December 1979 – 1 December 1981

No. 83

Letter from Mr Walden to Mr Alexander (No. 10), 30 January 1981[1]
Confidential (ENS 020/1)

Dear Michael,

Relations with the Soviet Union

There has been some recent press interest in the trade talks now being held in Moscow between officials from the Department of Trade and their Soviet opposite numbers. The news that we are to negotiate a new Anglo-Soviet Cultural Agreement may also attract attention (there has already been a not unhelpful article in the *Daily Telegraph* of 28 January). You will have seen the material provided for the Prime Minister's use at Question Time[2] recently but you may find some additional background helpful, in particular on how these developments fit with our policy on relations with the Soviet Union post-Afghanistan.

David Wright's letter to Stuart Hampson of 28 October[2] recorded the Prime Minister's approval for the resumption of inter-governmental trade contacts with the Soviet Union. We have consistently said that normal trade with the Soviet Union which benefits British exporters should continue. This involves a degree of governmental support, through the mechanism of the Anglo-Soviet Joint Commission which meets annually to review progress in implementing our 1975 Agreement on the Development of Long Term Economic Cooperation (the meeting has normally been held in May; in 1979 this slipped to October and in 1980 no date was in fact arranged). Without this framework, our exporters would find themselves at a disadvantage compared to their Western competitors. As you will see from the enclosed table,[2] we export much less to the Soviet Union than our main West European competitors. (Our exports to the Soviet Union rose last year because a number of major contracts were signed before the invasion of Afghanistan. They are expected to drop this year.) Some of our partners have already resumed full-scale inter-governmental trade relations with the Soviet Union, and others plan to do so soon. We therefore believe it right to begin preparing for a meeting of the Anglo-Soviet Joint Commission, perhaps in the late spring. A necessary part of this preparation is the review at official level of the Programmes for Economic and Industrial, and Scientific and Technological Cooperation. This is the purpose of the current talks in Moscow.

There are no plans to relax the specific measures on trade with the Soviet Union which we took following the invasion of Afghanistan. We do not intend to replace the inter-governmental credit agreement which we decided not to renew when it expired on 16 February 1980. Credit for trade with the Soviet Union is now available on a case by case basis, but at interest rates not more favourable than those laid down by the International Consensus. In addition, together with our partners, we have since January 1980 refrained from submitting to COCOM any major exceptions to the rules governing the transfer of sensitive technology. There has been some amendment of the COCOM lists to cover specific items of new

---

[1] In light of interest aroused in the press by UK/Soviet trade talks in Moscow, it was decided at one of the PUS's morning meetings to send a Private Secretary letter to No. 10 outlining the current state of relations with the Soviet Union. Mr Fergusson recognised that the case for sending a letter was essentially defensive, given that the Prime Minister had already approved the policy over trade contracts, and there was a risk of reopening the argument.

[2] Not printed.

UK-Soviet Relations, 1979-82

technology not previously covered. We have also discussed with our partners proposals for widening the scope of COCOM to cover areas such as know-how. But here the prospects for agreement are not good, given the wide divergence of views between the Americans on the one hand and the French and Germans on the other. Discussions continue, however, and there may be some small extensions of the embargoed list. Moreover the European Community has maintained its policy of not substituting supplies of agricultural products from the Community for those denied to the Soviet Union by the United States, subject to 'traditional' trade. This decision did not go as far as we should have liked. We have consistently argued for an end to all subsidised food sales by the Community to the Soviet Union. And exports of some products in 1980 were higher than even the Commission's estimates of 'traditional' trade. The Community's action in supporting the Americans has nonetheless had some impact, and appeared to satisfy the previous US Administration.

We also decided after the invasion of Afghanistan to avoid any major cultural event which might be used by the Russians to claim that we were carrying on business as usual. We cancelled or withheld support for a number of such events during 1980, and none are in prospect for 1981. At the same time we decided not to abrogate the 1979/81 Anglo-Soviet Cultural Agreement, nor to stop the routine exchanges of students, teachers and academics for which that agreement provides. This is the balance we want to maintain, and Lord Carrington has decided that it would be right to negotiate a new two-year Cultural Agreement to replace the one expiring this year and to allow for our routine exchanges to continue. There are good arguments, in terms of what we are attempting to do in the CSCE meeting in Madrid, for renewing this agreement since it translates into practical terms our efforts to promote freer exchanges with the Soviet Union of people and information. We think these work on balance to our advantage in the battle of ideas. The new Agreement will not commit us to any major cultural event during its lifetime, and there is therefore no question of our being obliged to go back on the policy we adopted in January 1980.[3]

Yours ever,

G. G. H. WALDEN

[3] In a covering note to the Prime Minister Mr Alexander observed: 'The Community aspect is unsatisfactory but our own line looks about right—assuming no further deterioration in relations e.g. as a result of intervention in Poland'. The Prime Minister noted that she was very sorry a new cultural agreement was being negotiated with the USSR. 'They will gain from it. We shall not. So much for Afghanistan' (PREM: UK-Soviet Relations).

No. 84

Lord Carrington to HM Representatives Overseas, 3 February 1981
Guidance Tel. No. 15 Confidential (ENS 020/1)

Anglo-Soviet Relations
1. We continue to be guided in our contacts with the Soviet Union by the line set out in Guidance Telno 95 of 8 September 1980.[1]

[1] No. 76.

7 December 1979 – 1 December 1981

2. You will have seen references in the press to the trade talks with the Soviet Union which took place in Moscow at official level from 26-28 January. There has also been public reference to the negotiations on a new Anglo-Soviet Cultural Agreement which will take place in Moscow from 16-23 March (we assume that this was made known to the press by the Soviet Embassy). There may be a similar leak once dates have been confirmed for the political consultations at senior official level which are likely to take place in Moscow at the end of March (see paragraph 12 below). Finally, the British-Soviet Joint Commission, which is expected to meet in London at Ministerial level at the end of May, will provide a further focus for publicity.

Line to Take

3. You may draw freely on paragraphs 4 to 7 below in response to questions. Paragraphs 8 to 12 give background which may be used as necessary (paragraph 12 only if news of Bullard's visit leaks).

4. The talks which took place in Moscow from 26-28 January between officials of the Department of Trade and the Soviet Ministry of Foreign Trade were to review the implementation of the 1975 Anglo-Soviet Long-Term Programme for the Development of Economic and Scientific Cooperation in preparation for the forthcoming meeting of the Anglo-Soviet Joint Commission. These are part of a regular series of meetings designed to provide British companies trading with the Soviet Union a similar degree of official support to that provided by other Western governments. The Government believe that normal trade between the UK and the Soviet Union which brings benefit to our exporters should continue. This was made clear when the Government's measures following the invasion of Afghanistan were announced in January 1980 (Verbatim 010/80).

5. None of these economic measures has been relaxed. We have not renewed the Anglo-Soviet Credit Agreement which expired in February 1980. Credit is now available on a case by case basis but not at rates more favourable than those agreed internationally. The application of COCOM rules governing the export of strategic and sensitive technology has been tightened. In common with our Allies, we have not submitted to COCOM any major exceptions cases since the invasion of Afghanistan. There are no plans to change this policy. The EC decided in January 1980 to support the US embargo on grain exports to the Soviet Union by not substituting Community supplies for US products on the Soviet market, either directly or indirectly, subject to traditional trade flows. We have actively supported this decision which remains in force. Indeed we have consistently pressed for an end to all subsidised food sales from the Community to the Soviet Union.

6. A new Cultural Agreement will be negotiated at talks at official level in Moscow in March.[2] The Agreement which, like its predecessors, will be for 2 years, will regulate and facilitate routine exchanges in the educational, scientific and cultural fields. No major cultural events under governmental auspices or sponsorship have been held since the invasion. None are in prospect for 1981 and we shall not be obliged under the terms of the new agreement to hold any such major events. But to cut off all cultural exchanges with the Soviet Union would be inconsistent with our policy of working, both bilaterally and through the CSCE process, for a freer flow of people, information and ideas.

7. We should of course review the entire range of our contacts with the Soviet

---

[2] A new agreement was signed in Moscow on 23 March 1981 by Sir C. Keeble. At British insistence, the term 'friendship' was removed from the preamble to the agreement which now only served to strengthen understanding and mutual cooperation.

UK-Soviet Relations, 1979-82

Union should there be a Soviet invasion of Poland.

Background

8. The trade talks come at a time when the Soviet Union is about to embark on a new Five-Year Plan and is the first intergovernmental meeting on trade matters since October 1979. Soviet trade with the FRG, Italy and France expanded rapidly in 1980. These and other West European countries have already held their Joint Commission meetings with the Soviet Union or plan to do so soon. It is therefore necessary for the inter-governmental activities providing the framework within which British exporters operate to be kept in repair if the competitive position of our companies is to be protected.

9. British exports to the Soviet Union in 1979 and 1980 were £419m and £453m respectively. Imports from the Soviet Union were £827m and £786m respectively. The 1980 figures are provisional. The increase in British exports in 1980 reflects deliveries under major contracts signed in earlier years. These have now largely been completed, and, since few major contracts were signed in 1980, UK exports are expected to decline in 1981 (although British firms are engaged in discussions of a number of large deals, there is strong competition from continental rivals).

10. The first Cultural Agreement was signed with the Soviet Union in 1959 and agreements are renegotiated every two years. Our aims are to secure a sure but steady expansion in facilities for British academics and others in the Soviet Union in order to promote fuller and freer exchanges in all fields, including wider dissemination of British newspapers and printed matter in the Soviet Union and increased sales of British books there.

11. Following the invasion of Afghanistan routine exchanges under the Cultural Agreement were not stopped, the agreement itself was not abrogated, but we discouraged major events. During 1980 this resulted in the cancellation of a UK tour by the Red Army Choir. We also withheld official support for a Soviet film week, cancelled a visit to the Soviet Union by the English Chamber Orchestra, and withheld support for an exchange of music festivals with the Soviet Union in 1981 and 1982.

12. Subject to confirmation of dates Bullard (DUSS) will visit Moscow in late March for political consultations with Deputy Foreign Minister Zemskov.[3] No announcement has been made but news may leak before the visit. These consultations are part of a regular series, but there has been a longer gap than usual because of Afghanistan. They should be seen in the wider context of our wish to keep open the channels of communication with the Soviet Union on important international and bilateral issues.

[3] See Nos. 90 and 91.

No. 85

Minute from Sir John Graham to Mr Humfrey[1], 12 February 1981
Confidential (FSA 021/3)

Afghanistan

1. Our present policy is to give full support to Pakistani efforts to set up meetings under UN auspices with representatives of the Babrak Karmal regime in

[1] Private Secretary to Mr Hurd.

7 December 1979 – 1 December 1981

their Party capacities, with Pakistani and Iranian participation, on condition that subsequently the Soviet Union will also be involved with the UN Special Representative and that the objective is the withdrawal of Soviet troops. Despite the appointment announced today of De Cuellar as Dr Waldheim's Special Representative, it looks increasingly unlikely that the Pakistani effort will get anywhere; and my own fear is that, even if it does, the Pakistanis will have found it necessary to make so many concessions that the whole process could be dangerous, ending up with virtual recognition by Pakistan of the Karmal regime, no involvement of the Soviet Union and in particular no commitment by them to withdraw troops. I note, for example, that in New Delhi's report of proceedings in the Non-Aligned Meeting Agha Shahi is quoted as referring to 'the representatives of the People's Democratic Republic of Afghanistan'; and it is clear from what the UN and the Pakistanis have told us that the furthest Russians have been prepared to go is to agree to consider receiving Dr Waldheim's Special Representative after the meeting between the Pakistanis and the Karmal representatives. They used a similar technique when they were negotiating the resolution in the General Assembly last autumn, holding out the possibility that they would accept it if it spoke only of a hope that the Secretary General would appoint a special representative and did not require him to do so: when this point had been conceded, they rejected the resolution root and branch. I fear that they will do the same on this occasion.

2. If I am right, I wonder whether we should not consider a new approach and pick up President Giscard's proposal for a conference of neighbours and other concerned governments, but excluding the Afghanis.[2] This French proposal has a nice logic in that all parties maintain that the primary cause of the trouble in Afghanistan is foreign interference—we differ only on the source and nature of that interference. It would have been better if the French had engaged in some consultations with those of us involved, notably the Pakistanis, in advance of springing the idea on us. Nevertheless their objective, an understanding or agreement between the outside powers to cease interference and not to interfere in the future in the internal affairs of Afghanistan, non-interference to include the withdrawal of any foreign troops that there may be there, and their proposed procedure are consistent with, and, as it were the other side of the coin to, our original proposal that Afghanistan should be declared neutral and non-aligned through a procedure to be defined, but probably including a conference. Thus it would not be impossible to present a new approach on these lines as an Anglo-French proposal.

3. If there is thought to be merit in this the necessary first steps would be to discuss it with the Americans, the Pakistanis and the French. I am not sure that it matters in which order these are approached although the Pakistanis should be brought in fairly early. I could discuss it in general terms with the Americans when I am in Washington next week.

---

[2] On 27 January President Giscard announced on French television a proposal for an international conference, under UN auspices, aimed at ending external intervention in Afghanistan, to be attended by the Soviet Union, other permanent members of the Security Council, Iran, Pakistan and India. The Afghan government need not participate since the conference would deal exclusively with the question of ending external interference, so that Afghanistan could re-affirm its non-aligned status. There was no consultation with Western allies who were given little, if any, notice and there was speculation that the proposal was an attempt by President Giscard to demonstrate that France was still capable of seizing the diplomatic initiative and pursuing an independent foreign policy in the run up to the forthcoming presidential election.

UK-Soviet Relations, 1979-82

4. In talking to the Pakistanis we could take the line that we have watched with admiration their skilful handling of the follow-up to the UN General Assembly resolution, but that it now seems that, given the attitude of the Soviet Union and the Iranians, it is not going to be possible to carry this forward without undue risk. We have been wondering therefore whether there would be merit in a conference on the lines of the French proposal. We recognise very clearly Pakistan's interest in a settlement which would involve withdrawal of Soviet troops, the establishment of good relations with Afghanistan and the return to their own country of the Afghan refugees. A conference on the lines suggested which did not involve recognition of the Karmal regime, but led to a declaration or agreement by all the outside Powers, both immediate neighbours and states otherwise more or less directly concerned, to eschew interference in the current affairs of Afghanistan, could achieve precisely the objective which we ourselves proposed in the spring of last year, namely a neutral and non-aligned Afghanistan, in effect guaranteed by its neighbours and the great Powers.

5. In speaking to the French we would say that we had been considering carefully President Giscard's proposal. We had not wished to cut across Pakistani efforts and from their explanations to us we noted that the French have had the same thought in mind. Now however it seemed that Pakistani efforts were not likely to be successful and we had therefore been considering whether we should not exploit the opening made by President Giscard in an attempt to achieve through a conference on the lines he suggested the objective that we all share, namely the withdrawal of Soviet troops and the establishment of an Afghanistan that is neutral and non-aligned as proposed by Lord Carrington in 1979.

6. I think it unlikely that the Soviet Union could agree to take part in any such conference, but it would be difficult for them to argue convincingly against it since they themselves have claimed that the problem is caused by outside interference and indeed declarations of non-interference by outside powers form part of their 14 May proposals. An initiative on these lines would therefore serve to head off the dangers which I foresee in the present Pakistani efforts and at the same time continue to keep pressure on the Russians.

7. I have discussed these ideas with Mr Donald who is in general agreement.[3]

JOHN GRAHAM

[3] Mr Hurd minuted: 'I think this is worth considering'. Mr Blaker also agreed that the French proposal had some 'real attractions' but he did not want to alienate the Pakistanis by cutting across their own efforts to initiate talks. The Foreign Secretary was, in principle, attracted by the ideas set out in the minute but agreed with Mr Blaker that these should be discussed in substance first with the Pakistan government. Sir J. Graham proposed allowing the current initiatives from Pakistan and the Secretary General's personal representative to run their course before taking any action. Mr Hurd agreed—a recent conversation he had had, in the Omani desert, with Mr Waldheim and Mr de Cuellar showed that they and the Pakistanis were still active.

7 December 1979 – 1 December 1981

No. 86

Sir C. Keeble (Moscow) to Lord Carrington, 5 March 1981
Confidential (ENS 011/1)

The 26th Congress of the Communist Party of the Soviet Union
(23 February-3 March 1981)

Summary . . . [1]

My Lord,
    This was a staid Congress, a formal rededication of the Soviet Party to its existing policies and a confirmation in office of its present leadership. Symbolic of it was the sight of the entire Soviet leadership, old, infirm and muffled against the February cold, paying their collective tribute at Lenin's mausoleum.
    2. The proceedings themselves were tidily and efficiently conducted. The leadership was clearly in command. The fraternal parties, albeit with some significant exceptions, paid their tribute. The organisers and drafters may relax content. Yet this was not a triumphal celebration. Five years ago at the 25th Congress Brezhnev could say 'The world is changing before our very eyes and changing for the better'. This year there was still talk of victory, but I would take as more typical his characterisation of the international scene as 'rough and complicated' and his disclaimer 'Far be it for us to paint the present day picture of the socialist world in exclusively radiant colours'. I enclose a copy of the report which he delivered on behalf of the Central Committee together with a summary of the main foreign policy proposals.[2] A number of detailed points have been the subject of separate correspondence with the Department. My purpose in this despatch is to assess the significance of the Congress as a whole in relation to the development of Soviet policy.
    3. In 1976 Brezhnev spoke with confidence of the changing balance of world forces. He could celebrate victory in Indo-China, recognition of the German Democratic Republic, a rise in the fortunes of some Western European Communist parties, and the conclusion of CSCE with its implied confirmation of European frontiers, together with a significant development of Soviet-US relations which he could hope would bring détente on Soviet terms. In 1981 he could not sustain the confident tone. Vietnam was bogged down in Cambodia and proving expensive both economically and politically. Other commitments in the Third World, for example in Angola, Ethiopia and the Yemen, were expensive too. The intervention in Afghanistan had failed to produce quick results and a price had to be paid in terms of relations with the Islamic States and other members of the Non-Aligned Movement. CSCE had turned sour. The Belgrade meeting was not a success from the Soviet point of view and Madrid did not look like producing results. The Euro-Communists were an embarrassment, Poland a worry and China unremittingly hostile. The military buildup and the interventions, direct or by proxy, in the Third World had bolstered Alliance willingness to stand up to Soviet pressure,

---

[1] Not printed.
[2] Not printed. The proposals included a moratorium on the deployment in Europe of new medium range nuclear missiles, extending CBMs to the European USSR and negotiating CBMs with all interested countries in the Far East, the continuance of the SALT negotiations and limitations on new submarines and SLBMs.

UK-Soviet Relations, 1979-82

facilitating the NATO decisions on increased defence spending and TNF modernisation. Above all the US, recoiling at last from the humiliation of Vietnam, the shame of Nixon and the muddles of the Carter Administration, seemed set to resist further Soviet expansion. SALT II had not been ratified and there was the prospect of a harsh contest for global strategic supremacy.

4. So, as Gromyko indicated in his January *Kommunist* article (my despatch of 5 February)[3] the 26th Congress was taking place in a colder political climate than its predecessor. The chances of giving positive content to US-Soviet relations were in effect limited to the one area where movement might be both desirable and possible: arms control. Even there, the Soviet leadership had to recognise they must wait until the US Administration had formulated a position. For the time being there was not much Brezhnev could do. He would not sacrifice Afghanistan. He had to be ready to hold Poland, but with any luck he could avoid intervention for a time at least. What he could do meanwhile was to signal his desire to do business where it could be done without sacrificing any of his positions; and to avoid unnecessary exacerbation of the international scene elsewhere. This broadly was the course he chose. He was clear, if not totally explicit, in avowing to the outside world that the Soviet Union was in practice ready to contemplate renegotiating SALT. The key phrase here was that the Soviet Union was ready to 'continue the relevant negotiations without delay, preserving all the positive elements that have so far been achieved'. The Russians would no doubt maintain as an opening position that SALT II ought to be ratified. But it is clear enough that they would be ready to enter into new talks if it appeared possible to preserve the substance of SALT II, while adding in an acceptable agreement on other systems, especially theatre nuclear forces.

5. Thus far one may say that Brezhnev was taking a constructive line. The trouble is that the more specific he became the clearer he made his objective of maintaining the strategic relationship between the Soviet Union and the US at essentially its present level. This is nowhere more apparent than in the proposal for a moratorium on the deployment of theatre nuclear forces and forward based systems, where the insertion of the word 'qualitative' seems carefully designed to re-emphasise that a Soviet force modernised by the inclusion of the already deployed SS20s should be balanced against an unmodernised NATO force. The proposal relating to submarine deployment may in turn be designed to provide a negotiating counter to enable the Soviet Union to reject a claim for a reduction of Soviet land based systems in the SALT context.

6. I argued in my despatch of 5 February[3] that the Soviet leadership needed a working relationship with the US and that they needed it in the arms control area. This is now explicitly recognised, but there is no hint of readiness to make the concessions which might bring agreement and indeed the clear Soviet objective of maintaining its position is so far at variance with the American and NATO desire to improve the Western position that, on the basis of what has been said at this Congress, one cannot discern a basis for eventual agreement.

7. Some of the groundwork for splitting Western Europe from the US was laid in Brezhnev's speech but it was again consistent with his desire to establish a working relationship that he did not at this stage point it up. The offer to extend confidence building measures to all the European territory of the Soviet Union in an exchange for an unspecified extension on the Western side was no doubt an

---

[3] Not printed.

7 December 1979 – 1 December 1981

attempt to woo Europe and perhaps especially France and this is one area which we can expect to see actively pursued. Of Britain, Brezhnev said only that stagnation of relations was not through any fault of the Soviet Union and was in the interests of neither party.

8. In relation to other areas of actual or potential international tension Brezhnev's report was more interesting for the things it did not say than for the things it did. He maintained his proposals for a conference on the Gulf as he did for Afghanistan. One would need considerable optimism to see, in his offer to link the two problems—itself essentially a debating riposte to Western linkage—a recognition that there could be discussion among the major powers of the 'international' aspects of the Afghanistan problem. The French may want to explore whether there is here a nibble at the Giscard proposal,[4] but I doubt it. The Soviet Union cannot afford to do other than continue the attempt to consolidate its hold on Afghanistan and it cannot do this without Soviet troops in the country. On the Middle East there was nothing new in the proposal for a new conference. When he spoke more generally of the 'newly free countries' Brezhnev's description of a 'fairly motley picture' was at least honest and it is here that one senses, from the absence of arguments about the changing correlation of forces, a desire to avoid exacerbation of East-West tensions. The absence of references to Latin America cannot have been accidental and only in relation to the 'mounting intensity of the liberation struggle' in Namibia and South Africa were the old doctrines proclaimed in the old tones.

9. As with the international scene, the internal development of the Soviet Union offered little cause for complacency. The machine was running reasonably smoothly and overt dissidence was being repressed. But three bad harvests during the past five years gave no cause for optimism as to the prospects for Soviet agriculture and the performance of the economy as a whole was disappointing. The 1961 Party Programme had declared proudly that the next two decades would lay the material basis for Communism and that the Soviet Union would catch up with the US in a variety of important fields by 1981. It had not happened. The preparation and implementation of the economic plan takes a major place in the Party's concerns but does not lend itself to a summary. I have already reported the draft plan guidelines, with their general impression of a slowing of the rate of growth. Brezhnev's report and Tikhonov's subsequent more detailed exposition added little of significance and the plan was formally confirmed. There was as expected an emphasis on fuel and power, transport, metallurgy and agriculture, but the point where Brezhnev doubtless touched a sensitive nerve was when, discarding the jargon, he said simply 'People go to shops, canteens, laundries and cleaners every day. What can they buy? How are they welcomed? How are they spoken to? How much time do they spend on all sorts of household chores? It is on the strength of how these problems are solved that people largely judge our work.'

10. In internal political terms too, the Congress was essentially an exercise in stocktaking rather than in inspiration. Part of Brezhnev's appeal to the Party has been precisely that he has stood for continuity and order after the disturbing initiatives taken by Krushchev. But it is also the business of a Congress to point the way forward. Although Brezhnev touched on some potentially difficult issues, including the problems of labour resources and population distribution, and dealt well with the needs of the consumer, he did not develop any new ideas and other

---

[4] See No. 85, note 2.

UK-Soviet Relations, 1979-82

speakers preferred on the whole to avoid difficult areas. Neither the Central Asians nor the speakers from the Russian Republic took up Brezhnev's remarks on labour resources and population distribution, presumably because the Russians do not particularly want Central Asians coming North and the Central Asians would be happier to see investment come their way in the shape of new industries than to try to persuade their people to move to colder climates. It was of some interest that the Central Asians also called for the waters of the rivers of the North to be partially diverted South, a project with a long back history which was not mentioned either by Brezhnev or by RSFSR[5] spokesmen. The role of trades unions in Soviet society was only briefly dealt with and there was very little beyond routine exhortation about the relationship between the Party and the people as a whole. Both these might have been expected to be in delegates' minds after what has happened in Poland. The leadership are perhaps occasionally and uneasily aware of the degree to which they are cut off from popular concerns. At any rate Brezhnev felt it necessary to call—once again—for a better propaganda and ideological effort to put across the Party's policies and ideals and for a serious response to the concerns expressed by private citizens in their letters. He also suggested that the 1961 Party Programme be brought up to date, but his suggestion was not echoed with much fervour by other speakers and a draft of the revised programme will not be considered until the next Congress in 1986. When it does appear, its main purpose may be to make the programme less specific in its goals.

11. It is not surprising that a cautious leadership concerned about the international scene and eschewing experiment at home should also be reluctant to contemplate new ideas in the international Communist movement. Foreign delegations were here to pay tribute, not to contribute new ideas. The East Europeans had of course to be represented at the highest level but others were less constrained. The leaders of the French, Spanish and Italian parties all stayed away, the French for electoral reasons and the Spanish and Italians because of disagreement with the Soviet Party. The Italian delegate, although representing the largest of the Western Communist parties, was not allowed to speak to the Congress itself and although his speech, with its critical comments and emphasis on the need for independence of individual parties, was carried in full by *Pravda*, the Soviet leadership had made their disapproval clear. By contrast, Castro was the first of the guest speakers and although his appearance was curiously morose he said the right things. The treatment accorded him was, however, not especially fulsome and the Russians may well be concerned to see that no Cuban-inspired adventure cuts across their broader policy interests. The Vietnamese came next and Pham Van Dong's[6] 75th birthday on 1 March was suitably marked.

12. In dealing with inter-Party relations Brezhnev acknowledged that there could and had to be differences between Communist parties as regards tactics. He refrained from referring to the proletarian internationalism (or in plain language the right of the Soviet Union to dictate policy), but balanced this by saying that all Communists shared a common approach and that criticism of other parties should be constructive, a clear dig at the Italian and Spanish parties. Divisions within the movement are of course reasonably familiar, but the impression I was left with was that the Soviet leadership are less prepared than ever to listen seriously to those they regard as less than whole-heartedly on their side.

[5] Russian Socialist Federative Soviet Republic.
[6] Prime Minister of the Socialist Republic of Vietnam.

7 December 1979 – 1 December 1981

13. The Kremlin was lucky that Poland was quiet during the Congress. There was therefore no need for the majority of delegations to address the subject. Brezhnev underlined the Soviet commitment to preserving socialism in Poland. Kania[7] too declared this as a firm intention of the Polish Party, but there was no echo of his insistence that this was something for the Poles themselves to work out. The East Germans and Czechs were silent. The Polish issue was however a major consideration in the background. One of the few occasions the Congress really came alive was during Kania's speech, when even the Party ideologist, Suslov, stopped fiddling with his papers. The thrust of Soviet foreign policy as enunciated at the Congress was to contain East-West tension, but nothing said there changed my assessment that they are determined to maintain their control over Eastern Europe, even if the result of events in Poland is to force them into yet another major commitment which will frustrate their wider international objectives. If there could have been any doubt on this point it was removed by a meeting with Kania and Jaruzelski, immediately after the Congress, at which the Soviet requirement for a reversal of the trend of events in Poland was put more bluntly than at any time previously.

14. Thus in all areas of home and foreign policy one feels that a cautious leadership is seeking, above all, stability. But although the stridency and the zeal may be missing there is no suggestion of relaxation in any area where power is now held, any loosening of orthodox doctrine or any serious intent to reduce military spending. 'We must rest assured' said Tikhonov 'that our valorous armed forces will have everything they need to counter any attempts of the imperialist forces to gain military superiority'. The prevailing search for stability was reflected also in the re-election unchanged of all the full and candidate members of the Politburo, as well as all the Party Secretaries. With the expansion of the Central Committee which took place at the Congress, there could be room for the development of those who may come to the fore in 1986, but for the present we see only the consolidation of the supremacy which Brezhnev has been establishing over the years. Many must have watched with some cynicism the contrived staging of the Congress as an expression of unity in policy behind a revered leader. There are zealots who seek an alternative to this deadening bureaucracy, but I suspect that in this essentially sluggish society a majority may find the absence of adventure reassuring.

15. If we are to draw conclusions for Western policy they can contain a measure of encouragement. Brezhnev's tone reflected a recognition that such appeal as there may have been in the Soviet example has waned, while resistance to the Soviet threat has strengthened. The Soviet Union is at least temporarily on the defensive, but Soviet doctrine is based on the concept of an offensive defence. We should not therefore expect a period of quiescence, but if the West continues to combine the search for a safe and mutually beneficial relationship where it can be obtained with a resistance to Soviet expansion wherever it occurs, the historians of the future may see this Party Congress as marking a significant stage in the safe containment of Soviet power.

16. I am sending copies of this despatch to Her Majesty's Representatives at Washington, Paris, Bonn, Rome, Warsaw, East Berlin, Prague, Budapest,

---

[7] See No. 81, note 3.

UK-Soviet Relations, 1979-82

Bucharest, Sofia, Belgrade, Helsinki and New Delhi; and to the UK Permanent Representative at NATO.[8]

I am, Sir,
Yours faithfully,
CURTIS KEEBLE

[8] In a minute of 22 April Mr Fall noted that for all the insight it provided on where the Soviet Union might go next, the Congress might well not have taken place. He commented: 'The Soviet Union now finds itself in a reactive rather than an initiatory posture. For the leaders of a "revolutionary" state committed to active measures to expand the sphere of communist influence, this is an uncomfortable situation. For the leaders of a Panglossian state, the problems are not much less. The garden is not responding well to the techniques which the system requires; and, if the US declines to pursue measures of arms control, either because of Soviet misbehaviour or because the improvement of American defence capability is considered more pressing, the Russians fear that they will find themselves in a renewed and more expensive arms race.' In addition to this was the problem of Poland: 'With a shadow like that over-hanging the Congress, it is not surprising that Brezhnev remarked on a certain lack of radiance in the prevailing colours.'

Mr Fall's reply to the despatch (also 22 April) went further regarding Poland: 'If Brezhnev invades, his epitaph will be the doctrine named after him in 1968 and the years in between will be trapped in that context. If he does not, he risks being remembered for permitting the Poles to break the mould. Either way, the idea of building socialist victory by détente must suffer. No wonder there was not much buoyant self-confidence; and, as you concluded, the West is entitled to draw a little cautious encouragement.'

No. 87

Letter from Mr Alexander (No. 10) to Mr Walden, 9 March 1981
Confidential (PREM: UK-Soviet Relations)

Dear George,

Message from President Brezhnev

The Soviet Ambassador called on the Prime Minister this morning to deliver a message from President Brezhnev. He was accompanied by Mr Ouspenski. Mr Bullard was also present.

I enclose the Russian language text of the message together with an unofficial translation provided by the Soviet Embassy. At the Ambassador's request, the Prime Minister read the text of President Brezhnev's message in full before the discussion began. She told him that the message would be studied very carefully and a reply sent in due course.[1]

The Prime Minister told the Ambassador that HMG were very anxious to reduce the level of armaments provided they could be certain that the Warsaw Pact countries would also do so, permanently, on a basis which could be trusted and with adequate verification. The Soviet Union must find its present arms programme a major drain on its resources. The West also wished to spend less on armaments provided that this did not damage its security. They wanted the military balance to be stabilised at a much lower level than presently obtained.

As regards détente, the Prime Minister said that she was anxious to pursue this provided it was a genuinely reciprocal process. It would be much easier to discuss this, and other matters, once the Soviet Union had withdrawn its forces from

[1] No. 92.

7 December 1979 – 1 December 1981

Afghanistan. To have an independent country occupied by a major power inevitably damaged confidence. It gave rise to the question: 'who next?' The Soviet occupation therefore remained a source of grave concern to HMG.

NATO was anxious to discuss the control of theatre nuclear forces. NATO's wish to negotiate arms control measures in this area had been announced at the same time as their decision to deploy Cruise missiles. The Soviet Union was far ahead of the West in the number, design and sophistication of their theatre nuclear forces. The SS-20 was still being deployed at a rate of one every five days.

People in the West were genuinely peace-loving. They valued freedom and the right to pursue their own lives in their own way. They wanted other countries to be free to determine their own destinies. The Prime Minister recognised, however, that other countries did not see things the same way. Therefore HMG would continue to seek adequate defences, to maintain the Alliance, and to develop cooperation with allies. She saw these as prime duties of the Government. Hers was the last generation that remembered the horrors of World War II. She and her contemporaries would therefore take particular care to try to ensure that it did not happen again. This meant maintaining a military balance.

A new factor in the situation was that conflict seemed to encircle the globe. Hostilities were, or had recently been, in progress in Vietnam, Cambodia, Afghanistan, the Middle East, Ethiopia, Somalia, Angola and the Caribbean. All these situations were extremely dangerous and must not be allowed to expand. The activities of the Cubans and the supply of arms to the Third World were a source of concern. These matters could all be the subject of fruitful discussion. But the Prime Minister said that she would need assurances that such discussions were genuine. While the situation in Afghanistan persisted, the West would have to look at any proposal with 'extreme care'. President Brezhnev had proposed a summit meeting. She had suggested to President Reagan that if there was to be a summit, it would have to be very carefully prepared. If it were rushed into, it would not succeed. Summits always raised expectations and caused proportionate disappointment if they did not achieve anything.

The Prime Minister summarised her position as being that if President Brezhnev wanted to maintain the military balance at a reduced level; if he was prepared to withdraw Soviet forces from Afghanistan; and if he was willing to engage in 'two-way' détente, then he would find that HMG were very anxious to discuss these matters.

The Soviet Ambassador said that he had found the Prime Minister's remarks very interesting. There were of course differences between the British and Soviet points of view, but there were also some points in common. The Prime Minister was concerned to resolve the difficult questions that faced both countries. He agreed with her that solutions could not be achieved without contacts, talks and negotiations. Failing such contacts, the problems would not be solved. Indeed, they would get worse. Problems could be tackled at different levels. The most difficult could only be dealt with at the highest level. The Soviet Union regarded the UK as a great power with influence in Europe and indeed in the world as a whole. Hence President Brezhnev's message. Any meeting at any level of course required careful preparation. But some of the most difficult questions got more complicated with the passage of time. As a consequence it was necessary to tackle them urgently.

Turning to disarmament questions, Mr Popov said that neither side could win a victory in a nuclear war. Limited nuclear war was not possible. Any such war would lead to the destruction of civilisation. For this reason, the Soviet Union gave

UK-Soviet Relations, 1979-82

the highest priority to curbing the arms race. The Soviet Government had taken numerous initiatives and were prepared to discuss any approach to the problems. Mr Popov quoted the experiences of his own family during the last war in support of his claim that the Soviet Union was deeply sincere in its approach to the problem of disarmament. He added that the Prime Minister was right about the damaging effects of the present level of defence expenditure on the Soviet economy. The Soviet Government would prefer to devote more money to economic development. The arms race was of no advantage to either side.

On Afghanistan, Mr Popov said that the decision to send troops in to Afghanistan had been a difficult one for his Government. Three Afghan Governments had asked that Soviet troops should be sent; only the third request had been accepted. The Soviet Government wanted a political solution. Their troops would be withdrawn immediately if:

(*a*) attacks by bands of bandits from outside the country ceased; and

(*b*) a guarantee was given that the attacks would not be resumed.

The more arms that were supplied to the rebels fighting against a legitimate Government, the longer delayed the Soviet withdrawal would be. The Soviet Government was anxious to see a political solution achieved either in Afghanistan alone or together with the Gulf. Such a settlement would not only resolve the situation in Afghanistan but would lead to improved relations between the Soviet Union and the UK.

Mr Popov said that his entire career had been spent in the field of Soviet/British relations. The relationship was 'close to his heart' and he had come to London to seek an improvement in it. He was concerned to see trade relations between the Soviet Union and France, the Federal Republic, Finland and Italy expanding while those with the UK diminished. He was equally concerned to read of meetings at the highest level between the Soviet Government and the Governments of France and the Federal Republic and to note the absence of such meetings between the Soviet and British Governments.

The Prime Minister said that she was anxious to see more Anglo/Soviet trade where this was mutually beneficial. This, like all other aspects of the bilateral relationship, would flourish if it was clear that there was on the Soviet side a genuine wish for peace, and for the according to others of the freedom to decide their own destiny. Ours was an open society while that in the Soviet Union was not. She did not agree with the Ambassador about Afghanistan. She was worried about some aspects of the implementation of the Helsinki Final Act: the treatment of Mr Orlov[2] was one example of the sort of thing that was unacceptable. She could not divine the motives for Soviet actions. She could only judge the Soviet Government by its actions. If Soviet deeds matched Soviet words, the Soviet Government would find in the British Government very willing partners. For the moment they would remain watchful.

The Prime Minister ended the meeting by expressing her regret at the death of Mr Kosygin[3] and by recalling how impressed she had been when she met him in Moscow in 1979.

I am sending copies of this letter to Brian Norbury (Ministry of Defence), Stuart Hampson (Department of Trade) and David Wright (Cabinet Office), together with

---

[2] On 5 February, Dr Yuri Orlov, the former leader of the Moscow Helsinki Group (see No. 81, note 6) began a hunger strike to mark the resumption of CSCE talks at Madrid. In May 1978, he had been sentenced to seven years hard labour for 'anti-Soviet agitation'.

[3] Alexei Kosygin, the former Soviet Prime Minister, died on 18 December 1980.

7 December 1979 – 1 December 1981

copies of the enclosure.

Yours ever,
MICHAEL ALEXANDER

Enclosure in No. 87

Unofficial translation of message from Mr Brezhnev to Mrs Thatcher,
6 March 1981

Dear Madame Prime Minister,

I found it necessary to approach you on the most pressing problems created by the present situation in the world. The Congress of our party paid the paramount attention to its analysis, assessment and practical conclusions. The question was about what should be done to preserve peace, to ensure the primary right of every man—the right to live for the present and future generations. This is the essence of the adopted decisions which determine the course of the Soviet Union in foreign policy for years ahead.

We are realists, and certainly we understand that the improvement of international situation, the diminishing and elimination of military threat depend not only on us, but on the will of other states. It also depends on whether it would be possible to create the proper mutual understanding and effective co-operation on the bilateral and multilateral basis in solving vital problems of the present time.

We are convinced that the attitude towards the existing military-strategic balance between the USSR and the USA, between the Warsaw Treaty states and NATO is of a principled [*sic*] importance. The Soviet Union was not seeking and is not seeking military superiority. But we would not permit to create such superiority over us.

The attempts of that sort as well as the attempts to speak to us from the position of force have absolutely no perspective.

The existing military-strategic balance objectively serves to preserve peace on Earth. We are standing for the consistent decreasing of this balances' level without tipping it. To try to win in the arms race, to rely on the victory in the nuclear war, is a dangerous folly. It is necessary to realise that the endless competition in accumulating newer and newer weapons, the existing tension in the world—that is the real source of the military threat which hangs over all countries. We are ready to act hand in hand with all states in the resolute struggle against this threat.

We would like to express hope, Mrs Prime Minister, that by joint efforts the present stagnation in Anglo-Soviet relations will be overcome and they will get a new positive impetus in the interests of the peoples of our countries and of the cause of strengthening peace.

We believe that, in spite of the aggravated international situation, there still remain real opportunities to preserve and to strengthen peace so that all nations can live in security and develop mutually advantageous co-operation. In particular, this can be referred to the situation on the European continent where, despite the efforts of the enemies of détente, peaceful co-operation among the countries with two different systems is developing not badly on the whole and where we manage to find common language on a number of major foreign policy issues. Of significant importance—both as such and for strengthening the political dimension—is the fact that the ties among European countries in various fields are widening and

UK-Soviet Relations, 1979-82

assuming new qualities.

As never before, in contemporary conditions consistent advancement is needed along those lines of principle which were defined by joint efforts during the last decade. Vital interests of peoples demand that Europe should follow the path laid down in Helsinki.

It is necessary to continue and to strengthen the process initiated by the European conference. Every form of talks—multilateral, bilateral—should be used to resolve the problems of concern for its participants. From these positions the Soviet Union approaches the Madrid meeting. The adoption in Madrid of a decision to convene the European conference to discuss and resolve the military détente and disarmament issues in Europe would be of a particular importance.

It is known that in recent years the Soviet Union put forward a number of proposals, aimed at diminishing military threat, strengthening international security, many of which had been approved by the UN and other representative forums. All of them remain valid and we will strive for their implementation.

However the situation today is such that it is necessary to increase further the efforts in order to radically improve the international situation, to give people the certainty of a reliable future. Guided by this urgent necessity the Soviet Union is advancing new major initiatives imbued with the deep concern in containing the arms race, deepening détente, strengthening peace.

I found it necessary to draw your personal attention, Mrs Prime Minister, to these proposals, made, as you know, at the Congress of our party. Apart from the scope and far-reaching character of these initiatives I would like to emphasize particularly their realistic nature, the fact that they take into account both our own and our partners' interests.

The experience shows what a difficult and complex task it is to eliminate hot-beds of military conflicts. It is important therefore to do the preventive work, to forestall the emergence of such hot-beds.

In this context a positive role in Europe is played by the confidence-building measures in military field, undertaken by decision of the European conference. The Soviet Union made proposals to expand considerably the range of such measures.

Now we propose to extend considerably the zone of application of such measures as well. We are prepared to apply them to the entire European part of the USSR, provided the Western states too extend the confidence-building measures' zone accordingly.

We also think that the elaboration and the application of confidence-building measures could be useful in the region of the Far East too. Here it would be necessary to take into account the specifics of this region.

The view is expressed in some countries that our recent proposals concerning Persian Gulf could not be taken apart from the question of the stay of the Soviet military contingent in Afghanistan. Our position is as follows: being prepared to reach an agreement on Persian Gulf as an independent problem and to participate separately in a settlement of the situation around Afghanistan, we at the same time have no objection either to the matters connected with Afghanistan being discussed together with the questions of Persian Gulf security. Such discussions naturally can concern only the international aspects of the Afghan problem and not the internal affaires of this country. The sovereignty of Afghanistan as well as its status as a non-aligned state must be fully protected.

Proceeding from the extreme importance of the strategic armaments limitation issue not only for the USSR and USA, but for other countries as well, we on our

7 December 1979 – 1 December 1981

part are prepared to continue without delay relevant talks with the United States preserving all the positive elements that have so far been achieved in this field. Such talks understandably can be conducted only on the basis of equality and equal security of both sides.

Trying to prevent the dangerous stockpiling of nuclear missile weapons in Europe and to contribute to a speedy decision on such weapons, we propose to reach an agreement that as of now a moratorium should be set on the deployment in Europe of new medium-range nuclear-missile weapons of the NATO countries and the USSR, that is to freeze the existing quantitative and qualitative level of these weapons, naturally including the US forward-based nuclear weapons in the region. The moratorium could enter into force as soon as the negotiations begin on this score and could be in force until a treaty is concluded on limiting or, still better, reducing such nuclear systems in Europe.

We believe that the knowledge by the wide public, all people of those consequences that nuclear war is fraught with, would be of major importance also from the point of additional influence on governments with a view to achieve agreements, aimed practically at preventing such a war. For this end we propose that an authoritative international committee should be set up, which would demonstrate the vital necessity of preventing a nuclear holocaust. The committee should be composed of the most eminent scientists from different countries. Probably appropriate part in implementing this goal could be played by the UN Secretary General. The whole world should be informed about the conclusions the committee draws.

Furthermore, to resolve numerous international problems existing today, a far-sighted approach, political will and courage, authority and influence are needed. That is why, in our view, it would be useful to call a special session of the Security Council with the participation of the top leaders of its member states—both permanent and non-permanent—in order to look for ways of improving the international situation and preventing war. If they so wish, leaders of other countries could evidently also take part in the session. Certainly, thorough preparations would be needed for such a session to achieve positive results.

Coming back to the hot-beds of tension and the task of their elimination, I would like to single out the question of the situation in the Middle East. No matter what one's attitude is to what has been done up to now in this region, it is clear that the political settlement there has been recently pushed backwards. The present situation urgently demands the return to the collective search for a comprehensive settlement on a just and realistic basis, which could be done, say, within the framework of the specially convened international conference.

The Soviet Union is prepared to participate in a constructive spirit in such a work and to do it together with other interested sides—with the Arabs, including, of course, the Palestine Liberation Organization, and with Israel. We are ready to search together with the United States, with whom we had in the past a certain experience on this score, we are prepared to co-operate with European countries, with every one who is sincerely striving for a lasting and just peace in the Middle East. Presumably the United Nations Organization can continue to play a useful role here.

These are the questions which I would like to raise in this message. We hope that you, Mrs Prime Minister, will treat our proposals with all attention. As you can see they cover the wide range of problems, envisage measures of political and military nature, concern different types of arms and armed forces, touch upon the

UK-Soviet Relations, 1979-82

situation in different areas of the world.

We understand of course, that it will take some time to study and to analyse them. Obviously a necessity will be arising in some consultations, in exchanges of opinions, in short in various forms of dialogue. We are prepared for it.

Yours sincerely,
L. BREZHNEV

No. 88

Letter from Mr Walden to Mr Alexander (No. 10), 16 March 1981
Confidential (ENS 026/2)

Dear Michael,

Anglo-Soviet Contacts

The Prime Minister is aware of the Foreign and Commonwealth Secretary's view that it is important for us not to cut ourselves off from all dealings with the Russians at Ministerial level or to allow our contacts with Moscow to become visibly inferior to those of our major allies. Were we to do so, our friends would be less inclined to give weight to our views on East/West relations, and our ability to promote British and wider Western interests would be diminished. Our close ties with the Reagan Administration, and our impending assumption of the Presidency of the Community, make it important to ensure that our judgement of the Soviet scene at this stage is well founded and seen to be well founded. The Russians will have noted the impact made on American thinking by the Prime Minister's visit to Washington[1] (e.g. on TNF negotiations; the Mexico Summit; and Central America). The Americans, for their part, would no doubt prefer not to leave European contacts with the Russians entirely in German (Herr Genscher goes to Moscow on 4 April) and French hands.

Lord Carrington therefore feels that the time is approaching when he should himself re-establish contact with Moscow and explore at first hand what substance there may be behind the conciliatory facade set up by Brezhnev in his speech to the CPSU Congress and his subsequent messages to Western leaders.[2]

As the Prime Minister knows, Julian Bullard is going to Moscow on 25 March for talks with the Soviet Deputy Foreign Minister.[3] This is part of an established though erratic pattern of consultation between the two Foreign Ministries and provides the occasion for a review of points of current interest in international and bilateral relations; but it is not a substitute for access to the Russians at policy-making level. Lord Carrington believes that it would be useful to take the opportunity of Bullard's visit to indicate to the Russians that he would welcome a businesslike meeting with Mr Gromyko in the near future.

Formally it is Gromyko's turn to come to London on an official visit. This would however involve more protocol and publicity than Lord Carrington thinks appropriate in present circumstances, and his idea would be to go instead for a short working visit to Moscow. We think that the Russians would be prepared to

---

[1] Mrs Thatcher, accompanied by Lord Carrington, visited Washington for talks with President Reagan and Congressional leaders on 25-28 February.
[2] See Enclosure in No. 87.
[3] No. 84, para 12. For the visit see Nos. 90 and 91.

218

7 December 1979 – 1 December 1981

accept a meeting on this basis, and that the programme could be so organised as to emphasise business and exclude frills.

There are reasons of substance why such a visit would be particularly useful before we take over the Presidency and while the US Administration is still in the process of formulating its policies towards the Soviet Union. These factors could also be used in public to explain the limited but important purpose of the visit and to rebut any criticism that we were changing the policies which we and our allies have followed since the invasion of Afghanistan.[4]

Yours ever,

G. G. H. WALDEN

[4] Mr Alexander observed to the Prime Minister: 'I am very conscious of the distaste you will feel for this proposal. But the arguments . . . seem to me powerful and on balance I would have thought it made sense for Lord Carrington to see Mr Gromyko.' Mrs Thatcher noted: 'I am very unhappy indeed. We should have to consult with the US. Can we not keep contacts to meetings in the margins of international fora' (PREM: Anglo-Soviet Relations). The Prime Minister wanted to discuss the issue with Lord Carrington before taking a decision as to whether or not Mr Bullard should say anything to the Soviet authorities during his visit to Moscow but no time could be found during the European Council meeting at Maastricht. In the event the question of a meeting between the Foreign Secretary and Gromyko was not mentioned during Bullard's visit.

No. 89

Record of a conversation at the Soviet Ministry of Foreign Affairs on 18 March 1981, 4 p.m.
Confidential (ENS 020/10)

Present:

Mr A. A. Gromyko	Sir Curtis Keeble
Mr V. P. Suslov	Mr A. M. Wood
Mr V. M. Sukhodrev	

1. After some opening banter in which Mr Gromyko agreed with Mr Suslov that the appropriate mark for Anglo-Soviet relations at present would be one, the lowest given to Soviet schoolboys, and after Mr Gromyko had recounted a story from Gogol with the apparent moral that the English were looking the other way when important matters were proceeding, the *Ambassador* was asked to open the discussion. He said he was glad of the opportunity to talk to Mr Gromyko. His three years in Moscow had not been as fruitful as he would have wished but he was grateful for the help he had received from the Foreign Ministry. He had asked for a call to set out the British position at a critical time for the development of international relations after the Soviet Party Congress and the installation of a new US Administration. *Mr Gromyko* interrupted to say in a sarcastic tone that the Administration should be described as 'beloved'. The *Ambassador* commented on this remark that he had been glad to see the Prime Minister and President Reagan had established a good relationship. He went on to point out that a number of events had deeply affected the way the British public and government viewed the Soviet Union. Two focal points in this process were the development of the Soviet military capability directed against Western Europe, and secondly, Soviet policies in the third world culminating in the introduction of Soviet military forces into

UK-Soviet Relations, 1979-82

Afghanistan. He did not propose to argue the rights and wrongs but simply wanted to point out as a matter of personal knowledge the deep effect which these events had had and their significance for the future. Since he had asked for the call the Prime Minister had received a message from Brezhnev and had had a talk with the Soviet Ambassador in London.[1] The Ambassador said that the Prime Minister had spoken in similar terms to those used by Mr Brezhnev on 23 February[2] when she said in New York on 28 February that the preservation of peace was vital. She said on that occasion the supreme task of modern statesmanship was the prevention of war. She had called for genuine two-way détente and said it was essential to continue to deal with the Soviet Union on a realistic and consistent basis. She did not believe the Soviet Union contemplated direct aggression against the West, but noted there was a conflict of interest which had to be dealt with. The Ambassador said he wanted to repeat to Mr Gromyko the essential points of what the Prime Minister had said to the Soviet Ambassador in London on 9 March: that détente must be genuine and two-way; that HMG were anxious to reduce the level of armaments provided this could be done on a permanent, trustworthy and verifiable basis in order to arrive at a military balance at a lower level than at present; that détente would be easier to discuss once Soviet forces were withdrawn from Afghanistan; and that NATO was anxious to discuss TNF but the fact was that the USSR was far ahead of the West in number, design and sophistication. HMG wanted a dialogue if the Soviet Union really wanted to maintain a military balance at a reduced level, to withdraw its forces from Afghanistan and to engage in pursuit of genuinely reciprocal détente. He invited Gromyko to offer any comments which might help in assessing the prospects for progress.

2. *Mr Gromyko* said that the report delivered by Mr Brezhnev to the Soviet Party Congress on 23 February had given a clear description of Soviet foreign policies. Mr Brezhnev had made important proposals for peace and the prevention of war. These had been conveyed to a number of governments of the world, including that of the UK. The Soviet leadership much regretted that the United Kingdom, or rather HMG, adopted such an unfriendly attitude towards the USSR. In general, one could say that the British position in international affairs supported the unconcealed militaristic course followed by Washington and especially by the new US Administration. The Americans did not even have to finish speaking before London actively and automatically supported them. This caused surprise in the Soviet Union. There were, for example, statements made at the highest levels in the United States that the US ought to be the leading military power in the world and that the USA should not refrain from using force if it felt that what it considered to be its vital interests were threatened in this or that region, whether near to the United States or far from them. There were other examples of London's immediate support for Washington's line. The Soviet Union was convinced that the UK had less and less independence in foreign affairs, including Anglo/Soviet relations. He could remember that things had been different in the past. It was of course HMG's business what policies they followed but the Soviet Union was entitled to express its opinion. The idea that the US should be the first military power in the world was ridiculous. Mr Brezhnev and others had pointed out at the Congress and on other occasions that it was impossible in today's world for any country or side to acquire and maintain the dominant position. The USSR and its allies would do all that was necessary so as not to fall behind the United States and

[1] No. 87.
[2] See No. 86.

7 December 1979 – 1 December 1981

NATO. The Soviet Union did not want such competition but Washington and London should realise the facts.

3. Mr Gromyko said that the Ambassador had referred in his opening statement to a number of problems and had reverted to the thesis which was repeated daily in London and the West, that the USSR represented a threat. He categorically denied this as an illusion and a fiction. The Soviet leaders were even inclined to think that Western leaders did not always believe what they themselves said about the Soviet Union being a threat. They needed to make such statements to justify their armaments programmes, the deployment of new arms, the arms race, the militarisation of Western Europe and the US attempt to become the world's leading military power. If anyone really was in continuing doubt about Soviet intentions he could only express regret at this and try to explain the facts. The Soviet Union needed no-one else's land and had no expansionist plans. The Soviet leadership had made it clear at the 26th Congress that their efforts were directed to fulfilling grandiose plans for the Soviet economy, agriculture and the life of the Soviet people. They needed to spend money on armaments only because the Western Governments forced them to do so. The Soviet side had made repeated proposals for arms reductions, including budget cuts, cuts in armaments, banning of weapons of mass destruction, and the reduction of forces in Central Europe. They were still prepared to pursue these ideas but all their proposals had been rejected both in public and in private. The West was not even prepared to discuss matters. Mr Brezhnev had proposed a dialogue at the highest level but leaders in Washington continue to circle the problem and engage in gymnastics over wording. The reaction the Soviet side wanted to hear, 'let us discuss matters', had yet to emerge. He could understand that Soviet ideas might be differently assessed in different capitals, but really it was a simple question of talking or not talking and Western reactions were extremely odd. He did not know how to judge the Western claim that one could not discuss matters unless one knew in advance that the results would be positive. He had not taken this line in agreeing to receive the Ambassador.

4. The Ambassador, continued Mr Gromyko, had mentioned TNF. He could think of only one explanation for the Western reaction to the idea of a moratorium—that the Soviet Union should freeze its programmes while the West fulfilled the December 1979 decision taken in Brussels. This was no way to proceed in an important matter affecting Western European security. The United States did not apparently want to change NATO's decision but to force theatre nuclear forces on Western Europe. This was all Washington thought of. He realised that this would be denied but we lived in a world where much was denied which was as obvious as the five fingers of a hand. If the position in Europe were to improve, this apparently would not suit Washington. This undermined the real security of Europe and the world in general. The Soviet Union believed that the US people did not need or want tension, or war, but there was a limit to what they could do if NATO and Washington were not prepared to play their part. He would like to hope that London—and Washington—would take a cool and restrained approach to this question and react appropriately to Mr Brezhnev's recent messages.

5. Mr Gromyko said the Ambassador had raised the question of Afghanistan. For his part he believed there was much in the Western position that was artificial. The Soviet Union had said many times what its policy was and would not change it. It wanted an independent Afghanistan, not one with a regime forced on her by

UK-Soviet Relations, 1979-82

foreign intervention. The present regime was one chosen by the Afghans themselves. The problem to be discussed was outside intervention by the Chinese and others and it was insulting to suggest otherwise. So far as the Soviet Union was concerned it had said a hundred times that as soon as intervention from Pakistan and part of Iran, but particularly Pakistan, would cease her troops would be withdrawn. He had explained the position to Lord Carrington who was a man of understanding but who was drawing the wrong conclusions about this question because he started from unrealistic premises. If a way could be found to stop intervention, Soviet troops would leave Afghanistan. Why could the UK, USA, FRG and so on not accept this? It was often said that Afghanistan ought to be non-aligned. The Soviet Union agreed. The United Kingdom would be more true to itself if it adopted a more realistic position towards Afghanistan. There ought not to be foreign troops there and there ought to be no foreign intervention. Soviet troops were in the country because armed bands had rushed in from all sides in an attempt to topple the regime simply because it was not to the taste of other governments and countries. If that problem could be solved Soviet troops would leave. The Soviet Union always kept its word. He sometimes wondered whether Western governments, including HMG, believed what they said about the problem but were, rather, inclined to maintain tension to cover aggressive political steps in the region such as the establishment of US bases and the Rapid Deployment Force. He could not believe that Western governments failed to understand that Soviet troops would be withdrawn if there was no outside intervention. It was a policy of deceit to pretend that the West was pre-occupied by what was happening in Afghanistan itself.

6. In describing Western policies towards Afghanistan, Mr Gromyko continued, he had used fair words in comparison with the language being used in Washington these days, for example in relation to the USSR. He hoped the Americans might learn to rise to a higher and more human level instead of employing gutter language. Perhaps the British could advise them in this sense, although he was not sure whether they could get up sufficient breath to say that. Even in hard times in the past, correct language had been used. The *Ambassador* interrupted to say that he could recall picturesque language being used by Soviet leaders. *Mr Gromyko* concluded his exposition by saying that the Soviet side would like its ideas studied carefully and without prejudice. Their wish for détente and better international relations was continuing and reflected the real interests of all peoples. He had noted that some people had said there were higher interests than peace. He hoped those employing such phrases did not believe they could frighten the Soviet Union into taking its hat off to Washington. If such statements reflected real intentions the future looked bleak. One could see a bottomless abyss. Everybody should understand this, even Washington. Mr Brezhnev had pointed out that he wanted Anglo/Soviet relations to improve. Mr Gromyko was convinced that it was in the objective interests of both sides that they should have better relations in political, economic and other fields. Recalling US/UK/Soviet cooperation in World War II, there was still a common interest, as only lunatics would deny, in avoiding war.

7. The *Ambassador* said HMG shared Mr Brezhnev's interest in better Anglo-Soviet relations. Mr Brezhnev had said that their present state was not the fault of the USSR. That was why he had set out in his opening statement the reasons as they appeared in Britain for the present poor state of relations. He knew Lord Carrington would welcome an effective political dialogue but in looking for genuinely better relations, we should also look to the means of curing the problems

7 December 1979 – 1 December 1981

which had caused the present stagnation. As regards a possible Afghanistan settlement there were at least in words points of agreement, for example over non-alignment. Lord Carrington had presented ideas on a neutral and non-aligned status for Afghanistan, a status which would be freely chosen by the Afghans themselves. The Soviet position had been that Afghanistan presented a potential security threat to the Soviet Union. If there were a threat Lord Carrington's proposals would have removed it. But the Ambassador's talks last year with Mr Zemskov,[3] conducted in an effort to work out how general propositions endorsed by the European Community could be made more precise in making certain there was no interference in Afghanistan from any quarter and providing for a Soviet withdrawal, had revealed a basic difference about the causes of the present situation. The British side did not then and did not now believe the essence of the matter was internal interference against a freely chosen regime. There was an internal problem which the Afghans themselves should resolve. But so far as external interference was concerned Lord Carrington's proposals had envisaged guarantees by Afghanistan's neighbours and perhaps others. The linkage with the timing of Soviet withdrawal could have been discussed. *Mr Gromyko* interjected that the Pakistanis should talk to the Afghan government and there should also be talks with Iran. The Pakistanis knew this was the right course to follow but did not want to do so. The *Ambassador* replied that bilateral talks with Babrak Karmal were not the way to a solution. But perhaps the UN Secretary-General's Personal Representative could make some progress. *Mr Gromyko* said the question was frozen at present because of Pakistan. He urged HMG to treat the political disease from which Pakistan was suffering. Today they wanted something, tomorrow they did not. The *Ambassador* reminded him that the solution of the Zimbabwe problem had shown what could be achieved in an apparently impossible situation. There was a lesson here for Afghanistan. *Mr Gromyko* repeated that we should advise Pakistan to cease intervention. It would then be easy for Soviet troops to withdraw. Pakistan was not following an adult policy in refusing to talk to Karmal, who held the power in Afghanistan. The *Ambassador* said that if this were really the case there might be less of a problem. Pakistan understood perfectly well that the basic issue in Afghanistan was an internal one in the first place: the Afghan people should be allowed to choose their own government. He simply could not accept the thesis that the Afghan question was kept alive as a cover for other aims. *Mr Gromyko* said he had set out the Soviet position fully.

8. The *Ambassador* said he wanted to revert to Mr Gromyko's opening remarks. Anglo-American relations and interests were indeed close. He hoped they would remain so. He did not believe this was a negative factor. The UK had an important role to play in trans-Atlantic and European affairs. His country would be taking on the Presidency of the Community from the middle of the summer. He repeated that the Prime Minister had said we needed to prevent war, control armaments and if possible reduce their level. Serious Soviet proposals would be looked at seriously. But the moratorium idea looked like an attempt to perpetuate an imbalance. In making its decision in December 1979 NATO had also called for negotiations on TNF. He welcomed the Soviet readiness to negotiate and knew that Soviet proposals were being fully studied in NATO. But the call for a moratorium was a call to halt change in an area of marked Soviet preponderance. *Mr Gromyko* said he did not wish to elaborate what he had said but that if one looked at the overall

---

[3] No. 71.

UK-Soviet Relations, 1979-82

picture one could not say that the Soviet Union had an advantage. The *Ambassador* said there had been constructive elements in the Brezhnev report, for example, over confidence-building measures. The Soviet Union had gone some way to meet the French proposals and would, he hoped, go the rest of it. *Mr Gromyko* said he hoped the West would propose something as the necessary concession for what Mr Brezhnev had suggested. The *Ambassador* said he did not think this was for the West to do. Europe was already covered on the Western side. He concluded by repeating that serious Soviet proposals would be examined seriously and said a reply to the Brezhnev message would be sent in due course. The meeting ended at 5.15 pm.[4]

[4] Sir C. Keeble reported on his meeting in Moscow telegram No. 143 of 19 March. He noted: 'Gromyko was ready enough to talk, but without developing any new points. His tone was serious, but the content was largely negative and he spent much of the time attacking the Reagan administration. It was clear that the language used in public by members of the administration rankled and there was an underlying note of frustration about the difficulty of establishing serious contact.'

No. 90

Record of Mr Bullard's call on Mr Kornienko[1] at the Soviet Foreign Ministry, 27 March 1981, 10 a.m.[2]
Confidential, UK Eyes A (ENS 020/2)

Present:

G. M. Kornienko	Mr Bullard
V. P. Suslov	HM Ambassador
V. M. Semeonov[3]	Mr Fall
G. G. Gventsadze	Mr Thomson

1. *Mr Kornienko* welcomed the British side. He noted that Anglo-Soviet political consultations in accordance with the relevant protocol had proved of mutual benefit. They were useful, even if the sides did not always come to common views on all points. It was of course even better when consultations resulted in the closing of positions and he hoped that the present round would lead to positive results. Regrettably, he could not help but note that in recent years there had been a certain stagnation in Anglo-Soviet relations, as had been stated by the Soviet leadership at the 26th Congress. The Soviet Union was unconditionally in favour of altering this situation. This had been expressed with crystal clarity in President Brezhnev's message to the Prime Minister.[4] He noted with some satisfaction that recently there had been some positive movement in bilateral relations.

2. After thanks, *Mr Bullard* replied that Mr Kornienko's assessment of the value of Anglo-Soviet consultations corresponded exactly with the British assessment and he would not try to add anything to it. He described the subjects covered in

[1] Georgiy Kornienko, Soviet First Deputy Foreign Minister.
[2] Mr Bullard requested copies of the record be circulated to Ambassadors in Eastern Europe, in the capitals of the Ten and NATO.
[3] Viacheslav Semeonov, Deputy Head, Second European Department, Soviet MFA.
[4] Enclosure in No. 87.

7 December 1979 – 1 December 1981

discussion yesterday morning with Mr Kovalev[5] and in the talks yesterday afternoon between Mr Fall and Mr Semeonov. There were no points he wished to raise arising from those talks. Instead, he would like to talk first about Soviet relations with the United States. These were especially important and at the same time complex.

3. It was often said that elections in the West were lost, not won. Certainly, there were aspects of President Carter's policies which had contributed to his defeat. But this was not the whole story. The attitudes which had led to the election of President Reagan had also been influenced by Soviet actions over recent years. Mr Bullard firmly believed that if the Soviet Union had not transported Cuban troops from Angola into Ethiopia instead of back to Cuba, had not launched development of the SS-20, had not withheld support from the US on the hostages in Iran, had not waited 6 months before responding to the NATO call for TNF negotiations, had not acted as it did over the strange incident in Sverdlovsk[6] and had not invaded and stayed in Afghanistan, then the US President today might be someone other than Mr Reagan.

4. There was always a transitional stage between Administrations. That of the Reagan Administration was an exceptionally long one for two reasons. First, Mr Haig was a man of strong character, determined to make the State Department the main instrument of US foreign policy. This had led to conflicts with individuals in the White House that were not yet concluded. Second, there was the fight by the Republican extreme right wing, personified by such as Senator Helms, to exercise a controlling voice in government appointments. The appointments of several Assistant Secretaries in the State Department had not yet been confirmed. It was therefore not surprising that US policy on important issues, such as the Middle East, South Africa, and SALT, was not yet fully formed. The corollary was that US policy was still open to influence from outside, both from America's allies and from other countries, including the Soviet Union. Soviet statements and actions during this time would have particular effect. Tone was relevant and the tone of President Brezhnev's message to President Reagan was certainly more likely to have a favourable influence than that of the recent article in *Pravda* by Alexandrov.[7] But actions were even more important. We needed more concrete proposals than those in Mr Brezhnev's speech to the 26th Congress. If there was one way of ensuring that any hawks there might be in Washington would triumph over the doves, then all the Soviet Union had to do was to intervene in Poland.

5. Mr Bullard understood why Mr Kovalev had yesterday said that third parties should not discuss Poland. But the latest news made it clear that the situation in Poland was potentially the most serious crisis in Europe.[8] Yesterday Britain and Poland's other creditors had been asked for a complete postponement of debt repayments. We were therefore involved, just as the Soviet Union was. Polish Deputy Prime Minister Rakowski had said he feared both East and West would come to believe that Poland could not govern itself. The British Government were

[5] Anatoly Kovalev, Soviet Deputy Foreign Minister.

[6] A reference to the accidental release of anthrax spores from a biological facility in April 1979 which resulted in over 100 'unexplained' deaths.

[7] I. Alexandrov was a pseudonym used for officially sponsored articles.

[8] A reference to the incident in which several prominent members of Solidarity and local councillors were attacked violently by Polish police, leading to calls for a general strike. A statement issued by the US National Security Council on March 26 warned that the Polish authorities were preparing to use force to deal with the continuing differences between the state and the labour unions.

UK-Soviet Relations, 1979-82

convinced that the Poles could, and that they should be allowed to do so. Britain and the Soviet Union had a strong common interest in letting the Poles solve their problems by their own efforts. Finally, Mr Bullard drew attention to the statement on Poland by the European Council meeting in Maastricht which he had already outlined yesterday to Mr Kovalev.[9]

6. Taking Poland first, *Mr Kornienko* said he would simply confirm what Mr Kovalev had already said. The British side said it proceeded from the premise that Poland could and must solve its internal affairs itself. It must certainly be aware of the outcome of the Warsaw Pact Heads of Government meeting on 5 December 1980 and the meeting of Polish and Soviet Heads of Government at the beginning of March this year where confidence was expressed that the Polish people and workers could solve their own problems and where at the same time it was stressed that Poland was, is, and would remain a Socialist state. Both Britain and the Soviet Union believed the Poles themselves should solve their problems and had expressed confidence that they could do so. There was therefore no call at all to discuss Poland's problems and internal affairs.

7. Turning to the points referred to by Mr Bullard in connection with the election of President Reagan, Mr Kornienko said he would take Angola as an example. When Angola received independence at the beginning of 1975 it had a tripartite government consisting of representatives from the MPLA, UNITA and the FNLA. The Soviet Union had supported that tripartite government. It had done nothing to destroy that government. But it was a historical fact, supported by official US documents that the US government and the CIA had destroyed that tripartite coalition and, by supplying US weapons to UNITA and the FNLA, had caused the Angolan civil war. It was only then that the Soviet Union and Cuba, fulfilling their international duty, began to aid Angola's legitimate government. These facts were turned completely upside down in the West, and everything was now presented as a Soviet master plan for expansion in Africa.

8. Mr Bullard's other points could be considered in the same way. Ethiopia was another example. US documents showed that Siad Barre undertook aggression against Ethiopia in the hope and expectation of US support. Though the Soviet Union lost its position (and valuable naval facilities) in Somalia as a result, it was a moral duty to aid Ethiopia which was the victim of aggression by a country using Soviet weapons for the purpose.

9. Sverdlovsk was another example. In 1979 the United States and the United Kingdom were perfectly clear about what had happened and had made no complaint. This was clear to the Soviet side (at least as far as the US was concerned). It was also clear when it had been decided to distort the story: at the start of 1980 just after events in Afghanistan. It was clearly a political decision to make an issue of Sverdlovsk. The Soviet Union could therefore only consider it a political provocation.

10. It was the Soviet Union's profound conviction that the international situation had worsened as a result of something Mr Bullard had not mentioned. During the first half of the 1970s SALT I had been signed and a series of other agreements on limiting nuclear weapons were agreed, though not signed. There were successes in reducing international tension, above all in Europe. All this was based on a mutual understanding of the existence of practical equality and an approximate balance of forces. The process of solidifying this balance and then

[9] See final paragraph of No. 92.

proceeding to a reduction of forces without upsetting the balance offered a promising future. But then the West, and above all the US; adopted a different view: that there was not an equality of forces between East and West and that the trend to détente should be halted. This was long before Afghanistan. And it was this that was the root of the evil.

11. *Mr Kornienko* recalled that President Carter's Administration had begun with Secretary Vance's visit to Moscow in 1977 with the proposal for deep cuts in strategic nuclear forces. This had been dressed up as a positive move, but the proposal in fact was designed to abolish the principle of approximate balance. Discussion, even in the US, had shown it was not a serious proposal and certainly not one that the Soviet Union could accept. This was the first break in the trend towards détente. Then, in May 1978, long before Afghanistan, NATO had taken long-range decisions on military spending aimed at upsetting the military balance. There had followed the agreement on SALT II between President Carter and President Brezhnev in Vienna, but the negotiating process had been difficult and even in Vienna the Soviet Union had feared the United States was not determined to secure ratification. Facts soon confirmed this fear. The episode over the Soviet brigade in Cuba had destroyed hopes of SALT II ratification. And the US Administration had created this incident themselves. The Soviet Union had had a training establishment in Cuba since 1962. Its numbers and its function had not changed over 17 years and the Russians knew that the US was aware of this. The US had therefore clearly generated this crisis in order to break SALT II.

12. The root of the problem, *Mr Kornienko* repeated, was that the United States and many politicians in Western Europe had come to the conclusion that building relations with the East on the basis of equality was not beneficial and should be changed. Two years before Afghanistan, in November 1977, President Brezhnev, on the occasion of the 60th Anniversary of the Revolution had said that international relations stood at a crossroads, leading either to the reinforcement of peace or to balancing on the edge of war. Why had he said this then? Because the Soviet Union had already encountered the US tendency to back away from the single sensible principle for the governing of East-West relations, that of an equal balance of force. It was a balance in the broad sense that was meant. It was only on the basis of considering each other as equal partners that there could be good relations. But the Reagan Administration had abandoned this principle completely. It sought military superiority, though it did not always express itself in those terms, sometimes referring to 'a margin of security'—anything could be hidden under that phrase. In practice, it was absolutely clear that the US was increasing its forces so as to speak to the Soviet Union from a position of strength.

13. Mr Bullard had mentioned the SS-20. Mr Kornienko wished to remind him of a few facts. Chancellor Schmidt, in an interview with a German magazine on 19 February 1981 and in answer to the question whether the Soviet Union had broken the balance of power, replied that the balance was not already broken but on the verge of being so. He said that he had been saying this for many years (a paradoxical admission); and yet on 25 February 1981, it was said in an FRG government statement that the Soviet proposal for a TNF moratorium was not acceptable because it would consolidate an existing imbalance. The Germans had contradicted themselves within a week. How could this be taken seriously? Again, on 23 February 1981 Mr Haig, in an interview with the French television station *Antenne 2* declared that he and the majority of Western observers considered that East and West were in a position of approximate balance but that by the mid 1980s

UK-Soviet Relations, 1979-82

the Soviet Union might achieve superiority. Mr Kornienko asked why, therefore, the West would not accept a moratorium now if they believed there was approximate balance at present but feared it would disappear soon. On that reasoning a moratorium would hardly be to the advantage of the West. He offered one further example: NATO had declared that their military spending decisions should preserve the balance of forces. But Defence Secretary Brown (at a secret Senate hearing subsequently made public) had said that present NATO programmes would secure 'a net military advantage' for NATO in the second half of the 1980s. As long as NATO maintained such a position, it was hard to talk of improving relations and returning to the principles of a balance of force and equal, mutually beneficial, and constructive relations. That was the Soviet assessment of the situation and of what was necessary to improve it. The contradictions existed because the heads of NATO governments were in fact seeking to change the equation of forces to their advantage.

14. *Mr Bullard* thanked Mr Kornienko for this long exposition. On Poland, he took what Mr Kornienko had said as a clear statement that the Soviet Union had no intention of interfering in that country's affairs. Mr Kornienko had said that Poland was and would remain Socialist. That was for the Poles to decide: they could choose socialism, military dictatorship or whatever they wished. It was not Mr Bullard's affair or Mr Kornienko's. The British Government had no interest in trying to weaken Poland's links with its allies in the Warsaw Pact and its partners in the CMEA. But the British Government was involved politically because of potential consequences of interference and economically because of its financial links with Poland. If political consultations were to be serious discussion of Poland could not be excluded.

15. What Mr Kornienko had said about Angola and Ethiopia illustrated how the Soviet perception of US policy influenced Soviet policy, just as US perceptions affected US policy in reverse. The British position on Southern Africa was clear. Mr Bullard pointed to the record of Zimbabwe. It had had the most democratic election in Southern Africa for many years. HMG had offered altogether £125 million at the Conference on Aid for Zimbabwe which, incidentally, the Soviet Union had chosen not to attend.

16. There was no question whatsoever of using the issue of Sverdlovsk for political advantage. HMG had approached the Soviet Government on the basis of a treaty which both states had signed and had been disappointed at the reply. The Soviet Union should not be surprised at the resulting reaction in the UK.

17. On the subject of the military balance, Sir Curtis Keeble might wish to follow up particular points later, but it was important to stress now the significance of super power relations for middle power states such as the United Kingdom. It was important to get the relationship right or the world would grow even more dangerous. Mr Kornienko's interpretation of events in Angola, the NATO Summit of May 1978, and the Soviet brigade in Cuba were completely wrong and a disturbing indication of the lack of mutual understanding between the United States and the Soviet Union. It was indeed the case that President Carter had sometimes been hard to understand, but the US found it even harder to understand the Soviet Union. Soviet secrecy created an enormous problem. The most serious confidence-destroying measure of recent years had been the Soviet Union's SS-20 programme, undertaken without warning to the United States or even apparently to its own allies. On the subject of military balance, Mr Bullard said he subscribed to the joint declaration four years ago by Chancellor Schmidt and President Brezhnev

7 December 1979 – 1 December 1981

on 'approximate equality and parity' and to the form of words used in the recent joint declaration by Chancellor Schmidt and President Giscard calling for *'equilibre'*. As to what this meant in practice, the Soviet side needed to be more sophisticated in its interpretation. It should not rely on extracts from magazine interviews. Also, it should distinguish between the military balance in Europe and at the global level. The UK placed some reliance on the unclassified publications of the International Institute for Strategic Studies. These showed that the world balance was sufficient to deter war, but that in Europe, in terms of 'arriving warheads', the Warsaw Pact had an advantage of 3.1 to 1, and this was increasing,

18. The proposal for a moratorium had been ridiculed even at the meeting of the Socialist International in Oslo, which might have been expected to take a more favourable line. It was true that the equation of forces might worsen to the West's disadvantage, but NATO had taken a decision that would in time rectify this. It was totally unrealistic to suppose that the Soviet Union could deploy SS-20s without any Western reaction. In conclusion, Mr Bullard said that he expected that the US would in time pick up the threads of the central relationship with the Soviet Union. It would adopt the usable parts of the SALT II agreement and make new proposals and in due course no doubt there would be a new agreement (it did not matter to us whether this was called SALT II or III). Mr Bullard was equally certain that the TNF talks in Vienna would be resumed. But what was needed at the moment was as clear an understanding between the two super powers as possible. He hoped that Mr Kornienko had had the opportunity to speak as frankly to the Americans as he had done to the British today. Looking forward, Mr Bullard asked what possibilities in Soviet-American relations Mr Kornienko saw, and what contributions the UK could make.

19. *Mr Kornienko* answered that he found it hard to say anything definite about the future development of Soviet-American relations. The problem was not due to any lack of clarity in the Soviet position. That remained as before: the Russians were ready to have a dialogue with the US Administration on the widest possible range of questions. This had been stated with absolute clarity by President Brezhnev at the 26th Congress. The US position however remained unclear, though it was evident that they were not yet ready to start negotiations on any question. For example, the US had refused to have a meeting even of the Permanent Consultative Commission on SALT I, postponing the meeting of 25 March. As an optimist, Mr Kornienko said he believed the present US Administration would come to take a more reasonable approach. Perhaps America's allies would persuade Reagan's Administration away from the futility of the present hard line, but it was hard to say when the US would be ready to discuss things seriously.

20. *Mr Bullard* said that the postponement of the meeting of the Permanent Commission was no doubt not unprecedented and was rather a good sign. It showed the US Administration's intention to think hard about serious international problems and its wish to draw the right conclusions. He wanted once again to stress that the Soviet Union could make an important contribution to US thinking.

21. In drawing the meeting to an end Mr Bullard invited the Soviet side to a continuation of political consultation talks in London. He regretted that the last round had been two years ago (though the reasons for this were known) and hoped that the next round would take place sooner. *Mr Kornienko* replied that he was in favour of Anglo-Soviet political consultations, and hoped that there would be a meeting in London, maybe even in the shorter time Mr Bullard had mentioned.

UK-Soviet Relations, 1979-82

Even if the two sides did not reach agreement, such meetings were of value in leading to better understanding of each other's points of view.

22. The meeting ended at 11.35.

No. 91

Minute from Mr Bullard to Mr Burns, 28 March 1981
Confidential (ENS 020/2)

Anglo-Soviet Consultations: Moscow 26-27 March

1. I got more out of this visit than I had expected.

2. In the absence of Zemskov (sick) I had two hours of talks with Deputy Foreign Minister Kovalev, who normally handles France and Italy, and 90 minutes with First Deputy Foreign Minister Kornienko. There were also some social engagements at which other Russians appeared, e.g. 'Professor' Gromyko, ex-Ambassador in East Berlin and now head of the African Institute, who has his father's combativeness without the wit.

3. After going through the motions of barring Poland as a subject unsuitable for discussion with third parties, the Russians allowed me to say what I liked, neither rising to deliberate provocations nor seeking to provoke me in return. The meetings were thus mellower than is usual. I assume the Russians wanted to be in a position to say that, only 15 months after Afghanistan, Anglo-Soviet consultations had taken place normally. This permits them to ask for more understanding from France and the FRG, on the grounds that Moscow and Bonn have traditionally been ahead of London in what Pompidou once said should not be seen as a bicycle race; and from the United States, where Reagan's policy of deliberately creating uncertainty in the Soviet mind seemed to me to be having considerable effect in Moscow, not all of it helpful.

4. The main subjects covered were the following:

(a) Poland

5. See Moscow telegram no. 172.[1] The Maastricht statement gave me the opportunity to repeat the warning against Soviet intervention, and the news from Warsaw made this timely.[2] The Russians clearly had instructions to say as little as possible.

(b) US/Soviet relations

6. I told Kornienko that the mood in Washington would not be as it is if the Soviet Union had taken a different line on Somalia/Ethiopia; the SS-20, the American hostages in Iran, TNF negotiations, the Sverdlovsk affair and Afghanistan. At the moment there were several matters on which the American position had not yet been decided. If the Russians wanted to influence it, they had better come up with offers more interesting to Washington than those in the Brezhnev letter. And if they wanted to ensure victory for the hawks, all they needed to do was intervene in Poland. Kornienko's reply to this was to dispute my

---

[1] Not printed.

[2] The statement, issued following the European Council meeting in Maastricht on 22-23 March, reaffirmed the Council's position that, in the interest of the Polish people and the stability of Europe, Poland should continue to face her internal problems in a peaceful manner and without outside interference. The threat of military intervention in Poland had been heightened by the fact that Warsaw Pact manoeuvres in Poland, East Germany, Czechoslovakia and Soviet Union from 19-26 March were extended to 7 April.

version of the events in question. I said this only illustrated my point that the perception by one super-power of the policies of the other was all-important. I hoped that the diplomatic channel between Washington and Moscow was in daily use. (In fact of course it is not, Dobrynin having been deliberately downgraded by Mr Haig and the American Embassy in Moscow awaiting a new incumbent.)

(*c*) *Politico-Military questions*

7. Kornienko made a heavy pitch, with dates and quotations to support it, for the theory that Western statesmen know very well that there is at the moment a military balance between East and West—a balance which the Pershing II and Cruise missile programmes would disrupt—and that a moratorium would thus be in everybody's interest. I urged him to be more sophisticated and to distinguish between a sufficient global balance, which existed, and a European equilibrium, which did not and was in any case being further disturbed by the SS-20 programme.

(*d*) *The Madrid Conference*

8. Kovalev pressed hard for a Western concession to match Brezhnev's acceptance of CBM extending to the Urals. But he refused to say whether this concession must be of a geographical kind. His remarks neither confirmed nor disproved the categorically negative conclusion drawn by the French as regards the prospects for Madrid.

(*e*) *Anglo-Soviet relations*

9. The Russians extolled the value of meetings such as this one, and referred once or twice to the 1975 Protocol on Consultations, as if to say that they regard it as still in force; I did not comment. (It provides for contact between Foreign Ministers or their representatives 'whenever the need arises and in principle at least once a year'.) They did not suggest a visit by Gromyko to London, nor invite the Secretary of State to Moscow.

10. HM Embassy's contacts with the Soviet Foreign Ministry seemed to me in excellent repair, considering the limited use which it has been possible to make of them since the invasion of Afghanistan. I left enough loose ends for the Embassy to follow up.

11. In other words the 'stagnation' in Anglo-Soviet relations, to use the words of Brezhnev's recent letter to the Prime Minister, has been given a bit of a stir. The experience was useful for the other meetings which I will be having in the coming weeks, and for the eventual British Presidency.[3]

---

[3] Sir Michael Palliser minuted: 'I'm glad you went. It was clearly well worth while.'

UK-Soviet Relations, 1979-82

No. 92

Letter from Mrs Thatcher to President Brezhnev, 3 April 1981[1]
T 59/81 Confidential (PREM: UK-Soviet Relations)

[No Salutation]

Thank you for your letter of 6 March.[2] As I said in response to a question about it in Parliament, it is important that there should be effective consultation between East and West. I see your message as a useful contribution to this process. I have also read with interest Sir Curtis Keeble's account of his recent conversation with Mr Gromyko.[3] I hope that there will be occasion for further such conversations. You will find the British side ready to play its full part in a business-like and constructive dialogue on questions of mutual interest.

I welcome your assurance that the Soviet Union is not seeking military superiority. As you know, there are differences between us as to whether an overall balance of forces now exists. But the objective of striking an even balance and of seeking to do so at a lower level is one which the British Government support and will strive to achieve. I hope that we shall be able to work together to this end. The overriding priority of all governments must be the preservation of peace. This can only be assured if international relations are conducted with the restraint necessary to the creation of a climate of confidence and trust. In the absence of such a climate, efforts to promote arms control agreements and to cut military spending, both of which are of the greatest importance, will not prosper.

There is a pressing need for a solution to the problem of Afghanistan in accordance with the resolutions of the United Nations General Assembly. I note with interest the reference in your letter to the need to protect fully the sovereignty and the non-aligned status of Afghanistan. This approach contains elements which are to be found in earlier proposals for resolving the problem. The aim should be to build on these proposals and to construct a political settlement which provides for the withdrawal of Soviet troops and the freedom of the Afghan people to have a government of their own choosing.

Such a settlement would need, of course, to take into account the legitimate interests of Afghanistan's neighbours, including those of the Soviet Union. Dr. Waldheim's appointment of Señor de Cuellar could be helpful in this connection and I hope that the Soviet Union will be willing to receive him. Whether achieved in these or other ways, there is no doubt that progress on Afghanistan would be of immediate benefit to East/West relations. I note your statement of willingness to take part in a settlement of the situation.

I also welcome your acceptance of the principle that Confidence Building Measures should cover the whole of the continent of Europe, including the European part of the USSR. If the question of territorial application is thus

---

[1] A draft of this letter was sent to No. 10 on 26 March by Mr Walden, who noted that 'all our Allies' had received messages from President Brezhnev similar to that in No. 87, and that there had been broad agreement in the North Atlantic Council on the points to be made in reply. Mr Alexander noted to the Prime Minister on 27 March that it was an odd moment to despatch the reply, suggesting that it should be delayed 'until the situation in Poland is a little clearer'. Mrs Thatcher agreed: 'Yes—wait at least a few days or more', and thought that the offer of 'talks at all levels', proposed in the FCO draft, should be removed. The letter was despatched on 3 April.
[2] Enclosure in No. 87.
[3] No. 89.

7 December 1979 – 1 December 1981

satisfactorily resolved, I hope that we can all move quickly to endorse the other criteria put forward in the French proposal at Madrid for a Conference on Disarmament in Europe. If we are really determined to increase confidence, it is obviously essential that the measures to be agreed should be militarily significant, verifiable and mandatory. I do not underestimate the difficulties which we shall face when we come to negotiate detailed measures at the Conference. But there is a good chance of success and the importance of the matter is such that we should not be content to set ourselves any lesser task.

I cannot, on the other hand, accept your suggestion that there should be a moratorium on the deployment of new medium range nuclear missiles in Europe. Such a moratorium would serve merely to contractualise the serious imbalance of theatre nuclear forces which exists today. We remain committed to the double decision which we took with our Allies in December 1979. This provides both for the deployment of American theatre nuclear forces in Europe and for negotiations on this vitally important subject. We believe that any agreed limitation on these systems should be consistent with the principle of parity. That is the only basis for long term stability.

You referred in your letter to stagnation in Anglo-Soviet relations. I do not disagree with this diagnosis, nor with your prescription of joint efforts as the remedy. Some of these efforts will have to be made in the wider international field, some in the purely bilateral. And it is by these efforts, much more than by words, that we shall judge and are ready to be judged. The British Government's policy is to pursue a consistent and constructive approach on all East/West issues. The challenge before us, and before other governments, is to translate the desire of our peoples for peace and cooperation into concrete action to build up confidence, strengthen security and develop our relations on a sound basis of mutual advantage. I am ready to work with you to this end. But I must conclude by emphasising that the situation in and around Poland continues to be in the forefront of my concerns. You will be aware of my position on this from the statement issued by me and my colleagues in the European Council in Maastricht on 23 March. We underlined the obligation of all States signatory to the Helsinki Final Act to base their relations with Poland on the strict application of the Charter of the United Nations and the principles of the Final Act. We emphasised that any other attitude would have very serious consequences for the future of international relations in Europe and throughout the world.[4]

---

[4] The heads of government also responded to a Polish request for food aid and a re-scheduling of the country's debt by stating that they were willing to act 'within the limits of their means and in collaboration with others'.

No. 93

Record of meeting between Mr Bullard and the Soviet Ambassador (Mr Popov), 9 April 1981, 11 a.m.
Confidential (ENS 020/1)

Present:
Mr J. L. Bullard   Mr V. I. Popov
Mr S. J. Wordsworth   Mr N. N. Ouspenski [Uspensky]

UK-Soviet Relations, 1979-82

1. The Soviet Ambassador called on Mr Bullard at the latter's request on 9 April.

2. After a discussion on the importance of developing relations and contacts on which there had been agreement during his visit to Moscow last month, *Mr Bullard* noted that conversations between the two sides could not be separated from the background of world events. It could be seen from the Prime Minister's speech of 8 April that she was worried about events in Europe.[1] *Mr Popov* replied that there were some questions concerning Europe which worried him as Ambassador. Statements by politicians about hypothetical threats of an invasion of Poland could not improve the atmosphere. Such pronouncements, and warnings to the Soviet Government, did not bode well for better relations.

3. *Mr Bullard* replied that Mr Popov should not pretend that the cause for the present atmosphere lay in London. The extended Warsaw Pact manoeuvres in Europe, military movements and speeches which openly drew a parallel between 1981 and 1968 led to a disagreeable climate, and to a response, not just by the British Government but also, as at Maastricht, by the other members of the Ten.

4. *Mr Popov* replied that it was important to interpret facts correctly. Troop manoeuvres were the business of the Warsaw Pact, but they were in any case now over, and were no cause for concern. In Brezhnev's speech the parallel drawn between Czechoslovakia and Poland was that in both countries Western countries had tried to change the situation. When asked which countries he was referring to, Mr Popov said that the British press contained many examples.

5. *Mr Bullard* said that he would repeat what he had said in Moscow: the British Government was not seeking to use this crisis to weaken Poland's links with its allies and partners. He believed that, as he had told Mr Kornienko, it was not anybody else's business what political system the Poles chose. Mr Kornienko had not commented on this point.

6. *Mr Popov* said he did not know why Mr Kornienko had not replied. Each people should choose its own system of government. It was his belief that each nation should have the best possible government. If a country had, for example, a Fascist government, then this was in his view not the best government, but it was the business of the people of that country to decide whether to overthrow it.

7. *Mr Bullard* went on to refer to Soviet press coverage of the Secretary of State's Far Eastern tour,[2] in particular his visit to Pakistan. He was sorry, he said, at the tone used by TASS and especially in an article in *Izvestia* of 20 March, which had represented Lord Carrington as following American orders and had portrayed UK aid to Afghan refugees, of whom there were now 1.8 million in Pakistan alone, as aid to counter-revolutionary terrorists. *Mr Popov* replied that he had not read the article as he had been in Malta at the time. But the article was the responsibility of the journalist. Many articles in the British press had criticised him personally, but he had not taken them up with the Foreign Office. *Mr Bullard* commented that Mr Popov's reply showed how far there was still to go in improving understanding.

---

[1] In a speech to the Diplomatic and Commonwealth Writers Association at New Zealand House, Mrs Thatcher re-stated her belief that 'an external intervention in Poland would be a disaster for Poland, for Europe, for East-West relations, and for all peoples" and expressed the hope that the Soviet leadership also realised that intervention would be a disaster for the Soviet Union. A copy of the speech can be found on the Margaret Thatcher Foundation website:
http://www.margaretthatcher.org/.

[2] Between 29 March and 8 April, Lord Carrington visited Pakistan, Hong Kong, China and Japan.

7 December 1979 – 1 December 1981

No. 94

Text of a message delivered by the Soviet Ambassador (Mr Popov), 23 April 1981[1]
Confidential (ENS 020/11)

1. The Soviet side notes with satisfaction the readiness of the British government to develop a political dialogue on topical international problems. The Soviet Union's view on ways of solving these problems is contained in the specific foreign policy proposals put forward in L.I. Brezhnev's Report at the 26th Congress of the CPSU and set out by him in the message to Prime Minister M. Thatcher.[2] The main import of the new Soviet initiatives is to eliminate the danger of war, to open the way towards stopping the arms race, and to strengthen détente.

An arms race unleashed with the purpose of achieving unilateral military advantages gives no answer to the crucial problems facing mankind, but only aggravates them and—what is more—to an immeasurably greater degree than before. The interests of preserving peace call for the maximum of restraint and for a sober and far-sighted approach to the conduct of international affairs and for not permitting disagreements to escape from the bounds of the peaceful settlement of disputes and from being transformed into military conflict situations. In our view, the complex and at times conflictual nature of the realities of today's world emphasise the importance of a responsible inter-state dialogue with a view to easing the situation.

A realistic approach to the solution of international problems leaves no room for the so-called concept of 'linking' truly urgent issues with contrived ones. Attempts to put such a concept into practice in fact divert away from constructive negotiations and businesslike cooperation.

The Soviet Union considers it necessary to conduct an active dialogue with other states, using for this purpose all existing possibilities up to and including the convocation of a special session of the Security Council with the participation of the highest leaders of the Council's member states, to discuss urgent international problems existing in and beyond Europe, and to seek keys for the improvement of the situation in the world.

Having made new foreign policy initiatives, the Soviet Union does not consider that it is, as it were, laying down the only possible formula for bringing about a turn for the better in world affairs. In his speech in Prague on 7 April,[3] L.I. Brezhnev noted that 'if anyone else has other reasonable proposals, we are ready to examine them too'.

All Soviet proposals for limiting the arms race and strengthening international security remain in force. This applies fully to the whole complex of problems which have at various times been discussed between the Soviet Union and United States and above all the problems of limiting strategic armaments.

---

[1] This message was delivered personally to the Foreign Secretary by Mr Popov at a hastily arranged meeting at 7.30 a.m. in the morning at Northolt airport prior to Lord Carrington's departure to Bonn. The above text is a translation undertaken by Mr Bishop, FCO Research Department, who commented that the Soviet translation provided by the Embassy 'contained one or two mistranslations as well as numerous infelicities'.

[2] Nos. 86 and 87.

[3] President Brezhnev was speaking at the Czechoslovak Communist Party congress where he stated that he was confident that the Polish leadership would be able to check 'the designs of the enemies of the socialist system' (*The Times*, 9 April, p. 6).

UK-Soviet Relations, 1979-82

2. In order to prevent the nuclear missile confrontation in Europe passing to a new and more dangerous level, the Soviet Union has proposed the establishment of a moratorium on the deployment in Europe of new medium-range nuclear missile weapons of the NATO states and the USSR, i.e. to freeze quantitatively and qualitatively the existing level of these systems, including the US forward-based nuclear systems in this region.

The Soviet Union is prepared here and now, without awaiting the outcome of the relevant negotiations, to halt the implementation of its current plans for modernising medium-range nuclear weapons in Europe. This reinforces our proposals on the possibility of reducing such weapons as a result of negotiations, and the scope of this reduction, moreover, could even be quite considerable, if our partners were prepared for this. The moratorium would enter into force immediately after the opening of negotiations on the limitation of nuclear weapons in Europe and would remain in force throughout the entire negotiations. The obligations of the sides in connection with the moratorium could be agreed even before the opening of the official negotiations.

We cannot agree with the assertion that the moratorium would perpetuate the allegedly 'serious imbalance' in favour of the USSR in medium-range nuclear weapons in Europe.

First, at the present time there exists in Europe an approximate equality in the relevant types of weapons. NATO has here a powerful grouping of nuclear systems capable of reaching the territory of the USSR. The Soviet Union's nuclear weapons in Europe do not exceed this level. In analysing the correlation of nuclear forces of the sides, one should not take in isolation one single type of weapon, for example, ground-based missiles. Nuclear potentials should be considered as a complex, since only on this basis can the principle of the equal security of the sides be maintained.

Secondly, the Soviet Union, in replacing old missiles with new ones for the purpose of preserving nuclear parity, not only did not increase by a single unit the aggregate number of medium-range nuclear weapon carriers but even decreased that number—with the deployment of each new (SS-20) missile one or two old missiles in the Soviet Union were simultaneously withdrawn.

Thirdly, as regards the number of the nuclear charges of medium-range weapons in Europe, the advantage currently favours NATO by approximately 1.5 to 1. The replacement undertaken of old missiles by new ones has not led to the Soviet Union acquiring superiority in this field. And the aggregate yield of the charges of Soviet medium-range missiles has not increased but even diminished.

Consequently, the introduction of a moratorium would only entrench the existing approximate equality and would open the way for the establishment of such equality at a lower level. Conversely, if, as planned, the NATO countries deploy additionally in Europe 572 medium-range missiles, then a more than 1.5 superiority in medium-range nuclear weapon carriers will be created on the NATO side. Moreover, we cannot but take into account the fact that in relation to the Soviet Union this US weapon is strategic in nature. It is common knowledge that the Soviet Union does not possess on the territory of other countries such weapons capable of striking targets on US territory. Thus, the deployment of further American medium-range missiles in Europe would disrupt the strategic parity between the USSR and USA and would make the situation less stable. Such a turn of events would compel the Soviet Union to take the necessary countermeasures so as to not to permit the worsening of the strategic situation and in order to re-

7 December 1979 – 1 December 1981

establish the balance, but at a higher level.

In drawing attention to the moratorium proposal, the Soviet side expresses the hope that the British government will carefully analyse once again all its aspects.

As regards the Soviet/American negotiations on the limitation of nuclear armaments in Europe the first round of which had took place in October/November last year, the Soviet side is prepared to resume them at any time, so it is now only up to the American side.

3. The Soviet Union considers it important to ensure that the Madrid meeting ends with results and it favours adopting understandings on all sections of the Final Act. We attach great importance to reaching agreement on convening a conference on military détente and disarmament in Europe and are ready for reasonable compromises. We could accept the option whereby a single conference would be held, with confidence-building measures being discussed at the first stage and issues of actual disarmament at the second. But we would also be agreeable to the holding of 2 conferences, having in mind that the first conference would be devoted to confidence-building measures and the second to disarmament issues.

The Soviet Union has expressed its agreement to a considerable expansion of the zone of application of confidence-building measures, applying them to the entire European part of the USSR,—subject to a corresponding extension of the zone by Western states. The specific parameters of the zone of application of confidence-building measures can be determined at the conference itself. What is required now is clarity on the approach in principle. Firstly, this means mutuality of obligations. Secondly,—their balance and the impermissibility of infringing the security interests of participating states.

The equality of states participating in the All-European Conference must be ensured in their rights and duties regarding confidence-building measures and in the All-European process as a whole. No one must have any privileges in comparison with others. Unilateral extension by the Soviet Union of the zone of confidence-building measures to the entire European part of its territory without reciprocal steps from the West would not correspond with the principle of equal rights and duties of all states participating in the All-European Conference.

In the decision on the convocation of the conference it would be possible to envisage, alongside the extension of the zone of confidence-building measures, an increase in the number of these measures (notification not only of major exercises by ground forces but also of major naval and air exercises and also of major troop movements, and the renunciation of military exercises involving the participation of more than 40-50,000 men). This would give the confidence-building measures a more important and more militarily significant nature as compared with the measures applied at present. Furthermore, the possibility would not be excluded of participants in the conference undertaking political obligations to carry out some of the confidence-building measures and of establishing, in certain circumstances, forms of verification making use of national means which would correspond with the nature of the specific confidence-building measures and which could be agreed between the sides.

At present, when the Madrid meeting is in recess, it is necessary to give serious thought to the current situation, bearing in mind the need for further development of the All-European process in the interests of peace and détente. In our view, the draft final document tabled by the neutral and non-aligned countries facilitates to some extent the achievement of mutually acceptable solutions. In Moscow it is hoped that the British government will make efforts for the constructive

UK-Soviet Relations, 1979-82

completion of the Madrid meeting.

4. The Soviet side is convinced that even the most acute problems in East/West relations can be solved, given the preservation of the legitimate interests of the sides. This applies also to the Middle East problem on which, in our view, there are, and could be found, new points of coincidence between the positions of the Soviet Union and Britain, and also to the settlement of the situation around Afghanistan, on which serious differences persist. A subject of real solutions could also be questions relating to the ensuring of peace and security in the Persian Gulf, if all interested parties show a desire to seek such solutions and to refrain from actions, particularly of a military nature, which might complicate the situation in that area. Specific proposals on this matter have been made by L.I. Brezhnev, including also those in his recent message to Prime Minister M. Thatcher.

5. There is satisfaction in Moscow with the statement by the British government of its readiness to pursue a constructive course in East/West relations and to cooperate with the Soviet Union, on the basis of joint efforts, in specific actions to strengthen confidence, consolidate international security and develop mutually advantageous relations between our countries.

Such an approach meets with understanding on the part of the Soviet Union. We are in favour of putting to work the considerable potential for cooperation created over the years in order to seek solutions to the urgent problems of curbing the arms race and strengthening détente, and of using existing opportunities in various fields of bilateral Soviet/British relations, giving them full development and translating them into specific actions. We are in favour of giving the political dialogue between our countries a level and content which would be in keeping with the requirements of the aggravated international situation.

No. 95

FCO to Sir J. Taylor (Bonn), 23 April 1981, 2 p.m.[1]
Tel. No. 164 Immediate, Confidential (ENS 020/11)

For Private Secretary[2]

Meeting with Soviet Ambassador at Northolt
1. The most striking aspect of the communication delivered by Popov[3] is its indication of willingness to develop the bilateral political dialogue, by implication at a higher level. The significance of this will be clearer when we know whether or not the communication is a round-robin delivered to all Western countries and have had a chance to compare notes if (as seems likely) it is. At the least, the communication gives us an opening to put forward proposals to the Russians if we choose, and the Russians will no doubt consider that the ball is now in our court.

2. We have the following comments on other points:
(*a*) TNF Moratorium: basically a restatement of the moratorium proposal put forward in Brezhnev's CPSU Congress speech in February, and repeated

---

[1] Repeated to Moscow as FCO Tel. No. 240 and UKDEL NATO as FCO Tel. No. 94.
[2] Lord Carrington visited the FRG between 23 and 25 April for talks with Chancellor Schmidt and Hans Dietrich Genscher to coordinate the Western position prior to the NATO ministerial meeting in Rome on 4-5 May.
[3] No. 94.

frequently since. If the communication is a round-robin, the timing would fit nicely with that of the NAC [North Atlantic Council] meeting in Rome. The only new element is the suggestion that 'the obligations of the sides in connection with the moratorium could be agreed upon even before the opening of the official talks.' Any such agreement could hardly be reached without a meeting, and it is conceivable that the Russians have the idea of a multilateral one in mind. The aim may be to make it harder for Ministers in Rome to reject the moratorium in standard terms, by offering the prospect of discussion on the points in dispute.

(*b*) Theatre Balance: generally standard, except for the specific claim that NATO has a medium range warhead advantage of 1.5:1. As far as we know this is the first time the Russians have made comparisons of numbers of warheads rather than delivery systems, but the figures are meaningless without details of the data base. The claim cannot be substantiated on any base that we would regard as reasonable but the aim may once again be to encourage discussion of this and related questions.

(*c*) CSCE: a cautious assessment of the NNA [Neutral and Non-Aligned] paper, but specific points all concentrated on CBMs and the prospects for a disarmament conference. Soviet offer to apply CBMs to the whole of the European part of the Soviet Union is repeated, but with more than usual emphasis on the need for reciprocal steps by the West and clear implication that the precise scope of the area of application may be for the conference itself rather than Madrid. The criterion of 'military significance' is identified with existing Soviet proposals for new CBMs. Confirmation of the equivocal nature of Soviet references at Madrid to the other two criteria ('political obligation' and 'verifiability') by indicating that only 'some' CBMs should be binding and by restricting the scope of verification. All this is pretty tough, though there is an indication of flexibility over the 'firebreak' in the suggestion that there might be either one conference in two stages, dealing with CBMs and disarmament respectively, or two conferences to deal with the two subjects in turn. Too early to tell whether this on the whole discouraging section is a tactic intended to lessen Western expectations on the resumption at Madrid or a substantive indication of lack of flexibility in the Soviet position. Experience suggests that the former is more likely.

(*d*) Afghanistan/The Gulf: nothing new.

3. We shall repeat this telegram to NATO and other posts to coincide with the addressees of your telegram giving the text of the communication.

UK-Soviet Relations, 1979-82

No. 96

Minute from Lord Carrington to Mrs Thatcher, 20 May 1981[1]
PM/81/28 Confidential (FSA 021/6)

Prime Minister

Afghanistan

1. It remains our aim to bring about a solution to the Afghanistan problem involving Soviet military withdrawal, freedom for the Afghans to have a government of their choosing and satisfactory arrangements for the return of the refugees. To this end we and like-minded countries have been trying to encourage two forms of pressure on the Soviet Union: resistance activity in Afghanistan and international diplomatic pressure. Resistance activity continues at a high level and shows no sign of slackening. But international pressure has been reduced. The US decision to lift the grain embargo and the consequent EC decisions may be interpreted as a weakening of the Western attitude. Pakistan is preoccupied with a new US aid offer and is no longer leading diplomatic activity. Waldheim's current efforts to find a way forward are unlikely to come to anything. No major UN or other discussion of Afghanistan is planned before the UN General Assembly in the autumn. With the change of President in France Giscard's earlier proposal for an international conference is not likely to be pressed.

2. I have therefore concluded that the United Kingdom should take the initiative to stimulate fresh diplomatic activity. My aim is that after careful initial consultations with our principal allies and the Pakistanis, and wider consultations later, the Ten would propose at the end of June that an international conference on Afghanistan be convened, perhaps in Geneva, in October/November. It would be presented as a conference in two stages. Stage One would be very much like Giscard's proposal and would involve discussions by the Permanent Members of the Security Council, Pakistan and certain others of external factors such as the cessation of external intervention and the establishment of guarantees for an independent Afghanistan. Stage Two would be attended additionally by representatives of Afghan opinion and would aim to reach agreement on the international arrangements proposed by Stage One and all other matters necessary to promote the return of Afghanistan to independence and non-aligned status. This proposal would avoid some of the difficulties of Giscard's proposal e.g. by making provision for Afghan opinion to be involved in the second stage. The difficult question of who should represent the Afghans does not have to be settled now. But it is clearly essential for them to participate in any settlement of the problem and

---

[1] The idea of reviving the French proposal for an international conference (see No. 85) was taken forward in early May by Mr Coles of South Asia Department. His submission of 13 May for a two-stage international conference was endorsed throughout the Office. The plan was for the proposal to be announced as an EC initiative in June (at a meeting of Foreign Ministers) with the UK, as President of the Community, conducting any further diplomatic efforts. The Secretary of State, in approving the recommendation, stated that he wished to inform OD colleagues. The original draft had a final paragraph, subsequently deleted, stating: 'The launching of the proposal may have some impact on the development of East/West relations and also on relations between the UK and the Soviet Union. There may be merit in my visiting Moscow at a suitable moment to impress upon the Russians the need to give it serious consideration. This would have the more general advantage of allowing me to exchange views with Soviet leaders in a context which did not imply business as usual.'

7 December 1979 – 1 December 1981

any proposal which does not recognise that from the outset is likely to encounter much criticism both from the Afghans and more widely.

3. The likelihood is that the Soviet Union will reject the proposed Conference. It has so far shown no serious disposition to negotiate. The primary purpose of the proposal is therefore to renew diplomatic pressure and rekindle interest. But there is an outside chance that the Russians will be prepared to consider a device which offers them a chance of withdrawal without loss of face. We shall in any case present the proposal as a serious attempt to promote a solution.

4. Much more work will be necessary on the details but my colleagues should be aware of the basic idea before we begin consultations about it with selected countries next week.

5. I am sending copies of this minute to the members of OD and to Sir Robert Armstrong.[2]

CARRINGTON

[2] The following day Mr Whitmore at No. 10 indicated, in a letter to Mr Lyne, that the Prime Minister was content to take the first steps towards launching a British initiative.

No. 97

Minute from Sir M. Palliser to Mr Walden, 29 May 1981
Confidential (ENS 020/12)

Anglo/Soviet Relations

1. Mr Suslov, Head of the Soviet Foreign Ministry Department responsible for Anglo-Soviet relations, called on me on 29 May[1]. I mentioned the call to the Secretary of State in advance as it was clear that Mr Suslov's main purpose would be to reinforce the carefully phrased message in the Popov Memorandum[2] about continuing and raising the level of Anglo-Soviet political dialogue.

2. Mr Suslov was quite candid in confirming that his only instructions were to probe my thoughts on this question. During our talks he refrained from comment when I mentioned Soviet actions in Afghanistan and the need for the Poles to settle their own affairs.

3. Mr Suslov wanted to ensure:

(*a*) that we were aware that the Popov Message had the imprimatur of the Soviet leadership; and

(*b*) that we had fully hoisted in the Russians' willingness to engage in dialogue at the political level.

On the second, he said that the impression in Moscow was that Lord Carrington 'had a pragmatic approach to the solution of certain problems and practical questions'.

4. As discussed earlier with the Secretary of State, I told Mr Suslov that Lord Carrington had read the Popov Message, including the concluding passage, with

[1] Mr Suslov was visiting London for a meeting of the Anglo-Soviet Joint Economic and Scientific Commission. He also met Mr Fergusson on 28 May, when Mr Broomfield noted Suslov was at his blandest. 'The Soviet instructions were clearly not to rock the boat. Although some progress was made on one or two bilateral points nothing particularly startling emerged.'

[2] No. 94.

UK-Soviet Relations, 1979-82

care and interest, and that we would continue to reflect carefully on it. At this stage I would say no more that that the Secretary of State saw the value of discussion and dialogue, which were particularly important at times of difficulty in the international situation.

5. The upshot of this encounter is that the Russians will now regard the path as having been cleared as thoroughly as they can for a possible visit by Lord Carrington to Moscow.

6. Considered advice on the timing and the other details affecting a visit (e.g. the initiative on Afghanistan) will be submitted early next week.

No. 98

Submission from Mr Broomfield to Mr Fergusson, 2 June 1981
Confidential (ENS 026/2)

Anglo/Soviet Relations

Problem

1. Would there be advantage in a visit by the Secretary of State to Moscow for talks with Mr Gromyko?

Recommendations

2. (*a*) That the Secretary of State should plan to visit Moscow; and that the visit should be discussed with the Russians in the near future. If possible, dates in July might be found.

(*b*) That the Secretary of State should speak to the Prime Minister on the lines of the attached Speaking Note[1] when they meet on 3 June.

3. SAD agree.

Background and Argument

4. The Russians have put out a number of feelers over the past few months about the possibility of the Secretary of State visiting Moscow. The memorandum delivered by Ambassador Popov on 23 April[2] contained a clear implication in the concluding paragraph that the Russians wanted to raise the political dialogue to the Foreign Minister level. This message was confirmed during the calls last week on the PUS and yourself by Mr Suslov, Head of the Soviet MFA's Second European Department which is responsible for Anglo/Soviet relations. The PUS's minute of 29 May is attached.[3]

Policy After Afghanistan

5. Our policy has been that we should not return to 'business as usual after only a perfunctory pause' (Lord Carrington's lecture in Stockholm, 19 August 1980).[4] At the same time we have made it clear publicly that political dialogue with the Russians on international questions should be continued. The Secretary of State has taken the view that a visit to Moscow at the appropriate time would serve the objective of keeping channels of communication open. In his speech at Stuttgart on 23 April,[5] the Secretary of State said that one of the elements of a common Western strategy was that of political communication between East and West and

---

[1] Not printed.
[2] No. 94.
[3] No. 97.
[4] No. 76, note 1.
[5] See No. 95, note 2.

242

the requirement to keep channels 'open and active' especially at times of uncertainty.

6. There are good reasons, set out in the attached Speaking Note, for an early visit to Moscow by the Secretary of State, especially with the Presidency in mind.

Afghanistan

7. We shall need to consider how a visit might be linked to our initiative on Afghanistan should this be endorsed by those countries which we are now consulting.[6] SAD would not wish to cover the possible effects of an early visit to Moscow on the Afghanistan initiative until the prospects for the latter are clearer. But in general they consider that effects of an early visit could be beneficial rather than detrimental to the Afghanistan initiative. Mr Coles is submitting separately today on how and when the initiative should be presented to the Russians.[7]

Other Factors: Poland/CSCE

8. A visit in July would take place while the CSCE is still in progress. The Secretary of State could be exposed to pressure on outstanding difficult points in the CSCE. On the other hand it would give a good opportunity to make the West's position quite clear over our requirements for a successful conclusion. A visit before the Polish Party Congress (14-18 July) would also give an opportunity to warn the Russians against intervention. If, however, the situation had altered radically, the visit would of course have to be reconsidered. On balance, however, I think these two factors argue for a visit before 14-18 July if possible. They would strengthen the presentation of the visit as one by a representative of the West putting agreed views to the Russians on matters of major international importance.

Timing of an Approach to the Russians

9. If a visit is agreed, soundings with the Russians about possible dates would begin next week (8/9 June). If we were prepared to suggest dates in early July and the Russians agreed, there should still not be a problem over an announcement of the Afghanistan initiative. The normal Soviet practice is not to announce a visit until a week before it takes place. If, as Mr Coles argues in his submission, we decide to inform the Russians about our Afghanistan initiative on or about 19 June (2/3 days before Foreign Ministers of the Ten meet) this will avoid the problem of announcing the visit before informing the Russians of the initiative.

10. If a decision is taken that a visit should be discussed with the Russians we should tell the Americans what we intend to do.[8]

N. H. R. A. BROOMFIELD

[6] See No. 100.

[7] Not printed.

[8] Mr Bullard commented that he was strongly in favour of the idea and hoped the Prime Minister would respond positively. He added: 'Of course they [the Russians] have wedge-driving in mind, but there is no reason why this should turn out to be the result'.

On 3 June Mr Fall minuted that Lord Carrington had discussed the idea with the Prime Minister and agreed the visit would go ahead, but very much in the context of the initiative on Afghanistan. A close eye would also have to be kept on developments in Poland. At an office meeting on 8 June the Secretary of State was clear—'no initiative, no visit'. However, as Mr Broomfield noted in a letter to Sir C. Keeble of 10 June, if a visit did take place, it would give an opportunity for discussion of other international topics as well as bilateral relations.

UK-Soviet Relations, 1979-82

No. 99

Minute from Mr Bishop (Research Department) to Mr Johnson, 8 June 1981
Confidential (ENS 020/2)

The Soviet Desire for 'Dialogue'

1. The 'Popov letter' of 22 April[1] ended with a thinly-disguised offer of a high-level Anglo/Soviet political dialogue. This was reinforced, though-still obliquely, by V. P. Suslov in his discussion with the PUS on 29 May.[2]

2. I am sure there are perfectly good reasons relating peculiarly to the UK for this Soviet interest in resuming business with us soon at such a level. But there is also a general and I believe wider Soviet interest in dialogue with the outside world and particularly with senior Western figures. This has to do with trying to improve the chances of drawing the Americans into talks with the USSR; regaining international respectability (in effect, 'getting away with Afghanistan'); regaining some Soviet sense of control of events; restoring a peaceful image and in particular trying to avoid Brezhnev's 'Peace Programme for the 1980s' dying a premature death; reassessing the costs intervening/not intervening in Poland, etc.

3. Not only are the Russians trying to maintain a flow of important visitors to Moscow (Khaddafi, Hussein, the Mexican Foreign Minister, etc.) on more or less empty business, but plans continue for a Soviet/FRG summit in Bonn in September (and Brandt visits Moscow on 29 June). But my feeling persists that all of this is largely for optical effect and that Soviet hearts are not in it.

4. Further evidence for this came in the handling of the visit to Moscow by Mladenov, the Bulgarian Foreign Minister, on 1-2 June. The Communiqué was as empty as it was long and seemed designed expressly to show that Brezhnev's peace proposals live and that the Russians are eager to talk to anyone. In case this message was missed, *Pravda* on the same day (3 June) gave 30 column-inches to a report of a press conference by Mladenov, in which he did nothing but make the same two points. Both this and the Communiqué contain language similar to the Popov message on the pressing need for dialogue, as the following quotations show:

(*a*) 'Both sides expressed the conviction that *the current situation in the world requires a cardinal change*, demands a turn from tension and confrontation to the improvement of the international climate, *a move to contacts and an extensive dialogue and constructive negotiations at all levels* with the aim of achieving mutually acceptable agreements on contentious problems, on key issues of strengthening peace and security' (Communiqué).

(*b*) [T. Zhivkov recently][3] 'gave a high appraisal of the peace initiatives of the Soviet Union and of *L I Brezhnev personally...who will go down in history as one of the major builders of peace and détente in our days. I note that Comrade Brezhnev is not letting the momentum of the Soviet peace initiatives slacken—* witness his speeches in Kiev and Tbilisi. But unfortunately one has to note that such concepts as dialogue and negotiations are currently not at all fashionable among the leaders of the USA and certain of its allies.' (Mladenov's press conference).

---

[1] No. 94.

[2] No. 97.

[3] Todor Zhivkov, General-Secretary of the Bulgarian Communist Party. (The brackets appear in the original text.)

7 December 1979 – 1 December 1981

5. The call for dialogue and negotiations at *all levels* is so unspecific as to subject-matter, and the attempt to blow more wind into Brezhnev's sails is so patent, that the impression created is of a Soviet Union devoid of ideas but hoping against hope that somebody outside will step in and provide some.[4]

K. A. BISHOP

[4] In a marginal comment Mr Johnson noted: 'I find this persuasive. If Mr Bishop is right, the chances of Gromyko agreeing to receive the S[ecretary] of S[tate] at fairly short notice are good'.

No. 100

Letter from Mr Lyne to Mr Alexander (No. 10), 9 June 1981
Confidential (EN 021/6)

Dear Michael,

Afghanistan

Clive Whitmore's letter of 21 May[1] conveyed the Prime Minister's agreement to the Foreign and Commonwealth Secretary's minute of 20 May[2] in which he described the steps he would be taking to promote a proposal by the Ten for an international conference on Afghanistan.

First reactions to the proposal have been most encouraging. Genscher and Cheysson have both said that they support it. The Americans have also said that they see no difficulty and we understand that a message to this effect will shortly reach us from Haig.[3] We made a particular point of carefully consulting the Netherlands Presidency who again reacted favourably. Sir John Graham visited Pakistan at the end of last week to present our ideas to the President and Foreign Minister. President Zia (who asked Graham to convey his good wishes to the Prime Minister) and Agha Shahi were also attracted by the proposal and said that Pakistan would support it—but they will be careful as to how they react initially to the announcement to avoid the appearance of collusion. They made no objection to the participation of India, although they hope this can be presented as representation of the Non-Aligned Movement.

The Prime Minister may wish to be aware of the further action that Lord Carrington contemplates. We shall be giving the rest of the Ten an outline of our proposal today in the hope that they will have time to study it and convey their agreement at the next meeting of Political Directors on 16 June. Before the formal announcement of the proposal at the meeting of the Foreign Ministers of the Ten on 22 June we propose to brief the Saudi Foreign Minister (on 10 June), the Australian Foreign Minister (on 12 June), and the Japanese Foreign Minister (on 17 June). On 17 June we would also brief NATO and, in capitals, New Zealand, Canada and Australia. On the following day we shall brief the UN Secretary-

[1] Not printed.
[2] See No. 96.
[3] Mr Haig wrote to Lord Carrington on 12 June giving the United States' enthusiastic support for the proposal for a conference. He added a number of considerations: Pakistan's attitude would be crucial; the agenda should not be enlarged to include the Gulf or the Indian Ocean; 'We should anticipate Soviet refusal to participate and try to move forward with a conference despite Moscow's obstructionist tactics'; the West would need a strong accompanying strategy for the UN General Assembly; a conference on Afghanistan refugees might be desirable at some stage (FSA 021/6).

UK-Soviet Relations, 1979-82

General, the Secretary-General of the Islamic Conference, the Saudis (in Jedda), India, Iran and Japan. We are still considering the best time to brief the Chinese.

The important step, however, is the approach to the Soviet Union. The Foreign and Commonwealth Secretary intends to instruct HM Ambassador, Moscow, to reply on 19 June to the message passed to Lord Carrington by Ambassador Popov on 23 April. Sir Curtis Keeble would tell the Soviet Union that Lord Carrington was interested in a meeting with Gromyko at which he would discuss a number of subjects, in particular, Afghanistan, on which we had some ideas about a possible solution. He would then describe in outline the proposed international conference in Afghanistan and suggest that Gromyko and Lord Carrington should meet on 3/ 4 July.

An approach on these lines would, as agreed, tie the visit to Moscow clearly to the Afghanistan initiative. It would give the Russians advance notice before the Foreign Ministers of the Ten announced the proposal on 22 June. We believe that some advance warning is desirable since our general approach is to give the Russians no easy excuse for rejecting the proposal (if they were simply informed by public announcement they could the more easily reject it as a propaganda move). But the proposed timing should be insufficient for the Russians to make disparaging public comment or to come back with a formal rejection, before 22 June; and the offer of a visit to discuss it should have a similarly inhibiting effect on Soviet public comment.

Lord Carrington believes that a visit at the time proposed (there is no easy alternative in the first half of July) would have the additional advantage of creating another reason for the Russians to hesitate over intervening in Poland. As the Prime Minister knows, Lord Carrington has invited the Polish Foreign Minister to come here next week, partly for the same purpose.[4]

Yours ever,
RODERIC LYNE

[4] The Prime Minister minuted her agreement with the arrangements—'Poland permitting' (PREM: Afghanistan: Internal Situation: Soviet Military Intervention). Mr Alexander, in a letter to Mr Lyne of 10 June, stated that the Prime Minister remained very conscious that the proposed visit was being arranged against the background of a deteriorating situation in Poland. 'She assumes that if the Soviet Union were to take any overt action against the Poles, Lord Carrington's visit to Moscow would be cancelled at once' (FSA 026/1).

Sir J. Graham, minuting on 2 June, thought there was a risk that all the activity would encourage expectations which were bound to be disappointed. 'But to do less', he added, 'would irritate friends who were omitted and lend colour to the accusation that it was purely a cold-war propaganda move' (FSA 021/6).

No. 101

Submission from Mr Broomfield to Mr Fergusson, 11 June 1981
Confidential (ENS 026/2)

Afghanistan: Secretary of State's Proposed Visit to Moscow

Problem

1. (*a*) When and how should we present to the Russians the initiative on Afghanistan and the proposal that the Secretary of State should visit Moscow?
(*b*) When should we inform our partners of the proposed visit?

7 December 1979 – 1 December 1981

Recommendations

2. (*a*) That HM Ambassador at Moscow be instructed to deliver on 19 June at the highest level he can achieve a communication from the British Government. I submit two self-explanatory draft telegrams.[1]

(*b*) That Mr Bullard should inform the Americans, French and Germans of the visit on Monday, 15 June, and that the remainder of the Ten be informed by the Secretary of State on 22 June. SAD and ECD(E) agree.

Background and Argument

3. The following papers, which have a bearing on the question of political dialogue with the Russians on Afghanistan and other international problems, are attached:

– President Brezhnev's letter to the Prime Minister of 6 March;[2]

– The Prime Minister's reply of 3 April;[3] and

– The message delivered by the Soviet Ambassador in London to the Secretary of State on 23 April.[4]

4. The Prime Minister has now agreed to the proposal in Mr Lyne's letter to No. 10 Downing Street of 9 June[5] that Sir C. Keeble should tell the Russians on 19 June that the Secretary of State was interested in a meeting with Mr Gromyko to discuss in particular Afghanistan, and outline our proposals for the international conference. We shall, therefore, be informing the Russians of the Afghanistan initiative three days in advance of its public announcement following the meeting of the Ten Foreign Ministers on 22 June. The manner of the approach and the brief intervening period are intended to minimise the possibility of the Russians attempting to kill the initiative at birth by an immediate negative public reaction.

5. The best method of getting the message across to the Russians would be for Sir C. Keeble to ask to see Mr Gromyko (or a senior deputy minister). There is, however, no need for a personal message from the Secretary of State. The draft is therefore in the form of a communication from the British Government (similar to the Popov Memorandum), which Sir C. Keeble would make clear he was conveying on instructions.

6. Mr Gromyko is by temperament and experience unlikely to reject the proposals on the spot. It would be clear to him that, if he were to do this, he would forego a visit by Lord Carrington to which the Russians clearly attach importance. This argues for beginning the message with a reference to the Popov Memorandum and the suggestion of a visit by Lord Carrington before going on to outline our proposals on Afghanistan. We should also pick up the Russians' stated willingness to hold discussions about the international aspects of the Afghanistan problem separate from any discussion of the Gulf.

7. Sir C. Keeble should be instructed to propose 3-4 July orally, and his draft instructions stress the importance we attach to the earliest possible meeting. We shall, however, need to have at least one set of alternative dates to offer the Russians if Sir C. Keeble is so asked. I understand that the only such alternative is 16/17 July. Although the Secretary of State's diary for 17 July is at present free, a number of important engagements on 16 July might need to be cancelled. An alternative would be 17/18 July, but 18 July is a Saturday and the Secretary of

[1] Not printed.
[2] Enclosure in No. 87.
[3] No. 92.
[4] No. 94.
[5] No. 100.

UK-Soviet Relations, 1979-82

State would have very little time between returning from Moscow and his departure for Ottawa on 19 July.[6] Despite the difficulties I hope that we shall be able to offer 16/17 or 17/18 July as alternatives. Both fall during the Polish Party Congress and would still afford an opportunity to warn the Russians against intervention. 3/4 July would, however, be preferable from this point of view. If the Russians agree to 3/4 July, I hope the Secretary of State will be able to depart for Moscow immediately after Cabinet on 2 July. If he were able to leave at 1.30 pm, he would arrive in Moscow just after 8 pm local time which would allow dinner and a briefing meeting with the Ambassador that evening.

8. Apart from dates, the draft telegram of instructions covers the questions of agenda and communiqué, as well as additional instructions on the presentation of the initiative on Afghanistan.

9. We will wish to give the Americans advance notice of the Secretary of State's intention. We had hoped that a reply by Lord Carrington to the expected message from Mr Haig on the Afghanistan initiative would have provided a vehicle for this. Mr Haig's message has, however, been delayed. Mr Bullard could use the opportunity of a meeting in London on 15 June to speak to Mr Eagleburger.[7] I think there would also be advantage in informing the French and Germans at the same time. This seems particularly important in view of M. Cheysson's statement in Washington on 6 June that he had decided not to go on to Moscow after visiting Washington because of Afghanistan.

10. There is a choice between informing the remainder of the Ten at the meeting of Political Directors on 16/17 June, or at the Foreign Ministers' Meeting on 22 June. I would favour the latter date, which would reduce the risk of premature leaks. Mr Bullard might, therefore, confine himself on 16 June to telling his colleagues we propose to outline our ideas on Afghanistan to the Russians on 19 June, leaving it for the Secretary of State personally to inform his colleagues on 22 June of his intention to visit Moscow to carry forward the initiative.

11. I hope that it may be possible to send the message and the covering telegram of instructions to Moscow on Monday, 15 June. This would be subject to a telegram from The Hague after the Political Directors' dinner on 16 June confirming that Sir C. Keeble may proceed to seek an appointment with the Russians and, if necessary, amending the language used to describe the Afghanistan initiative in the communication to the Russians so that it accords with that agreed by the Ten.

---

[6] The seventh G7 summit was held in Chateau Montebello on the Quebec side of the Ottawa river from 20-21 July.

[7] Mr Eagleburger, US Under-Secretary of State for Political Affairs, called on the Secretary of State on 15 June and confirmed that the proposed visit to Moscow would give Washington no problems (FSA 021/6).

No. 102

Lord Carrington to Sir C. Keeble (Moscow), 15 June 1981, 10.30 a.m.[1]
Tel. No. 365 Immediate, Confidential (ENS 026/2)

Afghanistan: Proposed Visit to Moscow
1. I should like to pay a short working visit to Moscow in early July to help

---

[1] Repeated Information to Washington, Paris, Bonn, The Hague (Personal for Ambassadors).

7 December 1979 – 1 December 1981

carry forward our initiative on Afghanistan.

2. You should therefore seek a call on Friday 19 June on Gromyko or a Deputy Minister to hand over the text in MIFT.[2] You should not, however, ask for the appointment until receipt of confirmation by telegram from The Hague that the Ten Political Directors have agreed on 16 June that our proposals can go forward for endorsement by Foreign Ministers on 22 June. It may also be necessary to amend the language used to describe our proposals for an international conference on Afghanistan in the light of discussion by Political Directors.

3. The communication in MIFT is not a personal message to Gromyko. You should, however, make it clear that you are delivering it on instructions. The message makes no specific proposal on dates. You should suggest 3-4 July as my strong first preference and seek to avoid suggesting alternatives. If pressed, however, you may mention 16-17 July but should make it clear that this is very much our second best. You should explain that I see advantage in a visit as early as possible in July and that it will be extremely difficult to find alternative dates later in our Presidency.

4. If the Russians ask about the agenda, you should say that I would wish to focus on Afghanistan and to explain the thinking behind our proposals. Other subjects which could be discussed include the Middle East, current problems in Europe, arms control issues including TNF, and CSCE, as well as bilateral relations. But I see no need for a formal agenda. You should stress that I see this as a working visit with the absolute minimum of protocol and formality which is why the proposed visit will not be following the strict protocol sequence. My objective, which I hope Gromyko will share, is to hold wide-ranging and frank discussions in the spirit of the recent correspondence between the British and Soviet governments.

5. If the Russians request advance information on travel arrangements, size of party etc, you should say that we will be in a position to give an early indication of these once we have the Soviet response on the proposal itself and on dates. For your own information, I should wish to arrive in Moscow on the evening of Thursday 2 July and depart on the morning of Saturday 4 July.

6. FCO telno 739 to Washington[3] sets out the main points of our proposal on Afghanistan, but the communication in MIFT contains somewhat different language on some aspects which we shall be putting to our EC colleagues on 16 June. In presenting the proposal you should draw on MIFT and explain that:

(*a*) The proposal is in accord with Brezhnev's statements that the Soviet Union is ready to hold separate discussions about the international aspects of Afghanistan. The first stage is limited to proposing international arrangements. You should nevertheless make clear that the second stage is an integral part of the proposal and that the ultimate purpose is a comprehensive settlement endorsed by representatives of Afghan opinion.

(*b*) The proposal is a serious attempt to find a way towards a political settlement acceptable to all the countries concerned, including the Soviet Union.

(*c*) While the ideas outlined in the proposal are of British origin, they have been discussed with our EC partners and the Ten are likely to announce the proposal

---

[2] Not printed. The telegram contained a draft communication to the Russians from the British Government outlining proposals for an international conference on Afghanistan. Following the meeting of EC Foreign Ministers on 22 June the language was amended to accord with that agreed by the Ten (see No. 103).

[3] Not printed.

UK-Soviet Relations, 1979-82

on 22 June as a proposal of the member states of the European Community.

7. If Gromyko probes our ideas, you should in general decline to be drawn and take the line that I should be glad to discuss them in greater detail during my visit. But you may say that:

(*a*) Our discussions with Third World and Islamic countries in recent months have revealed a continuing widespread interest in a negotiated settlement of the Afghanistan problem.

(*b*) I am putting our ideas to the Russians with the agreement of the rest of the Ten in advance of their announcement as a contribution to achieving the objectives set out in the exchange of messages between President Brezhnev and the Prime Minister, and in the spirit of the references in the Popov memorandum to the need for political consultation at the appropriate level between us. If you think it appropriate, you could also refer to the specific remarks about a bilateral dialogue over Afghanistan made by Suslov in London in late May.

8. Bullard will inform the American, French and German Political Directors on 15 June of my intention to visit Moscow, but will tell other Political Directors of the Ten on 16 June only that we shall be briefing the Russians on the Afghanistan initiative on 19 June.[4] I shall tell my colleagues in the Ten on 22 June of the proposed visit.

---

[4] In telegram No. 188 of 17 June from The Hague, Mr Bullard reported that there had been unanimous support at the Political Directors' Dinner on 16 June for the idea of a new initiative and a two-stage conference. However the French had argued strongly for the launch to be postponed until 29 June to give time for proper discussion and to allow the proposal to be launched by the European Council—rather than Foreign Ministers—for greater impact. The French suggestion was 'unfortunately seized upon by the other Political Directors, some of whom had already shown signs of nervousness at the pace of events'. The meeting ended with partners appealing to the UK to draw encouragement from the strong support given to the suggestion of an initiative by the Ten and not to abandon this in favour of a national proposal (FSA 021/6).

Despite the increased risk of leaks, the Secretary of State agreed to delay the announcement, as set out in a submission from Mr Coles of 17 June, in order to carry the Ten with him. It was felt that to revert to pursuing the initiative alone would be less effective and a bad start to Britain's EC Presidency (FSA 021/6).

No. 103

Lord Carrington to HM Representatives Overseas, 24 June 1981, 4.30 p.m.[1]
Tel. No. 81 Priority, Restricted (FSA 021/6)

MIPT
Begins.

1. The European Council notes with deep concern that the situation in Afghanistan remains an important cause of international tension, that Soviet troops remain in Afghanistan and that the sufferings of the Afghan people continue to increase.

2. The Council recalls its earlier statements, notably those issued at Venice on 12-13 June 1980, and Maastricht on 24 March 1981, which stressed the urgent need to bring about a solution which would enable Afghanistan to return to its

---

[1] This telegram contains the final text of the statement on Afghanistan issued by the EC Heads of State on 30 June following their Luxembourg summit.

7 December 1979 – 1 December 1981

traditional independent and non-aligned status free from external interference and with the Afghan people having the full capacity to exercise their right to self-determination. In keeping with the resolutions voted by the United Nations, the Islamic Conference and the New Delhi conference of the Non-Aligned Movement, the Council has made it clear on several occasions that it will support any initiative which could lead to the desired result.

3. The European Council considers that the time has come for a fresh attempt to open the way to a political solution to the problem of Afghanistan. They therefore propose that an international conference should be convened as soon as possible, for example in October or November 1981, and that the conference should consist of two stages, each stage being an integral part of the conference.

4. The purpose of stage one would be to work out international arrangements designed to bring about the cessation of external intervention and the establishment of safeguards to prevent such intervention in the future and thus to create conditions in which Afghanistan's independence and non-alignment can be assured.

5. The Council proposes that in due course the Permanent Members of the United Nations Security Council, Pakistan, Iran, India and the Secretary-General of the United Nations and the Secretary General of the Islamic Conference, or their representatives be invited to participate in stage one of the conference.

6. The purpose of stage two would be to reach agreement on the implementation of the international arrangements worked out in stage one and on all other matters designed to assure Afghanistan's future as an independent and non-aligned state.

7. Stage two would be attended by the participants in stage one together with representatives of the Afghan people.

8. The member states of the European Community will be ready at a later stage to make further proposals on the detailed arrangements for the proposed conference.

9. The European Council firmly believes that the situation in Afghanistan continues to demand the attention of the international community. It is convinced that this proposal offers a constructive way forward and therefore calls on the international community to support it fully with the aim of reducing international tension and ending human suffering.

Ends.

No. 104

Sir C. Keeble (Moscow) to Lord Carrington, 25 June 1981, 2.10 p.m.
Tel. No. 373 Immediate, Confidential (ENS 026/2)

My Tel No 369: Afghanistan[1]

1. Kornienko asked me to call this afternoon. He read a prepared statement to the effect that Gromyko was ready to meet you for an exchange of views on questions of mutual interest touched on in the recent correspondence between the British and Soviet leaderships. He confirmed that it would be convenient if you arrived for your short working visit on 5 July with a view to discussions with Gromyko on 6 July. He continued 'as far as the question of Afghanistan is

---

[1] Not printed. This telegram reported that Sir C. Keeble had transmitted the text of the agreed communication to the Soviet Foreign Ministry.

UK-Soviet Relations, 1979-82

concerned, while agreeing to an exchange of views on this question, at the same time we consider it necessary to say straight away that the proposal to call an international conference on Afghanistan as it was conveyed to us on 23 June appears unrealistic principally because it is proposed to exclude the Government of the Democratic Republic of Afghanistan from the participants in such a conference'.

2. I said that I was glad to have this quick confirmation of the dates. Since my discussion with Suslov I had obtained telephone confirmation from London and they could therefore be regarded as firm.[2] We would work out the details of the visit with the Second European Department.

3. So far as the subject matter was concerned I noted that in addition to the reference to the matters dealt with in the earlier exchange Mr Gromyko specifically agreed to a discussion of Afghanistan. I regretted, and I knew that you would, the description of our proposal as 'unrealistic'. I would however leave the substance for discussion between the Ministers.

[2] Sir C. Keeble saw Mr Suslov in the morning to go over the points in the telegram and the latter agreed to the 5-6 July for a visit. Keeble commented: 'It was in all respects a very Suslovian encounter. Before lapsing into silence he remarked "Your Secretary of State is a magician". I fear that it would be over optimistic to see this as a comment on the Afghanistan proposal' (Moscow telegrams Nos. 369 & 370 of 25 June).

No. 105

Letter from Sir C. Keeble (Moscow) to Lord Carrington, 25 June 1981
Confidential (ENS 026/2)

Dear Secretary of State,

The Russian Scene

1. I hope that we shall soon have a positive response from Gromyko to your suggestion that you should pay a short working visit to Moscow.[1] The Afghanistan proposal will not be welcome but they badly need to improve their dialogue with the West and I am fairly sure Gromyko will try hard to accept one of the possible dates. I thought therefore that it might be helpful to send by this bag a few thoughts on the current scene here.

2. First, a rather obvious point but one sometimes overlooked. In this type of socialist state the leadership are responsible literally for everything. The sheer business of running, from a central government apparatus, 260 million people scattered over eight million square miles means that the leadership is beset with endless internal problems. Foreign policy is therefore liable to take second place to internal political preoccupations and is I suspect often an unwelcome intrusion— the more so now when there is so little to comfort them as they scan the outside world.

3. In this situation I think they see the primary aim of their foreign policy as being the safeguarding of the rather favourable situation which they have built up over sixty years or so—years marked by bad relations with most of the world's powers for most of the time. They saw the conclusion of the Helsinki Final Act as putting the final seal of approval on the 1945 frontier in Europe. With the defeat of the United States in Vietnam and the attainment of strategic nuclear parity and

[1] See No. 104.

7 December 1979 – 1 December 1981

military superiority in Europe they saw a very satisfactory position in which, provided they exercised reasonable caution, they could expect gradually and safely to extend Soviet power. Over the last few years that position has begun to crumble. Their economic and internal political problems have been considerable. The threat of revolution in Afghanistan was something which they thought they could easily put down. They were proved wrong and are tied down in an old style colonial war. The NATO decision on Theatre Nuclear Forces threatened their superiority in Europe. The failure to secure ratification of SALT II meant that they might need a massive new effort if they were not to lose strategic parity. Now the ferment in Poland faces them with the choice between losing what they have publicly described as a cornerstone of the socialist system or engaging in the hazardous enterprise of once more subjugating the Poles by force.

4. All this is well trodden ground. I restate it only to explain why I think you will find Gromyko reflecting a leadership in Moscow who, behind their normal apparent self-confidence, are men who, in the last few years of their power, see their achievements threatened. They must be worried, uncertain and, by turns, belligerent. This is one reason why they will be glad that Gromyko is to talk to you and possibly also why they may be open to influence. The snag is that on the subjects that matter they have left themselves very little room for manoeuvre.

5. Afghanistan is the focus of your visit. If, like an ageing imperial power, the Russians really wanted to get out we could help them to do so honourably. But they are not yet quite at this stage and I do not see how they can suppose that any arrangement under which both the Afghan exiles and the Soviet army returned home could be compatible with retention of a shred of the communist regime. The one hope the Russians possibly still cherish is that they will gradually wear down the Afghan opposition to the point at which a garrison of a couple of divisions or so will suffice to maintain reasonable stability. After all, they may say to themselves, the Soviet Central Asian Republics were acquired by force, took a long time to subdue, and are now stable enough; Czechoslovakia has given no real trouble since 1968; Afghanistan is different but with patience it can be brought to heel. Some in the leadership will certainly argue that they have already invested so much military effort there and lost so much Third World sympathy that they should now stick it out till they get what they want. In these circumstances, while it may suit the Russians to talk of a political settlement, they will wriggle as hard as they can to avoid being dragged into one as a direct participant. (Incidentally, even if we judge that the present initiative is of value only as a means of exerting public pressure, I hope we shall do everything possible in public to present it as a constructive and realistic attempt to find a solution.) Kornienko's immediate response was to be expected. His points reflected the essential elements of previous Soviet statements and I would not see them as anything more. But Afghanistan is a nuisance and the less they are forced to talk about it the happier they will be. Which is not to say that happiness, in this context, is our objective!

6. There are two external issues which really worry them at present:

(_a_) _US/Soviet Relations_

Soviet external and internal policy both require that there should be no deterioration in the current ratio of strategic forces and that this ratio should be sustained at tolerable cost. To this end the Russians would like to see the beginning of discussions on Theatre Nuclear Forces in Europe and the establishment of some form of SALT agreement which would not be very different from the abortive SALT II. They may not be very hopeful of securing any results, but they probably

UK-Soviet Relations, 1979-82

feel that even the start of negotiations might help them with their major aims of preventing the implementation of the NATO programme, holding back the pace of American development and creating difficulties between the US and Western Europe. They were not too worried that the Reagan Administration should take some time to make up its mind, but they are now beginning to ask themselves whether their policies have any chance of success or whether they must accept that they can only sustain their present strategic position at the price of a further major effort in arms development and production. There is no reason why the West should ease their concern. What is more, if they fear American unpredictability they are more likely to be cautious. In this sense Haig's visit to China may have done no harm. Yet there must be some risk that public opinion in the West will see the inherent danger of an unstable super power relationship and swing in a way from which the Soviet Union could draw significant profit. It is difficult to know what to make of Brezhnev's latest grand appeal for peace. Clearly it is a propaganda gimmick and I assume that the main purpose is to encourage just this trend in public opinion. But it may equally be designed to prepare public opinion here for a hard time and to provide an international platform for the tension which will follow action in Poland. In any case, this whole area of policy is one where I believe the Russians will wish to talk seriously to you and although I know that our own options are severely limited, you may find room to exercise some influence.

(b) Poland

It was some months ago that a Soviet official described it to me as a Greek tragedy. It still looks that way. The logic of Czechoslovakia must be so compelling—and so compellingly argued within the Politburo by those like Suslov and Ponomarev who dealt with Dubcek—that it is remarkable that the Russians have not intervened before now. They must have been held back not so much by fear of the Western reaction—though this was a factor—as by realisation that a Poland subjected once again by military force would be even more of a nuisance than the present unruly Poland. They may also have the faint hope that somehow the Polish situation will be stabilised in such a way as to leave a reasonable prospect that in due course a sufficiently reliable communist regime may be re-entrenched, thus assuring continued CMEA and Warsaw Pact membership. A relatively moderate Congress, if that is the prospect, combined with Poland's economic problems, would encourage such hopes. But it may be that the decision has already been taken, perhaps with action planned after the Polish Party Congress. The current military intelligence seems to suggest that intervention is not imminent. The public campaign against the failures of the present Polish government has certainly stepped up in recent days and it has been linked with increased references to Western subversion. There may still be a little room for the exercise of influence, but in the last resort Soviet intervention will be determined by the situation in Poland itself, not by anything we can say or do.

7. Of the other possible areas for discussion I would make only a couple of points:

(a) CSCE

I think the Russians may be prepared to pay a little more here—and in particular not to expect substantial payment for their extension of CBMs to European Russia—if they think this will help to get Western agreement to attend a conference; agreement to hold a conference would be seen by them as a move to stabilise the East/West relationship and to encourage differences between the USA and Western Europe.

7 December 1979 – 1 December 1981

(_b_) _Middle East_

They are intrigued by the European initiative[2] and hopeful that they may, in current circumstances, be able to isolate the United States. This is therefore an area where they are likely to make encouraging noises for basically unhelpful reasons. The positive element could be that, while they enjoy making mischief for the West they do not want an explosion. So at that point there could be a genuine coincidence of interest.

8. I am sorry it is not a cheering picture, but I do not think you expected it to be. I shall however be disappointed if Gromyko does not rise above the sterile and essentially trivial acrimony with which you are only too familiar. I think he may. He ought to. And Brezhnev ought to want him to. Brezhnev may not mean very much when he proclaims (most recently on 23 June) Soviet readiness to negotiate on all issues of peace and security and to consider any constructive idea, but he must recognise that the Soviet Union now faces major problems which it cannot solve alone.

Yours sincerely,
CURTIS KEEBLE

[2] The European initiative on the Middle East was launched at the Venice Summit on 13 June 1980. The Venice Declaration recognised _inter alia_ the legitimate rights of the Palestinian people to self-determination, accepted that the PLO would need to be involved in future negotiations and considered that Israeli settlements in the West Bank and Gaza constituted a serious problem to the peace process in the Middle East.

No. 106

Note of a meeting between the Lord Chancellor[1] and the Soviet Ambassador (Mr Popov), 30 June 1981
Confidential (ENS 020/1)

1. The Ambassador began, speaking in English, by outlining his personal career, including the many studies he had made of diplomacy and of Anglo-Soviet relations, and emphasised his friendly attitude towards the United Kingdom. Then, speaking in Russian and with his Private Secretary translating, he formally delivered, to the Lord Chancellor in his capacity as Speaker the message from the Supreme Soviet of 23rd June.[2] He spoke at some length of President Brezhnev's desire for world peace, but his commentary did little but repeat the points made in the message from the Supreme Soviet.

2. The Lord Chancellor thanked the Ambassador for delivering this message. In his capacity as Speaker of the House of Lords he would ensure that it was delivered to the Clerk of the Parliaments who would lay it before the House. Both in that capacity, and as a Cabinet Minister, he warmly welcomed the stated desire for world peace and disarmament, as must any sensible country. His last close

[1] Quintin Hogg, Baron Hailsham of St Marylebone.
[2] Speaking at the opening session of the Supreme Soviet, Brezhnev declared that the Soviet Union did not threaten anyone and was not seeking confrontation with any state in the West or East. It was not pressing for military superiority and was ready to limit or ban any type of weapon by agreement with other states provided that negotiations were honest and equal and without preconditions. He further called on legislative bodies in the West to speak up vigorously in favour of talks that would stop a new round in the nuclear arms race.

UK-Soviet Relations, 1979-82

involvement with disarmament was when he had visited Moscow in 1963 to negotiate the Test Ban Treaty.[3] He felt (and the Ambassador agreed) that that Treaty had made a worthwhile contribution to the continuation of peace.

3. At the same time, the Lord Chancellor pointed out that genuine negotiations on disarmament could take place only in an atmosphere of mutual trust, if each side was convinced of the sincerity of the other. The Soviet Union had nothing to fear, first because the West had no desire to attack it, secondly because even if it had such a desire the Soviet Union had an overwhelming arms superiority, and lastly because the geography of the Soviet Union showed what small prospect of success any such attack would have—as Napoleon and Hitler had both discovered to their cost. Conversely, the United Kingdom and Western Europe could not feel safe from attack while the Soviet Union had such a superiority unless they were convinced that the Soviet Union had no intention of using their arms; and here the experiences of both Afghanistan and Poland did little to reassure. History showed that wars between the great powers seldom began directly, but more often as an escalation of a dispute involving smaller powers, if one of the great powers was ambitious.

4. The Ambassador disclaimed any such ambitious intent on the part of the Soviet Union, but agreed that instability in other parts of the world might well precipitate a crisis. His country was particularly anxious about the situation in the Middle East, and much deplored the Israeli bombing of the Baghdad nuclear reactor.[4] The Lord Chancellor agreed that it had been an unfortunate occurrence, but said that from his knowledge of the Middle East, where he had served for much of the war, he could well understand the state of mind which had led Israel to launch this attack. It was the inevitable consequence of a country being surrounded on all sides by hostile countries which, even if they did not intend to attack it, gave the impression that they might do so.

5. The Ambassador said that his Government very much welcomed the forthcoming visit of Lord Carrington to Moscow. The Lord Chancellor said that he had spoken to Lord Carrington, who was equally looking forward to the visit. He knew that, given the right constructive atmosphere, constructive proposals could emerge which would benefit world peace.

6. The Lord Chancellor concluded by thanking the Ambassador for his visit; he had very much enjoyed meeting him, was sure the meeting had been fruitful, and hoped that the Ambassador would feel free to call back at any time he wished.

---

[3] In July 1963, Lord Hailsham, Minister for Science and Lord President of the Council, and Averell Harriman, the former US Ambassador to the Soviet Union, visited Moscow to negotiate the Partial Test Ban Treaty which came into force in August 1963.

[4] On 7 June 1981, the Iraqi nuclear reactor at Osarik was destroyed in an attack undertaken by the Israeli air force.

7 December 1979 – 1 December 1981

No. 107

Record of meeting between Lord Carrington and Mr Gromyko, Ministry of Foreign Affairs Guest House, 6 July 1981, 10.30 a.m.[1]
Confidential (FSA 021/6)

1. *Mr Gromyko* welcomed Lord Carrington and expressed the hope that the talks would take place in a businesslike atmosphere. There were many questions which could be discussed. They should not be bound by any formal agenda. He invited Lord Carrington to state the questions he would like to discuss.

2. *Lord Carrington* thanked Mr Gromyko for his welcome and for arranging to meet at such short notice, not least because he had only just returned from Poland.[2] It was a good time to meet, because even in Mr Gromyko's experience of 23 years as a Foreign Minister he could hardly have found the world with more problems than now. By no means all were problems of East/West relations, there were others such as the Arab/Israeli dispute, the Iran/Iraq war, Cambodia, and Namibia. It was necessary to seek solutions, for all such problems carried within them the seeds of dangerous escalation. There were also East/West problems, of NATO and the Warsaw Pact, of TNF modernisation, of the CSCE Conference, all of which he hoped could be discussed later.

3. But he had been charged to speak about one particular item on behalf of the Ten Heads of Government who met on 29/30 June in Luxembourg. That was the problem of Afghanistan. He wished to give Mr Gromyko the text of a statement which the Ten issued on 30 June about Afghanistan.[3] As Mr Gromyko would be aware, the European Community had been following closely events in Afghanistan over the last 18 months. The European proposal was a genuine effort to find a solution acceptable to all. There had been various past proposals for a settlement. They had had little impact. Recently, we had noted with particular interest two statements by Mr Brezhnev. The first was to the CPSU 26th Congress on 23 February when he had said that the Soviet Union was ready to 'participate in a separate settlement of the situation around Afghanistan'. The second was his statement in Tbilisi on 22 May that 'The Soviet Union is for a political settlement that would end the undeclared war against Afghanistan and give it dependable guarantees on non-interference'. These two statements had given the Community hope that there was sufficient common ground between the various parties involved in the Afghanistan situation to make realistic the prospect of a negotiated settlement.

4. Lord Carrington pointed out that paras 3-7 of the paper he had handed to Mr Gromyko gave the essence of the Community's proposal. It was a fresh attempt to open the way to a political solution. There should be an international conference, perhaps as soon as October or November. The conference would be in two stages, each stage an integral part of the whole. Stage One would be confined to the international and external aspects of the situation. The aim would be to work out international arrangements and not to take decisions. Since Afghan representatives

---

[1] Those also present at the meeting were, on the British side, Sir C. Keeble, Mr Bullard, Mr Fall, Mr Coles, Mr Fenn, Mr Broomfield, Mr Wood, Mr Bishop and Mr Thomson; on the Soviet side, Mr Zemskov, Mr Komplektov, Mr Suslov, Mr Makarov, Mr Semeonov, Mr Posilyagin, Mr Chernenko, Mr Gventsadze, Mr Mazur and Mr Gusarov.

[2] Mr Gromyko returned on 5 July from a visit to Poland where he had sought reassurances from the Polish leadership that the reform movement would not undermine Communism in Poland.

[3] See No. 103.

257

UK-Soviet Relations, 1979-82

would not be present at that stage, it would be neither possible nor appropriate to take decisions. Mr Gromyko would note that the proposal referred to 'safeguards'. Mr Brezhnev had referred to 'guarantees'. This had a narrower legal meaning in English, though the sense was the same. Stage Two would reach agreement, taking decisions on the international arrangements worked out in Stage One. Obviously in Stage Two there were other matters which were as yet undefined but which would need to be decided. Stage Two would of course be attended by representatives of the Afghan people. Who they would be was not at present defined; first because it was still uncertain when Stage Two would meet; second and more importantly, because it would cause obstacles to the conference's progress. The Community believed the important thing was to launch the negotiating process. If Stage One met and made progress it might be possible to create a climate in which the problem of representation could be solved.

5. As Mr Gromyko would know, the Community had already made clear their views about Soviet intervention. In their view military withdrawal was an essential part of a solution. But the Soviet Union had a legitimate interest in a stable and friendly Afghanistan.

6. In conclusion, this proposal, which had been canvassed with others, was being put to the Russians as a serious attempt to solve a problem which had caused serious difficulty in East/West relations. The intention was certainly not to make propaganda but to make a genuine attempt to solve this difficulty. Of course, what was being proposed was not inflexible. The Secretary of State assured Mr Gromyko that if he could clarify any points or answer any questions he would be glad to do so. If time was needed to study the proposal, there was no difficulty in this.

7. *Mr Gromyko* agreed that the question needed to be discussed and suggested a break for a few minutes so that he could study the paper Lord Carrington had given him.

8. When the meeting resumed after a pause of ten minutes, *Mr Gromyko* observed that the contents of the paper did not appear to differ in fundamentals from that transmitted by the British Ambassador a few days ago. He understood, of course, that the paper today was given on behalf of the European Community and the previous one on behalf of the UK Government.

9. *Lord Carrington* confirmed that though some words differed there was no difference in the basic sense of the two papers. *Mr Gromyko* stated that he had to say the Soviet Union considered the proposal to be an unrealistic way of settling the Afghanistan question. Of course nobody disagreed that Afghanistan should be an independent and non-aligned state. Both the Soviet Union and the Government of Afghanistan had on many occasions stated that this is what they wished to see. On this there was no difference between the Soviet Union, Britain and the other Governments for whom Lord Carrington was speaking. If the authors of the present proposal really stood for the independence and non-alignment of Afghanistan then the Soviet Union was in agreement with them. The Soviet Union wanted to see Afghanistan independent and non-aligned and nothing else.

10. But how was this to be achieved? How to bring about the recognition of Afghanistan's independent and non-aligned status? The only correct way to arrive at a solution was to end the military interference from outside in the internal affairs of Afghanistan. For there was military intervention from foreign countries into Afghanistan, there was training of forces on the territory of other countries, the supply of weapons and aid to these forces. This had become the official policy of

7 December 1979 – 1 December 1981

some countries. The time was past when certain governments tried to prove that there was no interference in the internal affairs of Afghanistan, or tried to pretend that this was not taking place. Everyone with eyes to see who was not politically biased could see that there was blatant interference and that the time had come to put an end to this.

11. If military intervention against Afghanistan ceased and did not resume, and if there were political guarantees that it would not resume, then the Soviet Union would go home, with the agreement of the Government of Afghanistan. So in the process of considering the cessation of military intervention and of considering the implementation of appropriate arrangements to secure this, it would be possible to consider the withdrawal of Soviet troops. But this was not the only point. The Soviet Union could not settle the question of dates for the withdrawal of the Soviet contingent in the absence of a guaranteed settlement and the end of military intervention in the internal affairs of Afghanistan. Mr Gromyko was inclined to think that the British Government and the other governments who were the authors of the present proposal could be in no doubt that the Soviet Union would withdraw if military intervention ceased, provided, that was, they were prepared to consider the problem seriously. This would be the reliable basis for a settlement.

12. In the Soviet Union's view, and in the view of the Government of Afghanistan, a settlement should start with negotiations between representatives of Afghanistan and of Pakistan. He did not yet see any readiness on Iran's part to take part in similar talks, but in the final analysis there would have to be such talks. But the most important thing was negotiations between Afghanistan and Pakistan.

13. Turning to another aspect of the Community's proposal, Mr Gromyko suggested that many of the participants in the proposed conference were hostile to Afghanistan. Pakistan was, so too was Iran; the US position was quite clear; and the UK was a supporter of the US policy. China was not only a supporter but a co-participant in the military intervention since it helped with the military training of hostile bands. Some of the other participants were not without sin. In this respect, therefore, would the proposal really be called a realistic one? Not at all.

14. Even without the problem of participants, the proposal lacked a realistic basis. It was proposed that in the first stage representatives of Afghanistan would not take part. This seemed very strange to the Soviet Union. It seemed a proposal completely divorced from reality, as sky from earth. It was a bureaucratic approach. How was it possible to conduct a conference without Afghanistan representatives? It was impossible to conduct a conference on such a basis. It was possible to solve Afghanistan's problems but only when there was a genuine desire to do so. All that he had said, remarked Mr Gromyko, gave grounds for the conclusion that the authors of the present proposal were guided not by a desire to see Afghanistan as an independent and non-aligned country but by a desire to topple the existing regime in Afghanistan and to establish a reactionary regime there imposed from outside by other countries. It followed that the proposal envisaged that the Afghan Government would be hostile to the Soviet Union. The authors of the proposal stated that Afghanistan should be friendly and not hostile towards the Soviet Union but unfortunately this could not be believed. All the rest of the proposal suggested the contrary. The final and definitive Soviet conclusion was that the present proposal was unrealistic and could not lead to a solution by way of agreement. The Soviet Union did not think that the authors of the paper genuinely hoped to obtain the agreement of the Soviet Union and the Democratic Republic of Afghanistan to a settlement. Mr Gromyko assured Lord Carrington

UK-Soviet Relations, 1979-82

that what he had said was a conclusion reached after purely objective analysis. He expressed the hope that Lord Carrington understood this and understood that the Soviet Union would not adopt any other position. If the present situation continued then the Soviet Union would continue to discharge its duty to Afghanistan.

15. The Soviet Union had no designs upon Pakistan nor did the leadership in Afghanistan. Pakistan now had a unique opportunity to acquire a safe and stable boundary with its northern neighbour. But it had not expressed any interest. This was difficult to understand. It was perhaps the result of external interference or some other kind of pressure. Perhaps Lord Carrington could explain.

16. Mr Gromyko said that some time ago the leadership of Pakistan had come up with the idea that *de facto* representatives of Pakistan and Afghanistan should meet; both the Soviet Union and Afghanistan had received this proposal favourably. But after a short time Pakistan had made a U-turn. One part of Pakistan's proposal had been the idea that the UN Secretary-General or his representative should take part. Afghanistan had reacted favourably to this too but the idea had suffered a set back. Pakistan was not sufficiently mature politically to make progress on what the Soviet Union regarded as a realistic proposal. The Soviet Union should perhaps give a formal reply to the proposal, but from what he had said their position should be clear.

17. Mr Gromyko assured Lord Carrington that any British thinking that would contribute to a realistic solution of the Afghanistan problem would always find great understanding on the Soviet part. He was inclined to think that if the United Kingdom genuinely wished to contribute to a solution it could do so.

18. *Lord Carrington* replied that the proposal would certainly not have been put forward if its authors had considered it unrealistic. Many other ideas had been tried which had not been successful, notably the one of bilateral talks between Pakistan and Afghanistan mentioned by Mr Gromyko. That particular approach no longer appeared open.

19. Much of the thinking behind the proposal was based on Mr Brezhnev's message to the Prime Minister of 6 March 1981,[4] from which Lord Carrington quoted. The present proposal was formulated precisely to meet Mr Brezhnev's points. There would be first a provisional settlement of the international problems and then a settlement in Afghanistan itself. This explained why in the first stage there would be no representative of the Afghanistan people, though he again emphasised that no decisions would be taken at the first stage. It was certainly not the intention of the British Government or of the other nine Community Governments to propose a settlement which would establish an Afghanistan Government hostile to the Soviet Union. Indeed, it was hard to conceive of any sensible Afghan Government which would be hostile to the Soviet Union. Though the difficulties should not be underestimated, what we sought to achieve was a government in Afghanistan acceptable to the people of Afghanistan. Facts should be remembered including the fact that there were over 2 million Afghanistan refugees in Pakistan who did not find the present Government in Afghanistan acceptable. Since this problem was clearly difficult, it was better to start by trying to settle the international aspects. The proposed participants in the conference were only suggestions but seemed the obvious candidates. There was certainly no intention of weighting the membership one way or the other. The question of composition could be discussed in advance.

[4] Enclosure in No. 87.

7 December 1979 – 1 December 1981

20. As well as giving the Soviet Union advance notice of the proposal, Britain had talked to a number of non-aligned and neutral countries to see if they thought it could be successful. Most of them encouraged Britain to go forward on the basis of the proposal, though China was rather non-committal. He urged Mr Gromyko, that, before making a formal reply (which he understood he was not now doing) he should talk to other countries about the proposal.

21. *Mr Gromyko* said that Lord Carrington had presented the proposal admirably. The Soviet Union had already discussed its position with other countries and made clear its views on what a settlement of the international aspects of the Afghanistan problem should comprise.

22. He wished to emphasise a difference of principle. The Soviet Union did not believe other countries had any right to say what regime in Afghanistan was acceptable. This was the prerogative of the people of Afghanistan themselves. To question this was tantamount to questioning whether the October Revolution in Russia should have taken place. He could provide many arguments to undercut those who interfered in Afghanistan. They did not tolerate interference in their own affairs. Chile was an example. It was a regime of hangmen there. But the Soviet Union had never urged outside interference in Chile. It did not matter if interference was direct or round-about. It remained interference.

23. Lord Carrington had mentioned Mr Brezhnev's statement on the desirability of discussing the external aspects of the Afghanistan situation. The Soviet Union was indeed prepared to do this. But it was not prepared to discuss Afghanistan's internal affairs. This was unacceptable to Afghanistan and, from principle, unacceptable to the Soviet Union. Some had suggested that those taking part in armed struggle against Afghanistan should participate in the conference. That would be wholly unacceptable. He thought Lord Carrington had made the best possible case for the proposal he was recommending. That was not the problem: the very basis of the Community approach was unacceptable.

24. *Lord Carrington* replied that he did not believe there was any difference of principle over non-interference in a country's internal affairs. The difference was one of perspective. In the Soviet perspective interference came from one direction, in the Western perspective, from another. The proposal was designed to remove external interference from wherever it came, and to allow the people of Afghanistan to decide their own future. Thus, the first stage would be about the external situation. This accorded with Mr Brezhnev's message to the Prime Minister. *Mr Gromyko* reiterated that outside military interference was taking place against Afghanistan and asked rhetorically whether this was not a problem which concerned the Afghanistan regime and people. He could imagine a situation where Soviet or Afghanistan representatives would wish to present in a document a list of the atrocities by armed bands in Afghanistan. How could it be imagined that this could be presented at a conference without representatives of Afghanistan? It was impossible to say they had no right to speak on behalf of their people. *Lord Carrington* reiterated that it was precisely the object of the first stage to arrange that outside interference should be stopped. If Mr Gromyko excluded such things from the context of international questions concerning Afghanistan it was not clear what was left. *Mr Gromyko* complained again of the armed interference from outside and said that the killing which resulted could not be separated from a settlement. *Lord Carrington* said that if it could be decided which aspects of the situation were international and which were internal to Afghanistan then perhaps some progress could be made. *Mr Gromyko* agreed that there should be agreement

UK-Soviet Relations, 1979-82

about the international aspects. These included the organisation of hostile military groups, their arming and training. There was no need for a conference about that, for the question of what were the international aspects—the organisation and arming of military bands—could be discussed bilaterally. *Lord Carrington* pointed out that the two stages of the conference comprised a whole. What Mr Gromyko had spoken of was one part of the international aspects. Views differed on the nature of the interference. But it was agreed that there was a need to discuss with interested parties how to stop external interference. Pressing his theme, *Mr Gromyko* argued that matters of substance would be worked out in the first stage and the second stage would merely stamp them with a seal of approval. It was impossible to prepare all the steps of the first stage without the participation of Afghanistan. How could Afghanistan sign what had been agreed without its participation?

25. Why was it that Britain and some other governments were so scared of the Afghanistan regime and its leaders? The regime had emerged with full institutions and organs such as the Revolutionary Council; it had the broad participation of the population, including groups such as the tribes, in the State Government. Afghanistan had no warlike designs. It wished to remain non-aligned. It would be natural for Lord Carrington to invite an official Afghanistan representative to the United Kingdom or for a British representative to visit Afghanistan to see what was happening at first hand. Instead Britain went on scaring itself and others over the Afghanistan regime. Karmal was not a frightening figure, he had strictly peaceful intentions.

26. *Lord Carrington* said that he would reflect carefully on what Mr Gromyko had said and report it to his colleagues and other countries of the Community. If they had any comments he would arrange to convey them to Mr Gromyko. In the recent Polish/Soviet joint communiqué Mr Gromyko had talked of the problem of Afghanistan. There was a problem. It was likely to be a problem when he met Mr Gromyko in New York in September. Perhaps then they could discuss further what had been said today. *Mr Gromyko* replied that the discussion should certainly continue in New York. But any proposals should steer more closely to reality than the present proposals.

27. The meeting ended at 12.50.

No. 108

Record of a meeting between Lord Carrington and Mr Gromyko, Ministry of Foreign Affairs Guest House, 6 July 1981, 3 p.m.[1]
Confidential (ENS 026/2)

TNF

1. *Mr Gromyko* invited Lord Carrington to open the afternoon's discussion on European matters. *Lord Carrington* said he would like to begin with two points on nuclear weapons in Europe: the Soviet readiness for arms limitation talks on theatre nuclear forces, and American agreement to have talks before the end of the year. Lord Carrington said he had recently talked with Mr Haig about this. He was

---

[1] Those also present at the meeting were, on the British side, Sir C. Keeble, Mr Bullard, Mr Fall, Mr Broomfield, Mr Bishop and Mrs Jackson. The Soviet delegation had the same participants as the morning session (see No. 107, note 1).

262

7 December 1979 – 1 December 1981

convinced the US agreement to talks on TNF review was genuine. At the May meeting in Rome all fifteen NATO countries had been of the firm opinion that there should be negotiations between the US and the USSR.

2. There seemed to be two difficulties: the Soviet belief that the NATO TNF decision, if implemented, would give NATO a nuclear advantage, and the NATO belief that a moratorium as proposed by President Brezhnev would perpetuate a Soviet nuclear superiority. The figures, as the UK analysed them, did not seem to bear out the Soviet Union's view. But equally no doubt the Soviet Union would say the same thing in reverse. Would it not be possible for experts to get together and discuss frankly their data, what they were counting and why, so that they could analyse, before negotiations began, the basis on which the negotiations were to take place?

3. *Mr Gromyko* said that these were important matters which should be discussed in the actual course of negotiations. That was the purpose of negotiations. The US had stated several times that it was prepared to exchange views with the Soviet Union (and it had since been expressed even more cautiously) on how to conduct talks on nuclear weapons in Europe at the end of the year. The Soviet Union regretted the delay. They would see at the negotiating table what political baggage the US would be carrying and whether or not the US was ready to agree on these matters.

4. He was aware of NATO views on the correlation of nuclear forces between the US, NATO and the USSR. But the information given came from the Pentagon and was far from reality. It was a distortion of the real position, that the US and NATO had a considerable superiority in actual nuclear warheads with one and a half times as many as Warsaw Pact countries. Modernisation of Soviet missiles in Europe, the installation of SS-20s, would change this correlation very little indeed. Allegations about a Soviet nuclear superiority in Europe were completely false. A compelling illustration of this was the fact that the US excluded from their figures aircraft carriers (for example in the Mediterranean) with aircraft whose weapons could reach almost all the European part of the Soviet Union, but did include equivalent Soviet aircraft. Similarly the US excluded from their figures US bombers based in Europe. The US knew what they were doing. It was perhaps a plan based on counting methods calculated to mislead the ill-informed: while the truth remained unknown the US could proceed for months and even years with its plans and perhaps implement them fully. The 'US military and Washington' were no friends of the truth. It was a firm Soviet conviction that European statesmen were victims of deceit, or to put it more mildly, wrong information.

5. Mr Gromyko said it might be possible for Lord Carrington to look more closely at this question, taking into account the data of British military experts. The Soviet Union was in favour of an 'approximate equality' of nuclear weaponry in Europe and the continual observance of the principles of equality and equal security. The Soviet Union was prepared for negotiations on TNF, in natural conjunction with American forward based systems in Europe, and the sooner the better.

6. *Lord Carrington* said the problem was that no one agreed on figures. His briefing included many arguments which sought to refute what Mr Gromyko had said. For example Soviet statistics included American FBS but overlooked the equivalent Soviet systems; the Soviet Union included in their calculations European systems which could not reach Soviet territory. It was not profitable for the two Foreign Ministers to discuss this. But obviously before any negotiations

UK-Soviet Relations, 1979-82

could be successful there had to be agreement on data for the negotiations. It would probably be necessary for the first part of the conference to decide what the facts were. Arms limitation talks were not possible if one side felt unfairly treated or disadvantaged. This was why, broadly, NATO found it impossible to accept the Brezhnev moratorium proposal. An agreed basis was essential.

7. *Mr Gromyko* said that allegations that the Soviet moratorium proposal would perpetuate Soviet superiority were not possible because no such superiority existed. The facts showed a different picture. The only superiority was in NATO's favour. He denied that the Soviet Union included in its calculations systems which could not reach Soviet territory. He added that there was another factor which should be taken into consideration, which was that Soviet medium-range nuclear weapons could not reach American territory, whereas American TNF could reach Soviet territory. It did not show American 'kindness of heart' to place such systems on European soil when Soviet weapons reached only Europe and not the US. The US liked this situation. These American weapons should therefore be considered as tantamount to intercontinental strategic weapons, as both types reached Soviet territory. According to these criteria, medium-range missiles should have been considered in SALT I along with intercontinental missiles. The purely geographical factor here played an important strategic role.

8. *Lord Carrington* commented that both sides had been repeating standard arguments. Mr Gromyko had said there was a 1.5:1 superiority in NATO's favour; his own figures showed a 4:1 superiority for the Soviet Union. Mr Gromyko would of course say that this was not so. Only Soviet and American experts could discuss these questions and decide on them, taking into account each other's arguments. The US was in favour of talks. The new Administration would take some time to absorb the necessary knowledge and weigh the options, but would be prepared for discussions when it had its facts and figures right.

9. *Mr Gromyko* thought that the US was not working to discover the true state of affairs. It was on the road of deceit and maybe this suited some of its allies, who did not make the effort to inform themselves about the relevant facts. Asked by Lord Carrington how best to proceed, Mr Gromyko said that when the two sides sat down to negotiations, they should put their cards on the table. Before that, agreement was difficult. The Soviet Union was firmly convinced that the US liked the deceit it was practising while awaiting implementation of the NATO decision. The USSR was in favour of a solution to the problem, but if the US with the help of its allies pursued a policy disrupting the existing balance, the Soviet Union would be compelled to safeguard the security of itself and its allies.

10. *Lord Carrington* remarked that none of the new Western missiles, Cruise or Pershing, could conceivably be operational for two years. The Americans had agreed to start negotiations before the end of the year and intended to do so. So there was time to solve the problem and he hoped that it would be solved.

11. *Mr Gromyko* said that no progress could be made on the basis of the false data supplied by the US. It would not be in the interests of the USSR to supply false information, which would be easily discovered. The Soviet Union could not indulge in American behaviour, Soviet morals were different. SALT I and II had been agreed on the basis that both were verifiable with the national means of detection at the disposal of both sides. These means continued to give each side knowledge of the other's situation. *Lord Carrington* concluded that the best thing would be to start talks before the end of the year and get the figures settled by experts.

7 December 1979 – 1 December 1981

CSCE

12. *Mr Gromyko* said that the Soviet Union was not satisfied with the way things were going at Madrid. Progress was very slow. Some participants were switching their attention to matters of secondary or tertiary importance, leaving important primary questions aside. If it were possible to reach agreement on the zone of application for CBMs, then the conference could be concluded with a Conference on Military Détente and Disarmament (CMD&D). The Soviet Union expected NATO to make a counter-proposal to the Soviet statement on Soviet readiness to extend the zone to the Urals. Perhaps the UK could help the US and others to formulate this proposal. If agreement was reached, the main difficulty would be removed.

13. *Lord Carrington* said his understanding was that the Soviet Union had accepted a proposal to extend the geographical area to the Urals and suggested that a corresponding response should be made from the West. Since then the non-aligned countries had suggested a formula for that response, referring to the 'adjoining sea area and air space' in Western Europe. A French statement of 3 July had said the non-aligned proposal needed further clarification in the context of CBMs. A number of texts were circulating for agreement in NATO countries. The UK hoped before too long that agreement would be reached on the text, which would then be introduced into the conference. If the Soviet Union had its own ideas on how to make the phrasing more precise, he would be happy to hear them.

14. *Mr Gromyko* said that there had been no proposals at all from the West so far. We were still at the same point that we had been when the Soviet Union made its proposal. Lord Carrington said this was partly true as regards the other side of the proposal on linkage between a conference and CBMs. But a large measure of agreement had been reached in other baskets.

15. *Mr Gromyko* said it would be good if Madrid were to finish in a constructive atmosphere. There were allegations that the Soviet Union was more interested in the convocation of CMD&D than in a successful conclusion to Madrid. The Soviet Union did indeed wish for a positive result to Madrid but they believed that all countries should be interested in a CMD&D.

16. *Lord Carrington* said that disarmament proposals were not the only part of the conference which interested the UK. Another principle which interested us as much was human rights. He had discussed this previously with Mr Gromyko. When his visit to Moscow had been announced in Britain, he had received many letters on human rights, and on personal cases, of which the Foreign Ministry had the details. A delegation of Soviet Jewry had called on him. He looked to the Soviet Union to consider these matters and make relevant proposals.

Middle East

17. Lord Carrington said there were three problems in the Middle East which, if they went wrong, could have serious consequences for all of us. The first was the Arab-Israeli dispute in which Western Europe had been trying to play its part. As the new President of the EC Council of Ministers, it would now fall to him to continue the Community's efforts to move towards a Middle East settlement. He would be less than honest if he did not acknowledge that the situation had changed considerably for the worse in the last six weeks. The Israeli raid on Iraq's nuclear reactor[2] and the re-election of Begin[3] were two factors which were not conducive

[2] See No. 106, note 4.

[3] Menachem Begin retained his position as Prime Minister of Israel following elections held on 30 June.

265

UK-Soviet Relations, 1979-82

to a settlement. But it was necessary to proceed on the basis that some settlement was possible. He did not think it would be soon, but he hoped they could go some way towards making it easier. In a recent conversation, Mr Benyahia, the Algerian Foreign Minister, had said he thought the Community were going in the right direction with the Venice Declaration.[4] But no problem could be solved unless all the pieces were in the right place at the right time, and he did not think that they were, or were even getting there. The Community were considering further steps and would meet later in the month to discuss possibilities.

18. The Soviet Union had suggested an all party conference on the Middle East. Lord Carrington thought that this was likely as an eventual outcome, but at present there was little prospect that all the parties would come to a conference. It would be best to try to persuade all parties (although Begin would prove difficult) to recognise the existence, albeit qualified, of other parties. In the other two problem areas, the Iran-Iraq war and the internal situation in Iran, it seemed at present there was no useful role for us in either situation.

19. *Mr Gromyko* said that many of Lord Carrington's ideas were not at variance with his own, but certain things were not seen in the same light. The situation in the Middle East had become worse. Israeli actions in Iraq and Syria could lead to serious conflict, which was not in the interests of our two countries, or of peace generally. Begin and his government had crossed out any reasonable approach to the situation. They did not want a peaceful solution, they were not prepared to co-exist with their neighbours. The reason was that they had a strong patron in Washington without whom they would not act as they did. It was surprising in the middle of the twentieth century to see a country behave in this way. If the rules were strictly obeyed, the Security Council should adopt sanctions against Israel. But the US would not move a finger to introduce sanctions. The American President had stated after the raid that Israel possibly had grounds for doubts about Iraqi motives. Such reasoning, if generally accepted, would lead to chaos in international relations with no dividing line between war and peace. For appearances sake, the US had said they did not approve of the Israeli raid. But the President's words represented real US policy. It was therefore good that the UK and the Soviet Union should try to remove the possibility of conflict in the Middle East. The US had said it wished the Soviet Union to exercise a moderating influence in Syria. But the Soviet Union was acting in that way anyway as regards Syria, whereas the US were condoning Israel.

20. Turning to the Soviet proposal for a Middle East conference, Mr Gromyko said that reactions had been varied. The majority of Arab countries had reacted positively, others had raised the question of Egyptian participation. Egypt was a traitor to the Arab cause for its part in the separate deal.[5] The Soviet view was that if Egypt took part, it would by its very participation have renounced participation in Camp David and would be ready to take part in a settlement on a completely different basis, one acceptable to all parties. Participating countries must not be bound by Camp David. Not all Arab countries were happy about Egyptian participation. Mr Gromyko said he doubted the conference would take place in the very near future but it would be necessary to work for it. The only other way to a settlement was using arms. Better three years of negotiations than one day of war. The Soviet Union was firmly convinced that a peaceful solution through a

[4] See No. 105, note 2.
[5] In March 1979 Egyptian President Anwar Sadat concluded a peace deal with Israel in return for the latter's withdrawal from the Sinai peninsula and economic aid from America.

conference would relax tension in the Middle East. If the UK had any comments, he would be pleased to listen.

21. *Lord Carrington* said he was sure that a conference would be necessary in the end for a settlement. But he was doubtful that the time now was right for a conference. There was no way that Egypt would join in before April 1982 when it would get the rest of the Sinai back from Israel. After that the Egyptian attitude might change. And personally he did not think that a conference without Israeli participation would produce a satisfactory conclusion. Begin would not accept the idea, for the reasons which Gromyko had mentioned. There was therefore a need for some political activity to lead up to the conference to avoid an outbreak of fighting. The UK and its partners would be thinking of possibilities over the next few weeks.

22. *Mr Gromyko* agreed that the question needed more thought. It was difficult to argue against Lord Carrington's opinion that a conference would not take place in the near future. But even 1982 was not too far away. *Lord Carrington* agreed and said that there would be a need for a political initiative of some kind in the next few months or else the Arab countries would feel that Israel had got away with something it shouldn't.

23. On the Iran-Iraq war, *Mr Gromyko* said that the Soviet Union's main desire was the earliest possible termination of the war. They had expressed this viewpoint, more to Iraq than to Iran, where communication was difficult. But at present he saw no end to the war: prestige as well as interests, real and supposed, were involved. The Soviet Union would continue to do its utmost to this end by advising the sides to end the conflict. *Lord Carrington* noted that this was also the British position. We had a good dialogue with Iraq, but dialogue was impossible with Iran. Mr Palme's commission[6] had now run into the sand and there were few prospects of a speedy settlement.

Poland

24. Lord Carrington said that he had one other matter to raise, which had in fact already been done over lunch, and that was Poland. Mr Czyrek,[7] who had recently visited the UK, had seemed very worried about the economic situation. The UK had an interest as they had been asked by the Poles to provide credit. He would be interested to hear Mr Gromyko's views.

25. *Mr Gromyko* said this had been touched on over lunch. It was not Soviet practice to discuss Poland with countries, other than allies. But he would say strictly off the record that the situation was complicated. As Polish leaders themselves said, there had been miscalculations in the past, and the main problem lay in Polish debts to the West. The optimism of the Polish leaders was based on the existence of a sound productive base, many re-equipped factories and the promise of a very good harvest this year. The Poles were sure that they could overcome their problems and move on to a stable path to recovery. There were grounds for such optimistic assessment, but it was difficult to judge how long it would take.

26. Summing up, Mr Gromyko said that the four questions which he had discussed with Lord Carrington had all been major questions and worth considering. They had agreed to continue the dialogue. The Soviet Union had expressed their viewpoint sincerely and fully to the British side. They had tried to

---

[6] On 11 November 1980, the Swedish politician, Olof Palme was appointed the UN Secretary-General's Special Emissary to open peace negotiations between Iran and Iraq.

[7] Jozef Czyrek, Polish Foreign Minister.

UK-Soviet Relations, 1979-82

be as clear as possible on Afghanistan. He was very grateful to Lord Carrington for these useful and 'perhaps even necessary' discussions, and to all colleagues who had helped.

27. *Lord Carrington* said that he reciprocated every word of what Mr Gromyko had said. He looked forward to seeing Mr Gromyko in New York in September.[8] *Mr Gromyko* agreed they should provisionally schedule that meeting here and now.

28. The meeting finished at 5.05 pm.[9]

[8] See No. 111.

[9] In FCO telegram No. 88 of 8 July to HM Representatives Overseas, Lord Carrington declared he was disappointed but unsurprised by the Soviet reaction to the Afghan proposal. He thought it important that as many governments as possible should now make their support known, both publicly and privately, to the Soviet Union and he stressed the offer 'remains on the table as a reasonable proposal for negotiations'. In a message to Mr Haig, Herr Genscher and M. Cheysson (Rome telegram No. 266 of 7 July) Carrington summed up his trip as: 'All in all a tiring, not particularly pleasant, but not wholly unproductive visit.'

Mr Haig, replying in a letter of 15 July, supported Lord Carrington in his decision to continue pursuing the EC initiative. He believed it essential to point out that the initial Soviet response contradicted the Soviet line that Moscow was interested in a political settlement. The US would keep raising the issue in bilateral exchanges, 'pressurising hard for total Soviet withdrawal to make clear that this issue will not go away.' He thought the Foreign Secretary's visit to Moscow underlined that the proposal was a serious effort to initiate negotiations towards a settlement and not just a propaganda effort designed to embarrass the Soviets. He contemplated further action at the Ottawa Summit and in the UN, adding: 'We should not permit them to avoid the consequences of their current position or to avert the growing international pressure for their compliance with the UN resolutions calling for total Soviet withdrawal' (FSA 021/6).

Lord Carrington reported back to EC Foreign Ministers at a meeting on 13 July and was given discretion to continue promoting the proposal, in consultation with partners, as necessary (telegram No. 2659 of 13 July from UK Rep Brussels; FSA 021/6).

No. 109

Letter from Sir C. Keeble (Moscow) to Mr Broomfield, 16 July 1981
Confidential (ENS 026/2)

Dear Nigel,

Secretary of State's Visit

1. Thank you for your letter of 8 July.[1]

2. It was indeed a fairly hectic programme. It was a relief that all went well, even if substantively the results did not provide much basis for enthusiasm.

3. Since we have now reaffirmed the link between Afghanistan and our bilateral relationship by the Secretary of State's visit it is inevitable that one should continue to colour the other. Had we had a good response from Gromyko we could have settled down to the agreeable task of giving a new impetus to Anglo-Soviet relations. As it is, the task is to secure our interests as well as we can, while making clear that it is not 'business as normal'.

4. As I see it our current objectives are three-fold:

(*a*) If we conclude that there is no real possibility of the Soviet Union being brought to explore the chances of a political settlement on the lines we have suggested, we want nevertheless to preserve as much of the Afghanistan initiative as we can with the primary object of exposing the fallacy of Soviet claims and

[1] Not printed. This letter conveyed the Secretary of State's thanks for organising a successful visit.

7 December 1979 – 1 December 1981

keeping up the political pressure for Soviet withdrawal. With this in mind I certainly shall not be too activist with the Russians on Afghanistan. My worry if we push them too hard is not so much that we shall get the 'unrealistic' response but rather that we shall drive them into a formal reply of an even more negative character.[2] Gromyko himself has now added 'unacceptable' to 'unrealistic' (my telno. 447)[3] and an authoritative commentary in Pravda of 14 July (my telno. 452)[3] made it clear by implication that the Russians are not prepared to budge from the 14 May 1980 DRA proposals.[4] The more we press our ideas in the next few weeks and the better our arguments the more likely we are to inspire a formal rejection. I am therefore more inclined to work on our diplomatic colleagues here in the hope of influencing their own reporting in the direction of keeping the proposal alive. I have already had two sessions with the Indian Ambassador (my telno. 453).[3]

(*b*) Our second objective is to prevent the Soviet Union manoeuvring us into a position where they could pretend that our reaction to their invasion of Afghanistan is a thing of the past. We have already received the first bilateral follow-up in the shape of a reminder to David Downing that there is an outstanding invitation to the regular Anglo-Soviet meeting on environmental questions which should have taken place in Moscow in March 1980 (his letter of 10 July to Rowcliffe, DOE[3]). We shall of course continue to disabuse the Russians of any idea that it can now be business as usual. Public statements in the UK will help to do the same.

(*c*) Lastly we have to consider how best to protect British interests. There are some relatively minor bilateral matters for you to take into account here, of which the one with the most potential for trouble is the question of Embassy sites. I do not envy you the task of negotiating a third site in London for the Soviet Embassy. There is also the possible Parliamentary visit in October,[5] as well as the Round Table in November,[6] and the Petrovsky talks in January to consider.[7] I assume that the first two of these might be used in order to put across our basic case on Afghanistan and its effect on East-West relations, while the last is of no great political significance. Our commercial interests may need more thought. Had things gone differently I would have been recommending some high level attention to this area, perhaps in the context of the Neftagaz exhibition beginning on 21 October.[8] As it is, all I would argue is that we should continue to do what we can to separate non-strategic commerce and politics. Apart from the substantial regular business we do with the USSR through major British companies like ICI or Courtaulds, we have a number of important contracts coming up where we are well placed to gain useful returns. These include the big West Siberian project, where gas pipeline deals could reach £350 m; the Mixed Acids project (Davy/BP), up to £125 m; and others such as a brick-making plant (£60 m), Methanol plant (£60 m),

---

[2] Mr Broomfield had written to Sir C. Keeble on 8 July stating: 'On Afghanistan, as far as the Embassy is concerned, we would not want you to be too activist in pressing the case with the Russians. For the time being, the more we press the more clearly we are likely to get an "unrealistic" response from the Russians.'

[3] Not printed.

[4] See No. 63, note 1.

[5] See No. 113, note 9.

[6] This took place in Moscow on 16-17 November. The British team was led by Lord Harlech (replacing former Prime Minister, James Callaghan, who withdrew due to illness) and included politicians, academics and businessmen.

[7] Mr Petrovsky visited the UK in January 1982 for expert level consultations on disarmament questions and other UN matters.

[8] An oil and gas trade exhibition in Moscow.

UK-Soviet Relations, 1979-82

and airport cargo handling facility (£45 m) which could add a further £165 m (i.e. £640 m plus in total). There are of course also various useful potential items of business in the £10 m bracket and below.

5. I do not think it should be too difficult for us to pursue these objectives concurrently. After all we are now closely in line with our Community and NATO partners and if we do need to move to a harder line on Afghanistan, which would be reflected in the bilateral relationship, we ought to be doing this in good company.

Yours ever,
CURTIS KEEBLE

No. 110

Lord Carrington to HM Representatives Overseas, 21 July 1981, 3.53 p.m.
Tel. No. 95 Confidential (FSA 021/6)

Afghanistan: EC initiative

1. Our aim in the next few weeks, prior to the UN General Assembly, is to continue quietly to build up support for the European proposal, especially in the Third World. We hope that during the UNGA Third World countries will again take the lead on Afghanistan as they have done in the past.

2. So far, despite the expected Soviet attitude, the results of our lobbying have been encouraging. We have had a definitive reaction from over 60 non-EC countries. Of these six have been opposed to the initiative: the USSR, Afghanistan, Bulgaria, Cuba, Ethiopia, Hungary. Thirteen non-EC countries have made individual public statements of support (Austria, Egypt, Japan, Korea, Nepal, Norway, Pakistan, Portugal, Spain, the Sudan, Switzerland, Tunisia and the United States). On 26 June Mr Chatti made a statement of support on behalf of the Islamic Conference. On 2 July the Committee of Ministers of the Council of Europe made a statement supporting the proposal. (The Council of Europe comprises the EC countries plus Austria, Cyprus, Iceland, Liechtenstein, Malta, Norway, Portugal, Spain, Sweden, Switzerland and Turkey). We expect further public statements of support shortly from a number of other countries including Australia, Canada, New Zealand and Turkey.

3. Several countries in the South Asian region have welcomed the proposal. Pakistan and Nepal have given public support. Bangladesh has warmly welcomed the initiative, but has not yet made a public statement. The attitude of two key countries, India and Iran, is still non-committal. We await a report on the Indian Foreign Minister's recent visit to Moscow.

4. ASEAN countries have been pre-occupied with the Cambodian conference but are likely to make clear soon their support for the proposal. We have had private support from Indonesia, Singapore and Thailand. Burma remains non-committal. China supports the initiative, so far only privately.

5. A number of African countries have given private support. These include Botswana, Ivory Coast, Kenya, Sierra Leone, Somalia and Zimbabwe.

6. We are still awaiting a response from a number of South American countries, though Argentina, Brazil, Chile, and Venezuela have stated their support privately.

7 December 1979 – 1 December 1981

7. When you judge it appropriate, and not likely to be counter-productive, please use any opportunity which arises to continue to press the government to which you are accredited to make:

(*a*) A public statement of support (if they have not yet done so).

(*b*) To lobby the Soviet Union bilaterally in favour of the EC proposals.

You may draw on the above information in general terms, but should not inform the government to which you are accredited of the private responses made to us by specific countries. We do not wish to get into the position of passing on to one country the private response of another. You should continue to keep your EC colleagues closely informed and make your representations in the name of the Presidency. At the meeting of Political Directors in London on 16 July it was agreed that our EC partners would support the Presidency's efforts where appropriate.

8. If you are asked for a more detailed account of my discussion with Gromyko, please draw on the following:

(*a*) The three arguments which Gromyko used were:

(i) The main problem in Afghanistan was external interference by other countries, not by the Soviet Union.

(ii) The Karmal regime should be present from the start.

(iii) The proposed composition of the conference was unsatisfactory for the Soviet Union.

(*b*) I told Gromyko that I did not find his arguments convincing and made the following points in reply:

(i) The main cause of the problem was the invasion by 85,000 Soviet troops (Gromyko's objection was tantamount to saying that this should not be subject to discussion). The European proposal envisaged discussion of all forms of external intervention. What had the Soviet leaders meant when they said earlier this year that they were willing to discuss international aspects of the situation? Mr Gromyko had no convincing answer to this point.

(ii) The problem of Afghanistan representation would be easier to solve when negotiations had started, and an atmosphere of confidence and trust had been established. It could not be solved now in a way acceptable to all potential participants.

(iii) The proposed participants in the conference were the obvious people to invite: Namely the Permanent Members of the Security Council, and those countries in the region which were most closely involved. But we should consider adjustments.

9. Please report any action taken by the government to which you are accredited in response to your lobbying. Except where a response is particularly significant, you should report by means other than telegram from now on.

UK-Soviet Relations, 1979-82

No. 111

Sir A. Parsons (UKMIS New York) to FCO, 23 September 1981, 4.35 a.m.[1]
Tel. No. 895 Immediate, Confidential (ENS 020/13)

Following from Private Secretary

Secretary of State's Meeting with Gromyko

1. The Secretary of State called on Gromyko at the Soviet Mission. Kornienko and Dobrynin[2] were also present. The meeting lasted for an hour and forty minutes. Gromyko took a hard line, notably on Afghanistan, but was courteous and almost relaxed throughout.

2. On relations with the United States, Gromyko made no comment on President Reagan's message,[3] although given a clear opportunity to do so by Lord Carrington. He contrasted his own speech to the General Assembly (which he said had dealt with the major questions at issue, albeit ones on which there were divergences) with that of Haig which had bypassed them. If Haig pursued in their forthcoming bilateral talks the line in his speech, there would be nothing to talk about. US-Soviet relations were in disarray, and not through the fault of the Soviet Union. Lord Carrington had been right to mention the key question of arms limitations. If the Americans were prepared to discuss that, they would be able to talk business. But the Americans had taken far too long to prepare their position and even now wanted to discuss what should be talked about and when, rather than get down to substance. This was not because it required a super-human effort to address the substance, but because the Americans had decided that they gained advantage from delay.

3. Lord Carrington replied that the Americans were genuinely committed to negotiations. There had been a significant change in the policy of the new administration, which had come in with the idea that US-Soviet differences had to be looked at overall before negotiations could begin on individual subjects like arms control. That was no longer the American position. It was surely helpful to define the subject matter of the TNF negotiators at the outset. Meanwhile, it was the Russians who had been building up their weapons while policy was being assessed by the new administration. Gromyko concluded by saying that the Russians did not lack patience. It was necessary to build a bridge and then find a point on it where the two sides could agree. The Soviet Union was ready to do this. It had been drawn to his attention that the British Government wanted the process to get under way and what Lord Carrington had said confirmed this. This was a positive fact and was appreciated by the Soviet side.

4. Discussion then turned to Afghanistan (see MIFT).[4]

[1] Repeated Priority Bonn, Paris, Washington, UKDEL NATO and Moscow. This telegram was dated 22 September but not sent until early the next morning. Lord Carrington was in New York for the 36th session of the UN General Assembly where he delivered a speech on behalf of the EC strongly critical of the South African government's racial policies and its position on Namibian independence.

[2] Anatoly Dobryrin, Soviet Ambassador in Washington.

[3] Addressing a Republican rally in Chicago on 2 September, President Reagan stated that unless the Soviets agreed to verifiable arm reductions, the result would be an arms race that they could not win. See *Public Papers: Reagan (1981)*, pp. 745- 7.

[4] Not printed. The telegram relayed proposals put forward by the Afghan government and reiterated Gromyko's position that no progress would be forthcoming until outside interference ceased.

7 December 1979 – 1 December 1981

5. At the end of the meeting Gromyko said that the Soviet Union wanted businesslike and normal relations with the United Kingdom and saw possibilities for their development in the economic and other fields including the political (where there remained virgin land and vast opportunities). The Soviet Union was ready to play its part. Lord Carrington said that it would be useful if Sir C. Keeble could call on Gromyko to discuss other points which he would have liked to pursue had there been time. He mentioned as an example what Brezhnev had told Mr Foot[5] about the area of application of CBMs. Gromyko replied that he and his colleagues were of course ready to discuss such matters with the Ambassador, as no doubt Lord Carrington was ready to do likewise with the Soviet Ambassador in London. He also agreed with Lord Carrington that the two Ministers should meet more often.

[5] Michael Foot, leader of the Labour opposition, accompanied by a nine-member delegation of Labour MPs, visited Moscow between 16-18 September for talks with Brezhnev and senior officials to discuss arms control including the Soviet offer of a moratorium on the deployment of nuclear missiles in Europe.

No. 112

Sir C. Keeble (Moscow) to Lord Carrington, 29 September 1981
Confidential (ENS 014/1)

My Lord,
The Soviet Union: Will it Change?

1. A certain quality of immobility seems natural to this country. It suits their geography. It probably, for all their flashes of charm and violence, kindness and brutality, suits the people. But today's Soviet state is not just immobile. Of the features which are most apparent to the foreign observer—the dead litany of the revolution, the frozen international postures, the eternal polemic in which language loses contact with reality, the brutal repression of dissent, the grandiose images and the creaking reality of the bureaucracy—some have their roots deep in the history of the Russian church and state, but others seem alien here. In combination they make a pattern of such sterility that it is hard for a foreigner to believe that even Russia could sustain it indefinitely and unchangingly. Yet it is a characteristic of this system that an ideologically based power structure combines with the policy-perpetuating instincts of a bureaucracy to respond to stress with rigidity rather than flexibility.

2. In the early years of the Soviet state there was dramatic enough change and there are those who yearn for it now. I have heard an elderly member of the Soviet establishment reminiscing nostalgically about Lenin's New Economic Policy. By another I have been given the badge circulated among those who look to a Stalinist revival. Cynical contempt for the Brezhnev regime is not restricted to the intellectuals. There is, however, no evidence that among the mass of the people there is anything more than the kind of grumbling which exists in more open societies and there is indeed a certain patriotic pride in Soviet socialism. Nevertheless, it is appropriate to ask whether, with the ending of the Brezhnev years there may not come another period of change in the policies of the Soviet state, even if not in its essence. In the accompanying memorandum my Head of Chancery considers this question and concludes that, in the face of growing

UK-Soviet Relations, 1979-82

problems, new leaders will have little room to experiment with new solutions, at home or abroad. There can be no confident predictions, but I find Mr Wood's arguments convincing. In some ways, I wish I did not. I would like to be able to argue with conviction that in time some of the finer instincts of the Russian character will permeate its political philosophy. But, if change does come, there must be as great a risk that it will be characterised by brutality as by humanity. So, while endorsing the broad lines of Mr Wood's prognosis, I would add only the thought that there may come a point in the next five years or so when the Soviet Union has the potential for change and that, although the potential may not be realised, the ability of the West to handle its relationship at that point with flexibility and imagination may make a difference to the outcome. There could be a lot to play for.

3. I am sending copies of this despatch and memorandum to Her Majesty's Ambassadors at Bucharest, Budapest, Sofia, Warsaw, Prague, East Berlin, Belgrade, Helsinki and Washington; and to the United Kingdom Permanent Representative at UKDEL NATO.[1]

I am, Sir,
Yours faithfully,
ALAN BROOKE TURNER
(for Curtis Keeble)

ENCLOSURE IN NO. 112

The Soviet Union: Will it Change?[2]

1. Stalin, Krushchev and Brezhnev were once travelling together in a train, so the story goes, when the train driver decided to go on strike. Stalin said he should be shot. Krushchev wanted to negotiate. Brezhnev pulled down the blinds and claimed the train was still moving. The story illustrates the way Soviet political life has developed after 17 years of Brezhnev's rule.

2. I want in this memorandum to look at some of the problems of the present day Soviet system and to guess at the way Brezhnev's successors will approach them. I hope I may be forgiven if some of my comments are impressionistic, and if, in the interests of brevity, I do not always argue out the premises on which they are based. Where necessary and possible I have referred to earlier despatches which fill in the background.

3. The essential characteristic of the Brezhnev regime has been to preserve the essence of the Stalinist legacy, shorn of its revolutionary brutality, against 'hare-brained' experiments such as those attributed to Krushchev by his successors. In this it has had its successes. The economy has grown significantly, the intelligensia has remained largely quiescent, the empire has not only been preserved but has acquired new military strength and new clients and both bureaucratic and political upheavals have been avoided. There has, however, also been a price for resisting change and I believe it to have been a major one.

4. The price has been evident in the way the Soviet economy has developed and in particular in the way its growth has slowed (Sir Curtis Keeble's despatch of 8

---

[1] For Mr Broomfield's reply see No. 139.

[2] The paper was written by Mr Wood, Counsellor and Head of Chancery at the British Embassy, Moscow.

April 1981).[3] One does not have to be a Marxist to see coping with the resulting strains as the critical question for the future of the USSR. The basic problem lies in the fact that the central planning system is unable adequately to control and motivate a complex modern economy but remains too closely bound up with the political structure to make real reform anything other than very difficult. Attempts at reform under Brezhnev have been half-hearted and have amounted to little more than tinkering. The outlook remains for a continued effort to muddle through and therefore more disappointing results. The one relatively efficient and modern sector is the defence industry. The Soviet Union seems determined to continue its arms build up at the current pace, with the prospect therefore of a continuing and probably sharpening competition for resources. The energy demands of Eastern Europe will continue to grow and cannot be satisfied as hitherto by the USSR. Brezhnev remarked at the 26th Party Congress on 23 February (Sir Curtis Keeble's despatch of 5 March 1981)[4] that it was on how economic problems of everyday life are solved that 'people largely judge our work'. He cannot happily reflect on the fact that the Soviet Union of today is a far cry from Krushchev's boasts of 25 years ago—one reason why he proposed at the last Party Congress to change the CPSU programme, which recorded those boasts.

5. The price of Brezhnev has also been all too evident in what one might broadly call the creative field. Mr Brooke Turner described in his despatch of 30 July 1980[3] the torpid state of Soviet culture, a telling monument to a system of government which came to power in a Russia which was then at the forefront of European culture. It is satisfactory to the KGB that all forms of unorthodox thought, especially political dissent, are monitored and kept in check but I cannot believe it is healthy for Soviet society as a whole to be permitted as a regular diet only the most boring and trivial intellectual fare. It is a damaging feature of life here that innovation as such is distrusted, a situation illustrated, for example, by the often lamented fact that the enormous Soviet scientific research effort is so rarely reflected in industrial use.

6. The Soviet Union is faced with major social problems which have proved increasingly difficult to contain and to which no solutions have been found. Consumption of alcohol is still rising and drunkenness is a major disease. The astonishing number of divorces reflects problems of city living which the west is also faced with, but in addition I think a lack of commitment to longer term purposes which mirrors the life of the ordinary man in the Soviet Union and will mean even greater problems for the next generation. The laziness of the Soviet worker is legendary and absenteeism from work a significant factor in delaying that increase in productivity which is central to the further growth of the economy. In the longer term the central leadership will need to consider more deeply problems of the nationalities and of the demographic structure of the country. They are at present conscious of these and similar issues but appear to have little idea of what to do about them. Open-minded discussion of them is notable mainly for its absence. The 26th Party Congress was essentially an exercise in stocktaking, and failed either to inspire or to point the way forward in those contentious areas which were touched upon.

7. Despite the increase in Soviet military strength under Brezhnev the effort to ward off adverse change has also given rise to problems for the Soviet Union in the international arena. The increase in military strength may itself have contributed to

[3] Not printed.
[4] No. 86.

UK-Soviet Relations, 1979-82

this desire, given that greater strength has also brought greater liabilities, coupled with concentration on the question of relative advantage in comparison with the United States. Even if military figures have not increased their weight in political decision making—and so far as I can see there is little evidence one way or the other—I think it undeniable that military considerations have become more important in Soviet policy making over the past 17 years.

8. It may at first sight seem odd to write of Soviet resistance to change in the international scheme of things after their adventures in the Third World. But Soviet foreign policy in that area has been aptly compared to the attitude of the Soviet consumer: if it is on shelves, grab it—it may be gone tomorrow. The result has been to acquire, and in some cases subsequently lose, a disparate collection of client states now ranging from Angola to Vietnam. The rationale behind such policies has been essentially opportunistic, and the Russians have mostly been more concerned once an opportunity has been seized with protecting their acquisition than with exploiting it. The Soviet Union might benefit from a more flexible approach or even perhaps the occasional retreat, but is only prepared to adopt such policies when compelled to do so, as by Sadat. In South East Asia or Afghanistan the Soviet leadership is seemingly incapable of making the necessary effort to moderate Soviet liabilities. Cuba, Vietnam and other client states are a drain on the Soviet economy so major as to limit the Soviet ability in future to take advantage of new openings in the Third World. The Soviet leadership under Brezhnev has also proved notably, and foolishly, inflexible with regard to China. They have kept to the main lines of their policies towards the United States even while the world in which they have to be implemented has changed (Sir Curtis Keeble's despatches of 8 February 1980[5] and 5 February 1981).[6] And if we are considering the nature of Soviet foreign policy as a whole it is important to remember that their fundamental preoccupation is not the Third World, or even the West, but Eastern Europe, where the whole purpose of their policies since the War has been to preserve their grip on the area. The difficulties inherent in resisting change here have been especially clear (Sir Curtis Keeble's despatches of 3 September 1980 and 23 July 1981)[7] and the attempt to preserve the Soviet model against economic, sociological and nationalist pressures may well become increasingly hard. Poland is of course the current but by no means only example.

9. I have listed the avoidance of bureaucratic and political upheavals among Brezhnev's achievements. The *Apparat* certainly have every reason to be grateful to him and his colleagues for that. The country and party probably needed a respite after Krushchev. But the respite has now become a way of life. Apart from the costs I have sketched above, the result has been to put a question-mark at the heart of the system, whether it is possible in the Soviet Union to provide a mechanism for significant changes or reviews of policy. The bureaucracy does not like them and the current leadership is prejudiced against them. Reform can be dangerous in an organisation as rigid as the Soviet Union. In our societies we achieve the necessary flexibility through elections, in others there are *coups d'etat*. In the Soviet Union it is not even possible to agree on an effective method for choosing a successor to Brezhnev, let alone for retiring a man whose health is questionable at best. The result is that the Soviet Union is at present ruled by an ageing collection of mediocrities whose main preoccupations are not losing their power and privileges on the one hand and avoiding experiments on the other.

[5] No. 50.
[6] Not printed.

7 December 1979 – 1 December 1981

10. Public flattery of Brezhnev is pervasive. It is as though the authorities hope by claiming for their leader virtues he does not have and can scarcely be expected to have, among them erudition, that they will be able to cover up the inadequacies of their rule and conjure up a degree of popular enthusiasm. If this is their calculation they have got it wrong. For the glorification of Brezhnev represents no substitute for true leadership and fools no-one. One has only to hear the number of cracks that are made about the domination of the old or to note the bizarre nostalgia for Stalin to realise that this is so. Whether or not the top leadership have entirely lost their ideological faith there is precious little belief to be found among the population as a whole that the Soviet system represents a new and qualitative advance in the history of mankind. Several decades of official pretence that everything Soviet was the best in the world have come home to roost. In a situation where the state is responsible for everything but unable to control everything or for that matter at present to change much, cynicism about the regime's ideological pretensions is inevitable. The gap between the reality and the myth is uncomfortably wide. I also believe that the incidence of corruption has risen not just in the sense of various forms of bribery but also in the sense that wheeling and dealing has become an even more important factor in allowing the system to operate at all.

11. I have so far looked at the state of affairs under Brezhnev. I am, however, conscious that many of the problems to which I have referred are ones which have existed for longer than that. Sir John Killick wrote in his Valedictory Despatch of 29 October 1973[7] that it often seemed to him that the Russian Revolution had not yet taken place. It has been a favourite game of Western observers of the Soviet scene more or less since the Revolution to speculate on how long such a system can possibly survive. At the same time for practical purposes we have generally had to operate on the assumption that the known will continue in however modified a form. With this in mind I propose now to look at whether a new leadership is likely to arise which might be able to give a badly needed fresh impetus to the Soviet system.

12. In a sense we are already in a succession crisis. Brezhnev is at any rate helped to remain where he is by the fact that no-one else dares move against him lest others then gang up to prevent a new guard consolidating its position. The same mechanism is liable to operate immediately after Brezhnev goes which is why Kirilenko or even Chernenko are generally regarded as the best bets to follow him. It is anyone's guess what will happen after that but the assumption that a decisive generational change will take place after an interim period under a figure like either of the two above has been generally accepted. It may not happen that way of course, for we cannot rule out the possibility that some individual may be able to take control immediately after Brezhnev for more than a relatively brief interim period. Such a figure might want to put his personal stamp on history by pursuing individual rather than consensus policies. But even if this happens it will take time for a new leader to establish his dominance and it would be against the odds. If the succession is in stages its effect may not in fact be particularly evident even when men who are younger now take over in several years' time. It would be natural for today's dominant group to pick successors in their own image. The new generation may be better educated and more able technically than their

---

[7] Not printed.

UK-Soviet Relations, 1979-82

predecessors but the continuity between generations will be very strong. I believe the next one, too, is likely to be biased against change.

13. If there is a continuing reluctance to accept change it will be encouraged by the fact that anything other than tinkering with the existing system is likely to prove difficult and even disruptive. Poland is only the latest example for the Soviet Politburo to consider in feeding their already considerable fear of the speed with which changes can get out of control and the apprehensions of self-appointed men about what ordinary people may do once the power of the authorities is reduced. The Soviet authorities seem at least as impressed by the fragility of their system as by its strength. Even if these fears did not exist it is a fact of life that Soviet leaders would be bound to disagree, for example, over any proposals to make real reforms which would affect the central planning system, over possible concessions to local authorities or other interests which might dilute the present system of total Party control, or adjustments in foreign policy—especially if these involved the Soviet position in Eastern Europe. Such disagreements might arguably seem particularly dangerous in a post-Brezhnev period given that a struggle for power usually crystallises around specific policy issues and given that a struggle for power means a period of weakness in the leadership.

14. The fact that most Soviet problems are chronic rather than acute will also make it easier, if not necessarily safer in the longer run, for Brezhnev's successors to succumb to the temptations of the cautious approach. This is particularly true of the central problem, that of the management of the economy. The patience of the Soviet people with their rulers is remarkable, and so has their capacity been, so far, to put up with minimal jam today in return for promises of a feast tomorrow. The Soviet Union is a huge country with a correspondingly wide economic base which can tolerate a high degree of incompetence. But there are penalties in putting off necessary changes too long. Sir Howard Smith remarked in his Valedictory Despatch of 9 January 1978[8] that advisors to a post-succession leadership might see more clearly than their present counterparts the need for changes, especially in the economic system. He went on to write 'The leadership might then be faced with the horrid truth, which is that if they refuse to yield anything on the issues of total Party control and totally centralised planning, the Soviet Union will get stuck at around its present economic and industrial level, will fall ever further behind the industrialised West and will have increasing difficulty in meeting its internal needs'.

15. There could also be a further danger—that change will become progressively harder to achieve without sending the whole Soviet system into shock. There is I think at present a widespread sense among educated people in the Soviet Union, probably not shared at the highest levels, that reforms are necessary. I have economic reforms particularly in mind. I doubt, however, whether there is any consensus as to what those changes should be. The effect of most I can think of would be to dilute the power and privileges of the Community Party and particularly its leadership. The longer the latter are dedicated to inertia the more their claim to rule will be questioned if change is seen by others as increasingly desirable or necessary. But Brezhnev's successors will have good reason to cling to the hope that somehow the familiar can be made to work better. The present leadership are already isolated from their own population: the next may be even more cut off. If so, they may have all the more grounds for fearing that, for

[8] Not printed.

7 December 1979 – 1 December 1981

example, reforms which made a determined attempt to decentralise the economy and allow market forces to operate more freely would have a dangerously destabilising effect throughout the system.

16. 'Life itself' (to borrow a phrase from Pravda) may not of course permit the Soviet leadership to continue to stand as pat as they might like. It is not too hard for example to imagine serious difficulties for them after further harvest failures. I believe, however, that they face a particular and more immediate danger in Eastern Europe, and that their problems there may become acute rather than chronic. Almost any scenario in Poland is horrid for them. Even on the best of assumptions, that the Polish Party can still somehow or other wear Solidarity down, the cost to the Soviet economy will be considerable, and the solution can hardly be final. And it is not only Poland—the others have their problems too, with even East Germany heading for economic difficulties in this decade, at a time when the Soviet capacity to supply oil or aid is limited. Radical change in Russia has been the product of disaster often enough, and a major failure in the Bloc could prove to be 1905, if not 1917.

17. I remarked earlier that it has traditionally been a favourite game to speculate on how long this system can survive—that it ought not to do so is I suppose clear enough. It will be dangerous for us all when it goes. Only a fool, however, would now care to put a date on that. There are various possibilities, so far as the foreseeable future is concerned, ranging from continuation of the Soviet system in its present form to collapse under stress. My own belief is that Brezhnev's effort to preserve what he inherited has made the structure so rigid that his successors too will find they more or less have to follow similar policies but that the problems they will face in doing so will mount. The new generation may have greater ability and knowledge than the present but the effort to defend their position could all too easily make them more cynical, more dangerous, and even harder for the rest of us to live with.

No. 113

Sir C. Keeble (Moscow) to Lord Carrington, 27 October 1981, 6.45 a.m.[1]
Tel. No. 657 Immediate, Confidential (ENS 020/13)

Call on Gromyko
1. I saw Gromyko on 26 October for just over an hour. I said that you had asked me to follow up your discussion with him in New York[2]. Afghanistan had been dealt with at length both there and in Moscow, but I wanted to say a few words on it before turning to other subjects.

Afghanistan
2. I recalled Gromyko's description of the European proposals on Afghanistan as unrealistic. There had been progress towards indirect talks under UN auspices involving Afghan representatives and the Pakistanis but the main problem was the

---

[1] Repeated Information Immediate to Luxembourg (For Private Secretary).

[2] See No. 111. Mr Broomfield, in a letter of 20 October, thought that Gromyko was 'unlikely to be expansive' but asked Sir C. Keeble to check the importance the Russians still attached to establishing a working relationship with the US, following two recent meetings between Gromyko and Haig in New York, and probe particular current issues like CSCE/CDE and Southern Africa.

UK-Soviet Relations, 1979-82

presence of Soviet troops. The 24 August proposals from Kabul[3] also failed to take account of the fact that the Soviet military presence was an essential cause of the problem. They ignored too, the attitude of the Afghan people to the present regime. We still believed the European proposals provided a framework which would allow progress towards a peaceful settlement and hoped that the USSR would reflect further upon them. Until a peaceful settlement was achieved, Afghanistan would remain a substantial block on the way to better East/West relations.

3. I had not expected much discussion but in fact Gromyko took the opportunity to restate the Soviet position, without introducing any new element. He said he had hoped I had come with more than the meagre baggage of the European proposals, which had been discussed in New York. They were cut off from reality. The only subject for discussion was the external aspects of the problem. This could be either between two governments or five or six or seven. That did not matter. But talks could only be about the external aspects and the presence of the Afghan government was essential. There could be no question of breaking the principle of non-interference in internal affairs. This ruled out questions like that of the structure of the Afghan government. The European proposals were in conflict with this essential principle. He had no real need to repeat the Soviet position on troops. Once external military interference was over they would be withdrawn. This was absolutely clear and if someone claimed the contrary that could only be because they were being sly. He had agreed with you that Afghanistan should be independent and non-aligned.

4. I said I did not wish to take up time in going over sterile ground. The fact was, however, that there was an internal problem and there was also an external problem caused by the presence of Soviet troops in Afghanistan. I had seen a ray of hope as I thought you had in the expressed Soviet readiness to consider the external aspects. This had provided a starting point for the European proposals. Gromyko re-emphasised that Afghan government representatives had to be present at any conversations, the simplest way of approaching the matter was bilateral negotiations with Pakistan and/or Iran. I repeated that this ignored the presence of Soviet forces. Gromyko said that once interference was over and really over that was—not just on paper—Soviet forces would be withdrawn in agreement with the Afghan government. It was important not to confuse the matter. A Soviet staged withdrawal would begin by agreement between Afghanistan and the USSR—once an agreement on external interference was signed and implemented. The Soviet Union was not willing now to talk about stages or times for withdrawal, in the right conditions withdrawal would begin and would finish. I said we did not of course expect Soviet troops to withdraw all at once, but believed it would help if the military aspects of the problem could be discussed at the same time as other matters. He replied that Pakistan and Iran should sit down with Afghanistan. The Soviet Union would agree matters afterwards with Afghanistan. External interference had to stop in reality. There was no need to raise artificial problems about this whole question. Where, he asked himself, was traditional British diplomatic flexibility? We used only steel and concrete and oak. Would we not

---

[3] The proposals included: acceptance of trilateral talks with Iran and Pakistan; acceptance of the UN Secretary General at these talks; mention of a timetable for the withdrawal of Soviet forces; and the implied linkage of the trilateral talks with those between guarantors (including the USA and the USSR) in terms similar to the EC proposal. However the proposals rested on the assumption that the Karmal regime was the only legitimate representative of the Afghan people and that Soviet troops did not constitute external interference.

7 December 1979 – 1 December 1981

find some other materials. I said that I remembered Lenin commending flexibility. I thought we had shown it, but there was room for it on the Soviet side.

East/West Relations

5. I said that this was an important time in East-West relations. A central field was the US-Soviet relationship which he had discussed at length with me in March, there had now been his meeting with Haig in New York, which we had welcomed. We were glad that talks on TNF were to begin on 30 November and that there was the prospect of resumption of the SALT process. These questions were a matter for bilateral US/Soviet negotiation in the first place. NATO Defence Ministers had drawn attention at Gleneagles on 21 October to the imbalance in TNF and their hopes for a successful outcome to the talks in Geneva. Gromyko made no comment.

6. I told Gromyko we wanted progress at Madrid, particularly over the proposal for a Conference on Disarmament in Europe and human rights. We had been disappointed at the Soviet reaction to Western proposals on the area of application of CBMs. Was the Soviet Union now ready to accept without insisting on preconditions the main point that the zone should apply to the whole of the European land area? Gromyko said the question was not well founded. There could be no question but that the adjacent sea and air areas of Europe must be of concern to the Soviet side. They were organically linked to the situation in Europe. The Soviet Union would therefore be waiting to hear Western proposals or ideas from the neutral and non-aligned countries. These could be official or unofficial. The present cat and mouse game was no good. So far the Soviet delegation had heard nothing. It was no good waiting for the USSR to give everything while the West produced nothing. Was not Britain part of the European continent? So was it not necessary to put one's foot in the water? I also put it to Gromyko that on human rights there had been signs of some Soviet flexibility before the summer break. Was the Soviet Union prepared to be specific about its apparent readiness to agree to a human rights experts meeting and to accept language confirming the undertakings at Helsinki for the individual to know and act on his rights and duties and to exercise freedom of religion? Gromyko merely reverted to his thesis that what was needed was more flexibility. The NNAs had proved a little more flexible than the West but even they had made no proposals yet. We should see how matters turned out in the negotiations at Madrid. (I do not think anything should be read into what may appear to have been Gromyko's tacit acceptance that there should also be flexibility on human rights. He probably still had CBMs in mind.)

Poland

7. I told Gromyko I had been instructed also to say a word about Poland, whose crisis was a matter of serious concern for the whole of Europe. Gromyko interrupted to ask whether I believed he really wanted to discuss this subject. I said I recalled what he had said to you about it during your visit. I did not propose to discuss the political problem. That was for the Poles. But we and the Soviet Union were directly concerned in the economic sphere, we were doing what we could to help resolve Poland's problems. We knew the Soviet Union had given help too. We had also heard, however, that she might be thinking in terms of balancing her trade with Poland. It would be useful to exchange views about what each side was doing to help. Gromyko said it was true the Soviet Union had been giving a certain degree of assistance. There had been public statements about this. What the West did was a matter for them and the Poles, the main thing was that no-one should interfere in internal Polish politics. The Soviet Union condemned Western attempts

UK-Soviet Relations, 1979-82

to put pressure on Poland. I said I found it hard to listen to accusations of Western pressure against the sort of things I had read in *Pravda*. We nevertheless shared the view he had just expressed that the Poles themselves should sort out their own problems.

Southern Africa

8. I told Gromyko I believed we were agreed on basic objectives in relation to Namibia as expressed in Security Council Resolution 435.[4] I mentioned the work of the Western Group and in particular the current visit to Africa which would include a meeting with SWAPO[5]. I had been specifically instructed to raise a question we had discussed with the Angolan government, that progress towards a Cuban withdrawal would improve the atmosphere for progress towards a Namibian settlement and vice versa. President dos Santos had spoken helpfully to Mr Luce. The prospects for a settlement would be further improved if the Angolan government could make still clearer statements about their intentions including the possibility of reductions in the Cuban presence even before Namibian independence. Such steps might be taken in parallel with progress on implementing Security Council Resolution 435. We hoped for Soviet cooperation. Would the Soviet government be prepared to use its influence with the Angolan and Cuban governments? Gromyko said he was not prepared to discuss Cuban/Angolan relations. This was a matter for those governments, to whom we should turn. He was concerned about the situation in Southern Africa. South African aggression should stop and that country should cease to impede Namibian independence. The problem was to get South African troops out. It was strange that HMG should concentrate on academic questions of Cuban/Angolan relations and not on South African aggression against Namibia and Angola. If that aggression stopped and aid to UNITA ceased it would then be easier to discuss other problems which interested some states, such as Cuban/Angolan relations. I commented that we were in agreement on the substance, the necessity to terminate the South African presence in Namibia. In this case however, as in many other areas, the basic negotiating position could be made more susceptible to resolution if the surrounding circumstances could be eased. We all knew what we wanted and with luck might not be far off achieving Namibian independence. A gesture from Angola on this matter would help.

Middle East

9. I said that the public account of Gromyko's recent talks with Arafat reflected a large measure of agreement between them. Part of the Soviet position, as I understood it, was that all states in the area including Israel had a right to exist and that all interested parties including Israel should attend the conference proposed by the Soviet Union. Did Arafat in endorsing Soviet positions say anything during his talks in Moscow which might be relevant to conditional recognition by the PLO of Israel? Gromyko said that the problem had not been discussed as such, the PLO knew that the right of Israel to exist was part of the Soviet position. PLO leaders had not attempted to argue with that position. Countries which had fears for Israel's rights should also argue for the right of the Palestinians to their own state. If the United States or even Britain denied Palestinian rights, it was hard for the Palestinians to speak of Israel's right to exist. I commented that European statements had gone some way to provide the PLO with the sort of encouragement

---

[4] This resolution, adopted on 29 September 1978, called for a cease fire in South-West Africa (Namibia) leading to free elections to be carried out under the supervision of the UN.
[5] South West Africa People's Organisation.

7 December 1979 – 1 December 1981

they needed to make a helpful statement themselves. Even a conditional statement by the PLO would help. Perhaps progress could be made through the Saudi proposals. You would shortly be going to Saudi Arabia in an effort to find common ground between the European and Saudi positions.

10. Gromyko interrupted to say that he wanted to draw attention to US statements made after Sadat's assassination that the USA would not allow changes in the Middle East.[6] Speaking with some heat he said it was not a question of what regimes were sympathetic, but of Washington claiming the right to interfere in other countries' internal affairs. This was an extraordinary thesis which trampled on the US [*sic* ?UN] Charter. What remained of US statements that they would not interfere in other governments' affairs, as for example in Poland, when they claimed the right to dictate in the Middle East? He noted I had no instructions from my government to speak on this matter. I said that I had intended to ask for his views on the possible improvement of relations between Egypt and the other Arab states. What he had said brought us back to the fact that the lack of confidence in East/West relations was the result of international events. I thought the United States had good reason to feel concern when the head of a friendly state was killed. It was reasonable for the Americans to wish to see a peaceful succession. Gromyko said it was no good making the argument that because events in a certain country raised doubts that gave the right to others to dictate that there should be no internal changes. I questioned his quotation of the Americans and recalled Soviet statements, for example over Iran. Gromyko said that he had toned down what the Americans had said.

11. Reverting to the wider Arab-Israeli problem I commented that Egypt would presumably wish to proceed at least until the whole of Sinai had been returned. Meanwhile the EC countries had been considering possible measures to increase a sense of confidence between the Arabs and Israel for instance by improving practical conditions in Israeli occupied areas. Such confidence building measures were under discussion among the Ten and we believed they could help create a better climate for solution of the main problem.

Bilateral Affairs

12. Gromyko said the hitch in our bilateral relations should be corrected. This of course would have to depend on a mutually positive approach. We had useful contacts and trade which could be expanded. Cultural contacts were a field worth tending.[7] (He did not react to my observation that a recent Soviet action had not been helpful in this regard.)[8] I said that the substance of our relationship depended on the wider international picture. So far as bilateral arrangements were concerned I knew you had valued your meetings with him and we looked forward to sustaining a political dialogue at appropriate levels on subjects of common interest. It was a pity there had been no real progress on substance, especially on the main obstacle, Afghanistan. We hoped that Deputy Foreign Minister Zemskov could visit London for further discussions in the second half of February or March next year. There were proposals for discussions on UN, disarmament and Middle East questions. A party of MPs was arriving today.[9] We had a good team for the Round

---

[6] Muhammad Anwar Sadat was assassinated on 6 October 1981.

[7] The Anglo-Soviet cultural agreement was extended for two years on 23 March 1981.

[8] A reference to the expulsion, announced on 20 August, of the British Cultural Attaché, John Gordon, in retaliation for the expulsion of the Soviet diplomat, Viktor Lazin.

[9] On 27 October, John Osborn, Conservative MP for Sheffield Hallam, and a group of British parliamentarians (Mr Arthur Bottomley, Mr John Smith and Mr Peter Temple-Morris) visited

UK-Soviet Relations, 1979-82

Table discussions in mid-November. Mr Callaghan was looking forward to meeting him at that time.[10] We were keen to expand trade, as witness the major delegation the London Chamber of Commerce would be sending. Gromyko checked the dates of Mr Callaghan's visit and appeared to confirm the meeting, remarking that the Soviet approach to the bilateral relationship was positive.

Moscow under the auspices of GB-USSR Association. They had talks with academics and officials and called on Deputy President Kuznetzov.

[10] See No. 109, note 6.

No. 114

Letter from Sir C. Keeble (Moscow) to Mr Broomfield, 28 October 1981
Confidential (ENS 020/13)

Dear Nigel,

1. You will have seen my telno. 657 reporting my call on Gromyko.[1] There is really not a very great deal to add. After all the discouraging preliminaries from the Second European Department it was a pleasant surprise that the call came through so quickly.

2. Gromyko looked tired and seemed content that I should make nearly all the running. I started with Afghanistan, since this was the main subject dealt with during the Secretary of State's visit to Moscow and the meeting in New York and I had thought that it would be disposed of as a fairly brief preliminary. I was surprised that Gromyko took the opportunity for a longish statement of the Soviet position and I had hoped that this might contain some new element. But in fact he merely made it absolutely clear that the Soviet Union did not envisage either doing anything about troop withdrawals or even talking about them until, as a result of bilateral discussions, the 'interference' had ceased (i.e. Babrak Karmal's position had been stabilized) and Afghanistan had requested a Soviet withdrawal. I could not help thinking that there was an element of uneasy conscience in Gromyko's harping on the subject, but there was certainly no sign or readiness to contemplate any change of policy. The fact is that there is no choice open to the Soviet Union other than that between soldiering on in a long colonial war or admitting defeat. They are not yet ready for the latter.

3. It was slightly odd that on the question of US-Soviet relations and arms control negotiations Gromyko had nothing to say, particularly since the TASS account contained some standard Soviet sentiments and one might have thought it worth his while to utter them, if only for the sake of making the TASS account look a little more like an account of what actually happened in respect of a part of the discussion where the Russians had an interest in public presentation. It was during this part of the discussion that Suslov handed Andrew Wood a note saying 'When is he going to get on to CSCE/CDE?' and it may be that this was the area on which the Russians were looking for a more substantial discussion. Certainly Gromyko seemed reluctant to abandon it and I was sorry that my own instructions precluded any exploration of his remarks about putting one's foot in the water around Europe.

4. The discussion of the Middle East proceeded on a constructive note until

[1] No. 113.

7 December 1979 – 1 December 1981

Gromyko decided to let loose his blast about the United States and Egypt. He was well up to form and having started his remarks by saying that he noticed that I had no instructions to raise the matter with him (to which I replied that indeed I did have instructions to discuss the Egyptian situation) he concluded by remarking 'Perhaps you would do better just to stick to the line that you had no instructions'. But it was, I suppose, only fair that there should be some part of the discussion which he could enjoy. It was for the most part an agenda which offered him little joy and I was glad to be able to go through virtually the whole of the brief without interruption. I would have been happier had I been able to elicit a little more by way of response on various points. The available time did not of course make it possible to go into any one subject very deeply. We worked without an interpreter (though Sukhodrev was present), with Gromyko speaking Russian and I English, so that we made full use of the time but even so it was tight. More important than lack of time, however, was the fact that on virtually all the subjects my instructions were to restate a position already well known to Gromyko and even, for instance in relation to CBMs, to go less far than we had gone in the multilateral forum in Madrid. There is a general point in this, that if a discussion with an Ambassador is to seem worthwhile to a Foreign Minister—and I think the point is valid in most countries—the Ambassador needs to have something which, even if not palatable to his interlocutor, is at least calculated in some way to arouse his interest. It was with this in mind that I suggested the reference to confidence building measures in the Middle East and it was disappointing that this produced no reaction from him. However by then I think he was beginning to feel that he had had about enough.

5. There is nothing to add to the telegram in relation to Southern Africa or bilateral questions. On the latter he was deliberately taking a constructive position, but he did not pick up the reference to continued contacts with any remark which in any way implied that he hoped for an invitation to visit London. I do not think he caught the sense of my implicit reference to John Gordon's expulsion when he was talking about cultural exchanges but it will not have escaped Suslov.

6. My call was referred to on *Vremya*[2] and given relatively prominent treatment in *Pravda*, so it has aroused a certain amount of interest here and this may be slightly heightened by my call on Patolichev[3] yesterday. It possibly suits the Russians to give an impression of a degree of normality in our relations, though they cannot have many illusions on the substance.

Yours ever,
CURTIS KEEBLE

---

[2] *Time*, a Russian television news programme.
[3] Nikolai Patolichev, Soviet Foreign Trade Minister.

No. 115

Mr Brooke Turner (Moscow) to Mr Broomfield, 12 November 1981
Confidential (ENS 014/1)

Dear Nigel,

The Soviet Leadership

1. The Kremlin reception on the eve of the November 7 anniversary of the October Revolution afforded a rare opportunity for Heads of Mission to have a

UK-Soviet Relations, 1979-82

close look at Brezhnev and other members of the Soviet leadership. The Ambassador will no doubt have given you his personal impressions; Art Hartman, the US Ambassador, commented that despite all he had heard about the effects of age on them he was astonished at their decrepitude. He simply could not imagine how they could manage to run a country of the size of the Soviet Union without relying heavily on decisions prepared for them by the *apparat*.

2. Brezhnev in particular gave the impression of detachment to the point of being mentally absent from the proceedings. This may have been due to the effects of deafness; the Chief of Protocol had to shout twice with great emphasis when introducing the Federal German Chargé in order to elicit from Brezhnev a mumbled message of good wishes to Chancellor Schmidt, and the introduction of the French Ambassador elicited no reaction whatever, in contrast to last year's function when Brezhnev asked that his greetings be sent to President Giscard. The Federal German Minister, who accompanied Rau, the Minister-President of North Rhine-Westphalia, on his call on Brezhnev a few weeks ago, noted that before uttering even the most standard replies to Rau's points Brezhnev waited to receive a handwritten slip of paper from his aide Alexandrov-Agentov.

3. None of this necessarily means that Brezhnev is not still quite firmly in charge or that he will not get through the Bonn visit in reasonably good shape, though it is significant that the visit has been extended by a day to make it less exhausting[1]. But it suggests that Brezhnev's health and performance are more than usually subject to ups and downs and therefore that his standard of performance on any particular day is unpredictable. As recently as mid-September, Denis Healey reported him to be in good health.

4. The only conclusion I would draw from all this is that, at a time when in domestic affairs, in intra-bloc relations and in East-West relations difficult and sometimes rapid decisions will be called for, the Soviet leadership does not give the impression of ability to act rapidly and decisively. The handling of the Karlskrona submarine incident[2] was neither swift nor deft, but the Russians may have decided to play the hand slowly to put maximum pressure on the Swedes. In all probability a clash of interests (the Defence Ministry, the Foreign Ministry and the KGB/GRU) had to be reconciled in an unforeseen and acutely embarrassing situation and there were indications that this was no easy task. It maybe that over Poland hesitancy and indecisiveness in the counsels of the Soviet leadership have been helpful to Poland and the West; a more resolute and decisive group of men might have taken effective action a year ago to stop the rot in Poland, calculating that the price to be paid in terms of East-West relations was worth paying. But if hard choices on, say, SS-20 reductions have to be faced next year to avoid a failure of the TNF talks which could be convincingly ascribed by the West to Soviet inflexibility, Brezhnev and his colleagues may display that fatigue and hesitancy in

[1] Following the Bonn visit, the Head of the Soviet Department of the Federal German Foreign Ministry reported that Brezhnev, although still in control, looked constantly to Gromyko for advice and approval and relied on written notes from officials during the *tête-à-tête* sessions. Mr Bullard thought his performance was much worse. Brezhnev was only 'in control' in the formal sense, in which he would remain nominally in charge until he died or was incapacitated. But this did not mean Gromyko or others were dominant: 'The whole structure is a mass of pretence and double-talk even at the best of times. Western terminology scarcely applies' (minute of 13 December; ENS 010/2).

[2] On 27 October a Soviet submarine was discovered deep in Swedish territorial waters outside the naval base.

7 December 1979 – 1 December 1981

taking important decisions which is a not uncommon characteristic of ageing leaders.

Yours ever,
ALAN BROOKE TURNER

No. 116

Record of meeting between Lord Trefgarne and the Soviet Ambassador (Mr Popov), 23 November 1981
Restricted (ENS 020/2)

Present:
Lord Trefgarne[1]   HE Mr Popov
Mr D. Johnson   Mr Ivanov
Mr J. Macgregor

1. After initial courtesies, *Lord Trefgarne* asked Mr Popov how he thought the imminent TNF talks would go. *Mr Popov* said that the Soviet Union attached great importance to these negotiations and were ready for serious talks. There could be compromise provided each side's interests were preserved. He asked for Lord Trefgarne's impressions of how seriously the Americans would enter the talks in view of the pronouncements by some US politicians which suggested that they wished the negotiations to be brought quickly into deadlock. Mr Popov added that the outcome of the negotiations could depend in large degree on the United Kingdom since the Americans paid attention to UK attitudes in this field. *Lord Trefgarne* replied that we naturally hoped the talks would be successful. HMG had, however, been disappointed by the initial Soviet reaction to President Reagan's recent speech.[2] He recalled that when the NATO double decision had been announced in January 1979 there had been strident denunciation by the Soviet Union. He was therefore surprised that there had been such a swift, forthright and negative reaction to President Reagan's speech. He hoped that the Soviet approach would be different when the talks began. *Mr Popov* said that the speed of the Soviet reaction had been partly due to the fact that the British press had characterised President Reagan's proposals as a mere propaganda ploy and had speculated that they would not lead to a positive result. The Soviet reaction had been rapid also because there had been nothing new in what President Reagan had said: his proposals were aimed at upsetting an existing balance. The Soviet reaction had been critical, but not negative. *Lord Trefgarne* said that the zero option was an excellent starting point for negotiations. Such an outcome would be difficult to achieve, partly because of differences between the two sides as to the numbers of weapons now deployed, but it should be the ultimate goal of the negotiations. The UK was strongly behind the US advocacy of the zero option. *Mr Popov* rejoined

---

[1] Following the Cabinet reshuffle on 14 September, Lord Trefgarne was appointed Parliamentary Under-Secretary of State with responsibility for East/West relations and United Nations matters.
[2] On 18 November, in an address to the National Press Club, President Reagan announced the so-called zero option, whereby the US would cancel plans to deploy Pershing II and cruise missiles in Europe in return for the Soviets dismantling all of their intermediate range missiles (SS-20, SS-4 and SS-5). See *Public Papers: Reagan (1981)*, pp. 1062-67.

UK-Soviet Relations, 1979-82

that the Reagan proposals were not a good basis for beginning the talks. President Brezhnev's recent interview in *Der Spiegel* had set out the Soviet position fully.

2. Turning to bilateral relations, *Lord Trefgarne* said that Anglo-Soviet trade was below the level which it could and should reach. We had been pleased to learn of the contracts won by John Brown and Rediffusion for the Western Siberian gas pipeline. We had however been surprised to learn of the remarks made by a Soviet Deputy for Foreign Trade to the effect that Britain was an unreliable trade partner. *Mr Popov* replied that in a speech a few days previously he had said that the Soviet Government placed much value on trade with the United Kingdom. There had recently been some improvement in trading relations but the Soviet Union was not satisfied that these had reached the optimum level. Soviet trade with the FRG, France and Italy was much greater than that with Great Britain.

3. *Lord Trefgarne* said that Anglo-Soviet trade, and indeed political, relations could not be divorced from the broader international picture. Afghanistan was a major stumbling block. HMG had been disappointed that the European Council's initiative for a political settlement of the Afghanistan problem had not been received in Moscow more constructively. Those proposals remained on the table and the UK was ready to talk about them further. He asked Mr Popov how we might move forward together. *Mr Popov* replied that he did not see a direct connection between Anglo-Soviet trade and Afghanistan. The situation in Afghanistan did not apparently prevent Britain's competitors from developing their trade with the Soviet Union. As to the Ten's proposals, he recalled that when Lord Carrington had asked to visit Moscow in the summer, he was immediately received by Mr Gromyko even though the Soviet Government knew that he wanted to talk about Afghanistan and that his proposals would be unacceptable. Those proposals were unrealistic because they did not take into account the interests of the legitimate Government of Afghanistan. The way to a solution of the problem lay in the proposals put forward in May 1980 and August 1981 by the Government in Kabul.[3] It merely complicated the problem to introduce too close an interconnection between Afghanistan and other, unrelated, issues.

4. *Lord Trefgarne* said that the proposals made by the regime in Kabul were fatally flawed because they did not address the central issues: the need for Soviet troops to withdraw and for the Afghan people to decide their own fate free from outside interference. The United Kingdom could not agree to confer legitimacy on a regime which had been placed in office by a column of troops. The only basis for negotiations had to be the withdrawal of Soviet forces and the freedom of the Afghan people to choose their own Government. Lord Trefgarne added that nothing would do more for East/West relations than some progress in this matter and he referred to the recent vote in the UN General Assembly which demonstrated that 116 Member States shared the UK view.[4] The United Kingdom was always ready to listen to sensible proposals as to how the problem might be solved: but those put forward by the Karmal regime did not fall within this category.

5. *Mr Popov*, after referring to President Brezhnev's recent letter to President Reagan, said that there was a legitimate republican Government in Afghanistan whether some people liked it or not. There had been foreign intervention, statements by the US Government that they did not like the Karmal regime and

[3] For the May 1980 proposals see No. 63, note 1. The August 1981 proposals were similar, calling for tripartite talks on a political settlement between the DRA, Pakistan and Iran under UN auspices.
[4] In a vote at the UN General Assembly on 18 November, 116 delegates voted for a Soviet withdrawal from Afghanistan (with 23 voting against and 12 abstentions).

7 December 1979 – 1 December 1981

wanted it to be overthrown: arms had been sent to the so-called Mujaheddin: the longer this support continued the more difficult would be the solution. The Soviet military contingent had been sent to Afghanistan at the repeated request of the Government there and would remain in the country until the reasons for its presence had been eliminated. Referring to the refugees in Afghanistan, Mr Popov said that many were being kept on Pakistani territory by force and were being drawn by force into attacks against Afghanistan. *Lord Trefgarne* interjected that he presumed that Mr Popov did not expect him to believe that. Mr Popov continued that the Soviet Union was determined to solve the problem in a political way but only provided the interests of the legitimate government of Afghanistan were respected and that no deals were made behind its back.

6. *Lord Trefgarne* said that HMG did not accept the Karmal regime as a legitimate government. It had been installed by Soviet troops and was kept in office by them. He said that the United Kingdom had been particularly disturbed by reports of attacks by helicopters from Afghanistan on refugee camps in Pakistan. *Mr Popov* said that the question of the Soviet military contingent in Afghanistan was not a matter for Anglo-Soviet bilateral relations nor indeed for international discussion. This was a purely Soviet-Afghanistan issue. He claimed that there had been an open admission by United States politicians that arms were being sent to the rebels, and said that there had been appeals in the United Kingdom for money to be given for such arms supplies. The sooner this support for intervention ended, the sooner a political solution would be possible. Mr Popov said that there had been no Soviet troops in Afghanistan until foreign intervention had begun, to which *Lord Trefgarne* rejoined that the person alleged to have requested Soviet military support was dead the day before he was alleged to have made that request. There was no evidence that the Afghan people accepted the Kabul regime or that it took account of their interests. *Mr Popov* disputed this.

7. *Lord Trefgarne* then referred to press reports that a new prison sentence had recently been imposed upon Anatoly Shcharansky for alleged breach of prison rules.[5] Mr Shcharansky's continued ill-treatment was a source of great disappointment to the British Government and an irritant in the development of Anglo-Soviet relations. There was much public anxiety in this country about Mr Shcharansky's state of health. He hoped the Soviet Government understood this, and referred to the applicability of the CSCE Final Act in this and similar cases.

8. *Mr Popov* said that he would not discuss this question which was wholly within Soviet competence. He referred to Principle VI (on non-interference in the internal affairs of States) of the Helsinki Final Act and to the UN Charter. If the Final Act was to be raised then he would cite recent outrages against Soviet establishments in the United Kingdom. He mentioned the attack on the TASS office in London, the earlier attack on Aeroflot premises and the occasion when shots were fired at the Soviet Embassy. These were the obstacles to better relations and merited discussion; Shcharansky did not.

9. *Lord Trefgarne* said that the police would treat attacks on Soviet establishments in the United Kingdom as they would attacks on any other building. HMG defended the freedom of people to express their views but did not condone criminal acts. The United Kingdom did not wish to intervene in Soviet affairs but felt obliged to state its views when faced with reports about the inhumane treatment of prisoners in the Soviet Union.

[5] In 1977 Anatoly Shcharansky, a human rights activist, had been arrested on charges of spying for the US and sentenced to 13 year's forced labour in a Siberian labour camp.

UK-Soviet Relations, 1979-82

10. Turning to other elements of the bilateral relationship, *Lord Trefgarne* mentioned the recent visit of Mr John Osborn MP and three colleagues, the recent session of the Anglo-Soviet Round Table, and the invitation which had been extended to Mr Zemskov to visit London next year. *Mr Popov* said that he knew that Mr Zemskov would visit London but dates remained to be agreed. In general any indication of a willingness on the part of the British Government to improve relations would be positively received. It would be possible to develop, for example, cultural, educational and scientific relations. Despite the differences of a political and ideological nature between the two countries, there were no obstacles to a further development of relations. He handed to Lord Trefgarne a copy of President Brezhnev's letter to President Reagan of 25 May 1981 and stressed the passage which referred to the Soviet Union's wish to improve relations not only with the US but with other Western countries which, Mr Popov said, included in particular the United Kingdom.[6]

11. The meeting ended at 11.35 a.m.

[6] President Brezhnev proposed that the US and other Western countries enter into 'honest and constructive negotiations' to search for mutually acceptable solutions to 'practically all major questions existing between us.' The letter is reproduced at http://www.thereaganfiles.com/.

No. 117

Paper by Mr Gordon on British Cultural and Information Policy in the USSR, 1 December 1981[1]
Confidential (ENZ 291/11)

Summary

Introduction

1. Post-Afghanistan policy for restraining the Soviet Union has so far concentrated [on] action outside Soviet borders. The possibilities of action inside them to influence the Soviet population, hitherto relatively neglected, also need consideration since in the long-term cultural and information policy can play a significant part in encouraging Soviet evolution along more civilised lines. This paper looks at the various instruments available for the conduct of this policy, their effectiveness so far and possible changes for the future. But because of lack of concrete additional evidence much of its analysis is subjective (paras 1-3).

Historical Background

2. Western information programmes started only after the War, cultural programmes considerably later. Both have grown in size, but their original shape has altered little. Western expectations of results have varied greatly. *With the disappointing outcome of CSCE, they are now again low* (paras 4-8).

Objectives and Targeting

3. Policy objectives should be to project Britain, break the Soviet Government's monopoly of communication with its own people, promote knowledge of the

[1] Only the summary of this paper is reproduced here. It was prepared by Mr J. Gordon, after discussion with Mr Broomfield and Mr Fergusson, following his tit-for-tat expulsion from Moscow where he had been Cultural Attaché (see No. 113, note 8). It was produced on a personal basis, although comments on earlier drafts had come from his predecessor in Moscow, Mr Roland Smith, and also from Mr Sheinwald. Copies were sent to the Embassy in Moscow and the British Council.

7 December 1979 – 1 December 1981

respective language, culture and developments and build links between individuals and between institutions. The process is bound to seem in part ideologically subversive to the Soviet Government. But exchanges are, and must be, non-political in content and justifiable in terms of increased mutual understanding (paras 9-11).

4. Our main target is the educated classes, especially government and Party advisers and policy-makers, students and teachers and others professionally concerned with ideas. Other groups of interest are scientists, youth, workers and peasants and national minorities. The major area in which information from the West is required is political news. International affairs are seen primarily in terms of Soviet relations with the rest of the world. There is widespread acceptance, even among many disaffected, of official 'peace' propaganda (paras 12-23).

Effectiveness of Policy

5. It is useful to distinguish between (*a*) non-political activities undertaken in agreement with the Soviet Government; (*b*) political activities undertaken without such agreement; and (*c*) political activities undertaken with such agreement (para 24).

6. The first category covers all cultural and much information work. Visits to the UK are relatively few and cultural exchange visitors comprise mainly scientists, technologists and English language specialists. The impact of visits the other way is probably greater, notably from the large number of British (and Western) students. These lead to some long-term links. Inward non-academic exchanges work well, but outward ones are having to be reconstructed by the British Council to increase the element of personal contact. The inward flow of Soviet cultural personalities is reasonably satisfactory, and contacts between members of this group and our Embassy are generally good. But visits of leading British writers, composers etc the other way are hard hit by the political climate. Scientific exchanges are similarly affected by disillusionment on the part of British scientists and institutions (paras 25-36).

7. English language teaching is our major entry point into the Soviet system, particularly in view of the overwhelming popularity of English *vis à vis* other Western languages and the fact that no other foreign government is involved in its promotion. Our limited efforts suffer from a number of technical deficiencies and are small by comparison with the French programme. But our teachers nonetheless achieve very considerable results, particularly with Soviet teachers who have no other contact with Westerners (paras 37-40).

8. The promotion of British books is also a major success area; imports and number of sales points have increased considerably. British Council book exhibitions and increased translation of British literature by the Russians themselves also help spread influence. By contrast almost nothing has been done to increase imports of British newspapers and magazines. However *Anglia*, our second largest means of influence after the BBC, circulates widely, is in great demand, and spreads a favourable image of modern Britain. Our exhibitions policy has been successful but limited in recent years. Purely cultural 'events' [are] highly desirable on general grounds; their post-Afghanistan absence is misunderstood by most ordinary Russians (paras 41-48).

9. The GB-USSR Association has suffered not only from generally bad Anglo-Soviet bilateral relations but also from competition. Its position is notably stronger in some areas of the UK than others, and there is a similar uneven pattern in its

UK-Soviet Relations, 1979-82

contacts in the Soviet Union. It has been more successful in bringing over individuals than delegations (paras 49-51).

10. The only significant constituent element of the second category is BBC broadcasting. The World Service is theoretically preferred by the Soviet authorities and is still unjammed. But the Russian language service is far more important. Estimates of its listeners vary considerably, and are all unreliable. Nonetheless Western radio is now a regular and openly admitted source of information for Soviet officials and has succeeded in putting the regime partly on the defensive by forcing it to explain policies criticised by the West. The resumption of jamming is the best tribute to its effectiveness. The BBC has reacted by increasing the hours and frequencies of broadcasts and is helped in the longer term by earlier decisions to increase its transmitting power. There is also the possibility of closer cooperation with other Western services to overcome the problem. But for the present its effectiveness in urban areas is greatly diminished (paras 52-61).

11. The only example of the third category of programme is the Anglo-Soviet Round Table, which only very partially serves our purposes. The ability to reach the other side's population on political issues is the area of greatest imbalance in cultural and information policy (paras 62-64).

Conclusions

12. Progress has so far been limited. The Soviet Government is still under no constraints in the conduct of foreign policy as a cumulative result of our policies. Nonetheless, there have been significant changes in attitude which have implications for the future. The relevant provisions of the Final Act have helped. Increased contact with foreigners, the impact of increased study of foreign languages and our own efforts in promoting the English language have had effect. *Anglia*, the BBC and their Western analogues are very widely read or listened to. Western broadcasts have undoubtedly had the greatest impact in terms of opening up the Soviet Union to Western criticism of Soviet policies and at present our most important priority should be to weaken the effectiveness of securing the suspension of jamming. Western broadcasting, along with other aspects of cultural and information policy, may become more important as Soviet problems multiply in the 1980's. Our interests lie however not just in making the Soviet Union less dangerous but also in exploiting the assets of our existing programme to build up our position in the Soviet Union (paras 65-71).

13. These aims can be realised only through an adequately financed long-term policy. This would involve giving relatively greater attention to routine rather than high-profile activities and greater priority to improving the scope and effectiveness of our information work. The ways in which policy is formulated and administered should be re-examined, regular consultation with allies established, help for English language teaching and contacts with national minorities and probably also scientists expanded, efforts to disseminate printed information and exhibitions strengthened, the effectiveness of BBC broadcasting increased and the Soviet Government challenged to a political dialogue in ways which would involve the Soviet population being informed direct of our views. Of these proposals (which are set out in more detail in the attached annex), the extension of English language teaching and the improvement of BBC broadcasts are perhaps the highest priorities. Some of the proposals are relatively cheaper than others. But the total cost of implementing them all is likely to be under 0.000009 per cent of our national defence budget (paras 72-75).

Chapter II

17 December 1981 – 9 December 1982

In 1980, with the West in recession and rising oil prices, Poland was in economic difficulty. In August a wave of strikes broke out across the country as workers protested against price increases. The strikers, supported by Catholic intellectuals and academics, also began to make political demands: freedom of speech, the lifting of censorship, release of political prisoners, new labour laws, access of the church to the media and the establishment of independent trade unions. A new, free trade union, Solidarnosc *(Solidarity), led by Lech Walesa emerged and was recognised by the Government. Solidarity became a political opposition movement and the Government, undecided in how to deal with the situation, vacillated between taking repressive measures and making concessions. Moscow put increasing pressure on the Polish government to suppress Solidarity. In December Soviet and other Warsaw Pact countries mobilised forces on Poland's borders. President Carter and NATO foreign ministers warned that any move against Poland would have serious consequences for East-West relations.*

Protests continued during 1981 in response to attacks by the police on Solidarity members and food shortages. The first Solidarity national congress met in Gdansk in September and put forward plans to restructure the state and economy on a democratic basis. By now the union had an estimated 9 million members. At midnight on 13 December General Jaruzelski, the Prime Minister and leader of the Communist Party, declared martial law and established a Military Council of National Salvation to run the country. Solidarity was banned, its leaders arrested, and strikes and demonstrations were put down by force. On 15 December EC Foreign Ministers warned Moscow against any direct military intervention in Poland.

No. 118

Letter from Sir C. Keeble (Moscow) to Mr Fergusson, 17 December 1981
Confidential (RS 014/2)

Dear Ewen,

Poland

1. The Soviet leadership has been calling for well over a year for the Polish Party to take decisive action to set its house in order. Now it seems the Polish army is committed to breaking Solidarity by force. The part which the Soviet Union has played in this decision is very unclear and it is not easy to see how Soviet policy may develop. It may however be useful to examine such shreds of evidence as we possess.

2. We have all rehearsed *ad nauseum* the arguments against Soviet intervention—the effect on the US/Soviet strategic relationship, the setback to the

UK-Soviet Relations, 1979-82

whole détente policy, to which Brezhnev has committed himself, the additional economic burden on an overstrained Soviet economy, the damage to Soviet standing throughout the world and finally the fact that Soviet military intervention would do little to persuade the Poles to go back to work. The American Embassy here have a story that, according to a Polish diplomat, a Soviet delegation visited Warsaw secretly on Thursday December 10 and told Jaruzelski that unless he now took decisive action the Soviet Union would intervene. The Americans are rather doubtful about the story and so am I. Had it been wholly accurate, one would have expected some indication of increased Soviet military preparedness. However, whether or not the military threat was used, there can be little doubt that the Soviet Union wanted firmer action; even if the timing was determined in effect by Solidarity and the form by Jaruzelski. To the extent that the situation can be resolved by military power, it suits the Soviet Union very well that it should be the Poles who do it and as long as the Polish army will obey orders there is no need for the Russians. Afanasiev, the editor of *Pravda*, spoke to my German colleague about the 'restrained' Western reaction, remarked that it would no doubt have been different had Soviet tanks been used, and went on to say that there was no need for them, because the Poles had enough of their own. This, I think, encapsulated the Soviet position.

3. Now, however, the Soviet Union faces two problems. Jaruzelski having chosen a solution by force, can the Polish army be relied on to carry it through and, if they do carry it through, will the Soviet Union end up with the kind of Poland it wants?

4. On the first, I would think that the Soviet assessment is that the situation is, in military terms, under control, at least for the time being, and that there is no immediate need for their own military involvement or that of other Warsaw Pact countries. If however, for any reason, the military action goes wrong they can scarcely see room for a political solution and will expect to intervene at short notice.

5. The question of the longer-term political outcome must look rather more problematical to them. Speaking to Semeonov last night, I commented on the restrained support for Jaruzelski in the Tass statement of 14 December. Somewhat to my surprise, he readily agreed, saying that it struck him as cautiously worded and as indicating that the Soviet Union needed to wait and see how things developed. I then commented on the apparent absence of a role for the Polish Party. He said that it was mentioned in Jaruzelski's speech, but when I said that one would have expected the Politburo to be more openly associated with Jaruzelski's action, he went on to explain the 'moral' disintegration of Poland as a result of the Party's earlier errors and the infiltration of Solidarity into the lower reaches of the Party. At this point he decided he had said enough and changed the subject. He probably had good reason. The Russians can scarcely fail to have noted the national element in Jaruzelski's appeal and to have observed (as did JIC tel 142)[1] how the Polish Party has been left on one side—possibly deliberately, possibly merely overtaken by events. There are other slight signs of Soviet sensitivity about the fact that it has been necessary to declare martial law in a fraternal socialist state. The media have emphasised that it was necessary in order to avoid the actual threat of civil war and Tass has rerun a PAP[2] article pouring scorn on the idea that a military takeover had occurred. Also of interest in this

---

[1] Not printed.
[2] *Polska Agencja Prasowa* (Polish News Agency).

17 December 1981 – 9 December 1982

respect were the changes in the first three Tass reports of Jaruzelski's speech mentioning the detention of Solidarity leaders and former Party activists. The first report referred to both groups as having been 'detained'; the second stated that both had been 'isolated' but the third said that Solidarity activists had been 'detained' and the Party ones only 'isolated'.

6. If we assume that Jaruzelski remains able to control Poland in military terms and to prevent a resurgence of Solidarity—perhaps rather large assumptions at this stage—the Soviet Union might not worry too much about a long drawn-out stalemate, with Jaruzelski maintaining physical supremacy over a sullen population, even though this would mean that Poland would remain a burden on the CMEA. Their main long-term requirement will be that an orthodox system of Party control in Poland, obedient to direction from Moscow, should be re-established.

7. At that stage, we could be faced with a new Polish-Soviet crisis, but this is to look much further forward than one can reasonably do at the moment. It is Jaruzelski and the Polish people who now hold the cards. The Soviet Union is to a remarkable extent in their hands. With the other options now used up, direct Soviet intervention—despite all the arguments against it—could have been brought closer. We are therefore going through the contingency arrangements here in order to ensure that, so far as action lies with Moscow, they are up to date. I have considered whether there is much we might do to influence Soviet policy. At the moment, I do not think there is. The public statement by Community Foreign Ministers put our position adequately on record. The Soviet Union will not now intervene unless Jaruzelski's effort collapses and in that event Western remonstrances are unlikely to dissuade them.

8. I am copying this letter to Kenneth James and Clive Rose.

Yours ever,
CURTIS KEEBLE

No. 119

Mr Duncan (Moscow) to Mr Roland (Research Department), 17 December 1981
Restricted (ENS 015/1)

[No salutation]

1. You may care to have a brief indication of the current position on dissidents, even though most of the following is already known.

2. The KGB has stepped up its campaign against dissidents, with the result that surviving dissidents are either lying low or protecting themselves with anonymity. Thus, the recent, second number of the dissident journal *Poiski*—unlike its predecessor—consists of anonymous contributions. The KGB is particularly anxious to stamp out all group manifestations. Indeed, the only dissident group that continues to have some residual existence is the one dealing with the Protection of the Rights of Invalids. The measures taken against previous group members are

UK-Soviet Relations, 1979-82

draconian: Koryagin[1] has been undergoing a six-month confinement in a punishment cell in Perm; and Nikitin,[2] also of SMOT, after prolonged drug treatment in the Dnepropetrovsk Psychiatric Isolator is in danger of losing his sight. A number of young, Moscow-based writers, including Evgeny Kizlovsky, have been recently arrested and a trial is in the making. Kizlovsky is apparently to be charged under Article 190,[3] but apparently one of his main offences is the recent publication in Paris of a satirical book by him called 'The Dissident and the Detective'. On a minor tack, the annual mini-meeting in Pushkin Square on 10 December was policed by a large number of militiamen, and ended with a score of demonstrators being taken into custody.

3. [...][4]

4. The upshot of it all seems likely to be that dissidents will increasingly seek refuge in anonymity. There are, I am told, quite a number of leaflets being distributed. There will, of course, be exceptions: I enclose a copy of one such—an open letter to European Peace Movements from Vadimov about the Sakharov hunger strike, now overtaken by events.

5. On the refusenik front, the latest figures given to me in confidence by my Dutch colleague for November are:

USSR	336
of which RSFSR	154 (including Moscow 82, Leningrad 67)

Other sub-figures are:

Minsk	4
Moldavia	14
Kiev	22
Odessa	24

This means no overall change; the small improvement in Moscow/Leningrad figures is compensated by the poor returns from the republican city centres. Even given some minor improvement for December, the year's total is likely to be under the 9,500 mark.[5]

M. J. F. DUNCAN

---

[1] Anatoly Koryagin, psychiatrist and human rights advocate, was given a 12 year sentence in June for investigating the political abuse of psychiatry. His findings had been published in an article in *The Lancet* under the title 'Unwilling Patients' in April.

[2] Aleksey Nikitin was imprisoned in 1980 for trying to form a free trade union.

[3] Article 190 of the criminal code covered political offences such as 'the dissemination of deliberately false fabrications slandering the Soviet state' and 'organisation of, or active participation in, collective actions disrupting public order'.

[4] This paragraph, relating to dissident activity, has been omitted.

[5] On 14 October Mr Roland, of the Research Department, produced a paper on the future for Soviet dissidents following the KGB's latest purge. Whilst he expected to see continued signs of political dissent amongst certain national and ethnic groups, sectarians, and 'the mass of "insulted and injured" individuals who are an inevitable by-product of the Soviet system', there would be fewer 'coherent intellectuals' to articulate general grievances. While there had never been much chance of domestic dissent generating significant political change, the main impact of Soviet dissent had been abroad. Despite there being fewer dissidents to 'gain the ear' of Western journalists, their revelations of Soviet malpractices would still continue to irritate and embarrass the authorities in international fora.

17 December 1981 – 9 December 1982

No. 120

Sir N. Henderson (Washington) to Lord Carrington, 2 January 1982, 5.40 p.m.[1]
Tel. No. 3 Immediate, Secret (RS 014/2)

MIPT: Poland[2]

1. The Americans are appreciative of the action you have taken to achieve a meeting of the EC Foreign Ministers and a NATO Ministerial meeting and support for the US call for an early special session of the CSCE Review Conference.[3] The Prime Minister's statement has been widely reported here as the first and almost the only encouraging indication that there will be an Allied response.

2. On consultation, the Administration consider that in deciding the measures to be taken they had regard to the concerns expressed by the Allies that arms control negotiations should not be broken off and that the United States should not withdraw from the CSCE. There was no adequate advance consultation about the specific measures eventually decided against the Soviet Union.[4] The timing of their announcement was strongly influenced by the President's reaction to Brezhnev's message.[5] There certainly has also been a feeling that the Europeans are reluctant to contemplate any action. There would have been no domestic support for inaction. The public mood here is reflected in the *Washington Post* cartoon of Reagan telling a Soviet bear that, if it does not stop strangling Poland, 'you are going to have to deal with me and my staunch group of European allies' which are depicted as pygmies.[6]

3. Although the press are reporting extensively the fact that the Allies do not look likely to support many of the steps taken by the United States, the tone has been relatively restrained, largely because the Administration in its own briefings and statements has been trying to play down the differences. There is an understanding here that Europe is in a different position and that our trade with the Soviet Union is predominantly in manufactured goods. I do not believe there is any disposition here to expect that the Europeans would be prepared to consider

---

[1] Info Immediate to Paris, Bonn, UKDEL NATO (Personal for Ambassador).

[2] Not printed.

[3] EC Foreign Ministers met on 4 January and the NATO Foreign Ministers on 11 January. Both issued statements calling for the lifting of martial law, the release of those detained and the resumption of genuine dialogue between the Polish authorities and the Church and Solidarity. They also noted with concern and disapproval the pressure exerted by the Soviet Union against the efforts for reform in Poland. There was no special session of the European security review conference which reconvened in Madrid as planned on 9 February.

[4] These measures included the suspension of Aeroflot flights to the US; the closure of the Soviet Purchasing Commission; the suspension of licences for the export of high technology equipment; the postponement of a long-term grain agreement; restrictions on Soviet vessels visiting US ports; the extension of licensing requirements covering the Siberian pipeline; and the suspension of bilateral exchange agreements. See *Public Papers: Reagan (1981)*, p. 1209.

[5] On 23 and 25 December President Reagan and President Brezhnev exchanged letters each accusing the other of interfering in the internal affairs of Poland contrary to the principles of the Helsinki Final Act (the letters are reproduced at http://www.thereaganfiles.com/).

[6] During a National Security Council meeting held on 22 December 1981, President Reagan referred to European leaders as 'chicken littles' and went on to say: 'if we really believe that this is the last chance of a lifetime . . . a revolution started against this "damned force", we should let our Allies know that they, too, will pay a price if they don't go along; that we have long memories' (minutes reproduced at http://www.thereaganfiles.com/).

UK-Soviet Relations, 1979-82

economic measures affecting a higher proportion of their trade with the Soviet Union than the proportion of US trade so far affected.

4. The Americans are not asking us to take the same measures as those they have announced (I do not, for instance, believe that they think it likely that the Europeans would be prepared to suspend air services or take the same action in relation to maritime agreements). What we are being asked to do is to take some measures which would have an equivalent effect and to avoid under-cutting or circumventing the measures the United States have taken.

5. Whatever our judgement on the US action, as you suggested to the Political Directors we must take account of the long-term effects on the Alliance and European relations with the Americans of what could be perceived as a complete failure to support them.

6. The problem we will face in the meeting next week and in the subsequent NATO meeting may be not so much in the attitude to be adopted to the individual measures decided here as to avoid the general impression gaining ground here that the European Allies have been unwilling to take any specific steps to support the United States. As suggested in my telno 3954[7] I believe that the overall political impression here could be strongly influenced by:

(*a*) The working out of a coherent strategy to use the CSCE process to harry the Soviet Union and the Polish authorities over a return to dialogue in Poland.

(*b*) An agreement to tighten the rules for technology transfers. This is the point to which Haig and Weinberger have both stressed to me they attach great importance. If, furthermore, we are not reasonably supportive of US moves in this direction at the high level COCOM meeting,[8] this could compound the difficulties over US components for and the manufacture under licence of European equipment sold to the Soviet Union.

(*c*) A public undertaking not to undermine or circumvent the American measures (your telno. 162 to Brussels).[9]

7. This will not meet the American demand for measures having an equivalent effect, but would serve to demonstrate some action and that there will be an Allied response.[10]

---

[7] Not printed.

[8] This meeting took place in Paris on 19/20 January where the British delegation supported a measure to conduct further study of the US list of defence priority industries with a view to future inclusion in the COCOM lists (Paris telegram No. 82 of 20 January, EN 087/1).

[9] Not printed. This telegram, dated 31 January 1981, reported on an informal meeting of EC economic directors where discussion of the latest US measures was described as 'very guarded' with most countries reluctant to take a position. The idea was put forward for further consideration that Ministers of the Ten, at their meeting on 4 January, might undertake publicly not to undermine or circumvent the American measures.

[10] On the same day Mr Haig wrote to Lord Carrington to express his appreciation for the efforts the UK had made with regard to Poland. However he went on to stress that the West had a right—even an obligation—under the Helsinki Accords to act to ensure that the process of reform, supported by the overwhelming majority of the Polish people, was resumed. There was also a critical role to play in making clear to the Soviets the consequences of their continuing to prevent a process of reconciliation and negotiation in Poland. Otherwise there was a danger the Soviets would interpret European inaction as indifference or, still worse, as weakness in the face of covert and overt intervention. Mr Haig warned that the Atlantic relationship must be more than a one-way street and the United States would have no choice but to take more drastic measures if the Europeans took no specific actions of their own or undermined US measures, adding: 'Of course the consequences will not be borne by the United States alone'. He underlined the need for more than just rhetoric from Europe in the coming weeks and wanted to see specific economic and political measures directed at the Soviet Union as well as Poland.

17 December 1981 – 9 December 1982

No. 121

Extract from a brief by East European and Soviet Department for an informal meeting of Foreign Ministers, 2 January 1982[1]
Confidential (RS 014/2)

Brief No. 3: Relations with the Soviet Union

Points to Make

1. The Russians must be made to understand that we hold them partly responsible for what has happened. We should reiterate at every opportunity the need for them to stay out of Poland and stress the costs to them if they go in.

2. Our stance is not made any easier by the measures announced by the US on 29 December.[2] Alliance had always envisaged sanctions against the Soviet Union following military intervention in Poland: broad agreement has been reached on the economic and political measures we would take. But had not envisaged, and still not fully convinced of the arguments for strong measures against the Soviet Union in circumstances short of direct armed intervention.

3. US measures so far largely demonstrative, with the exception of the suspension of licences for high technology and, more importantly, the extension of controls on oil and gas equipment. The latter could prevent delivery under existing contracts of pumping equipment for the gas pipeline which is very largely dependent on US General Electric technology. This should be reviewed urgently with the US. Could Herr Schmidt do this during his meeting with President Reagan on 5 January?[3]

4. Main problem now is how to maintain alliance cohesion. US opinion apparently strongly behind Reagan; and now watching the Ten's reaction. We must do enough to reassure American Government and people that we are not soft. But that we have different interests and investment in trade with Soviet Union. US is mainly agricultural, European mainly industrial.

5. Need to look at sanctions US have announced, and how we might respond, in this light. Though also need to bear in mind the need for 'equality of pain'. Cannot be expected to adopt measures which will hurt us much more than the US. Nor should only some of the Ten act leaving others free to contribute as though nothing had happened.

6. Agree the lines proposed by Political Directors:

(*a*) avoid action or comment which would make Western disunity worse or seem worse than it really is: some degree of complementarity inevitable and even desirable in Western reactions;

(*b*) make maximum use of the possibilities in the political field, where the Ten are less constrained than in economic. Use Madrid lever in most effective

---

[1] The meeting was due to take place in Brussels on 4 January. In his covering minute Mr Broomfield stated that the brief aimed at damage limitation, against the background of Mr Haig's specific request for action against both Poland and the Soviet Union and his assertion that declaratory support from Western Europe would not be considered sufficient.

[2] See No 120, note 4.

[3] Washington telegram No. 38 of 6 January reported Chancellor Schmidt's visit to America. The Germans were not pressed to take specific measures, the pipeline issue was not raised and both sides agreed that the current US sanctions were economic and limited in nature, mainly intended to send a strong political warning to the Soviets. Herr Schmidt had made known that he was unhappy about the lack of consultation over the US sanctions.

UK-Soviet Relations, 1979-82

manner, arguing that Polish events undermine assumptions on which East/West relations have developed since Helsinki Final Act. Public statement to be issued after Foreign Ministers' meeting on 4 January should be suitably firmer than those made before Christmas. Not underrate Soviet sensitivity to well judged diplomatic pressure.

(*c*) Each of the Ten should look for ways to reflect disapproval of the Soviet role in Poland, e.g. by

– postponing/cancelling political consultations with Soviet Union.

– advising Parliamentarians to postpone/cancel their contacts with Moscow.

7. Do not need to decide economic measures today. But possibilities might include:

(*a*) raising tariffs or reducing quotas on Soviet products imported into the Community, as floated by the Commission at the officials' meeting on 30 December.

(*b*) imposing limits on activities of Soviet fish factory ships in Community waters. UK already considering this.

(*c*) reducing or ending work of Soviet oceanographic vessels in waters of the Ten (suggested by Italy at officials meeting on 30 December: note promised).

8. Not only the Ten involved. Need to involve others too, e.g. Japan, Australia, New Zealand.

9. The Ten might now declare publicly that they will consider measures on their own account which would show the seriousness with which they view the situation in Poland; though these would not be the same as those adopted by the US.[4]

---

[4] The communiqué issued following the meeting reiterated the Ten's disapproval of developments in Poland and warned that the already grave situation would be further aggravated if it led to open intervention by the Warsaw Pact. The Ten did not impose immediate sanctions but promised to undertake positive consultations with the US and other Western states. Reporting on the meeting in a letter dated 6 January to Mr Coles at No. 10, Mr Fall stated that there had been no fundamental disagreement over the Soviet Union's complicity in, and responsibility for, the imposition of martial law in Poland and most Ministers spoke firmly of the need for Western unity and non-undermining of US measures. But it was also recognised that an intense period of consultation both within NATO and the Community lay ahead.

No. 122

Extract from Sir C. Keeble (Moscow) to Lord Carrington, 7 January 1982[1]
Confidential (ENS 014/1)

Soviet Union: Annual Review for 1981

5. By the end of the year, with the eruption of the Polish crisis, the scene had changed once again. Earlier, as the Polish Government failed to stem the growth of Solidarity's power, there had been an oddly unreal period in which one might legitimately wonder whether the inconceivable might yet happen and the Soviet Union find itself compelled to accept a substantial weakening of its political control over a key sector of its Eastern European empire. At the Party Congress in February, the Soviet requirement for a reversal of the trend of events in Poland had been bluntly stated. It had been reiterated in a letter from the Soviet Central

---

[1] The summary and paras 1-4 and 7-12 (covering relations with the US, the internal situation and international outlook) are not printed.

17 December 1981 – 9 December 1982

Committee on 5 June and again on 18 September. The Soviet press for months had spoken of counter-revolution in Poland. As the year wore on, Kania had failed to act and had been replaced by Jaruzelski, but still there was no sign that the Soviet Union was able to enforce its demands. Finally, on 13 December, martial law was declared in Poland.[2] The evidence of the Central Committee letters, Brezhnev's own speeches and the whole Soviet press treatment of the Polish crisis shows clearly enough that Jaruzelski's action was in accordance with Soviet wishes. We may also assume that there was collusion between the Soviet and Polish military and security authorities in drawing up the plans for the imposition of martial law.[3] It may be that the final decision was Jaruzelski's and the timing was dictated by the Radom and Gdansk meetings of Solidarity rather than by a prearranged Soviet plan.[4] In a sense however these are secondary issues. What matters is that, at Soviet behest, Polish force has been used in an attempt to crush a movement which threatened to bring a real measure of freedom to Poland—and, incidentally, in so doing, to change the balance of power in Europe.

6. It has been a sad experience to be reminded so brutally of the reality of Soviet imperial power, of what it means when the Soviet Union proclaims that Poland 'was, is and will remain a Socialist state'. It must be for Her Majesty's Ambassador in Warsaw to assess how matters may develop, but I do not think that anyone in Moscow believes that 13 December marked more than the beginning of a stage. If Jaruzelski fails, we can expect the Soviet Union to use its own forces rather than let Poland slip out of control. If he succeeds he might just acquire a degree of authority and freedom of manoeuvre which might not be wholly welcome to Moscow and the Soviet struggle to reassert full political control might not be quickly and simply accomplished. If there is a prolonged, indecisive struggle, the drain on Eastern Europe's resources—and in particular on the Soviet Union—will be significant, both in economic terms and in terms of the will and cohesion of the bloc. Meanwhile, the conclusions to be drawn about Soviet policy are not wholly discouraging. The determination to maintain control over Eastern Europe was to be expected. What was interesting was that, faced in Poland with a remarkable assortment of inhibiting factors (some of them not unfamiliar to earlier imperial powers) they hesitated for a surprisingly long time before eventually inspiring action which, harsh though it has been, may yet prove to be less than fully effective.

---

[2] The issue of UK relations with the Soviet bloc, including Poland, will be covered in a forthcoming *DBPO* volume.

[3] On 4 January the State Department released a paper on Soviet pressure against Poland which, according to a spokesman, revealed 'a consistent pattern of pressures, threats and intimidations against Poland, a pattern that lays blame for the ultimate crack-down squarely on the Kremlin' (RS 014/2).

[4] On 12 December in Gdansk the Solidarity leadership had put forward proposals for a new power-sharing agreement with the Communist Party, a nationwide referendum on a non-Communist government for Poland, free elections and a redefinition of the military relationship with the Soviet Union.

UK-Soviet Relations, 1979-82

No. 123

Letter from Mrs Thatcher to President Reagan, 8 January 1982
Secret (RS 014/2)

Dear Ron,

I was grateful for your letter of 24 December about your messages to General Jaruzelski and to President Brezhnev.[1]

Before replying, I wanted to see what progress was made in our discussions with our European partners in the New Year. You obviously had a good meeting with Helmut Schmidt earlier this week, and he will have given you an account of the meeting of the Ten Foreign Ministers in Brussels on 4 January.[2] The task of reconciling views and interests among ten different countries is never easy and you will be aware of some particular difficulties in this case. Nevertheless, the outcome as reflected in the Ten's Communiqué is better than seemed likely at one stage and reflects ideas for which we fought hard.

I hope we shall be able to go further in the consultations which lie ahead. The statement in the Communiqué that: 'other measures will be considered as the situation in Poland develops, in particular concerning credit and economic assistance to Poland and measures concerning the Community's commercial policy with regard to the USSR' will be helpful in this connection. The last word has not been said. We shall certainly be pushing in the same direction as you, believing as I do in the importance of the Western Alliance and the way of life for which we stand.

We must ensure that the focus of attention is directed where it belongs—at a blatant example of the failure of the Soviet system and Soviet ideas—and not at differences between Alliance partners whose aims are identical.

1981 was an eventful year for us all. I send you my warm regards and best wishes for 1982.

Yours ever,

MARGARET

[1] Not printed. In these letters, President Reagan reaffirmed the need for a firm stance and stated that the US administration was considering the full range of issues affecting relations with Poland and the Soviet Union.

[2] See No. 121, notes 3 and 4.

17 December 1981 – 9 December 1982

No. 124

Lord Carrington to Sir N. Henderson (Washington), 18 January 1982, 4.15 p.m.[1]
Tel. No. 59 Immediate, Secret (RS 014/2)

Poland: Economic Measures towards the Soviet Union

1. I am concerned that the unity achieved among the Allies at the NATO Ministerial meeting on 11 January may already be in danger, because of the US position about existing export contracts and German reluctance to take measures against the USSR.[2]

2. There seems to be a real risk that the Americans will apply their own measures towards the Soviet Union in such a way as to prevent the inclusion of US items in equipment supplied by the Europeans to the Soviet Union under existing contracts (your Telnos 132 and 133).[3] That would of course prevent or greatly delay the pipeline project. Yet the Germans intend to persevere with the pipeline (para 6 of Paris Telno 27)[3] and many Europeans have strong views about not interfering with existing contracts. And such chances as there are that the Germans and some others will take worthwhile measures of their own towards the Soviet Union, in accordance with the NATO declaration of 11 January, would probably be destroyed by US interference with existing European contracts.

3. The UK has an interest in the pipeline going ahead, notably because of the John Brown contract. Cancellation of the pipeline might cost UK firms £170 million. We also have the important general interest that NATO's response to the Polish crisis should be seen to be adequate and reasonably united. The question is whether we can do anything to avert the serious problems ahead.

4. The following are some of the considerations:

(*a*) Several other Europeans, and notably the Germans, have a far greater interest than the UK in the pipeline project.

(*b*) We cannot be sure that, even if the Americans were to exempt existing European contracts from their measures, all the European members of NATO would take worthwhile measures under the NATO declaration.

(*c*) Yet such European measures, coupled with the American wish for a united allied response on Poland, are the only leverage available for pressing the Americans to exempt existing European contracts.

(*d*) We assume that Haig realises that interference with existing European contracts will cause a major transatlantic row. Subject to your views, we therefore wonder whether anyone in Washington except the President could

---

[1] Repeated Immediate to Paris, Bonn; Information Immediate to UKREP Brussels, UKDEL NATO. At the PUS's morning meeting there was a discussion about the danger of new Allied differences over Poland. After considering the situation with the Secretary of State the PUS favoured approaching embassies in Washington, Bonn and Paris for advice on how to try to avert a transatlantic row.

[2] The communiqué issued after the meeting of the Special Ministerial session of the NAC on 11 January condemned the imposition of martial law in Poland and deplored the concerted campaign mounted by the Soviet Union against efforts by the Polish people for national renewal and reform which could not be reconciled with the principles of the Helsinki Final Act. It further supported action by each ally to place restrictions on the movement of Polish and Soviet diplomats and to impose energy, agricultural, financial and technological sanctions if the situation in Poland did not improve.

[3] Not printed.

UK-Soviet Relations, 1979-82

take the decision to exempt European contracts (assuming that European ones can be separated from purely American ones in such a decision).

5. We should be grateful for your views. One course would be to wait for the Germans to realise fully that a major row is looming, in the hope that they will themselves decide to tackle the Americans. But during the delay the media might well direct much more attention to transatlantic differences. Another approach would be for us to discuss the matter at a high level with the Germans and French, and then to make separate approaches to the Americans. Yet such concertation [*sic* ?consultation] might alienate the latter. Alternatively, we might suggest that Schmidt should approach Reagan, following up their recent successful meeting (even though the pipeline was not then discussed). In any case, an approach to the Americans would probably need to imply a deal whereby the Americans would relax their position on existing European contracts in return for European undertakings to take worthwhile action towards the Soviet Union in line with the NATO declaration. The nature of such action would no doubt need to be indicated. One of the supporting arguments would be that the NATO contingency planning about Poland foresaw no interruption of existing export contracts.

6. Paris please pass copy to Bridges and UKREP to Bullard.

No. 125

Minute from Mr Goodison to Mr Bullard, 20 January 1982
Confidential (RS 014/2)

British Action against the Soviet Union

1. At the lunch I gave today for Mr Petrovsky, the Director for International Organisations at the Soviet Ministry of Foreign Affairs, I was pressed very hard by Mr Bykov, the Minister-Counsellor at the Soviet Embassy, on our intentions for action against the Soviet Union in the context of Poland. I understood him to say that they had had someone present at the meeting yesterday between the Secretary of State and the Foreign Affairs Committee on this topic. They had been confused because at various points in the discussion Lord Carrington had said that:

(*a*) we should act with the USA;

(*b*) we should act in the framework of NATO and the Community; and

(*c*) national action was to be determined by each country separately.

Could I tell him what action we contemplated; how this was to be reconciled with what Lord Carrington had said; and how I envisaged Anglo-Soviet relations in the future?

2. I said that Lord Carrington had said what he meant. These were all considerations that must be present in our minds. We were seriously concerned about Poland; we stood by the NATO Declaration and he must certainly expect us to take action. I was not willing to specify what action we might take. That was for decision in cooperation with our allies. I could not be optimistic at present about Anglo-Soviet relations if there was to be no movement from their side over Poland.

3. Mr Bykov said that we must understand that the Soviet Union would retaliate if we took action against them. They did not understand why we were so worked up about Poland. (In historical digression I was unwise enough to allude to Catherine the Great and the 1939 Treaty of Brest-Litovsk [*sic*].) He said that there

304

17 December 1981 – 9 December 1982

were plenty of things which they could invoke against us; he had recently visited Northern Ireland. I did not rise to this fly.

4. Mr Petrovsky, who is concerned among other things with the CSCE, asked me how I foresaw the discussions there. I said that again I was not optimistic about the atmosphere. He must understand the strength of feeling on the topic of Poland in Western Europe. He would be aware that a large number of our Foreign Ministers were proposing to attend and to discuss this topic. He said that the Soviet Union attached considerable importance to a successful outcome of the Madrid Conference. I said 'Ah, yes!'

A. C. GOODISON

No. 126

Sir N. Henderson (Washington) to Lord Carrington, 23 January 1982, 1.25 a.m.[1]
Tel. No. 206 Immediate, Confidential (RS 014/2)

Poland, the USA and the Alliance

1. Let me try to take stock of where the US government are heading over Poland, the motives for their actions and the consequences for the Alliance.

2. You will have noticed the conviction the Americans have that the situation in Poland is deteriorating. They do not see much prospect, whatever they do, of martial law being quickly ended, detainees released and a dialogue resumed with Solidarity. Herein lies the difference between their view and that of the Europeans who believe that all is not completely lost in Poland, and that, even if is pretty hopeless, it is better to behave as though there is still some entity in Poland that is worth having dealings with.

3. The US view is increasingly that they must show the Soviets unequivocally the unacceptability of what is happening in Poland at Soviet instigation, that the Soviets must be punished and that this punishment must be such as will deter Moscow from undertaking anything comparable in the foreseeable future.

4. You will hear a lot about various pressures at work upon the Administration: you will know of Kissinger's criticism:[2] and there is undoubtedly a widespread feeling in this country that the government cannot just sit back and let Poland be

---

[1] Repeated Information Immediate to UKDEL NATO, Paris, Bonn; Priority Moscow, Warsaw, Rome; Routine other NATO Posts. This telegram was dated 22 January but not sent until early the next morning.

[2] In two lengthy articles in *The New York Times* (reprinted in *The Times* on 22 and 23 January), Dr Kissinger ridiculed the idea of holding summit meetings and arms talks with Moscow while the Soviet Union continued to underpin martial law in Poland. He further criticised the US administration for its failure to take decisive action over Poland. Dr Kissinger suggested that the Europeans could not be expected to embark on a tough round of sanctions as long as America continued to supply large quantities of grain to the Soviet Union, and advocated that the West should use Poland's debt as political leverage with the Soviet Union.

Washington telegram No. 210 of 23 January reported that, according to a source in the State Department, Mr Haig had been particularly upset by Dr Kissinger's attack. Mr Haig was therefore advocating a complete embargo on trade with the Soviet Union, to call the bluff of those advocating stronger measures. Mr Bullard noted: 'If the Allies are going to be told that we have to do X & Y to support something done by Haig merely to ward off criticism from arch-conservatives, heaven help us.'

UK-Soviet Relations, 1979-82

crushed. I would not say that the Congressional elections at the end of this year are a dominant factor in US decision making on the issue. What is undoubted is that the American public is worked up and that the Reagan Administration have to give practical fulfilment to their commitment to stand up to the Russians and not to acquiesce in the further spread of Soviet influence. The Americans are aware of the scepticism of their allies about the efficacy of sanctions. As I suggest, they do not claim that even if fully implemented they would arrest the crackdown in Poland but they do believe that the Soviet Union and the Eastern bloc are in a particularly vulnerable economic situation and that a concerted exercise of economic pressure at the present time could give the Russians a hiding that they would not forget for a long time.

5. To the argument that the European allies will suffer more from the imposition of sanctions than the USA, the Americans, from a wide political spectrum, will retort that that is all very well but they, the Europeans, will tend to suffer most if the Soviets can get away with yet another victory in Europe and that in any event the path of economic involvement with the Communist bloc is a hostage to fortune. They are, hence, unsympathetic to the gas pipeline, asserting that regardless of the present Polish issue, the Europeans will be laying up trouble for themselves in the future if they become heavily dependent upon Soviet gas. To counter by saying that this economic interdependence between the Soviet bloc and the West was at the core of détente policy prompted by the US government is to invite the counter argument that that was 'Kissingerism' in which few in the United States now believe.

6. What then in practical terms do the US have in mind to do as their next stage of economic pressure against the Soviet Union? There is much to-ing and fro-ing about the grain issue and it is difficult to be categorical about US intentions. But on present evidence it does not look as though the Americans intend going in for a complete grain embargo. This is not only because of the economic and political difficulties of doing so, but also because they know that it would be circumvented by grain exports from Canada, Argentina, etc. Nor will they sever all diplomatic contacts with the Soviet Union even assuming, as is likely, a dusty meeting between Gromyko and Haig on 26 January. They will not set a date for the opening of START[3] talks but on present reckoning they will continue with the INF meetings. They also hope to have the chance at Madrid on 9 February to lambast the Soviets across the table.

7. What they are considering on the economic side is to extend the existing measures to cover a wider range of exports, in particular all those for the oil and gas industries, and applying them to US subsidiaries overseas and to manufacture under licence. It seems unlikely that any exceptions will be tolerated for items hitherto obtained from the USA and destined to go to the Soviet Union under existing contracts.

8. In addition, they are considering invoking the so-called Tank clause which will mean in practice pushing Poland into formal default on its debts. They calculate that the consequences of this would be to cause other creditors to take similar action. In turn this would provoke the banks into declaring Poland in default on bank credits which would be likely to result in denial of short term credit for other Eastern European countries, particularly Romania, Czechoslovakia

[3] Strategic Arms Reduction Talks began in Geneva in June 1982.

17 December 1981 – 9 December 1982

and Yugoslavia. They also recognise that such action would be very costly for the German banking system in particular.

9. As you know they are also seeking to tighten up COCOM.

10. The Americans would certainly like to coordinate their actions with those of Western Europe. They have said repeatedly that there will be consultations before they move. But in their present mood it would be foolhardy to assume that if the Europeans object, or do not wish to go along the same sort of path, they, the Americans, will refrain from doing so. Haig has always said that whatever the outcome for Poland of present events it must not lead to the impairment of the Alliance. This is certainly the American desire but unless the Europeans make some sort of noises and take some sort of measures that can be regarded here as impinging upon the Soviets I do not see how significant damage is going to be avoided, and I am not sure that it does good to agonise over whether it will be the Europeans or the Americans who are most to blame. But I think that the Europeans should be in no doubt that their interests may suffer.

11. Hitherto I have tended to take a conservative view about the development of Mansfield-like tendencies[4] in this country but in circumstances in which the Europeans were being highly criticised by the Americans for inadequate response to the Soviet Union, and when there is a readiness in the capitals of Europe to indulge in superior criticism of the Americans coupled with demonstrations of unilateralism, it would be unwise to assume the anti-European tendencies will not develop in this country.

12. Looking a bit further ahead it is a fair assumption that Washington and Moscow, unless they go to war, are eventually going to engage in some sort of dialogue. What we must avoid surely is a state of affairs in which they do so over the heads of and without regard to Western Europe, a danger that could be enhanced if Europe, in American eyes, abdicated its responsibilities over the issue of Poland. The temptation that exists in Europe at the present time to make some sort of parallel between El Salvador and Poland and to suggest that what the Russians are doing in Poland is not all that different from what the Americans are trying to do in Central America, has the effect of infuriating the Americans who do not have any divisions in Central America.

13. Of all the dangerous shifts that seem to me to be stirring in the Alliance, the most disturbing at the present time is the evolution of German opinion and the reaction of the Americans towards it. To say that there is common incomprehension is unhelpful, however true. But just as, for a long time, the Americans looked upon the Germans as the sheet-anchor for the defence of Western Europe, so the new tendencies in the Federal Republic, not to mention the scathing criticisms by the Chancellor about the Americans and their armed forces, will play into the hands of those here who toy with the idea of some reduction of US military involvement in Europe.[5]

---

[4] The extent of US military commitment to Europe was strongly questioned by Senator Mansfield and others who between 1966 and 1973 sponsored a series of amendments to Senate bills (none of which proved successful) designed to reduce the number of American troops serving in Europe.

[5] In a minute to Mr Mallaby dated 25 January, Mr Broomfield stated that if the Americans followed the course described by Sir N. Henderson they would be challenging the basic tenets of *Ostpolitik* as practised by the Germans since 1968. Moreover, unless the Americans compromised or the Germans agreed to defer the pipeline, there was no way of avoiding a major and public transatlantic row. Also commenting to Mr Mallaby on the same day, Mr Bullard thought the West was more likely to suffer harm as a result of mistakes made by themselves than of 'master strokes by the Russians'. The East had mishandled Poland for 35 years and the imposition of martial law was a

UK-Soviet Relations, 1979-82

defeat for them, not the West. 'The worst danger at the moment is that the US will split the Alliance by setting a pace too fast for the Alliance to follow, or loyalty tests which some of the Allies are bound to fail, or targets grossly disproportionate to the situation.' He thought that the answer, as always, was to consult, 'free of arbitrary deadlines and the unilateral adoption of extreme positions'. He concluded: 'Would it not be better to draw a lesson from Afghanistan, accept that actions by the West are not likely to reverse the course of events in Poland and concentrate on making the Soviet situation as uncomfortable as possible, materially and politically?'

No. 127

FCO to Sir N. Henderson (Washington), 29 January 1982, 6.50 p.m.[1]
Tel. No. 154 Immediate, Secret (RS 014/2)

MIPT[2]

Dear Ron

1. I was most grateful to Al Haig for rearranging his plans at short notice to call here today.[3] It gave us an invaluable opportunity to hear from him how he had got on in Geneva and in the Middle East: and we were able to have a good discussion of the Polish situation.

2. I know that Al will give you a full account of our talk but I thought nevertheless that I should send you this personal message, to underline my deep concern at the danger that the unity of the Western Alliance could be seriously damaged by the current differences over how to react to the repression in Poland.

3. We must at all costs avoid a demonstration of disunity in the Alliance which would give Moscow a first class propaganda victory and impair our efforts to check further adventurism on their part in the future. We must also avoid measures which would do more harm to the West than to the Soviet Union.

4. I have taken a close interest in the preparation of a package of British measures both towards Poland and towards the Soviet Union. We have already said in NATO that we would be willing to take a number of measures as part of an Allied reaction to complement your own resolute stand, provided that we can all agree about not undermining each other's measures.

5. The measures which the United Kingdom has taken, or would in principle be

---

[1] Personal for Ambassador. Repeated Immediate Jakarta (Personal for Private Secretary). Lord Carrington was visiting South East Asia.

This telegram contains the text of a letter from Mrs Thatcher to President Reagan. The Foreign Secretary and the Lord Privy Seal were concerned about the growing risk of a public transatlantic dispute which would have lasting consequences for relations amongst the Allies and for Western security. As there was little indication either that the Europeans were willing to take more serious measures towards the Soviet Union or that the Americans were willing to discuss the problem of existing contracts, they thought the time had come for an urgent message from the Prime Minister to President Reagan to draw the President's personal attention to the situation.

[2] Not printed.

[3] Mrs Thatcher invited Mr Haig to stop over in London on his way back to the US from the Middle East. Mr Haig sent a telegram giving President Reagan a read-out of the meeting and prior warning of the letter, in case it arrived before he and the President had chance to speak. He said Mrs Thatcher had spoken with 'unusual vehemence' on the subject of the extra-territorial reach of the sanctions already imposed and rumours of additional extreme measures (including calling Poland to default on its debts), and predicted 'dire consequences for the Western Alliance should we preceed [*sic*] in that direction' (Haig to Reagan telegram of 29 January 1982; Reagan Library: NSA Head of State File: Box 35, reproduced on the Margaret Thatcher Foundation website: http://www.margaretthatcher.org/).

17 December 1981 – 9 December 1982

willing to take, include:

Towards Poland: restrictions on Polish diplomatic missions; increased broadcasts, already begun, to Poland; suspension of commercial credit except for contracts already concluded; the placing in suspense of negotiations about debt rescheduling for 1982; the suspension with our partners in the European Community of food exports at specially subsidised prices; and increased humanitarian aid to the Polish people. Towards the Soviet Union: significant new restrictions on Soviet diplomats; reduced activity under technical co-operation agreements; clear exposure in the Madrid Review Conference of Soviet complicity in the repression in Poland; readiness to move with our European Community partners to increase the interest rates on export credit and to restrict certain imports from the Soviet Union; termination, in concert with others, of our bilateral maritime agreement; and new restrictions on Soviet factory ships.

6. I am sure that our joint objective now should be a credible and united Allied position, to demonstrate our rejection of martial law and of the Soviet hand in it. We must not allow the Soviet crisis in Poland to bring about a crisis in the Western Alliance which would suit only Soviet purposes.

7. I know you agree with this aim. The question is how to attain it. I can well understand why some of your people may be growing impatient and thinking of a second set of American measures against the Soviet Union. My fear is that further measures taken unilaterally would not carry the Allies with them but would greatly deepen and expose the divisions within the Alliance. That could advance Soviet interests more than your new measures would set them back. I hope therefore that you will feel able to hold back on further measures until we have thoroughly explored the possibility of a united Allied position.

8. I understand that new measures under consideration in Washington may include steps such as denunciation of the 1981 Agreement on rescheduling Polish debt, which would lead to a Polish default. But the immediate effect of that would be that the Poles would give up their present efforts to make such payments as they can under the rescheduling arrangements, either to Western Governments or to Western banks. That in turn would take pressure off the Soviet Union to help them. On the other side, the effects on the international banking system would be unpredictable, and probably very severe, particularly if other defaults followed. These effects would certainly not be confined to Europe. The damage to the West could be at least as great as the damage to the Soviet Union. The health of the international financial system is a Western, not a Soviet interest. They have every reason to rejoice if it is impaired.

9. What we need now is a reasonable set of measures, jointly agreed. This is the direction in which we should all be working. My own view is that the most promising basis for agreement would be an arrangement whereby the European allies took measures comparable to yours, both in their effects on the Soviet Union and in their domestic implications, and took positive action to meet their commitments not to undermine your measures with respect to future contracts, while existing European contracts would go ahead. I realise that this last consideration is a difficult one for you. But the French, Germans and Italians cannot and will not give up the gas pipeline project, whatever one may think of its merits. We too have important contracts at stake, notably one held by John Brown

UK-Soviet Relations, 1979-82

Engineering, the cancellation of which would cause additional unemployment.[4] An accommodation on existing contracts is therefore essential to allied unity over Poland.

10. Your measures of 29 December sent a clear signal to the Soviet Union without seriously compromising your own interests.[5] We should all be following suit. Although the NATO discussions have so far been frustratingly slow, it should surely be possible, if you could move on existing contracts, for the rest of us to reach agreement on measures comparable to yours. We should look resolute and united and we should still have some shots left in our lockers.

11. I suggested to Al Haig that the best approach now would be for the US to arrange secret consultations in the very near future between senior officials from the allied countries most closely concerned—you, UK, the French, the Germans, and I think in this case the Italians.[6] This should enable us to make progress at the NATO meeting on 3 February. But I think that a further NATO meeting may well be needed a few days after that.

12. It will also be important to carry the Japanese and others in our plans. It would not be tolerable to ask our own industries to forgo opportunities only to see them seized by Japan.

13. We have the opportunity to show the Soviet Union a firm united front. What we can achieve together in this can give a lasting boost to allied unity and a setback to Soviet ambitions. We have embarked on this course and should make every possible effort to carry it through to a successful conclusion. The crisis in Poland looks like being a prolonged one. We risk losing the prize if we act hastily or out of step.

With warm personal regards
Margaret[7]

---

[4] The original draft made no mention of John Brown Engineering which the Foreign Secretary found too disingenuous. He considered that the effect of the message would risk being diminished if Britain did not 'make a clean breast of our concern for John Brown', of which the Americans were already well aware (Jakarta telegram No. 53 of 29 January, not printed).

[5] See No. 120, note 4.

[6] A five-power meeting took place on 2 February at the US Embassy attended by Economic and Political Directors. In a short note of the meeting Mr Mallaby reported that the Americans thought the political situation in Poland was being set back to the 1950s but additional measures could bring effective pressure to bear on the Polish regime and on the Soviet Union. The Europeans argued strongly against moves which could affect European industry through US subsidiaries in Europe or even European countries holding manufacturing licences from the US. Lord Bridges pointed out that such measures might be seen in Europe as being directed more at the Europeans than the Russians.

[7] The personal intervention of the Prime Minister was credited with bringing about a mood of greater patience in Washington (FCO telegram No. 198 to Washington of 5 February, ENZ 020/5).

No. 128

Letter from Mr Goodison to Sir C. Keeble (Moscow), 1 February 1982
Confidential (RS 014/2)

Dear Curtis,

Poland

1. Many thanks for your letter of 21 January to Ewen Fergusson, and for your

17 December 1981 – 9 December 1982

follow-up telegram 55 of 26 January.[1] Both were received here with great interest and were particularly timely in view of the assessment we are now trying to make of where Poland in particular, and East/West relations in general, are heading.

2. We find ourselves very much in agreement with you. Like you, we think the Russians had long since reached the conclusion that developments in Poland were a grave threat to their political and security interests, and that something had to be done. The international penalties of direct Soviet intervention were no doubt judged to be so great that 'the internal route' of a Polish military crackdown was vastly preferable from the Russians' point of view. But by early December, when the collapse of party authority in Poland was plain for all to see, there must have been those in Moscow who were arguing that the situation had become so dangerous that, whatever the international costs, if the Poles would not take action themselves, the Russians would have to. Fortunately for them, Jaruzelski acted.

3. Since Jaruzelski's crackdown, the Russians have, of course, done all they can to justify his actions and have counter attacked in the propaganda war by suggesting, on lines familiar from Afghanistan, that it is the Western reaction that amounts to interference in Poland's affairs rather than any actions of theirs. They have also accused us of hypocrisy by reciting El Salvador, Chile, Turkey, Northern Ireland etc as examples of Western double standards. But there is a defensive and unconvincing note in all this which suggests that the Russians are embarrassed by a military takeover in a Communist country and uncertain how to move on to a more orthodox model of 'advanced socialism'.

4. At present they are engaged in a damage limitation exercise, hoping that economic interests will drive deep divisions between Western Europe and the United States and that Western European nuclear sensitivities will insulate the INF talks and keep the Americans at the table. They should be both encouraged and discouraged by developments so far: encouraged because the sanctions issue is causing the Alliance considerable difficulties; discouraged because those difficulties have so far proved manageable, and because the START talks have been linked with events in Poland and postponed. Their hope will be that the strains among the Allies will prove too great and provide them with a double prize: the successful reassertion of control over Poland at very little practical cost, and a seriously divided and damaged Western Alliance. We must of course do all we can to make sure that they are disappointed.

5. So far as re-establishing firm control over Poland is concerned, we agree that they will be reasonably satisfied so far. But they must be aware of the possibility that this has been the easy bit and that the long, difficult and expensive haul is only just beginning. Their aims will, as you say, be to ensure the total emasculation of Solidarity, the rebuilding of the party, and the revitalising of the economy. None of these will be easy. Solidarity may manage to reorganise underground (and there are signs that it is doing so); the rebuilding [of] the party will take time. Revitalising the economy will prove hardest of all. It may, as you say, give the Russians a certain satisfaction to see the Poles cold and hungry, as just deserts for their behaviour. But they may wonder whether the effect will be to cow the population as they would like, or to fuel resentment and opposition which could lead to a

---

[1] Not printed. In this correspondence, Sir C. Keeble commented on Sir N. Henderson's reporting of US policy (see No. 126), contending that Moscow viewed the imposition of Western counter-measures as a lesser evil than the renewed loss of control in Poland, and that any damage inflicted on the Soviet economy 'can hardly begin to compare with the damage which would be represented by the collapse of the Soviet position in Poland'.

UK-Soviet Relations, 1979-82

renewed confrontation between the people and the Polish authorities, and one which it could require direct Soviet intervention to contain. I assume they will wish to avoid such intervention in future just as much as they have in the past; they may therefore realise that it would be wise to restrain their punitive pleasures and not to allow the Polish population to suffer too much.

6. We would add a further aim to the list of Soviet objectives you mention: to diminish the authority and influence of the Polish Church. The Russians know that even if the Polish authorities win what promises to be a long battle of attrition with Solidarity, there is still another alternative power structure in Poland and one which will continue to command the loyalty of the vast majority of Poles. They may well therefore urge Jaruzelski to cut back on the Church's privileges and increase the administrative pressures upon it. For his part Jaruzelski will have to decide how far he can afford to take such a risk without provoking the sort of popular (and Papal) confrontation he needs to avoid. Yet another possible objective to the list is private agriculture, one more anomaly which Soviet ideologues and economists would no doubt wish to see removed. Once again the calculation for Jaruzelski is a nice one. In the long term, larger state-run farms might be more efficient; in the short term he would run the gauntlet of the peasants' wrath and the likelihood that they would try to withhold supplies from Poland's depleted market. What to do with rural Solidarity may prove just as big a headache as industrial Solidarity.

7. Assuming that the Russians will not want a return to a genuine dialogue in Poland, they will, as you say, steel themselves to a long process of 'normalisation' in Poland, even though this will complicate their relations with the West. They will hope nevertheless that these complications will have little if any effect on their economic and arms control interests and that beneath the barrage of polemics, cooperation will continue. The question, of course, is how realistic this hope will prove to be. It is still uncertain how the sanctions question will be resolved but they will certainly suffer some appreciable damage at the end of the day; as for arms control negotiations, our hunch is that, barring a direct Soviet intervention and assuming the Administration can withstand right-wing pressure in Washington, INF talks will continue. (So far as START is concerned, it is still too soon to venture a guess.)

8. But the equation is not simply an East/West one; there is also the question of the impact of the crisis on the CMEA and the Soviet system. For even if the West is unable to agree on a very far reaching package of economic sanctions against the Soviet Union, it is reasonably certain that there will be no new Western money for Poland. Until now the Soviet Union's most intractable satellite has been subsidised by the West; but from now on the Soviet Union and the CMEA will have to shoulder the very considerable burden of the Polish economy alone. Given the economic difficulties all the Socialist countries are suffering, the additional strain will be considerable. And even if the system can stand it, by accepting lower growth and a measure of disruption, there is good reason to doubt that the political normalisation of the Poles will be a smooth process. Poland could yet prove to be an economic liability and an indigestible political problem for a long time to come, materially, psychologically and perhaps politically weakening the system. The Russians may argue that what has happened in Poland is the result of too little socialism incorrectly applied. But more socialism, more rigorously applied, is unlikely to meet with any greater acceptance from the Poles, who made their feelings known in 1956, 1968, 1970, 1976 and 1980. The most the Russians may

17 December 1981 – 9 December 1982

be able to look forward to is slow economic recovery in Poland and grumbling political acquiescence. History suggests they will be lucky to achieve this, anyway for long.

Yours,
A. C. GOODISON

No. 129

Minute from Mr Heap to Mr Adams, 3 February 1982[1]
Confidential (ENS 163/1)

West Siberian Gas Pipeline Project
1. You asked, in your note on Rome telno 37,[2] for an updated assessment of the energy implications of the Soviet gas pipeline.

Current Situation
2. Present Soviet gas exports to Europe are currently estimated at 24-30 billion cubic metres (bcm) per annum. The West Siberian pipeline will enable the USSR to export a further 40 bcm. France and the FRG are the only two Western European countries of those planning to take Siberian gas which have so far reached agreement with the Soviet Union on the amount to be imported and the price to be paid. After the events in Poland, other Western nations decided in late December to take a 'pause for reflection'.

3. The current position country by country is as follows:

FRG. The FRG gas utility, Ruhrgas, signed a 'Heads of Agreement' in November last year with Soyuzgasexport to take 10.5 bcm of gas per annum over a 25 year period from 1984. This is a reduction from the 12 bcm originally contemplated. An additional 0.7 bcm will go to West Berlin. The basic price agreed was about $4.70 per million British thermal units (MMBTU).[3] This relatively low price has been regarded as a victory for Ruhrgas in their negotiations with Soyuzgas (as a comparison if Statfjord gas was flowing, it would currently be priced at $5.70 per MMBTU). The price was generally believed to reflect the Soviet keenness to make progress with the project, even if this meant accepting less than their original target. This Heads of Agreement has not so far been turned into a full contract.

France. An agreement was reached in January under which the French will import 8 bcm of gas per annum over 25 years from 1984. No price has been revealed; but we understand the French settled for a slightly *lower* price than that agreed by the FRG to take account of the additional transmission costs. A figure of 8 bcm is lower than the original amount of 10 bcm which the French were intending to take. This follows a French re-assessment of the level of dependence on Soviet gas which they regard as acceptable. The agreement is subject to final approval by the French Government. When the pipeline is fully operational, Soviet gas supplies to France and the FRG will amount to 25 percent of gas consumption and 4 percent of total energy consumption.

Italy. Although there have been reports that agreement has been reached at

---

[1] Peter Heap, Head of the Energy, Science and Space Department, FCO; William Adams, Assistant Under-Secretary of State.
[2] Not printed.
[3] M=1,000.

UK-Soviet Relations, 1979-82

technical level between the Italian gas utility SNAM and Soyuzgasexport the Italians continue to maintain that the 'pause for reflection' still holds good. Now that the French have signed an agreement the Italian Government, which is facing Parliamentary opposition to the project, may decide that they should, if they are to remain in the running for future contracts, follow suit. They are expected to take 8.5 bcm per annum.

Other West European Countries. The other European countries which had planned to take Soviet gas, the Netherlands, Belgium, Luxembourg, Austria and Switzerland continue to delay negotiations with the Soviet Union. There has been no suggestion, however, that this will lead to any decisions against participation in the project. The Spanish Government has recently taken a decision in principle to import Soviet gas at a level of about 4 bcm per annum. A major technical problem is the absence of a pipeline link between Spain and France. The French have said that if the Spanish want a pipeline to the French frontier, then Spain should pay for it: the Spanish, understandably, have difficulty with this idea.

Implications

4. These developments are still in accord with the main conclusion in the JIC paper—'Western Dependence on Soviet Energy'[4]—that dependence on Soviet gas 'should not involve an unacceptable risk to Western coherence and freedom of action'. The JIC also assessed that by 1990 in overall terms Western European dependence on Soviet energy would decline from about 5 percent of total energy consumption to about 3 percent, as Soviet oil exports fall. By 1990 only gas would be imported from the Soviet Union. Dependence within NATO Europe on Soviet gas would then reach some 20 percent of total gas consumption. However, if, as some forecasters predict, the level of gas demand in Western Europe is lower over the next 20 years than was originally forecast, then Western European dependence on Soviet imports will rise proportionately. But this should be set against the conservation of indigenous European gas supplies (particularly Dutch Gas), which the import of Soviet gas will allow. The existence of these supplies will leave Europe in a strong position to withstand a cut-off.

5. France and the FRG hope that the favourable prices obtained in their agreements with the Soviet Union will have the additional benefit of strengthening their hands in their negotiations for gas supplies from other sources. The French appear to be confident that the Soviet deal will enable them to strike a better deal with Algeria. If so, the Italians would be keen to follow suit. It would be logical for the Algerians, faced with a European surplus of gas supplies by 1990 to moderate their line on prices for long term export contracts. But there is no sign at present of their backing off their aim that gas prices should have parity with crude oil prices.

6. A surplus, brought about by Soviet gas exports, could also have implications for the UK. Pressures to export gas to Europe would presumably diminish; while our access to Norwegian gas (which, as mentioned in paragraph 2 above, is more expensive than Soviet gas) could improve if its attraction to continental Europe decreases.

7. The US can be expected to remain concerned about the pipeline and the level of European dependence on Soviet gas supplies.[5] It would be useful in future

---

[4] Not printed.

[5] Sir N. Henderson reported that the Americans considered the pipeline a 'grave error', not necessarily because it would increase Western European energy dependence upon the Soviet Union but because it would provide the Soviet Union with so much hard currency. As a consequence the

17 December 1981 – 9 December 1982

discussions to bring out the point that imports from the USSR will enable European gas supplies to be conserved for longer term and contingent use. The points in paragraphs 5 and 6 could be used defensively, although they are unlikely to cut much ice with the Americans. The latter are also likely to continue to press their requests for the UK and Norway to install oil and gas surge capacity in the North Sea against the contingency of a cut off of Soviet supplies. We should continue to resist this on economic as well as technical grounds.

P. W. HEAP

US administration was determined to do everything within their power to prevent the Europeans from constructing the pipeline (Washington telegram No. 386 of 5 February, RS 014/2).

No. 130

Record of meeting between Lord Trefgarne and the Soviet Ambassador, 5 February 1982, 11.45 a.m.
Restricted (ENS 020/5)

Present:
Lord Trefgarne   HE Mr V. I. Popov
Mr J. Macgregor   Mr Ouspensky
Mr N. Sheinwald

1. *Lord Trefgarne* said that the Ambassador would know HMG's views and those of our NATO allies concerning Soviet involvement in the recent events in Poland. These views had been made public in the Communiqué following the meeting of Foreign Ministers of the Ten on 4 January and of Foreign Ministers of the North Atlantic Alliance on 11 January.[1] We had deplored the sustained campaign mounted by the Soviet Union against the Polish people's efforts for national renewal and reform, and its active support for the subsequent systematic suppression of those efforts. We had called upon the Soviet Union to respect Poland's fundamental right to solve its own problems free from foreign interference and to respect the clear desire of the Polish people for national renewal and reform. We regretted that there had been no sign of any cessation of Soviet pressure on Poland.

2. Against this background, Lord Trefgarne had asked the Soviet Ambassador to call in order to inform him of the measures HMG had decided to adopt towards the Soviet Union. They were as follows:

(*a*) The free travel area for Soviet officials in London would be reduced from 35 to 25 miles;

(*b*) Activity under four bilateral technical cooperation agreements would be reduced;

(*c*) A licensing system had been introduced which controlled Soviet Union factory ships 'trans-shipping' fish caught in United Kingdom waters; and

(*d*) We were giving notice of our intention to re-negotiate the terms of the 1968 Anglo-Soviet Treaty on Merchant Navigation.

[1] See No. 124, note 2.

UK-Soviet Relations, 1979-82

3. Lord Trefgarne handed the Soviet Ambassador a Note (attached)[2] on travel restrictions and asked him to draw its contents to the attention of his authorities and all Soviet personnel subject to the travel notification scheme. The reduction of the free travel area was being implemented with immediate effect. Lord Trefgarne continued that the new radius would bring our practice more into line with the restrictions placed on our travel in Moscow. He pointed out, however, that in view of the large prohibited areas in Moscow within the free travel zone, the total free area in London would still be significantly larger. In addition it had been noted that travel within the so-called open areas of the Soviet Union was, in practice, much restricted by refusal of permission for journeys by members of our staff on what were described as temporary grounds. There were also large areas of the Soviet Union permanently closed to foreigners. Lord Trefgarne said that we would keep travel restrictions in Britain under review in light of future Soviet practices.

4. Lord Trefgarne handed the Soviet Ambassador a *bout de papier* (attached)[2] which, he said, gave notice of HMG's intention to re-negotiate the terms of the bilateral Treaty on Merchant Navigation. We regarded this as an important and urgent requirement.

5. The *Soviet Ambassador* said that he was surprised by Lord Trefgarne's treatment of this question. He resolutely rejected as unfounded the linkage which the Minister had made. The question of Poland had nothing to do with the measures Lord Trefgarne had just announced. Poland was a sovereign state and adopted its decisions by itself. These decisions were taken by the highest organs of Poland's state power. Efforts to attribute to the Soviet Union some form of complicity in events in Poland were an attempt to shift to others responsibility for the actions of Western countries which had, for a long time and in various ways, interfered in Poland's affairs. To the extent that the Polish problem existed, it was a problem of Western interference in Poland's affairs. Furthermore, events in Poland were being used as a means to poison the atmosphere of international dialogue. The Ambassador had thought that the United Kingdom supported such dialogue. The West was using Poland to divert attention away from questions of disarmament, war and peace.

6. Mr Popov stated that the measures conveyed by Lord Trefgarne were discriminatory. He had to express his regret that Britain had not learnt the lessons of the past. It was well known that it was futile to talk to the Soviet Union in such language. The measures could only damage British interests and completely contradicted the repeated statements of senior FCO representatives that Britain wished to develop relations with the Soviet Union. The measures were totally unfounded and contradicted existing understandings between Great Britain and the USSR, the UN Charter and the Helsinki Final Act. Mr Popov quoted from Article 9 of Chapter 1 of the Helsinki Final Act concerning 'Cooperation among States' in which participating states undertook to develop their cooperation as equals, to promote understanding and confidence, and friendly and good neighbourly relations among themselves. The parties had also pledged themselves to cooperate in the economic, scientific, technological, social, cultural and humanitarian fields.

7. The Ambassador continued that the United Kingdom's unilateral curtailment of ties which had developed over the decades would harm British interests. It was easier to cut than to restore such links.

8. There was, he said, no foundation whatsoever in the argument concerning the

---

[2] Not printed.

17 December 1981 – 9 December 1982

move to restrict the movements of Soviet diplomats in London. This reduced, even further, the possibilities for travel, for example to the Ambassador's country residence (sic) and, so far as he understood, certain areas in London would also now be restricted. There was no justification for this, and it contradicted understandings between the two countries.

9. In conclusion, the Soviet Ambassador emphasized that the responsibility for these actions and consequences lay with the British Government alone.

10. The meeting ended at 12.05.

No. 131

Teleletter from Mr Sheinwald to Mr Wood (Moscow), 11 February 1982
Confidential (ENS 020/5)

[No salutation]
Anglo-Soviet Relations

1. Keline's[1] departure has prompted a re-shuffle in the Soviet Embassy. Dolgov has been promoted to Minister-Counsellor and his previous job as Counsellor on the Anglo-Soviet side has gone to Posilyagin (who we had first imagined would be placed on the British foreign policy side of the Embassy). Dolgov brought Posilyagin in to see Nigel Broomfield on 9 February for an introductory call. I was also present.

2. They used the call, which [was] set up before the LPS' Parliamentary statement on 5 February,[2] to probe our views on the prospects for Anglo-Soviet relations. In brief, Nigel made the following points:

(*a*) Unlike some others, we did not disguise our views, on international or bilateral matters. This might be disagreeable to the extent that it provoked disagreement but it was salutary in the long run for the Russians to know exactly what we thought.

(*b*) Poland had dealt a severe blow to East/West confidence. Without such confidence or mutual trust relations would inevitably be more strained and less productive. We noted that the Soviet Union took a fundamentally different view from ourselves and our Western partners about events in Poland, their causes and their relation to the Helsinki Final Act. The opposing views would no doubt be aired at Madrid. But the Soviet Union should be under no illusions that until it gave grounds for restoring trust by the exercise of restraint, the prospect for concrete agreements, in which either side trusted the other to fulfil its commitments, would remain bleak.

(*c*) It would take time to recreate the necessary confidence. In the meantime there might be a lean period in Anglo-Soviet relations before both sides were able to identify areas where movement or contact would be useful. This had happened too following Afghanistan.

3. Dolgov for his part said he was more optimistic. The Soviet Union still wanted political dialogue with Britain, and hoped it would continue. He referred to Popov's recent conversation with Julian Bullard (on 28 January, at which Popov

---

[1] Vladimir Keline, Charge d'Affairs, Soviet Embassy, London.
[2] On 5 February, the Lord Privy Seal, Humphrey Atkins, informed Parliament of the measures HMG had adopted in response to the introduction of martial law in Poland (see No. 130).

UK-Soviet Relations, 1979-82

had mentioned Zemskov's prospective visit).[3] Posilyagin, not content with the polished oblique approach, then asked directly about Zemskov's visit. Nigel Broomfield said that we were giving this some thought. In reply to his question, Posilyagin said that Zemskov was about to return from his month's holiday outside Moscow, and was well.

4. Dolgov's pitch (i.e. dialogue to continue, more of the same generally) duplicates on the political side of the relationship the reaction in other areas to last week's announcement of measures. The scientific section of the Soviet Embassy here were in touch early this week with the Departments of the Environment and of Health to fix up meetings to discuss the future programme. DOE have stalled, but Joe Hallowell will be seeing them later this week and will convey personally the line given in his recent telegram to Moscow. It would appear therefore that the Soviet tactic will be to proceed on a business as usual basis and note for future reference each instance where the British partner was unwilling to reciprocate. It will, in such circumstances, be important to maintain the maximum unity on the Western side in terms of our responses over visits, joint commissions etc. We will be working in the Eastern European working group in POCO and the Political Committee to get the best result we can.

5. Posilyagin, on this first sighting, seemed pleasant enough and his 2ED[4] background will serve him well. But he does not have Dolgov's highly anglicised manner, nor as yet Dolgov's ability to use the carefully telegraphed language of Anglo-Soviet relations. Perhaps his natural disposition is towards directness.

6. We shall be writing separately about Zemskov's visit in time for the Ambassador's lunch with him next week.

N. E. SHEINWALD

[3] Not printed (see No. 113, para 12).
[4] Second European Department, Soviet MFA.

No. 132

Minute from Mr Bullard to Mr Broomfield, 19 February 1982
Confidential (ENS 020/5)

Anglo-Soviet Relations

1. Mr Dolgov, now Minister-Counsellor at the Soviet Embassy, called on me this morning, accompanied by Ivanov as note taker.

2. Dolgov had found a sentence in the Secretary of State's recent speech in Harrogate about the need to continue dialogue.[1] He said that this was also the Soviet view and wanted to know what proposals we had to make.

3. I said that the Secretary of State had come to Harrogate fresh from Madrid, where the prospects for the conference looked less rosy than they had been in December.[2] He had no doubt wanted to make it plain that, whatever might happen in Madrid, the principle of East/West dialogue was one to which we attached importance. This applied also to the INF talks, notwithstanding some differing voices in the West.

[1] At the Young Conservatives' Annual Conference, 14-16 February.
[2] The first plenary session of the CSCE Review Conference opened in Madrid on 9 February.

17 December 1981 – 9 December 1982

4. Coming down to brass tacks, I said that the Soviet Embassy must understand the degree of shock caused in Britain and elsewhere by the events in Poland. The crisis there was still dominating the foreground and affecting East/West relations, of which Anglo-Soviet relations were a part. We had therefore judged it wise to send a message to Zemskov that we did not think that March would be appropriate for the proposed consultations. I would not like to offer a new date: it depended largely on the course of events in Poland, which Dolgov would be better able to predict than I was.

5. He made only a very half-hearted attempt to argue first that the Soviet Union was not involved in any way in Poland; and second, that Anglo-Soviet contacts should continue regardless. I rejected the first point and said that the second was unfortunately impossible.

6. On the way out Dolgov gave me the Ambassador's compliments and asked whether I would be willing to be his guest at lunch or dinner, perhaps with one or two colleagues. I accepted in principle, but suggested that the Soviet Embassy should wait until the situation in Madrid had clarified before ringing up to remind us.

J. L. BULLARD

No. 133

Record of a meeting between Lord Trefgarne and the Soviet Ambassador, 22 February 1982, 12 p.m.
Confidential (ENS 020/5)

Present:
Lord Trefgarne   Mr Popov
Mr Macgregor   Mr Ouspenski

1. After an exchange of courtesies *Mr Popov* said that he wished to raise two points concerned with arms control and disarmament. The first was to bring Lord Trefgarne's attention to a draft agreement on Mutual Reduction of Forces and Armaments which had been tabled in Vienna by the Soviet Union, GDR, Poland and Czechoslovakia. The draft's main aim was a reduction in Soviet and American forces in Central Europe and a commitment by both sides to maintaining the new reduced level of forces in Central Europe for the duration of the agreement, i.e. 3 years. The draft also suggested *inter alia* the prior notification of all movements of land forces involving more than 20,000 men and other large scale exercises in Central Europe, and the establishment of a temporary joint commission to administer these arrangements.

2. Mr Popov said that the draft would provide a balanced basis for proceeding in Vienna, and was designed to overcome the present stalemate there. It asked nothing of the Western countries which the Soviet Union itself was not prepared to carry out. The Soviet Union hoped that the United Kingdom would give the paper constructive consideration, and anticipated UK support for the proposal in Vienna.

3. *Lord Trefgarne* assured the Ambassador that the Western Alliance was committed to achieving agreement on MBFR, which would enhance mutual security in Central Europe at reduced force levels. The Soviet draft would be

UK-Soviet Relations, 1979-82

studied with care but since it had been put forward so recently it would take some time to give a considered response. On first sight, it would appear that an agreement on the lines proposed would be defective as regards data and Associated Measures i.e. verification; the Soviet draft appeared to contain no new ideas to solve these problems. The UK side had put forward a paper in 1979 proposing solutions to the verification question. It was unfortunate that these seemed not to have been taken into account during the drafting of the Soviet paper.

4. *Mr Popov* said that the Vienna talks had been under way for 8 years, and that it was now time for some real progress to be made. Given the necessary political will, results could be achieved speedily. As to the problem of data, figures had been exchanged in 1976 and 1980, but these still remained on the table.

5. Mr Popov said that the second point he wished to raise was the dismay with which the Soviet Union viewed the US decision to commence production of a new generation of chemical weapons. This decision rekindled the arms race. The Ambassador referred to a TASS statement on 18 February.

6. *Lord Trefgarne* replied that the US decision was understandable, in view of the massive Soviet capability in chemical weaponry. The United States Government had restated its commitment to an overall ban on chemical weapons. The UK had been pursuing such a comprehensive ban in Geneva for some time. He hoped that the Soviet Government would study with care the paper on verification problems tabled by the UK delegation in Geneva on 18 February. It would be a mark of good faith if the Soviet Government would facilitate access by members of the UN Experts Group to areas in which it had been alleged that toxin weapons had been used.

7. *Mr Popov* replied that the Soviet Union had never used chemical weapons, whereas the United States had used them frequently in Indo-China. The alleged incident in the Soviet Union had no foundation whatsoever, as had been explained many times before in the past.[1] The Soviet Union had gone on record as being in favour of banning chemical weapons. He had not seen the UK proposal but assured Lord Trefgarne that it would be studied closely.

8. The meeting ended at 12.35 p.m.[2]

---

[1] See No. 90, note 6.

[2] Reflecting on the meeting in a note of 27 February, Mr Sheinwald thought the Russians had oversold themselves by requesting a ministerial appointment for a piece of business that should have been conducted at departmental level. He advocated in future offering ministers only if the issue was known to be of real importance or urgency.

No. 134

Paper by Mr Mallaby on the Western Response to the Polish Crisis: Assessment and Prospects, 1 March 1982[1]

Confidential (RS 014/2)

1. This paper describes the West's political aims in the Polish crisis and the measures adopted in pursuit of them, and examines the likely consequences for Poland and the Soviet Union, for East/West relations and finally for the Allies

---

[1] An earlier version of this paper was discussed at a DUS's meeting on 23 February. This revised version, by Mr Mallaby, was seen by EESD, ERD, the Defence Department and ECD(E). It was again discussed at the DUS's meeting on 2 March.

17 December 1981 – 9 December 1982

themselves.

I. *Western Aims: Poland*

2. The West would ideally like to promote a return to Renewal[2] in Poland. What they *can* seek to do by measures towards Poland is to increase the pressures on Jaruzelski to relax the repression and to leave elements of the Renewal in place, in the hope that liberalisation may revive at some future time. The West also wants the burden of supporting Poland's economy to fall to the greatest extent possible upon the Soviet Union and CMEA and, unless economic and political circumstances change, to limit further Western economic exposure.

3. In pursuit of their political aims the Allies have called for the lifting of martial law, the release of those detained and the restoration of genuine dialogue between the Government, the Church and the legitimate representatives of Solidarity. These requirements have been stated in general terms, so that the West is in a position to say whether Jaruzelski's future actions satisfy them. The UK has backed these demands with the measures towards Poland listed in Annex A.[3]

II. *Western Aims: USSR*

4. The West has no single position on this aspect. The Americans sometimes seem to have very ambitious ideas about what can be achieved by pressure on the Soviet Union. For instance, Mr Haig in a letter of 26 January to Lord Carrington[3] wrote 'the stakes go far beyond Poland and our economic ties to the East. They extend to the very basis for constructive dialogue with the Soviet Union and its allies in every area'. This may be inconsistent not only with continued US grain sales to the Soviet Union but also with the European view that arms control negotiations remain desirable and that East/West trade can be to mutual advantage and should not be halted. Mr Haig also wrote that 'a secure future can be assured only when the Soviet Union recognises . . . that it is in its interests to accept peaceful change within an internationally acceptable framework of law and obligation in Eastern Europe'. This is unrealistic.

5. The European governments, for their part, would probably see the purpose of their measures against the Soviet Union as being to give the latter such motives as we can for allowing the repression in Poland to be reduced and some elements of the Renewal to endure; though some Europeans regard economic sanctions against the Soviet Union in present circumstances as inappropriate, partly because they may be ineffective, partly because of doubts about the principle of applying sanctions where vital interests are at stake, and partly because of a continuing belief in the principles of détente.

6. However the Americans and the Europeans (less Greece) would agree on four further purposes: to discourage the Soviet Union from invading Poland; to achieve a reasonably united response and thus prevent the Soviet Union's crisis in Poland from becoming a crisis of Western unity; to respond to the abhorrence in Western public opinion at Soviet complicity in the clampdown in Poland; and to add somewhat to the factors that may argue in Moscow against expansionism and for restraint in foreign policy in future.

7. The measures taken by the UK against the Soviet Union are listed in Annex B.[3]

III. *The Effects of the Western Measures*

8. The measures have had a number of short-term effects. Because of the suspension of new credit to Poland, livestock production has been hit by a shortage

---

[2] The process of political change that took place in Poland during 1980-81.

[3] Not printed.

UK-Soviet Relations, 1979-82

of food grains and industrial production by a shortage of Western components and spares. Jaruzelski, unlike Husak in Czechoslovakia after 1968, will be unable to use gestures to the consumer in order to distract the population's attention from the repression. The measures will also have unwelcome side-effects. The Poles will look to the Soviet Union and other CMEA countries to make good the shortages and provide new credits. This will increase still further Soviet leverage on Poland.[4]

9. As regards the Soviet Union, our measures have demonstrated that the West holds Moscow accountable for developments in Poland and that such Soviet actions have a significant effect on East/West relations. Press articles and public statements in the Soviet Union suggest that this message has been clearly registered and that the Russians are disappointed at the degree of unity that the NATO countries have so far displayed. This was also the impression gained by Mr Haig when he last met Mr Gromyko.

IV. *The Prospects for Poland and Eastern Europe*

10. Martial law has ended the Polish Renewal without a breakdown in public order. But passive resistance and resentment persist and could still break out in active resistance. The Polish authorities might be able to deal with this. If not, the Soviet Union would no doubt intervene militarily.

11. There is no prospect in the foreseeable future of a return to genuine Renewal. But Poland in 1982 is not Czechoslovakia in 1968. The national temperament and the role of the Church will see to that, even if the regime manages somewhat to curtail the political voice of the latter. Poland will not be reconciled to Soviet domination. It has resisted it at frequent intervals (1956, 1968, 1970, 1980/81) and will remain a weak link in the Soviet glacis as well as a drain on the Soviet economy. The political weakness of the Soviet grip in Eastern Europe has again been demonstrated, but so also has Soviet determination to maintain that grip. The Soviet domination of the region is unnatural and unpopular, but unlikely to end for many years. There will be crises again, in Poland or elsewhere in Eastern Europe.

12. There is no prospect of any early recovery of the Polish economy after a fall of 13 percent in output last year. Output could stabilise at current levels, provided that assistance from the Soviet Union and other CMEA partners continued, or could decline further.

13. Even if Poland's debt repayments due in 1982 are rescheduled, the country will need about $4.7 billion in new credit in 1982 to meet residual debt service payments. Neither the West nor the USSR, or the two together, are likely to provide this very large sum. (Both Haig and Herr Genscher have referred to the possibility of large scale economic aid if the process of renewal is resumed. But to be of any real attraction to the Poles the sums involved would have to be significantly greater than $4.7 billion.) Before long, therefore, the Poles will almost certainly give up such attempts as they are making to meet repayments on the debt. This would probably enable them to keep their economy going at a depressed level by trading on a cash basis. But it would also produce a formal default or a moratorium. It would then be out of the question for Western countries to resume export credits. It would also be very difficult for many reasons to provide governmental financial aid to Poland.

---

[4] Commenting on an earlier draft Mr Green, of the Economic Relations Department, noted 'we must be very careful not to exaggerate the likely effects of our measures against Poland. Mr Wilson made himself look extremely foolish over Rhodesia; we must not place our own Ministers in a similar position in 6-12 months time'.

17 December 1981 – 9 December 1982

14. However, in so far as, and for as long as, Jaruzelski believes there is the possibility of Western financial assistance, he may be somewhat more inclined than he would otherwise be to moderate repression when he feels it safe to do so. (Mr Haig's and Herr Genscher's references to possible aid may help in this connection.)

15. This rather gloomy analysis suggests four considerations for policy:

(*a*) Ideas of Marshall Plans for Poland would be too costly to merit serious consideration; although references to them may serve some political purpose.

(*b*) Once Poland has defaulted, Jaruzelski is likely to realise that prospects for Western help are minimal and any remaining leverage will be correspondingly reduced.

(*c*) The Poles have asked for negotiations about rescheduling in 1982. The Americans in their present mood are likely to refuse. The Europeans may wish to agree, in order to avoid a disorderly default with harmful effects on banking confidence. (These issues will be discussed at a meeting of creditors alone, probably on March 18.)

(*d*) Jaruzelski predictably has blamed the Western measures for making the situation worse in Poland. If widespread hunger develops, voices in the West may accuse governments of having precipitated it by withholding credit. Providing humanitarian aid will help to answer this charge, but we should avoid giving it all now, with nothing left to give should conditions in Poland deteriorate. We must also bear in mind that it will not amount to more than a fraction of the food assistance given in 1981/82.

V. *The Effect on East /West Relations*

16. With repression likely to continue for many months in Poland the outlook for East/West relations is bleak. Many kinds of East/West contacts and exchanges, already cut back after the invasion of Afghanistan, will be further reduced. The recent resumption of contact between the superpowers, consisting of the INF talks and the regular meetings between Messrs Haig and Gromyko, is now unlikely for some time to develop further; indeed it may regress.

17. The *CSCE Meeting* in Madrid may still be suspended until the autumn. Prospects thereafter are uncertain. Mr Haig has suggested that the Polish crisis may prove fatal to the CSCE process. But in the European view, and nominally in the American also, it is in the interests of the West that this process should continue, as a long term influence for change in Eastern Europe. The East Europeans also have an interest in the resumption of the process, once Poland is no longer a dominant issue in Europe. The neutral and non-aligned countries will almost certainly favour resumption in due course. The Soviet position may be as uncertain as the American.

18. In *arms control*, developments which we had hoped would have a positive influence on public opinion in Western Europe—the beginning of START and moves towards a CDE—have already been delayed. The interests of the European governments point towards beginning the START negotiations as soon as possible. For the moment, the US administration is still talking of announcing a date at the NATO Summit on 10 June. But US public opinion may remain critical of such a move for many months, so the Europeans should not relax the pressure. If the chances of an early beginning to START fade, the Europeans should concentrate on persuading the US to press on with the INF negotiations, despite the general deterioration of other areas of East/West relations. This case may become increasingly hard to make in Washington. Two arguments which the Europeans

UK-Soviet Relations, 1979-82

might use are that the Soviet Union, having an interest in East/West business as usual, might conceivably be brought to make limited concessions in INF; and that a complete shutdown in East/West business would remove a factor for restraint in Moscow. If the Americans insist on some further negative move in the field of arms control, it would be preferable to interrupt MBFR than INF.

19. If the situation in Poland were to deteriorate, with increased violence and repression, the West would have to consider further measures and East/West relations would suffer more. A Soviet invasion of Poland would cause the Americans to interrupt the INF negotiations. It might also put an end to the gas pipeline contract. East/West relations would then reach their lowest ebb for many years.

VI. *The Effects on the Western Alliance*

20. The US measures against Poland caused relatively few immediate problems for the Europeans, although they were taken largely in response to domestic pressures and after little consultation with allies. The US measures against the Soviet Union were taken without consultation and apparently without calculating their effect on the Europeans. This contributed to deep strains in the West over Poland. An open clash has so far been averted, but is still very possible. Since the US is primarily an agricultural exporter to the Soviet Union, and Western Europe primarily an industrial exporter, it is not surprising that the greatest difficulty has concerned economic measures towards the USSR. If the Americans, under continuing domestic political pressure and in order to exert political leverage at a time of Soviet economic weakness, were to take further unilateral measures, or to refuse to exempt existing European contracts from their measures of 29 December 1981, the resulting transatlantic row could be very serious. It might well stimulate anti-Americanism in Europe and isolationism in America. The prospect of carrying out INF deployments, especially in Germany, might be prejudiced and talk of US troop withdrawals from Europe could spread.

21. Intensive consultation, such as Britain has been promoting, is the main tool for averting such a row. But the NATO Summit provides a major opportunity to reassert and project the unity of the Alliance. The UK is therefore exploring the idea of a Summit Declaration setting out an overall Alliance policy in East/West relations. Whether this can be negotiated will become clear as discussion proceeds, but initial signs are hopeful. The text would no doubt have to paper over some differences. But, by recording agreement on major areas of the subject, it might be able to reduce the scope for future disagreements.

VII. *Conclusions*

22. (*a*) No significant part of the Polish Renewal is likely to survive the present clampdown. Repression will continue for many months. Active resistance may possibly grow. Soviet invasion is still possible. Poland will remain a weak and troublesome province in the Soviet empire.

(*b*) Western measures towards Poland and the Soviet Union cannot reverse the repression. But in the short term the measures have some effect. And in so far as Jaruzelski believes there is a possibility of further Western financial assistance he will have a somewhat greater interest in relaxation than would otherwise be the case.

(*c*) Poland is virtually certain to default on its debts. Thereafter there will probably be no question of new Western money for Poland, with a corresponding lessening of influence on Jaruzelski.

(*d*) East/West relations face a bleak period. The Europeans should concentrate, in

17 December 1981 – 9 December 1982

discussion with the Americans, on arguing for START to begin and the INF talks to continue.

(*e*) There is still a serious risk of a Western split about Poland. The UK should continue to act as a catalyst for unity, concentrating initially on persuading the Americans to refrain from further unilateral measures and to exempt existing European contracts from the US measures of 29 December and on convincing the US that official credit to the USSR should not be suspended in the short term.

(*f*) The NATO Summit should be used to project Alliance unity. It is worth trying to negotiate a Declaration about policy in East/West relations.

No. 135

Submission from Mr Broomfield to Mr Goodison, 2 March 1982
Confidential (ENS 020/5)

Anglo-Soviet Relations

1. It may be worth attempting to look at our relations with the Soviet Union through the other end of the telescope to see what the picture might look like to an official Soviet observer.

2. I attach a note on measures we have taken or are about to take.[1] All of them have been taken for good reasons, even if some of the reasons were somewhat peripheral to Anglo/Soviet relations. But their cumulative effect will last for some while. We have yet to get into the maritime treaty renegotiation, nor have we yet introduced discriminatory licensing against Soviet fish factory ships.

3. I think there are a number of points which can be made:

(*a*) although not all our recent moves have been caused by events in Poland, that is how they will probably look to the Russians. Popov immediately related the expulsion of Zadneprovsky[2] to our Polish measures;

(*b*) even though a number of our allies have now announced measures against the Soviet Union, the UK contribution stands out, because of both its timing and scope, and because some of our partners have made it known that they were reluctantly doing the minimum possible. (See Abrasimov's predictable comments to Sir J. Taylor, BMG telno. 20);[3]

(*c*) as a result of the measures adopted after Afghanistan and now Poland, the Anglo/Soviet relationship has been stripped of any fat. If a situation short of a Soviet military intervention were to arise requiring politically demonstrative action, we would have to move to termination of agreements under which activities have already been suspended, or action in areas previously deliberately excluded (e.g. the Cultural Agreement) or measures of a type more appropriate to Soviet military action, e.g. trade embargo, arbitrary or large-scale expulsions of Soviet officials.

4. The Russians will of course continue to have an interest in the UK even when our bilateral relations are bad. They recognise that the UK is an influential member of the international community. They know that our views carry weight with the

---

[1] Not printed (see Nos. 127 and 130).

[2] Vadim Zadneprovsky, a KGB officer attached to the Soviet Trade Delegation in Highgate, was expelled from Britain on 22 February for attempting to obtain classified information through agents.

[3] Not printed.

UK-Soviet Relations, 1979-82

Americans, in the European Community and in NATO; and they are also interested in us as a nuclear power and as a permanent member of the Security Council. The potential value to them of a dialogue with us increases at times when their relations with the US are strained.

5. It does not, however, follow that Anglo/Soviet bilateral relations are unimportant. We have a continuing interest in a realistic and reasonably substantial political dialogue with the Soviet Union. Such a dialogue cannot be purely multilateral and confined to discussions in New York or Geneva. We also need bilateral exchanges, not for their own sake, but in order to put over our views at senior levels and obtain an authoritative account of Soviet thinking at first hand. This is important to our position as informed observers of Soviet policy in discussions with our Allies, in particular the French, Germans and Americans, and helps us at times in attempts to bridge transatlantic differences. Thus far, despite the thinning down of Anglo/Soviet relations since Afghanistan, we have still managed to retain Soviet interest in political discussions on what, for them, have been unpromising themes (e.g. they accepted a visit by Lord Carrington in July last year to present the Afghanistan initiative).[4]

6. We also have other objectives. One of them is to increase British exports to the Soviet Union, within whatever framework emerges from the debate on non-undermining and the long term conduct of East/West economic relations. Although trade with the Soviet Union represents only 1 percent of our total foreign trade, some British firms and particular industries would be badly hurt if, for political reasons, the Russians were further to cut down their allocation of contracts to Britain.

7. Thus I believe both our political and economic interests could be damaged if the Russians formed the view that we had adopted a totally negative attitude towards Anglo/Soviet bilateral relations. It follows that we must take care to avoid completely demolishing the bilateral framework. Soviet willingness to talk at a high level depends in part on a degree of structural underpinning. Lord Carrington's visit last year, for example, although not strictly bilateral and very much 'in the context of the European Council proposals on Afghanistan', was from the Soviet point of view under-pinned by other contacts like Mr Bullard's meetings in Moscow in March[5] and discussions between Sir C. Keeble and Gromyko and Popov's meetings here.

8. I would therefore suggest that, without in any way modifying our overall policy, we might look at ways of ensuring that the Russians did not draw the conclusion that we have given up any attempt to achieve a measured and constructive approach to bilateral relations. For this reason I think it important that the *Joint Commission Meeting* should go ahead and be preceded by the *Economic and Industrial Review*. I also suggest that we might consider putting dates to the Russians in about four weeks time for a *visit by Zemskov* in November or so. At a technical level I would hope that in a few weeks time we may be able to take forward the *visa discussions*. Finally at the level of our *relations with the Soviet Embassy here* I think it is helpful that you and Mr Bullard plan to attend the introductory cocktails for Mr Dolgov and Mr Posilyagin today and it would also be helpful if Mr Bullard were able to have a lunch with the Soviet Ambassador in the next few weeks thereafter.

N. H. R. A. BROOMFIELD

[4] No. 107.
[5] No. 90.

17 December 1981 – 9 December 1982

No. 136

Minute from Mr Goodison to Mr Bullard, 2 March 1982
Confidential (ENS 020/5)

1. I agree with Mr Broomfield[1] that the cumulative effect of the measures we have taken or are taking may be misjudged by Soviet analysts. I agree that we have a difficult task if we are to ensure, and to make it clear to the Russians, that our current actions are reversible and limited in intention and scope. I agree that we must not let them think we are totally negative.

2. Part of the trouble is that since a major motive of our current policy is to influence United States opinion, inside and outside the Administration, we have been obliged to give the measures connected with Poland considerable publicity. This adds to their force as negative signals.

3. It looks as if some of the measures are not in fact going to add up to very much, e.g. licensing of fish factory ships, and even Community action on Soviet exports, where we are having second thoughts on grounds of economic self-interest. But we cannot tell the Russians that, and we still do not want to make any positive gesture (like reaching agreement on double taxation) which will receive publicity. Inviting Mr Zemskov to come in November is a risk; we may still not want him by then. We must concentrate on gestures which do not attract public attention, like most of those suggested by Mr Broomfield. (In this connection, I should note that I have been obliged to refuse an invitation to a musical evening on 15 March from the Soviet Ambassador.)

4. But there is a limit to the extent to which we can distance ourselves from American policy, and we may yet be forced into inflicting further damage on Anglo-Soviet relations.

A. C. GOODISON

[1] See No. 135.

No. 137

Minute from Mr Bullard to Mr Macgregor, 4 March 1982
Confidential (ENS 020/5)

Anglo-Soviet Relations

1. I have some reservations on points of detail in Mr Broomfield's minute of 2 March:[1]

(*a*) I do not believe for a moment that the Soviet Ambassador supposes that our expulsion of Zadneprovsky, an obscure official in the Soviet Trade Delegation at Highgate, has anything to do with events in Poland. He pretended to believe this because this fitted conveniently into the show of bluster which was his only possible response to my communication;

(*b*) The Soviet Ambassador in East Berlin has been there on and off for many years and his periodic statements on Anglo-Soviet relations, of which he knows

[1] No.135.

UK-Soviet Relations, 1979-82

nothing, have always been a mere gramophone record and a pretty dull one at that.

On the whole I am relieved that the British contribution to measures against the Soviet Union in the Polish context has not been more conspicuous.

2. But I strongly endorse Mr Broomfield's main thesis that Anglo-Soviet relations matter, for the reasons he gives; and that we are getting close to the point where there is too little substance left in these relations to give the Russians even a marginal incentive for good behaviour or to give us further weapons for use e.g. in the event of a Soviet military occupation of Poland.

3. It follows that I also endorse Mr Broomfield's point about the need to intersperse our current disapproving line with at least one or two concrete signs of interest. I made a point of going early to the Soviet Ambassador's reception last week and of showing a smiling rather than a frowning face. I should have accepted the invitation to some kind of chamber music concert on 15 March if I had not been due to go to Brussels on that day. I would recommend that the technical talks on visa arrangements for the Joint Commission (downgraded from Ministerial to senior official level) should also go ahead. I am not sure about my talks with Zemskov: I would rather have at least some company in the Ten for contact with the Soviet Union at Deputy Foreign Minister level.

4. I hope Lord Trefgarne may have time to read these minutes and give us some guidance.[2]

J. L. BULLARD

[2] See No. 141. The PUS noted his agreement with Mr Bullard.

No. 138

Sir C. Keeble (Moscow) to Lord Carrington, 4 March 1982
Confidential (ENS 020/5)

The Relationship between Britain and the Soviet Union

Summary . . . [1]

My Lord,

1. It is now nearly three years since in my despatch of 3 April, 1979[1] I addressed your predecessor on the question of British-Soviet relations. They were, I said, thin in substance and sour in flavour. No doubt many of my predecessors over the past sixty years have been saying the same thing and arguing, as I did, that there was a case for seeking a more substantial relationship. Now, with the Afghan and Polish crises, we have reached a point at which, beyond the barest formality of diplomatic relations, a trickle of trade and a handful of students, Britain has at present almost no contact with the Soviet Union, the world's second power. I am not sure whether the present state of relations could correctly be described as 'cold war'. The term still sounds over-dramatic, but it is not wholly inappropriate. Whatever terms we use, there is no doubt about the profound change in the climate of relations, albeit less in the underlying realities, which has occurred since the

[1] Not printed.

17 December 1981 – 9 December 1982

high noon of détente. It may be useful to examine how this has come about, the extent to which the present situation is compatible with British interests and the case for trying to change it. If I tread ground which I have trodden before, I ask your indulgence. There are two reasons for treading it again at this time. The first is the current state of East/West relations. The second is the state of the Soviet Union as it begins to condition itself to the prospect of the post-Brezhnev period.

2. If there is one single point which must be stated at the outset, it is the relationship between Britain and the Soviet Union cannot now and indeed never could be determined in isolation, or even on its own merits. It is the product of a whole complex of other policies and relationships, above all the superpower relationship between the Soviet Union and the US. Nevertheless, the fact that it cannot be determined in isolation is no excuse for failing to examine it and, in concert with our allies, if necessary to adapt it.

3. It was seven years ago, in February 1975, that the then Prime Minister, Sir Harold Wilson, engaged in talks with Mr Brezhnev which, in the words of their joint statement 'marked the opening of a new phase in Anglo-Soviet relations and would make a positive contribution towards consolidating international peace and security, especially in Europe'.[2] An agreement on co-operation in the field of medicine and public health was concluded; long-term programmes of economic and industrial co-operation and scientific and technological cooperation were drawn up; a joint declaration on the non-proliferation of nuclear weapons was signed, in which, *inter alia*, the two sides expressed their aim as 'the discontinuance of all test explosions of nuclear weapons for all time'; and, in a separate joint protocol, the two Governments made arrangements for regular political consultations as well as stating their intention that, in the event of 'a situation arising which, in the opinion of the two sides, causes international tension [they] . . . will make contact without delay in order to exchange views on what might be done to improve the situation'. There were references to stable peace, good neighbourliness and co-operation in Europe. There was agreement on the provision of credit, on cultural links, Parliamentary contacts, exchange of visits by representatives of the armed forces, references to the settlement of the Cambodian problem 'without any outside interference' and a commitment to general and complete disarmament. Much of the language was overblown. No doubt many of the aims were unrealistic and it all has, to say the least, a dated feel. Nevertheless, it was not without effect, even as late as 1981. Trade grew. British exports to the Soviet Union were worth £97 million in 1973. In 1977 they were worth £347 million and by 1980 £452 million. Bilateral exchanges flourished and gave evidence of at least a healthy mutual curiosity. Political consultations were held. The deterioration in relations, however, began very quickly. In the summer of 1978 the dissident trials in the Soviet Union brought a sharp reaction from the British Government, including the cancellation of a proposed Soviet Ministerial visit. There was a cautious renewal in 1979 and indeed the Prime Minister's meeting with Mr Kosygin at Moscow airport shortly after she assumed office gave hope for a relationship which, realistically rough though it might be, would not be devoid of substance. It might be said that with your visit to Moscow in the summer of 1981, the commitment to exchange views on situations causing international tension was honoured in the case of Afghanistan. However, relations had in effect been suspended with the Soviet occupation of Afghanistan at the end of 1979 and had

---

[2] For an account of the visit see *DBPO*, Series III, Vol. III.

UK-Soviet Relations, 1979-82

barely begun to resume when the imposition of martial law in Poland brought them to the present minimal level.

4. At each step, the deterioration in relations was brought about by Soviet action—the repression of free opinion within the Soviet Union itself, the occupation of Afghanistan and the insistence that the Polish Government should crush the Solidarity movement—to which the British Government and in varying degrees other governments responded by a reduction in contacts. Considered individually, the measures we and others took were slight in character and, for the most part, ephemeral in duration. They were, however, effective in demonstrating to the Soviet Union that the policies typified by their actions in Afghanistan and Poland were not compatible with the détente spirit of the mid-seventies and, if continued, could prejudice wider Soviet objectives. At the same time, they gradually eliminated the chance of a political dialogue.

5. A Soviet theorist, N. I. Lebedev, analysed the structure of international relations in 1978 in the following terms: 'The struggle between two systems, which represent the axis of international life, conditions not merely the external policy of states with different social structures, but also the development of the whole system of international relations.' In this struggle as Lebedev saw it, there was an obligation on both sides to avoid nuclear war. Bilateral political consultations with Western Governments were the means by which this could be achieved. There is in Soviet political literature much talk of co-operation between states with opposing political systems, but such co-operation is seen as no more than a means of ensuring that the Soviet Union secures its material needs from the West while conducting its struggle without threat to its own security. I believe that over the period since 1978 Western policy has gradually brought the Soviet Union to realise that this concept of détente, in which it remained free to pursue destabilising policies worldwide and repression within its own sphere; to develop military superiority in Europe and a world-wide intervention capacity, while maintaining a stable strategic relationship with the US; and to draw as necessary on Western technology, finance and markets, was not sustainable. The repression of dissent alienated those in Western countries who saw East-West contacts and scientific and cultural relations as a way of bridging the ideological gulf as well as those usually inclined to give the Russians the benefit of doubt. The military build-up produced the NATO response in 1978 and an even more dramatic one from the American electorate in 1980. The direct action in Afghanistan and indirect action in Poland led to a reduction in the availability of Western credit and technology at a time when both were badly needed. All these consequences flowed from the Soviet attempt to have their cake and eat it. I have from time to time commented on the Soviet Union's own recognition, most recently at the 26th Party Congress,[3] of the way in which its position in the world has changed since the heady days of the early 'seventies. The Western response to Soviet measures has seemed a gloomy, essentially negative and unrewarding process—particularly in terms of the role of this Embassy—but there was no realistic alternative and, accompanied as it has been by the widespread condemnation of Soviet policy among Third World countries and by the NATO measures to improve the defence capability of the Alliance, it has made the world a somewhat safer place today than it might have been. The talk of war is high, but the risk of it is, I believe, very low, so far as the two alliances are concerned. So we have reached today's situation in which the

[3] See No. 86.

17 December 1981 – 9 December 1982

essential mutual hostility of the Soviet and Western systems is displayed with full clarity; in which each has the military capacity to annihilate the other; and in which the political relationship is deadlocked. Among the various sets of East-West negotiations the Madrid review of CSCE is close to adjournment in acrimony and in the field of arms control only the Soviet-American negotiations on intermediate-range nuclear weapons in Europe can at present be said to have any substance. It is a chilly situation, but the chill is healthier and safer than the false optimism of 1938 [*sic* ?1978].

6. Is this situation harmful to British interests? In some respects, the answer must be that it does us no great harm. If relations were better we could get a little more business, but the state of the Soviet economy and the essentially autarchic nature of Soviet economic policy are significant limiting factors and even in 1978, when political relations were relatively good, 270 million Russians bought from the UK only one-fifth as much as did six million Swiss. It is primarily on the balance of political interest that the relationship with the Soviet Union needs to be judged. There is little doubt about current Soviet objectives. Their main preoccupation is in the field of internal policy where their need is to improve the economy, particularly in relation to food and consumer goods and to prevent dissent. Externally they wish to maintain at minimum cost political and military control over the empire; and where possible to move the balance of political influence in its favour elsewhere. At the same time they wish to hold the present favourable ratio of nuclear and conventional armaments between the two alliances and, if possible, reduce the absolute level on both sides without losing their existing superiority in many fields. These objectives do not exclude the destabilisation of areas not already under Soviet control or even the physical acquisition of new territory, but I do not believe that the latter at least is a direct objective. If I am right, we can expect Soviet policy in the coming years to involve, as it has done over the past three years, affront to internationally accepted concepts of human rights and acute tension in relations, but not necessarily a direct threat to vital Western interests. On this last point we cannot be certain. We may reasonably assume that a Government which bases its authority upon force in its own country, on force in the areas which it occupies and on a doctrine which sees the Western democracies as an imperialist enemy doomed to inevitable decline and final extinction, will not refrain from challenging vital Western interests if it thinks that it can without risk profit by doing so. We should therefore proceed upon the basis that the principal restraining factor is the demonstration by the West of the ability and will to defend its interests, by political and if necessary by military means, and thus to make it plain that Soviet encroachment will involve excessive risk. It is on this basis that we have reached the present uneasy but relatively stable relationship. In that relationship of continuing tension, one basic premise of Western policy should be that the confrontation should be so controlled as to promote Western interests without incurring a risk of direct armed conflict. In pursuing this aim we also need to avoid directly challenging important Soviet interests since otherwise we shall face the choice, as in Poland, between unacceptable risk and disagreeable reverse. Within such a policy there is room for debate whether the emphasis should be upon the reality of confrontation or the search for co-operation, but it will in either case be to our advantage to seek a better understanding of Soviet policy and to try to ensure that the Soviet leadership understand our own policy. If, at one extreme, our aim is the kind of 'peaceful co-existence' of the 1975 agreements, it goes without saying that we need to develop contact. If, at the other, our aim is the

UK-Soviet Relations, 1979-82

gradual break up of the Soviet empire, a precise assessment by both sides of the degree of risk at any point becomes even more necessary. Only if we were resigned to the eventual resolution of the conflict by force might there be a case for a long-term policy in which the avoidance of political contact with the Soviet Union could perhaps have a part.

7. The second reason which I cited as necessitating a review of our policy is the current state of the Soviet Union. It is not what it was even when I addressed your predecessor in 1979. Kosygin and Suslov are dead, Brezhnev himself seems only just capable of exercising power. Those around him are more obviously aging, the economy is in a bad way and the whole system is showing the stress of its imperial burden. We see only the barest murmur of popular discontent and no sign at all of a younger generation of leaders preparing to take over, but there can be little doubt that the Soviet Union is approaching a time of transition, a time when new leaders will inherit a tired ideology, a strained economy, a restless empire, a hostile relationship with the major powers and a military power unparalleled in their history. The next few years could be the kind of period that occurs only rarely in history. We badly need to know the potential new leaders and to have them know us, if possible before rather than after they have taken over. Our mutual ignorance is almost total. I wish it were possible for Ambassadors to fulfil their proper role in this respect, but in the Soviet Union we cannot do so, except as a by-product of political contact at Ministerial level.

8. I have perhaps spent over long arguing the self-evident in terms of the need for political contact, but I see a certain risk that unless it is argued we may drift into a self-defeating and perhaps dangerous stagnation of policy. It is, however, one thing to argue in the abstract the case for dialogue with the Soviet Union. It is another to relate that argument to the Soviet concept of a dialogue; and another again to take account of the reality of East-West relations after the imposition of martial law in Poland. In the Soviet Union those who hold power and those who are responsible for expounding Soviet policy abroad have been brought up in a common tradition where discussion is essentially a means of securing acceptance of an approved position. A Soviet official has an exchange of views when a visitor arrives with his own erroneous view and leaves with the correct official view. You are only too familiar with Mr Gromyko's style. On the Parliamentary level, Shitikov and Rubin, the Presidents of the two Chambers of the Supreme Soviet, are worse. I have seen little evidence that the quality of discussion engaged in by Presidents Carter and Giscard d'Estaing or Chancellor Schmidt with Mr Brezhnev was noticeably more open. Nevertheless, even among the present leadership there are those who will listen and may absorb more than they are prepared to indicate. Certainly, it cannot have been a waste of time for Herr Schmidt, immediately after the Soviet occupation of Afghanistan, to be able to have most of the members of the Soviet Politburo following with attention his exposition of Western policy and it may not be fanciful to suppose that this was a factor in moderating Soviet policy towards Poland. Moreover, the Soviet style is not a Russian style. This is a people which loves to talk. At various levels within the Soviet apparatus there are men of power, intelligence and influence and I would not exclude the possibility that some, particularly among the younger generation, may be genuinely interested to understand more of the world outside the Communist bloc. Even Mr Brezhnev, in his speech to Jaruzelski, made the point that the Communist states could not live in isolation. The UK still has, I believe, a certain reputation here as a medium-sized power which is capable of talking sense and from that point of view we are well

17 December 1981 – 9 December 1982

placed as an interlocutor. It is to our advantage to encourage those who may be ready for a dialogue and it will be difficult to do this without starting by a resumption of the normal pattern of political consultation.

9. I recognise the difficulty of timing. Now, when Germany has agreed to reduce political contacts with the Soviet Union, when the whole question of the response to the Polish crisis is one of acute difficulty within the Alliance and when the Soviet Union is doing its best to exacerbate this difficulty, it is clearly unrealistic to envisage an early resumption of an Anglo-Soviet dialogue. Moreover, we must assume that the Soviet Union is not going to abandon control of Poland and that it will require a degree of political orthodoxy in Poland which will guarantee continuing tension within and in respect of that country for many years. One cannot, therefore, foresee a time at which resumption of a political dialogue will appear both appropriate and easy. I can only express the hope that we should recognise that it is in our interest to resume the dialogue as soon as we can, that we should be ready to take advantage of opportunities when they do occur and that meanwhile we should do what we can not to make eventual resumption even more difficult. In areas other than foreign policy the balance of interest may vary. There are areas, for instance medicine, where the product of previous exchanges was disappointing and there is little case for resumption. In the cultural area, student and teacher exchanges are to our benefit and continue, but major manifestations of a goodwill character are inappropriate. We have a clear interest in maintaining the formal intergovernmental trade arrangements, but the sanctions in the field of trade and finance should remain in force until there are substantive developments which justify their removal. A political dialogue is not necessarily a demonstration of good will and a Soviet interlocutor is more likely to treat his British partner with respect if he is operating against a firm policy background.

10. In all this I am suggesting nothing new or original. In its essentials the policy I recommend is that embodied in your despatch of 7 December, 1979.[4] My concern is simply that at a time when the short-term negative aspects of our relationship with the Soviet Union are necessarily dominant, we should not lose sight of the need for a positive longer-term policy, one directed towards the safe management of confrontation until eventually the Soviet Union can be brought to pursue responsible policies appropriate to its importance in the international community.

11. I am sending copies of this despatch to Her Majesty's Ambassadors at Washington, Bonn, Paris, Prague, Bucharest, Budapest, Sofia, East Berlin, Warsaw and Belgrade; and to the UK Permanent Representative at NATO.

I am, My Lord,
Yours faithfully,
CURTIS KEEBLE

[4] No. 1.

No. 139

Mr Broomfield to Sir C. Keeble (Moscow), 9 March 1982
Confidential (ENS 014/3)

Dear Curtis,

The Soviet Union: Will it Change?

1. My apologies for the long delay in commenting on your despatch of 29 September and Andrew Wood's extremely interesting memorandum[1]. In a sense the intervening months have provided confirmation of what you describe as the Soviet Union's 'frozen international policies'.

2. Certainly the problems facing the Soviet leadership pose deep conflicts of interest. An outside observer can readily identify many problems which in themselves are compelling reasons for change: sharply declining economic growth but continuing heavy demands by the defence industries; inadequate returns on investment, particularly in agriculture; a planning and management system incapable of coping with the demands of a sophisticated economy; the end of growth by extensive means yet persistent failure to improve productivity; the rising costs of the exploitation of untapped resources in the remoter areas; deficiencies in labour supply; the absence of incentives to improved individual and collective performance; an increasingly sterile domestic political climate; major social problems (work indiscipline, alcoholism, falling life expectancy, decline of the family as a stable unit of society); inability to meet consumer expectations; looming demographic change; failure to apply science to industry, etc. etc. All these point to a need to galvanise Soviet society if the momentum of the three post-War decades is to be renewed and the Soviet Union is not to fall further behind the West, let alone establish a basis for a superpower role consisting of more than just military might.

3. Speeches by the leadership over the past two years have made it clear that the Party recognises these failings and is casting about for ways to rectify them. In any society which allowed a free interplay of stimuli, recognition of failings as numerous and fundamental as those facing the Soviet leadership would take the country more than halfway towards decisions on the kinds of cure which should be attempted within the broad framework of society which that country has acquired. The problem in the Soviet Union is quite simply that the political structure and the range of permitted views are less flexible and the possible options therefore limited if that basic fabric is not to be destroyed. The temptation for any Soviet leadership is to resort to those half-measures which are politically safe while hoping that the underlying economic and social problems will not become intractable.

4. In the early years of declining growth and social stagnation tinkering with the system can have a marginal and palliative effect. The leadership can take comfort from the fact that some action is being taken to hold the situation. Although radical improvement is not achieved, things do not deteriorate too fast and there is always the hope that good fortune (e.g. favourable weather leading to good harvests, new methods of mineral exploitation) will combine to bring a slow improvement over the longer term. This, it seems to me, is what we have witnessed in the Soviet Union in the past three to four years. But assuming no miracles occur, will the leadership continue to ignore the need to encourage more far-reaching ways to

[1] No. 112.

17 December 1981 – 9 December 1982

stimulate the population and the economy to a better performance? Will the Soviet Union muddle through, muddle along or muddle down in a continuing decline?

5. Your despatch of 23 December[2] showed that the Party is not faced with an impending economic and social disaster. There is a basic underlying strength to the Soviet economy which should provide a cushion. But however good future harvests may be, and however much it may be possible to juggle with investments in order to satisfy conflicting priorities, the problems with which the leadership must now begin to grapple will not in the long term respond to the minor changes, which are all the leadership apparently contemplates for the moment. Pressure for change will build up—in the next two decades—which may well prove very strong. Those pressures will originate both within the Soviet Union and in its external relations. Unless the Soviet Union is going soon to pass its zenith, and never become a superpower except in the military sense, those pressures will have to be heeded, at least to a degree.

6. One might argue that a future leadership, not bound to policies with which the present ageing group is closely identified, would be more likely, once it had found its feet, to be willing to look positively at different ideas for stimulating Soviet society. No leader would wish for long to preside over a failing economy, which among other effects adds important constraints to Soviet freedom of action in foreign policy. In a collective leadership, one of the contenders to become top dog might copy Malenkov and Khrushchev and promise speedier improvements in the standard of living. Yet the ideological blinkers will still be in place. The leaders would be the heirs of Brezhnev used to his policies of stability. They might innovate but they might as easily revert to type and funk it.

7. We should not, however, take it as read that economic and social change can only be of the kind which carries with it the inevitability of political relaxation. Moves in the opposite direction are by no means inconceivable. There is probably a hankering in some Soviet circles for the order, discipline and 'progress' which marked the Stalin era. Is it to be ruled out that a future Soviet leadership would find it possible to contemplate a series of economic measures which, by channelling resources and energies more effectively, would promote revival while at the same time tightening the political screws to ensure that there are no undesirable side effects in terms of greater liberalisation? (I personally consider such a course as doomed to the same relative failure as present policies. Marxism/Leninism is a more or less coherent economic/political system. Both parts are deeply enmeshed, and changes in one part are not neutral as far as the other is concerned.) A Soviet Union which saw itself more under siege might additionally decide that greater autarky was the only solution even if this had to be accompanied by greater repression. I guess that the Soviet people would knuckle under. Such a scenario seems to me at least as likely as the relaxation of central control and stimulation by incentive for which the situation now cries out. It could be easier to get through the conservative Central Committee apparatus since it would involve no risky departures from basic ideological tenets and pose less of a danger to entrenched personal problems.

8. My assumption that the Soviet people would accept the hardships that would probably accompany a tightening of the political screw (and some loss of jeans and other identifiable signs of 'progress' in the seventies) is based on the difference between the Soviet people and their Eastern European neighbours. Change is

---

[2] Not printed.

UK-Soviet Relations, 1979-82

caused by necessity and desire and is usually imitative. The free market, democratic alternative corresponds albeit tenuously in a number of cases, to historical precedents in most East European states. It is therefore more understandable, in addition to their proximity and cultural ties with Western Europe, for those countries to desire a change in that direction. But the modern Soviet Union corresponds rather closely to its Czarist predecessors. Change may not necessarily mean something different, but more or better of the same.

9. Developments in the direction of tighter control, especially if autarky was involved, would pose considerable dangers for the West. A Soviet leadership which felt bound to embark on such policies would pay less heed to the need for a constructive East/West relationship and might therefore be not only less predictable in foreign policy but more hard-faced and aggressive. We should perhaps examine what action the West might take to avoid such a turn of events. In the short term we ought to seek more information: is anyone pushing for change, in what direction, and how much weight do they have? Before he left David Johnson suggested that we might consider inviting some eminent Soviet economists to this country to try to get a line on the kinds of ideas which are now being examined. Do you think this could be useful in a few months' time? We might, in addition, do more to tap the knowledge acquired by our principal commercial firms in the course of their commercial dealings with the Soviet bureaucracy and of academics like Michael Kaser who talks to Soviet economists. Assuming that we can, even in part, satisfy the need for information, what policies could the West pursue in order to move things in the right direction?

10. You will have seen from recent telegrams and letters that the subject you addressed in your despatch is likely to become very much the centre of discussion between the Americans and their European allies in the run-up to the NATO Summit and probably thereafter. We will be going back to fundamentals with the Americans and trying to discover what they really expect to achieve with their present policies towards the Soviet Union. And in what direction and in what time scale they consider the Russians are likely to respond to the pressures that are working on them. Your despatch has been a very useful contribution to our own mind-clearing exercise before engaging in these wider discussions.

11. I am sending copies of this letter to the recipients of your despatch.[3]

Yours,

N. H. R. A. BROOMFIELD

---

[3] In his reply, dated 25 March, Sir C. Keeble noted that it was easy to identify the problems facing the Soviet Union but more difficult to guess how the post-Brezhnev leadership would rise to the challenge. The most plausible prognosis was that radical change was unlikely, given the need of the leadership to preserve their own position and the difficulty of the problems faced. He went on to say that the US Embassy in Moscow was engaged in a similar 'crystal ball exercise' and had reached the conclusion that the new leadership would be so beset by problems that they would have little choice but to disown the Brezhnev legacy, brutally batten down the hatches, and eschew adventures abroad and experiments at home. Whilst this view was a little melodramatic for Sir C. Keeble, he felt it contained an essential truth: 'In circumstances when the Soviet Union feels sufficiently undermined by setbacks at home or abroad, its reflex may well be not to seek new and imaginative ways out of trouble, but to fall back on the tried and tested policies of brute force and discipline.'

17 December 1981 – 9 December 1982

No. 140

Sir C. Keeble (Moscow) to Lord Carrington, 11 March 1982[1]
Confidential (EN 020/1)

My Lord,

US/Soviet relations

1. In my despatch of 8 February 1980[2] I considered the relationship between the Soviet Union and the United States immediately after the entry of Soviet forces into Afghanistan. Now, with a new mood in America and a new crisis in Poland, it is appropriate to see how the bilateral relationship looks, when seen from a Soviet viewpoint, and how it may develop. My principal conclusions in 1980 were that the security of the Soviet state required a controlled relationship with the United States, that the Soviet Union would nevertheless continue its search for a surrounding belt of subservient or at least compliant states, and that Soviet expansion would continue unless the Soviet leadership became convinced that such expansion was incompatible with their nation's security. The prospect, I argued, was for continued confrontation, but realism in the United States could ensure that such confrontation was more controlled, limited and safer.

2. In the past two years, from the Soviet point of view, things have not gone well. The reasons for this lie partly within and partly outside the bilateral relationship. Soviet-American relations have not only a powerful influence on international politics; they are themselves largely a function of international politics as a whole, for the lack of mutual dependence other than in the arms control field remains a feature of the strictly bilateral relationship. This relationship is therefore all too frequently the victim of events, often enough outside the control of either of the partners, which bring the two into conflict more or less whether they like it or not. The conflict of interests is still there even if in particular instances (e.g. in Angola and Ethiopia) there is no direct countervailing US reaction to Soviet policies.

3. For all the talk here in the 1970s of a shift in the world 'correlation of forces' (Sovietese for balance of power) the Russians ought to have known that the post-Vietnam mood of the United States would not last forever. Perhaps they did, and merely misjudged the length of time during which the United States would remain turned in on itself. As I have remarked before, Soviet judgement of the United States is often inaccurate. Reviewing past history now, however, they cannot, if they are capable of objective assessment (and even if they are not, but are guided by Marxist logic of action and reaction), escape the conclusion that Soviet policies have done much to revive the United States' will to resist the Soviet Union. Some of these policies were ones which the Soviet Union was free to develop in slower time. In particular the Russians may wonder whether it would have been better to tread more cautiously in pursuing their military build-up on land, at sea and in the air and to have acted more circumspectly in trying to take advantage of troubled situations in the Third World. That way they might not so quickly have alerted US public opinion. It is, however, necessary to recognise that an essential element in the deteriorating relationship between the two superpowers has been the Soviet response to crisis which almost any Soviet leadership would be likely to see as

---

[1] Copied to Ambassadors in Washington, UKDEL NATO, Paris, Bonn, East European posts, Vienna and Helsinki.

[2] No. 50.

UK-Soviet Relations, 1979-82

affecting essential Soviet interests. To a large extent, both in Afghanistan and in Poland, the development of the crisis owed much to Soviet policy, but in both cases its immediate cause lay outside the control of either the Soviet Union or the United States.

4. From the Soviet point of view what was an issue in Afghanistan was whether or not to let an acknowledged client drown, a question with implications for the structure of Soviet power elsewhere. The effect on the United States was either misjudged or even, if judged correctly, held to be of lesser importance. With hindsight the Soviet leadership may regret that they did not abandon the Afghan revolution while they could still do so at not too great a price. At the time of their intervention, however, the risk of helping did not seem to be too great and the military assessment was no doubt that Soviet arms could achieve a swift success. Both expectations have proved wrong, but the result has been to make it still more difficult for the Soviet Union to consider a change of course, despite the damage to the Soviet standing in the world and the way in which intervention crystallised US perceptions of a renewed Soviet threat during an election year. Soviet policies in Afghanistan were and are reprehensible and dangerous. To us they may seem to have been self-defeating for the Soviet Union: although I suspect that some in the leadership are arguing that, in Afghanistan itself, the worst is already over. But we should recognise that it was not mere opportunism which inspired the Soviet leadership to act as they did. Soviet action reflected the sort of state the USSR is. The system, dogmatic yet anxious, has not learnt when to withdraw. Deputy Foreign Minister Kornienko has, within the last few days, made this plain to the American Ambassador.

5. The imperatives in the case of Poland are so strong that they may have largely blinded the Soviet leadership to the possibility of acting in any other way than to do all they could to suppress the dynamic manifestation of popular will and emotion represented by Solidarity. Indeed the remarkable feature of the Polish crisis has been the fact that, confronted with this phenomenon, the Soviet leadership hesitated to force an earlier repression. The effects on the Soviet relationship with the West, and the USA in particular, have been very much a secondary consideration, but the leadership see themselves as having acted with restraint and feel themselves wronged by US reactions. The fact that they did not intervene directly from August 1980 to December 1981 may have been because they felt it would not be the most effective course and hoped that somehow or other the situation would right itself, but compared to 1956 in Hungary and 1968 in Czechoslovakia they showed restraint. For the Soviet Union a threat to the Polish ruling class comes very close to being a direct threat to the Soviet Union—or rather its ruling class. In Soviet eyes this is so obvious that they can barely believe that others do not see it too and understand why Soviet action, whether direct or by proxy, is necessary to preserve stability in Europe. From that it is but a short step to seeing the suppression of Solidarity as a pre-condition for European peace. Alexander I preserving the Christian rulers against revolution a century and a half earlier would have understood it all very well. It is peculiarly difficult for the Soviet Union to understand Western, and more particularly United States, reactions as anything other than hostile to the Soviet Union and careless of the need, which is fundamental to a balanced relationship between the two superpowers, and enshrined in the 1972 US/Soviet agreement,[3] to take Soviet interests into account.

[3] See No. 8, note 4.

17 December 1981 – 9 December 1982

For what the United States appears in Soviet eyes to be asking is that a process should be allowed to resume in Poland which will inevitably lead to the disintegration of the Soviet position in that country and, in due course, in Eastern Europe as a whole.

6. It is not easy to disentangle what the Russians think from what they feel they ought to think and what they find it tactically useful to say, but there are probably those in the leadership who are wondering whether US policy is now going beyond an effort to contain and counter-balance Soviet power in Europe. Western Europe on the other hand is seen as still accepting the basic tenet of détente in the 1970s, that the balance of power in Europe cannot and should not be changed, except perhaps as the distant result of a long period of reduced tension. The Soviet leadership are alive to the possibility of using Western Europe to influence US actions and/or to play upon trans-Atlantic differences in order to make them worse. The peace movement in Western Europe was the one bright spot for them last year. They noted what it did to European political attitudes (Sir J. Taylor's despatch of 25 February on Federal German Security Policy—The Last Two Years)[4] and hence its influence on US willingness to talk about arms control. In a sense, the fear of driving Western Europe into a more whole-hearted endorsement of American policy has been a constraint on Soviet actions. They must now hope that Poland will remain reasonably quiet and that Western European pressure on the United States to negotiate on arms control will be kept alive by a resurgent peace movement.

7. When President Reagan took office, Soviet leaders hoped he would in practice prove not so different from President Nixon before him and that the rhetoric of the campaign could be more or less ignored as having been only the cynical exploitation of a popular mood for the purposes of achieving power. After what they saw as President Carter's unpredictability the prospect of a more stable relationship under his successor was welcome. But the language the new President used at his first press conference about the Soviet leadership probably went some way towards undermining such comfortable Soviet assumptions. Soviet observers have been more conscious throughout the past year of the continuing power of the extreme right wing in and outside the Congress, and of some figures of a markedly anti-Soviet cast of mind within the Administration itself. They have almost certainly also been disturbed for some time by the way the Administration has approached arms control. Arms control has for so long been so central to the Soviet-American relationship that the questioning by the US Administration of the concepts underlying past negotiations may be seen by the Soviet Union as possibly calling into question the essence of the strategic relationship between the USA and the USSR as it had evolved over the past decade. From a Western point of view, one might add 'and well it might'. In assessing the American attitude, Soviet thinking is almost certainly guided by the belief that, whatever may be said in Administration statements, the Americans will not be willing to negotiate in earnest on INF limitation because they are determined that nothing should stand in the way of NATO modernisation of theatre nuclear forces beginning in 1983. To frustrate this is a major Soviet aim, not only because, as they argue, the weapons would constitute a new and immediate threat to the territory of the Soviet Union itself but because the moral victory of preventing NATO from deploying weapons systems which it had decided were militarily necessary would deal a severe blow

---

[4] Not printed.

UK-Soviet Relations, 1979-82

to the Alliance and to American leadership of it. The only important bilateral negotiation now in progress between the two superpowers is therefore the one which the Soviet Union approaches with a blend of optimism and misgiving but little immediate hope of progress. The INF negotiations, moreover, are no substitute in their minds for continuation of the process of strategic arms limitation. The Soviet Union saw the withdrawal of the SALT II Treaty for the ratification process in the Senate after the invasion of Afghanistan as a symbolic turning point in its relationship with the United States and the postponement of the START talks in the aftermath of the imposition of martial law in Poland seemed to confirm the trend. Instead of START negotiations, the Soviet leadership found itself faced with a US defence budget which it claims and may indeed believe is evidence of a desire to acquire strategic superiority and a first strike capability. The arms control dialogue is now linked with other issues of East-West contention, especially Poland, on which the Russians are inhibited by ideological reasons from giving ground. They denounce this linkage arguing that they themselves did not allow their disapproval of the Viet Nam war to impede the SALT process and therefore that the Americans in their turn should insulate the process of strategic arms limitation from disagreements with them about Afghanistan and Poland.

8. I have little doubt that events of the past year, including the long-running Polish sore and the US handling of the CSCE review conference, have encouraged some here to argue that the Soviet Union has been made to wait on arms control because the Soviet Union is not really interested in seeking agreement but prefers to bring the overall Soviet-American relationship, and hence also that between East and West as a whole, into question. If this school of opinion exists, its arguments may be all the more persuasive to the Soviet leadership in a situation where the Soviet Union is under internal and external pressure. There is already some danger that the high pitch of anti-US propaganda may unduly affect policy-making as such, producing anti-American policies for their own sake, which could be exacerbated if the pressure on the USSR were to increase and foreign policy become an issue in the succession stakes. The Soviet economy is in a poor state and Soviet resources have been stretched to the point where its freedom of manoeuvre has been limited. Eastern Europe is in an even worse case. The gas pipeline project is threatened by US pressure on Western Europe—pressure which to the Russians appears provoked not merely by events in Poland but also by a desire in some quarters of the US establishment directly to undermine the Soviet Union. Internationally, the Russians are stuck in Afghanistan, have heavy and not necessarily promising commitments elsewhere (for example in South East Asia) and are landed with a Polish situation which is liable to get worse. If they further conclude that the United States is fully prepared for its relationship with them to be placed under strain, they may well see the future in terms of a reversion to the policies of the cold war.

9. I do not think that the leadership as a whole yet believe things have come to this pass. My impression is that the debate here continues and that there is as yet no definitive assessment in the Soviet Union of a permanent change in the US approach. They recognise that US foreign policy-making is not, as Sir Nicholas Henderson showed in his despatch of 15 December 1981,[5] always coherent. Despite the strain of anti-Sovietism for its own sake, there have been contrary indications, notably the lifting of the grain embargo, and the Russians may be

---

[5] Not printed.

17 December 1981 – 9 December 1982

somewhat cynical about the duration of an increased US defence effort on the scale currently being promoted. Some may also have been alive to the US tactical interest in making the Soviet Union wait for arms control talks to begin and see it as no more than the kind of tactic which they themselves might follow. It can, furthermore, be argued that, Poland apart, the United States has in fact, despite the rhetoric, done rather little to damage Soviet interests, and that even in the case of Poland, the Americans have stopped short of measures that would really hurt—in particular a new grain embargo. If this line is accepted, it would be reasonable to conclude that the Reagan administration is one with which it is still possible business can be done.

10. The development of the Polish crisis will obviously be an important factor in Soviet-American relations. It may be one which will operate independently of the wishes of either party and contrary to the interests of both, with the consequence that either may be forced into action or counter action which will appear to override any wider interest. There is, however, an important distinction to be drawn between preventative and dynamic aspects of Soviet policy-making. Even if Soviet policy-makers drew the worst conclusions about US intentions, it must be open to question whether there could be a fundamental alteration in the preventative side of Soviet policy towards the United States. By this I mean that the Soviet Union will still in any circumstances need to avoid an uncontrolled relationship and therefore retains vital interest in trying to maintain a dialogue in order to avoid a disastrous confrontation even when that dialogue cannot lead to fruitful cooperation. That may be compatible with a high degree of mutual hostility and abuse, for the constraint is the fear of a war which might escalate, not a desire to achieve harmony, but it cannot in any circumstances be in Soviet (or, I should have thought, American) interest to be in avoidable doubt as to the policies of the other side. So far as the second aspect is concerned, the Soviet Union is at present less free than the United States to pursue dynamic policies. It is trying too hard to keep what it has. In some of the world's trouble spots (Central America, Southern Africa) the Soviet Union, despite the great increase in its power to deploy military force at long range, could not face a military showdown. In others (South East Asia) there is the China factor to consider. In others (Iran), however tempting involvement may be, the risks of an open clash with the US are simply too great. Soviet interests are therefore for the time being at least better served by propaganda attacks on the United States than by policies which may add to Soviet problems and lead to further quarrels with the Americans. In short, to use Soviet language, the 'correlation of forces' has, during the past two years, turned against the Soviet Union.

11. The present Soviet position was well summed up by Brezhnev in his speech of welcome to Jaruzelski on 1 March.[6] Having referred to increased American pressure on Poland and 'socialism's' readiness to defend itself, he went on to speak of disarmament and in that context said 'there can be no doubt that the political climate of the world largely depends on the state of Soviet-American relations. But that is not the whole truth. In the settlement of world problems, the political weight and influence of other states including those of Europe is great. Their voice can indeed be decisive. We are in favour of continuing and enriching the dialogue between East and West, putting aside the masses of accusations and counter accusations and getting on with the settlement of urgent practical problems, in the

---

[6] General Jaruzelski paid a visit to the Soviet Union in March.

UK-Soviet Relations, 1979-82

first place disarmament'. This unremarkable passage in fact displays all the principal elements of current Soviet policy—the determination to maintain control over Poland, the priority on the wider scene of the relationship with the United States, the desire to concentrate that relationship on disarmament negotiations and the hope that European opinion will facilitate that process. The elements are familiar. They pull, as ever, at the same time towards confrontation and accommodation with the United States. Change could come, especially in the context of a change in the leadership of the Soviet Union, but the factors which have produced the present state of bilateral relations are not susceptible to quick or easy evolution.[7]

I am, My Lord,
Yours faithfully,
CURTIS KEEBLE

[7] For Sir J. Bullard's reply see No. 149.

No. 141

Minute from Lord Trefgarne to Lord Carrington, 11 March 1982
Confidential (ENS 020/5)

Anglo-Soviet Relations

1. You will wish to see Mr Broomfield's minute of 2 March, endorsed by Mr Bullard.[1] I agree with the main thrust. Coincidentally Sir Curtis Keeble has just sent a useful despatch on Anglo/Soviet relations.[2] He ranges more widely but reaches much the same conclusions as in the attached minute.

2. I am particularly concerned, as I know you are, to avoid risking any damage to Alliance solidarity or getting out of step with our major allies, especially the US.

3. While there is thus no scope for cordiality or even great substance in our strictly bilateral relations with the Soviet Union, and now is certainly not the right moment for major Anglo/Soviet initiatives, there are good reasons not to distance ourselves from the Russians so far that we put at risk our channels of political communication and openings for assessment of their policies. This will become increasingly important as both the economic strains of superpower ambition and the political strains of the Brezhnev succession struggle begin to tell.

4. I therefore now propose that we should:

(*a*) go ahead with the Joint Commission on schedule, but at senior official rather than Ministerial level on our side (a letter issued yesterday in this sense);

(*b*) go ahead with Zemskov's visit perhaps in early autumn provided that Mr Bullard's check with his colleagues in the Ten on 15/16 March shows that one or two of our other partners will be doing something similar;

(*c*) resume or maintain routine technical level discussions with the Russians on visa arrangements and a double-taxation agreement; and

(*d*) adopt a slightly less frosty attitude to the Soviet Embassy here. I might accept an invitation which has been extended more than once to dine with the Soviet Ambassador. This would not preclude taking a firm line on Afghanistan

[1] See Nos. 135 and 137.
[2] No. 138.

17 December 1981 – 9 December 1982

or Poland but would indicate an interest in keeping a dialogue going.

5. I do not believe that any of these proposals present the risks referred to in paragraph 2 above and I seek your agreement to them.[3]

DAVID TREFGARNE

[3] Lord Carrington commented on the minute that 'the line proposed strikes the right balance.'

No. 142

Minute from Mr Weston (Defence Department) to Mr Gillmore, 17 March 1982
Secret (DPN 083/4)

Soviet Moratorium on SS-20 Deployments

1. In advance of Ambassador Nitze's visit this afternoon,[1] it may be useful to summarise the likely Soviet motives that lie behind President Brezhnev's announcement yesterday (Moscow telno 136)[2] that no more SS-20s will be deployed in the European USSR. In the light of discussion with Mr Nitze, we shall also wish to give No 10 a considered view tomorrow, before the Prime Minister sees Chancellor Schmidt on 19 March.

2. The announcement of a unilateral moratorium was expected and follows a series of strong hints recently, from Zamyatin and other Soviet officials. It is obviously designed to take the high ground in public relations terms as the Geneva negotiations go into recess. It looks very likely that it will have little or no practical effect on Soviet plans. Since the construction of new SS-20 bases starts around the turn of each year and is completed about 12 months later we would not anyway have expected to see further SS-20 deployments in the European USSR until the end of 1982/beginning of 1983: at least one and possibly three SS-20 bases have recently been completed there.

3. Brezhnev has put a highly restrictive condition on maintenance of the freeze by saying that it may be lifted if practical preparations are made for the deployment of cruise and Pershing II missiles. Such preparations are, of course, already in hand (notably in the UK at RAF Greenham Common). He has therefore provided himself with ample excuse to lift the freeze in say, another 9-12 months time.

4. By making the announcement yesterday, the Russians were able to capitalise on the publicity generated by the last day of the first round of the INF negotiations and to produce what appears to be a concession for consideration by Western publics over the two month recess in the negotiations. They will also expect their announcement to be regarded sympathetically by the group of US Congressmen

[1] Paul H. Nitze was the chief US negotiator at the INF talks in Geneva. He was due to meet Mr Hurd, Lord Trefgarne and officials.
[2] Not printed. This telegram reported on a speech made by President Brezhnev on 16 March to the Congress of Soviet Trade Unions where he announced the Soviet Union would deploy no more SS-20 missiles in the European USSR. The moratorium was to be qualitative and quantitative, with no increase in existing numbers or any further replacement of the older SS4 and SS5 missiles by SS-20s. He also promised a unilateral reduction of Soviet medium range missiles provided the international situation did not worsen. In addition, President Brezhnev called for the renewal of strategic arms control, no deployment of GLCMs and SLCMs pending strategic arms talks, and restrictions on SSBN patrol areas.

who have recently spoken out in favour of a freeze on existing nuclear weapons levels.

5. We must assume that in the USSR East of the Urals SS-20 deployments will continue regardless. We know that there are sufficient bases under construction to raise the SS-20 total by a further 50 missiles (150 warheads).

6. Brezhnev made a number of further points when announcing the moratorium:
(*a*) He threatened that if cruise and Pershing II were deployed, the Soviet Union would take retaliatory steps which would put US territory in an analogous position to that of Soviet territory. If this statement were to be taken literally, it would suggest the deployment of Soviet long-range land-based INF within range of the continental US; Cuba comes to mind in this context, which would obviously be a very high profile response. But it seems more likely that the Russians are putting down a general marker designed to sound suitably impressive, without commitment as to any particular option at this stage. It would for example be open to them to portray the new type ICBM which we know they have under development (within SALT 2 provisions) as a direct counter-measure to GLCMs and Pershing. Another possibility would be the deployment of Soviet sea-launched cruise missiles (also under development) in waters close to North America. Their basic purpose here appears to be to raise the stakes and thereby widen misgivings among at least some Americans, as well as Europeans, about the likely political and military costs of proceeding with NATO's deployments.
(*b*) Some unilateral reductions by the Soviet Union. We must assume that these will be in the obsolescent SS-4 and SS-5 missiles since if there was any question of reducing SS-20s, the Russians would make maximum capital of the fact. Again there is an easy let-out, if the international climate is judged not to justify such reductions.
(*c*) A renewed plea for the resumption of strategic arms control. This is a familiar call, but we are on safe ground in referring publicly to the US commitment to strategic arms reductions which the Americans are happy to repeat in public themselves. The plea to go on observing SALT 2 Protocol limits on SLCM and GLCM deployments is designed partly to catch President Reagan's decision to deploy a strategic reserve of sea-launched cruise missiles.
(*d*) A call for restrictions on SSBN patrol areas. This is more explicit than hitherto, and reflects the known Soviet preoccupation with their relative disadvantage in the submarine-launched ballistic missile field and in anti-submarine warfare. The Russians rely less than the Americans on SSBNs for their strategic nuclear strength. But the proposal could have some appeal in terms of avoiding the risk of sneak SLBM attacks from close to the US coast.[3]

P. J. WESTON

[3] On 22 March the Soviet Ambassador called on Mr Hurd to hand over the text of President Brezhnev's speech that covered arms control. Mr Hurd said his preliminary reading was that the Soviet proposals did not go far enough, as public opinion demanded the total removal of this class of weapon as envisaged in the Western 'zero option' proposal. Mr Popov replied that the 'zero option' was not a serious offer as it would grant the US superiority. Mr Hurd also asked whether the reference to 'in an analogous position' implied the installation of Soviet missiles in Cuba. This was denied by Mr Popov who said President Brezhnev had frequently stated that the Soviet Union would not station weapons on the territory of others (FCO telegram No. 162 of 24 March to Moscow, not printed).

17 December 1981 – 9 December 1982

No. 143

Letter from Mr Broomfield to Sir C. Keeble (Moscow), 18 March 1982
Confidential (ENS 020/5)

Dear Curtis,

The Relationship between Britain and the Soviet Union

1. I have already thanked you briefly for your despatch of 4 March,[1] but am now doing so at greater length after submitting it within the Office. It has been sent for printing as a Diplomatic Report.

2. Your picture of the deterioration of the Anglo/Soviet relationship over the last few years is all the more vivid because (through no fault of yours let me hasten to add!) the period coincides so exactly with that of your own tour in Moscow. However, I am sure you are right that many of your predecessors over the past 60 years have also referred to the thinness of Anglo/Soviet relations. The Wilson/Brezhnev 'new phase' opened in February 1975 came after a period of poor relations dating back at least to the Soviet invasion of Czechoslovakia; and arguably, thin and sour relations have been the norm over the whole period since the War if not the Revolution. The brief honeymoons, such as that of 1975 and the earlier Macmillan visit in 1959, have never led to a sustained improvement, except of course for the unique circumstances of the Wartime alliance.

3. Bad relations are not, of course, co-terminous with thin relations. I think one has to recognise that because of the nature of the Soviet system, the respective national interests and other factors, there is always a tendency for Anglo/Soviet relations to be on the cool side of normal. This point is well illustrated every time people in London start looking around for things to axe to punish Soviet bad behaviour and equally when the search is for possible growth areas during the honeymoon periods. In both cases the possibilities have been limited because the bilateral strand of the relationship between Britain and the Soviet Union is limited, and in dealing with the Soviet Union very few things will flourish without regular injections of Government support. It is therefore not surprising that you have found yourself contemplating such a bleak situation at present.

4. With my earlier acknowledgement of your despatch, I enclosed a copy of my submission of 2 March[2] in order to show you that we shared your anxieties about the risks to British interests of a situation in which we had no dialogue with the Soviet Union, and that we had been giving some thought to practical moves designed to signal our continuing interest in Anglo/Soviet relations. The minute has now been through all the stages of submission and I enclose copies of minutes by Alan Goodison, Julian Bullard and Lord Trefgarne.[3] You will see that the Secretary of State commented that the line proposed strikes the right balance. I cannot pretend that going ahead with the Joint Commission, the Zemskov visit and discussions on visas and double taxation adds up to a very striking package, even with the addition of a slightly less frosty attitude to the Soviet Embassy here: moreover there is still a question mark over Zemskov, as you will see from the enclosed copy of a further minute by Julian Bullard recording views in the Ten.[4] Nor, of course, as you recognise, is this the time for exciting packages. But it

---

[1] No. 138.
[2] No. 135.
[3] Nos. 136, 137 and 141.
[4] Not printed.

345

UK-Soviet Relations, 1979-82

should be enough to help sustain the dialogue whose importance you rightly stress.

Yours,
N. H. R. A. BROOMFIELD

On 2 April 1982 Argentina invaded the Falkland Islands. The event was described by Lord Carrington as a 'humiliating affront' to the country and led to his resignation. A Committee of Inquiry into the handling of the dispute, chaired by Lord Franks, would later conclude that the invasion could not have been foreseen or prevented. However, in the immediate wake of the invasion, the Government faced strong criticism from Parliament and the press. Lord Carrington and the Defence Minister, John Nott, bore the brunt of this. At a meeting of Conservative backbench MPs they faced 'cat-calling, derision and jeers'. In an editorial, The Times *called on the Foreign Secretary to 'do his duty'. Carrington concluded his departure was necessary to unite Parliament and the country behind the Government. Despite initial attempts to dissuade him, Mrs Thatcher accepted his resignation on 5 April along with other senior members of his team—Humphrey Atkins and Richard Luce. He was replaced as Secretary of State by Francis Pym, the Leader of the Commons.*

Sir Michael Palliser retired as the Permanent Under-Secretary on 9 April and moved to the Cabinet Office as special adviser to the Prime Minister for the Falklands. His farewell party, arranged for 5 April, was cancelled in the light of the invasion and the resignation of the Foreign Secretary. Sir Antony Acland succeeded him as Permanent Under-Secretary.

A task force was assembled and sailed for the South Atlantic on 5 April. British forces landed at San Carlos Bay on 21 May. After fighting at Darwin and Goose Green, and around Port Stanley, the Argentines surrendered on 14 June.[1]

[1] *Falkland Islands Review* (Cmnd. 8787) January 1983; Margaret Thatcher, *The Downing Street Years* (London: HarperCollins, 1993) pp. 185-7; *The Times* leader, 5 & 6 April 1982; Lord Carrington, *Reflect on Things Past* (London: Collins, 1988), pp. 368-372; John Nott, *Here Today: Gone Tomorrow: Recollections of an errant politician* (London: Politico's, 2002), p. 268; Sir Lawrence Freedman, *The Official History of the Falklands Campaign. Volume II: War and Diplomacy* (London: Routledge, 2005), pp. 15-18.

No. 144

Briefing Paper on East-West Relations for Mr Pym, 8 April 1982[1]
Confidential (EN 021/6)

I. *The Background*
Afghanistan and Poland

1. East/West relations have deteriorated sharply as a result of the Soviet invasion of Afghanistan in December 1979, the continuing Soviet military build-up, and the imposition of martial law in Poland in December 1981 (see Annex A:

[1] Submitted by Mr Montgomery, EESD.

17 December 1981 – 9 December 1982

Poland).[2]

Soviet Difficulties and Attempts to Regain the Initiative

2. The Russians face other problems besides Afghanistan and Poland: domestically, economic and agricultural performance is disappointing, (see Annex C: Eastern European Economic Problems)[3] while externally they are confronted by a determined and assertive US Administration with which they would like to establish a stable relationship while being unwilling to exercise the degree of restraint necessary to do so. The Soviet Peace Programme articulated by Brezhnev at the 26th Party Congress last year,[4] is aimed at Western public opinion over the heads of Western Governments. The campaign against NATO's plans to deploy intermediate range nuclear weapons in Europe is the most obvious example of their efforts to weaken transatlantic unity.

II. *Western Aims and Policy*

3. Our aim is to maintain Western unity and impress on the Russians that stable and productive East/West relations are possible only on the basis of political and military restraint. Soviet economic and political difficulties should at least in theory make better East/West relations attractive to the Soviet leadership. At the same time we have sought to exercise a positive discrimination in our relations with the other Eastern European countries, with a view to encouraging trends towards liberalisation and independence.

4. The measures adopted against the Soviet Union after the crackdown in Poland are intended to reinforce these aims and give a clear signal to the Soviet Union that its policies are unacceptable.

III. *Current Problems*

US Measures: The Buckley Mission

5. Unfortunately the American measures against the Soviet Union have put the unity of the Alliance under severe strain. The Americans have extended and tightened up their licensing controls on the export and re-export of goods to the Soviet Union, and are considering further action. These measures raise serious difficulties for European firms, especially in connection with the Siberian gas pipeline. The Americans have also been exploring with their allies the possibility of restricting export credits to the USSR. The whole question of East/West economic relations is now under review, and the future of Western policy will be an important subject for the Versailles Summit, and perhaps in OECD and NATO (see Annex B).

Eastern European Economic Problems

6. Economic problems in Eastern Europe (highlighted by the Polish crisis) have led to a loss of confidence on the part of banks and governments, and an unwillingness to extend credits. In the Soviet Union an invisibles deficit and the need for large agricultural imports (grain and sugar) have forced massive gold sales (see Annex C).

IV. *Prospects*

7. East/West prospects are uncertain. If the situation in Poland does not deteriorate further, progress may be possible on some issues (e.g. INF, START) where there may be benefits to both sides. East/West relations will remain strained in the forseeable future. A Soviet military intervention in Poland would make the situation dramatically worse, but the Russians would accept the East/West costs of

---

[2] Not printed.

[3] Not printed, see para 6.

[4] See No. 86.

intervention rather than lose control.

The Leadership

8. A further factor making for uncertainty is the prospect of leadership changes in the Soviet Union. Brezhnev's health is poor and he could die at any time. After his departure, the Kremlin may be preoccupied with leadership struggles. Even when new leaders do emerge they are likely to have little experience of foreign affairs.

ANNEX B

US Measures: The Buckley Mission

1. Following the declaration of martial law in Poland, US trade measures against the Soviet Union were announced by President Reagan on 29 December 1981.

2. The effect of these measures falls most heavily on Europe. Unless exemptions are granted they will prevent the fulfilment of existing European contracts which depend on embargoed US goods. Existing contracts for the Siberian gas pipeline alone are worth about $4 billion. John Brown has a £100 million contract for turbines and spares which is threatened because it depends on parts from GEC. By contrast, the bulk of US sales to USSR consist of grain, which is not affected.

3. It originally appeared that the US would agree to exempt existing contracts of other Western countries, if the latter would agree not to undermine US measures by taking up contracts which would have gone to US firms. The Prime Minister has sent two messages to President Reagan advocating this solution.[5] But the US now appears less interested in non-undermining, and instead has turned to the question of Western credits for the Soviet Union.

4. A US Mission headed by Under-Secretary Buckley visited London on 17 March, and also visited Bonn, Paris and Brussels. Its purpose was to propose that governments should limit or ban subsidised credits and official guarantees for exports to the Soviet Union (and perhaps Eastern Europe). It was announced that further US action on the 29 December measures would be suspended pending the outcome of the Buckley Mission. As a first step an information-sharing exercise is now under way.

5. The Buckley Mission's view appeared to be that whether the Americans grant exemption for existing contracts should depend on action by the Europeans on credits. In our view, it is essential to break this linkage, since the problem of existing contracts is immediate, while the question of credits will take time. We are proceeding in close consultation with our European partners. The whole question will be discussed further during preparations for and at the Versailles Economic Summit (4-6 June) and in other appropriate forms (e.g. NATO, OECD).

[5] See No. 127.

17 December 1981 – 9 December 1982

No. 145

Mr Pym to Sir C. Keeble (Moscow), 15 April 1982, 4.31 p.m.[1]
Tel. No. 210 Priority, Confidential (ENS 020/5)

Falkland Islands: Soviet Ambassador's call on Mr Hurd

1. The Soviet Ambassador called, at his request, on Mr Hurd today to give the Soviet account of the last round of INF negotiations in Geneva (record by bag).

2. At the end of the meeting Mr Hurd drew Popov's attention to the remarkable degree of unity in the debate in the House of Commons on 14 April on the Falkland Islands crisis. He emphasised that we wished to reach a peaceful solution in accordance with SCR 502.[2] Mr Hurd said we had been following carefully the development of the Soviet attitude. We found it disturbing. Events were being presented as if the UK were behaving as a colonial power. But, for example, we had seen no references in the Soviet press to the fact that SCR 502 was mandatory and required the withdrawal of Argentine troops. No mention had been [made] of the fact that in decolonisation, the principle of self-determination lay at the heart of the UN Charter. What was happening in the Falkland Islands was of the greatest importance for international order.

3. Popov maintained that the Soviet position was 'principled' and not opportunist. It had not changed since the UN resolution of 1963 had included the Falkland Islands as one of the territories to be decolonised. The Soviet Union supported this resolution. As far as the present dispute was concerned, he hoped that both the UK and Argentina would adhere to the principles of the UN Charter and that the dispute could be resolved by peaceful means. In his speech on 5 April in Belgrade Mr Gromyko had said that the Soviet Union was against adding to existing hotbeds of international tension. Popov added that he personally sincerely hoped a peaceful settlement could be achieved. Mr Hurd pointed out that the Soviet line appeared to overlook the fact that force had already been used. The situation was dangerous. We hoped that the Soviet Union would be helpful over implementation of SCR 502.

4. MIFT[3] contains line taken by News Department on Popov's call.

[1] Repeated Information Routine to Bonn, Paris, UKDEL NATO, Washington, UKMIS New York; Information Saving to Budapest, Bucharest, Belgrade, Sofia, Prague, Warsaw.
[2] This resolution, approved by the UN Security Council on 3 April, demanded the immediate cessation of hostilities, the withdrawal of Argentine forces, and called on both governments to seek a diplomatic solution observing the principles of the UN Charter. The resolution was adopted by a vote of 10-1 with only Panama voting against. The Soviet Union, China, Poland and Spain abstained.
[3] Not printed.

No. 146

Mr Brooke Turner (Moscow) to Mr Pym, 17 April 1982, 10 a.m.[1]
Tel. No. 202 Immediate, Confidential (ENS 020/5)

FCO Telno 460[2] (not to all): Falkland Islands: Soviet Attitude.

[1] Repeated Information Immediate to Washington, UKMIS New York, UKDEL NATO; Information Priority Paris and Bonn.
[2] Not printed.

UK-Soviet Relations, 1979-82

1. I called this morning on Semeonov, Deputy Head of the Second European Department in the MFA, to carry out the instructions in your TUR, indicating that my call was a natural follow-up to my earlier notification of the maritime exclusion zone. I read, and gave Semeonov on a personal basis, a speaking note containing the language in para 2 of TUR, Semeonov undertook to report this immediately to higher authority.

2. Subsequent discussion covered the subjects below, the first three of which Semeonov raised in response to my speaking note.

(*a*) *Return of the Islands to British Administration.* Semeonov said that the Soviet Government considered that this intention amounted to an attempt to return the Falklands to a colonial status and that this was unacceptable. He subsequently read from a manuscript note a formal statement of the Soviet position:

'We consider impermissible the attempts by the United Kingdom to re-establish colonial status and we openly oppose such attempts. We qualify them as contradictory to the decision of the UN General Assembly on decolonisation of these islands and as creating a threat to peace and security'.

In reply I stressed that Britain had been negotiating in good faith right up to and beyond the New York meeting in February and in subsequent contacts. Throughout we had been guided by the principle of self determination and the paramountcy of the interests of the islanders.

(*b*) *UN Charter Article 51.* Semeonov disputed that Britain had full rights to use force. It would create a serious threat to peace. Semeonov claimed to find ambiguities in your speech in the Commons on 14 April over the status of the islands. It was not clear whether Article 51 was being invoked for the defence of Britain or the defence of the people of the Falkland Islands. I said I had noted the Soviet Government's attitude towards Article 51. I had read that article again and was quite clear that it covered the right of self-defence without making distinctions about what portion of territory had been attacked. The people living on the Falklands had been British for 150 years, and wished to remain so. It was for them that we would evoke [*sic* ?invoke] Article 51. The principle that force could be used while negotiations were in progress was one which Britain and many other countries did not want accepted. I thought that the Soviet Union too would not wish to see it endorsed.

(*c*) *British Responsibility.* Semeonov said that the Soviet Union considered Britain responsible for the conflict because its procrastination over 17 years had led to the present situation. I said I found his comment very disappointing. I could not see how, when the last communiqué of the Anglo/Argentine negotiations had referred to their cordial atmosphere and when the Falklands had shortly thereafter been subjected without warning to naked aggression, the Soviet Union could maintain the position that Britain was responsible. I would report Mr Semeonov's statement with great regret, the more so as the Soviet Union claimed to pursue a principled foreign policy. We looked for support from the Soviet Union for the full implementation of UN Resolution 502, for respect for the inhabitants' right to self-determination (a point the Soviet Union usually made much of), and condemnation of the use of violence as a way to settle territorial disputes.

(*d*) *Soviet Union's Principled Position.* Semeonov claimed that the Soviet Union did have a principled position, especially on decolonisation and against the use of force. The Soviet Union 'regretted that Argentina had used force' but it was Britain which had created the situation by bringing talks to stalemate. The Soviet position was clear. Semeonov again reminded me of the passage in Gromyko's speech in

17 December 1981 – 9 December 1982

Belgrade (my telno 181, para 2(1)),[3] calling for a considered approach to disputes. The Soviet Union stood for the fulfilment of UN resolutions and for the peaceful settlement of disputes. But now Britain threatened force and had already applied economic sanctions. Two wrongs did not make a right. I again stressed the need for implementation of SCR 502 in all its parts.

(*e*) *Press Comment*. I said I had been surprised to see that until two days ago there had been no reference in the Soviet press to the fact that Security Council Resolution 502 was mandatory and called for the withdrawal of Argentine troops and that there had been no account in the Soviet press of the wishes of the Falkland Islanders themselves. In subsequent discussion of press treatment of the crisis, Semeonov complained that the British press distorted the Soviet position and propagated flat untruths. For example, it was known that the US was supplying Britain with intelligence but now the press alleged that the Soviet Union was doing likewise for Argentina. This was simply an invention. When I pressed him on this, Semeonov confirmed that we could take this as a formal denial.

3. In conclusion Semeonov repeated the hope he had expressed at my last call that Britain would use its political wisdom and experience to find a peaceful settlement without threatening force. He feared that government speeches were tough and biased. Passion should not be allowed to overtake cold reason. The Soviet Union did not want more points of international tension. 25 April was already worryingly near.[4] Semeonov suggested that Israel might use the Falklands crisis as cover for aggression. I stressed HMG's serious search for a peaceful solution upon the pre-condition of Argentine withdrawal from the islands but formally rejected the suggestion that Britain did not have the right to use force in self-defence. I went on to stress the degree of unity shown in Parliament and throughout Britain for HMG's actions, and to draw attention to the extensive international support which we had received for our position, (by reading out the list of condemnations of Argentina action in paragraphs 2 and 3 of your guidance telegram no 51).

[3] Not printed.

[4] A possible reference to the Israeli withdrawal from the Sinai under the Camp David Accords which was due to be completed by 25 April.

No. 147

Record of a meeting between Mr Rifkind[1] and the Soviet Ambassador,
21 April 1982, 4 p.m.
Confidential (ENS 020/5)

Present:

Mr M. Rifkind	HE Mr V. I. Popov
Mr J. Macgregor	Mr N. N. Ouspensky
Mr N. Sheinwald	

1. *Mr Popov* extended his congratulations to Mr Rifkind. He looked forward to friendly personal relations and hoped that Mr Rifkind would contribute to better

[1] Malcolm Rifkind was appointed Parliamentary Under-Secretary of State for Foreign Affairs on 7 April.

UK-Soviet Relations, 1979-82

bilateral relations between Britain and the USSR in all fields. This, Mr Popov thought, was the aim of both Governments.

2. *Mr Rifkind* said that he had just returned from hearing the Secretary of State's Statement in the House on the Falkland Islands. There continued to be strong and extensive parliamentary support for the Government's policy. Mr Pym had indicated that some progress had been made in the negotiations, but that the proposals were not yet acceptable in terms of the conditions set down in Security Council Resolution 502. *Mr Popov* said that he had expressed the Soviet point of view at his meeting with Mr Hurd the previous week. The Soviet Union hoped for a peaceful solution by negotiation. He asked what would happen after Mr Pym's talks in Washington. *Mr Rifkind* said that Britain wanted a diplomatic solution. But force had been used by the Argentine to put British citizens under military occupation. This was not acceptable to us, any more than it would be acceptable to the Soviet Government if Soviet territory was occupied.

3. *Mr Popov* said that this was a question of decolonisation. He referred to the 1963 UN Resolution. *Mr Rifkind* said that the critical point was self-determination. There was no doubt of the wishes of the Islanders. *Mr Popov* suggested that basic principles of decolonisation were at stake. The problem should be resolved by negotiation. On 5 April Mr Gromyko had said that there were enough hot-beds of international tension. *Mr Rifkind* agreed. To this end it would help if the Soviet Union were to use its influence to persuade the Argentine to withdraw its troops. Before the invasion, there had been peace and negotiations. It was necessary to recognise who had caused the situation to deteriorate. *Mr Popov* asked what kind of Soviet assistance was meant. *Mr Rifkind* said that the Soviet position was moving close to justifying the Argentine contentions, which were in dispute. This was difficult to understand. *Mr Popov* repeated that the Soviet position was clear and unchanged. The Soviet Union participated actively in decolonisation questions at the UN.

4. *Mr Rifkind* noted that there were many territorial claims in the world. Decolonisation meant independence and self-determination of the colonial people. If the use of force was endorsed, grave damage would be done to the international order. He asked why the Soviet Union would not encourage the Argentine to withdraw its forces and support a diplomatic resolution of the problem. *Mr Popov* said that it was the Argentine and Britain who were in dispute. There were many means available to solve the problem diplomatically, some direct, some indirect, with UN help or not. The Soviet Union would not interfere.

5. *Mr Rifkind* said that he welcomed Mr Semeonov's assurance that the Soviet Union was passing no intelligence to the Argentine. *Mr Popov* said that he had expected his first meeting with the Minister to cover bilateral relations, but since the discussion had turned to this subject, he was authorised by Moscow to draw attention to the unfriendly statement made by the British Ambassador to Washington, Sir N Henderson.[2] This had been published in the British press and

---

[2] On 19 April, during the course of an interview on US television, Sir N. Henderson stated that 'the Soviet Union is giving extremely important help to the Argentinians at the moment by supplying knowledge about our fleet movements'. Henderson recorded in his diary for 10 April: 'My main aim is to expose the unholy alliance between the Soviets and the Argentinians. The playing of the anti-Communist card is the best way to win any game here. The pro-Argentinians in the State Department and Jeane Kirkpatrick are saying that the USA must not take sides for fear of driving the Argentinians into the arms of the Bear. My answer is that they are already there. The Russians are observing our fleet and notifying the Argentinians of our movements.' *Mandarin: The Diaries of an Ambassador 1969-1982* (London: Weidenfeld and Nicolson, 1994), p. 452.

17 December 1981 – 9 December 1982

carried on tapes, e.g. UPI. Mr Rifkind would know the statement being referred to. The Soviet side regarded it as inadmissible and provocative. *Mr Rifkind* noted the Ambassador's comment. He said that any remarks made by Sir N Henderson naturally reflected the British Government's views. And the Government spoke for the whole British public and Parliament. In Britain there was great strength of feeling on this subject. We had received much support from the Community, the Commonwealth, non-aligned and Third World countries and at the UN. This was not a peripheral matter for us. It was only right to draw the Ambassador's attention to it. *Mr Popov* repeated that Soviet policy gave no cause for inadmissible and provocative statements.

6. Turning to bilateral relations, Mr Popov said that the Soviet side had on many occasions expressed its readiness to develop Anglo-Soviet relations, if the British side was also willing. He referred to Mr Brezhnev's remark at the 1981 CPSU Congress that bilateral relations were stagnant. The Soviet Union wanted to develop relations in all fields—culture, science, trade and political relations. There were also relations in the arms control field. Mr Popov had the previous week discussed with Mr Hurd the Soviet view of the INF negotiations and Mr Brezhnev's recent proposals at the Soviet Trades Union Congress. These offered a good basis for the negotiations. Great Britain could play a very important role in disarmament and arms control. As far as bilateral trade was concerned, Mr Popov suggested that Britain had slipped behind its Western European competitors in trade with the USSR, despite having historically been the Soviet Union's first and leading trade partner. There had been a 12 percent decline in bilateral trade turnover in 1981. The Prime Minister had told Mr Popov that she supported mutually profitable trade relations.

7. *Mr Rifkind* asked what was needed to give impetus to bilateral trade. Mr Popov suggested that, first, there should be no artificial obstacles to trade, or discrimination. Second, both sides should show an interest. The official-level Review meeting had been successfully held in March. But now the Soviet Trade Counsellor could not obtain an answer from the Department of Trade about the Joint Commission which was due to begin on 17 May. The Soviet side needed something definite. As Ambassador, Mr Popov's job was to improve relations. He was envious of his Soviet colleagues in Western European capitals. *Mr Rifkind* said there was a mutual interest in improving trade. We agreed on the general objective, but the detail of how to achieve it was less straightforward. Trade could only benefit both countries. *Mr Popov* referred to the long-term character of Soviet trade planning.

8. Mr Popov handed over the section of Mr Brezhnev's recent interview dealing with the US-Soviet Summit. *Mr Rifkind* said that we hoped a meeting would be possible and would be mutually beneficial. He sought the Ambassador's assessment of the Geneva talks. *Mr Popov* replied that progress was possible, if the US was genuine about the negotiations. The zero option was not a reasonable proposal. The Soviet Union had always been a proponent of arms limitation. There were qualitative and quantitative aspects. As for new weaponry, of 25 new systems introduced since World War II, 22 had US authorship. The Soviet Union had to catch up, but was not the instigator. As far as the qualitative aspect was concerned, US assertions that the Soviet Union had superiority were unfounded. There was an approximate parity. Herr Schmidt and Mr Carter had said there was a balance, and

UK-Soviet Relations, 1979-82

in recent days Mr Warnke[3] had said that the Soviet Union did not have superiority and that the zero option was unrealistic, since it would force unilateral disarmament on the Soviet Union. The real purpose of the American position was to create US superiority by diplomatic means. It was therefore unacceptable.

9. *Mr Rifkind* asked why it was not possible to isolate the talks on medium range systems from the wider strategic context. Referring to the SS-20, he sought Mr Popov's confirmation that there was at present no comparable deployment of US systems. *Mr Popov* referred to a recent article by an ex-Deputy Director of the CIA who had stated that the West had enough weapons to counter the SS-20. The SS-20 was in any case simply a replacement for older types of weapon. The balance had not changed. Indeed, total megatonnage had decreased. Mr Popov also referred to the desire for peace in the Soviet Union as a result of Soviet losses in the War. He had lost five members of his family. Had he not been in the Siberian regiment, he might also have been a casualty.

10. The meeting ended at 16.35 hours.

[3] Paul Warnke, former Director of the US Arms Control and Disarmament Agency.

No. 148

Sir C. Keeble (Moscow) to Mr Pym, 18 May 1982, 3.08 p.m.[1]
Tel. No. 286 Immediate, Confidential (DPN 083/18)

MIPT: Brezhnev on nuclear arms.[2]

1. Europe. Brezhnev tries to present a constructive approach to the Geneva INF talks. His criticism of the US approach is restrained and there is no hint of the disillusionment with the talks which has crept into recent Soviet comment. The message is that the search for compromise should continue.

2. His attempts to answer criticism of the Soviet position as announced in his 16 March speech (my telno 136)[3] are clearly aimed at Western European, especially FRG, opinion. Brezhnev does not deny that there are SS20s (not mentioned by name) beyond the Urals, which could be aimed at Western Europe and by implication he admits a Western interest in not having any 'additional' ones there. But he deliberately uses different and vague geographical expressions: 'beyond the Urals' and 'eastern part of the country' and ends with the clearly intended implication that existing missiles in the 'eastern part' are aimed at China (also not mentioned by name), so putting them beyond the scope of the Geneva talks.

3. Two new points are the statement that the construction of missile sites has also been unilaterally frozen, and the claim that missiles are already being reduced by a considerable amount. The reduction is no longer tied to the state of the international situation (as it had been in the 16 March speech). But we are not told which or how many missiles are being reduced.

[1] Repeated Info Immediate Washington, UKDEL NATO, MODUK. Info Saving to NATO Posts, Dublin, Warsaw, Budapest, Bucharest, E. Berlin, Prague, Sofia, Belgrade, New Delhi, Tokyo, Peking, UKMIS New York, UKMIS Geneva in New York, UKDEL Vienna.
[2] Not printed. Moscow telegram No. 285 outlined the main points of a speech President Brezhnev gave at the opening session of the Soviet Youth League (Komsomol) in Moscow on 18 May. Much of the speech was devoted to the issue of nuclear weapons in Europe and strategic arms.
[3] Not printed. See No. 142 for analysis of the speech.

17 December 1981 – 9 December 1982

4. Strategic arms. Brezhnev has agreed to early commencement of talks on strategic arms while criticising the approach of President Reagan in his Eureka speech.[4] His remarks suggest a serious approach to the talks. The omission of specific reference to SALT II is notable but the intent to start from the SALT II position and probably use SALT II methods is clear in the references to 'preserving everything positive' and 'not starting from scratch'. The call for a quantitative and qualitative moratorium was expected, but not all qualitative improvements in strategic weapons are ruled out. Brezhnev is careful not to limit negotiating possibilities by either addressing Reagan's proposals in any detail or by putting forward specific counterproposals.

FCO please pass to all Saving addressees.[5]

---

[4] In this speech, delivered at Eureka College in Illinois on 9 May, President Reagan announced a two-stage process to reduce US and Soviet strategic arsenals. The first stage would entail a reduction in the numbers of land and submarine-launched ballistic missile warheads by at least one-third. The second stage would seek to achieve equal ceilings on ballistic missile throw weight. The President stated that the aim of the proposal was to enhance deterrence and achieve stability through significant reductions in the most destabilising nuclear systems. See *Public Papers: Reagan (1982)*, Book I, pp. 580-86.
[5] On 25 May the US Embassy delivered their assessment of the speech to Patrick Wright, DUSS (circulated to all NATO Foreign Ministers). In a minute to Mr Gillmore of 26 May, Mr Logan, of Defence Department, noted the American assessment agreed closely with the British view, in particular the judgement that President Brezhnev's tone was moderate and encouraging about the renewal of START talks. There was also agreement that in expanding the moratorium on Soviet INF missile deployments, the Soviets were responding to Western criticisms. The letter also asked for continued public support for the US position in the INF negotiations in Geneva and the forthcoming START talks. If the Soviets perceived that the Alliance firmly supported the US positions in these two negotiations, they would be more readily convinced of the need to negotiate seriously and to accept meaningful limitations and reductions of their own forces. Mr Wright assured the Embassy of the Government's continued support.

No. 149

Mr Bullard to Sir C. Keeble (Moscow), 26 May 1982
Confidential (EN 020/1)

Dear Curtis,

US/Soviet Relations

1. Many thanks for your admirable despatch of 17 March[1] which was particularly timely in view of the full programme of East/West discussions that lies ahead. President Reagan's Eureka speech on 9 May[2] with Brezhnev's response on 18 May[3] have set the scene for a six-month period which should include the Versailles and NATO summits, a further Haig/Gromyko encounter, and possibly the first meeting between Reagan and Brezhnev. It is also, of course, a period in which the START talks should begin.

2. Despite the Russians' critical reaction to the START proposals which the President put forward at Eureka, and their predictable hostility to his accompanying programme for East/West relations, I share your view (Moscow

---

[1] No. 140. The despatch was actually dated 11 March.
[2] See No. 148, note 4.
[3] See No. 148.

UK-Soviet Relations, 1979-82

telno 268)[4] that they will come to the START table and may well take a more positive line in due course, albeit to advance distinctly different proposals of their own. Their pressure to resume the SALT/START process has been genuine (whatever the propaganda benefits of such a stance); and among the reasons for their anxiety about the re-emergence of popular protest in Poland is that they will not want Polish developments to prejudice START prospects a second time (I doubt if they believe that the Eureka speech has really disposed of linkage). They probably recognise that the next few months are likely to determine whether there is to be any real content to the US/Soviet relations during the Reagan Presidency; and whatever the polemics, I have no doubt they would rather there was a substantive dialogue than not. They are, however, likely to remain suspicious about the genuineness of Reagan's commitment to dialogue, a suspicion that is not wholly without echo in the Alliance. Remarks made recently by Burt and others seem to indicate that the Americans are at least as much concerned with the public presentation of some of their proposals as with content. For example, it seems that references in the Eureka speech to Afghanistan etc. were not made on the basis of any private discussions with the Russians.[5]

3. Nevertheless such a dialogue, even if unproductive for much of the time, at least has an educative value; which in turn is relevant to your contention that the Russians often misjudge the Americans. It is a proposition with which I would agree, although I would equally add that the Americans frequently misjudge the Russians. The Russians certainly misread the likely reaction to their abuse of détente and their invasion of Afghanistan. It seems to me, for all that they sometimes try to exploit them, that the Russians usually fail to understand the popular pressures at work on the US Administration (and on other democratic governments). They misjudged the effect the Tehran hostage issue had on American attitudes and politics, and Suslov's apparent puzzlement over the Falklands issue (Moscow telno 238 of 29 April)[4] may be something of a parallel in our own case. For their part, the American misjudgements have less to do with ignorance and lack of imagination than, I would suggest, with a tendency to over-simplify. Social unrest and political upheaval are too easily held to be the product of Soviet meddling; increasing Soviet economic difficulties are too quickly seen to promise a radical weakening of the Soviet system; and the present state of flux in the Soviet leadership is being over-dramatised in itself and too readily assumed to presage policy changes. (We ourselves assume a large measure of continuity whoever succeeds Brezhnev.) In the American case the Alliance provides an opportunity for discussion, dissension and revision. The Russians have no such sounding-board. The conclusion of course is that communication between Washington and Moscow is to be encouraged, however shrill the tone. At present each side is suffering from under-exposure to the other. We very much hope therefore that the possible Haig/Gromyko and Reagan/Brezhnev meetings will go ahead.

4. I am sure you are right to suggest that the correlation of forces will appear to the Russians to have shifted against them in the last two years. 1979-81 may turn out to have been something of a watershed for Soviet foreign policy, the end of a

---

[4] Not printed.

[5] President Reagan stated that the United States was prepared to engage in a serious effort to negotiate an end to the conflict caused by the Soviet invasion of Afghanistan. The US was ready to cooperate in an international effort to resolve the problem, to secure a full Soviet withdrawal from Afghanistan, and to ensure self-determination for the Afghan people.

17 December 1981 – 9 December 1982

comparatively risk free expansionist period when the Americans were traumatised by Vietnam and Watergate, and the Europeans lulled by comfortable delusions about the nature of détente. Afghanistan, the Polish crisis and the advent of Reagan and bleak economic prospects have conspired to make it all look much more difficult from the Russians' point of view.

5. Poland has, in large measure, come to symbolise this shift in Soviet fortunes. A major foreign policy dilemma for the Russians, the crisis has at the same time raised fundamental questions about the relevance and viability of the Soviet political and economic system and the Russians' ability to find convincing answers to them. I do not mean to suggest by this that they cannot maintain control of Poland of course they can: but the knowledge that 30 years after transplanting it, rejection of the Soviet system in Eastern Europe can still only be overcome by force must have had a corrosive impact on Soviet confidence. The damage it has done in propaganda terms and the damage it will go on doing to the CMEA economic system (and also to Soviet standing in the international communist movement) presents the Russians with a heavy bill for their uneasy and debilitating maintenance of empire. It would be encouraging to think that recent experience may have prompted at least some in the leadership to consider whether Soviet long-term interests might not be better served by adopting a lighter touch in Eastern Europe, with an altogether more flexible and more sophisticated policy. But there is nothing to suggest that anyone in Moscow is yet ready to think in such terms.

6. One reason for this is the deeply held conviction that nothing must be risked that might disturb the post-war settlement in Europe. We have been struck here by Soviet sensitivity over any suggestion that it might be time to review the structure which emerged in Europe after the Second World War; the communiqué issued after Jaruzelski's March visit to Moscow is an obvious example. As you say in your despatch, the Russians are not about to take chances with anything they regard as a direct threat to the Soviet Union and its ruling caste, not least because, as their propaganda tirelessly repeats, the present arrangements were bought with 20 million Russian dead and it is sacrilege to question the fruits of such a sacrifice. On 9 May, Ustinov again reminded us and the Poles that the liberation of Poland cost over 600,000 Soviet lives. It is as well to remind ourselves that the last war continues not only to determine the political landscape of Eastern Europe but also to condition the psychology of its Soviet masters, and I would not expect the passing of the Brezhnev era to affect this very much.

7. I therefore agree that, with so much at stake, the Russians will consider they have acted with restraint over Poland, although it is a restraint motivated too by concern for their wider international interests, in particular pursuit of their 'peace programme' which they hope will prove the solvent of trans-Atlantic unity. It would be interesting to examine the Polish crisis simply from the perspective of the TNF/INF debate, and to assess just how far it affected the Soviet approach. The interplay of the two issues was neatly symbolised by the Czechoslovak Party Congress in April 1981;[6] waiting to see what Brezhnev's speech to the Congress would indicate about Soviet intentions towards Poland, we were treated instead to a further lecture on the merits of the Soviet Peace Programme and the iniquities of the NATO double decision. It was a speech to Western public opinion, not the Czech Party faithful, an example of how the Russians have missed no opportunity

[6] See No. 94, note 3.

UK-Soviet Relations, 1979-82

to encourage the Western 'peace movements'. As you say, these are the one bright spot on their horizon; Andropov[7] was at it again at the Leninfest on 22 April. But I suspect that despite their efforts, and some satisfactory results, they may now be beginning to wonder whether 'the peace movements' will, after all, do the trick. For a number of reasons, the moratorium on INF deployments has had less impact in the West than the Russians must have hoped for. Schmidt was successful in holding the line at his Party Conference last month; and the INF negotiations and the prospect of START talks have gone a fair way towards taking the edge off popular anxieties in the West. The Russians will still hope that, as the moment for INF deployment approaches, resolution will weaken. But my guess is it now seems more problematical to them whether the peace programme and the 'peace movements' will be enough to derail the NATO double decision.

8. It has taken a long time for the Reagan entourage to accept that the two superpowers need to take account of each other and to talk to each other, and that dialogue can be good for the West as well as the East. I doubt whether all those around Reagan still do accept it, although as far as the President himself is concerned the difficulty of reconciling the defence budget with his overall economic objectives, the mood in Europe and the growth of domestic opposition to his apparently confrontational stance towards the Soviet Union must have done much to persuade him to accept what Haig in his speech to the US Chamber of Commerce on 27 April called 'an American approach to the Soviet Union that balances strength and negotiations'.

9. Given that the pressures on Reagan coincide with a period of economic and political difficulty for the Russians, circumstances should, in theory, be propitious for a shift in the attitude of both sides towards accommodation and away from confrontation. This is not to say it will happen; logic is frequently a poor guide to events and, as you conclude, the factors determining the bilateral relationship will not evolve quickly or easily. But if in the next few months the Russians and Americans can establish a really serious dialogue on arms control issues, it might have a beneficial impact on the wider bilateral relationship and on the East/West climate generally. The bones of contention will of course remain; Afghanistan, Poland, and the arms build-up will still be there; the Russians will be no more inclined to surrender positions of advantage or pass up opportunities than before. Is there really a prospect that they will accept the sort of rigorous verification that the Americans have in mind? We shall still be faced with the task of trying to persuade the Russians, in Kissinger's words, 'that they cannot have everything, that there are no free lunches, that they cannot identify their security with imposing regimes against the will of the population, that they cannot subvert structures on our side of the line while maintaining by force those on their side of the line, all the time getting our economic help. They will have to choose'; or as President Reagan put it on 9 May: 'The Soviet Union must make the difficult choices brought on by its military budgets and economic shortcomings'.

10. Getting them to choose restraint will be as much a question of their own economic and domestic difficulties as of US policy. But a more substantial US/Soviet relationship might make them less inclined to go looking for trouble and more inclined to try to reach agreements which offer economic, political and military benefits. We shall continue to do what we can to encourage the Americans to pursue a dialogue, not only in the hope that the difficulties of the past two years

---

[7] Yuri Andropov, Chairman of the KGB.

17 December 1981 – 9 December 1982

may make the Russians more receptive to Western ideas about restraint and accommodation but also in the knowledge that such dialogue, even if unrewarding, is a crucial tool in the successful management of the Alliance.

N. H. R. A. BROOMFIELD
(for J. L. Bullard)

No. 150

Mr Broomfield to Sir C. Keeble (Moscow), 24 June 1982
Confidential (ENS 014/3)

Dear Curtis,

19th Komsomol[1] Congress

1. In my letter of 2 June[2] I promised you some further comment on your despatch of 26 May.

2. Drab, ritualistic and depressing are indeed the adjectives which come to mind in describing the recent *Komsomol* Congress. They are of course adjectives which would also characterise most other highly-staged Soviet events of this kind. The exhortations [to] constant and prepared applause and exploitation of the occasion to put over a specific foreign policy message are only too familiar. We agree that it is highly unlikely that this kind of presentation will inculcate the virtues of hard work, discipline, patriotism and ideological fervour in Soviet youth. And, *a fortiori*, it does not look like a message or style which will reap dividends once repeated at the lower *Komsomol* branch level round the country. The often self-righteous and moralising tone is, after all, precisely what annoys young people about their elders anywhere in the world.

3. But what are Soviet youth really like? In his despatch of 7 June 1977[3] your predecessor referred to a letter to a Soviet youth paper which said that the main thing for Soviet youth was 'to wear ragged jeans, make love and to be like everyone else'. Howard Smith[4] described the large majority of Soviet youth as politically apathetic and unlikely to oppose the regime as such. Instead they were interested in a higher standard of living, especially more consumer goods. We here have seen nothing in the intervening years to challenge these basic statements.

4. However, it is easy to overstate the point about materialism and political apathy. There is evidence of a yearning for spiritual values among a considerable section of Soviet youth. This may show even in their interest in Western pop music. The Moscow University students who gathered to honour the memory of John Lennon or the many young Muscovites and Leningraders who flocked to hear Elton John were, I suspect, seeking something more than a strong beat. The same certainly goes for the very large numbers who attend poetry readings or who stand outside or even inside churches at Easter, even if in many cases they may not find what they are looking for.

5. There is also evidence that ordinary Soviet people, young or old, can work

[1] Soviet youth organisation.
[2] Not printed. The letter of 2 June acknowledged the despatch of 26 May which reported on events at the Congress (see No. 148, note 2).
[3] Not printed.
[4] HM Ambassador in Moscow, 1976-78.

UK-Soviet Relations, 1979-82

out for themselves basic principles about the sort of political society they would prefer. This is clear from the *samizdat*[5] material reaching the West. This is not to say that in time a movement of a more widespread nature could develop in which political opposition to the regime was a feature. How could it, in the face of the omnipresent party and the KGB—and *Komsomol*? But we do not, I think, need to see the Soviet youth as divided into a majority looking cynically for improved material wellbeing, while the minority of careerists and future members of the *nachalstvo*[6] are equally cynically mouthing the dogma of the revolution with little personal commitment or conviction that the message will make an impact on others. There are, I believe, many who have considerable latent idealism which cannot find fulfilment in anything offered by the Party.

6. All this is, of course, relevant to Western cultural and information policy. There is no need for us to plug jeans and videos—they advertise themselves. Some of our effort needs to be directed specifically towards the reaffirmation of our own political and social values. But it seems to me that anything we do which demonstrates the infinitely greater scope offered to artistic and intellectual creativity in the West than the Soviet Union carries a message which will find a much readier response among Soviet youth than the weary sterility of the *Komsomol*. Having said that I realise that your mind will naturally turn to major cultural events. I accept your (unspoken) thought and should perhaps rephrase the sentence as anything we can do 'within the present constraints'.

Yours,

N. H. R. A. BROOMFIELD

[5] Underground literature.
[6] The 'bosses' or the 'elite'.

Throughout 1982 officials became increasingly concerned with the poor state of bilateral relations with the Soviet Union and saw a need to re-energise UK policy (Nos. 135, 136, 137). This was a view shared by Sir C. Keeble in Moscow (No. 138) and, to an extent, by Ministers (No. 141).

In July Mr Manning produced a draft paper entitled 'East-West Political Relations: UK Policy towards the Soviet Union' in which he advocated relaxing the policy of maintaining minimum political contact with the Soviet Union and suggested that the Prime Minister should visit Moscow (No. 151). He was supported in this view by Mr Broomfield (No. 152) and Mr Walden (No. 153). A submission and draft paper from Mr Broomfield, in which he proposed re-establishing political dialogue and cultural exchanges (No. 154), were put to Sir J. Bullard who agreed with the recommendations (No. 156). At the same time officials were engaged in drafting a paper dealing with British policy in East-West economic relations in the 1980s (No. 159).

Mr Broomfield's paper was discussed at a meeting with the Secretary of State on 15 September, during which the proposal for the Prime Minister to visit Moscow was dropped as too dramatic a gesture. Mr Pym circulated the final paper to No. 10 and OD colleagues on 27 September (No. 160). Mrs Thatcher remained unsure about such a significant change of policy and indicated that she wanted to discuss the issue with the Secretary of State. A briefing note was prepared by Mr Broomfield in preparation for the meeting (No. 162).

Meanwhile, on his arrival in Moscow the new British Ambassador, Sir Iain

17 December 1981 – 9 December 1982

Sutherland, expressed his surprise at the extent to which the UK had cut itself off from the Soviet Union (No. 164). Mr Broomfield reported that at a meeting on 14 October, to prepare himself for his discussion with the Prime Minister, Mr Pym still expressed himself strongly in favour of 'thickening up' dialogue with the Soviet Union but it remained to be seen whether his arguments would carry the day (teleletter from Mr Broomfield to Sir I. Sutherland, 19 October 1982; ENS 020/5). The meeting with Mrs Thatcher eventually took place on 17 November (No. 172).

No. 151

Draft Paper by Mr Manning on East/West Political Relations: UK Policy, 2 July 1982[1]
Confidential (EN 021/6)

Background

1. East/West political relations have been severely strained in the past three years by lack of Soviet restraint in the conduct of international relations. The Soviet invasion of Afghanistan provoked a sharp deterioration in the East/West climate, and Soviet complicity in the military crackdown in Poland further exacerbated tensions.

2. Like our Western partners, we have signalled our strong disapproval of Soviet behaviour during this period by taking a number of measures designed to restrict the scope of our bilateral relations. These have included *inter alia* curtailing high level political contacts and reducing cultural exchanges. But the Afghan and Polish crises seem likely to continue indefinitely, with no prospect of improvement in directions we would like to see. In the circumstances, this paper argues that it is time to reconsider our approach. The sharp reduction in the extent of our bilateral contacts made a strong impact in the immediate aftermath of the Soviet invasion of Afghanistan; but it is now suffering from the law of diminishing returns. It is doubtful whether the absence of bilateral political dialogue is any longer in our interests, or is likely to persuade the Russians to moderate their policies in ways we should like; the reverse is perhaps more likely to be the case.

Bilateral Political Contacts

3. Following the invasion of Afghanistan, we greatly reduced the frequency of our bilateral exchanges with the Russians, both at Ministerial and at Senior Official level. Our partners did likewise. There have been occasional bilateral meetings between Foreign Ministers in the margins of international meetings (e.g. the UN General Assembly), and one visit to Moscow by Lord Carrington to put forward the EC proposal for a settlement to the Afghan crisis. But there has been no regular pattern of discussion at Ministerial level nor any regular exchanges at the level of political directors. The lack of such dialogue deprives us of the chance to assess Soviet thinking at first hand, as well as denying us the opportunity of exposing senior Soviet foreign policy makers to our point of view.

4. Lord Carrington's visit to Moscow a year ago[2] (like Mr Haig's three bilateral meetings with Mr Gromyko since) was an occasion when plain speaking left the

---

[1] This paper was written following an Office meeting with Mr Broomfield on 30 June to reconsider whether HMG's policy of minimum political contacts with the Soviet Union should be modified.

[2] See Nos. 107 and 108.

UK-Soviet Relations, 1979-82

Russians in no doubt about Western views and policies, and which provided a useful opportunity for us to assess those of the Soviet Union. The Carrington and Haig meetings gave no impression that we had done the Russians a favour by bestowing a spurious respectability on them (as was the case with President Giscard d'Estang's ill-judged meeting with President Brezhnev in Warsaw in May 1980). On the contrary, these encounters were widely perceived to have provided the opportunity for some tough talking and to have enabled the West to register its opposition to Soviet policies, and the continuing strength of Western feeling over Afghanistan and Poland. Encounters of this kind, which put the Russians under pressure by challenging them to justify their actions and policies, are more likely to have an influence on the Soviet leadership than a refusal by Western leaders to conduct a dialogue.

5. We should therefore now seek to re-establish a regular pattern of political discussion with the Russians. Our aim should be to set this up on three levels. The first would be at Foreign Minister level: in principle we should aim for annual discussions alternating between London and Moscow, supplemented by the traditional bilateral meeting in the margins of the UN General Assembly. The second level would be talks between the Minister in the FCO responsible for East/West relations (Mr Rifkind) and a senior Soviet Deputy Foreign Minister (Kornienko). These should also be annually, alternating between capitals. And the third level would be talks between the Political Director (Sir J. Bullard)[3] and a more junior Soviet Deputy Foreign Minister (Ryzhov or equivalent) as his approximate analogue, again on an annual basis alternating between capitals.

6. We should aim to ensure that the rhythm of these exchanges was regular and, if on occasion we chose to interrupt it to signal our displeasure at Soviet behaviour, we should only do so as a symbolic gesture and on a temporary basis. We should make it clear that rather than break off our bilateral political exchanges we would want to use them to leave the Russians in no doubt about the extent of our displeasure. We would thereby avoid getting into our present position where we find it difficult to justify reopening a political dialogue with the Russians because there has been no resolution of the Afghan or Polish crises.

7. In addition to regular exchanges on the three levels described in paragraph 6 [*sic*], we should also remain alive to the possibility of exchanges at both higher and lower levels, on an *ad hoc* basis. The idea of the Prime Minister visiting Moscow and talking plainly to the Soviet leaders has much to commend it. Her ability to present the Western case forcefully and lucidly while eschewing false bonhomie, would be an educative process for the Soviet leadership. At non-Ministerial level, we should also be ready to hold expert level meetings where we believe these would be to our advantage. Nuclear issues (including non proliferation), Southern Africa, and the UN are all possible subjects.

8. It is increasingly clear that other Western governments are also reviewing the possibility of resuming bilateral exchanges with the Russians, a process that has been given additional impetus by the possibility of a Reagan/Brezhnev summit later this year. The French are a case in point. There have been hints that M. Cheysson may soon have talks with Gromyko, despite saying until recently that such a dialogue was ruled out by the Afghan and Polish crises; and it is rumoured that such an exchange might well pave the way for a visit to Moscow by President Mitterrand in 1983.

---

[3] Mr Bullard was awarded a KCMG in the Queen's birthday honours announced on 12 June.

17 December 1981 – 9 December 1982

9. The signs that the post-Afghanistan Western boycott of high level political exchanges with the Russians may be weakening is not surprising. The sense of outrage has inevitably dimmed, other issues have supervened, and our partners are gradually accepting the inevitability of rebuilding their links with the Russians not least so that they can try to impress their own views on the Soviet leadership. We should accept the inevitability of this process and rebuild our own. Given that East/West political exchanges are almost certain to increase, it is important that a firm British voice is one of the first the Russians hear when regular contacts are restored.

Cultural Contacts

10. We should also consider re-establishing the pattern of our cultural exchanges with the Russians, sharply curtailed after the Soviet invasion of Afghanistan. Apart from satisfying the immediate need to take action to register our displeasure at Soviet behaviour, it is doubtful whether this has achieved very much. On the contrary, it has prevented us from advertising British artistic and cultural excellence in the Soviet Union, thereby assisting the regime in its efforts to minimise outside influences in the interests of maintaining orthodox conformity. At the same time, the sharp reduction in government sponsored cultural exchanges has tended to leave the field open to the Communist front organisation[s], to the advantage of the Russians.

Relations with Eastern Europe

11. The same criteria should apply in principle to our relations with the Eastern European countries. We should aim to establish a regular pattern of political contacts, and promote cultural exchanges as the shop window for Western diversity and excellence. This approach should be tailored to our overall policy towards Eastern Europe of positive discrimination, whereby we devote more effort to East European countries with comparatively liberal internal policies (Hungary) or those which attempt to assert greater independence vis-à-vis the Soviet Union (Romania) than we do to the more orthodox loyalists (Czechoslovakia or the GDR). Poland is at present a special case. Since the imposition of martial law last year, we have co-ordinated our policies closely with those of our allies. We should continue to do so; but we should monitor the way our allies implement that policy carefully and be ready to review our approach if we detect signs of a breakdown of the Western consensus.

US/European Differences

12. Recent months have seen increasing differences between the Western Europeans and the Americans over East/West relations. We do not share the US view that Soviet economic difficulties will make the Russians particularly vulnerable to Western economic pressure during the 1980s nor do we accept US arguments against the Soviet/West European gas pipeline project. For as long as the Reagan Administration is in power, differences of emphasis and of analysis are likely to persist. This makes it even more important that we should establish a political dialogue with the Russians not only so that there is a distinct British voice heard in Moscow, but also to strengthen our position when discussing Soviet affairs with the Americans.

Conclusion

13. Our present policy towards the Soviet Union is hamstrung by the measures we adopted in the aftermath of the Afghanistan crisis. With no regular pattern of bilateral political exchanges and few major cultural exchanges, we are in effect minimising our impact on Soviet policies and reducing the possibility that we

UK-Soviet Relations, 1979-82

might be able to influence those policies, either in the short or long term. We should therefore re-establish a regular pattern of such contacts, not least because our allies are beginning to move in that direction, and because differences between ourselves and the Americans on some aspects of East/West relations make it all the more important that our own voice is heard.

No. 152

Draft Paper by Mr Broomfield on East/West Relations, 13 July 1982[1]
Confidential (EN 021/6)

Introduction

1. Policy towards the Soviet Union and the other Warsaw Pact countries of Eastern Europe should be based on a dispassionate view of a system which is fundamentally inimical to the values on which our own political system is based. We should not be surprised when, from time to time, the Soviet system is obliged to reveal more publicly than is usual its underlying nature. We should recognise, however, that the Soviet system is neither transient nor monolithic. Notwithstanding our fundamental opposition there will be issues on which it may be possible to influence the Soviet Union and its partners to adopt policies which are likely to be less damaging to our interests. To exploit these opportunities we need to maintain contacts. But the way in which we use such contacts and the starting point on the British side should be to recognise the basic differences in political objectives. If the Soviet Union, or its partners, backs away from a dialogue of this sort then it will be they who have revealed their weakness and disinclination to pursue the 'battle of ideas' and not the Western partner, which at present might appear to be the case.

2. Specifically we are now boxed in by our policy of having cut back contacts with the Russians. We need to restore a dialogue not only to put across our views but to assess Soviet thinking at first hand. Differences in perception on some issues make it important that we should have our own channels to the Russians and thereby increase the weight of our contribution in discussions with the Americans and others.

Propositions

3. We should maintain a regular *political dialogue* at least at DUS and junior Minister level. Contacts which would involve bilateral visits by the Prime Minister and Secretary of State could be less frequent and depend on the international climate and Soviet policies.

4. Such a dialogue should be presented as:

(*a*) ensuring that our views on all matters are put directly to the Russians and to assess their thinking at first hand;

(*b*) parliamentary statements and press briefings would bring out the frank nature of the exchanges on such issues as Afghanistan, Poland, human rights etc.;

(*c*) communiqués would be kept to a basic minimum—'frank and businesslike

---

[1] In a covering minute dated 13 July, Mr Broomfield informed Sir J. Bullard that the draft was a condensed version of a longer paper prepared by Mr Manning (No. 151) and that 'it would be preferable to obtain your views on the basic approach before deciding whether to submit anything fuller.'

17 December 1981 – 9 December 1982

on matters of mutual concern'.

5. In our *cultural relations*, in addition to exchanges of students and teachers we should also proceed with major cultural manifestations subject to the following conditions:

(*a*) we are satisfied that our outward exhibitions are genuinely representative of our music, literature, art etc. and not edited beyond recognition by the Russians (the Exhibition of Contemporary British Art falls into the former category);

(*b*) access in the Soviet Union would be genuinely open to the Soviet public.

6. In *presenting* this policy we would argue that:

(*a*) it was important to enable the Soviet public to see that there are societies in which individual expression, diversity and originality are allowed and encouraged;

(*b*) Soviet exhibitions in the UK will allow those who wish to attend to make their own judgements of the artistic merits of the Soviet system.

7. Our *information* effort should be maintained. We should continue to issue detailed background briefs on contentious issues, six-monthly reports on CSCE implementation etc. The BBC should continue their East European services as well as working for greater audibility of their World Service.

8. *Other contacts* should be judged on their merits. When, as in the political field (Middle East, UN), we have found advantage in exchanging views we should do so. The same approach should apply to all areas, e.g. if necessary we should renegotiate the Air Services Agreement, the Treaty on Merchant Shipping etc.

9. The same criteria should apply to our relations with the Eastern European countries. This would be complementary to our policy of positive discrimination.[2]

---

[2] Mr Manning, in a minute of 13 July, noted: 'arguments in the original draft which are not reflected in the condensed version (perhaps deliberately) are:

(*a*) that we are boxed in by our own policy of having cut back contacts with the Russians;

(*b*) that we need to restore dialogue not only to put our views across but to assess Soviet thinking at first hand;

(*c*) that some of our allies (e.g. the French) show signs of resuming a dialogue with the Russians, and that we should be in the vanguard of any resumption of Western contacts not in the rear;

(*d*) and that differences of perception between ourselves and the Americans about East/West issues make it all the more important that we should establish our own voice in exchanges with the Russians (thereby increasing the weight of our contribution in discussions with the Americans).'

He wondered whether Mr Broomfield's introduction 'might not rehearse these arguments rather more explicitly before the paper goes on to discuss the specific propositions that flow from them'.

Mr Goodison commented on 16 July that Ministerial contacts on neutral ground such as New York offered the opportunity for dialogue without the penalties of publicised visits. On paragraph 6(*b*) he added: 'Don't be too sniffy. Surely their musical interpretation at least is of world standard, and their dancing.'

Mr Beel, of Research Department, was in broad agreement with the paper but thought it was a moot point whether contact should be dependent on the international climate and Soviet policies. Whilst he suspected this might be the case for domestic political reasons it avoided the basic question as to whether Britain should only talk to the Russians when they were behaving themselves. 'There is a respectable view that contacts are even more necessary at times of international tension, in order to avoid possibly dangerous misperceptions on both sides.'

UK-Soviet Relations, 1979-82

No. 153

Minute from Mr Walden[1] (Planning Staff) to Mr Smith,[2] 22 July 1982
Confidential (EN 021/6)

East/West Political Relations

1. We discussed Mr Manning's draft[3] on the phone. I agree with the thrust, but the presentation to Ministers and eventually to No. 10 will need careful consideration.

2. Firstly, I think we should have a fixed objective and timetable in mind, e.g. a visit by the Prime Minister to Moscow in about a year's time, before we get into the run-up to British elections. Secondly, the argument should be put in the broadest and most positive way, in any draft minute to the Prime Minister and perhaps to other members of DOP.[4] Such a minute could point out:

(*a*) British policy should be active, confident and assertive. After the Falklands, no-one could reasonably suggest that we are going cap in hand to the Russians, (cf. Peter Blaker (i.e. Mr Bullard's) minute to the Secretary of State of 9.8.79 about seeking Soviet respect, not their good opinion.)[5]

(*b*) We cannot maintain the exacting stance of a middle-ranking country with world interests if we do not talk to one of the superpowers.

(*c*) If we remain on the sidelines, our weight in the councils of Europe will suffer accordingly, especially when the French edge back into a dialogue with Moscow. There is no question however of competing with the French or Germans: we are in a special position and can pursue our dialogue in our own way.

(*d*) We shall need first hand experience of the Russians (particularly if a new leadership emerges in the next year) if we are to influence American East/West policies, or fight our battles on e.g. East/West trade effectively.

(*e*) Potentially serious changes are looming in Eastern Europe. German reactions may need steadying. We shall be badly placed to do this if we are not in contact with Soviet prime movers.

(*f*) The Russians are weak politically and economically, but increasingly strong militarily. Both their strengths and their weaknesses are arguments in favour of a dialogue.

(*g*) Dialogue with the Russians could help to take the steam out of the disarmament lobby.

(*h*) The decline in the traditionally high level of Soviet studies in the UK is another sign of incipient marginalisation.

3. We should not labour the Afghanistan point too much, though we could mention that the fact that the Russians are bogged down there is an element of their weakness. Any continued liberalisation in Poland could of course be used as an argument for increased contacts with the Russians.

4. No misleading promises about increased trade, or indeed any practical benefits (apart from the routine handout of a few personal cases), should be dangled before DOP. The diplomatic case for high level contacts stands by itself.

---

[1] George Walden was appointed Head of Planning Staff in July.
[2] Roland Smith, Assistant (Soviet Union), EESD.
[3] No. 151.
[4] The Cabinet's Oversea and Defence Committee.
[5] Not printed.

17 December 1981 – 9 December 1982

Public and parliamentary opinion here would however need to be prepared for a resumption of these contacts, using some of the above arguments, to avoid leaving the field open to simplistic and petty right wing critics.

5. In putting forward our case, we should avoid any suggestion of promoting 'good relations' with Russia for their own sake. We should also avoid focussing on ticklish and emotive issues such as cultural contacts, though we would expect these to pick up slowly and as unobtrusively as possible as time goes by.

6. It may well be that the Secretary of State will decide not to send such a minute to the PM. But if we think it is the right line of action, there is nothing to prevent us putting forward a forcefully reasoned case. If we do not do this in the coming months, time will begin to run out as the 1984 elections approach.

7. The Secretary of State's invitation to Gromyko to lunch would be a natural first step. It will come too soon to be a convenient occasion for sounding him out on a visit by the PM, even if she agreed. But EESD may wish to include in Mr Pym's briefing some mention of the possibility as a culmination of this process, not for use with the Russians.[6]

G. G. H. WALDEN

[6] The paper on East/West Political Relations was redrafted to take into account the comments of Mr Walden, Mr Beel and others, and a draft minute prepared from the Secretary of State to the Prime Minister recommending that she should visit the Soviet Union in the summer of 1983. In submitting the documents to Mr Broomfield on 12 August Mr Smith thought this was the logical outcome of the policy being advocated and its inclusion gave the paper focus. In addition it might make the policy as a whole more attractive to the Prime Minister (ENS 020/5).

Further comments came from Mr Walden on 19 August who thought that trade should get more of a mention, if only to pre-empt the argument that a visit would not lead to more exports, and also that the minute should pre-empt the rejoinder that the Americans would not like it. The point that difficulties might arise with the Americans over a visit by the Prime Minister to Moscow was also picked up by Mr Goodison. Mr Broomfield, in a minute of 23 August, recognised that this point might be contentious and spelt out more clearly in the redrafted paper both the US and FRG current practice and proposals.

Mr Burton, head of the South Asia Department, was concerned that as the Soviet intervention in Afghanistan was the original cause of the freeze in Anglo-Soviet relations, the paper should consider the presentational impact of a proposed thaw on those countries—particularly Pakistan and other Muslim countries—who had taken a firm stance on Afghanistan via the Islamic Conference Organisation (minute of 25 August). A new paragraph was incorporated covering the attitude of other countries.

No. 154

Submission from Mr Broomfield to Sir J. Bullard, 26 August 1982
Confidential (ENS 020/5)

East/West Political Relations: UK Policy towards the Soviet Union
1. I submit a paper prepared in EESD[1] which argues that we should reconsider our policy of minimal political contacts with the Soviet Union. Among the paper's proposals is the suggestion that the Prime Minister should visit the Soviet Union. I therefore also submit a draft minute from the Secretary of State.[2] Planning Staff,

[1] Not printed. For the final version of this paper see No. 160.
[2] Not printed. The draft minute argued that there was no prospect of any early resolution of either the Afghan or the Polish crises and that Britain might have a greater impact on the thinking of the

UK-Soviet Relations, 1979-82

TRED, ECD(E), CRD and SAD concur.

2. As a consequence of the Soviet invasion of Afghanistan, and of Soviet complicity in the military crackdown in Poland, we sharply curtailed high level political contacts with the Russians to signal our displeasure at their conduct. We also curtailed cultural exchanges. Our allies adopted a similar policy, but (apart from the Americans) were less rigorous in implementing it. There is no doubt that this has had an impact on the Russians and that they have disliked the measure of international isolation imposed on them. But this policy is now suffering from the law of diminishing returns and for the reasons advanced in the attached paper the time has come when our interests are likely to be better served by re-establishing a political dialogue with the Russians than by refusing to conduct a dialogue at all.

3. The paper argues that we should seek to establish such a dialogue at three levels: Foreign Minister, Deputy Foreign Minister (Mr Rifkind) and Political Director. There should be other exchanges at both higher and lower levels on an *ad hoc* basis where we judge these to be in our interest. We should be ready to hold expert-level meetings when appropriate, and Mr Goodison[3] might also make an early familiarisation visit to the Soviet Union. At the same time, we should re-establish the pattern of our cultural exchanges insofar as these give us opportunities to project Western values to the Soviet people.

4. As far as high level visits are concerned, the paper argues that we should encourage the Prime Minister to visit Moscow, perhaps in the summer of 1983. The Prime Minister is recognised by the Russians as one of the most considerable of Western leaders (the more so since the Falklands Crisis). Despite the pro-Argentine line taken by their propaganda, the Russians have a healthy respect for the successful use of military force. A visit by her to Moscow would be valuable to the Alliance as [a] whole, as well as enabling us to assess Soviet policies and personalities at first hand. This is particularly important in view of the uncertainty surrounding the succession to President Brezhnev. There is no reason why such a visit need be seen as representing a 'softening' of our attitude to Afghanistan, Poland, the Soviet military build-up etc; rather it would offer an opportunity for the Prime Minister to be seen conducting the argument face to face with the Soviet leaders.

5. Apart from the benefits such a visit might bring to Anglo-Soviet relations,

Soviet leadership by talking frankly and directly to them, rather than continuing to avoid political exchanges. The reasons set out were: '*First*, the political uncertainty surrounding the eventual departure of President Brezhnev makes it important for us to have first hand experience of Soviet thinking and of as many members of the Soviet leadership as possible. This will be valuable to us not only for our own understanding of developments in the Soviet Union but also in discussing East/West prospects with our allies. *Second*, the uncertainty about Soviet prospects is matched by a similar uncertainty about the prospects for the Soviet Union's Eastern European neighbours. The Polish crisis is likely to be with us for some time yet, and could prove the precursor of serious economic and political upheavals elsewhere in Eastern Europe. In these circumstances we may well find ourselves trying to exert a steadying influence on our European partners, particularly the FRG, a role we shall be better able to play if we are a recognized and knowledgeable interlocutor of the Soviet Union. *Third*, with serious transatlantic differences over East/West trade policy, and over the Soviet Union's economic prospects, the greater our first hand knowledge of the Soviet Union, the better placed we shall be in discussing these issues with the Americans: and *fourth*, a renewed dialogue with the Russians could help to demonstrate our continued interest in genuinely balanced and verifiable measures of arms control at a time when pressure from the disarmament lobby is likely to be building up significantly as the deployment date for American INF approaches at the end of next year.'

[3] Alan Goodison (AUS) was given responsibility for European and Soviet affairs following Ewen Fergusson's appointment as British Ambassador to South Africa in April 1982.

17 December 1981 – 9 December 1982

and the impact it might have on East/West relations, it would also have a wider value for us internationally. It would enhance our importance in the eyes of our European partners, as well as the Americans, and would add to our weight in alliance counsels. At the same time it would serve to demonstrate that we have a voice of our own to which the Russians are prepared to listen. The Americans can scarcely accuse us of breaking ranks. They have had three long meetings at the Haig/Gromyko level. President Reagan suggested a meeting with Brezhnev in the margins of the UNSSOD in June[4] and the proposal for a summit is still on the table.

[4] The UN Second Special Session on Disarmament took place in New York from 7 June to 10 July.

No. 155

Letter from Mr Thomas[1] (Washington) to Sir J. Bullard, 27 August 1982[2]
Confidential, Eclipse (EN 020/1)

Dear Julian,

US/Soviet Relations

1. In a meeting last month with your colleagues from the Community, you described President Reagan's views on international affairs, and especially East/West relations, as exceptionally crude. I agree and we had a shot, earlier this year, at developing the theme in a paper. But the work fell victim of the Falklands crisis and we have only now brought it up to date and completed it. Michael Pakenham[3] has done most of the work. As you will see, he sets out the present state of US/Soviet relations weighed against the philosophy of the Administration when it entered office. Perhaps it is worth adding a few thoughts of my own to set the paper in context.

2. President Reagan's view of international affairs is, as you say, crude, or at least simple. It is much of a piece with the rest of his policies, in harking back to the relatively clear-cut black and white concepts of earlier eras. It is deeply conservative and deeply mistrustful of the Russians. His speech to Parliament in London was a good illustration.[4] It reflected his own conviction that Western democracy and communism represent good and evil, Christ and anti-Christ. This conviction has not changed and will not do so.

3. What has changed is the way these concepts are translated into policy, at least on arms control negotiations. Throughout the rest of the world, United States policy remains run on much the same guidelines as were established in January 1981. But in the strategic balance, strengthened defence is no longer the single pillar on which security policy rests, though it is still the pre-requisite for dialogue. This degree of movement is partly due to the efforts of ourselves and other Europeans to get across our real concerns, and partly due to the domestic political

[1] Derek M. D. Thomas, Minister, British Embassy, Washington.
[2] Copied (without enclosure) to UKREP Brussels, UKDEL NATO and HMA in Moscow.
[3] The Hon. Michael Pakenham, First Secretary, British Embassy, Washington.
[4] In his speech to both Houses of Parliament on 8 June, President Reagan spoke of his hope that 'the march of freedom and democracy . . . will leave Marxism-Leninism on the ash-heap of history as it has left other tyrannies which stifle the freedom and muzzle the self-expression of the people'. See *Public Papers: Reagan (1982)*, Book I, pp. 742-48.

UK-Soviet Relations, 1979-82

need, which borrows something from European movements, to reduce the perceived increase in the threat of a global nuclear war. Needless to say, the battle is not won (as demonstrated by the last-minute revisions in the United States negotiating position for START). We shall need to maintain our efforts and, where necessary, speak forcefully to the Americans when we perceive their negotiating position stretching beyond the bounds of the attainable or desirable.

4. In economic policy, the picture is somewhat different. A greater realisation by this Administration of the economic and political limitations on America's freedom of action constrained the innate desires of the hard-liners to 'crack the whip' over the Russians in the early days after the crackdown in Poland. But the essential lines of policy—no trade on subsidised terms, cut back on exports of high technology, and economic sanctions of increasing severity to demonstrate Western disapproval of Soviet policy and determination to effect a change—all these remain in place and have become a greater factor in the Administration's foreign policy since June. I do not perceive any grounds for optimism that this will change in the near future. Indeed the reverse. The President believes that it is important to make clear his resolve both to the Russians and to the rest of the world. Ironically, the more the allies complain the more this helps to emphasise the strength of his resolve.

5. Evolution in policy will depend to a large extent on the ability and readiness of the Europeans to provide a bridge for the President to re-cross the present choppy waters of the Alliance. It is admittedly unfair that we should be called upon to haul the Administration's chestnuts out of the fire which they themselves have stoked. Nonetheless, you do not need me to point out the necessity of our doing so. The Americans can, in the last resort, do without us. At the present stage of the Alliance and the evolution of the Community, we cannot do without them.

6. Evolution will also depend on other factors; developments in Poland; a spreading of Community influence in Central America; the consequences of the Israeli invasion of Lebanon,[5] which arguably gives the United States more of a role to play in the Middle East and reduces Soviet credibility there as a major player in the game. A change of leadership in Moscow might in due course open up new possibilities for mutual exploration and the development of new attitudes here. Certainly President Reagan has spoken about the possibility of influencing the post-Brezhnev succession by a judicious application of particular United States policy lines (though you will have noticed that Shultz[6] said the opposite last Sunday). Within the United States, the speed of progress towards a strengthened defence posture, which will be to some extent a function of the outcome of the battle over the budget and the performance of the United States economy, will certainly be an important factor in influencing readiness to make progress on arms control. In addition, as the 1984 elections approach (and perhaps before then), domestic political pressures will influence the Administration's approach to arms control. Once Reagan has met the Soviet leadership and recognised them as human beings there may be some tendency to inch towards direct dealing between the super powers. This could seem attractive as one way of asserting, or re-asserting the world leadership role of the United States—again with an eye on domestic

[5] On 6 June 1982, Israeli forces invaded Southern Lebanon in 'Operation Peace for Galilee'. The *casus belli* was the attempted assassination in London on 3 June of Israel's Ambassador to London, Shlomo Argov, by a PLO splinter group under Abu Nidal. Israeli forces soon encircled Beirut, forcing the PLO leadership to evacuate the city and establish new headquarters in Tunis.

[6] In July George Shultz replaced Alexander Haig as US Secretary of State.

17 December 1981 – 9 December 1982

politics. A more developed bilateral relationship might become tempting, if the Russians ever show any signs of willingness to strike a bargain which involved the curb on activities of surrogates around the world.

7. As to our own role the Americans will listen to us on this range of issues. But they will make up their own minds according to how they see their own interests. They will not necessarily be influenced by what we say. In the central field of security this means that, at the end of the day, we have little choice but to defer to their views, however reluctantly. In developing any political relationship with the Soviet Union we perhaps have more scope to manoeuvre within the agreed Alliance guidelines, though in practice our views and those of the Americans seem unlikely to diverge too far (though we will be more influenced by our need not to fall out with our European partners). Even in the economic and trade field, where our judgments differ considerably, our policy differences (e.g. on COCOM, credit, etc) are probably manageable. Only where (as with the pipeline) the Administration's attempts in pursuit of its simple vision of East/West relations, to impose its own restrictions on our pattern of trade will we have to resist—on wider grounds going well beyond issues of policy towards the Russians. This may mean reducing, as far as we can, our dependence on the United States of the supply or licensing of important components.

8. I was fascinated to see a recent report from Mexico City about López Portillo's[7] current feelings towards President Reagan. He described him as a man wedded, for all his surface charm and civility, to certain untenable convictions about the world and the place of the United States in it; and as the person who took nearly all the aggressive decisions which now marked United States foreign policy. This is something that, with his amiable image, people are sometimes inclined to forget about the present President of the United States. We should not make this mistake.[8]

Yours ever,
DEREK THOMAS

ENCLOSURE IN NO. 155

US Policy towards the Soviet Union: Theory and Practice

'The Russians may not be firing, but they are at war with us'
(President Reagan at the NATO Summit, 10 June 1982)

Introduction

1. The global role of the Soviet Union is the prime focus of this Administration's foreign policy. Relations between Washington and Moscow are at their lowest point for twenty years. Détente, the diplomatic goal of three Administrations, has been publicly scorned and pronounced extinct. According to the polls, and in contrast to widespread doubts about his domestic policy, President Reagan has the support of almost two-thirds of the country for his policy towards the Soviet Union.

US Attitudes

2. US policy is based on the personal convictions of the President and his senior

---

[7] José López Portillo, President of Mexico.

[8] For Sir J. Bullard's reply see No. 158.

UK-Soviet Relations, 1979-82

advisers. In his first press conference Mr Reagan created a sensation when he accused the Russians of 'reserving unto themselves the right to commit any crime, to lie, to cheat, in order to further their cause'. Several times this year he has confirmed that he has not changed his mind; nor had the Russians changed their habits. 'What', he asked this May at Eureka College,[9] 'can we expect from a world power of such deep fears, hostilities and external ambition?' Far from accepting the Carter thesis that it was time to do away with America's 'inordinate fear of communism', he and his colleagues believe that communism must be confronted wherever it threatens the interests of the free world. However, as he explained to Parliament in London this June, he remains optimistic that freedom and the role of the individual as encouraged in the Western democracies will prevail. A year ago he proclaimed that 'the West will not contain communism, it will transcend communism . . . it will dismiss it as a sad, bizarre chapter in human history whose last pages are now being written'. He still feels this, encouraged by Communism's failures (Poland, Afghanistan and the Soviet economy); at Eureka College he spoke of the Soviet Empire beset with malaise and resentment, and faltering because rigid, centralized control had destroyed incentives for innovation, efficiency and individual achievement.

3. The President's personal feelings are shared by his closest advisers and friends, by most of Congress, and by large parts of the country. Secretary Haig saw Moscow as 'the greatest source of international insecurity today'. Like others at the top of the Administration, he also tended to see the world in terms of a US-Soviet zero-sum game. His successor, George Shultz, has so far been careful, or reluctant, or both, to reveal his own philosophy. His views remain something of an unknown factor. Defense Secretary Weinberger, steeped in the history of the 1930s and the respective roles of Churchill and the appeasers, is determined that the errors of the détente era must not be repeated. The conservative wing of the Republican Party, whose political influence outweighs its size, has been another factor in strengthening the determination of the Administration to give no quarter to Moscow in the global battle.

4. The Republican platform for the 1980 election spoke for the majority of Americans when it condemned Soviet aggression, expansionism and violation of international agreements; and described the premier challenge facing the United States, its allies and the globe as the checking of the Soviet Union's global ambitions. US moves against the Soviet Union over Poland have won just as much support from the left-wing of the Democratic Party and from the labour unions as from the right. Events in Angola, Ethiopia and Afghanistan have enhanced the traditionally low American opinion of Soviet trustworthiness.

The Policy in Theory

5. During his first year the President focussed his mind and political efforts on getting the economy right. Foreign policy had to wait for attention. Hence, there was relatively little development of the policy towards Moscow beyond the stark outlines of the campaign and the personal beliefs of Administration leaders. Their attitudes were reinforced by the dearth of experience among senior officials outside the State Department in practical dealings with Moscow. In the White House the *troika* (Meese, Baker, Deaver) still view foreign policy almost exclusively through the prism of its domestic impact (usually short-term).

6. The attitudes of other senior members of the Administration are based on

[9] See No. 148, note 4.

17 December 1981 – 9 December 1982

certain rather simpler principles. As Churchill—whose influence over the thinking and speeches of this Administration is striking—said, the key to the Soviet riddle is to be found in Soviet national interest. The Russians should be offered, and Mr Reagan specifically put this in an April 1981 letter to Brezhnev, a constructive and beneficial relationship so long as they behave themselves. Denied the Western trade and credits which have enhanced the prosperity of Eastern Europe for a decade and concealed the inherent weakness of the communism system, the Soviet leaders may conceivably adjust their approach. That however is a long-term process. There can be no fond hopes of the Politburo changing of its own accord. Soviet intentions do not demonstrate at present any shared basis of interest with the US in global stability. The only shared interest at present is the avoidance of nuclear war. The West cannot count upon a convergence of Soviet and our own political principles or strategic doctrines; and should avoid 'dangerous optimism about the prospects for more benign Soviet objectives'. Responding to US leadership, the West should keep our military guard up, and our purses closed (but granaries must remain open since the mid-West vote cannot be sacrificed to the demands of this philosophy). Of the twin clauses in the 1967 Harmel Report[10]— détente and deterrence—the accent once again must be placed on deterrence, following the disappointments of détente.

7. The conclusion, which began to be publicly disseminated fifteen months ago, was that Soviet-American relations, the pre-eminent element in US foreign policy, were to be governed by a strategy of neo-containment. This was to be encapsulated in three key points:

(*a*) The need for Soviet *restraint*, i.e. rejection of armed interventions in other countries either directly or through proxies (Cuba and Libya, in particular);

(*b*) The need for Soviet *reciprocity*, i.e. compliance with undertakings e.g. on arms control and under the Helsinki Final Act; and

(*c*) *Linkage*—'not a theory, a fact of life'. The Soviet Union must satisfy US requirements in other policy areas if it wanted a satisfactory bilateral relationship, especially over arms control and economic exchanges with Washington.

Of these other areas the most important was that described as geopolitical issues i.e. the numerous conflicts arising between the US and the Soviet Union beyond their direct bilateral relations, as a result of Soviet intervention in regional conflicts. Détente, if it was to be pursued at all, must be indivisible.

The Policy in Practice

8. As theoretical propositions, none of these differ[s] markedly from the ideas of Kissinger, now seen by right-wing Republicans as the villain of détente. What is crucially different is the style. As always in Washington, the process of translating principles into practice has been subject to internal conflicts between senior officials, and between the Administration and Congress. Nonetheless the Administration's approach has been remarkably (if inconveniently) consistent (except for grain). In bilateral relations they were determined to avoid the mistake which Carter was seen as making, of running after the Russians. Direct contacts were restricted to a minimum. Haig met Gromyko on only three occasions during his 18 months in office. Shultz and Gromyko will probably meet again in New York this September. A meeting between Presidents Brezhnev and Reagan (if the

---

[10] The Report examined the future tasks of the NATO Alliance and its procedures for fulfilling them with a view to strengthening the Alliance as a factor for durable peace. It was commissioned on the initiative of the Belgian Foreign Minister Mr Pierre Harmel.

UK-Soviet Relations, 1979-82

former survives that long) must, the Administration emphasise, be carefully prepared and will not take place before the autumn at the earliest, even though President Reagan continues publicly to speak in favour of the benefits of a face-to-face meeting.

Economic Relations

9. Economic exchanges and discussions on arms control have formed the central content of bilateral relations. Of the former, the predominant element for the United States (some two-thirds of US exports to the Soviet Union) is grain exports. The embarrassment from the lifting of the Carter embargo, a decision taken entirely for domestic political reasons and against the advice of all senior foreign policy advisers but in fulfilment of a much publicized campaign pledge, was made no easier to bear by European criticism of American self-interest. But it did not persuade the Administration to change course. As a result of the grain trade, US exports to the Soviet Union last year doubled to a value of $1.5 billion. They still only represent less than 1 percent of total US exports; while Soviet exports to the US represent only 0.1 percent of total US imports. Following Carter's embargo American grain farmers, who used to dominate the Soviet market, now share it with the farmers of Argentina, Canada and Australia. The Food and Agriculture Act of 1981 lays down that future bans would have to be part of a total embargo. Although another long-term agreement is at present unlikely, President Reagan has agreed to a further, one-year extension of the present arrangements; and the Russians have picked this up.[11]

10. In other areas of economic relations, however, the Administration have been at pains not only to maintain the post-Afghanistan restraints but to persuade their Allies to do more. President Reagan secured a commitment from his partners at the Ottawa Economic Summit to restrict the flow of high technology to the Soviet Union; and a high level meeting of COCOM was held in January 1982 to consider how the rules of that organisation might best be tightened.[12] America's allies accepted that the process is in the common interest, and cooperated accordingly.

11. But it was over the linked questions of the Siberian pipeline and subsidised credits to Eastern Europe that this Administration and the Western Europeans have really come into conflict. The growing economic difficulties of the Soviet Union and the Soviet bloc, and the growth of East/West trade financed by Western credit, raised issues for which the Administration had no easy solution vis-à-vis the Allies. A significant body of American opinion has always held that any trade with the Soviet Union—even goods with no conceivable military application—gives comfort to the potential enemy and releases resources within the Soviet economy which can be diverted to the military sector. Those in the present Administration who hold this view (mostly in the Department of Defense and the NSC staff) consistently pressed the President for the first six months of this year to go beyond the economic sanctions he imposed in December 1981. They argued that the instrument lay to hand: the substantial hard currency debts of the Soviet bloc, and the evident Soviet need for further loans. Call in the debt, deny new loans, and the Russians would at last be forced to choose between guns and butter. Moreover, the risk of Soviet indebtedness becoming a form of reverse leverage over Western

---

[11] In announcing this decision, on 30 July, President Reagan stated that the Soviets should not be afforded the additional security of a long-term agreement as long as repression continued in Poland. But he also concluded that grain sales had little impact on Soviet military and industrial capability and absorbed hard currency earnings. See *Public Papers: Reagan (1982)*, Book II, p. 994.

[12] See No. 127.

17 December 1981 – 9 December 1982

policies would have been averted. The allies must follow suit, cutting back on their trade and credits—with particular reference to the Yamal pipeline[13]—both in their own best interests and as a test of their loyalty to Western interests. The President's second statement to the NATO Summit, quoted at the beginning of this memorandum demonstrates where his own personal preferences lay.

12. On the other hand, another school within the Administration, largely represented in the State Department, part of the Commerce Department, and the Treasury, accept that East/West trade cannot simply or effectively be used as an instrument of pure politics, that trade benefits not only the Russians, and that some at least of America's allies have substantial and legitimate, political and economic interests involved. These people understood that too much pressure on their partners to change course was more likely to damage the Alliance than the Russians. They therefore advocated pursuing the more modest aim of persuading the allies to be more prudent about the level of lending to the Eastern bloc, to reduce the subsidised element in their loans, and to think seriously about the degree of economic and therefore political dependence on the Soviet Union they risked building up through the gas pipeline or in other ways. In this they reflected one of the themes of the Kissinger era; that Governments should not leave the shaping of policy to businessmen and bankers. More control by Governments would provide policy makers with a choice which would depend in turn on Soviet responses.

13. Until the Versailles and Bonn Summits, the moderates prevailed, and not only for the political reasons of Alliance management. Treasury officials feared the damage to the international financial system that could be done by too ruthless a treatment of bloc debtors. And substantial domestic industrial and commercial interests were involved as well. The result was that at Versailles the Western Europeans believed that they had reached some sort of compromise with President Reagan, which would enable them to continue their contribution to the Yamal pipeline without fearing further US sanctions, while for their part they would adopt some, admittedly minor, adjustments in their credit regimes for Eastern Europe. This uncomfortable but workable compromise was brusquely overturned by the President's announcement of 22 [*sic* 18] June, less than 2 weeks after the NATO Summit, of further, more stringent measures against the Soviet Union and in particular against any US involvement in the pipeline project. Such an involvement was defined in terms to imply extraterritorial jurisdiction by the US Government over US technology previously exported to Western Europe, over US firms incorporated in Western Europe, and over existing contracts already negotiated between Western Europe and the Soviet Union.[14]

14. It has been suggested that the President was persuaded to take these further steps as a result of the ill-advised post-Summit comments by Chancellor Schmidt and President Mitterrand. In the eyes of the hard liners in Washington, these made a mockery of any claims by the President that he had achieved at least some of his aims at the Western Summits. As a result, the hard-line school in Washington was immeasurably strengthened and the President was able, with support from at least some senior advisers, and in the belief that this would be a clear signal to the Russians—and to the Europeans—of his strength of purpose, to proceed with the more stringent measures. On the other hand, such an interpretation may underplay

---

[13] See No. 129.

[14] For a copy of the US statement announcing the extension of sanctions, see *Public Papers: Reagan (1982)*, Book I, p. 798.

UK-Soviet Relations, 1979-82

the importance of the President's own philosophy. There are many in Washington who are convinced that, even had his European Allies not spoken out in the aftermath of the Summits as they did, the President would still have acted as he did. What is clear is that he was badly advised about the likely reaction of the Europeans, and sadly underestimated their concern at these new measures and their unwillingness to accept them.

15. The Administration now finds itself in a most uncomfortable box, from which there is no easy exit. The President has linked a loosening of current sanctions with an improvement in the situation in Poland, a linkage which lacks both conviction and logic, particularly when he has also linked the extension of the grain agreement with the Soviets to an alleged improvement in the internal regime in Poland. Others, including Weinberger, have linked the US action against the pipeline to the wider considerations of Western European energy dependence, the opportunities offered by Soviet economic weakness, the scope for restricting Soviet hard currency earnings and the dangers of strengthening of the Soviet military industrial complex. Whatever rationale is chosen, there are no signs that the President will be easily budged from his present position over sanctions. The task of both Administration officials and the Allies will be to construct a suitable package of measures which will enable the President to claim some impact on Soviet policies while reducing the current damage to the internal fabric of the Alliance. The underlying problem is the President's determination to avoid one of the chief Carter weaknesses, the impression of continual flip-flopping in foreign policy. With the new agreement with Peking over Taiwan arms, with some possible adjustments in Middle East policy in the wind, with tax increases following a short year after tax cuts, the President and his political staff are keenly aware of the dangers they face of identification with his predecessor. In this sense, his present obduracy in the face of Allied complaints serves some domestic political interest. It also demonstrates to Moscow that—despite his problems with the Allies—his resolve is unbroken and he remains determined to press them for the necessary concessions. Even if the allies continue to squeal the Russians must see that they will pay a price for Poland.

Arms Control and Defence

16. Initially, the prime concern of the Reagan Administration in relation to arms control was to avoid such discussions, especially on strategic arms, forming the centrepiece of relations with the Soviet Union or representing a major element in the enhancement of Allied security. Arms control could do something to help. But the prime contribution must come from increased defence efforts in the West. Some in the Administration suspected that negotiating on arms control meant nothing more than doing the Russians a favour, and feared that its pursuit would enfeeble the Western determination to match Soviet military efforts. Consequently, the US have focussed on areas of arms control which, whatever their objective merits, present particular difficulties for the Russians: the achievement of parity narrowly defined, the insistence on adequate verification and compliance by the Soviet Union, and the requirement for reductions, rather than simple limits on all forms of weapons. At present there is still great emphasis on the desirable, as demonstrated by the position on SS-18s presented to the Russians in the START negotiations; less attention is paid to the negotiable. The attitude towards multilateral disarmament, for example in the Geneva Committee on Disarmament, remains offhand; there is little real interest in MBFR; and total opposition to negotiations on a comprehensive test ban. President Reagan has separated the

17 December 1981 – 9 December 1982

search for a military balance from arms control, as discrete elements of US policy. But in practice the two remain closely linked.

17. He has concentrated on building up US forces to match what is seen as comprehensive Soviet advantages. A search for military superiority over the Russians is not an objective, despite the demands for it in the Republican platform. But the President and Secretary Weinberger are determined to re-establish what they perceive as parity, and to demonstrate to the Russians that they are prepared to pay the price necessary to achieve this end. Last year there was a widespread belief here that in any arms race America, by virtue of her financial, technological and political advantages could win. The growing doubts in Congress about the practicability in present economic circumstances of the Administration's plans for increased defence spending over the next five years (which could reach $1.6 million billion) has begun to induce a more sober assessment. The President will have to accept some cuts in projected defence spending in this and future years. But there has been no let-up in his own insistence on substantial increases in the defence effort.

Political Relations

18. The Administration do not believe that the Soviet military position now makes the Russians more likely to engage in a military confrontation with the US. But they do fear that the Soviet build-up has provided them with greater confidence to engage and confront the United States throughout the world in the political arena. They see the military balance casting a shadow over every significant geopolitical decision, and affecting the daily conduct of American diplomacy. Thus, apart from the effects of US economic sanctions, the main content of US-Soviet relations over the past eighteen months has emerged in an indirect form, reflecting the battle for influence and position in third countries. This battle, and the perceived need to defeat the Soviet advance, have formed the prime focus of US attention.

19. US efforts to establish a strategic consensus in South West Asia; their bolstering of Pakistan, Saudi Arabia, Egypt and Israel; their struggle to resist left-wing influences in Central America; their support for the dictatorships of South America; their renewed interest in the Namibian negotiations, which by removing the Cubans from Angola would provide a real setback to the Russian's cause; their determination, exemplified by Mrs Kirkpatrick, to denounce double standards at the UN; their enhancement of the International Communication Agency as an organ to broadcast the anti-Soviet gospel; and the greater freedom provided to the CIA to counter Soviet subversion overseas; all these reflect the main theme of US foreign policy: counter-measures against the Soviet threat. Even in relations with China, the commitment of the President to Taiwan and his own antagonism to a communist regime have not prevented the Administration from making a special effort to develop relations with Peking, essentially in order to contribute to the overriding objective of containment of the Soviet Union.

20. In Europe, the same ambitions and the same concerns apply. Persuaded that part at least of the present transatlantic problems stemmed from Carter's failure to provide proper leadership, the new Administration was determined to demonstrate leadership from the outset. There has been a disposition—ironic in its practical results—to see East-West relations as a function of Alliance management rather than a chance to establish a new dialogue between the two sides. The US have so far succeeded in neither objective. Determined to pursue their own view where necessary against the advice and wishes of the allies, they have created problems

UK-Soviet Relations, 1979-82

within the Alliance which tinkering with the mechanisms of consultation will not resolve. As they demonstrated over the INF negotiations there are circumstances in which they are prepared to modify their policies when that is necessary to avoid gratuitous damage to transatlantic relations. But there is a limit to their readiness to meet the Europeans half-way, as the pipeline saga has shown so clearly.

21. Events in Poland served to convince the Administration of the correctness of their approach to the Soviet Union, and of the errors of the European attitude. Carter claimed to have learned an enormous amount about the Russians from the invasion of Afghanistan; President Reagan said just before the June Summits that 'what I have come to learn (in the Presidency) has not changed in any way how I felt about the Soviet Union'. Moscow's evident unwillingness to move against the Poles before December 1981 reinforced the judgement that the stick, not the carrot, was the proper treatment for an international bully. The crack-down confirmed their judgements about the nature of communist regimes and the Soviet Union in particular. Solidarity could not, even to a minor extent, be held responsible, since this would amount to an admission that the Russians were not the prime villains of the piece. They did not accept the argument of some at least of the Europeans that sanctions against the Soviet Union were not the appropriate response; and that continued pressure on the Polish regime was not justified.

22. Poland now presents the Administration with a new dilemma. They have no reason to expect a significant change in the Soviet or Polish position in the foreseeable future. They are dedicated, under the linkage doctrine, to maintaining the pressure on the Poles to meet the three Western conditions. They are also dedicated to seeking compensation elsewhere for this Soviet-backed oppression. But domestic political pressures require that US grain exports to the Soviet Union should not be singled out for an embargo, just as European domestic pressures insist that trade in areas of importance to them should continue. While theory demands that relations with the Russians are frozen even tighter, political reality requires that despite Poland more substance is injected into the bilateral relationship.

23. It is here that the confusion in current policy is most apparent. The President agrees to an extension of the grain agreement on the grounds that the situation in Poland has marginally improved, and existing contracts should be fulfilled. But his Administration takes punitive action against companies which defy US claims to extraterritorial and retroactive jurisdiction over their exports, so long as the situation in Poland remains so dire. It is unclear whether the Administration intend their sanctions to be punitive (and against whom) or merely corrective. Most people would favour the latter. But there is a significant body who prefer the former and even may welcome events in Poland as providing the US with the opportunity (or excuse) to re-establish an appropriate basis for East-West trade.

Conclusion

24. The Administration launched themselves twenty months ago on a quest for a new relationship with the Soviet Union which would overthrow the accepted fabric constructed since the early 1960s. The policy of neo-containment reflected a desire to revert to less complex policies of 30 years ago. The real dilemma is that these policies are no longer applicable in the world of the 1980s, in a multi-polar world in which Soviet ambitions can no longer be inhibited by the simple application of the stick. Perhaps more important, the Administration (and indeed most Americans) do not accept that a Western Europe whose GNP is now greater than that of the United States, whose technological sophistication is comparable, and

17 December 1981 – 9 December 1982

whose political cohesion is growing, is no longer disposed to follow the US lead so readily. If they are to manage successfully the Alliance of which they will remain the dominant member, the Americans will have to learn to compromise with their allies' views of their own particular interests even where they think these views are wrong. The Americans would not be human if they did not find this a hard lesson to learn.

25. At the heart of the dilemma lies a misunderstanding about the nature of détente. Even at its peak, the economic element of the US-Soviet relationship was thin. The denial by Congress of most favoured nation treatment to the Russians destroyed a key building block. The supposed benefits for the Russians never fully materialized; the web of interlocking relationships was only half-spun. The centrepiece remained, as it had been since the 1960s, the negotiation of arms control agreements. But as Soviet expansionism became more blatant, and American confidence—in the White House and on Capitol Hill—declined, so the remaining bilateral strand of cooperation became more isolated and strained, to break in late 1979. What former President Nixon recently described in the *New York Times* as the search for 'hard-headed détente' was no longer a political option, even if the arguments in its favour remained, and remain today, eminently valid.

26. The Alliance should recognise US determination to redress and maintain— at considerable sacrifice—the military balance with the Soviet Union. There is no doubt about the commitment to the Alliance of the current Administration, despite the flirtation of some of the civilian ideologues within it with less Euro-centric strategies. The danger that current US military strategy, designed to create a credible defence capability throughout the world, may lead to a decline in the primary emphasis on the defence of Europe, is appreciably less than the obverse: that fortress America will be re-established behind her ocean barriers and Western Europe will be left to look after itself. This danger has been increased by the pipeline row: a few Americans now argue that, if the Allies are unwilling to accept American judgements about the sort of policies needed to contain the Russians, there is not much reason why the United States should put itself out to keep costly forces in Europe to defend their Allies there. There is also the consideration that in the super-power world nurtured by Kissinger, there was always the temptation for the Americans to deal exclusively with the Russians over the heads of the Europeans. This temptation will always remain. But in the present climate the present Administration are less likely to listen to Soviet blandishments.

27. In his April 1981 letter, written from his hospital bed to Brezhnev, President Reagan was expressing a sincere wish to put the world on a more peaceful footing. On arms control, there has been an important and striking evolution in the Administration's policy, starting with the 18 November proposal for a 'zero option' in the deployment of intermediate-range nuclear weapons in Europe.[15] Haig stated that the President clearly considered the subject of arms control in a special category of normal bilateral relationships with the Soviet Union. Later, the unmet Western conditions on Poland notwithstanding, the US proposal for a resumption of strategic arms talks duly appeared.

28. Linkage is still alive as a factor in the US approach to Moscow. But in another sense, not publicised by the Administration, it has also been confirmed in

---

[15] His proposal for NATO to cancel its planned deployment of Pershing II and cruise missiles if the Soviet Union scrapped all of its long-range theatre nuclear forces (SS-20, SS-5 and SS-4 missiles) was outlined in a televised address to the nation. See *Public Papers: Reagan (1981)*, pp. 1062-67.

UK-Soviet Relations, 1979-82

striking fashion. SALT II failed because public and Congressional opinion in the United States could no longer accept business as usual with the Russians in a particular area while US interests elsewhere were being progressively eroded by the actions of the Russians (and others). In other words, artificial isolation of the SALT process was politically unattainable. In 1982 the same was true, in reverse. Public and Congressional pressures, stimulated by the nuclear freeze movement in the US and anti-nuclear campaign in Europe, drove the President back to the SALT process, despite the reluctance of some of his senior advisers and the unfulfilled preconditions, including the prior re-establishment of US military strength.

29. The strategy remains the drive to get the Russians back to the negotiating table on arms control and geo-political issues, suitably chastened and readier to do business realistically. Putting the economic squeeze on them is expected to exert pressure towards this end. A 'return to the Cold War'—an irrelevant expression twenty years after the Cuba crisis—was not, and is not on the cards. The temptation on the European side may now be to assume that, with suitable camouflage, détente will be revived with all its old objectives—political convergence, stimulated trade, increased contacts, greater cooperation from Moscow in resolving regional conflicts. But this is unlikely to happen. When this Administration came into office there were some hopes among the Soviet leaders that it would turn out to be another Nixon Administration, coming into office on the basis of harsh anti-Soviet rhetoric, but quickly resolved to do business with the Soviet Union and tempted indeed to look for ways of dividing the world into mutually accepted spheres of influence. The present Administration is not of that character. It remains profoundly distrustful of Soviet behaviour and intentions and what has happened in Poland has done nothing to increase its confidence. It has been prepared to modify its policies in some areas in response to the advice of its principal allies and a predictable shift in the political mood here. It is now under strong pressure to adjust its policies in other areas. There is, however, a point beyond which it will not go. Neither this, nor perhaps a future administration, will pursue détente in the manner in which it was conceived and sold to American opinion in the 1970s.

No. 156

Minute from Sir J. Bullard to Mr Macgregor, 31 August 1982
Confidential (ENS 020/5)

East/West Political Relations: UK Policy towards the Soviet Union.
1. I contributed to Mr Broomfield's paper in draft and am strongly in agreement with all his recommendations. I hope that these will be welcome to the Secretary of State, who commented at Chevening[1] in July on the absence of serious contact between Britain and the Soviet super power.

2. The fact is that the natural 'angle of repose' of Anglo-Soviet relations is rather flat, so that positive effort is required to keep things alive. In the period of Afghanistan and Poland there has been no impulse for this from the British side; while in Moscow the machine is burdened with the inertia of Brezhnev's incapacity, Gromyko's lack of receptiveness to new ideas and the gap left by the

---

[1] Chevening House, in Kent, the official residence of the Foreign Secretary.

17 December 1981 – 9 December 1982

death of Deputy Foreign Minister Zemskov.[2] The result is that Anglo-Soviet contacts, through the Embassies as well as direct, have atrophied by comparison with say 5 years ago. So we risk being out of touch with the real nature of Soviet society and Soviet policy, and thus losing authority with our allies on the points of greatest importance where we need to have a view and to be able to back it.

3. I particularly welcome the suggestion that the Prime Minister be encouraged to go to Moscow to meet Brezhnev next year. She was very effective with Kosygin at Moscow airport in 1979 and I have no doubt as to who would carry off the honours in any meeting with Brezhnev. I was sorry to hear that Sir I. Sutherland's appointment with her had been cancelled:[3] I cannot help wondering whether a new French or German Ambassador to Moscow would be allowed to set off to his post without having seen Mitterrand or Schmidt.[4]

[2] Mr Zemskov's death was announced at the beginning of April. His responsibilities for supervising Anglo-Soviet relations were temporarily transferred to Mr Ryzhov.
[3] Sir Iain Sutherland was appointed Ambassador to Moscow in September 1982. He did, in fact, see Mrs Thatcher before his departure (see No. 164, para 6).
[4] Commenting on Sir J. Bullard's minute, Sir A. Acland suggested that: 'An alternative would be to wait to make recommendations to the PM until after the meeting with Gromyko in New York.'

No. 157

Sir C. Keeble (Moscow) to Mr Pym, 8 September 1982
Confidential (ENS 014/7)

Valedictory Despatch

Summary . . . [1]

Sir,

After four and a half years in the Soviet Union a valedictory does not flow easily. I have come to have as much affection for the people of this country as I have distaste for their system. They are a people as capable of sustained endeavour as they are of sustained idleness, as kindly in private as they can be boorish in public, as generous as any I have met, but to whom savagery comes as easily as charity. They have endured more than their fair share of violence and tyranny, natural hardship and war. Now they have inflicted upon themselves a governmental system which combines lofty principle with evil application and monumental dullness. They have built themselves a military superpower. To run it, they have a group of old men, mediocre in spirit, who view the Western world with a malevolence, sometimes timorous, sometimes vengeful, always suspicious. I first encountered the Soviet system early in 1945, when I watched one junior Soviet officer with the power of the Kremlin behind him transform a squalid, stinking rabble of 2,000 Soviet prisoners of war, within the space of a few days, into a smart, disciplined unit, wild with joy at the prospect of returning to the motherland. They were met with a band on the quayside at Odessa, left to sit there for some days and then sent into exile—all, that is, except a dozen who slit their throats at the prospect ahead of them. All the emotions and all the contradictions are still there. It is tempting to write a valedictory in this vein and there would be some point to it, since we tend to see the Soviet Union too much in the image of *Pravda*

[1] Not printed.

UK-Soviet Relations, 1979-82

and too little in the image of its people. It is, however, the Soviet Government and its policies with which, at least in the medium term, we are confronted and which it is appropriate now to review.

2. When I arrived here early in 1978, British relations with the Soviet Union were active. So too were those of our allies. The Soviet Union itself was in one of its more confident and expansionist moods. Effective parity with the US had been obtained and détente was the fashionable doctrine. Now, as I leave, Anglo-Soviet relations are minimal in form and content, the Soviet Government is ill-tempered, unsure of itself and defensive. Détente is rarely spoken of. It is tempting to say that the high water of Communist pressure is past and that the boats are beginning to swing to the ebb. Perhaps they are, but history is too untidy an affair for its patterns to be clearly discernible as they develop. What one can say is that these years, with the collapse of the détente of the '70s, have seen a significant development in the relationship between the Soviet Union and the remainder of the world. To use Communist terminology, the correlation of forces has changed. It may be helpful therefore to look at what has happened and at its implications for the West.

3. By 1978 the Helsinki agreements probably still seemed to the Soviet leadership to provide a satisfactory basis for stability in Europe, reflecting the consolidation of the country's wartime gains. There was a price in terms of opening up the Soviet empire to Western ideas, but the Soviet intention was to avoid paying it. The search for a stable strategic relationship with the US remained a major task, but the SALT II negotiations were in progress and the prospects were not bad, despite some concern at the erratic nature of President Carter's policies. China represented a serious source of instability, which had still somehow to be controlled. Elsewhere, the international scene seemed encouraging enough to make an occasional foray into the Third World seem worth while. In Afghanistan and the Horn of Africa, the revolutionary process was producing gains. Viewed from the West, it was legitimate to see in Helsinki the augury of a certain relaxation of Soviet constraint upon human rights and a freer development of East-West relations, but both in Europe and outside it the doubts about the Soviet concept of détente—opportunistic expansion against a background of strategic stability—were already growing.

4. Looking back now over the events of the succeeding years, with the détente policy in tatters, the Soviet leaders have few successes to record, either in the stabilisation of their principal strategic relationships or, with the possible exception of Ethiopia, in the expansion of their influence in the Third World. At best, they have narrowly avoided major reverse. China's punitive raid on Vietnam showed that the Soviet Union was not willing to hazard its own security in defence of a distant socialist brother. The Soviet Union had little success in repairing its relationship with China and had to watch while the West began gradually to develop its own more positive relationship. In Afghanistan, an area which was already effectively under Soviet suzerainty, and where Western involvement was minimal, it must have seemed safer to try to hold on to revolutionary gain by military intervention than to risk seeing it lost by insurrection, but instead of a brief, limited, self-contained military operation, the Soviet Union found itself bogged down in a colonial war, faced with condemnation by an overwhelming majority of the UN and experiencing a significant loss of standing in the Third World. It may eventually win the war, but its best hope—and that a slender one—now can be to achieve by military means, at considerable cost, what it thought it had achieved cheaply by political means in 1978. In Africa, even Ethiopia seems

17 December 1981 – 9 December 1982

less of a strong point of Soviet influence than it was a few years ago and must seem progressively less relevant to the real interests of the Soviet Union. The Zimbabwe settlement was a reverse and Namibia could be another. Cuba remains a useful but expensive client and the Central American area could have further potential, but Grenada was a smallish sprat to land. With relations cooling elsewhere, the ability to maintain a moderately cordial relationship with India became the more important, but the Soviet Union found difficulty in resisting the temptation to overplay its hand. In Eastern Europe, with rising popular expectations in the post-Helsinki atmosphere, matched by Soviet inability to meet those expectations in either the economic or political sphere, there was a reasonable certainty of trouble. The remarkable feature of the Polish crisis was not the fact that it happened, nor the fact that eventually the Soviet leaders forced their Polish subordinates to declare martial law, but rather the fact that they hesitated so long, until one of the main Soviet strategic bastions in Eastern Europe had almost collapsed. Disaster was for the time being averted, but stability and reliability were certainly not achieved. There is a continuing trial of strength ahead and the mere maintenance of the Soviet empire in Eastern Europe represents a constant defensive preoccupation as well as an economic burden. In the critical central strategic relationship with the US, the Soviet leadership profoundly misunderstood the American mood. After the signature of SALT II, they had a chance to achieve the stability they sought, but their dislike of President Carter led them into policies which meant that the impetus was lost and, with the occupation of Afghanistan, the Reagan victory in the US and the adoption of a firmer anti-Soviet policy there, it was necessary for the Soviet Union to set out afresh on the search for a stable strategic balance, to drop its preconditions for INF talks and to accept that the NATO programme remained just intact, while the American defence programme moved ahead. The outcome they may now obtain can scarcely be as favourable—even at best—as had SALT II been ratified. The Iranian revolution destroyed a strong point of American influence, but it shows little sign of being exploitable and the current crisis in the Middle East illustrates the difficulty which the Soviet Union has in developing any policy initiative. The area is one which it has defined as 'close to the southern border', i.e. an area in which the Soviet Union regards its strategic interest as important. Yet, despite a friendship treaty with Syria, and despite the opportunity offered in terms of Soviet/Arab relations by the American identification with Israel, the Soviet Union remains cautiously on the sidelines, calling only for an international conference, while it is an American intermediary who brings about a ceasefire, a US-French-Italian force which, by agreement with the Lebanese and Israeli Governments and the PLO, moves into Beirut and Reagan who provides the major initiative towards a settlement for the Palestinians. The Head of Middle East Department of the Foreign Ministry summed it up at my farewell lunch: 'We can only watch'—not quite true, but none the less revealing. In short, the net effect of Soviet foreign policy over the last four years has been to leave the Soviet Union with a set of unstable and, from its point of view, unsatisfactory relationships in virtually all the areas of major interest to it.

5. Throughout this period of confrontation, the policies pursued by the West, disorganised and at times contradictory though they were, served on balance to heighten the Soviet perception of the fruitlessness of much of its policy and to reinforce the desire for a stabilisation of its principal strategic relationship. In the US the ideological element of Soviet policy began to meet an ideological counter-policy. It cannot be said that Western policies brought direct benefit to the West, or

UK-Soviet Relations, 1979-82

indeed, that wider Western interests have been promoted. The Helsinki process within Europe has been set back, there is less freedom in the Soviet bloc than there was in 1978 and tensions within the Alliance have been exacerbated. Yet, despite all the ineptness of policy implementation by the Carter and Reagan Administrations, the differences within NATO over TNF modernisation and now the deplorable wrangle over the pipeline contracts, there has been a checking of Soviet ambition and an unwillingness on the part of the Soviet leadership to precipitate any fresh challenge. It is in fact the West rather than the Soviet Union which today has the greater room for initiative.

6. If it is true that we have now held Soviet expansion and have some room for initiative, how can we best move forward? That depends largely upon our assessment of the kind of Soviet Union we are dealing with. Is it still a revolutionary power bent upon world domination, or is it just another country, very large, very powerful, with a repugnant ideology, but concerned essentially with its own interests, most of them domestic, and with the management of its untidy empire? Is it now, or could it soon become, ready for some kind of accommodation with the West, some genuine and balanced détente? I think it is reasonable to assume that the present leaders of the Soviet Union, although they may seek to expand their sphere of influence where they safely can, are not prepared to run the risk of nuclear war for the sake of it. Nor is it likely that they believe, in the light of 65 years' experience, that, for all its current economic troubles, the West will crumble under the sole impact of Marxist-Leninist logic. In short, they have neither a political nor a military strategy for world domination. Yet it would be wrong to treat them as simply a large power concerned with its own interests. Soviet foreign policy is a principled Leninist policy. Its theoretical foundation is the conflict between socialism and imperialism. Foreign policy issues are analysed and dealt with on this basis. It is a basis which does not exclude a deal with the enemy and if Soviet interests should clash with Leninist doctrine it would be the doctrine which would be adapted to accommodate the interest. Nevertheless, the effect of the doctrine is that international problems are viewed through a distorting mirror and, even when no direct Soviet interest is involved, Soviet analysis and policy reflect a philosophy of conflict, not of co-operation.

7. The opportunity for Western initiative must also be conditioned by the nature of the present and prospective Soviet leadership. Throughout these last few critical years, the Soviet Union has been led by a man who, powerful though he is, is clearly handicapped in his physical and mental processes, and surrounded by a tight little group of ageing Politburo members, whose inability to offer their country any inspiration must have been even more apparent to a Soviet observer than to a foreign Ambassador. Well before 1978, Brezhnev's infirmity was apparent and speculation was rife that he might not long retain the leadership. Since then, once or twice a year, the speculation has revived. It has not been without some foundation. Brezhnev himself said last year that he hoped to remain 'as long as I have the strength'. The end could well come at any time now. As the people of the Soviet Union—and, for that matter, of the world—wait uneasily in anticipation of a new leadership, there is in this country a distinct malaise. There are those, weary of a stale bureaucracy, who yearn for a new Stalin. There are probably some who, still inspired by the spirit of Helsinki, hope for a more open society. There is public recognition of widespread corruption. There is cynical disillusion among the young. The economy is still growing, but, as the requirements of a consumer society become ever more complex, its inadequacy

17 December 1981 – 9 December 1982

becomes correspondingly more apparent. This year seems likely to produce the third disastrous harvest in a row and Khrushchev's boast of overtaking the US in material welfare is long forgotten. The sense of frustration must be considerable, but the structure will not crack, and I doubt whether the policies will much change. This is a vast country and the patient resilience of its people makes for a massive inertia, but at the same time for an underlying strength. I doubt whether disaffection is serious and, wherever it may surface, repression will be swift. A different leadership and a different people might at such a time be ripe for significant changes, internally and externally, but I do not think this one is. The reaction to internal failings, or external pressures, is more of a laager mood, a prickly defensiveness. When Brezhnev goes, we can expect the remaining senior members of the Politburo to share out the principal offices among themselves and to continue essentially the present policies, perhaps even a little more cautiously externally and more oppressively internally, while they consolidate their grip. Within another five years or so this group, now for the most part in their 70s, may be replaced by men now in their 50s, men as yet wholly unknown to the West. These men may well decide to retreat into a 'fortress Russia' policy, but they could be tempted, either for better or for worse, into bolder policies at home or abroad. It will be with their arrival that there could be either the opportunity to develop a worthwhile détente or the need to face a more dangerous confrontation. Unknown though they now are to us, they must already be close to the Centre, observing the failure of the Brezhnev policies, pondering the options which will be open to them when they come to power and beginning to muster their supporters.

8. I have argued in earlier despatches, in particular that of 4 March, 1982,[2] that, whether our policy places the emphasis on the current reality of Soviet confrontation or the search for a more co-operative relationship, in either case we need to get back into dialogue with the Soviet Union. If we expect continued confrontation, we need dialogue, if only in order to provide a better estimate of Soviet intentions on which to found our own policy. If we hope for co-operation, the need is self-evident. The time when an empire begins to break up is a time both of great opportunity and great danger. The likelihood that, at this very time, the Soviet Union will come under new leadership makes the argument for dialogue the stronger. I doubt whether in present circumstances the dialogue will be productive. Even leaving aside the fact that the very nature of the Soviet system presupposes a state of continuing tension with those who assert Western values, the present Soviet leadership and their prospective immediate successors seem too tired, too old and too entrenched in their traditional ways of thought to be capable of developing substantially new policies, either in their own country or in their foreign relationships. Even if the will were there, it is difficult to see how they could conclude that a change of policy in relation to Afghanistan or Poland would serve Soviet interests. Either the Soviet army stays in Afghanistan or defeat has to be admitted. Either the Poles have to be held down by their own Government, or disorder may again erupt to a point to which the Soviet Union has to commit its own forces. I think the leadership see well enough the failings of their current policies but fear even more the consequences of abandoning them.

9. I took the opportunity of my farewell call on Mr Gromyko to explore whether a more optimistic prognosis of Soviet policy would be justified, not specifically in relation to Afghanistan and Poland, but more broadly in terms of the Soviet

[2] No. 138.

UK-Soviet Relations, 1979-82

Union's approach to relations with the West. In reply, he spoke time and again of the need to find a 'common language' with us, of the desire of the leadership and of Mr Brezhnev personally for a better relationship. He defined peaceful coexistence, not in the classic terms of a struggle in which only the use of armed force was excluded—as he himself had done last year—but in the language of the Anglo-Soviet declaration of 1975,[3] which spoke of mutually beneficial co-operation. At my farewell lunch, his deputy, Mr Ryzhov, pursued the same theme. In my reply I welcomed this, but pointed out that it is deeds rather than words that count. I believe both Gromyko and Ryzhov were genuine in wanting a better relationship but in nothing that they said could I sense any real readiness to move from existing Soviet positions. With Gromyko I chose the Middle East as an area where the conflict of interest between us ought not to be such as to prevent a common language from being found, but he offered nothing new—and the public Soviet reaction to President Reagan's major policy statement on the Palestinian problem is no better as an augury. When we moved to arms control there was only the old suspicion of American policy. There was less combativeness than there has been, more of a weary regret. In someone who has been Soviet Foreign Minister for the past quarter of a century, it was understandable enough.

10. Nevertheless, even if we accept that there is little prospect of developing, at least in the immediate future, a substantially more productive relationship, or even a productive dialogue with the Soviet Union, I still hold to the view that the initiation of the dialogue offers us some prospect of gain and none of loss. Moreover, if we are to be ready for the next generation of Soviet leaders, and if we are fairly to reflect widespread European aspirations, we need to develop our thinking and the exposition of our policy beyond the mere containment of Soviet expansion. We shall not break the Soviet Union by military or economic pressure, even if we were to take this as our objective. We need, today, to contain it, and we need to offer the prospect of a more positive relationship in the hope that there may, even now, be those who can be influenced by it. To begin to formulate a more positive policy is of course to run straight into the political realities which ended the détente of the 70s. If, for instance, the Eastern Europeans are going to run their countries as they wish, the Soviet Union is going to lose its main defensive *glacis*. We do, however, have in the INF and START negotiations important positive elements. In the Helsinki Final Act we already have as good a set of principles as we are likely to find. The trouble is that, by themselves, the unimplemented declarations of the past quickly acquire all the appeal of a rain-sodden deckchair in a public park. Merely to direct attention to them is not enough. It ought not however to be impossible to devise and to proclaim a policy in the wider area of East-West relations which would match what the NATO double decision did in a more limited area, offering on the one hand the confrontation of Soviet expansion, and on the other, a prospect of a relationship in which the emphasis is on interests rather than ideology and in which there is room for a greater degree of accommodation than at present.

11. I cannot usefully in this despatch take the argument further. The problem of our relationship with the Soviet Union carries with it many of the deepest problems of political life, the role of the individual and the state and the taming of imperial

---

[3] In February 1975 Harold Wilson and James Callaghan visited Moscow where they signed a protocol on regular political consultations, agreements covering industrial and economic co-operation and a joint declaration on the non-proliferation of nuclear weapons. See *DBPO*, Series III, Vol. III, No. 76.

17 December 1981 – 9 December 1982

ambition in an age where war among the major powers can no longer be accepted as a final arbitrament. There are no absolute answers, but, by a whole series of individual political acts, we can tip the balance one way or the other, towards or away from a more civilised world. The next few years may give us a chance to tip it a little in the right direction and I hope we shall use the flexibility which the Western system possesses and the Soviet Union lacks, to exploit whatever chance may exist. It happens that Britain is peculiarly well placed at the moment to take the lead on the Western side in this East-West relationship. For various reasons, neither France nor Germany has quite the influence it had a few years ago and, although the US can always secure a dialogue with the Soviet Union if it wants one, the reality of superpower confrontation and superpower pride may make the initiation of it more difficult. By contrast, the Prime Minister's standing is high and her words will carry weight here.

12. It has been a privilege for which I have been deeply grateful to be able to spend these past four years in Moscow supported by a staff whose understanding of the issues involved has been matched by the professionalism with which they have tackled them, and helped by a wife who, like so many Diplomatic Service wives around the world, has made my job her own and earned in her own right the respect and affection of many of these odd, hard-bitten, sentimental Russians. Throughout the period of my stay here, I have, too, been grateful for a degree of support from you, Sir, from your predecessors in both this and the previous Government, and from your Department, which my German, French and American colleagues, not to speak of others, have frequently envied.

13. I am copying this despatch to Her Majesty's Ambassadors at Washington, Paris, Bonn, New Delhi, Helsinki, Vienna, UKDel NATO, Belgrade, Bucharest, Budapest, Sofia, East Berlin, Prague, Warsaw, Peking and Ulan Bator.[4]

I am, Sir,
Yours faithfully,
CURTIS KEEBLE

---

[4] The despatch was submitted direct to the Foreign Secretary by Mr Broomfield to inform a discussion due to take place on 15 September between the Secretary of State and Mr Rifkind on policy towards the Soviet Union and Eastern Europe. He flagged paragraphs 10 and 11 on reopening dialogue with the Soviet Union as particularly relevant. In a minute of 29 September from Mr Jay, PS to Sir A. Acland, the PUS is recorded as finding Sir C. Keeble's despatch 'extremely interesting and persuasive' but lacking in any analysis of 'what the Russians think of *us*'. See No. 163 for the reply to this query.

No. 158

Letter from Sir J. Bullard to Mr Thomas (Washington), 17 September 1982[1]
Confidential, Eclipse (EN 021/1)

My dear Derek,

US/Soviet Relations

1. Thank you for your very interesting letter of 27 August, and for the valuable paper by Michael Pakenham which you enclosed with it.[2] There is very little in Michael Pakenham's analysis, nor indeed in your own comments, from which I would wish to dissent. But the subject is such an important one that it might be worth setting out the further thoughts which were sparked off in our minds by reading your letter.

2. You remind me in your opening paragraph that I described President Reagan's basic views on East/West relations as exceptionally crude. That crudeness is brought out in the paper. It was well illustrated by the speech at the Bonn Summit, a quotation from which appears at the head of the paper. But of course President Reagan made two speeches to the Bonn Summit. The quotation is from his second, *extempore*, intervention in which obviously he spoke from the heart and expressed his basic personal beliefs. The first, which had no doubt been drafted by officials and duly cleared, was much more moderate and balanced in its approach. One can see this dichotomy of approach running all through the Administration's East/West policies. The President's speech in the Royal Gallery at Westminster[3] lay somewhere in between, but perhaps closer in spirit to the second intervention in Bonn rather than the first. Incidentally Frank Giles[4] spoke to me with some apprehension recently about the follow-up conference to that speech to which he has been invited in Washington next week, and I look forward to hearing your impressions of that event.

3. It is some comfort to know that there are moderate forces within the Administration, and that their voice is sometimes heard. (This point is brought out in paras 12 and 13 of Michael Pakenham's paper.) On the other hand, the fact that others have very different views, which the President's deepest instincts incline him to share, means that there are fissiparous tendencies within the Administration which make it peculiarly difficult to deal with.

4. The difficulty is compounded by the problem that the basic precepts of what I may call the hard-line Reaganites have not been properly translated, and perhaps are not capable of translation, into a coherent overall policy, and are not fully supported by planning and analysis. The paper's discussion of 'The Policy in Theory' in paras 5-7 may perhaps be too kind to it in supplying it with an intellectual coherence which it does not really possess. Certainly our own experience has been that it is extremely difficult to debate the policy meaningfully with Administration representatives because it is based on a set of *a priori* assumptions rather than on a prior analysis and because many of the people whose

---

[1] Copied to UKDel NATO, UKRep Brussels, Moscow, Bonn and Paris. In a minute of 9 September covering a draft of the letter, Mr Broomfield commented that whatever the current difficulties over the pipeline might be they would 'pale into insignificance in 1983 if the European NATO allies begin to believe that the fault lies more on the US than the Soviet side for any lack of progress there might be [in arms control/INF deployment].'

[2] No. 155.

[3] *v. ibid.*, note 4.

[4] The Editor of *The Sunday Times.*

17 December 1981 – 9 December 1982

job it would be to supply the analysis do not themselves appear to believe in the policy. All too often the discussion runs up against rocks labelled 'The President feels strongly' or 'it would be politically impossible in the United States . . . .' As I think I recorded at the time, it struck me during the spring Ministerial meeting of NATO in Luxembourg that the Americans seemed to be approaching the US-Soviet relationship mainly as a problem of domestic and international public relations.

5. Recent conversations here with Burt and Weinberger have highlighted this difficulty of disentangling stated assumptions about the Soviet Union from the detailed implementation of policy. I attach a copy of Weinberger's interview with David Watt in *The Times* on 9 September[5] and have underlined the passages in his third and fourth answers which bring out this point. The first answer is right in line with the balanced prudential statements of President Reagan's first intervention at NATO.[6] The second brings out the confrontational nature of the US attitude.[7] Both are relevant to the current search for a package of concessions which may meet the four points put to the Secretary of State by Shultz on 26 August (FCO telno 1575 to Washington).[8] Whether or not we can get agreement to such a package and whether or not it will be adequate for Shultz's purposes, it seems most unlikely to pass the test of 'helping reconciliation in Poland' (President Reagan on 18 June).

6. You are of course absolutely right in saying that we cannot do without the Americans and that we have got to keep up our efforts to get across our concerns to them. In attempting to provide a bridge for the President to re-cross, the UK, as so often, will have a crucial and probably thankless role to play. Owing not least to the very good personal understanding between the President and the Prime Minister, we are probably better placed than any of our partners to interpret European concerns to the Americans. At the same time, whatever else the pipeline affair has done, it has at least demonstrated to the other Europeans that the British are Europeans too, and that we are prepared to stand up to the Americans when our interests demand it.

7. The task of trying to bridge the gap is not made easier by the reluctance of the French in particular to make even small concessions to the American viewpoint. Looking back over the pipeline issue, one cannot help being struck by the narrowness of the failure to bring the Americans and Europeans together. In the run-up to the Versailles summit, it was only French intransigence that prevented agreement on a credit mechanism which at that time probably would have been sufficient for the Americans to yield on existing contracts. (They might in fact have been prepared to concede the mechanism at Versailles itself, but they stressed that a political decision would be needed, and the Americans failed to press the point with Mitterrand for fear, ironically in the light of what has happened since, of making the summit a 'failure'). Even after Versailles, all might have been well if

---

[5] Not printed.

[6] This question asked whether there was a divergence between the US and some European governments over the policy of increasing economic pressure on the Soviet Union in order to minimise its war making potential. In response, Weinberger stated that limited economic warfare was not part of American policy but that it served nobody's interests to effectively subsidise the Soviet economy by providing 10 billion dollars a year.

[7] Mr Weinberger was asked where he drew the line in relation to trade with the Soviet Union. In his response, he stated that the West should not provide anything that would be of immediate military benefit, such as the Siberian pipeline, and that the US had to do something short of military action to discourage Soviet aggression and repression in Poland.

[8] Not printed. See No. 173, note 2.

UK-Soviet Relations, 1979-82

the Europeans had allowed the Americans to present what had been agreed on credit as more of an achievement than it really was: but Mitterrand removed this possibility by saying—in his interview on 11 June—that France was not obliged by the summit declaration to reduce the amount of credit extended to the Russians. I note that Michael Pakenham believes (para 14) that the President might still have acted as he did in any case, but Mitterrand's remarks clearly did not help. And recently it is the French who have been difficult about agreeing to a meeting *à cinq* on the pipeline issue. I see France at the moment as reverting to the normal posture of instinctive anti-Americanism after a honeymoon which I always found slightly artificial.

8. Despite the difficulty of keeping the French on board, we must continue trying to get across to the Americans, and in particular now to Shultz, a coherent European view. Ideally this should involve prior agreement between the Europeans as to our priorities, so that the Americans hear the same story from their various European interlocutors about the points of greatest concern to us. This will not be easy. It will require the best use of all the various mechanisms available to us—4, 5, 10, EC, NATO, COCOM etc. The most important issue, and one where because of lack of technical expertise the Europeans are often slow on the uptake, will be the START/INF talks. It will however be essential for the Americans to be seen to be making every effort to reach agreement in the INF talks, so that if there is no agreement and the Alliance is faced with going ahead with deployment, it is apparent that this is the result of Soviet and not American inflexibility.

9. Incidentally, we were mildly encouraged by Robin Renwick's teleletter of 3 September to Nigel Broomfield[9] about the Shultz/Gromyko meeting and a possible summit, which did seem to suggest that the Americans still believe in some effort at a dialogue with the Russians. Let us hope that Shultz's 'sphinx-like style' will prove more effective than Haig's lecturing. It could be that more will come out of this meeting than out of Haig's famous eleven hour encounters last year.

Yours ever,
JULIAN

[9] Not printed.

17 December 1981 – 9 December 1982

No. 159

Summary by Mr Broomfield of a paper on British Policy in East-West Economic Relations in the 1980s, 22 September 1982[1]
Confidential (EN 091/1)

1. The paper argues that trade with the Soviet Union and Eastern Europe should be considered as falling into two unequal categories. The first, governing the minority of trade of strategic importance, is covered by the COCOM regulations. The UK will be helpful over revising the COCOM list to include in it new technologies which would have a military application. We would not, however, wish to see the list expanded as the Americans appear to have argued on some occasions, to include items which, although clearly important in trade terms, do not have any military significance. If once these distinctions are blurred the chances are that the COCOM lists, which are widely respected by Western countries, will fall into disrepute and be more honoured in the breach than in their observance.

2. As to non-COCOM trade, the paper argues that in any circumstances short of a major East/West political crisis:

(*a*) The overriding principle should be commercial advantage. Trade should not be used as a political weapon (i.e. no economic warfare).

(*b*) Nor should trade be artificially encouraged for political reasons.

(*c*) We should abide strictly by the OECD credit consensus and encourage our partners to do likewise.

(*d*) The way in which trade is structured on the Eastern side makes governmental involvement on the Western side unavoidable. (Mr Rees will be meeting Mr Brezhnev (son) at the Anglo/Soviet Joint Commission when the Secretary of State will be in New York.) Such involvement should not, however, be taken to denote political approval of the regimes involved.

3. The paper makes certain recommendations about prudence in energy dealings with the Soviet Union and in other fields. It draws attention to the fact that a great deal of what the Americans have opposed in terms of 'subsidising' trade with the Soviet Union has now been corrected. The Eastern European countries are seen as much higher risk markets both by commercial banks and by official credit guarantee organisations and the premia and availability of credit have been adjusted accordingly. As far as the Soviet Union is concerned the change is striking. In one year the minimum official credit rate has risen from 8.5% to 12.25%.

4. The paper deals at some length (paragraphs 8-12) with differences of

---

[1] Mr Broomfield submitted this summary to accompany the latest version of a paper being put to FCO Ministers. He admitted the paper had become 'rather long and in the nature of collective efforts some of the drafting bears signs of inter-departmental compromises'.

Work began on the paper in January after the Planning Staff proposed developing long-term ideas on economic relations with Eastern Europe after Afghanistan and Poland. This was recognised as a topic which could lead to strains within the Alliance. In May a first version of the paper was submitted to MISC 64—the Cabinet Committee on economic policy towards Eastern Europe. It did not find favour with everyone. Mr Bull, from the Bank of England, wrote on 13 May: 'I find it a somewhat peculiar essay, containing a number of generalities, some somewhat dogmatic assertions and a few half truths and inaccuracies, and that the impression I get is of an attempt to rationalise past policies in rather a superficial way'. MISC 64 asked for the paper to be shortened and revised to concentrate on policy issues at stake, especially those of operational significance such as credit. A further version was considered by MISC 64 in September when additional amendments were called for.

UK-Soviet Relations, 1979-82

approach between the Americans and their partners in the Alliance to trade with the Soviet Union. While the Americans have maintained (most recently Mr Weinberger during his visit to London) that they are not engaged in economic warfare, some of their rhetoric would appear to indicate otherwise. There has also been a failure on the US side to distinguish clearly between the particular moves they have made in relation to the imposition of martial law in Poland and the overall plan they have for East/West trade. As far as Poland is concerned the US's NATO partners considered that they were sending a 'strong signal' to the Soviet Union. Some US statements have gone much further indicating a desire to 'punish' the Russians and to make them pay a price.[2]

[2] Events now overtook the completion of the paper. Whilst Mr Pym expressed sympathy with the argument in the paper he was concerned that nothing should cut across the line he had been taking with the Americans over their wish to bear down on the Soviet economy; namely, that the question should be discussed by the Allies and if they agreed it was a good idea, to conduct a study on how best to implement it. He believed such a study would be useful in its own right, but also helpful in finding a solution to the Siberian pipeline problem. With this in mind, there could be no suggestion that Britain had already drawn its conclusions and were not open to argument. Further circulation of the paper was stopped but it was felt that the work to date would provide a good basis for an agreed British line should an Allied study be agreed to.

No. 160

Minute from Mr Pym to Mrs Thatcher, 27 September 1982
PM/82/79 Confidential (EN 021/31)

Prime Minister

Eastern Europe and the Soviet Union

1. I have been reviewing our policy towards Eastern Europe and the Soviet Union and have approved the general lines set out in the enclosed papers[1] which I am now circulating to you, to colleagues in OD and to Sir R. Armstrong for information and for any comments which you or they may have.

2. Within the overall framework of our policy on Eastern Europe we have the particular problem of Poland. In the wake of the disturbances and deaths connected with the 31 August demonstrations,[2] now is clearly not the time to change our policy of seeking to hold the Polish authorities to their own statements about returning to the path of renewal and reform. But this is a long-term problem and it is almost certainly unrealistic to expect that the situation in Poland will ever return to the position exactly as it existed before martial law. I think therefore that, together with our Allies, we should be prepared to react to any partial moves by Jaruzelski towards reconciliation with the Polish people with an appropriate response.

3. In the meantime we have to deal with the increasingly urgent problem of the rescheduling of Poland's official debts in 1982. These amount to some $3.4 billion due to the 16 major creditors. We will continue to argue that the problem must be tackled very soon if the unity of the Western Creditors Group is not to break up.

[1] The paper on Eastern Europe has not been printed.
[2] Large-scale riots erupted throughout Poland to mark the second anniversary of Solidarity's formation.

17 December 1981 – 9 December 1982

ENCLOSURE IN NO. 160

East/West Political Relations: UK Policy towards the Soviet Union[3]

Background

1. Early in the life of the present Government, Ministers decided that our policy towards the Soviet Union should aim to secure the respect of the Russians, rather than their good opinion. They agreed that while we should not necessarily seek to match what the Americans, French and Germans did, it was self-evident that we needed a business-like relationship with the Soviet super-power, based on a realistic calculation of our respective interests. They also agreed that this would require an active programme of visits and exchanges at all levels.

2. Shortly after Ministers had reached these conclusions the Russians invaded Afghanistan, provoking a sharp deterioration in the East/West climate. This was further exacerbated in December last year by Soviet complicity in the military crackdown in Poland. Like our allies, we signalled our strong disapproval of Soviet behaviour by taking steps to restrict the scope of our bilateral relations. These included *inter alia* curtailing high level political contacts and visits, and reducing cultural exchanges. But with the Afghan and Polish crises likely to continue for the indefinite future, it is doubtful whether the absence of bilateral political dialogue is any longer in the British interest.

Bilateral Contacts

3. Since the Soviet invasion of Afghanistan there have only been occasional bilateral meetings at Ministerial level. Lord Carrington met Mr Gromyko several times in the margins of international meetings (e.g. the UN General Assembly), and paid one visit to Moscow to put forward the EC proposal for a settlement to the Afghan crisis. But there has been no regular pattern of discussion at Ministerial level nor any regular exchanges at the level of Political Directors. The lack of such a dialogue deprives us of the chance to assess Soviet thinking at first hand as well as denying us the opportunity of putting our views directly to the Soviet leadership.

4. Lord Carrington's visit to Moscow last year (like the three bilateral meetings Mr Haig had with Mr Gromyko) was an occasion when plain speaking left the Russians in no doubt about British and Western views and which provided a useful opportunity for us to assess those of the Soviet Union. The Carrington and Haig meetings were not seen as implying that we had done the Russians a favour by bestowing a spurious respectability on them (as was the case with President Giscard d'Estaing's ill judged meeting with President Brezhnev in Warsaw in May 1980). On the contrary, these encounters were widely understood to have provided for some tough talking enabling the West to register its strong opposition to Soviet policies. Meetings of this kind, which put the Russians under pressure by challenging them to justify their actions and policies, are more likely to have an influence on the Soviet leadership than a continuing refusal by Western leaders to conduct a dialogue.

5. We should now seek to re-establish a regular pattern of political discussion with the Russians. Our aim should be to set this up on three levels, involving on the British side the Foreign Secretary, the FCO Minister responsible for East/West relations (at present Mr Rifkind) and the Political Director in the FCO (at present Sir J. Bullard) respectively.

6. We should aim to ensure that the rhythm of these exchanges is regular and

[3] Memorandum by EESD dated 17 September 1982.

UK-Soviet Relations, 1979-82

roughly annual. If on occasion we choose to interrupt it in order to signal displeasure at Soviet behaviour, the break should be of limited duration: rather than break off bilateral political exchanges we should use them in order to leave the Russians in no doubt about the strength of our disapproval. We should thereby avoid getting into our present position where we find it difficult to justify reopening a political dialogue with the Russians because there has been no resolution of the Afghan or Polish crises. A pattern of Anglo-Soviet political discussions on these lines would be consistent with the Government's public commitments on contacts with the Soviet Union. We announced in Parliament, in January 1980 that high-level and ministerial contacts would be avoided for the time being. Mr Hurd's answer to a Parliamentary Question in June 1981 (Annex A)[4] however made clear that there were occasional high level and ministerial contacts where these were deemed advantageous. The same answer makes it plain that normal trade which was to mutual advantage would continue. The resumption of a political dialogue is unlikely of itself to make a great difference to UK/Soviet trade and in the present state of transatlantic disagreement over Western trade with the Soviet Union, we should be careful not to present any move on the political front as being linked to expectation of increased trade.

7. In addition to the regular exchanges outlined above, we should also encourage exchanges at an appropriate level on an *ad hoc* basis where we judge those to be in our interests. At non-ministerial level we should be ready to hold expert level meetings where we believe these would be to our advantage. The Middle East, nuclear issues (including non-proliferation), Southern Africa, and the UN are possible subjects; there could also be a meeting of Planning Staffs of the two Foreign Ministries.

The Attitude of Our Allies

8. A resumption of Anglo-Soviet political exchanges on this scale would not be out of line with the policies of our major partners. The FRG has maintained a summit-level dialogue with the Soviet Union. Chancellor Schmidt visited Moscow in June 1980 and received President Brezhnev in Bonn in November 1981, their seventh meeting. President Giscard met President Brezhnev in Poland in May 1980. The present French administration have so far adopted a more cautious approach towards the East, but this is unlikely to last indefinitely, nor would the French have any scruples about changing their policy abruptly if they judged it in France's interest to do so. The US-Soviet dialogue meanwhile continues. Mr Haig had extended talks with Gromyko in Geneva and twice in New York, an example to be followed by Mr Shultz. The proposal for a Reagan-Brezhnev summit remains on the table. The Russians did not take up the suggestion of a meeting in the margins of the UNSSOD[5] in July and the prospects of a meeting this autumn are receding.

9. The UK cannot maintain the exacting stance of a middle ranking power with world interests if we do not talk to one of the superpowers. If we remain on the sidelines, our weight in Western consultations will suffer. This is not to suggest that we should see ourselves as competing with the French or Germans; we have our own distinctive position and can pursue our dialogue in our own way. But given that East/West political contacts are almost certain to increase, it is important that a firm British voice is among the first the Russians hear when regular contacts are restored.

---

[4] Not printed.
[5] United Nations Special Session on Disarmament.

17 December 1981 – 9 December 1982

The Attitude of Other Countries

10. The reactions of some other governments need to be taken into account. In particular, Pakistan and some of the other Muslim countries in the Islamic Conference Organisation will be concerned lest the restoration of our contacts with the Soviet Union should imply a weakening of our position on Afghanistan. It will need to be carefully explained to them that this is not the case. In doing so we could argue that it was natural for us to include Afghanistan as an element in our resumed dialogue with the Soviet Union as a follow-up to Lord Carrington's visit to Moscow in 1981. Furthermore the Americans themselves have recently conducted discussions on Afghanistan with the Russians with the blessing of the Pakistanis.

Transatlantic Differences

11. It is strongly in our interests to pursue our own dialogue with the Russians at a time when changes in the Soviet leadership appear imminent, not least so that we are in a position to discuss Soviet affairs authoritatively with the Americans. Our current differences with the United States over East/West trade policy and our different judgement of Soviet economic prospects point to the importance of our being in a position to make our own analyses and reach our own conclusions, independently of the Americans.[6]

Cultural Contacts

12. We should also consider re-establishing the earlier pattern of our cultural exchanges with the Russians, sharply curtailed after the Soviet invasion of Afghanistan. While this satisfied the immediate need to demonstrate disapproval, it is doubtful whether it is now achieving very much. It is however preventing us from projecting Western values to the Soviet people: we are *de facto* helping the regime in its efforts to minimise outside influences and preserve orthodox conformity. For example, proposals for a major exhibition in Moscow and Leningrad of twentieth-century British painting have been held up for several years: such an exhibition would excite great interest among Russians and would demonstrate the vitality of British art, which contrasts strikingly with the barrenness of Soviet 'Socialist Realism'. Our guiding principle in such major exchanges should be that they must be genuinely open to the Soviet people and not just to selected audiences. The sharp reduction in government-sponsored cultural exchanges has tended to leave the field open to the Communist front organisations, to the advantage of the Russians: there is no lack of impresarios willing to bring to the UK Soviet musicians and dancers.

Consultations with Partners

13. If the policy advocated in this paper is adopted, there will be a need for us to inform our partners at an early stage and to formulate agreed common lines on important subjects, as was done in advance of Chancellor Schmidt's meeting with Brezhnev in 1981. This process of consultation might be taken in stages, starting with our closest allies before taking action with the Ten or in NATO.

Conclusion

14. We should not promote 'good' relations with the Soviet Union for their own sake. But there is a strong case for re-establishing a regular pattern of political discussion with the Russians at various levels in order to:

(*a*) assess Soviet policies and personalities at first hand;

(*b*) put UK views and policies directly to the Soviet leadership;

---

[6] See No 159.

UK-Soviet Relations, 1979-82

(*c*) ensure that if East/West political contacts continue to expand in the near future, as is likely, the British voice and style [is] among the first to be heard and seen in Moscow; and

(*d*) ensure that we are in a position to discuss Soviet affairs authoritatively with our European partners and with the United States.

There is no reason why such contacts should be seen as conferring respectability or a seal of approval on Soviet policies, but rather as a channel for whatever plain speaking policies may call for.[7]

[7] In a letter to Mr Bone, APS to the Foreign Secretary, of 4 October, Mr Coles indicated that the Prime Minister wished to discuss both papers with Mr Pym and that in the meantime no further action was to be taken. Mr Broomfield discovered that the Prime Minister thought the paper on the Soviet Union represented a major departure from present policy. She remained unsure about the merits of dialogue and even less sure about cultural contacts. In a letter to Sir I. Sutherland of 6 October, Mr Broomfield stated that he intended to brief the Secretary of State that dialogue and contact with the Soviet Union, if properly prepared and handled, could be a tougher and more challenging policy than the one currently being pursued (see No. 162).

No. 161

Mr Thomson (UKMIS New York) to FCO, 28 September 1982, 10.10 p.m.[1]
Tel. No. 1483 Priority, Confidential (ENS 020/10)

Following from Private Secretary

UNGA: Bilateral with the Soviet Foreign Minister, 28 September[2]

1. The Secretary of State invited Gromyko (who was accompanied by Kornienko, Dobrynin, Troyanovsky and Sudhodrev) to a working lunch, which lasted just under two hours.

Anglo-Soviet Relations

2. Mr Pym introduced discussion saying that it was to our mutual advantage to talk to each other more at a time when East-West relations were in a bad state. Gromyko replied that he had been glad to accept the invitation to lunch. He was by his standards relaxed throughout the proceedings, and he concluded the meeting by saying that the Soviet Union wanted good relations with Britain. We should work

[1] Repeated Information Priority to Moscow, Info Bonn, Paris, Washington, UKDEL NATO.
[2] In June the Secretary of State began considering ways in which he might make contact with Mr Gromyko. He raised the possibility of a working lunch, on neutral ground, in the margins of the annual meeting of the General Assembly. Mr Bullard agreed but noted on 21 June that the suggestion 'must not be made in such a way that we appear to be running after the Russians or copying Mr Haig'. An offer was made through the UK Mission in New York with the Embassy in Moscow taking supporting action with the Foreign Ministry. Topics for discussion proposed by officials included the Middle East, Southern Africa, nuclear issues, arms control and disarmament. These were considered to be areas where there was common ground or a possibility of movement by the Soviets. However Mr Pym wanted to avoid a formal agenda noting, on 25 July, 'I want to *talk* to Gromyko: so let us keep flexible.'
On the eve of the meeting Sir I. Sutherland, in Moscow telegram No. 550 of 24 September, reported: 'Gromyko is unlikely to be in a sanguine mood. Internally the atmosphere is uneasy: economic difficulties continue and as Brezhnev's strength fails the future of the leadership is increasingly uncertain. Abroad, the failures of Soviet diplomacy are at present more evident than its successes.' But he ended: 'I believe that, without damage to our position on Poland and Afghanistan, there is now an opportunity to develop the dialogue with the Russians on a realistic basis, without excessive expectations on either side, and on something like our own terms.'

17 December 1981 – 9 December 1982

together to seek solutions to problems. The Secretary of State agreed.

3. Gromyko said that there had been an extensive deterioration in our bilateral relations, with the exception of trade (and even there we were doing far less together than we could). This was not satisfactory, to say the least. He could not understand the tendency of the British and other Western governments to reject Soviet proposals almost before they were put on the table. There had been many examples since the war of the British acting to help find a way round differences between the United States and the Soviet Union, and he could name British Foreign Secretaries who had done so. But this way of proceeding seemed to have been forgotten. The Soviet Union was not begging for more contact and could survive without, but it would be in our mutual interest to return to previous patterns.

4. The Secretary of State said that he was prepared to consider any serious proposal by the Soviet Union and could not remember ever having turned one down out of hand. But when outrageous things were done, they could not but have consequences for our bilateral relations. There was a difference between the political and the commercial, but they could not be entirely divorced. We would continue to hope for progress on Afghanistan: for liberalisation instead of oppression in Poland: and for greater respect for the Final Act (in which context he mentioned Shchavansky [Shcharansky], Sakharov, Ida Nudel and telephone links). Gromyko responded on Afghanistan and the personal cases (see below) but did not take up the mention of Poland.

Arms Control

5. Gromyko argued on familiar lines that the Soviet Union was not seeking supremacy but regarded parity as a 'holy of holies' to which they would remain firmly committed. There was a tendency in Washington and elsewhere in NATO to disregard the facts and figures which made it clear that it was the West which had the advantage. The Secretary of State replied that we had our own view of the figures. If the Soviet Union accepted the need for balance we should get on with it and try to establish it at the lowest possible level. He could not understand how Gromyko, who knew the West well, could really believe that any Western government was planning to take offensive action against the Soviet Union. Gromyko claimed in reply that the Americans, by rejecting NOFUN [no first use of nuclear weapons], were seeking to maintain a first strike capability and the right to use it, which the Soviet Union could not afford to ignore.

CSCE

6. Gromyko said that the key question was whether to convene the CDE. Questions of substance would be for the conference itself to discuss. But there were those in Washington who did not want such a conference and who wanted to 'kill Madrid' by producing only a brief and empty final document. The European countries themselves would be the losers from such an outcome, and Britain should place its considerable weight in favour of a successful conclusion. The Secretary of State said that he wanted to seek agreement at Madrid and hoped that it would be possible. But we would need to reach through dialogue a clear understanding of what we meant. Events in Poland and elsewhere had shown that the Soviet view of what had been agreed at Helsinki was very different from that held in the West. The debate was about people, and we wanted an agreement which ensured that they were treated with respect and dignity.

Afghanistan

7. Gromyko argued that the presence of Soviet troops was the consequence and

UK-Soviet Relations, 1979-82

not the cause of the problem in Afghanistan. No one had the right to interfere in its internal aspects. Its external aspect was the continuation of armed incursions into Afghanistan from Pakistan (and to a lesser extent from Iran) which were encouraged mainly but not solely by the United States. If these incursions stopped and appropriate guarantees could be provided, Soviet troops would be withdrawn. If not, they would remain. He hoped that the Afghan and Pakistan representatives talking in Geneva through the good offices of the UN Secretary General might be able to make some progress on this point. The Secretary of State commented that Gromyko's line on non-interference in Afghan internal affairs seemed to apply to everyone except the Soviet Union. No one could believe that the Russians were there merely by invitation or accept the Soviet view of the problem.

Personal cases

8. With a rather contrived show of amusement, Gromyko said that the discussion of these matters had no place in a discussion of serious international problems. They were a purely internal affair. We no doubt had similar ones and would be the first to object if the Soviet Union or anyone else sought to raise them with us. The Secretary of State accepted that the Soviet Union would decide the treatment it accorded to its citizens, but this was a matter on which we and others had views which we would continue to express.

No. 162

Note by Mr Broomfield for Mr Pym on Policy towards the Soviet Union, 4 October 1982[1]
Confidential (ENS 020/5)

Points to Make

1. Policy advocated in the paper[2] is to restore some momentum in direct contacts with Soviet Union. You saw Kosygin in 1979. This was useful, as were Lord Carrington's talks with Gromyko in Moscow in July 1981.

2. British voice should be heard in Moscow. Not suggesting a cosy relationship or a 'new phase'. On the contrary, meeting would be an opportunity for frank and straight talking. Easier option is not to meet Soviet leaders, the greater challenge is to meet and impress on them firmness of Western positions and views. Britain well qualified to do this.

3. Should remember that because of closed nature of Soviet society, Soviet leaders are not normally exposed to differing views. Nor are they properly informed about the West or Western thinking. Not infrequent that information put to them about the West omits 'inconvenient' or difficult points. Meetings only way to be sure they are hearing what we are saying and to judge at first hand Soviet leaders and views. This particularly important at a time of transition and uncertainty in the Soviet Union.

4. No contradiction with policy of major allies. French and Germans have continued contacts (though some cut-back by French in Mitterrand's first year). CDU[3] Foreign Affairs spokesman has publicly confirmed continuation of dialogue with the East (although tone no doubt will be sharper than before).

[1] See No. 160, note 7.
[2] Enclosure in No. 160.
[3] Christian Democratic Union.

17 December 1981 – 9 December 1982

5. US contacts maintained. Haig had three lengthy sessions with Gromyko. Shultz has just had two extensive sessions with him in New York. In addition, continuing US/Soviet negotiations in Geneva on INF and START provide standing framework for contacts in security fields. Also unofficial US/Soviet channels, e.g., when senior US political and business figures are received at high levels in Moscow.

6. Before reopening dialogue we envisage consultations with our allies, starting with the closest (para 13 of the paper).

7. *Cultural exchanges* currently a one way street. Soviet Union is free to export cultural visits to UK under arrangements made by commercial impresarios e.g., Moscow Phil[h]armonic orchestra and Ukrainian State Dance Company in 1981. These carefully chosen representatives leave a good impression in the UK of Soviet cultural standards.

8. Since Afghanistan there have been no major British cultural manifestations in the Soviet Union. This makes KGB's life easier and cannot be in our interests if we take 'battle of ideas and values' seriously. Objective is to expose Soviet people to British and Western ideas and influences.

9. Accept American cultural policy towards Soviet Union at present in low gear, but France, FRG, Japan, Italy have all engaged in major cultural events since Afghanistan.

No. 163

Minute from Mr Broomfield to Mr Jay, 6 October 1982[1]
Confidential (ENS 014/7)

Valedictory Despatch from Moscow: The Soviet View of the UK[2]

1. Your minute of 29 September[3] recorded the PUS's enquiry about what the Russians think of us.

2. For the Soviet Union, the bilateral relationship with the UK is significant less in itself than as a factor in Soviet relations with the West as a whole.

3. There have been times in the past (e.g. the Macmillan visit to Moscow in 1958) when the UK has been seen as having a leading role on the Western side in the development of the East/West relationship. But in recent years, the Russians have given priority among European countries to their relations with Germany and France, in the belief that these offer the greatest potential for affecting the cohesion of the Alliance and for influencing its policies, as well as (particularly in the case of Germany) greater trade opportunities. The UK has not been regarded as a suitable case for wedge-driving because it is traditionally too close to the US and because it has no major interests dependent on Soviet goodwill (unlike the Germans, with their concern for Berlin and their relations with the GDR, or the French with their large communist party and their desire to play an independent role in world affairs).

4. The UK has nevertheless been cultivated to some extent, mainly for its influence with the US, within the Community and within the Commonwealth; and also because of its status as a nuclear power and as a permanent member of the UN

---

[1] The minute drew heavily on notes prepared by Mr Murrell of the Research Department.
[2] No. 157.
[3] Not printed. *v. ibid.*, note 4.

UK-Soviet Relations, 1979-82

Security Council. We are also recognised as playing an important role in Western defence generally, both because of our high level of defence spending and because of our strategic position. The affair of the 105[4] demonstrated that we were a major target for the KGB. I expect that we still appear high on their list.

5. But the lack of content in relations with the UK, dating at least from the Soviet invasion of Afghanistan, was probably not of great concern to Moscow until recently. However, a number of developments may have enhanced the UK's importance in Soviet eyes. I would summarise them as follows:

(*a*) growing Soviet pessimism about the prospects for doing business with the US, and about US intentions;

(*b*) cooling of relations with France since the accession of President Mitterrand;

(*c*) uncertainty about the policies of the Kohl Government in the FRG;

(*d*) the pipeline dispute, which showed that the UK does not automatically follow US policies, but has its own perceptions on East/West issues;

(*e*) the Falklands war when, despite their public line, there is no doubt that the Russians were impressed by UK resolve and military prowess.

6. Of these factors, the most important is the first. The Russians are undoubtedly concerned about the difficulties of developing a stable relationship with the Reagan administration. While they consider the UK to be basically hostile and hard line, they nevertheless regard us as more sensible and predictable than the Americans. They may hope that, given the standing of the UK in Washington, we may be able to influence the Reagan administration in the direction of an improvement in the overall East/West relationship. It is interesting that during his conversation with the Secretary of State in New York, Gromyko recalled that 'there had been many examples since the war of the British acting to help find a way round differences between the United States and the Soviet Union' (paragraph 3 of UKMIS New York telno 1483).[5]

7. Finally, it may be worth adding a word about how the UK appears to Russian people generally, which has some impact on the view taken of us by the leadership. More Russians learn English than any other foreign language, and the model is still British English. The BBC is probably the most trusted Western radio station. Despite jamming, the Russian language broadcasts can be received in many areas and many Russians also listen to the World Service in English. Our quarterly magazine *Anglia* although its nominal circulation is only 100,000, commands a high price on the black market and by passing from hand [to hand] is probably read by at least 500,000 people. For older Russians, memories of the war-time alliance still also mean something—this is of course a theme which Soviet propaganda sometimes tries to exploit, but it does give us a rather different standing from that enjoyed by the Germans or even the French.

---

[4] A reference to the expulsion of 105 Soviet intelligence officers from the UK in September 1971. See *DBPO*, Series III, Vol. I.

[5] No. 161.

17 December 1981 – 9 December 1982

No. 164

Sir I. Sutherland (Moscow) to Mr Pym, 14 October 1982, 3.30 p.m.
Tel. No. 598 Immediate, Confidential (ENS 020/5)

Policy towards the Soviet Union and Eastern Europe

Following for Bullard

1. I note from Broomfield's letter of 6 October[1] that our policies towards the Soviet Union stand as they were but are due to be discussed at a meeting between the Secretary of State and the Prime Minister on 15 October.[2] I also note from his letter of 28 September that the Soviet Union does not figure in the appended list of recommended bilateral visits.

2. Three weeks of Moscow at first hand finds me surprised and concerned at the extent to which we have cut ourselves off from sources of direct intelligence and opportunities to put across our views in a period when Soviet policy is both more active and more hesitant than for some time past and economic difficulties more acute and when, I judge, the pace of social change is accelerating and a new leadership could be not long delayed. The latest developments in Poland notwithstanding, I believe that the re-establishment of contacts and a dialogue in the political and certain other carefully chosen fields would better serve British interests. The arguments are well set out in the department's paper and also covered in my predecessor's valedictory despatch[3] and paragraphs 6 and 7 of my tel no 550.[1]

3. Most of our allies have been less inhibited and have already embarked on the kind of contacts we are now contemplating, without, so far as I am aware, any prior consultation. The following summary of recent exchanges is by no means exhaustive but demonstrates the point. Paragraph 8 of the Department's paper needs updating to take account of recent developments.

(*a*) *FRG*. In addition to the visits referred to in my telegram 586[1] (Solomentsev and Kostandov both in Germany this week for a major exhibition and the Soviet/FRG joint commission respectively. Both received by Kohl. An invitation from the Bundestag to the Supreme Soviet) there were discussions in Bonn in August on UN matters and, when they met in New York, Genscher renewed an invitation to Gromyko to visit Bonn.

(*b*) *France*. As reported in my despatch of 7 October,[1] Mme Cresson is in Moscow this week for the largest French exhibition ever staged in the Soviet Union and Chevènement is due next month. The delegation from the Foreign Affairs Commission of the National Assembly, led by Maurice Faure, has just left after a salutary row over the mention of Poland in the joint communiqué. Andreani was here in September, a new fishing agreement was signed in August, and in July Ilychev was in Paris for talks on Africa, and a group here from the Quai to discuss the Middle East.

(*c*) *The Italians* have kept to about the same level of activity as ourselves. The Dutch have perhaps been more restrictive. The Irish have been active with their Political Director and parliamentary delegation visiting the Soviet Union in

---

[1] Not printed.

[2] Although Mr Pym met the Prime Minister as planned on 15 October the discussion of policy towards the Soviet Union was deferred to a later date. The meeting eventually took place on 17 November (see No. 172).

[3] No. 157.

UK-Soviet Relations, 1979-82

July. Their Joint Commission met in September. The Danish PUS came last month and the Soviet Minister of Agriculture goes to Canada in late October.

(*d*) *The United States.* Moscow has seen a steady stream of Congressmen and senior business representatives throughout the year, arms control analysts two weeks ago and a very large delegation is expected for the non-official US/Soviet Trade and Economic Council in November. Although senior intergovernmental contacts have been limited, Shultz's meetings with Gromyko in New York, constituted, in the description of my US colleague who was present, seven and a half hours of serious, non-political discussion which did not exclude the most difficult and sensitive issues, including human rights. Hartman was struck by the contrast between this and what Arbatov and the Soviet pundits on the United States had been saying about the futility of discussion with the Reagan Administration. The superpower relationship is *sui generis* but I see no reason why, with the right interlocutors, we should not be able to achieve a similar hard-headed dialogue.

4. In cultural exchanges, the French, Germans and Italians at least have pursued a more active policy for the past year, with, for instance, the visits of the Hamburg Opera and the Teatro Veneto to Moscow, the Kirov ballet to Paris and the Bolshoi to Italy, a German sculpture exhibition at the Pushkin and a major Franco-Soviet art exhibition. The Dostoyevsky exhibition, which was to have been held first in London has gone to Dusseldorf. One consequence of our policies has been that the Russians have been able to send us, through commercial channels, a succession of first-class musicians and performers, while the flow of British artists to the Soviet Union has been reduced to a generally second-rate trickle of individuals and groups selected by the Russians.

5. I still think that we should not dismiss the idea of a visit by the Prime Minister, which could provide an opportunity to put some home truths to the Russians, much as Schmidt did in 1980 after the invasion of Afghanistan. But, if this is not accepted, I would hope that it would at least be possible to restore to working order some of the basic machinery of Anglo-Soviet relations including:

(*a*) a limited programme of ministerial visits;

(*b*) contacts at your or AUSS level (particularly now that we have dropped a broad hint about an invitation to Deputy Foreign Minister Ryzhov);

(*c*) the resumption of meetings between Foreign Ministry experts on international subjects;

(*d*) a more active, targeted brief for this embassy;

(*e*) the stepping up of our cultural activity in the Soviet Union, and

(*f*) as recommended in paragraph [*sic*] of my despatch on the recent British/Soviet Joint Commission,[4] a re-examination of agricultural and related exchanges with a view to exploiting commercial possibilities against the background of the food programme. A similar re-examination of other areas where we may have curtailed exchanges to the detriment of our commercial interest.

6. When I called on the Prime Minister before leaving London, I did not, as we agreed, anticipate the recommendations in the Department's paper, but I concluded from our conversation that she would recognise, against the background of a situation as described in my paragraph 2, the need for increased contact to obtain the fullest possible appreciation of developments in Soviet policy and as a means

---

[4] Not printed.

17 December 1981 – 9 December 1982

not only of putting across our views, but of projecting the attractions and advantages of our society.[5]

[5] Mr Broomfield wrote to Sir I. Sutherland on 26 October and confirmed that the Anglo-Soviet Cultural Agreement had been renewed on the 25 October but that the Secretary of State wished to make it clear that 'this should not be taken as committing him to any re-activation of cultural relations' and that policy towards the Soviet Union remained unchanged 'until such time as he has had an opportunity to discuss possible changes to it with the Prime Minister'. In a marginal note of 28 October to Sir J. Bullard, Mr Broomfield commented that 'Sir I. Sutherland is still full of hope for a different relationship with the Soviet Union. He should not however be under any illusions. I explained the difficulties to him before he went out and have kept him informed of "progress" since.'

No. 165

Mr Pym to HM Representatives Overseas, 20 October 1982, 12 p.m.
Guidance Tel. No. 191 Restricted (ENS 163/1)

West Siberian Gas Pipeline

1. FCO Guidance Telno 184 of 5 October[1] outlined the immediate causes of the transatlantic dispute over the West Siberian Gas Pipeline, and the UK line to take. This supplementary Guidance summarises the background to the pipeline deal, the deal itself, and gives the line to take on the wider issues of East/West Trade and economic relations raised by the pipeline argument. You should draw on it as appropriate.

Background

2. During the 1970s a number of West European countries opted to reduce the share of oil in their total energy requirements partly in order to lower their dependence on OPEC. This decision led *inter alia* to an increase in natural gas consumption at a time when indigenous EC production (mainly from the Netherlands) was levelling off. The Soviet Union, already a supplier of significant quantities of gas to Western Europe, was then developing the huge West Siberian gas fields and was prepared to sell the newly exploited gas in large quantities. Alternative sources e.g. Norway could not be developed in the same timescale to meet the needs of the European countries principally involved (France, FRG, Italy, Belgium). This was the origin of the pipeline project.

The Project

3. The scale of the pipeline project, the largest ever East/West trade deal, has contributed to the controversy over it. Agreements were signed in Autumn 1981 for various West European countries to provide materials, equipment and finance to the USSR to build a 4,500 kilometre large diameter gas pipeline from the Urengoy gas field in Western Siberia to Uzhgorod on the Soviet/Czechoslovak frontier. The line will run through Czechoslovakia, possibly with a spur through Hungary, to West Germany, Austria and Italy, linking up with existing West

[1] Not printed. Following the declaration of martial law in Poland, President Reagan announced measures that prevented the supply of US components to European companies (including John Brown Engineering) with existing contracts for the Siberian gas pipeline. On 18 June, the US administration extended measures to cover US subsidiaries and licensees. In response, the EC made it clear that extra-territorial and retrospective measures were unacceptable. The British Government approved an enabling Order under Section 1 of the Protection of Trading Interests Act 1980 that prohibited John Brown and other specified companies from complying with American regulations.

403

UK-Soviet Relations, 1979-82

European gas pipeline networks. The pipeline's design specification could permit a maximum flow of 50 billion cubic metres of gas a year but supplies at present definitely contracted by West European countries (France and West Germany) amount to only 21 billion cubic metres annually. A further 10 billion cubic metres could be delivered annually through the pipeline to Eastern Europe. The first gas is scheduled to come on stream at the end of 1984. The supply contracts price the gas at an average of $4.75 per million BTU compared with Algerian demands for $5.75 per million BTU and recent bids of $5.50 by British Gas for gas from the Norwegian Staatfjord [sic] field. The EC member states receiving the gas will be West Germany and France; the Italian State Gas Company (SNAM) has agreed to purchase 8 billion cubic metres but the agreement has yet to be ratified by the Government. The Netherlands and Belgium may also take some gas (gas will be supplied to Austria and Switzerland as well). The UK will not receive any from the USSR. It is expected that by 1990, West Germany will receive 27 percent of its total natural gas supplies from the Soviet Union, France 20 percent and Italy 29 percent. This would mean that altogether the USSR would be supplying about 20 percent of EC natural gas consumption (compared with 7 percent at present). Norway and Algeria would each provide about 10-15 percent. But with the expected decline in Soviet oil exports, which will not be fully compensated by the additional gas exports, energy dependence as a whole on the USSR will fall: in the case of the FRG, from 6.2 percent of total energy consumption in 1979 to less than 5 percent in 1990; for France, from 4.4 percent to just over 3 percent; and for Italy, from 7.1 percent to 5 percent.

The Orders

4. The total value of orders to the Western countries supplying for the pipeline is $4.0-$4.5 billion, including orders for 41 compressor stations. Contracts for 2.0-2.5 million tons of large diameter steel pipe required to complete the line should account for about $2 billion. There are many subsidiary contracts, for compressor station equipment, construction machinery, computerised communications and information systems, fire-fighting equipment etc. The main engineering contracts have been awarded to a consortium of Creusot-Loire (France) and Mannesman (West Germany) for 22 compressor stations, and to Nuovo Pignone (Italy) for 19 compressor stations. Nuovo Pignone is also to supply 57 turbines for its section of the pipeline, while AEG-Kanis (West Germany) and John Brown Engineering (UK) are to supply respectively 47 and 21 turbines to the Mannesman/Creusot-Loire section. John Brown Engineering, AEG-Kanis and Nuovo Pignone are all 'manufacturing associates' of the US firm General Electric (GE). They manufacture under licence turbines for the compressor stations, designed by GE and incorporating GE supplied parts, including rotor blades and shafts. The French company Alsthom Atlantique is tooling up to produce 40 sets of blades and shafts under GE licence. In value terms, West German companies secured initial orders of over $1,300 million, Italian $700 million, French $570 million and British $335 million. Interest on the finance for these orders was within the old OECD consensus rate of 8.6 percent. First deliveries under contract began in the second half of 1982, and continued in August, September and October with shipments from France, Italy, the UK and West Germany.

The Wider Argument

5. The pipeline dispute directly involves not only the four major European powers and the USA, but also the Netherlands and the EC as a whole. The Commission and member states jointly prepared a protest note criticising the US

17 December 1981 – 9 December 1982

measures, delivered by the Commission and Presidency on 12 August in Washington.

6. The dispute's widespread ramifications stem from the fundamentally different approaches of the USA and the Europeans towards East/West economic relations. The US believe that, in view of the Soviet Union's growing economic difficulties, concerted Western pressure, in particular denial of credits and technology, would heighten Soviet problems of resource allocation, and in the end lead to a reduction in defence spending. The West Europeans, Canada, and Japan, believe that the Soviet Union's economic problems are less serious than the Americans maintain (since the USSR is largely economically self-sufficient and has immense natural resources), that Western credits and technology have only marginal impact overall on its economy, and that Alliance economic pressure would lead to belt-tightening rather than changes in defence or foreign policy.

US Attitudes

7. The US Administration have not been consistent in explaining their case. They have argued that US measures over the pipeline are in response to Soviet complicity in events in Poland, but also that the real purpose of the embargo is to secure more far reaching changes in Soviet internal and external policy.

8. The immediate US objections are that West European countries should not buy more gas from the USSR, or supply equipment for the pipeline. Instead, the West should develop alternative Western energy resources. The EC could, for instance, import more coal from the US, and the Norwegians might increase substantially the rate of development of their gas reserves and gas exports to Western Europe. The US Administration has argued that:

(*a*) the West Europeans are in danger of becoming so dependent on Soviet gas that the USSR could influence their policy decisions by threatening to cut off the gas supplies;

(*b*) the additional gas sales will generate for the Soviet Union a considerable hard currency income, freeing resources for further military spending;

(*c*) export credit for the pipeline is officially supported and in some cases subsidised; such assistance is wrong, especially at a time when the USSR is in economic difficulties;

(*d*) Western economic and trade pressure should be brought to bear on the Russians, in the form of a tighter technology embargo and restricted credit, in order to induce more reasonable Soviet behaviour.

The European View: Line to Take

9. The British and Europeans believe that the benefits of a long-term secure supply of reasonably priced gas, which reduces European dependence on OPEC oil and obviates a potentially damaging energy shortage, outweigh possible problems inherent in the project.

In our view:

(*a*) it is for the West European Governments concerned to make their own decisions about security of energy supplies. Western Europe's overall dependence on Soviet energy will decline in the 1980s if Soviet oil exports fall as expected. The gas purchase diversifies energy sources (cf paragraph 3 above). This will tend to make gas supplies more, not less, secure. The West Europeans are also ensuring by a number of different means, including flexibility on alternative sources of supply, strategic gas storage schemes, and use of interruptable contracts to final consumers to circumvent any possible Soviet interruption of supplies. By the nature of the pipeline, the Russians could not cut off supplies to one country, but

UK-Soviet Relations, 1979-82

could only reduce the total volume supplied.

(b) Soviet net income from the gas would be greater if the West did not help to construct the pipeline. Even if supplies of Western equipment were stopped now, the Russians would still build the pipeline by diverting other resources. (Six pipelines from Urengoy are scheduled for construction in the current 5 year plan, of which only one is due for export.)

(c) Soviet oil sales to the West (which now provide about half Soviet hard currency income) are expected to decline substantially in this decade. The gas sales will not fully make up the difference. The Russians are probably earning about 30 percent more in real terms from energy sales now than they will in 1990.

(d) Only part of the credit for the pipeline was officially subsidised. The largest credit was raised by a consortium of West German banks; although this was within the old OECD consensus rate of 8.5 percent, it was in line with German market rates and contained no official subsidy. The support provided by ECGD involved only the normal subsidy available for all overseas markets. Cover for any new contracts with the USSR would now conform to the new OECD consensus guidelines so that the minimum rate for officially supported credit has been increased to over 12 percent (a rate almost the same as the sterling market rate at present).

(e) Trade sanctions are ineffective unless agreed and applied by all suppliers. Restriction of Western trade with the USSR in non-COCOM items would be unlikely to reduce Soviet military expenditure, aggression abroad, or repression at home. The Soviet leadership would be likely to blame economic problems on Western sanctions, thereby escaping responsibility for them. Against this background, it is improbable that they would allow Soviet defence spending to fall.

The Way Ahead

10. We believe it is essential to defuse the dispute. Together with other Western nations, we are working to achieve an agreed analysis of the Soviet economy and a coherent Alliance strategy on East/West trade and economic relations, as foreshadowed in the Versailles and Bonn NATO Summits in June. The informal meeting of NATO Foreign Ministers at La Sapinière on 2/3 October made useful progress. We are now working to follow this up in appropriate fora.[2]

11. Other issues have become caught up in the pipeline saga:

(a) *Grain Sales*

Large American grain sales to the Soviet Union continue, and the Americans decided in July to prolong their grain supply agreement with the Soviet Union until 30 September next year. We are not opposed to such sales but we regard them as inconsistent with attempts to enforce an embargo on European sales for the pipeline. The Americans claim that their grain sales are different because they are for cash or short term credit; a grain embargo would only divert sales to Canada, Australia, and others; and the sales use up Soviet hard currency instead of generating it. We do not accept this argument. Recent studies show that the USSR would be considerably worse off financially if it had to develop greater grain self-sufficiency since this would require significant resources to be diverted from efficient to inefficient sectors of the Soviet economy.

(b) *European Attitudes towards Poland, Afghanistan*

The US Administration has not criticised either the British or the European responses to Soviet responsibility for developments in Poland and the occupation

---

[2] See No. 170, note 4 and No. 173, note 2.

17 December 1981 – 9 December 1982

of Afghanistan. But the US press has various articles criticising European support over these issues. The reply to such criticisms is that the UK adopted significant economic and political measures towards the Soviet Union following both Afghanistan and Poland. These were intended to send a strong signal of disapproval of Soviet actions, rather than to inflict damage on the Soviet economy. Several other European countries and the EC took measures of their own, including EC support for the US grain embargo against the USSR after Afghanistan, and EC proposals to upgrade OECD consensus interest rates towards the USSR after martial law in Poland.

No. 166

Minute from Mr Walden (Planning Staff) to Mr Broomfield, 28 October 1982
Confidential (EN 021/6)

Prime Minister's Guildhall Speech: East/West Relations

1. I am increasingly unhappy about the tough stuff that we planners amongst others find ourselves drafting for the Prime Minister on the Russians. We try to balance it with reference to a dialogue, but this tends to be drowned by truculent noises. (The final draft of the Prime Minister's Berlin speech is pretty high pitched.)[1] Of course all this goes down well domestically: but there is another and perhaps growing audience who would like a little bit of reassurance, particularly as INF looms.

2. Brezhnev's growling speech yesterday[2] underlines how far the deterioration of the superpowers' relationship has gone. I know that the Prime Minister is not going to accept the FCO philosophy outlined in your Department's paper[3] by 15 November, let alone agree to go the Soviet Union next year. (As far as I know Mr Pym has not even discussed all this with her yet.) I wonder however whether she might not be persuaded to insert some cost-free and eye-catching gesture to the Russians in her speech to balance the hard stuff. I cannot quite think what this might be: is there something we can dress up in the chemical warfare field, where I gather progress is more likely than in other areas? I would welcome views and suggestions.

3. Independently of Mr Pym's talks with the Prime Minister, I suspect that East/West relations are getting to the stage where they would be a good subject for a DUS's discussion. Now we have dealt with the periphery, perhaps we should return to the centre! Perhaps such a discussion could pave the way for a very small

---

[1] Between 28 and 30 October, the Prime Minister visited West Germany and West Berlin for a two-day summit conference with Helmut Kohl. In a speech delivered in the Brandenburg Hall, Berlin, on 29 October Mrs Thatcher told city dignitaries that the Berlin wall was 'an ever present reminder that those who repress the liberties of our Eastern neighbours, seek also to extinguish our own. Let us resolve that they must never succeed.' A copy of the speech can be found on the Margaret Thatcher Foundation website: http://www.margaretthatcher.org/.

[2] On 27 October, President Brezhnev, in an address to Soviet military leaders on the eve of the twentieth anniversary of the withdrawal of Soviet nuclear missiles from Cuba, condemned ruling circles in the United States for launching an unprecedented political, ideological and economic offensive against socialism which strained the relationship between the two countries to breaking point.

[3] Enclosure in No. 160.

UK-Soviet Relations, 1979-82

seminar with the Prime Minister on East/West relations? There are quite successful precedents soon after she came to office.

G. G. H. WALDEN

No. 167

Minute from Mr Gillmore to Mr Walden (Planning Staff), 1 November 1982
Confidential (EN 021/6)

Prime Minister's Guildhall Speech: East/West Relations
1. Your minute to Mr Broomfield of 28 October.[1]
2. I understand and sympathise with your unhappiness about the tough language we inevitably find ourselves drafting for the Prime Minister when we mention the Russians. Nevertheless I would be strongly against trying to dress up something in the field of chemical weapons. The Prime Minister has seen a number of recent papers on this subject and will, I fear, be much more inclined to berate the Russians for their own modern capability than to hold out, as it were, the olive branch of constructive dialogue and arms control. We are trying to get the CD[2] to settle down to proper negotiations on CW;[3] but our main problem so far has been to bring the Americans and our own MOD along with us. In short, CW is a difficult subject where we have to tread delicately. I doubt if we would help ourselves by raising the Prime Minister's consciousness on it at this juncture.
3. Like you, I am pretty barren of ideas for other issues/gestures which could balance the hard stuff. Perhaps the idea of political dialogue, including confidence-building measures, is the right approach. But even here there is a risk that this will produce winces in Washington, unless of course in the end the Americans agree to go back to Madrid in a more constructive and positive frame of mind than at present seems likely.

D. H. GILLMORE

[1] No. 166.
[2] Conference on Disarmament.
[3] Chemical weapons.

No. 168

Sir I. Sutherland (Moscow) to Mr Pym, 5 November 1982, 2.45 p.m.[1]
Tel. No. 665 Priority, Confidential (EN 021/15)

Soviet foreign policy—A change in direction?
1. Since mid-September, Brezhnev and other members of the Politburo have delivered a series of speeches which have been characterised by:
(*a*) A renewed call for détente
(*b*) Increasingly sharp attacks on the US administration
(*c*) Conciliatory references to China and

[1] Info Priority to Washington, UKDEL NATO, Bonn, Paris and Peking; Info saving other EC posts, UKMIS New York, UKMIS Geneva, UKDEL Vienna, Ulan Bator and East European posts.

17 December 1981 – 9 December 1982

(*d*) Warnings of the need for military preparedness.

The degree of emphasis has varied. In his speech at Baku on 26 September (my telno 556)[2] Brezhnev concentrated on resurrecting the theme of détente linking this to the possibility of normalising relations with Peking. The other three themes were emphasised in his address to senior officers in the Kremlin on 27 October (my telno 643),[3] a speech which has been widely interpreted denoting a major change in Soviet policy and by some as the beginning of Brezhnev's swan-song. I think this goes too far. But the apparently inconsistent themes are, I believe, complementary and consistent with an increasingly negative assessment of American policies and a corresponding adjustment in the main lines of Soviet policy with a view to isolating the United States and neutralising a perceived ideological struggle and military challenge. This adjustment appears to be taking place against the background of an internal debate involving the armed forces and the party leadership about priorities in the allocation of economic resources.

2. Further intimations of an evolution in Soviet policy are provided in the speech made on 29 October by Chernenko, Brezhnev's closest colleague in the Politburo and one of his two most likely successors, when he presented the Order of Lenin to the City of Tbilisi, a ceremony which the General Secretary would normally have performed himself. A complicating factor which probably accounts for an unaccustomed hesitancy and some apparently conflicting signals about the direction of policy is Brezhnev's partial incapacity. The widespread expectation of changes in the leadership amongst Russians as well as foreigners here is certainly one reason for the call for unity and vigilance in the face of the American 'challenge'. But Brezhnev appears to be no worse if no better than he was, and my guess is still that he will hang on for a while.

Détente and anti-détente

3. The common thread in all three speeches referred to in my preceding paragraphs is an attempt to depict the current international situation as marked by two fundamentally different approaches.

(*a*) The Soviet line of bridling the arms race, strengthening 'peace' and defending the sovereign rights of nations.

(*b*) The United States' line of disrupting détente, escalating the arms race, and of threats and interference in other countries' affairs.

This Manichean thesis is not new. It was propounded in Brezhnev's Report to the 26th Congress in February last year.[4] But it has been much sharpened in recent pronouncements and accompanied by a vituperative campaign designed to discredit the administration in Washington. In Tbilisi, Chernenko spoke of two 'poles'—of those who stood for détente and those who wanted a return to the Cold War. Zamyatin, head of the information department of the Party Central Committee who will have a major hand in drafting Brezhnev's speeches, has characterised the two approaches as 'détente and anti-détente' (*Literaturnaya Gazeta*, 29 September).

What the Russians now mean by détente

4. After many months when the word had been scarcely mentioned in the Soviet press, in his Baku speech Brezhnev produced a long bland definition of détente in terms designed to appeal to anyone with good intentions. Ignoring the traditional endorsement of ideological struggle, it appears to be a different animal from the

---

[2] Not printed.
[3] Not printed. See No. 166, note 2.
[4] See No. 86.

UK-Soviet Relations, 1979-82

détente of the Nixon period. It differs in that it is not applied to relations with the United States. As Chernenko put it, the American ruling classes have not stood up to the test of détente and peaceful cooperation. With the same finality, Zamyatin wrote that the Reagan administration has completely broken with détente. It also differs in that it has the widest geographical application, being relevant to Asia as well as to Europe and, as such, related to the new opening in China. It is in Chernenko's phraseology a multi-aspect and multi-dimensional process. In effect détente is now a designation used for any international activity which can be held to accord with the line at 3(*a*) above. It is a catch-all for the non-aligned but it is particularly geared to current Western European concerns and the opportunities which they provide for wedge-driving. The aim is to isolate the present US administration, to neutralise INF modernisation and other alliance defence plans and generally to exploit the opportunities presented by transatlantic differences over East/West relations. It provides readily accepted slogans for the peace movements and others in the West held to be struggling against 'imperialism', but the new broad-based détente campaign is also manifest in some soft pedalling towards West European governments, even those very critical of Soviet policies. As reported in my telno 653[5] the reaction to the Prime Minister's speech in Berlin on 29 October was, for instance, surprisingly limited.[6]

The view of the United States

5. As early as the 26th Congress last January, Brezhnev had referred to disturbing signs in the policies of the Reagan administration but indicated that the Soviet government would wait and see how they worked out. A debate ensued as to whether it was possible to do serious business with Washington. President Reagan's turning of the ideological struggle against Moscow, in particular his crusade against socialism speech at Westminster last June,[7] struck a particularly raw nerve here. The public line became increasingly pessimistic and by 5 October this year *Pravda* was writing that those who were unremittingly hostile to the Soviet Union predominated in Washington. The message in Brezhnev's speech of 27 October appeared to be that there was no reason to expect any understanding of Soviet concerns there and that the Russians must accordingly be economically self-sufficient and devote every effort to matching US military strength. The thrust of Chernenko's subsequent remarks confirms that he wishes it to be understood that the Soviet leadership had concluded that there is no or almost no prospect of a constructive relationship with the present US administration. Like Brezhnev, Chernenko made no explicit mention of the arms control talks in Geneva. On 2 November General Chernov spoke of the complete lack of any progress in the INF or START talks. Chernenko had concluded 'if Washington cannot rise above primitive anti-Communism, if it is going to continue a policy of threats and diktat, well, we are sufficiently strong and can wait'. Like Brezhnev, he also made a direct link between US policies and recent Soviet attempts to establish a better relationship with Peking. Chernenko even referred to the Soviet Union's 'great' Chinese neighbour.

Shifts in policy and the need to reassure the armed forces

6. To whom is this message of Brezhnev and Chernenko primarily directed? In paragraph 7 of my telno 643[5] I concluded that Brezhnev's address of 27 October was probably a response to uncertainties within the armed forces about the

---

[5] Not printed.

[6] See No. 166, note 1.

[7] See No. 155, note 4.

17 December 1981 – 9 December 1982

implications for them both of the international situation and of domestic economic policies. My US colleague goes rather further in ascribing the markedly harsher tone towards the United States as almost wholly to internal considerations. Hartman believes that the military must have been seeking assurances now given to them by Brezhnev that at a time of economic difficulty when additional resources are being channelled into the food programme, they should nevertheless have first priority. He also points to some evidence that the military may be uneasy at certain aspects of the new wider definition of détente, in particular the theoretical justification which it gives for an opening to China. As the article by Ustinov, the Soviet Defence Minister, in *Pravda* on 12 July referred to in Moscow telno 410[8] indicated they may well also have had reservations about Brezhnev's 'no-first use' of nuclear weapons proposal at a time when the NATO deployment of Pershing-Cruise missiles is proceeding. A Moscow radio broadcast directed at Eastern Europe has, I understand, referred to letters from listeners criticising the proposal. Whether or not the military have been reassured, they will realise that Brezhnev's speech carried the full weight of the Party behind it, an impression reinforced by the presence of five heavyweight members of the politburo. Hartman agrees with me (contrary to the view expressed by some of my community colleagues) that, although the possibility of voluntary, honourable [retirement] by the General Secretary on the occasion of the 60th anniversary of the Union is not to be excluded (my telno 632, para 5),[8] the signal from the leadership has been 'here we stand, behind our leader, Brezhnev, and here we stay'.

7. It is too soon to say whether all this represents the beginning of a fundamental shift in Soviet foreign policy. So far what we have seen are significant changes in emphasis. And in the final analysis, however disillusioned the Russians may be with Reagan, they know that they have no choice but to deal with the Americans and that the other side of the triangle between Moscow and Peking cannot provide an alternative of equal weight. There will be a number of public occasions in the coming weeks for further elaboration of Soviet foreign policy, the first being the speech traditionally given by a member of the Politburo tonight on the eve of the 7 November holiday. Another will be next week when both the Americans and Russians will have an opportunity to put across their views when Senator Dole[9] and members of the US Trade Council go to the Kremlin.

8. FCO please pass to saving addressees.[10]

---

[8] Not printed.

[9] Republican Senator from Kansas, 1969–1996.

[10] Replying in a letter dated 10 November, Mr Broomfield largely agreed with the analysis provided by the Ambassador. However he wondered whether the Soviet definition of détente had really changed. The Soviet leadership seemed to argue that the US had rejected détente but at the same time stressed they were keeping the door open (in part to drive wedges in the NATO Alliance). The definition of détente had been stated in broad terms, perhaps to coincide with recent approaches to China. Nevertheless the dominant theme remained the Soviet Union's commitment to a peaceful foreign policy as endorsed at the 26th Party Congress.

UK-Soviet Relations, 1979-82

No. 169

Briefing note for Mr Pym, 11 November 1982[1]
Confidential (ENS 010/4)

Effects of Brezhnev's Death on Soviet Foreign Policy[2]

1. Brezhnev's successor as Party General Secretary will be drawn from present senior leadership, all of whom identified with policies of Brezhnev years. Successor will rely on same party apparatus. Watchword will be continuity because:

(*a*) Soviet tradition is to reassert collective principle when leadership changes;

(*b*) Soviet Union does not change course easily even in normal times;

(*c*) Brezhnev has for some time been in less than full command, and collective approach will already have been established.

2. Andropov and Chernenko front runners for General-Secretary. Neither has much experience of dealing with the West. Positions of General-Secretary and President likely to be split. Will take time for single dominant figure to emerge after period of rivalry.

3. Brezhnev's speech of 27 October showed importance attached by Party leadership to demonstrating continuing commitment to needs of armed forces. No doubt military under Party control. Ustinov (Minister of Defence) a Party, not a military figure.

4. Unusual number of recent speeches by Soviet leaders[3] have set out main themes of Soviet policy for the West:

(*a*) Soviet Union ready to match US armament programmes, even though resources tight;

(*b*) Soviet leadership ready for substantive talks with the US, but inclined to despair of Reagan administration.

(*c*) This message likely to be repeated.

5. No compromise likely on Poland or Afghanistan.

[1] The briefing note was written by Mr Sheinwald for a meeting the Foreign Secretary was due to have with the Prime Minister and Defence Secretary on 12 November.
[2] On 11 November at 11 a.m. local time, Soviet television announced that President Brezhnev had died suddenly at 8.30 a.m. on 10 November.
[3] See No. 168.

No. 170

Sir I. Sutherland (Moscow) to FCO, 15 November 1982, 9.43 a.m.[1]
Tel. No. 724 Immediate, Confidential (EN 021/6)

Following from Private Secretary[2]

Secretary of State's Meeting with Mr Shultz: East/West Relations

1. Shultz recalled President Reagan's message to the Prime Minister and her

[1] Telegram repeated Information Immediate to Washington, UKDEL NATO; Information Priority to Paris, Bonn.
[2] Mr Pym was in Moscow representing HMG at President Brezhnev's funeral (see No. 175).

412

17 December 1981 – 9 December 1982

reply.[3] It was time for the allies to demonstrate three things: realism, strength and readiness for a more constructive relationship. The US had been trying to emphasise the third element. Some people in Moscow appeared to see the lifting of the pipeline sanctions as a conciliatory act by the US.[4] There was a feeling abroad, voiced by Dr Kissinger among others, that an opportunity for a breakthrough existed. This might be so, but not simply because Brezhnev had died. It was not a moment for the West to change its policy, but to emphasise it, and meanwhile to maintain the necessary strength.

2. The Secretary of State agreed. He could not tell at this stage whether a new opportunity existed or not. But there was nothing to be lost by exploring, and much to be lost if this was not done. In Britain, the government was considering the question of the timing of the deployment of new INF systems in relation to the FRG. The whole country was determined, from the Prime Minister downwards, to stand by the double decision. Public attitudes in this matter would be very important. Western governments would be expected by their own people to take steps to find out what was the colour of Andropov's money.[5] There had been much speculation. Time would show. The note struck by President Reagan was exactly the right one.

3. Hartman (US Ambassador to Moscow), invited to speak about the Soviet internal situation, said that he saw Andropov as occupying the number one slot but not yet wielding Brezhnev's power. In his first speech he had doffed his cap to the military, to whom he owed his position. It was too early to assume that he would follow a tougher policy than Brezhnev's, if such a thing could be imagined. His speeches so far were directed mainly at the domestic audience. Resource decisions for the Soviet Government were going to be difficult whatever happened. It would be in the Western interest 'to keep Andropov's options tight'. Certainly Andropov would not cut back defence spending simply because he found himself in a resource pinch. But Soviet support for e.g. Ethiopian and Cuban adventures, and for Eastern Europe, might be reduced, and indeed there were signs of the latter already happening. Hartman detected an inability to take decisions because 'nobody knows how to make the system work'. The problems were institutional as well as economic. What the West should do in this situation was to paint a picture of how things could be if the Soviet leaders adopted the necessary attitude.

4. Shultz said he was more pessimistic than Hartman about the meaning of Andropov's first public statements. He saw him as a hard man. The time of opportunity for the West was more likely to come later than immediately.

5. The Secretary of State posed the question how any Soviet leader could reduce

---

[3] On 12 November President Reagan wrote to Mrs Thatcher suggesting how the West should conduct relations with the Soviets in the period following the death of President Brezhnev. The Prime Minister replied on 15 November agreeing strongly with President Reagan, in particular over the need to make it clear to the new Soviet leaders that a more constructive East-West relationship was available if they were prepared to act responsibly. She promised to make the point in her speech at the Guildhall in the City of London that evening. The more strident tones of the original draft were downplayed with the Prime Minister promising 'a ready welcome and quick response' to any solid evidence that the new Soviet leadership was willing to work for genuine multilateral disarmament (a copy of the speech can be found on the Margaret Thatcher Foundation website: http://www.margaretthatcher.org/). She also agreed with President Reagan about the overriding importance of Western unity at this particular time and to this end welcomed the progress that had been made in discussions over economic policy towards the East.

[4] On 13 November, the US administration announced its decision to lift sanctions on the supply of high technology equipment for the Siberian pipeline. See No. 173, note 2.

[5] Yuri Andropov was elected General Secretary of the Soviet Communist Party on 12 November.

UK-Soviet Relations, 1979-82

defence spending if he wished to do so, given the self-perpetuating nature of Soviet policies and of the system. He saw the Soviet Union as facing great problems abroad and at home, including a potential problem of Islamic fundamentalism. Provided the West retained sufficient strength to deter any attack and coordinated its policy, we had little to fear from the USSR.

No. 171

Mr Pym to Sir I. Sutherland (Moscow), 15 November 1982, 10 p.m.[1]
Tel. No. 676 Priority, Confidential (ENS 010/4)

Following from Private Secretary

Secretary of State's Meeting with Mr Gromyko, 15 November

1. At the end of the day before leaving for the airport I had a thirty minute bilateral meeting with Gromyko. He was studiously uncontentious, had nothing particularly new to say on any of the points I raised and raised none himself. At 73 he was no doubt tired after the funeral and a series of foreign callers.

2. I referred to the change in the Soviet leadership. We hoped that a more productive relationship would become possible. What conclusions should be drawn from the new leadership's initial statements. Gromyko replied that Andropov was a member of the same Politburo which would continue to follow the same internal and external policies. The latter would be characterised by peace and détente. The Soviet side was for an improvement in our bilateral relations including the political, cultural and economic fields. We should use our considerable influence positively in international affairs.

3. Mr Pym stressed the need for effective arms control and for the Madrid talks to reach a successful conclusion. Gromyko argued that the solution to the arms race lay in negotiations which, even if they did not reduce, would at least check arms levels. But the current negotiations in Geneva had made no progress, no headway. They were not proceeding as they should if both sides were showing real will.

4. Mr Pym asked if Gromyko saw any possibility of change in Afghanistan. He claimed that the position was now more stable. Unofficial Afghan/Pakistan talks were proceeding. If the UK wished to make a positive contribution we should support them. The Soviet Union was not itself directly engaged. There could be no question of negotiating with Pakistan, but they made their views clear as they had done earlier that day directly to the President of Pakistan.[2]

5. Gromyko refused to hazard a guess on when martial law might be lifted in Poland. The Polish leadership had made it clear that this would happen as soon as the situation returned to normal. An end should be put to efforts aimed at undermining the present regime.

6. Gromyko claimed that currently Iran was more stubborn than Iraq in resisting efforts to bring the war to an end.[3] Both sides were of approximately equal

---

[1] Repeated Information Priority to Copenhagen, Washington, Bonn, Paris, UKDEL NATO; Information Saving to Kabul, Baghdad, Tehran, Islamabad, Warsaw.

[2] General Zia-ul-Haq.

[3] A reference to the war between Iran and Iraq which started in September 1980.

17 December 1981 – 9 December 1982

strength. Unpredictable events could not be ruled out. But blood was flowing quite senselessly.

No. 172

Letter from Mr Coles (No. 10) to Mr Fall, 17 November 1982
Confidential (EN 021/6)

Dear Brian,

East/West Relations

The Foreign and Commonwealth Secretary discussed the above subject with the Prime Minister this afternoon.

Mr Pym said that there were three broad considerations to keep in mind. We needed to explore the possibility of change in Soviet policies, following the change of leadership; President Reagan's recent message to the Prime Minister was relevant.[1] We should do all we could to maintain the strength of our relationship with the United States. We needed to ensure that the Europeans remained firm during 1983 with regard to NATO's two-track decision on the stationing of intermediate-range land-based missiles.

He had it in mind to send a message to Mr Shultz on these matters.[2] This would refer to the changes in the Soviet Union, draw attention to the importance of the forthcoming meeting of NATO Foreign Ministers and suggest the adoption by that meeting of a declaration describing the West's attitude to East/West relations. The message would go on to say that we wished to pursue the considerations in the recently agreed paper on East/West economic relations and to set up the necessary machinery quickly. Finally, the message would float the idea of an early Summit between President Reagan and Mr Andropov. The discussions which Vice President Bush had had with Andropov in Moscow recently contained a hint that this idea might be worth pursuing. There had been a similar hint in the conversations between the President of the Federal Republic of Germany and Andropov. The thought might be that a very early meeting between the two would be easier to arrange, and would run less risk of raising expectations, than a Summit proposed in a few months' time. It would be seen publicly as a positive move at the beginning of a very difficult period. We should bear in mind that Andropov might himself make such a proposal. It would in any case be useful for us to float the idea with Mr Shultz. By doing so we could involve ourselves in the preparatory discussion for the Summit and thus keep our relationship with the United States in the best possible condition.

The Prime Minister recalled that President Reagan's position seemed to be that he was ready to respond if the Soviet Union provided genuine opportunities. Previously, we had always argued that a Summit should be very well prepared. It would be a very big departure from this position simply to urge that one should take place. Mr Pym said that he believed such a proposal would have a very helpful effect on European opinion. The Prime Minister said that her reading of Andropov was that he would need to demonstrate in his early weeks that he was tough. But he might propose one or two cosmetic moves which would lead some in the West to claim that there were new possibilities of détente and thus lower their

[1] See No. 170, note 3.
[2] See No. 173.

415

UK-Soviet Relations, 1979-82

guard. She agreed that it would be wise for there to be a US/Soviet Summit at sometime in the next two years. But she doubted whether there could be more than one. The Foreign and Commonwealth Secretary said that he thought this was not necessarily so, given the appearance of a new leadership. If Mr Shultz thought the idea was worth examining, we could do more detailed work.

The Prime Minister said that if the Foreign and Commonwealth Secretary thought that it would help his relationship with Mr Shultz to float such a proposal, she would not wish to object. But she believed the idea would get a much better reception if we did more work on it first. We needed to be clear as to what such a meeting could achieve, what the limitations and risks were, and where it would take place. It should certainly not be held in Moscow. The next US/Soviet Summit, whenever it took place, would set the scene for East/West relations for a long time ahead. When President Reagan met Andropov, he must not fail. She was not convinced that there was merit in an early meeting.

Mr Pym said that he also thought there could be merit in new contacts between the United Kingdom and the Soviet Union. For example, Mr Rifkind might pay a visit to Moscow. It might also be useful for contacts to take place at senior official level. We tended to do much less than our major allies in this respect. This was rather damaging since our allies knew that they had more contact than we did. The purpose of such meetings would be to put across our point of view on a range of subjects. There was nothing to lose.

The Prime Minister expressed some concern that such moves would harm our whole stance on East/West relations. Trade contacts at Ministerial level were a different matter. But we should have to be sure that any political contacts were consistent with the various understandings into which we had entered after the Soviet invasion of Afghanistan. She was opposed to a Senior Minister visiting Moscow but could perhaps envisage a visit at lower levels, provided it had a clear purpose. She thought we should give Mr Shultz advance warning of any such visits. In general, she was not enthusiastic about the prospect but would not raise objection if the points she had made were met.

Yours ever,
JOHN COLES

No. 173

Mr Pym to Sir N. Henderson (Washington), 18 November 1982, 7 p.m.[1]
Tel. No. 2037 Immediate, Confidential (EN 021/6)

East-West Relations

1. Please pass the following message from me to Shultz. Message begins: Dear George. I have been thinking about the conversation we had in Moscow when we were both there for President Brezhnev's funeral and about the prospects for East-West relations. Three things strike me:

(*a*) There have been significant shifts in the last week in the scenery of East-

[1] Repeated Information Priority to Bonn, Paris, UKDEL NATO, Moscow. This telegram was dated 17 November but not sent until the following day.
The message was drafted prior to Mr Pym's meeting with the Prime Minister and represented agreement reached at the Secretary of State's Office meeting on 16 November.

416

17 December 1981 – 9 December 1982

West relations. The change of leadership in Moscow gave the opportunity for the signal contained in President Reagan's message of condolence and for the important conversation which George Bush and you had with Andropov and Gromyko after the funeral:

(*b*) There has been a convergence of attitudes towards East-West relations among the major Western allies. This was for example reflected in the joint statement issued by President Reagan and Chancellor Kohl:

(*c*) The successful conclusion of the pipeline exercise on the basis of your 'non-paper'[2] has created both the opportunity and the urgent need for the Western allies to concert a common line on East-West relations, including but not merely the economic dimension.

It is very important that we should seize the chance which I believe these developments offer to us, and not lose a day more than is necessary. There is very little time before the December NATO Foreign Ministers' meeting, which will obviously be of exceptional importance this year. I should like to see that meeting adopt, in addition to the usual communiqué, a declaration on East-West relations, setting out in an eloquent and eye-catching form the basic Western approach, and repeating the various offers and proposals already made to the Soviet Union, so as to bring out President Reagan's point that a more constructive East-West relationship is there for the asking if the new Soviet leaders will only do what is necessary to grasp the opportunity. Such a declaration might have to be drafted by an inner group of allies rather than in the usual NATO drafting machinery.

At the same time, I also hope that we can move ahead rapidly on East-West economic relations. The French problem has, I hope, been largely ironed out as a result of a meeting I had in Moscow with Claude Cheysson and the others concerned. We ourselves take very seriously all our commitments in the 'non-paper', and have clear ideas on how to pursue them. I have sent instructions to Oliver Wright to help maintain the momentum.

One point struck me as being of particular interest in your Ambassador's account of your meeting with Andropov. I gather that Andropov dropped a hint about a possible summit. In normal times I would go along with the argument that summits need to be very carefully prepared if they are not to arouse and then disappoint public expectations. But in present circumstances, and with all the changes in the East-West scenery of which I have spoken, it seems to me that there could be something to be said for an early Soviet-American summit. It would need to be presented not as an attempt to reach comprehensive agreements, but as a chance for the two leaders to get to know one another, and also to enable President Reagan, as leader of the Western alliance, to spell out to Andropov the major areas of Western concern—the strategic balance, Afghanistan, Poland and human rights. Like the declaration on East-West relations which I have suggested, this would help to underline the point that a more constructive relationship is possible if the Russians want it and are ready to work for it. Ideally the summit would follow

---

[2] The term 'non-paper' is used to describe an unofficial or off-the-record presentation of policy often circulated to members of a multilateral organisation with the aim of sounding out a new policy. The Shultz 'non-paper' led to the suspension of US sanctions covering the Siberian pipeline and their replacement with a high level study agreed by all members to determine their future energy requirements. During the course of the study all parties agreed they would not enter into new contracts with the Soviet Union for the purchase of natural gas. It was also agreed that it was not in the West's interests to subsidise the Soviet economy but it was also not their purpose to engage in economic warfare against the Soviet Union. President Reagan made the announcement on 13 November (see *Public Papers: Reagan (1982)*, Book II, pp. 1464-65).

UK-Soviet Relations, 1979-82

soon after the NATO meeting, for example early next year.

I have considered the possible effect of a summit on European public opinion, and in particular the risk that it might encourage illusions about a better East-West relationship which would make it more difficult to go ahead with INF deployment. But I believe that, providing it were held really early in 1983, a summit could help to keep public opinion steady—perhaps especially in Germany—by demonstrating that the United States is doing everything possible to reach agreement on genuinely balanced measures of arms control, at the same time as putting the other half of the double decision into effect.

To put the idea in another form, would the President be able to reject a summit if Andropov were to propose one now, as could happen in connection with the Warsaw Pact meeting early next month? If the answer is no, perhaps the right course is for the United States itself to take the initiative.

I have not so far had an opportunity to talk these things over with Claude and Hans-Dietrich, but would like to do so when I see them on 22-23 November at one of our regular Community meetings. I hope you may be able to let me have a first reaction before then. Yours, Francis. Message ends.[3]

---

[3] Mr Shultz replied on 22 November. Whilst he agreed with Mr Pym on the need for a firm and positive restatement of the basic Western approach to relations with the Soviet Union in December's NATO communiqué he had reservations about expanding this into a separate declaration. He thought it was too early to draw any conclusions about Soviet behaviour in the post-Brezhnev era and such a declaration might prove counter-productive within the Alliance, with some governments seeking to take a more hopeful and positive line than circumstances yet dictated. He also believed a US/Soviet summit would be premature as he had seen nothing in his exchanges with the Soviets to date which suggested that the change in Soviet leadership would create a situation in which such a meeting might be productive (Washington telegram No. 2056 of 22 November 1982).

On 26 November Roger Harrison, of the US Embassy, called on Mr Weston following his return from a meeting in Washington of politico/military staff from US Embassies in Europe. The UK proposal for an early Reagan/Andropov summit had not gone down well in Washington where it was seen as over-hasty and ill-judged. Sir J. Bullard minuted: 'I have no regrets about our suggestion, but accept that it is no use pushing it in the face of US reluctance' (EN 020/1).

No. 174

Mr Pym to Sir I. Sutherland (Moscow), 18 November 1982, 7 p.m.[1]
Tel. No. 691 Priority, Confidential (ENS 020/5)

UK/Soviet Relations

1. You will have seen that I have decided to float the idea of a US/Soviet Summit with Shultz (my telno 2037 to Washington).[2]

2. I have been considering also future political contacts between the UK and the Soviet Union, including both talks at senior official levels and the possibility of a visit by Mr Rifkind to Moscow. The purpose of such meetings would be to put across our views clearly on a range of subjects. The following are possibilities:

(*a*) Talks at expert level between Planning Staffs (Walden) in Moscow and on the Middle East (Grinevsky) in London.

(*b*) A visit by Goodison to Moscow for talks with the Head of Second European

---

[1] Repeated Information to Washington, Bonn, Paris, UKDEL NATO; Saving Prague, Budapest, Bucharest, Sofia, East Berlin, Warsaw, Belgrade, UKDEL Madrid, Rome. This telegram was dated 19 November but sent the day before.
[2] No. 173.

17 December 1981 – 9 December 1982

Department.

(*c*) Confirmation of the invitation for Deputy Foreign Minister Ryzhov.

(*d*) Visit by Mr Rifkind to Moscow for talks with a First Deputy Foreign Minister (Kornienko or Maltsev).

3. Our policy over contacts with the Soviet Union is set out most recently in Mr Hurd's written reply to Mr Lawrence's PQ on 18 June 1981.[3] We had stated after the Soviet invasion of Afghanistan that high level and Ministerial contacts with the Soviet Union were to be avoided for the time being. Mr Hurd went on to say, however, there were occasionally high level and Ministerial contacts where these were deemed advantageous. These guidelines remain in force. The ideas suggested above fall within them. But we would clearly wish to avoid bunching them in order not to convey the impression of a sudden change of direction or policy. I am therefore inclined first to propose Planning Staff talks: Walden would be ready for these soon, possibly before the end of the year. I should welcome your advice on the timing and order of the other possible events. (Our initial view is that Ryzhov might be invited to come in January and that the proposal could then be made that Mr Rifkind visit Moscow in June 1983.)

4. For the time being also, and notwithstanding what may be the practice and intentions of our European partners, I should not (not) wish to increase the level or scale of our cultural activities. To do so might create an impression of total normality in Anglo-Soviet relations which I wish to avoid.

5. I shall want to inform the Americans, and probably our other close allies at the appropriate time, but I would not wish you to take any such action in Moscow at this stage.[4]

---

[3] *Parl. Debs., 5th ser., H. of C.,* 18 June 1981, vol. 6, col. 406W.

[4] Replying in Moscow telegram No. 772 of 23 November, Sir I. Sutherland welcomed the proposals. He thought that if the aim of any increase in contacts was to reinforce the concerns which had governed policy towards the Soviet Union since the imposition of martial law in Poland and the invasion of Afghanistan, it would be important to establish quickly with major allies and Community partners how far, if at all, the advent of Mr Andropov represented a 'window of opportunity'; and on this basis to ensure a consistent message was sent to the new Soviet leadership.

No. 175

Sir I. Sutherland (Moscow) to Mr Pym, 25 November 1982
Confidential (ENS 010/4)

The Funeral of President Brezhnev[1]

Summary . . . [2]

Sir,

In a civilised society an elderly man with a history of heart trouble, suffering from hardening of the arteries and respiratory problems, would be allowed to retire with dignity and conserve his waning strength. He would not be expected to stand

---

[1] In FCO telegram No. 678 of 16 November, Mr Broomfield reported that on the return flight the Foreign Secretary expressed the hope that the funeral, which had apparently made a deep impression on him, could be 'written up'. He appeared particularly impressed by his experience at the wreath-laying in the Hall of Columns.

[2] Not printed.

419

UK-Soviet Relations, 1979-82

for two hours in a temperature some way below zero and to inspect a military parade. But because the Soviet Union has not yet learnt how to provide its aged and ailing leaders with a graceful exit from public life or to evolve a predetermined procedure for succession to the highest posts, Leonid Ilyich Brezhnev was, at 75, obliged to carry on as General Secretary of the Party and Head of State until the rigours of office killed him. Since his return to Moscow after the summer holidays, Brezhnev had followed an exacting schedule, including an exhausting trip to Azerbaidjan [*sic*] and state visits to Moscow by leaders from India, South Yemen and Vietnam. The traditional 7 November parade was evidently the last straw. As I reported at the time, when I joined the queue to shake his hand at the subsequent reception in the Hall of Congresses in the Kremlin, he seemed in a daze, scarcely aware of what was going on around him. Three days later he was dead.

2. Brezhnev's death was far from unexpected. Rumour had frequently anticipated it. Throughout his 18 years at the apex of the Soviet pyramid there had been stories about ill health. By the late 'seventies these were fuelled by visible signs of physical deterioration: the stiff robotic walk, the increasingly slurred speech, the fish-like gasping for breath, an apparent inability in the final period to concentrate on anything but the simplest briefs. It was at the last a rather pathetic figure whose passing was announced at 11 a.m. on 11 November, 26½ hours after the stated time of death.

3. The last occasion when a General Secretary of the Soviet Party had died in office was in 1953. I was a junior secretary at this Embassy at the time and recall the extraordinary manner in which the populace of Moscow reacted to the announcement of Stalin's death. The people, who had been schooled for a generation to adulate the ruthless enigmatic tyrant were stunned. Many wept in the streets. On the day of his funeral vast throngs tried to reach Red Square and, as we learned later, many were trampled to death. When it was first announced that Brezhnev had died, life in Moscow went on as if nothing had happened. He too had been adulated and, in his later years, loaded with medals and prizes, but few reacted with any emotion. His funeral followed a similar pattern; the number of foreign representatives who attended was considerably larger; but there were no violent scenes and the arrangements were by and large quite efficient. Nevertheless, as you, Sir, witnessed on 15 November, the funeral of this unloved, unimaginative and in the final analysis not very successful ruler of the Soviet Union was, in its own way, an extraordinary event.

4. The authorities took no chances this time. After the four-day period of official mourning was announced late on the 11th and the red flags with black ribbons had been hung in the special, uniform iron brackets affixed since Tsarist days to the frontage of almost every Russian house and public building, the whole central area of the capital was closed off by a ring of police and troops. Troops were also present in large numbers in the streets and squares around the Kremlin. Passage through the central area and access by road to Moscow from the provinces were strictly controlled. Until after the funeral the city was invested by a cordon of security in depth.

5. Brezhnev's body had been taken to the Hall of Columns of the House of Trade Unions, the pre-revolutionary Nobles' Club, where those Soviet leaders deemed worthy of an official funeral have lain in state since Lenin's body was brought there in January 1924. The Central Committee of the Party, including members flown in from Republican capitals, were the first to pay their respects to their late Secretary-General. They did not stay to form a roster of pall-bearers

17 December 1981 – 9 December 1982

round the body as their predecessors had done for Stalin. They were to go straight to an extraordinary plenum after which it was announced that Yuri Vladimirovich Andropov had, by unanimous vote, been elected their new leader. Meanwhile, groups representing other organisations of Party and State began to converge on the Hall of Columns. Pimen, Patriarch of All the Russias, and a swathe of attendant bishops provided a flash of colour for the waiting TV cameras. The diplomatic corps was invited on the Saturday morning and by then a queue over a mile long and several deep had formed. Individuals were however not allowed. The mourners in the queue had been brought in batches by special buses. They were docile, awed and respectful but apparently little touched by grief, nor resentful of those like myself who were ushered ahead up the stairs and through a separate entrance to come into the crowded pillared hall with its chandeliers draped in black muslin and face the body of Brezhnev, propped up, face and neck exposed, on an elevated bier of flowers. The queue of citizens filed past in their winter overcoats and out by another door. The privileged visitors who had left their coats below could feel the chill of refrigeration. At the corpse's feet, displayed on individual red velvet cushions, were the many medals and orders which the Communist leader had accumulated over a lifetime of service to the party, but mostly in the later years when he himself could bestow them. On an elevated platform to the right a string orchestra played the strains of Chopin's funeral march. I said a silent prayer for the Russian people and, with the two members of my staff who accompanied me, returned through the dense throngs of people waiting on the stairs and in the halls on the floor below where hundreds of wreaths were stacked against the walls, the majority at that stage from Soviet organisations, but already many from foreign delegations to the funeral.

6. The great queue to view the lying-in-state continued throughout Sunday the 14th but the doors of the House of Trade Unions were closed that evening. Your special RAF aircraft with the wreaths from Her Majesty The Queen and the British Government was not due until later. An extension was, however, granted for some late arrivals. When we went the following morning, apart from an escort from the Protocol Department, we walked alone up the marble stairs and along the eerie corridors, preceded by two Soviet Frontier Guards bearing our wreaths. We were greeted silently in a dark ante-room by four people whose identity I never established, representing organisations with which the dead President had been associated. Emerging into the great Hall of Columns, it appeared deserted except for Brezhnev lying in his huge bed of flowers. But the orchestra was still there on its platform, still playing Chopin's funeral march. We were, I believe, the last foreigners to view the lying-in-state before the funeral.

7. The arrangements for the funeral were under the direction of a commission of forty-eight under Andropov's chairmanship. When its composition was announced on the evening of the 11th this was a pointer, but not a certain one, to his succeeding as Party leader. Khrushchev had been chairman of the funeral commission for Stalin but seven months were to elapse before he took over. The commission for Brezhnev included a significantly sizeable number of military officers, Khrennikov, the dreary time-serving President of the Musicians' Union and Bondarchuk, the creator of patriotic film epics.

8. In general, the arrangements had an air of improvisation which I had not anticipated. There must have been detailed contingency plans; the marshalling of the official Soviet mourners, the exclusion of other citizens and the publicity coverage were soullessly efficient. But one had the impression that, although

UK-Soviet Relations, 1979-82

Brezhnev's death must have been long expected, no one had ventured to update the plans for some time. A co-ordinating office for foreign delegations was established and, after their fashion, the officials there and in the Ministry of Foreign Affairs tried to be helpful. Nevertheless the details which the embassies in Moscow were able to obtain about the arrangements were minimal and belated. No doubt there was a party whip out to the leaders of those Communist parties which are, to a greater or lesser degree answerable to the CPSU, but no representatives of foreign governments were actually invited. The foreign press was confined to those resident in Moscow. In the event, the number of those who came from abroad was greater than the Russians expected. Including representation from Communist parties, there were, according to their count, a total of more than 150 delegations from over 100 countries. I enclose a list at Annex A.[3] The visitors included 27 Heads of State, 10 Vice-Presidents, 11 Prime Ministers and four princes. I regret that the Soviet restrictions on numbers prevented Sir Julian Bullard or the other officials in our party from attending the ceremonies in Red Square. But I am glad that we were able to put up all who came from London in the Residence and with members of my staff. (Mr Foot, representing the Labour Party and Mr Steel the Liberals, stayed, respectively, with my Defence and Naval Attachés.) Some delegations had brusque exchanges with the Soviet authorities over accommodation and who should get the official guest villas in the Lenin Hills.

9. You, Sir, observed the funeral from the right-hand side of the Lenin Mausoleum. I, with Michael Foot and David Steel watched from the stands on the other side. Those who saw the full sequence on television saw more but missed the portentous atmosphere of Red Square. They saw the coffin, closed now and draped in red, brought out from the Hall of Columns, set on a gun-carriage and hitched to the battle-green armoured scout car which was to draw it on its last journey. Mr Foot agreed that horses would have been more seemly. But the ungainly military vehicle, flanked by goose-stepping soldiers with fixed bayonets was not inappropriate for one who, in the same square, eight days before, had reviewed a parade of modern tanks and mobile rocket launchers and, boasting of Soviet armed might, had in his last speech threatened to deal a crushing blow against any imperialist aggressor. We saw the cortège emerge into the square itself some 15 minutes later. With the fantastic polychrome towers of St. Basil's Cathedral to the south, the red brick walls of the Kremlin behind us and as back-cloth the ornate 19th Century Russo-Byzantine facade of the building now occupied by the GUM department store, the square is an astonishing architectural stage. Rank upon rank of dark-clad citizens who had been there since the early morning stood in front of GUM, amongst them standard-bearers each with an identical black-framed portrait of the dead leader. Troops of cadets were drawn up in the foreground with a military band playing Chopin's funeral march now in slow time.

10. First in the funeral procession came a veritable Birnam Wood of wreaths carried by hundreds of soldiers. There followed a platoon of senior officers bearing Brezhnev's medals and orders, each on its red velvet cushion. Behind the coffin with its goose-stepping escort, with other family mourners walked Brezhnev's widow, who had seldom appeared in public during his years in power. She was followed by the leaders of Party and Government. As the English clock in the Kremlin's Spassky Tower struck midday, the coffin was placed in front of Lenin's Mausoleum and once more the lid was removed so that Brezhnev confronted his

---

[3] Not printed.

17 December 1981 – 9 December 1982

colleagues for the last time as they climbed to the tribune immediately above to pronounce the funeral orations. All the members of the Politburo stood there looking down except the 83-year-old Pelshe who was not however dead as many journalists had reported and the disgraced Kirilenko, who had once been first-runner for the succession and who was later spotted, a disconsolate figure, in the crowd by the graveside. The TV cameras focused on the five who had composed Brezhnev's 'inner cabinet' in the final months—Chernenko, Gromyko, Tikhonov, Ustinov the Minister of Defence and Andropov himself, the new General Secretary, the five who have kept together since.

11. It was Andropov, Ustinov, Aleksandrov President of the Academy of Sciences, a Moscow factory worker and the Secretary of the Party in Brezhnev's home town Dneproderzhinsk who spoke. Echoing the phraseology of the Orthodox liturgy but less directly and less effectively than Stalin had done at Lenin's funeral, Andropov spoke of Brezhnev as a worker and a soldier, an outstanding organiser and a wise political leader who was flesh of the flesh and bone of the bone of the people and was linked with them by unbreakable bonds. 'Comrades', he went on to say later in his oration, 'at this hour of grief, paying our last homage, all our Party and Central Committee declare their determination to pursue firmly and consistently the strategic line in home and foreign policy which was worked out under the beneficial influence of Leonid Ilyich Brezhnev'. As I am reporting in a separate despatch,[4] Andropov has thus far continued the same strategic line.

12. The speeches over, the leaders descended from the tribune and, now with only the coffin, the family and the most senior mourners, the cortège moved towards the Kremlin wall past the delegations from other Communist parties who had stood to the left of the Mausoleum. Members of the Politburo led by Andropov and Tikhonov helped carry the coffin to the grave, the family came forward to kiss the body and the lid was replaced for the last time. The coffin was lowered and hit the ground with a thud audible to TV and radio listeners throughout the Soviet Union. I am told that many considered this a bad omen. As it fell cannons fired and factory hooters sounded; a period of silence as Brezhnev's family and the Politburo members scrabbled on the ground to throw earth into the grave. As the leaders returned slowly to the Mausoleum we had once more the slow Chopin dirge. But as soon as Andropov and his colleagues were lined up again on the tribune the tempo changed. In quick time and fortissimo the band struck up a jaunty march which echoed across Red Square as several battalions of crack troops marched past in review. In the official record published next day in *Pravda* the march-past was described as a last tribute from the armed forces to Marshal Brezhnev Chairman of the Defence Committee. To many of us who were present it seemed more like a dramatic demonstration of 'The King is dead; long live the King!'

13. We had been advised in a note received the previous evening that after the funeral there was to be a reception in the Kremlin to which Heads of Delegations were invited. It had not been revealed whether, this being after 1 p.m., there would be refreshments after the long vigil in the square. Nor was it clear, despite my explanations that the British delegation had four heads, that Mr Foot, Mr Steel and I might not be barred. But the Head of the Department at the Ministry of Foreign Affairs responsible for the UK and the Old Commonwealth had earlier materialised on the terraces by the Mausoleum to advise that it was up to us to find our way. And so it proved; for within the security cordon round the central area of Moscow

---

[4] Not printed.

UK-Soviet Relations, 1979-82

that day, there appeared to be no controls as the long jostling line of Russians and foreign delegates filed past Brezhnev's grave past the wreaths now laid the length of the red brick wall and into the Kremlin through Spassky Gate. The grave had been filled in and piled with flowers and the medals set out again on the red velvet cushions.

14. In the Great Kremlin Palace, that vast monument to the 'autocracy, orthodoxy and rationality' of Tsar Nicholas I which faces this Embassy across the Moskva river, the grand staircase and vestibule were crowded with the heads of state, prime ministers, ministers and princes who had come for the funeral in such numbers. Most had brought other delegates but I noted President Kyprianou and Mrs. Marcos[5] both alone and lost in the throng. The Communists and one or two other favoured delegates had been ushered on ahead. As we waited on the stairs some were already coming down from the reception. For Arafat, a bear-hug from Papandreou[6] as they passed. From Mr Foot a greeting of recognition for Mr McLennan of the CPGB.[7] I caught up with you before you entered the Georgievsky Hall, the largest of the five reception halls on the upper floor of the Palace each named after one of the Grand Orders of the Russian Empire. Vice-President Bush and Mr Shultz were coming out. President Zia of Pakistan was immediately in front.

15. There were no refreshments in St. George's Hall. The foreign visitors advanced slowly towards the end of the vast ornate two-hundred feet long reception room where they were introduced to Andropov, Tikhonov, Gromyko and Kuznetsov, First Deputy Chairman of the Presidium of the Supreme Soviet. A brief handshake for most as they expressed their condolences. The press made much of the few minutes' conversation which Huang Hua, the Chinese Foreign Minister, had with the new General Secretary. A black-bordered portrait of Brezhnev like those carried by the crowds in Red Square was displayed on an easel and as they turned to leave the Hall most of the delegates paused to pay their respects to the man they had just seen buried. But the reception was Andropov's durbar and the funeral was over.

16. The dramatic events of 10-15 November—Brezhnev's death, his replacement by Andropov as General Secretary, his impressive but macabre funeral and the series of meetings with foreign statesmen which Andropov and other Soviet leaders held after the reception described above—have excited the keenest interest outside the Soviet Union. As the second annex to this despatch, I enclose a more detailed chronology of these days.[8] The irony is that within the country the reaction appears to have been one of relative indifference. As I have noted, this was in marked contrast to the emotional reaction to Stalin's death. Even the deaths of Khrushchev—in obscurity—and of Kosygin—a lesser political figure—seem to have aroused a great depth of sincere feeling. Why should this have been so? In part it was the reaction of a people long prepared for Brezhnev's death. In part it was the consequence of a style of leadership, adorned with grotesque forms of officially orchestrated adulation which, particularly in his later years, made him a Tsar-like figure removed from the concerns of ordinary people. But, most important, he reaped in death what he had sown in life. His legacy is a

---

[5] Spyros Kyprianou, President of the Republic of Cyprus; Imelda Marcos, First Lady of the Philippines.
[6] Andreas Papandreou, Prime Minister of Greece.
[7] Communist Party of Great Britain.
[8] Not printed.

17 December 1981 – 9 December 1982

society more prosperous and militarily stronger but one in which cynicism, boredom and materialism abound. How this has come about is the subject of another despatch on 'The Brezhnev Years'.[9]

17. I am copying this despatch with enclosures to Her Majesty's Ambassadors at Washington, Paris, Bonn and Peking and to the UK Permanent Representative on the North Atlantic Council.[10]

I am, Sir,
Yours faithfully,
IAIN SUTHERLAND

[9] No. 177.
[10] The Secretary of State commented on the despatch 'v. enjoyable' and asked for a personal copy.

No. 176

Mr Pym to Sir I. Sutherland (Moscow), 30 November 1982, 6 p.m.[1]
Tel. No. 717 Priority, Confidential (ENS 020/5)

Your Telno 772:[2] UK/Soviet Relations

1. You have authority to:

(*a*) Inform Ryzhov that Sir J. Bullard invites him to London on 1-2 February for talks (if these dates do not suit Ryzhov, perhaps he could propose alternatives):

(*b*) Propose 20-21 January to the Russians for talks between the Planning Staffs in Moscow. (Here too we would gladly consider alternative dates):

(*c*) Inform the Russians that we have it in mind to invite them to London for talks on the Middle East, perhaps in February or March. The dates could be fixed during Ryzhov's visit.

2. You may inform your American, French and German colleagues after taking action. You should present Ryzhov's invitation in a low key as a routine contact which had been somewhat delayed by the death of Deputy Foreign Minister Zemskov. This and the other proposals are, as you know, in line with what we understand some of our close allies to have been doing or to be intending to do.

3. Sir J. Graham should not (not) say anything to NATO colleagues at this stage. I will probably have a word with Shultz, and possibly other foreign ministers, in the margin of our meeting in Brussels on 9-10 December.

4. We leave it to you as to whether you leave taking action on Ryzhov until you meet Gromyko. Our preference would, however, be to proceed without undue delay.

5. For your introductory call on Gromyko we have no particular new points we would wish you to make. You should continue to be guided by the instructions in my telno 642[3], and by the line I took with Gromyko on 15 November (my telno 676).[4] You will also bear in mind what I said in Brussels on 23 November (my

[1] Repeated Information to Washington, Bonn, Paris, UKDEL NATO; Information Saving to Prague, Budapest, Bucharest, Sofia, East Berlin, Warsaw, Belgrade, UKDEL Madrid, Rome. This telegram was dated 1 December but sent the day before.
[2] Not printed. See No. 174, note 4.
[3] Not printed.
[4] No. 171.

UK-Soviet Relations, 1979-82

telno 157 to Copenhagen)[3] and by my speech of 25 November about arms control[5] (copy by bag) especially the final paragraphs. Please telegraph when the time of your call is confirmed so that we have an opportunity to let you have any last minute thoughts.

[5] In a speech to the English Speaking Union in Leeds on 25 November, Mr Pym indicated that HMG would review its refusal to negotiate with Moscow over Britain's strategic deterrent, if the Soviet threat to the UK was substantially reduced.

No. 177

Sir I. Sutherland (Moscow) to Mr Pym, 9 December 1982
Confidential (ENS 014/3)

The Brezhnev Years

Summary . . . [1]

Sir,

During Brezhnev's 18 years as First (later General) Secretary of the Soviet Communist Party, the Soviet Union came to full superpower status, and advanced towards the goal of creating a modern industrialised society. But it lost its position as the leader of the world socialist movement and to all practical purposes abandoned its goal of achieving full Communism at home. Under Brezhnev, the Bolshevik Revolution finally ran out of steam and for this Brezhnev was in part personally responsible. This despatch looks at Brezhnev's years as Soviet leader and assesses some of the main changes, achievements and failures. It is not intended to be a history, but concentrates on his legacy in three areas: foreign policy, the economy and the evolution of Soviet society.

2. The main features of Brezhnev's life are well known. They are recorded in an official autobiography, the first to be published by a Soviet leader. This describes Brezhnev's impeccable proletarian origins as the son of a steel worker in the Ukraine and his progress from factory worker to engineer; from local Party official to Dnepropetrovsk Party Secretary; from tank training school to Political Officer in the Army; to wartime Major General; and, after the war, to the Moscow power-house of the Central Party apparatus via Party jobs in the Ukraine, Moldavia and Kazakhstan, as well as a further stint in the political administration of the Ministry of Defence. In 1957 Khrushchev made Brezhnev (already a Secretary of the Central Committee) a full member of the Politburo (or Presidium as it was then known). From this position he was chosen to take over as Party leader when Khrushchev was ousted in 1964.

3. Brezhnev was an efficient and loyal Party man. He had a good war. In this there was not much to distinguish him from many of his peers who had also swiftly advanced their careers thanks to the purges and to the war. But he had wide experience in Party industrial and agricultural management (at Krushchev's behest he had gone to Kazakhstan in 1954 to help supervise the Virgin Lands scheme); he had good and long-standing contacts with the military; he was not erratic like Khrushchev; and he could be expected to respect the conventions of collective leadership and rule as the first among equals.

[1] Not printed.

17 December 1981 – 9 December 1982

Foreign Policy

4. The problems confronting the Soviet Union in 1964 have a familiar ring today. The need to do something about the dangerously unstable relationship with the US predominated. It had been the Soviet humiliation during the Cuban crisis of two years previously which had in part contributed to Khrushchev's downfall. The need to find a *modus vivendi* with the Federal German Republic and an understanding with the three Western powers on Berlin followed closely in importance. The Soviet economy, if it were to live up to the pretensions of the leadership, required the short-cuts which Western technology alone seemed able to provide. The Chinese threat to the Soviet Union's Asian borders and their challenge to the leadership of the world Communist movement had to be neutralised. The policy of détente elaborated at successive Party conferences was Brezhnev's answer to these problems. At first, the policy appeared brilliantly successful. In the early '70s a raft of agreement[s] was signed with the US, the most important covering arms control, and including the 1972 Treaty on Strategic Arms Limitation (SALT I). The relationship with the Americans was thereby put on a safer and more stable basis and the arms race apparently reduced to economically and technologically manageable proportions. At the high point of détente, the Soviet Union and the US briefly came near to agreeing to a tacit condominium in world affairs. The Moscow Agreement of 1970 marked the formal post-war reconciliation with the Federal Republic and opened the way to a rapid expansion in trade and economic relations. The Quadripartite Agreement of 1971 defused the Berlin problem.[2] A web of agreements of lesser importance, many of them economic, was signed with Western countries. The UK was not excluded from the process and the high point in bilateral relations was reached in 1975 with the Anglo/Soviet Summit in Moscow. A few months later Brezhnev reached the peak of his international prestige when the Final Act of the Conference on Security and Cooperation in Europe (CSCE) was signed in Helsinki by 35 heads of state and government. The CSCE had been a Soviet idea and the Final Act was interpreted by the Russians as sanctifying Europe's post-war borders, a long-standing objective of Soviet foreign policy.

5. But these successes did not endure. When détente was put rigorously to the test—in the Third World, in the field of human rights, in arms control—it began to break up on the fundamentally different approaches of East and West. For the Soviet leadership détente was, and remains, a refinement of the doctrine of peaceful co-existence which goes back to Lenin himself. Its ideological premise is that all forms of competition with the West, short of war, are inevitable and desirable. Brezhnev never abandoned the Marxist-Leninist precept that peaceful co-existence was a form of the class struggle on the world arena, allowing the Soviet Union to intervene in the affairs of Eastern European countries under the guise of 'socialist internationalism' (generally known as the Brezhnev doctrine); to support in one way or another 'national liberation' movements in the Third World; and to wage anti-Western propaganda. But the strategy of détente failed because its two main components, political and military competition and a stable and controlled relationship, were in basic contradiction. As Brezhnev pursued the former with growing assertiveness, so the latter began to slip from his grasp as American and Western alarm at Soviet behaviour sharpened. The measure of trust which had developed between Brezhnev and Nixon soon evaporated. The

---

[2] For an account of the Quadripartite negotiations on Berlin see *DBPO*, Series III, Vol. I.

UK-Soviet Relations, 1979-82

remorseless build-up of armed strength; the grasp for Third World clients; the cynical exploitation of the weakness of successive US Presidents; the running sore of human rights abuses; all conspired eventually to push US/Soviet relations back to where Brezhnev had found them in the 1960s, with the events in Poland and Afghanistan setting the seal on the process. Contrary to Brezhnev's confident assertions in the mid-'70s, life itself had shown détente to be anything but irreversible.

6. The Russians do not like Reagan but they have the US Administration which they deserve and which in part they helped to create. They are now confronted with precisely the situation which détente was intended to forestall: the possibility of a quantum leap in the arms race which they will be hard pressed to match and which poses crucial questions of priorities at a time of economic difficulty. This would have mattered less had Soviet foreign policy scored lasting successes elsewhere. But the 'correlation of forces' which is supposed by the Marxist laws of history to be moving Moscow's way has also gone into reverse. In the Middle East, for example, in an area of traditional Russian influence which touches the country's borders, the Soviet Union has repeatedly been shown to be a superpower of the second category, at a psychological, political, military and economic disadvantage with the US. Israel's repeated humiliation of the Arabs and its savagery in the Lebanon notwithstanding, the US is now the prime mover on the Middle East stage. The Soviet Union can only watch and wait. Similarly in Iran, despite the elimination of Western influence, the game for the Russians is long and the outcome uncertain.

7. All this has taken place against a background of political crises (especially Poland) and growing economic difficulties within the socialist camp. This has made it difficult politically to exploit the economic crisis in the West. Brezhnev, who at an early stage in his career as General Secretary had presided over the invasion of Czechoslovakia, must have found the disintegration of the Polish Party a particularly bitter experience in his twilight years. He did not even have the consolation of a united world Communist movement behind him. His successor has identified relations within the socialist community as his first priority, but will not, I think, be in a hurry to repeat the disastrous experience of 1975 and the failed World Communist Conference in Berlin.

8. By Brezhnev's last year there seemed only two exits from the blind alley into which Soviet foreign policy had driven: China and Western Europe. Both are problematical. Both are being pursued principally because of the breakdown of the central strategic relationship with the US and the apparent deadlock in the START and INF talks in Geneva. Both are attempts to exploit disenchantment with the US. It is no accident that détente as a slogan has been brought down from the shelf this year after a longish period of disuse and given a wedge-driving, Western European focus and a new definition to include the Chinese. The objectives are to block the NATO INF decision and to remodel Soviet policies in Asia. But this is a long way from the glittering prize which Brezhnev must have thought that he had within his grasp almost a decade ago. Brezhnev genuinely wished to go down in history as a man of peace. He will also have died disappointed, with his many peace initiatives forgotten in the West. The 'Brezhnev doctrine' will be his principal monument.

The Economy

9. While the economic progress achieved during the Brezhnev era may be counted as a solid success, he has left a legacy of economic problems to his successor. His contribution in this field was consistency and caution. After

17 December 1981 – 9 December 1982

Khrushchev's hare-brained economic experiments and the disruptive reorganisation that accompanied them, this was a relief. But on the other side of the coin, Brezhnev's approach could also be characterised as unimaginative and conservative, failing to get to grips with deep-rooted problems that now are probably ineradicable by gradual reform.

10. Under Brezhnev the bureaucrats took control of the economy, though within tight ideological constraints imposed by the Party. He achieved a degree of modernisation and streamlining of the system but set no new course, except perhaps in agriculture. One of his first moves was to restore to Gosplan[3] primary responsibility for economic planning and management, working through specialised Ministries staffed with the post-war generation of experts. Brezhnev saw the need for a scientific approach to the task of controlling an increasingly sophisticated economy, making it answer the growing, complex demands of military expansion, consumer needs and Soviet foreign clients. The aim was to make the existing economic machine work better, not to reform it.

11. According to national economic indicators, the effort has been broadly successful. Since 1965 national income has risen by 140 percent, industrial production by 170 percent. Energy production has doubled, gross agricultural production has risen by 35 percent. Despite a slowing down of growth in recent years, the Soviet economy is broad-based and has by no means exhausted its reserves of initiative and productive potential. Heavy industry has retained its leading role, supporting an armaments sector which has been the basis of the advancement to military parity with the West. The growing prosperity of the non-Russian republics under Soviet rule has contributed more to Soviet unity than the binding force of Party ideology. Soviet economic power has enabled it to support its increasingly expensive clients abroad, particularly Cuba and Viet-Nam, and to undertake costly adventures. It has also provided at least until recently, the economic backbone of the Warsaw Pact.

12. Under Brezhnev the development of Siberia achieved new momentum. Huge industrial complexes were established, based on vast reserves of minerals, fuel and hydro-electric power. In particular the development of oil and gas fields of Western Siberia, so important to the Soviet energy balance and export potential for the rest of this century, was accelerated. Construction of the BAM, the new trans-Siberian railway, was finally undertaken and, though delayed, is now nearing completion, making it possible to exploit other new reserves. Attempts were made to redress certain imbalances of the Khrushchev years, notably to arrest and reverse the decline of central Russia. Large-scale re-housing projects have been pushed through, the urban population has soared and the transformation of a backward, predominantly peasant society into a modern urban one has been advanced.

13. In an age of world-wide inflation, and unemployment, prices have been kept steady, and full employment, at least in formal terms, maintained. The Soviet consumer is now better clothed, better housed, better paid, better fed than 20 years ago. But here the first cracks in the picture of success appear. Despite the successes, consumer dissatisfaction is running high. Expectations have outstripped the gains and the present generation of consumers has forgotten the scarcities of the past. These were made tolerable by an unspoken acceptance of the need to tighten one's belt and a tradition of a communal and frugal being. That tradition has gone. The Soviet people no longer accept the need for austerity. The influx of

---

[3] Gosplan, or the State Planning Committee, was responsible for economic planning in the Soviet Union, including the creation of Five Year Plans.

UK-Soviet Relations, 1979-82

Western ideas and consumer goods, and foreign travel—some of the by-products of détente—have helped to illustrate how austere the Soviet life really is, at least in comparison with the US and Western Europe.

14. Dissatisfaction is perhaps greatest in the food sector, where the chronic inability of Soviet agriculture to raise productivity, coupled with bad weather, have produced four bad harvests in a row. The result has been widespread shortages and rationing in some areas. Brezhnev had been closely associated with agricultural policy, trading on his experience in the Virgin Lands scheme. He doubled investment in agriculture. He ended the petty persecution of private production that had been prevalent under Khrushchev. But despite initial gains, the results of this sustained effort were disappointing. This led on to the much vaunted Brezhnev Food Programme, launched with much noise at the Party Plenum this May. But the programme was set in the policy tradition established since 1965 and in a price structure established even earlier. It started badly and is unlikely by itself to succeed. If the Programme fails or is abandoned in its present form this will be a major element in the Soviet verdict on the Brezhnev era once the initial period of respectful remembrance is over. It may even be the specific vehicle for a longer term denigration of his memory and his achievements.

15. Agriculture has not been the only failure. At a time when foreign commitments and the burden of military expenditure have increased, there has, as I have noted, been a general slowing down in economic growth, with the sharpest fall in 1982. Among the causes have been an ageing capital stock, the exhaustion of traditional centres of raw materials and energy production and labour shortages especially in central Russia and Siberia. The Socialist economies have not been immune from the effects of the international recession and the capacity of the Soviet Union to support its expanding imports of grain and other commitments has been eroded recently by falling prices for its two staple exports, oil and gold.

16. The crucial challenge faced by the Soviet Union under Brezhnev which has now passed unsolved to his successor, is the need to overcome inertia and inefficiency. Brezhnev showed himself to be aware of the deep-seated nature of the problem. The obstacles include low levels of technology, excessive interference by the Party, managerial incompetence and indiscipline among the work force (especially absenteeism and theft) and cooking the books for better-seeming plan results. In his later years, Brezhnev addressed himself to these shortcomings and became increasingly strident in his criticism. But it had little effect and the basic issues of the incentives to work and to utilise capital to the best advantage were not faced. Even the modest reforms introduced at the July 1979 Plenum have been only slowly and incompletely introduced. Despite administering sharp reprimands for failure to deliver the goods, he allowed most of his Ministers to keep their jobs and rumble on as before. Perhaps Brezhnev's virtue as a conciliatory party co-ordinator told against him in later years, when he found himself incapable of taking firm action and overcoming the entrenched interests of his colleagues and lower-level party functionaries. It is a legacy of neglect and marking time which will be difficult for Brezhnev's successor to overcome.

The Social Scene

17. Inertia and lack of innovation and inspiration on the part of an ageing leadership has affected attitudes to authority throughout Soviet society. It is notoriously difficult for any foreigner to judge public attitudes in this country. The Russians have not lost their traditional patriotism, their resentment at criticism by outsiders, their strong sense of being a people with a mission and a nation apart.

17 December 1981 – 9 December 1982

Sixty years of instruction in the language of Marxism produces a conditioned response which is not confined to Party members. But at the end of the Brezhnev era one detects a prevailing mood of cynicism which is, I think, in large part the result of the premium which he and his associates placed on stability and predictability after the violence of Stalin and the zig-zags of Khrushchev. In the process, such idealism and revolutionary cutting edge as may have survived Stalin and the War all but evaporated. Public political activity became dreary beyond belief, its tired slogans unrelieved by originality or idealism. The response of the Soviet people, better educated and more critical than in the previous generation, was passivity and boredom with politics as they found them. Some have discovered a new romantic interest in the early years when the Revolution was revolutionary. Many opted out to cultivate their hobbies and their dacha gardens. A few, looking for metaphysical reliefs, turned to religion. But most turned to consumerism.

18. With few incentives to save and an economic system which produced an over-supply of money but failed to satisfy consumer expectations, the black market proliferated. Corruption increased and, despite severe penalties for those who were exposed, continued to grow. The abuse and entrenchment of privilege created an elite of party and state functionaries and their families, enjoying special shops, schools, access to jobs and foreign travel. Public morality was undermined by the knowledge that this new bourgeoisie does not have to share the hardships and frustrations of ordinary people. Other attributes of the consumer society, only too familiar in the West but which were rare when I first served in Moscow in the early '50s began to appear. Muggings and burglaries are not uncommon. Fighting among spectators at football matches occurs frequently. The new ills are exacerbated by the traditional Russian vice of alcoholism, which shows no sign of abating.

19. If increasingly cynical of authority, this is a society which under Brezhnev became relatively comfortable and, within prescribed limits, there was increased freedom of choice. A large percentage of the young went on to higher education. Those with special talents were encouraged. Travel abroad and tourism within the country increased. The Russian people were free to listen to Western pop music or even to Western broadcasts. They even felt free to crack jokes about the regime. Everyone did this including Brezhnev himself. Those who were not catered for were the dissenting individuals and minorities who dared to criticise openly the intolerant philosophy by which the regime justified its authority. Although the KGB and the law enforcement authorities became a little more polite and gave up some of their arsenal of dirty tricks, there was no reduction in the scope of their activity or in the reliance placed on them to put out any sort of fire at an early stage. There were few death sentences and, with the exception of Sakharov, few public martyrs were allowed to remain at large within the Soviet Union. But dissidents were dispersed and rendered largely leaderless by a variety of methods, including imprisonment, expulsion, exile, defamation and threats. Similar treatment was meted out to religious protesters, to some nationalist groups, and to some who explored a heretical line in Marxist theory.

20. I do not doubt that, but for the penalties, many more would have dared to step outside the prescribed limits for criticism and protest. But although the man in the street is not disposed to give his leaders much credit for what they have achieved, it would be a profound mistake to regard the mass of the Soviet population as disaffected. What you do not know, you do not miss. Russian man has never known a genuine Parliamentary democracy and he does not yearn for it

UK-Soviet Relations, 1979-82

now. Even the non-Russian nationalities are far from the state of critical discontent predicted by some. Life in the Asian and Caucasian republics compares favourably with that in Afghanistan and Pakistan or even Turkey, and the local populations know it.

21. Towards the end of his life, Brezhnev acquiesced in the development of an absurd personality cult and the orchestration of mass sycophancy. With the medals and titles, he collected personae: Brezhnev the war hero, Brezhnev the writer, Brezhnev the composer of verse. But in truth 'the most influential leader of the planet' (to cite the obsequious Aliev) remained till the end the hard-working, cunning and limited son from the Ukrainian backwoods. During his years as leader, despite the iniquities of Soviet behaviour in, for instance, Czechoslovakia and the suppression of human rights at home, it would be hard to portray this very fallible and human man as an evil tyrant. Brezhnev, however, never seized the imagination of the Soviet people and, as his successor must know, he bequeathed in most areas more problems than he was able to solve.

22. I am copying this despatch to Her Majesty's Representatives at Washington, Paris, Bonn, all posts in Eastern Europe and to the UK Permanent Representative to the North Atlantic Council.[4]

I am, Sir,
Yours faithfully,
IAIN SUTHERLAND

---

[4] Responding in a letter of 21 December, Mr Broomfield congratulated Sir I. Sutherland on his authoritative *tour de force*. He agreed with his description of the sterility of Soviet public and private life which evolved under President Brezhnev, whose style of management was to tinker with the system rather than go for structural reforms. The question now was whether Soviet political and cultural life would be freed from the constraints of Socialist patriotism and morality to help deal with the problems, especially in the economic sphere, the leadership faced. On the foreign policy side, he gave President Brezhnev slightly greater credit for the changes that took place and thought his overwhelming achievement, from the Soviet point of view, was in achieving military parity with America. He thought the quadripartite agreement on Berlin and the treaties with the FRG would continue to remain prominent features of the East/West landscape and, at a political and psychological level, détente made an impact on Western European attitudes.

APPENDIX

Note by the Joint Intelligence Committee, 10 January 1980
UK Confidential, Cabinet Office, JIC(80)(N) 4

Soviet Intervention in Afghanistan—An Interim Assessment

1. This note offers some preliminary views on the motives for the Soviet intervention in Afghanistan and on its implications.

2. Afghanistan occupies a strategic position on the southern border of the Soviet Union which has long regarded it as important for its own security that the country should be governed by a stable regime which is well disposed to the Soviet Union. It was the earliest recipient of Soviet aid, beginning in about 1954. The Daoud regime, which was in power before the Marxist takeover in April 1978, showed due consideration for Soviet interests and the Russians were probably content with the political and military influence they enjoyed in the country at that time and the standing it gave them in the region. Although we do not know whether the Russians engineered the Taraki coup which overthrew the Daoud regime or played any direct role in it, it provided them with an opportunity of which they were quick to take advantage, and changed the nature of the Soviet/Afghan relationship. This new relationship was formalised in the Soviet/Afghan Friendship Treaty signed in December 1978. The Russians now had the ideological motive of supporting a 'socialist' regime as well as that of pursuing their national interests in relation to Afghanistan. Military and civilian advisers were accordingly sent in increasing numbers to help Taraki consolidate his position and defeat the anti-Communist insurgents. Despite Soviet attempts to enable the regime to get on top of the security situation, this continued to deteriorate, first under Taraki and then under Amin. Contingency plans for large-scale Soviet military intervention in Afghanistan, should this become necessary, probably began to be made early in 1979 while Taraki was still in power. When Amin proved not only unable to deal with the insurgents or extend his power base, but also unwilling to listen to Soviet advice, the need to replace him must have appeared pressing.

3. Eventually the Russians concluded that they were faced with a choice between large-scale intervention or the continued instability and possible collapse of the pro-Soviet regime. This would be damaging to their prestige and could lead to anarchy in Afghanistan and perhaps the eventual emergence of a second fundamentalist Islamic state on their southern border in close proximity to the Muslim areas of the Soviet Union. Only by intervening could they establish control over Afghanistan and eliminate this risk. They may have calculated that in the process they would gain advantage by demonstrating the Soviet Union's capacity and readiness to use military force in defence of 'socialism' and its national interests. Furthermore, a military presence in Afghanistan would bring the Russians closer to the Indian Ocean (450 miles from Kandahar) and the Gulf and put them in a better position to exert influence in the area.

4. For the Russians these arguments for military intervention outweighed its likely costs in terms of the reactions of the rest of the world, particularly the other Moslem states, China and the West. They may have calculated that Western reaction would be limited and short-lived because the West would acknowledge that Afghanistan was within the Soviet sphere of influence and would in any case lack the cohesion and decisiveness to take effective action in respect of a country

UK-Soviet Relations, 1979-82

which their policies had indicated was not of vital interest to them. Soviet experience of the lack of effective Western reaction to the invasion of Czechoslovakia and, more recently, its involvement and that of its proxies in Africa and elsewhere, will no doubt have influenced this assessment. The Russians may have felt, too that, given the low ebb in East/West relations, they had relatively little to lose on that front by taking action in Afghanistan. They may even have hoped that various Western countries would continue to do business as usual, thus effectively acquiescing in the Soviet view of the geographical limits of détente. The most disturbing possibility the Russians will have envisaged is no doubt that of a move by the United States and China towards military co-operation; but they probably concluded that this would not assume significant proportions.

5. The Russians must have expected that their intervention in Afghanistan would cause short-term damage to their relations with other countries in the region, especially Iran and Pakistan. But they may have concluded that there could be long-term benefits in that these countries would become more vulnerable to Soviet pressure after such a show of force. The Pakistan government, which now has a Soviet presence on its border for the first time, has indeed reacted strongly, condemning the Soviet intervention and repeating earlier denials of Soviet allegations that Pakistan was aiding Muslim insurgents against the Afghan regime. Reports that Soviet troops are moving into areas of Afghanistan near the border with Pakistan and speculation that the Russians might support both Afghan claims to Pakistani Pushtunistan and Baluchi aspirations for separation from Pakistan have been particular causes of Pakistani concern. More immediately the Pakistanis must fear the possibility of Soviet reprisal raids on the Afghan refugee camps on their territory or hot pursuit over the border. The Indians have expressed disquiet over the prospect of increased Western arms supplies to Pakistan, and this issue could lead to tensions between the two countries. In Iran the Foreign Ministry has sent a protest note but Ayatollah Khomeini has not condemned the Soviet action in public. He probably believes that so long as Iran is confronting the United States it should not antagonise the Soviet Union. Nevertheless suspicions among Iranians of Soviet long-term intentions in Iran and of the motives for the support given to Khomeini by the Iran Communist Party must have been reinforced.

6. Having intervened in force in Afghanistan the Russians will wish to restore stability as soon as possible; this will require them to gain control of all population centres and communications routes, though not necessarily the remoter parts of the country. This immediate objective has already been virtually achieved. It is not yet clear how far the Soviet Union intends to go in committing its own forces to eradicating the insurgents. The Soviet leaders would no doubt prefer the Afghan government to take on the main role of countering the insurgency, both by taking political steps to placate some of the opposition and by military means. The Soviet forces at present in the country are not sufficient to conduct a full-scale counter-insurgency campaign though air power is available which could be used to attack insurgents in parts of the country into which the Russians may not want to send ground forces immediately. An extended campaign would in any case be difficult at this time of year. If the decision is taken to attempt to eliminate insurgency, and the Afghan forces do not prove willing and able to help in the task effectively, which is likely, the Soviet government will have to introduce the additional forces already available over the border and possibly other troops as well. How long the establishment of full control would take also depends on a number of other factors, including how many of the Afghan forces remain loyal to the government, how

Appendix

effectively the frontiers can be secured and the extent of resistance. Although it is unlikely that resistance in Afghanistan can be totally eliminated, the Russians should be able to assert effective control over the country within a matter of months. In due course the Russians will have to decide whether to withdraw their armed forces. Although we believe some might well be withdrawn for propaganda purposes, it is highly unlikely that there would be a total withdrawal. The Afghan regime will remain unstable, and if Soviet protection were withdrawn the threat from tribal dissidents would revive. Large numbers of Soviet military personnel will continue to be needed for the protection and maintenance of the regime and for keeping control over population centres and communications. The build-up of Afghan armed forces capable of taking over any of these tasks will take a considerable time and their reliability will remain uncertain. The Russians would in any case be unlikely in any foreseeable circumstances to give up their military presence in a strategically important area. The best solution from the Soviet point of view would probably be an Afghanistan with a reliable indigenous government enjoying at least the acquiescence of a docile population and with a reduced Soviet military presence available for use if necessary. But such a situation is a long way off.

7. We believe that the Soviet Union intervened in Afghanistan because the collapse of a client regime on its southern border, with unpredictable consequences, was considered by the Soviet leadership to be intolerable, particularly at a time when Iran was in chaos; and that they weighed up the price that might have to be paid in terms of world reaction and did not think it too high. We do not think that the move into Afghanistan was taken as the first of a series of pre-planned steps in a military advance into Iran and Pakistan. However, having established a military presence in Afghanistan, the Russians are well placed to take advantage of any opportunity to increase their influence in neighbouring countries. However, they recognise that these countries, unlike Afghanistan, are areas of strategic interest to the West, and this will affect their assessment of the likely cost of a Soviet move against them. In Iran the Russians have strong reasons for attempting to build up their influence as and when opportunity occurs. There are more immediate dangers in the situation in Pakistan and in the possible use by Afghan insurgents of Pakistan territory as a refuge. Clashes on the Afghan/Pakistan border could raise the prospect of Soviet/United States confrontation in view of the United States commitment to defend Pakistan. Western reactions to the Soviet intervention in Afghanistan are unlikely to cause the Russians to modify their intentions there; but they will help to determine the West's future credibility in Soviet eyes. The danger is that the Russians could conclude that their success in Afghanistan was cheaply bought and that this could lead them to underestimate the dangers of any future military adventure they might contemplate.

Index

Acland, Sir Antony 346, 381, 387
Afghanistan: 14 May 1980 proposals 147, 158, 162, 269; action at the UN 23-4, 27, 30, 33, 41, 43, 59, 69, 75-6, 159, 188, 206, 240, 268, 270, 279-80, 288; Afghan resistance 28-9, 30, 36-7, 71, 100-1, 111, 148, 187-9, 289, 187, 189; aid 24-5, 43, 76; international conference 205-6, 240-1, 245-52, 257-62, 269-71; non-recognition of Karmal regime 16, 24-5, 35, 205-6, 288-9; Soviet invasion 7-8, 10-12, 17-18, 45-8, 61-3; UK proposal for neutral and non-aligned status 101-2, 112, 122-3, 129, 131, 135-7, 144-7, 157-8, 162-3, 189, 223; USSR Treaty of Peace and Friendship 8, 12, 20, 37, 40, 53, 62, 83, 433
Alexander, Michael 51, 59, 77, 112, 128, 149, 202, 212, 219, 232, 246
Algeria 266, 314, 404
Amin, Hafizullah 8, 11-12, 15-18, 20, 33, 36, 44-7, 52, 61, 70, 73-4, 190, 433
Andropov, Yuri 358, 412-18, 421, 423-4
Anglo-Soviet Cultural Agreement 201-4, 283, 403
Anglo-Soviet Joint Commission 43, 171, 197, 199, 201-4, 326, 342, 345, 353, 391, 402
Anglo-Soviet Round Table 269, 282-4, 290, 292
Angola 3, 28, 31, 41, 52, 54, 107, 109, 116, 126, 150, 159, 207, 213, 225-6, 228, 276, 282, 337, 372, 377
Arafat, Yasser 282
Argentina 270, 306, 346, 349-52, 374
Arms control 4-5, 81, 172-3, 191-2, 207-8, 212-18, 219-21, 226-30, 235-8, 255-6, 262-5, 272, 281,

319-20, 323-4, 339-40, 343-4, 353-6, 358, 376-7, 379-80, 397, 410-11
Armstrong, Sir Robert 92, 101
Australia 6, 10, 35, 95, 152-4, 156, 172, 245, 270, 300, 374, 406
Austria 84, 101, 270

Bahrain 92-3
Bangladesh 24, 270
Beel, Graham 365, 367
Begin, Menachem 265-7
Belgium 49, 314, 402
Benyahia, Mohammed Seddik 266
Bishop, Anthony 235, 244
Blaker, Peter 28-9, 105, 117, 168, 171, 198, 200, 206, 366
Botswana 270
Braithwaite, Rodric 7, 83, 106, 149-50
Brandt, Willy 123-4, 244
Brazil 270
Brement, Marshall 28-9
Brewster, Kingman 34-5, 77, 98
Brezhnev, Leonid 170, 332, 357; 26th CPSU Congress speech 207-12, 220-4, 225, 235, 238, 409; Afghanistan 38-9, 51, 53, 73, 90-1, 128-30, 157, 166-7, 196, 216, 257-8; arms control 5, 55, 208, 215-18, 228, 235, 244-5, 254-5, 341-2, 343-4, 354-5; bilateral relationship with UK 222, 353, 386; 'Brezhnev Doctrine' 12, 83, 136, 212, 428; China 54, 275, 409-10; funeral 419-25; health 56, 72, 198, 286, 332, 348, 380, 384; internal situation 56, 74, 209-10, 274-9; Iran 54; legacy 426-32; Middle East 196, 217; Persian Gulf Zone of Peace 196, 200, 216; Poland 211-12; USA 107, 114, 116, 197, 208-9, 227, 290, 341-2, 368, 394, 407, 410-11

Index

British Broadcasting Corporation (BBC) 3, 42, 149-50, 156, 161, 186, 197, 292, 365, 400
British Council 3, 42, 60, 82, 291
British Olympic Association 89, 96, 99
British Olympic Committee 95-8
British-Soviet Credit Agreement 99
Brooke Turner, Alan 285, 349-51
Broomfield, Nigel 241, 269, 279, 290, 299, 307, 387, 403, 411, 419; assessment of Brezhnev 432; bilateral relationship with USSR 317-18, 325-8, 345, 364-5, 367-9, 396; Carrington visit to Moscow 242-3, 246-8; East-West economic relations 391-2; Soviet view of UK 399-400; views on USSR 334-6, 359-60
Broucher, David 7, 85, 143
Brown, Harold 67, 70, 82, 228
Brzezinski, Zbigniew 14, 67, 102, 116, 124, 138, 150, 164, 174
Buckley, James 347-8
Bulgaria 171, 244, 270
Bullard, Julian 1, 15, 112, 204, 243, 247-8, 305, 307, 396, 425; Afghanistan 149, 250; bilateral relationship with USSR 318-19, 327-8, 380-1; dissent 106; East-West relations 224-31, 234; Poland 228; US/Soviet relations 355-9, 388-90, 418; view of Brezhnev 286
Burma 270
'Burning Bush' 150
Burton, Michael 367
Butler, Sir Michael 194
Bykov, Vladimir 304

Callaghan, James 284
Cambodia 107, 213, 257
Camp David Agreement 93-4, 96, 115, 266
Canada 23-4, 26, 42, 29, 49-50, 81, 95, 121, 270, 306, 405-6
Carrington, Lord 98-9, 106, 234, 235, 238; Afghanistan 33-4, 36-8, 59-61, 111-13, 122-3, 144-7, 185-6, 199-200, 223, 240-1,

257-62; Alliance relations 112-13, 121-2, 298, 303; bilateral relationship with USSR 199-200, 202, 218, 222, 273, 343; CSCE 265; East-West relations 150-1, 159-62, 168, 174, 182, 194-5, 272; meetings with Gromyko 143-7, 185-6, 257-68, 272-3; Middle East 265-7; resignation 346; TNF 262-4; visit to Moscow 242-3, 245-6, 248-50, 361; visit to SW Asia/Gulf 92-6, 99, 106
Carter, 'Jimmy' 70, 114, 116, 131, 196, 225, 228, 293, 332, 339, 353, 372-8, 382-3; Afghanistan 8-9, 13, 30, 55, 60, 64, 66, 77-80, 121, 134, 177; arms control 21, 67, 78, 227; Olympics 81, 96, 125; Pakistan 82, 133-4
Castro, Fidel 210
Chatty, Habib 157, 183
Chernenko, Konstantin 277, 409-10, 412
Cheysson, Claude 245, 248, 362, 417
Chile 261, 270, 311
China 26-7, 30, 32, 163, 172, 261, 270, 349, 377; UK 94, 100; USA 67, 70; USSR 4, 52-4, 67, 84, 90, 106, 108-9, 130, 142-3, 192, 276, 382, 408, 411, 427-8; Vietnam 54
Christopher, Warren 10, 14-15, 20-8, 30, 31-3, 77, 79-82, 87-8, 118-19, 124
Churchill, Sir Winston 372-3
Coles, A. John 186, 239, 243, 250, 396, 415
Commonwealth 91
Comprehensive Test Ban (CTB) 67, 80, 192, 376
Conference on Security and Cooperation in Europe (CSCE) 5, 27, 71, 115, 207, 427; Madrid review meeting 19, 67, 71, 79-80, 108, 112, 143-4, 172-3, 183, 192, 239, 243, 254, 265, 281, 297-8, 318, 323, 331, 397, 414
Confidence Building Measures (CBM) 207, 232-3, 237, 239, 254, 265, 273, 281, 285
Cooper, Richard 81

Index

Coordinating Committee for Multilateral Export Controls (COCOM) 4, 43, 58, 60, 80, 88,97, 99, 132-4, 172, 201-3, 298, 374, 391, 406

Cornish, James 83

Cortazzi, Henry 15

Council for Mutual Economic Assistance (CMEA/ COMECON) 5, 16, 65, 228, 295, 312, 321-2, 357

Cuba 115-16, 159, 227, 270, 344; Angola 282, 377; NAM 26, 141; Soviet proxy 22, 37, 54, 73, 142, 150; USSR 110, 276, 383, 429

Cuban missile crisis 114, 174, 178, 380

Cyprus 270

Czechoslovakia 108, 171, 254, 306, 319, 357, 363; events in 1968 8, 15, 28, 31, 37, 66, 73, 121, 166, 169, 172, 177, 183, 190, 234, 322, 428

Daoud, Mohammad 15, 433

De Cuellar, J. Perez 205-6, 232, 260

Defence and Oversea Policy Committee (OD) 96-8, 111, 150, 159-62

Demirel, Suleyman 134

Denmark 50

Desai, Morarji 20

Diego Garcia 132, 138

Disarmament 67, 74, 90, 213-14, 256, 284; conference 5, 32, 108, 144, 173, 192, 233, 281, 319-20, 323, 376-7, 397, 408

Dissidents, Soviet 5, 99, 103-106, 181-2, 198, 289, 295-6, 397-8

Dolgov, Vyacachslav 317-19, 326

Duncan, Michael 295

Eagleburger, Larry 248

Economist 187

Egypt 4, 36, 138, 266-7, 270, 283, 285, 377

El Salvador 307, 311

English Chamber Orchestra 204

Eritrea 22

Ethiopia 22, 109, 116, 126, 270 372; USSR 52, 78, 130, 159, 207, 213, 226, 382, 413

European Community 5, 86, 153, 218, 223, 283; Afghanistan 60, 97, 99, 202, 240, 245-50, 257-62, 270-1; Pakistan 132, 189; Poland 297-300, 302, 309; USA 120, 370, 404-5

European Council 122, 137, 226, 230, 233, 250-1, 288, 326

Export Credit Guarantee Department (ECGD) 43, 171, 406

Falin, Valentin 166

Falklands War 346, 349-53, 356, 400

Fall, Brian 198, 212, 243, 300

Federal Republic of Germany (FRG) 121, 159-60, 171, 177; Afghan resistance 187, 189; Alliance relations 50, 64, 112, 138-9, 153, 178-80, 184; NATO 194-5; Olympics 81, 95, 124; *Ostpolitik* 1, 84, 100, 108, 126, 139, 154, 174-6, 194; Siberian gas pipeline 303-4, 309-10, 313-14, 403-7; USA 123-8, 307; USSR 169, 192, 394, 399-402

Fergusson, Sir Ewen 7, 58, 61, 81, 105-6, 109, 173, 198, 201

Finland 72, 84, 139, 214

Foot, Michael 273

Ford, Gerald 174

France 1, 195, 265, 366, 394; Afghanistan 22, 24-5, 27, 187, 189, 250; Alliance relations 112, 118-19, 139, 153, 159-60, 178-80, 389-90; Siberian gas pipeline 304, 309-10, 313-14, 375, 403-7; USSR 29-30, 50, 60, 63-5, 69, 71, 87-8, 108, 173-6, 399-402

François-Poncet, Jean 69, 121

Frost, Ellen 82

G7: Venice summit 127, 132, 172, 187, 266; Versailles summit 347, 389, 375

Gandhi, Indira 17, 20, 23, 63, 82, 100, 109, 129, 133

Garside, Roger 186

Index

Genscher, Hans-Dietrich 9, 95, 166, 174, 218, 238, 245, 322-3
German Democratic Republic (GDR) 108, 171, 191, 194, 196, 319, 363
Gillmore, David 408
Gilmore, Sir Ian 98, 194
Giscard d'Estaing, Valéry 29, 229, 332; Afghanistan 187, 205-6, 209, 240; Alliance relations 86, 139, 169; USSR 194, 197; visits 55, 148, 170, 184, 362, 393
Goodison, Alan 304, 310, 327, 365, 368
Gordon, John 283, 285, 290
Gottlieb, Alan 23-7
Graham, Sir John 204, 206, 245-6
Greece 50, 84, 321
Green, Andrew 322
Gromyko, Andrei 208, 380; Afghanistan 123, 148, 144-7, 185-6, 223, 257-62, 279-80, 397-8, 414; bilateral relationship with UK 273, 283-4, 385-6, 396-7, 414; CSCE 144, 265; East-West relations 219-24, 272, 281, 397, 414; India 129-30; Iran 185, 414; meetings with Carrington 143-7, 185-6, 253, 255, 257-68, 272-3; meetings with Keeble 219-24, 279-85; meetings with Pym 396-8, 400, 414-15; Middle East 115, 265-7, 282-3; Poland 267, 281; South Africa 282; TNF 262-4
Gulf States 94, 99, 103

Haig, Alexander 225, 227, 254, 272, 281, 305, 322, 373; Afghanistan 245, 268; Alliance relations 298, 307; meeting with Thatcher 308; USSR 321, 358, 372, 379, 390
Hailsham, Lord 255-6
Hartman, Arthur 286, 402, 411, 413
Heap, Peter 313
Helms, Jesse 225
Helsinki Final Act 3, 5, 103, 108, 112, 115, 173, 186, 191, 214, 233, 237, 252, 281, 289, 297-8, 300, 303, 316-7, 373, 382, 386, 397, 427

Henderson, Sir Nicholas 14, 190; Alliance relations 118-19, 138-40, 175; Falklands War 352-3; Siberian gas pipeline 314; US policy 19, 117, 137-40, 194-5, 297-8, 305-7
Heseltine, Michael 88
Hibbert, Reginald 175, 193-5
Hillier-Fry, William 7, 44, 45
Howard, Michael 149
Howe, Geoffrey 113
Hungary 3, 105, 171, 183, 270, 363; events in 1956 15, 22, 37, 96, 121, 180, 196, 338
Hurd, Douglas: Afghanistan 19-21, 23-8, 30, 34-5, 70, 79-83, 206, 344, 349, 419; Alliance relations 80; arms control 344; Falklands War 349; Olympics 35, 81
Hussein, Saddam 185, 244

Iceland 50, 270
India 86, 99, 194, 245, 270; China 112; reaction to Afghan invasion 17, 20-2, 27, 32, 82, 92-4, 100, 141; USSR 53, 109, 129, 383
Indonesia 23, 270
Intermediate range nuclear forces (INF) 311, 312, 318, 323-4, 339-40, 343, 354-5, 358, 378, 390, 413, 418, 428
International Olympic Committee 42, 88-9, 95-6, 131
Iran 9, 13, 20-2, 25, 27, 30, 32, 53, 54-5, 62, 70-1, 78; Afghan settlement 101, 112, 146, 149, 186, 205-6, 223, 246, 259, 270; USA 9, 20-2, 30, 138; USSR 16-17, 53-4, 71, 83-4, 109, 130, 145, 191, 341, 383, 434
Iran-Iraq War 185, 191, 196, 267, 414
Iraq 20, 267
Islamic Conference 20, 22, 111, 122, 137, 141, 157, 158, 166, 183, 270, 367, 395
Israel 129, 256, 265-7, 282-3, 351, 370, 377, 383, 428

Index

Italy 22-3, 25, 29, 88, 112, 179, 197, 204, 214, 288, 309-10, 313-14, 403-4
Ivory Coast 270

James, C. Kenneth 118
Japan 6, 95, 113, 127, 139, 152-4, 156-7, 161, 172, 234, 270, 310, 405
Jaruzelski, Wojciech 211, 293-5, 301, 311-12, 321-4, 357, 392
John Brown Engineering 288, 303, 309-10, 348, 403-4
Johnson, David 75, 141, 182, 245
Joint Intelligence Committee (JIC) 51, 314, 433

Kania, Stanislaw 197, 211, 301
Karmal, Babrak 21, 146, 262, 284; Afghan coup 11-12, 18, 20, 31, 33, 37, 40, 44-5, 47-8, 61, 83, 128
Kedourie, Elie 149
Keeble, Sir Curtis 104, 130, 157, 209-10, 336; Afghanistan 17-19, 53-4, 61-3, 71, 89-91, 128-30, 162-3, 165-8, 190-1, 196, 251-3, 268-9, 279-80; arms control 354-5, 385; bilateral relationship with USSR 102, 193, 197, 269-70, 328-33; East-West relations 71-2, 102-3, 163-5, 190-3, 197, 207-8, 219-24, 382-7; meetings with Gromyko 219-24, 279-85, 385-6; meetings with Zemskov 102-3, 162-3, 167-8; Middle East 282-3, 255, 385; Olympic Games 59; Poland 281, 190-1, 193, 196-7, 211, 254, 293-5, 300-1, 311; South Africa 282; US/Soviet relations 113-18, 208, 253-4, 337-42; valedictory 381-7
Kenya 121, 138, 270
KGB 104-5, 181, 275, 295-6, 399-400, 431
Khomeini, Ayatollah 16, 83, 93, 434
Killanin, Lord 131
Killick, Sir John 277
Kirilenko, Andrey 277, 423

Kissinger, Henry 68, 115, 154, 168, 175, 193, 305-6, 358, 373, 375, 379, 413
Kornienko, Georgi 224-31, 234, 251-3, 338
Kosygin, Aleksei 51, 56-7, 61, 72, 170, 198, 214, 329, 381, 398, 424
Kovalev, Anatoly 225-6, 230-1

Lankester, Tim 8
Leusse, Bruno de 22, 24-7, 30
Liechtenstein 270
Lithuania 104-5
Long Term Defence Programme 2, 32
Luce, Richard 103, 282, 346
Lunkov, Nikolai 35-8, 103
Luxembourg 314
Lyne, Roderic 245

Maitland, Sir Donald 135
Malfatti, Francesco 22-3, 25
Mallaby, Christopher 1, 89, 106, 109, 149, 173; Afghanistan 28-9, 51-3, 58, 147-9; bilateral relationship with USSR 58; dissent 104-5; Poland 310, 320-5; USSR in Developing World 6-7, 83, 109-10
Malta 270
Manning, David 361, 365
Mexico 95
Micronesia 129
Middle East 79, 120, 125; Soviet policy 83, 109, 140, 192, 196, 217, 255-6, 265-7, 282-3, 383, 386, 428
Mitterrand, François 362, 375, 389-90, 398, 400
Moi, Daniel arap 121
Mondale, Walter 81
Monro, Hector 95
Murray, Donald 82
Murrell, Geoffrey 72, 143, 399
Muskie, Ed 146, 148, 175
Mutual and Balanced Force Reduction (MBFR) 4, 32, 67, 78, 80, 130, 172, 183, 192, 319, 324, 376

Namibia 155, 209, 272, 282, 383
Nepal 270

Index

Netherlands 50, 245, 314, 404
New York Times 67, 118, 305, 379
New Zealand 10, 153, 245, 270
Nigeria 23
Nixon, Richard 113-14, 154, 191-2, 208, 339, 379-80, 427
North Atlantic Treaty Organisation (NATO): Afghanistan 31-3, 49-51, 60, 64-6, 69, 71, 80-1, 87-8, 94, 111, 169; arms control 213, 220-1, 223, 228-9, 236, 239, 262-5, 323, 339, 334, 386; long-range capability 132, 154-6, 160, 172, 195; Poland 293, 297-8, 303-4, 308, 310, 322, 324; review 194
Northern Ireland 304, 311
North Korea 84
Norway 50, 84, 270, 403-5
Nott, John 346

Olympic Games 19, 25, 42, 49-50, 58, 127, 131, 195-6; boycott 35, 59, 69, 77, 81, 88-9, 95-9, 117, 121, 124-5, 141, 160, 195-6
Oman 32, 43, 92-4, 99-100, 110, 120, 138, 161
'Operation Common Sense' 106
Organisation of Economic Cooperation and Development (OECD) 3, 42, 169, 391, 404, 406-7
Orlov, Yuri 214
Osborn, John 290
Ostpolitik 165, 173, 190, 307

Pakenham, Michael 369, 388, 390
Pakistan 97; Afghanistan 17, 20-3, 31-2, 93-4, 434-5; Afghan resistance 36, 71, 100-1, 111, 187, 189; Afghan settlement 145-7, 185-6, 204-6, 222-3, 245, 259, 270, 280, 288, 395, 414; refugees 17, 20, 25-6, 76, 82, 93, 189, 234, 245, 260, 289; threat from USSR 53, 71, 82, 130, 189; UK aid 132; USA 25, 32, 77, 81-2, 94, 133-4, 138, 240
Palestine Liberation Organisation (PLO) 217, 255, 282-3

Palliser, Sir Michael 60, 193-4, 231, 241-2, 346
Parkinson, Cecil 171
Parsons, Anthony 30, 69
Pavlovsky, Ivan 62, 73
People's Democratic Republic of Yemen (PDRY) 4, 37, 52, 55, 93, 109-10, 126, 130, 159, 207
Percy, Charles 198
Petrovsky, Vladimir 269, 304-5
Philippines 24
Poland 3, 85, 105, 171, 243, 254, 257, 293, 321-5, 378, 392; reaction of the West to martial law 297-300, 302, 303-10, 315-7, 320-2; USSR 190-1, 193-4, 195-7, 211-2, 225-6, 228, 230, 234, 267, 278-9, 281-2, 293-5, 300-1, 311-2, 338-9, 357, 383, 414
Pompidou, Georges 230
Popov, Viktor: Afghanistan 214, 288-9; arms control 213-14, 255-6, 287, 319-20; bilateral relationship with UK 199-200, 213-14, 288-90, 315-17, 353; Falklands War 349, 351-3; Persian Gulf 200; Poland 234, 315-17
Portillo, José López 371
Portugal 50, 270
Posilyagin, Nikolai 317-18, 326
Pym, Francis 346, 392; Afghanistan 397-8; arms control 397, 414; bilateral relationship with USSR 396-7, 414, 416, 418-19; CSCE 397; East-West relations 413, 415-18; meetings with Gromyko 396-8, 414-15; meeting with Shultz 412-14; personal cases 398; Poland 392

Qotbzadeh, Sadegh 16-17

Rakowski, Mieczyslaw 225
Reagan, Ronald 186, 192-5, 272, 287, 297, 302, 358, 412-13, 415-17; Alliance relations 297, 299; Eureka College speech 355-6, 372; political views 369-80, 388-9; Soviet opinion of 192, 339, 410, 428

Index

Reddaway, Peter, 104, 106
Rhodesia 4, 91, 129, 159, 178, 186, 322
Rifkind, Malcolm 351-4, 387, 418-19
Romania 3, 5, 9, 21-2, 32, 171, 306, 363
Rose, Clive 31, 34, 49, 64, 87, 194
Ryzhov, Nikita 381, 386, 402, 419, 425

Sadat, Anwar Al 188, 276, 283
Sakharov, Andrei 99, 103-4, 108, 115, 198, 296, 431
Saudi Arabia 43, 92-4, 97, 99-101, 138, 188, 245-6, 283, 377
Schapiro, Leonard 149
Schmidt, Helmut 194, 227-9, 332, 353, 375, 394; Alliance relations 86, 139; criticism of USA 124-8; Poland 299, 302, 304; visits 18, 25, 55, 166, 169, 170, 197, 394-5, 402
Semeonov, Viacheslav 225, 294, 350-2
Shahi, Agha 77, 81, 134, 185, 205, 245
Shcharansky, Anatoly 289
Sheinwald, Nigel 317, 320
Shultz, George 370, 372-3, 389-90, 402, 412-18
Siberian gas pipeline 288, 297, 299, 303-4, 306-7, 309, 313-15, 324, 340, 347-8, 363, 374-5, 388-9, 392, 403-7, 413, 417
Sierra Leone 270
Singapore 24, 270
Smith, Sir Howard 278, 359
Smith, Roland 296
Solidarity 191, 196, 225, 279, 293-5, 300-1, 305, 311-12, 321, 330, 338, 378
Somalia 32, 138, 213, 226, 230, 270
South Africa 141, 160, 209, 225, 272, 282
Soviet Union: 26th CPSU Congress 207-12; Afghan solution 144-9, 157-8, 162-3, 167-8, 185-6, 221-3, 232, 257-62, 280, 288-9, 397-8; dissidents 5, 99, 103-106, 181-2, 198, 289, 295-6, 397-8; economy

56, 75, 134, 142, 154-5, 198, 209-10, 274-5, 278, 428-30; influence in the Developing World 3-4, 6-7, 52, 73, 91-2, 109-110, 141-2; internal situation 252, 273-79, 334-6, 359-60, 384-5, 430-2; justification for invasion 8, 12, 13, 36-41, 44, 214, motives for invasion 21, 28, 51-3, 61-3, 72-5, 83, 90, 190, 433-5; subsidised credit for 3-4, 29, 35, 42-3, 49-50, 97, 99, 132-4, 169, 172, 201, 391, 407
Spain 270, 314, 349
Spiegel, Der 123, 288
Sri Lanka 24
SS-20 missiles 55, 115, 208, 213, 225, 227-31, 236, 263, 286, 343-4, 354
Strategic Arms Limitation Talks (SALT) 4, 9, 18, 19, 21, 28, 31-2, 49, 55, 63, 66-7, 73, 90, 114-17, 165, 172, 183, 190-2, 196-7, 207-08, 225-9, 252, 264, 281, 340, 344, 355-6, 380, 382-3, 427
Strategic Arms Reduction Talks (START) 306, 311, 323, 325, 340, 355-6, 358, 370, 376, 386, 399, 410, 428
Sudan 156, 270
Suslov, Mikhail 72-3, 211, 254, 332
Suslov, Vladimir 219, 241-2, 244, 252, 284-5
Sutherland, Sir Iain 361, 381, 396, 401, 408, 412, 419, 426
Sverdlovsk submarine incident 225-6, 228, 230
Sweden 270
Switzerland 270, 314, 404
Syria 196, 266, 383

Tabeyev, Fikryat 44
Taraki, Nur Muhammad 8, 11, 17, 22, 24, 45, 52, 61, 73, 433
Thailand 270
Thatcher, Margaret: Afghanistan 9, 13, 36-8, 77, 97-100, 111-13, 121, 125-6, 131, 187, 212; Alliance relations 125, 302, 308-10; arms control 57, 212-13; bilateral

Index

relationship with USSR 202, 214, 219, 407, 416; East-West relations 132-3, 149-50, 161, 213, 413, 415-16; FCO 106, 149; FRG 100, 123-8; Olympics 59, 77, 97, 99, 121, 125; Poland 234, 246, 302, 308-9; potential visit to Moscow 362, 366-8, 381, 402

Theatre Nuclear Force (TNF) 2, 19, 21, 32, 62, 67, 73, 78, 103, 117, 131; negotiations 172, 183, 190-2, 197, 213, 220-1, 223, 229, 238-9, 262-4, 281, 287

Thomas, Derek 369

Thomas, Hugh 149

Thomson, Sir John 194

Tikhonov, Nikolai 170, 209, 211, 423

Times, The 36, 96, 187-8, 305, 346, 389

Tito, Josip Broz 5, 84, 109, 141

Trefgarne, Lord 287-90, 315-7, 319-20, 342

Trudeau, Pierre 121

Tunisia 270

Turkey 50, 78, 84, 97, 117, 130, 270, 311; aid 92-4, 131-2, 134, 157

United Kingdom (UK): analysis of Soviet invasion 15-18, 21, 51-3, 433-5; bilateral relationship 42, 58, 91, 102,170-1, 182-3, 193, 197, 199-202, 209, 218-19, 222, 229-31, 238, 241-5, 269-70, 273, 283-4, 290, 316-9, 325-33, 342-3, 345-6, 353, 361-9, 380-1, 385-6, 393-7, 396-403, 414, 416, 418-19; cultural policy 3, 58, 159, 201-4, 290-2, 360, 363, 365, 395, 399-400, 403; Eastern Europe 2-3, 71-2, 171, 183, 363; measures against the USSR 41-4, 49, 58, 59-60, 75-6, 87-8, 91, 97-100, 308-10, 315-7; prevention of Soviet expansion in the Developing World 2-4, 6-7, 109-110, 151, 155-6, 159-61, 171-2; trade 3 160, 57-8, 197, 199, 201-4, 214, 269-70, 284, 288, 303, 326, 329, 353, 371, 391-2

United Nations (UN): Afghanistan 12, 23-4, 27, 30, 33, 41, 59, 69, 75-6, 159, 188, 204-6, 232, 240, 245, 251, 268, 270, 279-80, 288; Falklands War 349-53

United States of America (USA) 1, 20-2, 24-5, 62, 88, 93-5, 100, 112, 133-5, 144, 148-9, 153-7,159-61, 166, 173, 187-9, 194, 202, 218, 270, 283, 402; Alliance relations 118-121, 138-40, 174-5, 178-9, 297-8, 302-4, 307-10, 324, 348, 377-8, 389-90, 392, 404-6; grain sales to USSR 4, 29, 35, 42, 80, 85, 91, 141, 160, 196, 203, 240, 306, 340-1, 373-4, 378, 406; measures against the USSR 79-80, 297, 299, 305-7, 309-10; reaction to Soviet invasion 10-14, 20-8, 31-3; relations with USSR 66-8, 102-3, 106-7, 113-18, 140, 192, 208, 220-2, 224, 225, 227, 253-4, 263-4, 272, 337-42, 355-9, 369-80, 388-90, 410, 428

USSR *see* Soviet Union

Vance, Cyrus 9-10, 114-15, 118, 121, 124-5, 131-3, 227

Van Well, Günther 22, 24-6

Venezuela 270

Vietnam 18, 22, 54-5, 63, 107, 114, 130, 150, 157, 159, 213, 276, 382

Walden, George 106, 149, 201, 218, 232, 366-7, 407, 419

Waldheim, Kurt 33, 188, 205, 232, 240, 251, 260

Warsaw Pact 2, 3, 5, 43, 65, 117, 158, 173, 183, 196, 212, 226, 229, 234, 254, 263, 294, 300, 364, 418, 429

Washington Post 297

Weinberger, Casper 298, 372, 376-7, 389, 392

Weston, P. John 66, 343

Whitmore, Clive 241, 245

Wilson, Sir Harold 42, 170, 322, 345, 386

Wood, Andrew 181, 274, 284

Wright, Oliver 139, 175, 190, 193-5

Index

Yalta memorial 147
Yemen Arab Republic (YAR) 93-4,
   99-100, 109, 125
Yugoslavia 5, 26, 70, 171, 196, 307;
   threat from USSR 9, 21, 32, 78,
   84, 95, 109

Zagladin, Vadim 195
Zambia 156, 161
Zemskov, Igor 204, 223, 283, 290,
   318-19, 326-8, 342, 345;

Afghanistan 162-3, 167-8;
   bilateral relationship 102; death
   381, 425; East-West relations
   102-3; Sakharov 103
Zhivkov, Todor 244
Zia-ul-Haq, M. 31, 93-4, 97, 110,
   133-4, 187, 189, 245
Zimbabwe 157, 196, 223, 228, 270,
   383
Zorin, Valerian 91